"…The folks who wrote this book know what they're talking about, and can write rings around most of the other certification writers."

William Steinmetz, from the Official Editorial Review on Amazon.com

"Don't Hesitate to Purchase This Book! GREAT! This book does it all…Don't stand around and wish you had that certification, order this book and start studying!"

Five-Star Review on Amazon.com

"Excellent…It is easy to understand and I like the "real" world examples. Buy it!"

A reader from Phoenix, AZ
Five-Star Review on Bookpool.com

"I am now A+ Certified and I would not have done it without this book! I highly recommend this as your first study platform then using A+ Exam Cram to polish your knowledge before taking the tests!"

Five-Star Reader Review on Amazon.com

A+® Complete

Study Guide
Third Edition

David Groth

San Francisco • London

Associate Publisher: Neil Edde
Acquisitions Editor: Elizabeth Hurley Peterson
Developmental Editor: Colleen Wheeler Strand
Production Editor: Susan Berge
Technical Editors: Andre Paree-Huff, Craig Vazquez, Warren Wyrostek
Copyeditor: Tiffany Taylor
Compositors/Graphic Illustrators: Rozi Harris, Bill Clark, Interactive Composition Corporation
CD Coordinator: Dan Mummert
CD Technician: Kevin Ly
Proofreaders: Emily Hsuan, Laurie O'Connell, Nancy Riddiough, Sarah Tannehill
Indexer: Ted Laux
Book Designer: Bill Gibson
Cover Designer: Archer Design
Cover Photographer: Natural Selection

Library of Congress Card Number: 2003106713

ISBN: 0-7821-4243-5

How to Become CompTIA Certified:

This training material can help you prepare for and pass a related CompTIA certification exam or exams. In order to achieve CompTIA certification, you must register for and pass a CompTIA certification exam or exams.

In order to become CompTIA certified, you must:

(1) Select a certification exam provider. For more information please visit http://www.comptia.org/certification/test_locations.htm.

(2) Register for and schedule a time to take the CompTIA certification exam(s) at a convenient location.

(3) Read and sign the Candidate Agreement, which will be presented at the time of the exam(s). The text of the Candidate Agreement can be found at www.comptia.org/certification

(4) Take and pass the CompTIA certification exam(s).

For more information about CompTIA's certifications, such as their industry acceptance, benefits, or program news, please visit www.comptia.org/certification

CompTIA is a non-profit information technology (IT) trade association. CompTIA's certifications are designed by subject matter experts from across the IT industry. Each CompTIA certification is vendor-neutral, covers multiple technologies, and requires demonstration of skills and knowledge widely sought after by the IT industry.

To contact CompTIA with any questions or comments:
Please call + 1 630 268 1818
questions@comptia.org

SYBEX

To Our Valued Readers:

Thank you for looking to Sybex for your A+ certification exam prep needs. We at Sybex are proud of our reputation for providing certification candidates with the practical knowledge and skills needed to succeed in the highly competitive IT marketplace, and are pleased to have helped thousands of A+ certification candidates prepare for their exams over the years.

With the latest update to the A+ exams, CompTIA has raised the bar for IT certifications yet again. The new exams better reflect current technologies and accurately address the skills needed to succeed in the highly competitive IT industry.

The author and editors have worked hard to ensure that the Study Guide you hold in your hands is comprehensive, in-depth, and pedagogically sound. We're confident that this book will exceed the demanding standards of the certification marketplace and help you, the A+ certification candidate, succeed in your endeavors.

As always, your feedback is important to us. Please send comments, questions, or suggestions to support@sybex.com. At Sybex we're continually striving to meet the needs of individuals preparing for IT certification exams.

Good luck in the pursuit of your A+ certification!

Neil Edde
Associate Publisher—Certification
Sybex, Inc.

Software License Agreement: Terms and Conditions

The media and/or any online materials accompanying this book that are available now or in the future contain programs and/or text files (the "Software") to be used in connection with the book. SYBEX hereby grants to you a license to use the Software, subject to the terms that follow. Your purchase, acceptance, or use of the Software will constitute your acceptance of such terms. The Software compilation is the property of SYBEX unless otherwise indicated and is protected by copyright to SYBEX or other copyright owner(s) as indicated in the media files (the "Owner(s)"). You are hereby granted a single-user license to use the Software for your personal, noncommercial use only. You may not reproduce, sell, distribute, publish, circulate, or commercially exploit the Software, or any portion thereof, without the written consent of SYBEX and the specific copyright owner(s) of any component software included on this media.

In the event that the Software or components include specific license requirements or end-user agreements, statements of condition, disclaimers, limitations or warranties ("End-User License"), those End-User Licenses supersede the terms and conditions herein as to that particular Software component. Your purchase, acceptance, or use of the Software will constitute your acceptance of such End-User Licenses.

By purchase, use or acceptance of the Software you further agree to comply with all export laws and regulations of the United States as such laws and regulations may exist from time to time.

Software Support

Components of the supplemental Software and any offers associated with them may be supported by the specific Owner(s) of that material, but they are not supported by SYBEX. Information regarding any available support may be obtained from the Owner(s) using the information provided in the appropriate read.me files or listed elsewhere on the media.

Should the manufacturer(s) or other Owner(s) cease to offer support or decline to honor any offer, SYBEX bears no responsibility. This notice concerning support for the Software is provided for your information only. SYBEX is not the agent or principal of the Owner(s), and SYBEX is in no way responsible for providing any support for the Software, nor is it liable or responsible for any support provided, or not provided, by the Owner(s).

Warranty

SYBEX warrants the enclosed media to be free of physical defects for a period of ninety (90) days after purchase. The Software is not available from SYBEX in any other form or media than that enclosed herein or posted to www.sybex.com. If you discover a defect in the media during this warranty period, you may obtain a replacement of identical format at no charge by sending the defective media, postage prepaid, with proof of purchase to:

SYBEX Inc.
Product Support Department
1151 Marina Village Parkway
Alameda, CA 94501
Web: http://www.sybex.com

After the 90-day period, you can obtain replacement media of identical format by sending us the defective disk, proof of purchase, and a check or money order for $10, payable to SYBEX.

Disclaimer

SYBEX makes no warranty or representation, either expressed or implied, with respect to the Software or its contents, quality, performance, merchantability, or fitness for a particular purpose. In no event will SYBEX, its distributors, or dealers be liable to you or any other party for direct, indirect, special, incidental, consequential, or other damages arising out of the use of or inability to use the Software or its contents even if advised of the possibility of such damage. In the event that the Software includes an online update feature, SYBEX further disclaims any obligation to provide this feature for any specific duration other than the initial posting.

The exclusion of implied warranties is not permitted by some states. Therefore, the above exclusion may not apply to you. This warranty provides you with specific legal rights; there may be other rights that you may have that vary from state to state. The pricing of the book with the Software by SYBEX reflects the allocation of risk and limitations on liability contained in this agreement of Terms and Conditions.

Shareware Distribution

This Software may contain various programs that are distributed as shareware. Copyright laws apply to both shareware and ordinary commercial software, and the copyright Owner(s) retains all rights. If you try a shareware program and continue using it, you are expected to register it. Individual programs differ on details of trial periods, registration, and payment. Please observe the requirements stated in appropriate files.

Copy Protection

The Software in whole or in part may or may not be copy-protected or encrypted. However, in all cases, reselling or redistributing these files without authorization is expressly forbidden except as specifically provided for by the Owner(s) therein.

For Ryan the Fierce

Acknowledgments

Thanks first of all to you, the reader, for buying this book. You could've spent your money on any A+ book, but you chose mine. Thank you.

Thanks very much to all those who supported me while I was writing and developing this book. A very special thanks to my wife, family, and friends for understanding when I was under deadlines and didn't have as much time as they wanted to spend with them.

Also, many thanks to all the talented people at Sybex who published this book. In particular, thanks to my acquisitions editor, Elizabeth Hurley. We've worked on quite a few books together now and I always appreciate the hard work she puts forth. And of course, many, *many* thanks to the fine editors who produced the book: Colleen Strand, Tiffany Taylor, Warren Wyrostek, Andre Paree-Huff, Craig Vazquez, and Susan Berge. Thanks also to the rest of the book team: Rozi Harris, Bill Clark, Dan Mummert, Kevin Ly, Emily Hsuan, Laurie O'Connell, Nancy Riddiough, Sarah Tannehill, and Ted Laux. As usual, everyone did a perfect job.

I hope all of you enjoy this book and that it is useful to you. If you have questions or comments, positive or negative, please e-mail me at `dgroth@cableone.net`. I'm always striving to make my books better.

—David Groth

Contents at a Glance

Contents

Table of Exercises

Introduction

Welcome to the *A+ Complete Study Guide*. This is the third edition of our best-selling study guide for the A+ certification sponsored by CompTIA (Computing Technology Industry Association).

This book was written at an intermediate technical level; we assume that you already know how to *use* a personal computer and its basic peripherals, such as modems and printers, but we also recognize that you may be learning how to *service* some of that computer equipment for the first time. The exam covers basic computer service topics as well as some more advanced issues, and it covers some topics that anyone already working as a technician, whether with computers or not, should be familiar with. The exam is designed to test you on these topics in order to certify that you have enough knowledge to fix and upgrade some of the most widely used types of personal desktop computers.

We've included review questions at the end of each chapter to give you a taste of what it's like to take the exam. If you're already working as a technical service or support person, we recommend you check out these questions first to gauge your level of knowledge. You can use the book mainly to fill in the gaps in your current computer service knowledge. You may find, as many service technicians have, that being well versed in all the technical aspects of the equipment is not enough to provide a satisfactory level of support—you must also have customer-relations skills. We include helpful hints to get the customer to help you help them.

If you can answer 80 percent or more of the review questions correctly for a given chapter, you can probably feel safe moving on to the next chapter. If you're unable to answer that many correctly, reread the chapter and try the questions again. Your score should improve.

Don't just study the questions and answers—the questions on the actual exam will be different from the practice ones included in this book and on the CD. The exam is designed to test your knowledge of a concept or objective, so use this book to learn the objective *behind* the question.

What Is A+ Certification?

The A+ certification program was developed by the Computer Technology Industry Association (CompTIA) to provide an industry-wide means of certifying the competency of computer service technicians. The A+ certified "diploma," which is granted to those who have attained the level of knowledge and troubleshooting skills that are needed to provide capable support in the field of personal computers, is similar to other certifications in the computer industry. For example, Novell offers the Certified Novell Engineer (CNE) program to provide the same recognition for network professionals who deal with its NetWare products, and Microsoft has its Microsoft Certified

Systems Engineer (MCSE) program. The theory behind these certifications is that if you need to have service performed on any of their products, you would sooner call a technician who has been certified in one of the appropriate certification programs than you would just call the first "expert" in the phone book.

The A+ certification program was created to offer a wide-ranging certification, in the sense that it is intended to certify competence with personal computers from many different makers/ vendors. You must pass two tests to become A+ certified:

- The A+ Core Hardware Service Technician exam, which covers basic computer concepts, hardware troubleshooting, customer service, and hardware upgrading
- The A+ Operating Systems Technologies exam, which covers the DOS and Windows operating environments

You don't have to take the Core Hardware and Operating Systems Technologies exams at the same time; you have 90 days from the time you pass one test to pass the second test. The A+ certified "diploma" is not awarded until you've passed both tests.

Why Become A+ Certified?

There are several good reasons to get your A+ certification. The CompTIA Candidate's Information packet lists five major benefits:

- It demonstrates proof of professional achievement.
- It increases your marketability.
- It provides greater opportunity for advancement in your field.
- It is increasingly a requirement for some types of advanced training.
- It raises customer confidence in you and your company's services.

Provides Proof of Professional Achievement

The A+ certification is quickly becoming a status symbol in the computer service industry. Organizations that include members of the computer service industry are recognizing the benefits of A+ certification and are pushing for their members to become certified. And, more people every day are putting the "A+ Certified Technician" emblem on their business cards.

Increases Your Marketability

A+ certification makes individuals more marketable to potential employers. A+ certified employees also may receive a higher base salary, because employers won't have to spend as much money on vendor-specific training.

What Is an AASC?

More service companies are becoming A+ Authorized Service Centers (AASCs). This means that over 50 percent of the technicians employed by that service center are A+ certified. At the time of the writing of this book, there are more than 1,400 A+ Authorized Service Centers in the world. Customers and vendors alike recognize that AASCs employ the most qualified service technicians. As a result, an AASC gets more business than a nonauthorized service center. And, because more service centers want to reach the AASC level, they will give preference in hiring to a candidate who is A+ certified over one who is not.

Provides Opportunity for Advancement

Most raises and advancements are based on performance. A+ certified employees work faster and more efficiently, thus making them more productive. The more productive employees are, the more money they make for their company. And, of course, the more money they make for the company, the more valuable they are to the company. So if an employee is A+ certified, their chances of being promoted are greater.

Fulfills Training Requirements

A+ certification is recognized by most major computer hardware vendors, including (but not limited to) IBM, Hewlett-Packard, Apple, and Compaq. Some of these vendors apply A+ certification toward prerequisites in their own respective certification programs. For example, an A+ certified technician is automatically given credit toward HP laser printer certification without having to take prerequisite classes and tests. This has the side benefit of reducing training costs for employers.

Raises Customer Confidence

As the A+ Certified Technician moniker becomes more well known among computer owners, more of them will realize that the A+ technician is more qualified to work on their computer equipment than a noncertified technician is.

How to Become A+ Certified

A+ certification is available to anyone who passes the tests. You don't have to work for any particular company. It's not a secret society. It is, however, an elite group. To become A+ certified, you must do two things:

- Pass the A+ Core Hardware Service Technician exam
- Pass the A+ Operating Systems Technologies exam

The exams are administered by Prometric and can be taken at any Prometric or Pearson VUE Testing Center. If you pass both exams, you will get a certificate in the mail from CompTIA saying that you have passed, and you will also receive a lapel pin and business card. To find the Prometric training center nearest you, call (800) 755-EXAM (755-3926). To find the nearest Pearson VUE center, go to www.vue.com.

To register for the tests, call Prometric at (800) 77-MICRO (776-4276) or register online at www.2test.com. For Pearson VUE, call (877) 551-PLUS (7587) or go to www.vue.com. You'll be asked for your name, Social Security number (an optional number may be assigned if you don't wish to provide your Social Security number), mailing address, phone number, employer, when and where (which Prometric testing center) you want to take the test, and your credit card number (arrangement for payment must be made at the time of registration).

Although you can save money by arranging to take more than one test at the same seating, there are no other discounts. If you have to take a test more than once in order to get a passing grade, you must pay both times.

It is possible to pass these tests without any reference materials, but only if you already have the knowledge and experience that come from reading about and working with personal computers. But even experienced service people tend to have what you might call a 20/80 situation with their computer knowledge—they may use 20 percent of their knowledge and skills 80 percent of the time, and they have to rely on manuals, guesswork, the Internet, or phone calls for the rest. By covering all the topics that are tested by the exams, this book can help you to refresh your memory concerning topics that, until now, you might have only seldom used. (It can also serve to fill in gaps that, let's admit, you may have tried to cover up for quite some time.) Further, by treating all the issues that the exam covers (problems you may run into in the arenas of PC service and support), this book can serve as a general field guide that you can keep with you as you go about your work.

In addition to reading the book, you might consider practicing these objectives through an internship program. (After all, all theory and no practice makes for a poor technician.)

Who Should Buy This Book?

If you are one of the many people who want to pass the A+ exam, and pass it confidently, then you should buy this book and use it to study for the exam. The A+ Core Hardware Service Technician exam is designed to measure essential competencies for an entry-level PC technician. The Operating Systems Technologies exam is intended to certify that the exam candidate has the necessary skills to work on microcomputer hardware and typically has at least six months of on-the-job experience.

This book was written with one goal in mind: to prepare you for the challenges of the real IT world, not just to pass the A+ exams. This study guide will do that by describing in detail the concepts on which you'll be tested.

How to Use This Book and CD

We've included several testing features throughout the book and on the CD-ROM. At the beginning of the book (right after this introduction) is an assessment test for each A+ module that you can use to check your readiness for the actual exam. Take both of these exams before you begin reading the book. Doing so will help you determine the areas you may need to brush up on. The answers to each assessment test appear on a separate page after the last question of the test. Each answer also includes an explanation and a note telling you the chapter in which this material appears. To test your knowledge as you progress through the book, there are review questions at the end of each chapter. As you finish each chapter, answer the review questions and then check your answers—the correct answers appear on the page following the last review question. You can go back to reread the section that deals with each question you got wrong to ensure that you answer correctly the next time you are tested on the material. You'll also find 150 flashcard questions for the A+ Core exam and 150 flashcard questions for the Operation Systems Technologies exam. You can use these handy exams for on-the-go review. Download them right onto your Palm device for quick and convenient reviewing.

In addition to the assessment tests and the chapter review tests, you'll find four sample exams. The first two exams are dedicated to the Core Hardware exam, and the next two focus on the Operating Systems Technologies exam. Take these practice exams just as if you were actually taking the A+ exams (without any reference material). When you have finished the first module, move on to the next three exams to solidify your test-taking skills for the second module. If you get more than 90 percent of the answers correct, you're ready to take the real exam.

If you are going to travel but still need to study for the A+ exam, and you have a laptop with a CD-ROM drive, you can take this entire book with you just by taking the CD-ROM. This book is in PDF (Adobe Acrobat) format so it can be easily read on any computer.

The Exam Objectives

Behind every computer industry exam you can be sure to find exam objectives—the broad topics in which the exam developers want to ensure your competency. The official CompTIA exam objectives are listed here.

Exam objectives are subject to change at any time without prior notice and at CompTIA's sole discretion. Please visit the A+ Certification page of CompTIA's website (www.comptia.org/certification/aplus/index.htm) for the most current listing of exam objectives.

The A+ Core Hardware Service Technician Exam Objectives

As mentioned previously, two tests are required to become A+ certified: the Core Hardware Service Technician exam and the Operating Systems Technologies exam. The following are the areas (or *domains*, according to CompTIA) in which you must be proficient in order to pass the A+ Core Module exam:

Domain 1 Installation, Configuration, and Upgrading   The objectives in domain 1 test your knowledge of the basic service practices of installing, configuring, and upgrading computer hardware. You will learn the basic parts of a computer and how they work, as well as how to properly remove, configure, and install the components of a computer. Questions from this domain make up 35 percent of your final exam score:

1.1   Identify the names, purpose, and characteristics of system modules. Recognize these modules by sight or definition.

1.2   Identify basic procedures for adding and removing field-replaceable modules for desktop systems. Given a replacement scenario, choose the appropriate sequences.

1.3   Identify basic procedures for adding and removing field-replaceable modules for portable systems. Given a replacement scenario, choose the appropriate sequences.

1.4   Identify typical IRQs, DMAs, and I/O addresses, and procedures for altering these settings when installing and configuring devices. Choose the appropriate installation or configuration steps in a given scenario.

1.5   Identify the names, purposes, and performance characteristics of standardized/common peripheral ports, associated cabling, and their connectors. Recognize ports, cabling, and connectors by sight.

1.6   Identify proper procedures for installing and configuring common IDE devices. Choose the appropriate installation or configuration sequences in given scenarios. Recognize the associated cables.

1.7   Identify proper procedures for installing and configuring common SCSI devices. Choose the appropriate installation or configuration sequences in given scenarios. Recognize the associated cables.

1.8   Identify proper procedures for installing and configuring common peripheral devices. Choose the appropriate installation or configuration sequences in given scenarios.

1.9   Identify procedures to optimize PC operations in specific situations. Predict the effects of specific procedures under given scenarios.

1.10   Determine the issues that must be considered when upgrading a PC. In a given scenario, determine when and how to upgrade system components.

Domain 2 Diagnosing and Troubleshooting   Questions on the objectives in this domain test your knowledge of troubleshooting. These objectives cover troubleshooting practices, common problems, how to begin troubleshooting, and how to diagnose and fix a problem. Questions from this domain make up 21 percent of your final exam score:

2.1 Recognize common problems associated with each module and their symptoms, and identify steps to isolate and troubleshoot the problems. Given a problem situation, interpret the symptoms and infer the most likely cause.

2.2 Identify basic troubleshooting procedures and tools, and how to elicit problem symptoms from customers. Justify asking particular questions in a given scenario.

Domain 3 PC Preventive Maintenance, Safety, and Environmental Issues   Questions based on the objectives in this domain test your knowledge of various preventive maintenance, safety, and environmental topics. You should know how to perform preventive maintenance tasks on a computer, which products to use and how to use them, how to ensure safety when working on a computer, and how to protect the environment when servicing a computer. Questions from this domain make up 5 percent of your final exam score:

3.1 Identify the various types of preventive maintenance measures, products, and procedures and when and how to use them.

3.2 Identify various safety measures and procedures, and when/how to use them.

3.3 Identify environmental protection measures and procedures, and when/how to use them.

Domain 4 Motherboard/Processors/Memory   In this domain, questions test your knowledge of the details of motherboards, processors, and memory. You should know the specifications of PC CPUs and the differences between them. You should also be familiar with the different types of RAM and what differentiates them from each other. Finally, you should know the different motherboard types, what makes motherboards different from one another, and how they are configured. Questions from this domain make up 11 percent of your final score:

4.1 Distinguish between the popular CPU chips in terms of their basic characteristics.

4.2 Identify the types of RAM (Random Access Memory), form factors, and operational characteristics. Determine banking and speed requirements under given scenarios.

4.3 Identify the most popular types of motherboards, their components, and their architecture (bus structures).

4.4 Identify the purpose of CMOS (Complementary Metal-Oxide Semiconductor) memory, what it contains, and how and when to change its parameters. Given a scenario involving CMOS, choose the appropriate course of action.

Domain 5 Printers   Questions from this domain test your knowledge of the different types of printers, their parts, the problems they have, and how to fix/install/upgrade them. Questions from this domain make up 9 percent of your final exam score:

5.1 Identify printer technologies, interfaces, and options/upgrades.

5.2 Recognize common printer problems and techniques used to resolve them.

Domain 6 Basic Networking   As more computers are networked at home, the networking domain has become increasingly important. Therefore, this domain now counts for 19 percent of your final exam score. Questions from this domain test your knowledge of the physical connections and layout of a network, as well as how networks work and how to connect a PC to the Internet:

6.1   Identify the common types of network cables, their characteristics and connectors.

6.2   Identify basic networking concepts including how a network works.

6.3   Identify common technologies available for establishing Internet connectivity and their characteristics.

Operating Systems Technologies Exam Objectives

The following are the areas in which you must be proficient in order to pass the A+ Operating Systems Technologies exam.

Domain 1 Operating System Fundamentals   This domain requires knowledge of the Windows 95/98/Me (a.k.a. 9x), Windows NT, Windows 2000, and Windows XP operating systems. You need to know the way they work, as well as the components that compose them. You also need to understand topics relating to navigating the operating systems and, in general, how to use them. Operating system fundamentals make up 28 percent of the exam:

1.1   Identify the major desktop components and interfaces, and their functions. Differentiate the characteristics of Windows 9x/Me, Windows NT 4.0 Workstation, Windows 2000 Professional, and Windows XP.

1.2   Identify the names, locations, purposes, and contents of major system files.

1.3   Demonstrate the ability to use command-line functions and utilities to manage the operating system, including the proper syntax and switches.

1.4   Identify basic concepts and procedures for creating, viewing, and managing disks, directories, and files. This includes procedures for changing file attributes and the ramifications of those changes (for example, security issues).

1.5   Identify the major operating system utilities, their purpose, location, and available switches.

Domain 2 Installation, Configuration, and Upgrading   This domain tests your knowledge of the day-to-day servicing of operating systems. This includes topics such as installing, configuring, and upgrading the various operating systems (Windows 9x, NT Workstation, 2000 Professional, and XP Professional). You are also expected to know system boot sequences. These topics make up 31 percent of the exam:

2.1   Identify the procedures for installing Windows 9x/Me, Windows NT 4.0 Workstation, Windows 2000 Professional, and Windows XP, and bringing the operating system to a basic operational level.

2.2   Identify steps to perform an operating system upgrade from Windows 9.x/ME, Windows NT 4.0 Workstation, Windows 2000 Professional, and Windows XP. Given an upgrade scenario, choose the appropriate next steps.

2.3   Identify the basic system boot sequences and boot methods, including the steps to create an emergency boot disk with utilities installed for Windows 9x/Me, Windows NT 4.0 Workstation, Windows 2000 Professional, and Windows XP.

2.4   Identify procedures for installing/adding a device, including loading, adding, and configuring device drivers, and required software.

2.5   Identify procedures necessary to optimize the operating system and major operating system subsystems.

Domain 3 Diagnosing and Troubleshooting   Questions in this domain test your ability to diagnose and troubleshoot Windows 9*x*/NT/2000/XP systems and make up 25 percent of the test:

3.1   Recognize and interpret the meaning of common error codes and startup messages from the boot sequence, and identify steps to correct the problems.

3.2   Recognize when to use common diagnostic utilities and tools. Given a diagnostic scenario involving one of these utilities or tools, select the appropriate steps needed to resolve the problem.

3.3   Recognize common operational and usability problems and determine how to resolve them.

Domain 4 Networks   This domain requires knowledge of the networking capabilities of the various versions of Windows and how to connect them to networks. It includes what the Internet is, its capabilities, basic concepts relating to Internet access, and generic procedures for system setup. Network questions make up 16 percent of the exam:

4.1   Identify the networking capabilities of Windows. Given configuration parameters, configure the operating system to connect to a network.

4.2   Identify the basic Internet protocols and terminologies. Identify procedures for establishing Internet connectivity. In a given scenario, configure the operating system to connect to and use Internet resources.

Tips for Taking the A+ Exams

Here are some general tips for taking your exam successfully:

- Bring two forms of ID with you. One must be a photo ID, such as a driver's license. The other can be a major credit card or a passport. Both forms must have a signature.

- Arrive early at the exam center so you can relax and review your study materials, particularly tables and lists of exam-related information.

- Read the questions carefully. Don't be tempted to jump to an early conclusion. Make sure you know exactly what the question is asking.

- Don't leave any unanswered questions. Unanswered questions are scored against you.

- Some questions have multiple correct responses. When there is more than one correct answer, a message at the bottom of the screen will prompt you to "Choose all that apply." Be sure to read the messages displayed.

- When answering multiple-choice questions you're not sure about, use a process of elimination to get rid of the obviously incorrect options first. Doing so will improve your odds if you need to make an educated guess.

- On form-based tests, because the hard questions will eat up the most time, save them for last. You can move forward and backward through the exam. (When the exam becomes adaptive, this tip will not work.)

- For the latest pricing on the exams and updates to the registration procedures, call Prometric at (800) 755-EXAM (755-3926) or (800) 77-MICRO (776-4276), or Pearson VUE at 877-551-PLUS. If you have further questions about the scope of the exams or related CompTIA programs, refer to the CompTIA website at www.comptia.org.

Assessment Test: Core Hardware Service Technician Exam

1. Which of the following computer components can be safely disposed of in regular trash?

   A. Monitors

   B. Printer toner

   C. Laptop batteries

   D. None of the above

2. Which of the following components is especially dangerous to repair and should only be opened by specially trained professionals?

   A. Printer

   B. Mouse

   C. Monitor

   D. Computer

3. Which of the following information is not stored on a computer's CMOS chip?

   A. Hard drive configuration

   B. Printer configuration

   C. Memory information

   D. Date and time

4. Which type of memory is typically upgraded on a computer when you add memory?

   A. DRAM

   B. SRAM

   C. VRAM

   D. QRAM

5. Which of the following interfaces are considered serial interfaces? (Select all that apply.)

   A. IEEE 1294

   B. FireWire

   C. USB

   D. ECP

6. Which of the following standards is commonly referred to as a FireWire port?

   A. IEEE 1294

   B. IEEE 1394

   C. ISO 1294

   D. IEEE 1666

7. Which of the following memory types offers the highest transfer rate and bandwidth rate?

   A. FPM DRAM

   B. EDO RAM

   C. DDR SDRAM

   D. RIMM

8. What is the main purpose of a video card?

   A. To play videos

   B. To provide additional functions to the CPU

   C. It is a special type of memory

   D. It provides video display capability to a computer

9. What type of cable is used by floppy drives?

   A. 18-pin ribbon cable

   B. 21-pin ribbon cable

   C. 34-pin ribbon cable

   D. 40-pin ribbon cable

10. How much disk capacity is supported by the original IDE specification?

    A. 528MB

    B. 640MB

    C. 628MB

    D. 1.2GB

11. What type of cable is used by internal SCSI devices?

    A. 21-pin ribbon cable

    B. 34-pin ribbon cable

    C. 40-pin ribbon cable

    D. 50-pin ribbon cable

12. Which ends of a SCSI bus should be terminated?

    A. Neither end should be terminated; termination is for IDE buses.

    B. The beginning of the chain should be terminated.

    C. The end of the chain should be terminated.

    D. Both ends of the chain should be terminated.

13. Which bus feature allows devices to bypass the processor and write their information directly to main memory?

    A. DMA channels

    B. IRQs

    C. I/O addresses

    D. Bus mastering

14. Which IRQ is typically assigned to LPT2?

    A. IRQ 3

    B. IRQ 5

    C. IRQ 10

    D. IRQ 15

15. Which bus architecture is typically associated with IBM PS/2 computers?

    A. ISA

    B. EISA

    C. MCA

    D. VESA

16. What type of bus architecture is commonly used with Pentium-class computers and supports 64- and 32-bit data paths?

    A. ISA

    B. EISA

    C. PCI

    D. VESA

17. What type of PCMCIA card is 5mm thick and is commonly used with modems and LAN adapters?

    A. Type I

    B. Type II

    C. Type III

    D. Type IV

18. Which of the following connector types are not typically associated with mice?

    A. Serial connector

    B. Parallel connector

    C. Bus mouse interface

    D. PS/2 interface

19. What is the maximum resolution supported by the VGA standard?

    A. 320×480

    B. 480×600

    C. 640×480

    D. 800×600

20. Which type of cable is commonly associated with parallel printers?

    A. DB-25F on the first connector and male Centronics 36 on the second connector

    B. DB-25F on the first connector and male Centronics 50 on the second connector

    C. DB-25M on the first connector and male Centronics 36 on the second connector

    D. DB-25M on the first connector and male Centronics 50 on the second connector

21. What is the primary purpose of the transfer corona assembly in a laser printer?

    A. It charges the paper so that the toner sticks to the paper.

    B. It fuses the toner to the paper.

    C. It moves the paper through the printer.

    D. It is a laser that scans the image to the printer.

22. Which of the following options offers the slowest transfer speed between a printer and a computer?

    A. Serial

    B. Parallel

    C. USB

    D. Network connection

23. Which of the following physical network topologies offers the most fault tolerance in terms of cable interruption, while balancing requirements for the amount of cable required?

    A. Bus

    B. Ring

    C. Mesh

    D. Star

24. Which IEEE specification is responsible for defining fiber optic standards?

    A. 802.1

    B. 802.4

    C. 802.6

    D. 802.8

25. What is the maximum data rate that can be transmitted over 2 pairs of UTP Category 3 cable?

    A. 4Mbps

    B. 10Mbps

    C. 16Mbps

    D. 100Mbps

26. Which DMA channel is typically assigned to the hard disk controller?

    A. DMA 1

    B. DMA 2

    C. DMA 3

    D. DMA 4

27. What will most likely happen if you leave the blank (the piece of metal or plastic that covers the space where expansion cards are placed) off the computer when an expansion card is removed?

    A. More airflow will be added.

    B. Less airflow will be added.

    C. More static will be present in the computer.

    D. Less static will be present in the computer.

28. Which universal command is used to access a computer's CMOS settings?

    A. During the computer's startup, press F1.

    B. During the computer's startup, press the Delete key.

    C. During the computer's startup, press Ctrl + Shift + Esc.

    D. There is no universal way of accessing CMOS.

29. Which DOS command is used to create a bootable diskette that can be used for troubleshooting?

    A. `FORMAT A: /S`

    B. `FORMAT A: /B`

    C. `FORMAT A: /Q`

    D. `FORMAT A: /T`

30. Which DOS configuration file would you check if a device driver was not loading properly?

    A. `AUTOEXEC.BAT`

    B. `SYSTEM.INI`

    C. `CONFIG.SYS`

    D. `BOOT.INI`

Answers to Assessment Test: Core Hardware Service Technician Exam

1.   D.   Many consumer electronic components, including monitors, printer toner, and batteries, are considered hazardous material and should be disposed of properly. Check your local waste disposal service for detailed disposal instructions. See Chapter 9 for more information.

2.   C.   The monitor is one of the most dangerous components to repair. It can retain a high-voltage charge even when it is not turned on. Monitors should only be opened by specially trained professionals. See Chapter 9 for more information.

3.   B.   The computer has a special chip called CMOS (Complimentary Metal Oxide Semiconductor) that saves important configuration information when the computer is turned off. This includes date and time, hard drive configuration, and memory settings as well as other options. See Chapter 1 for more information.

4.   A.   Dynamic random access memory (DRAM) is the type of memory that is expanded when you add memory. Static random access memory (SRAM) is often used for cache memory. See Chapter 2 for more information.

5.   B, C.   The three main types of serial interface are Standard serial, Universal Serial Bus (USB), and FireWire. IEEE 1294 and Enhanced Capabilities Port (ECP) are considered parallel standards. See Chapter 1 for more information.

6.   B.   The FireWire standard was adopted by the Institute of Electronic and Electrical Engineers in 1995 as IEEE 1394. See Chapter 1 for more information.

7.   D.   Direct Rambus (RIMM) is a relatively new technology that uses a fast (up to 800MHz) technology. See Chapter 2 for more information.

8.   D.   The function of a video card is to convert signals from the computer into signals that can be displayed on a monitor or other display device. See Chapter 1 for more information.

9.   C.   Floppy drive cables use a 34-wire ribbon cable with three connectors. See Chapter 3 for more information.

10.   A.   The original IDE specification only supported drives up to 528MB and speeds to 3.3MBps. See Chapter 3 for more information.

11.   D.   SCSI internal devices use a 50-pin ribbon cable. IDE devices use a 40-pin ribbon cable. See Chapter 3 for more information.

12.   D.   Both ends of a SCSI bus must be terminated for signals to be properly maintained. See Chapter 3 for more information.

13.   A.   Direct Memory Access (DMA) channels allow a device to write directly to memory. Bus mastering allows devices to write directly to each other. See Chapter 2 for more information.

14.   B.   IRQ 5 is assigned to LPT2. Most computers do not use LPT2, so this IRQ is typically available for use with other devices. See Chapter 2 for more information.

15. C. The Micro Channel Architecture (MCA) bus was developed by IBM for its PS/2 computers as an upgrade to the ISA architecture. See Chapter 5 for more information.

16. C. Peripheral Component Interconnect (PCI) is a bus type commonly used with Pentium-class computers. This bus type supports 64- and 32-bit data paths and can be used in 486 and Pentium-class computers. See Chapter 2 for more information.

17. B. Type I cards are 3.3mm thick and are commonly used for memory cards. Type II cards are 5mm thick and are used for modems and LAN adapters; they are the most commonly used cards. Type III cards are 10.5mm thick and are commonly used as PC hard disks. See Chapter 7 for more information.

18. B. Common mouse interface standards include serial connectors, bus mouse interfaces, and PS/2 interfaces. See Chapter 1 for more information.

19. C. The maximum resolution supported by VGA is 640 × 480. The SVGA standard supports up to 1024 × 768 resolution. See Chapter 1 for more information.

20. C. Parallel printer cables use a DB-25M connector to connect to the parallel port on the computer and a male Centronics 36 connector to connect to the printer. See Chapter 4 for more information.

21. A. After the laser writes the image to a photosensitive drum, the transfer corona wire charges the paper so that the toner is pulled from the drum to the paper. See Chapter 4 for more information.

22. A. Serial is the slowest option for printer communication. With a serial connection, data is sent one bit at a time with the overhead of communication parameters. See Chapter 4 for more information.

23. D. With a physical star topology, each network device connects to a central hub. This prevents the entire network from failing in the event of a single cable segment failure. The mesh topology is technically more fault tolerant, but is not practical due to the amount of cable that would be required. See Chapter 5 for more information.

24. D. The IEEE 802 workgroup has designated 802.8 as the Fiber Optic Technical Advisory Group. See Chapter 5 for more information.

25. B. Category 3 UTP cable contains four twisted pairs of wires and has three twists per foot. It is only capable of transmitting data at 10Mbps. See Chapter 5 for more information.

26. A. DMA 1 is the default assignment for the hard disk controller. See Chapter 6 for more information.

27. B. Blanks are used to promote proper airflow to the internal components of a computer. Introducing a new hole often results in less airflow, which could cause your computer to overheat and burn out components. See Chapter 6 for more information.

28. D. Each computer manufacturer has a specific way of accessing the computer's CMOS settings. This procedure varies from computer to computer. See Chapter 6 for more information.

29. A. The FORMAT A: /S command is used to create a floppy disk that has the system files installed so that the disk is considered bootable. See Chapter 10 for more information.

30. C. In a DOS environment, the CONFIG.SYS file is the main configuration file for memory management and device configuration. See Chapter 10 for more information.

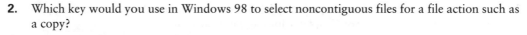

Assessment Test: Operating Systems Technologies Exam

1. Which Windows 98 command-line utility is used to delete files and directories, even if the subdirectories contain additional files?

   A. DEL

   B. REMOVE

   C. DELTREE

   D. REMTREE

2. Which key would you use in Windows 98 to select noncontiguous files for a file action such as a copy?

   A. Ctrl

   B. Shift

   C. Alt

   D. F5

3. Which Windows 98 utility would you use to check a disk drive for disk-related errors?

   A. Disk Cleanup

   B. Disk Manager

   C. Disk Defragmenter

   D. SCANDISK

4. What is the minimum amount of RAM a computer must have to run Windows 98?

   A. 8MB

   B. 12MB

   C. 16MB

   D. 32MB

5. Which of the following commands would you use to partition your disk drives prior to a Windows 98 installation?

   A. PARTDISK

   B. FDISK

   C. MAKEPART

   D. FORMAT

6. What is the purpose of the MSCDEX.EXE file on the Windows 98 startup disk?

    A. Memory manager

    B. Video manager

    C. Provides hard drive support

    D. Provides CD-ROM support

7. Which Windows 95 option would you use if you did not want your system checked for Plug-and-Play devices?

    A. SETUP /pi

    B. SETUP /np

    C. SETUP /-np

    D. SETUP /-npnp

8. Which of the following options best describes what happens when you install Windows 95 with the portable configuration?

    A. No networking is installed.

    B. PCMCIA support and APM support are installed.

    C. The minimum Windows 95 files are installed.

    D. The GNP components are installed.

9. Which of the following options is not an upgrade enhancement when upgrading from Windows 95 (original version, not OSR2) to Windows 98?

    A. Better Internet support through the integration of Internet Explorer

    B. Support for newer hardware such as USB, AGP, and DVD

    C. Support for the FAT32 filesystem

    D. DOS 6 replaced by DOS 7

10. Which Windows 98 startup file allows the rest of the operating system and its programs to interact directly with the system hardware and the system BIOS?

    A. MSDOS.SYS

    B. BIOS.SYS

    C. IO.SYS

    D. OSIO.SYS

11. Which Windows 98 utility is used to easily edit configuration files such as CONFIG.SYS and WIN.INI?

    A. MSCONFIG

    B. WINCONFIG

    C. W98CONFIG

    D. REGEDIT

12. Which Windows 98 utility would you use if you wanted to upgrade a FAT16 partition to a FAT32 partition?

    A. Drive Converter

    B. FDISK

    C. Disk Manager

    D. Disk Administrator

13. How much free disk space is required on a computer that will have Windows 2000 Professional installed?

    A. 650MB

    B. 1.2GB

    C. 1.6GB

    D. 2GB

14. You want to install Windows 2000 on a computer that has just had its hard drive formatted. What command would you use to make Windows 2000 startup disks on a Windows 98 computer that had the Windows 2000 Professional CD?

    A. BOOTDISK

    B. MAKEBOOT

    C. MAKEBT16

    D. MAKEBT32

15. What command would you use to install Windows 2000 Professional on a computer that needs to have the accessibility options installed?

    A. SETUP /A

    B. SETUP /H

    C. WINNT /A

    D. WINNT /H

16. Which of the following operating systems can be upgraded directly to Windows 2000 Professional? (Select all that apply.)

    A. Windows 3.1

    B. Windows 95

    C. Windows 98

    D. Windows NT Workstation 4.0

17. Which Windows 2000 boot file is used in a dual-boot configuration to keep a copy of the DOS or Windows 9x boot sector?

    A. NTBOOT.SYS

    B. NTBOOT.DOS

    C. BOOTSECT.SYS

    D. BOOTSECT.DOS

18. The _____ is used to provide virtual memory functions within Windows.

    A. Kernel

    B. Swap file

    C. GUI

    D. DOS window

19. Which of the following options provides the most reliable way to uninstall a Windows 98 application?

    A. Control Panel ➢ Windows Configuration

    B. Control Panel ➢ System Configuration

    C. Control Panel ➢ Add/Remove Programs

    D. Delete the application files with Windows Explorer and remove any Registry entries

20. Which printer option is used to bypass printer spooling?

    A. Print Directly to the Printer.

    B. Bypass Print Spooling.

    C. Disable Spooling.

    D. This option can only be set by directly editing the Registry.

21. Which feature of Windows helps to conserve disk space by making more disk space available?

    A. File compression

    B. Disk defragmentation

    C. Explorer

    D. Backup

22. Which of the following commands is not located on a Windows 98 startup disk?

    A. FDISK

    B. FORMAT

    C. SYS

    D. DELTREE

23. What command-line utility would you use to create a Windows NT Emergency Repair Disk?

   A. ERD

   B. MAKEERD

   C. RDISK

   D. MAKEDISK

24. Which of the following network protocols is not a default protocol that can be loaded with Windows 98?

   A. NetBEUI

   B. DLP

   C. NWLink

   D. TCP/IP

25. What software must be loaded on a Windows 98 client so that the computer can access other Microsoft network clients?

   A. Microsoft Client for Microsoft Networks

   B. Client Connect

   C. TCP Connect

   D. File and Print Sharing Manager

26. What UNC path would you use to connect to a folder called DATA and a share called ACCT on a computer called WS1 on a domain called ACME?

   A. \\ACME\WS1\ACCT\DATA

   B. \\ACME\WS1\ACCT

   C. \\WS1\ACCT\DATA

   D. \\DATA\ACCT\WS1\ACME

27. Which service is responsible for managing Internet host names and domain names as well as resolving the names to IP addresses?

   A. DHCP

   B. WINS

   C. DNS

   D. SMS

28. What key do you press to access Safe mode when Windows 98 is booting?

   A. F1

   B. F2

   C. F6

   D. F8

29. Which utility would you use to troubleshoot hardware problems on a Windows 98 computer?

   A. Task Manager

   B. Device Manager

   C. SCANDISK

   D. System Services Manager

30. What command is used on Windows 98 computers to check the consistency of the Registry and to back up the Registry?

   A. REGEDIT

   B. REGEDT32

   C. SYSREG

   D. SCANREG

Answers to Assessment Test: Operating Systems Technologies Exam

1. C. The DEL command is used to delete files. RD is used to remove empty directories or subdirectories. DELTREE is used to delete files and directories, even if they contain files. See Chapter 12 for more information.

2. A. The Ctrl key is used to select noncontiguous files; the Shift key is used to select contiguous files. See Chapter 12 for more information.

3. D. SCANDISK is used to check a disk drive for errors or problems. Disk Cleanup is used to delete unneeded files. Disk Defragmenter is used to arrange data so that it is more easily accessed. See Chapter 12 for more information.

4. C. Although 16MB is the bare minimum to load the operating system, Microsoft recommends at least 24–32MB of memory. See Chapter 14 for more information.

5. B. The FDISK utility is used to manage disk partitions. With FDISK you can create, delete, and mark the active partition. See Chapter 14 for more information.

6. D. The MSCDEX.EXE file is used to provide CD-ROM drive support prior to Windows 98 being loaded. You also need to load the proper CD-ROM driver. See Chapter 13 for more information.

7. A. The SETUP /pi switch skips the check for any Plug-and-Play devices. See Chapter 14 for more information.

8. B. When you install a portable or laptop computer and use the portable configuration, PCMCIA support is added as well as Advanced Power Management for when the laptop is running from battery power. See Chapter 14 for more information.

9. D. When you upgrade from Windows 95 to Windows 98, DOS 7 (16-bit) is replaced by DOS32 (32-bit). See Chapter 14 for more information.

10. C. The IO.SYS file allows the rest of the operating system and its programs to interact directly with the system hardware and the system BIOS. Part of this file's code is hardware drivers for common devices (such as serial and communication ports and disk drives). See Chapter 13 for more information.

11. A. The MSCONFIG utility is used to edit configuration files easily and graphically. See Chapter 13 for more information.

12. A. The FAT32 filesystem offers several enhancements to the FAT16 filesystem. You can convert existing FAT16 partitions to FAT32 partitions by using the Drive Converter wizard. See Chapter 18 for more information.

13. D. Windows 2000 installations require a minimum of 2GB of free disk space for the installation process. See Chapter 14 for more information.

14. B. The MAKEBOOT command is used from Windows 9x computers, whereas the MAKEBT32 command is used from Windows NT/2000 computers. See Chapter 13 for more information.

15. C.   Windows 2000 uses the WINNT command to start the installation process. The /A switch specifies that the accessibility options should be installed. See Chapter 14 for more information.

16. B, C, D.   If the hardware requirements for a Windows 3.1 computer meet the Windows 2000 requirements you can install Windows 2000, but there is no supported upgrade path for this operating system. See Chapter 14 for more information.

17. D.   If your computer has an operating system installed and you install Windows 2000 (as opposed to an upgrade), your computer will be capable of dual-booting. The previous operating system's boot information is stored in a file called BOOTSECT.DOS. See Chapter 13 for more information.

18. B.   Swap files are special files used to provide virtual memory to Windows. Windows creates them and manages them. See Chapter 17 for more information.

19. C.   The best and safest way to remove Windows applications is through the Add/Remove Programs applet within Control Panel. See Chapter 12 for more information.

20. A.   When you access a printer's properties, you can bypass printer spooling by selecting the Print Directly to Printer option. See Chapter 15 for more information.

21. A.   File compression compresses individual files to free up drive space. See Chapter 12 for more information.

22. D.   The Windows 98 startup disk is a bootable disk that contains most of the commands needed to set up the computer prior to the Windows 98 installation. However, this disk does not contain the DELTREE command by default. See Chapter 12 for more information.

23. C.   The RDISK command is used in Windows NT computers to create the ERD. This disk is not bootable and is specific to the computer that it was created on. See Chapter 12 for more information.

24. B.   Windows 98 does not support a protocol called DLP. See Chapter 16 for more information.

25. A.   The Microsoft Client for Microsoft Networks software is used to allow the computer to access network resources located on other Microsoft computers. See Chapter 16 for more information.

26. C.   Universal Naming Convention (UNC) paths specify the computer name, followed by the share name, followed by the path. See Chapter 16 for more information.

27. C.   The Domain Name System (DNS) is used to resolve Internet host names or domain names to IP addresses. See Chapter 16 for more information.

28. D.   When prompted during the Windows 98 boot process, press the F8 key to access Windows Safe mode. This mode is useful for troubleshooting purposes. See Chapter 18 for more information.

29. B.   The Device Manager utility can be used to see all of the devices recognized by the Windows 98 operating system, along with their status. See Chapter 18 for more information.

30. D.   The SCANREG command is used to check and back up the Registry. It also attempts to fix any problems it diagnoses with the Registry structure. See Chapter 18 for more information.

A+ Hardware Service Technician Exam

PART

I

Chapter

1

PC Architecture

THE FOLLOWING OBJECTIVES ARE COVERED IN THIS CHAPTER:

✓ 1.1 Identify the names, purpose, and characteristics, of system modules. Recognize these modules by sight or definition.

✓ 1.5 Identify the names, purposes, and performance characteristics, of standardized/common peripheral ports, associated cabling, and their connectors. Recognize ports, cabling, and connectors, by sight.

A *personal computer (PC)* is a computing device made up of many distinct electronic components that all function together in order to accomplish some useful task (such as adding up the numbers in a spreadsheet or helping you write a letter). By this definition, note that we're describing a computer as having many distinct parts that work together. Most computers today are modular. That is, they have components that can be removed and replaced with a component of similar function in order to improve performance. Each component has a very specific function. In this chapter, you will learn about the components that make up a typical PC, what their function is, and how they work together inside the PC.

Unless specifically mentioned otherwise, throughout this book the terms *PC* and *computer* can be used interchangeably.

The components in most computers include:

- The case
- The power supply
- The motherboard
- The processor /CPU
- Memory
- Storage devices
- The adapter cards
- Display devices
- Ports and cables

As you read this chapter, please keep in mind that many of these parts will be covered in more detail in later chapters. Figure 1.1 shows an example of a typical PC and illustrates how some of these parts fit together.

FIGURE 1.1   The components of a typical PC

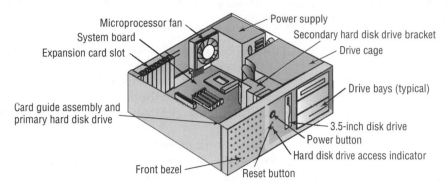

The Case

A *computer case* is the enclosure that encases all the components of a computer. All the computer's components mount to the inside of the case—the case is essentially the mounting platform for all the electronic devices that make up the computer. Typically, cases are square or rectangular boxes, usually beige in color (although the current trend is for all-black cases and matching peripherals), and made of steel, aluminum, or plastic. Figure 1.2 shows an example of a typical computer case.

FIGURE 1.2   A typical computer case

To see some examples of many different styles and colors of computer cases, visit www.pimprig.com.

Cases are primarily categorized in two ways: by their physical size (full tower, mini tower, and so on) and by the type of motherboard they are designed for (such as AT, ATX, or Mini-ATX). We'll talk more about motherboard designs in a later chapter. For now, just remember that in addition to their type, cases must also be designed for the motherboard type. You could have two cases with the same physical dimensions and look, but with completely different internal layouts suitable for their motherboards.

Case styles vary in the way they normally sit (vertically or horizontally) as well as the number of device bays they support. A *device bay* (or *bay* for short) is a large slot into which an expansion device fits (usually a disk drive of some sort). There are two bay sizes: $5\frac{1}{4}$-inch (typically used for CD-ROM and similar drives) and $3\frac{1}{2}$-inch (used for floppy, Zip, and hard disk drives).

Several common PC case styles are in use today. Let's take a quick look at each of these and how they differ. These styles include:

- Full tower
- Mid tower
- Mini tower
- Midi tower
- Desktop
- Slimline
- Proprietary

It is important to note that these are general guidelines. What one manufacturer calls a tower, another may call a mid tower. When you're determining whether a particular case will fit your needs, it is more important to note its physical size and specifications than its labels.

Full Tower

A *full tower case* is a computer case that stands approximately 20–25 inches tall, has at least five $5\frac{1}{4}$-inch drive bays, and is designed to stand vertically on the floor next to a desk (instead of on the desk). This type of case usually has wheels so you can move it easily when you need to unplug a cable or do other work on the computer. Often, because of its sheer size, it will have stabilizing feet to prevent it from tipping over. Figure 1.3 shows an example of a full tower case.

Full tower cases are often used for server computers because of the number of disk drives a server needs to hold. If a computer you are building or buying needs lots of drives, you may want to look into a full tower case.

FIGURE 1.3   A full tower case

Such a case also has a lot of room inside. This space allows components to be separated and provides good airflow around them. People who need many different components inside their computer and need to keep temperatures in check for reliability might also consider a full tower case.

You Get What You Pay For

As with any other product, there are varying degrees of quality and design among full tower cases. You could find two cases that look exactly the same outwardly but are built completely differently. They might differ in metal type and thickness, fastener type, and whether the motherboard mounting plate can be removed to make motherboard mounting easier. As you look at the various types of available cases, remember that generally speaking, you get what you pay for. Cheaper cases are made of thinner gauge metal, use inferior fastening mechanisms, and generally don't have the fit and finish of the more expensive cases. The quality of the case is especially important when you are building the computer yourself.

The full tower case has a couple of drawbacks. The most obvious is sheer size. The case's large size makes it awkward to place anywhere but on the floor next to your desk (which may not always be possible). Also, because full towers are the largest type of case, they are usually the most expensive you can buy.

Mid Tower

A *mid tower case* is a computer case that stands between 16 and 19 inches tall, has at least three 5 1/4-inch drive bays, and is designed to stand vertically either on the floor or on a computer user's desk next to the monitor. This type of case doesn't have quite as much room inside as a full tower case, but it still has significant room for airflow and component layout. And, these cases are less expensive than full tower cases. At the time of this writing (early 2003), the mid tower case is probably the most popular case being sold for computers. Figure 1.4 shows an example of a mid tower case.

FIGURE 1.4   A mid tower case

About the only drawback to a mid tower case is that it doesn't quite fit well on either the floor or a desk. It's a bit too big for a desk and a bit too small for the floor. But, because it is more convenient, most people make room for the case on their desk.

Mini Tower

A *mini tower case* is a computer case that stands about 12 to 15 inches tall, has one or two 5 1/4-inch drive bays, and is designed to stand next to a computer monitor. It was designed to keep the small form factor of a desktop case but also keep the look of a tower, which is more visually appealing. Mini towers are often used in low-end or entry-level computer systems to keep the price down. They are the cheapest possible tower-style case you can buy. Figure 1.5 shows an example of a mini tower case.

FIGURE 1.5   A mini tower case

The main drawback to mini tower cases is their relatively small size. Most components are packed inside these cases with relatively little room for airflow, so the cases tend to be used for computer configurations that don't have many components (housing all-in-one motherboards, for example).

Midi Tower

Midi tower case is a term used to describe a computer case that's between a mid tower and a mini tower in size. The term is used (mostly in Europe) interchangeably with the term *mid tower*. It's primarily a marketing term, and not really a case type. (This case type has nothing to do with Musical Instrument Digital Interface [MIDI], the technology used to interface computers with digital musical instruments.)

Desktop

A *desktop case* is designed to lie horizontally, with at least three 5 1/4-inch bays oriented horizontally and the 3 1/2-inch bays oriented vertically. The original IBM PC used this style of case (although the case for the original PC was much bigger). Currently, the dimensions for a typical full size desktop case are about 15 to 17 inches wide and 5 to 7 inches high. Figure 1.6 shows an example of a desktop case.

FIGURE 1.6   A desktop case

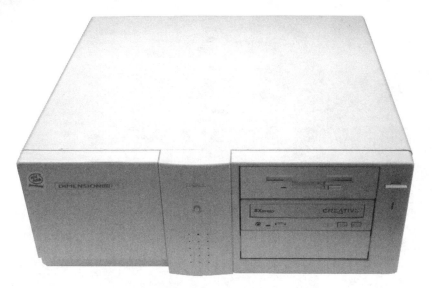

This case design usually saves floor and desktop space and was the design of choice for corporate America for several years for this reason. However, this case costs about the same as a similarly configured mini tower case and has less internal space. Desktop cases also don't necessarily cool as well as their vertically oriented cousins (and it didn't help that people were putting monitors on top, adding to the internal heat level). For these reasons, sales of desktop systems today are much slower compared to similarly configured mini tower versions.

Slimline

Because desktop space is always at a premium, case designers continually develop new designs that hold the most components in the least amount of space. Toward that end, designers have come up with the *slimline case*. A slimline computer case usually has only one 5 1/4-inch drive bay, mounted horizontally (or possibly two, side by side). It's designed to take up the least amount of desktop space, and is the smallest standardized form factor. Figure 1.7 shows an example of one type of slimline case.

FIGURE 1.7   A slimline case

The only advantage of the slimline case is its small size. However, this small size leads to one major disadvantage: heat. Heat shortens the life of computer components, and due to the small size of slimline cases, they require specialized cooling design (and they still do a poor job of cooling). Even so, sales of slimline cases continue to rise as people try to make their PC as unobtrusive on their desk as their pencil cup.

Proprietary Case Designs

The cases we have listed so far are only some of the styles available. Many PC manufacturers (such as Dell and Gateway) don't use standardized cases, but rather manufacture their motherboards and cases together to keep costs down. This results in what are known as proprietary case designs. A *proprietary case* is a computer case that is designed to work with only one particular motherboard and set of components and is typically designed for a specific purpose.

Dell's computers are a perfect example of PCs that use proprietary cases. Although Dell's cases could be classified as mid tower or mini tower, they only work with Dell motherboards designed for the particular case and are therefore usually classified as proprietary.

You can check out some of Dell's computers at www.dell.com.

Comparison of Case Designs

Now that we've discussed the styles of cases, let's take a quick look at the different designs available. Table 1.1 compares the case designs you have read about in this chapter.

TABLE 1.1   Case Design Comparison

Case Design	Number of 5 1/4" Bays	Footprint Size	Cooling	Cost
Full tower	5 or more	Largest	Excellent	$$$$
Mid tower	3 or more	Large	Good to excellent	$$$
Mini tower	1 or 2	Medium	Good	$$
Desktop	3 or more	Medium	Poor to good	$$
Slimline	1	Smallest	Poor	$
Proprietary	Varies	Varies	Varies	Varies

The Power Supply

The computer's components would not be able to operate without power. The device in the computer that provides this power is the *power supply* (Figure 1.8). A power supply converts 110 volt or 220 volt AC current into the DC voltages that a computer needs to operate. These are +3.3 volts DC, +5 volts DC, –5 volts DC (ground), +12 volts DC, –12 volts DC (ground), and +5 volts DC standby. The 3.3 volts DC and +5 volts DC standby voltages are used only by ATX motherboards, not AT motherboards.

You may frequently see *volts DC* abbreviated as *VDC*.

FIGURE 1.8   A power supply

WARNING   Power supplies contain transformers and capacitors that carry *lethal* amounts of current. They are not meant to be serviced. *Do not* attempt to open them or do any work on them.

Power supplies are rated in watts. A *watt* is a unit of power. The higher the number, the more power the power supply (and thus your computer) will use. Most computers use power supplies in the 250- to 400-watt range.

Power Supply Connectors

Power supplies use four types of connectors to power the various devices within the computer (Figure 1.9): floppy drive power connectors, AT system connectors, ATX power connectors, and standard peripheral power connectors. Each has a different appearance and way of connecting to the device. Additionally, each type is used for a specific purpose.

FIGURE 1.9   Standard power supply connectors

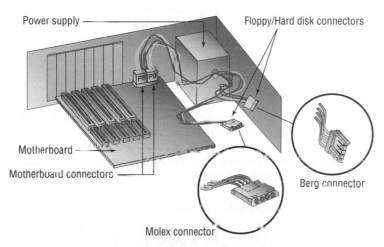

Let's take a quick look at each type of power connector and what it is used for.

Floppy Drive Power Connectors

Floppy drive power connectors are most commonly used to power floppy disk drives and other small form factor devices. This type of connector is smaller and flatter (as shown in Figure 1.10) than any of the other types of power connectors. These connectors are also called *Berg connectors*. Notice that there are four wires going to this connector. These wires carry the 2 voltages used by the motors and logic circuits: +5VDC (carried on the red wire) and +12VDC (carried on the yellow wire) plus 2 black ground wires.

FIGURE 1.10   Floppy drive power connector

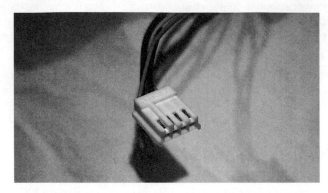

AT System Connectors

The next type of power connector is called the *AT system connector*. There are two 6-wire connectors, labeled P8 and P9 (as shown in Figure 1.11). They connect to an AT-only mother-board and deliver the power that feeds the electronic components on it. These connectors have small tabs on them that interlock with tabs on the power connector on the motherboard. If there are two connectors, you must install them in the correct fashion. To do this (on most systems), place the connectors side by side with their black wires together, and then push the connectors onto the receptacle on the motherboard.

Although it's easy to remove this type of connector from the motherboard, the tabs on the connector make it difficult to reinstall it. Here's a hint: Place the connector at a right angle to the motherboard's connector, interlocking the tabs in their correct positions. Then tilt the connector to the vertical position. The connector will slide into place easily.

FIGURE 1.11   AT Power supply system board connectors

It is important to note that only computers with AT and baby AT motherboards use this type of power connector. Most computers today use the ATX power connector to provide power to the motherboard.

ATX Power Connector

The *ATX system connector* (also known as the *ATX motherboard power connector*) feeds an ATX motherboard. It provides the six voltages required, plus it delivers them all through one connector: a single 20-pin connector. This connector is much easier to work with than the dual connectors of the AT power supply. Figure 1.12 shows an example of an ATX system connector.

FIGURE 1.12   ATX power connector

Standard Peripheral Power Connector

The *standard peripheral power connector* is generally used to power different types of internal disk drives. This type of connector is also called a *Molex connector*. Figure 1.13 shows an example of a standard peripheral power connector. This power connector, though larger than the floppy drive power connector, uses the same wiring color code scheme as the floppy drive connector.

FIGURE 1.13   A standard peripheral power connector

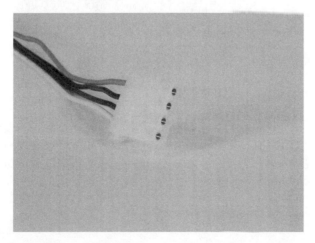

The Motherboard

The spine of the computer is the *motherboard*, otherwise known as the *system board* (and less commonly referred to as the *planar board*). This is the olive green or brown circuit board that lines the bottom of the computer. It is the most important component in the computer because it connects all the other components of a PC together. Figure 1.14 shows a typical PC system board, as seen from above. All other components are attached on this sheet. On the system board, you will find the Central Processing Unit (CPU), underlying circuitry, expansion slots, video components, random access memory (RAM) slots, and a variety of other chips.

FIGURE 1.14   A typical system board

Types of System Boards

There are two major types of system boards: integrated and nonintegrated:

Nonintegrated system board   Each major assembly is installed in the computer as an expansion card. The major assemblies we're talking about are items like the video circuitry, disk controllers, and accessories. Nonintegrated boards can be easily identified because each expansion slot is usually occupied by one of these components.

Integrated system board   Most of the components that would otherwise be installed as expansion cards are integrated into the motherboard circuitry. Integrated system boards were designed for simplicity. Of course, there's a drawback to this simplicity: When one component breaks, you can't just replace the component that's broken; the whole motherboard must be replaced. Although these boards are cheaper to produce, they are more expensive to repair.

With integrated system boards, there is a way around having to replace the whole motherboard when a single component breaks. On some motherboards, you can disable the malfunctioning onboard component (e.g., the sound circuitry) and simply add an expansion card to replace its functions.

System Board Form Factors

Nonintegrated system boards are also classified by their form factor (design): AT, ATX, or NLX (and variants of these). AT system boards are similar to the motherboards found in the original IBM AT. The processor, memory, and expansion slots are all in line with each other. Because of advances in technology, the same number of components that were on the original AT motherboard (now called a *full AT* board) were later compressed into a smaller area. This configuration is known as the *baby AT* configuration.

The baby AT used to be the most commonly used design, but it has some fundamental problems. Because the processor and memory were in line with the expansion slots, only one or two full-length cards could be used. Also, the processor was far from the power supply's cooling fan and therefore tended to overheat unless a heatsink or processor fan was directly attached to it. To overcome the limitations of the baby AT design, the ATX motherboard was designed. The *ATX motherboard* has the processor and memory slots at right angles to the expansion cards. This arrangement puts the processor and memory in line with the fan output of the power supply, allowing the processor to run cooler. And, because those components are not in line with the expansion cards, you can install full-length expansion cards in an ATX motherboard machine. AT motherboards are rarely found for sale because ATX (and its derivatives) are the primary motherboards sold today.

Also, because the AT and ATX have different board layouts for their components and expansion slots, they will have different case layouts for the cutouts where expansion ports and slots go at the back of the case. Therefore, an ATX motherboard will not fit into a case designed for an AT motherboard (and vice versa).

The line between integrated and nonintegrated system boards is quickly becoming blurred. Many of what would normally be called nonintegrated system boards now incorporate the most commonly used circuitry (such as IDE and floppy controllers, serial controllers, and sound cards) onto the motherboard itself.

A fairly new motherboard form factor that has been gaining popularity in the last couple of years is *NLX*. This form factor is used in low-profile case types. NLX motherboards are unique because the expansion slots are placed sideways on a special *riser card* (as shown in Figure 1.15) to use the space optimally.

FIGURE 1.15   An NLX motherboard with riser card

These motherboard form factors are usually found in what are known as *clone* computers (those not manufactured by a Fortune 500 PC company). Some manufacturers (such as Compaq and IBM) design and manufacture their own motherboards, which don't conform to either the AT or ATX standard. This style of motherboard is known as a *proprietary design* motherboard.

There are other motherboard designs, but these are the most popular and also the ones that are covered on the exam.

System Board Components

Now that you understand the basic types of motherboards and their form factors, it's time to look at the components found on the motherboard and their locations relative to each other. Figure 1.16 illustrates many of the following components found on a typical motherboard:

- Expansion slots
- Memory slots
- CPU and processor slots or sockets
- Power connectors
- On-board disk drive connectors
- Keyboard connectors
- Peripheral port and connectors
- BIOS chip

- CMOS battery
- Jumpers and DIP switches
- Firmware

FIGURE 1.16 Components on a motherboard

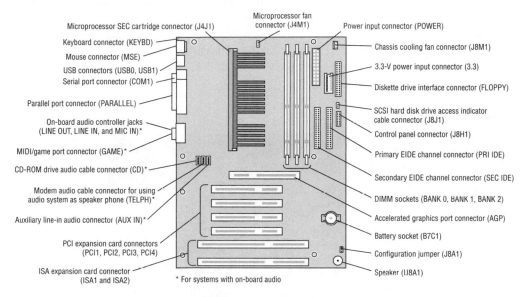

In this subsection, you will learn about the most used components of a motherboard, what they do, and where they are located on the motherboard. We'll show what each component looks like so you can identify it on any motherboard you run across. Note, however, that this is just a brief introduction to the insides of a computer. The details of the various devices in the computer and their impact on computer service practices will be covered in later chapters.

Expansion Slots

The most visible parts of any motherboard are the *expansion slots*. These look like small plastic slots, usually from 3 to 11 inches long and approximately 1/2 inch wide. As their name suggests, these slots are used to install various devices in the computer to expand its capabilities. Some expansion devices that might be installed in these slots include video, network, sound, and disk interface cards.

If you look at the motherboard in your computer, you will more than likely see one of three main types of expansion slots used in computers today:

- ISA
- PCI
- AGP

Each type differs in appearance and function, as you'll learn more about in Chapter 2, "Motherboards, CPUs, and RAM." In this chapter, we will cover how to visually identify the different expansion slots on the motherboard.

ISA Expansion Slots

If you have a computer made before 1997, chances are the motherboard has a few *Industry Standard Architecture (ISA) expansion slots*. They're easily recognizable, because they are usually black and have two parts: one shorter and one longer. Computers made after 1997 generally include a few ISA slots for backward compatibility with old expansion cards (although most computers are phasing them out in favor of PCI). Figure 1.17 shows an example of ISA expansion slots.

FIGURE 1.17   ISA expansion slots

  VL-Bus, an expansion of ISA, was designed to provide 32-bit, processor-direct capabilities to ISA. You will learn more about ISA and VL-Bus in Chapter 2.

PCI Expansion Slots

Most computers made today contain primarily *Peripheral Component Interconnect* (PCI) slots. They are easily recognizable, because they are short (around 3 inches long) and usually white. PCI slots can usually be found in any computer that has a Pentium-class processor or higher. Figure 1.18 shows an example of several PCI expansion slots.

FIGURE 1.18   PCI expansion slots

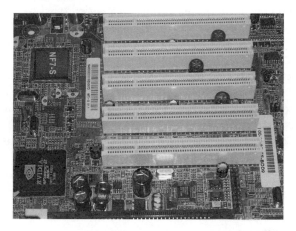

AGP Expansion Slots

Accelerated Graphics Port (AGP) slots are becoming more popular. In the past, if you wanted to use a high-speed, accelerated 3D graphics video card, you had to install the card into an existing PCI or ISA slot. AGP slots were designed to be a direct connection between the video circuitry and the PC's memory. They are also easily recognizable, because they are usually brown, are located right next to the PCI slots on the motherboard, and are shorter than the PCI slots. Figure 1.19 shows an example of an AGP slot, along with a PCI slot for comparison. Notice the difference in length between the two.

FIGURE 1.19   An AGP slot compared to a PCI slot

You will learn more about the details of the various expansion bus types and the expansion cards that go in them in Chapter 2.

Memory Slots

Memory or random access memory (RAM) slots are the next most prolific slots on a motherboard, and they contain the memory chips. Many and varied types of memory are available for PCs today. In this chapter, you will learn the appearance of the slots on the motherboard, so you can identify them. You will learn more about the details of the different types of PC memory in Chapter 2.

For the most part, PCs today use memory chips arranged on a small circuit board. These circuit boards are called *Single Inline Memory Modules (SIMMs)* or *Dual Inline Memory Modules (DIMMs)*, depending on whether there are chips on one side of the circuit board or on both sides, respectively. Aside from the difference in chip placement, memory modules also differ in the number of conductors, or *pins*, that the particular memory module uses. Some common examples include 30-pin, 72-pin, and 168-pin (the 168-pin modules are most often DIMMs). Additionally, laptop memory comes in smaller form factors known as Small Outline DIMMs (SODIMMs). Figure 1.20 shows the popular form factors for the most popular memory chips. Notice how they basically look the same, but the memory module sizes are different.

FIGURE 1.20   Different memory module form factors

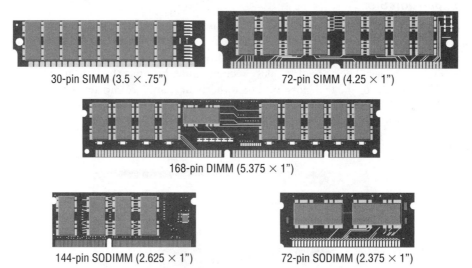

30-pin SIMM (3.5 × .75")   72-pin SIMM (4.25 × 1")

168-pin DIMM (5.375 × 1")

144-pin SODIMM (2.625 × 1")   72-pin SODIMM (2.375 × 1")

Memory slots are easy to identify on a motherboard. SIMMS are usually white; DIMMS are usually black and placed very close together. The number of memory slots varies from motherboard to motherboard, but the appearance of the different slots is similar. Metal pins in the bottom make contact with the soldered tabs on each memory module. Small metal or plastic tabs on each side of the slot keep the memory module securely in its slot.

Central Processing Unit (CPU) and Processor Socket or Slot

The "brain" of any computer is the *Central Processing Unit (CPU)*. This component does all the calculations and performs 90 percent of all the functions of a computer. There are many different types of processors for computers—so many, in fact, that you will learn about them later in this chapter in the section "The Processor/CPU."

Typically, in today's computers, the processor is the easiest component to identify on the motherboard. It is usually the component that has either a fan or a heatsink (sometimes both) attached to it (as shown in Figure 1.21). These devices are used to draw away the heat a processor generates. This is done because heat is the enemy of microelectronics. Theoretically, a Pentium (or higher) processor generates enough heat that without the heatsink, it would self-destruct in a matter of hours.

FIGURE 1.21 A processor with a fan and a processor with a heatsink

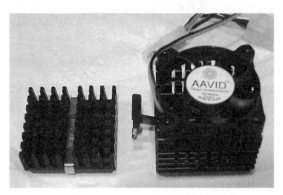

Sockets and slots on the motherboard are as plentiful and varied as processors. Sockets are basically flat and have several rows of holes arranged in a square, as shown in Figure 1.22. The processor slot is another method of connecting a processor to a motherboard, but one into which an Intel Pentium II or Pentium III–class processor on a special expansion card can be inserted (as shown in Figure 1.23). To see which socket type is used for which processors, examine Table 1.2.

FIGURE 1.22 An example of a CPU socket

FIGURE 1.23   A Slot-1 connector slot

TABLE 1.2   Socket Types and the Processors They Support

Connector Type	Processors
Socket 4	Pentium 60/66, Pentium 60/66, OverDrive
Socket 5	Pentium 75-133, Pentium 75+ OverDrive
Socket 6*	DX4, 486 Pentium OverDrive
Socket 7	Pentium 75-200, Pentium 75+ OverDrive, AMD K6-2, K6-3
Socket 8	Pentium Pro
Slot 1	Pentium II, Pentium III, and all SECC and SECC2
Slot 2	Pentium XEON only
Slot A	Early AMD Athlon
Socket 370	PPGA processors, including Celeron
Socket A (socket 462)	AMD Athlon/Thunderbird/XP/Duron
Socket-423	Early Pentium IV
Socket 478	Pentium IV

*Socket 6 was a paper standard only and was never implemented in any systems.

Power Connectors

In addition to these sockets and slots on the motherboard, a special connector (shown in Figure 1.24) allows the motherboard to be connected to the power supply to receive power. This connector is where the ATX power connector (mentioned earlier in this chapter in the section "The Power Supply") plugs in.

FIGURE 1.24   An ATX power connector on a motherboard

On-Board Floppy and Hard Disk Connectors

Almost every computer made today uses some type of disk drive to store data and programs until they are needed. You'll learn the exact details of how they work later in Chapter 3. Most drives need a connection to the motherboard so the computer can "talk" to the disk drive. These connections are known as *drive interfaces*, and there are two main types: *floppy drive interfaces* and *hard disk interfaces*. Floppy disk interfaces allow floppy disk drives to be connected to the motherboard and, similarly, hard disk interfaces do the same for hard disks. When you see them on the motherboard, these interfaces are said to be *on board*, as opposed to being on an expansion card (*off board*). The interfaces consist of circuitry and a port. Most motherboards produced today include both the floppy disk and hard disk interfaces on the motherboard.

The differences and compatibility between the different types of hard disk interfaces will be covered in Chapter 2.

Keyboard Connectors

The most important input device for a PC is the keyboard. All PC motherboards contain a connector (as shown in Figure 1.25) that allows a keyboard to be connected directly to the motherboard through the case. There are two main types of keyboard connectors: AT and PS/2. The AT connector is round, about 1/2 inch in diameter, and has five sockets in the DIN-5 configuration.

FIGURE 1.25   An AT connector on a motherboard

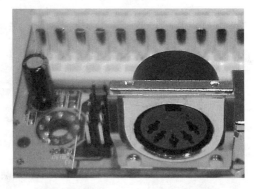

The PS/2 connector (as shown in Figure 1.26) is smaller and more common than the AT connector. Most new PCs you can purchase today contain a PS/2 keyboard connector as well as a PS/2 mouse connector right above it on the motherboard. Compare your PC's keyboard connector with Figures 1.25 and 1.26.

The newest motherboards have color coded the PS/2 mouse and keyboard connectors to make connection of keyboards and mice easier. PS/2 mouse connectors are green (to match the standard green connectors on some mice) and the keyboard connectors are purple.

FIGURE 1.26   A PS/2-style keyboard connector on a motherboard

Peripheral Ports and Connectors

In order for a computer to be useful and have the most functionality, there must be a way to get the data into and out of it. Many different ports are available for this purpose. We will discuss the different types of ports and how they work later in this chapter.

Briefly, the seven most common types of ports you will see on a computer are serial, parallel, Universal Serial Bus (USB), video, Ethernet, sound in/out, and game ports. Figure 1.27 shows an example of the two different types of *serial ports*: 9-pin male and 25-pin male. Figure 1.28 shows a typical *parallel port* (also called a *printer port*, because the most common peripheral connected to it is a printer). *Universal Serial Bus (USB)* ports look slightly different, as shown in Figure 1.29. *Video (SVGA) ports* (as shown in Figure 1.30) are found on motherboards that have built-in video circuitry to allow the computer to display images on a monitor. The video port is typically a 15-pin, three row, female connector. If your motherboard has an Ethernet network adapter integrated into its circuitry, you may see an *Ethernet port* (Figure 1.31), an RJ-45 port, attached to the motherboard. Finally, Figure 1.32 shows an example of a *game port* (also called a *joystick port* because that's the most common device connected to it). Game ports are used to connect peripheral devices to the computer and use a 15-pin female connector.

FIGURE 1.27   Typical 9-pin and 25-pin serial ports

FIGURE 1.28   A parallel port

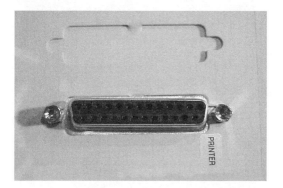

FIGURE 1.29   A Universal Serial Bus (USB) port

FIGURE 1.30   A video port

FIGURE 1.31   An Ethernet port

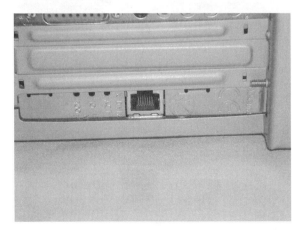

FIGURE 1.32   A game port

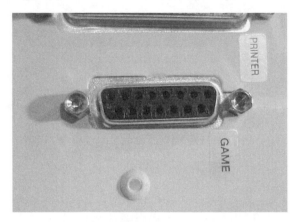

There are two ways of connecting these ports to the motherboard (assuming the circuitry for providing these functions is integrated into the motherboard). The first, called a *dongle connection*, allows you to mount the ports into the computer's case with a special cable (called a *dongle*). The dongle for each port connects to the respective pins on the motherboard for that port (as shown in Figure 1.33).

FIGURE 1.33   Connecting a port to the motherboard with the dongle method

The second method of connecting a peripheral port is known as the *direct-solder method*. With this method, the individual ports are soldered directly to the motherboard. This method is used mostly in integrated motherboards in non-clone machines. Figure 1.34 shows peripheral ports connected to a motherboard with the direct solder method. Notice that there is no cable between the port and the motherboard and that the port is part of the motherboard. As discussed earlier, these onboard ports can be disabled in the BIOS setup if necessary.

FIGURE 1.34   Peripheral ports directly soldered to a motherboard

BIOS Chip

Aside from the processor, the most important chip on the motherboard is the basic input/output system (BIOS) chip. This special memory chip contains the BIOS software that tells the processor how to interact with the rest of the hardware in the computer. The BIOS chip is easily identified: If you have a non-clone computer (Compaq, IBM, HP, and so on), this chip has on it the name of the manufacturer and usually the word *BIOS*. For example, the BIOS chip for a Compaq has something like *Compaq BIOS* printed on it. For clones, the chip usually has a sticker or printing on it from one of the three major BIOS manufacturers (AMI, Phoenix, or Award).

If you can't find the BIOS chip with these guidelines, look for a fairly large chip close to the CPU.

CMOS Battery

Your PC has to keep certain settings when it's turned off and its power cord is unplugged. Some of these settings include:

- Date
- Time
- Hard drive configuration
- Memory

Your PC keeps these settings in a special memory chip called the Complimentary Metal-Oxide Semiconductor (CMOS) chip. Actually, CMOS (usually pronounced *see-moss*) is a type of memory chip; it is the parameter memory for the BIOS. But that doesn't translate into an easy-to-say acronym. So, because it's the most important CMOS chip in the computer, it has come to be called the CMOS.

To keep its settings, the memory must have power constantly. When you shut off a computer, anything that is left in main memory is lost forever. To prevent CMOS from losing its information (and it's rather important that it doesn't), motherboard manufacturers include a small battery called the *CMOS battery* to power the CMOS memory. The batteries come in different shapes and sizes, but they all perform the same function. CMOS batteries come in different styles and sizes, but most look like either large watch batteries or small, cylindrical batteries.

Jumpers and DIP Switches

The last components of the motherboard we will discuss in this section are jumpers and DIP switches. These two devices are used to configure various hardware options on the motherboard. For example, some processors use different voltages (either 3.3 volts or 5 volts). You must set the motherboard to provide the correct voltage for the processor it is using. You do so by changing a setting on the motherboard with either a jumper or a DIP switch. Figure 1.35 shows both a jumper set and DIP switches. Motherboards often have either several jumpers or one bank of DIP switches. Individual jumpers are often labeled with the moniker JP*x* (where *x* is the number of the jumper).

FIGURE 1.35 Jumpers and DIP switches

Jumper   "Rocker-type" DIP switch   "Slide-type" DIP switch

Many of the motherboard settings that were set using jumpers and dip switches are now either automatically detected or set manually in the CMOS setup program.

Firmware

Firmware is the name given to any software that is encoded into a read-only memory (ROM) chip and can be run without extra instructions from the operating system. Most computers use firmware in some limited sense. The best example of firmware is a computer's CMOS setup program, which is used to set the options for the computer's BIOS (time/date and boot options, for example). Also, some expansion cards (like Small Computer System Interface [SCSI] cards) use their own firmware utilities for setting up peripherals.

The Processor/CPU

Now that you've learned the basics of the motherboard, you need to learn about the most important component on the motherboard: the CPU. The role of the CPU, or central processing unit, is to control and direct all the activities of the computer using both external and internal buses. It is a processor chip consisting of an array of *millions* of transistors.

Older CPUs are generally square, with transistors arranged in a Pin Grid Array (PGA). Prior to 1981, chips were found in a rectangle with two rows of 20 pins known as a Dual Inline Package (DIP). See Figure 1.36. There are still integrated circuits that use the DIP form factor. However, the DIP form factor is no longer used for PC CPUs. Most CPUs use either the PGA or the Single Edge Contact Card (SECC) form factor. SECC is essentially a PGA-type socket on a special expansion card.

FIGURE 1.36 DIP and PGA

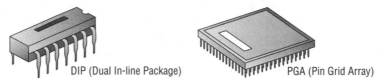

DIP (Dual In-line Package)   PGA (Pin Grid Array)

You can easily identify which component inside the computer is the CPU, because it is a large square lying flat on the motherboard with a very large heatsink and fan (as shown earlier in Figure 1.21). Or, if the CPU is installed in a Slot 1 motherboard, it is a large 1/2-inch thick expansion card with a large heatsink and fan integrated into the package. It is located away from the expansion cards. Figure 1.37 shows the location of the CPU in relation to the other components on a typical ATX motherboard. Notice how prominent the CPU is.

FIGURE 1.37 The location of a CPU inside a typical computer

CPU chips, their manufacturers, and their specifications will be covered in much more detail in Chapter 2.

> ### 🌐 Real World Scenario
>
> #### What's Your CPU?
>
> The surest way to determine which CPU your computer is using is to open the case and view the numbers stamped on the CPU. However, you may be able to get an idea without opening the case, because many manufacturers indicate the type of processor by using a model number that contains some combination of numbers for the processor type and speed. For example, a Whizbang 466 could be a 486 DX 66MHz computer. Similarly, a 75MHz Pentium computer might be labeled Whizbang 575.
>
> Another way to determine a computer's CPU is to save your work, exit any open programs, and restart the computer. Watch closely as the computer returns to its normal state. You should see a notation that tells you what chip you are using. If you are using MS-DOS, you can also run Microsoft Diagnostics to view the processor type (that is, unless your computer has a Pentium, in which case it will report a very fast 486).

Memory

"More memory, more memory, I don't have enough memory!" Today, memory is one of the most popular, easy, and inexpensive ways to upgrade a computer. As the computer's CPU works, it stores information in the computer's memory. The rule of thumb is, the more memory a computer has, the faster it will operate. In this brief section we'll outline the four major types of computer memory: DRAM, SRAM, ROM, and CMOS. (Memory will also be covered in more detail in Chapter 2.)

To identify memory within a computer, look for several thin rows of small circuit boards sitting vertically, packed tightly together near the processor. Figure 1.38 shows where memory is located in a system.

DRAM

DRAM is dynamic random access memory. (This is what most people are talking about when they mention RAM.) When you expand the memory in a computer, you are adding DRAM chips. You use DRAM to expand the memory in the computer because it's cheaper than any other type of memory. Dynamic RAM chips are cheaper to manufacture than other types because they are less complex. *Dynamic* refers to the memory chips' need for a constant update signal (also called a *refresh* signal) in order to keep the information that is written there. If this signal is not received every so often, the information will cease to exist.

SRAM

The *S* in SRAM stands for *static*. Static random access memory doesn't require a refresh signal like DRAM. The chips are more complex and are thus more expensive. However, they are faster. DRAM access times come in at 80 nanoseconds (ns) or more; SRAM has access times of 15 to 20 ns. SRAM is often used for cache memory.

FIGURE 1.38   Location of memory within a system

ROM

ROM stands for read-only memory. It is called read-only because it can't be written to. Once information has been written to the ROM, it can't be changed. ROM is normally used to store the computer's BIOS, because this information normally does not change.

The system ROM in the original IBM PC contained the Power-On Self Test (POST), basic input/output system (BIOS), and cassette BASIC. Later IBM computers and compatibles include everything but the cassette BASIC. The system ROM enables the computer to "pull itself up by its bootstraps," or *boot* (start the operating system).

CMOS

CMOS is a special kind of memory that holds the BIOS configuration settings. CMOS memory is powered by a small battery so the settings are retained when the computer is shut off. The BIOS reads information such as which hard drive types are configured for this computer to use, which drive(s) it should search for boot sectors, and so on. CMOS memory is usually *not* upgradeable in terms of its capacity.

Storage Devices

What good is a computer without a place to put everything? Storage media hold the data being accessed, as well as the files the system needs to operate and data that needs to be saved. The many different types of storage differ in terms of their capacity (how much they can store), access time (how fast the computer can access the information), and the physical type of media used.

These storage devices will be covered in depth in Chapter 3.

Hard Disk Systems

Hard disk systems are used for permanent storage and quick access (Figure 1.39). Hard disks typically reside inside the computer (although there are external and removable hard drives) and can hold more information than other forms of storage.

FIGURE 1.39   A hard disk system

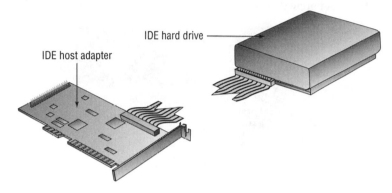

The hard disk system contains three critical components:

Controller   Controls the drive. It understands how the drive operates, sends signals to the various motors in the disk, and receives signals from the sensors inside the drive.

Hard disk   The physical storage medium. Hard disk systems store information on small disks (between three and five inches in diameter) stacked together and placed in an enclosure.

Host adapter   The translator, converting signals from the hard drive and controller to signals the computer can understand.

Most of today's hard disk technologies incorporate the controller and drive into one enclosure. (For more information on disk types, see Chapter 3.) In addition, most motherboards incorporate the host adapter into the motherboard's circuitry.

Floppy Drives

A *floppy disk* is a magnetic storage medium that uses a flexible diskette made of a thin plastic encased in a protective casing. The floppy disk itself enables the information to be transported from one computer to another very easily. There are two main types of floppy disks. The floppy disk, which is 5 1/4 inches square, is the older style; the *diskette* is a disk that is 3 1/2 inches square. Most computers today use diskettes.

Generally speaking, throughout this book we will use the term *floppy drive* to refer to a 3½-inch diskette drive.

A *floppy drive* (shown in Figure 1.40) is used to read and write information to and from these drives. The advantage of these drives is that they allow portability of data (you can transfer data from one computer to another on a diskette). The downside of a floppy disk drive is its limited storage capacity. Whereas a hard drive can store hundreds of gigabytes of information, most floppy disks were designed to store only about one megabyte. Table 1.3 shows the five different floppy disk drive formats you may run into, with five corresponding diskette sizes supported in PC systems.

FIGURE 1.40   A floppy disk drive

Drives that offer anything less than 1.2MB are increasingly rare, because most computers today do not carry the 5¼-inch size. Some are even eliminating floppy drives altogether in favor of larger capacity CD-R and CD-RW drives (as well as other larger capacity removable media drive like the ZIP drive).

TABLE 1.3   Floppy Disk Capacities

Floppy Drive Size	Number of Tracks	Capacity
5¼"	40	360KB
5¼"	80	1.2MB
3½"	80	720KB
3½"	80	1.44MB
3½"	80	2.88MB

CD-ROM Drives

Most computers today have a CD-ROM (Compact Disc Read-Only Memory) drive. The compact disks are virtually the same as those used in CD players. The CD-ROM is used to store data for long-term storage. CD-ROMs are read-only, meaning that once information is written to a CD, it can't be erased or changed. Also, it takes much longer to access the information than it does to access data residing on a hard drive. Why, then, are CD-ROMS so popular? Mainly because they make a great software distribution medium. Programs are always getting larger and requiring more disks to install. Instead of installing a program using 100 floppy disks (a real possibility, believe me), you can use a single CD, which can hold approximately 650MB. (A second reason they are so popular is that CD-ROMs have been standardized across platforms, with the ISO 9660 standard.). Figure 1.41 shows an example of a typical CD-ROM drive.

FIGURE 1.41   A typical CD-ROM drive

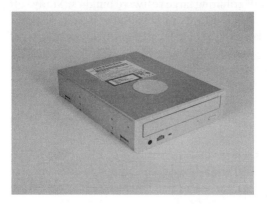

CD-ROM drives are rated in terms of their data transfer speed. The first CD-ROM drives transferred data at the same speed as home audio CD players, 150KBps. Soon after, CD drives rated as "2x" drives that would transfer data at 300KBps appeared (they just increased the spin speed in order to increase the data transfer rate). This system of ratings continued up until the 8x speed was reached. At that point, the CDs were spinning so fast that there was a danger of the CDs flying apart inside the drive. So, although future CD drives used the same rating (as in 16x, 32x, etc.), their rating was expressed in terms of theoretical maximum transfer rate. The drive isn't necessarily spinning faster or transferring data at 40 or 50 times 150KBps, it is just theoretically possible using the drive's increased buffers and so on.

CD-R and CD-RW Drives

CD-Recordable (CD-R) and CD-Rewriteable (CD-RW) drives (also known as CD *burners*) are essentially CD-ROM drives that allow a user to create (or *burn*) their own CD-ROMs. They look very similar to CD-ROM drives, except the front panel of the drive includes a reference to either CD-R or CD-RW.

The difference between these two types of drives is that CD-R drives can write to a CD only once. A CD-RW can erase information from a disk and rewrite to it multiple times. Also, CR-RW drives are rated according to their read, write, and rewrite times. So, instead of a single rating like 40x, they have a rating of 32x-16x-4x, which means it reads at 32x, writes at 16x, and rewrites at 4x.

DVD-ROM Drives

A new type of drive is finding its way into computers: the DVD-ROM drive. You have probably heard of DVD (Digital Versatile Disc) technology in use in many home theater systems. A DVD-ROM drive is basically the same as the DVD player's drive in a home theater system. As a result, a computer equipped with a DVD-ROM drive and the proper video card can play back DVD movies on the monitor.

However, in a computer, a DVD-ROM drive is much more useful. Because DVD-ROMs use slightly different technology than CD-ROMs, they can store up to 4.3GB of data. This makes them a better choice for distributing large software bundles. Many software packages today are so huge they take multiple CD-ROMs to hold all the installation and reference files. A single DVD-ROM, in a double-sided, double-layered configuration, can hold as much as 17GB (as much as 26 regular CD-ROMs).

A DVD-ROM drive looks very similar to a CD-ROM drive. The only difference is the DVD logo on the front of most drives.

DVD Burners

A DVD burner operates it a similar manner to a CD-R or CD-RW drive: It can store large amounts of data onto a DVD. However, there are many different standards for DVD burners; as they mature, we hope a clear leader will emerge.

Other Storage Media

Many additional types of storage are available for PCs today. However, most of them are not covered on the A+ exam, so we'll just discuss them briefly here. Among the other types of storage are Zip drives, tape backup devices, and optical drives. There are also external hard drives like the Kangaru drives, and new storage media like the USB memory sticks that can store 128 to 256MB on a single small plastic device that can be carried on a keychain.

Zip Drives and Jaz Drives

Iomega's Zip and Jaz drives are detachable, external hard disks that are used to store a large volume (around 100MB for the Zip, 1 and 2GB for the Jaz) of data on a single, floppy-sized disk. New Zip drives hold up to 250MB of data. The drives connect to either a parallel port or a special interface card. Internal Zip drives are IDE. Zip and Jaz drives are used primarily to transport large amounts of data from place to place, a task that used to be accomplished with numerous floppies.

Tape Backup Devices

Another form of storage device is the tape backup. Tape backup devices can be installed internally or externally and use a magnetic tape medium instead of disks for storage. They hold much more data than any other medium, but are also much slower. They are primarily used for archival storage.

With hard disks, it's not a matter of "if they fail"; it's "when they fail." So, you must back up the information onto some other storage medium. Tape backup devices are the most common choice in larger enterprises and networks, because they can hold the most data and are the most reliable over the long term.

Optical Drives

Optical drives work by using a laser rather than magnetism to change the characteristics of the storage medium (typically an aluminum-coated plastic disk). Optical drives look similar to and are used for the same applications as Zip drives (archival storage and large file transport). However, optical drives can store more information and have slower access times than Zip drives.

Adapter Cards

An *adapter card* (also known as an *expansion card*) is simply a circuit board you install into a computer to increase the capabilities of that computer. Adapter cards come in many different kinds, but the important thing to note is that no matter what function a card has, the card being installed must match the bus type of the motherboard you are installing it into (for example, you can only install a PCI network card into a PCI expansion slot).

Four of the most common expansion cards that are installed today are as follows:

- Video card
- Network interface card (NIC)
- Modem
- Sound card

Let's take a quick look at each of these cards, their functions, and what they look like.

Video Card

A *video adapter* (more commonly called a *video card*) is the expansion card you put into a computer in order to allow the computer to display information on some kind of monitor or LCD display. A video card also is responsible for converting the data sent to it by the CPU into the pixels, addresses, and other items required for display. Sometimes, video cards can include dedicated chips to perform certain of these functions, thus accelerating the speed of display.

With today's motherboards, most video cards are AGP expansion cards that fit in the AGP slot on a motherboard. Figure 1.42 shows an example of a video card.

FIGURE 1.42   A video expansion card

Network Interface Card (NIC)

A *network interface card (NIC)* is an expansion card that connects a computer to a network so that it can communicate with other computers on that network. It translates the data from the parallel data stream used inside the computer into the serial data stream of packets used on the network. It has a connector for the type of expansion bus on the motherboard (PCI or ISA) as well as a connector for the type of network (such as RJ-45 for UTP or BNC for coax). In addition to the NIC, you need to install software or drivers on the computer in order for the computer to use the network. Figure 1.43 shows an example of a NIC.

FIGURE 1.43   A network interface card (NIC)

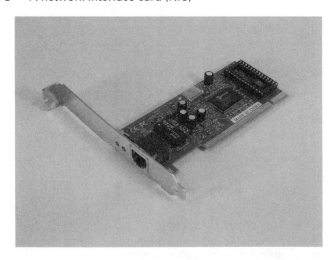

Some computers have NIC circuitry integrated into their motherboards. Therefore, a computer with an integrated NIC wouldn't need to have a NIC expansion card installed, unless you were using the second NIC for load balancing or fault tolerant applications.

Modem

Any computer that connects to the Internet via a dial-up connection needs a modem. A *modem* is a device that converts digital signals from a computer into analog signals that can be transmitted over phone lines and back again. These expansion card devices have one connector for the expansion bus being used (PCI or ISA) and another for connection to the telephone line. Actually, as you can see in Figure 1.44, there are two RJ-11 ports: one for connection to the telephone line and the other for connection to a telephone. This is the case primarily so that putting a computer online still lets someone hook a phone to that wall jack (although they won't be able to use the phone while the computer is connected to the Internet).

FIGURE 1.44   A modem

Sound Card

Just as there are devices to convert computer signals into printouts and video information, there are devices to convert those signals into sound. These devices are known as *sound cards*. Many different manufacturers make sound cards, but the standard has been set by Creative Labs with its SoundBlaster series of cards.

A sound card typically has small, round, 1/8-inch jacks on the back of it for connecting to microphones, headphones, and speakers as well as other sound equipment. Many sound cards also have a DB-15 game port which can be used for either joysticks or Musical Instrument Digital Interface (MIDI) connections (allows a computer to talk to a digital musical instrument, like a digital keyboard or similar). Figure 1.45 shows an example of a sound card.

FIGURE 1.45 A typical sound card

Display Devices

The second way of getting information out of a computer is to use a computer display. Display systems convert computer signals into text and pictures and display them on a TV-like screen. As a matter of fact, the first personal computers used television screens because it was simple to use an existing display technology rather than to develop a new one. Several types of computer displays are in use today, including the TV. All of them use either the same *cathode ray tube (CRT)* technology found in television sets (almost every desktop monitor uses this technology) or the *liquid crystal display (LCD)* technology found on all laptop, notebook, and palmtop computers.

Display Concepts

Several aspects of display systems make each type of display different. However, most display systems work the same way. First, the computer sends a signal to a device called the *video adapter*—an expansion board installed in an expansion bus slot—telling it to display a particular graphic or character. The adapter then *renders* the character for the display—that is, it converts the single instruction into several instructions that tell the display device how to draw the graphic—and sends the instructions to the display device. The primary differences after that are in the type of video adapter you are using (monochrome, EGA/CGA, VGA, or SuperVGA) and the type of display (CRT or LCD).

Video Technologies

Let's first talk about the different types of video technologies. There are four major types: monochrome, EGA/CGA, VGA, and SuperVGA. Each type of video technology differs in two major areas: the highest resolution it supports and the maximum number of colors in its palette.

Resolution depends on how many picture units (called *pixels*) are used to draw the screen. The more pixels, the sharper the image. The resolution is described in terms of the screen's dimensions, indicating how many pixels across and down are used to draw the screen. For example, a resolution of $1,024 \times 768$ means 1,024 pixels across and 768 pixels down were used to draw the pixel grid. The video technology in this example would use 786,432 ($1,024 \times 768 = 786,432$) pixels to draw the screen.

Monochrome

The first video technology for PCs was *monochrome* (from the Latin *mono*, meaning one, and *chroma*, meaning color). This black-and-white video (actually, it was green and white or amber and black) was fine for the main operating system of the day, DOS. DOS didn't have any need for color. Thus, the video adapter was very basic. The first adapter, developed by IBM, was known as the Monochrome Display Adapter (MDA). It could display text but not graphics, and used a resolution of 720×350 pixels.

The Hercules Graphics Card (HGC), introduced by Hercules Computer Technology, had a resolution of 720×350 and could display graphics as well as text. It did this by using two separate modes: a *text mode* that allowed the adapter to optimize its resources for displaying predrawn characters from its onboard library, and a *graphics mode* that optimized the adapter for drawing individual pixels for on-screen graphics. It could switch between these modes on-the-fly. These modes of operation have been included in all graphics adapters since the introduction of the HGC.

EGA and CGA

The next logical step for displays was to add a splash of color. IBM was the first with color, with the introduction of the Color Graphics Adapter (CGA). CGA could display text, but it displayed graphics with a resolution of only 320×200 pixels with four colors. It displayed a better resolution (640×200) with two colors—black and one other color. After a time, people wanted more colors and higher resolution, so IBM responded with the Enhanced Graphics Adapter (EGA). EGA could display 16 colors out of a palette of 64 with a resolution of 320×200 or 640×350 pixels.

These two technologies were the standard for color until the IBM AT was introduced. This PC was to be the standard for performance, so IBM wanted better video technology for it.

VGA

With the PS/2 line of computers, IBM wanted to answer the cry for "more resolution, more colors" by introducing its best video adapter to date: the Video Graphics Array (VGA). This video technology had a whopping 256KB of video memory on board and could display 16 colors at 640×480 pixels or 256 colors at 320×200 pixels. It became widely used and has since become the standard for color PC video; it's the starting point for today's computers, as far as video is concerned. Your computer should use this video technology at minimum.

One unique feature of VGA is that it's an analog board. Thus the 256 colors it uses can be chosen from various shades and hues of a palette of 262,114 colors. VGA sold well mainly because users could choose from almost any color they wanted (or at least one that was close).

SuperVGA

Up to this point, most video standards were set by IBM. IBM made the adapters, everyone bought them, and they became a standard. Some manufacturers didn't like this monopoly and set up the Video Electronics Standards Association (VESA) to try to enhance IBM's video technology and make the enhanced technology a public standard. The result of this work was SuperVGA (SVGA). This new standard was indeed an enhancement, because it could support 256 colors at a resolution of 800×600 (the VESA standard), or $1,024 \times 768$ pixels with 16 colors, or 640×480 with 65,536 colors.

XGA

In the final development in this tale of "keeping up with the Joneses," IBM introduced a new technology in 1991 known as the Extended Graphics Array (XGA). This technology was only available as an Micro Channel Architecture (MCA) expansion board and not as an ISA or EISA board (MCA, ISA, and EISA are expansion bus technologies discussed in more detail in Chapter 2). (It was rather like IBM saying, "So there. You won't let me be the leader, so I'll lead my own team.") XGA could support 256 colors at $1,024 \times 768$ pixels or 65,536 colors at 640×480 pixels. It was a different design, optimized for GUIs like Windows or OS/2. It was also an *interlaced* technology, meaning that rather than scan every line one at a time to create the image, it scanned every other line on each pass, using the phenomenon known as *persistence of vision* to produce what appears to our eyes as a continuous image.

Table 1.4 details the various video technologies, their resolutions, and the color palettes they support.

TABLE 1.4   Video Display Adapter Comparison

Name	Resolutions	Colors
Monochrome Display Adapter (MDA)	720×350	Mono (text only)
Hercules Graphics Card (HGC)	720×350	Mono (text and graphics)
Color Graphics Adapter (CGA)	320×200	4
	640×200	2
Enhanced Graphics Adapter (EGA)	320×200	16
	640×350	
Video Graphics Array (VGA)	640×480	16
	320×200	256

TABLE 1.4 Video Display Adapter Comparison *(continued)*

Name	Resolutions	Colors
SuperVGA (SVGA)	640 × 480	65,536
	800 × 600	256
	1,024 × 768	16
Extended Graphics Array (XGA)	800 × 600	65,536
	1,024 × 768	256

Monitors

As we have already mentioned, a monitor contains a CRT. But how does it work? Basically, a device called an *electron gun* shoots electrons toward the back side of the monitor screen (see Figure 1.46). The back of the screen is coated with special chemicals (called *phosphors*) that glow when electrons strike them. This beam of electrons scans across the monitor from left to right and top to bottom to create the image.

FIGURE 1.46 How a monitor works

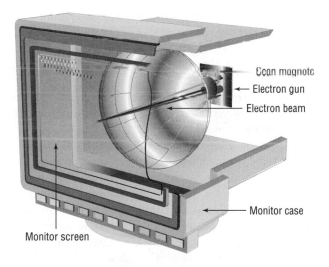

Scan magnets
Electron gun
Electron beam
Monitor case
Monitor screen

There are two ways to measure a monitor's image quality:

Dot pitch The shortest distance between two dots of the same color on the monitor. Usually given in fractions of a millimeter (mm), the dot pitch tells how "sharp" the picture is. The lower the number, the closer together the pixels are, and, thus, the sharper the image. An average dot pitch is 0.28mm. Anything smaller than 0.28mm is considered great.

Refresh rate   (Technically called the *vertical scan frequency*.) Specifies how many times in one second the scanning beam of electrons redraws the screen. The phosphors stay bright for only a fraction of a second, so they must constantly be hit with electrons to stay lit. Given in draws per second, or Hertz, the refresh rate specifies how much energy is being put into keeping the screen lit. The standard refresh rate is 60Hz for VGA. However, some monitors have a refresh rate of 72Hz, which is much easier on the eyes (less flicker is perceived).

One note about monitors that may seem rather obvious: You must use a video card that supports the type of monitor you are using. For example, you can't use a CGA monitor on a VGA adapter.

 To use a 72Hz monitor, your video card must also support the 72Hz refresh rate. Most video cards sold today support this faster 72Hz refresh rate but are configured as 60Hz out of the box. If you intend to use the 72Hz rate, you must configure the card to do so. Check the documentation that came with the card for details on how to configure it.

Liquid Crystal Displays (LCDs)

Portable computers were originally designed to be compact versions of their bigger brothers. They crammed all the components of the big desktop computers into a small, suitcase-like box called (laughably) a *portable computer*. No matter what the designers did to reduce the size of the computer, the display remained as large as the desktop version's. That is, until an inventor found that when he passed an electric current through a semicrystalline liquid, the crystals aligned themselves with the current. It was found that by combining transistors with these liquid crystals, patterns could be formed. These patterns could represent numbers or letters. The first application of these *liquid crystal displays* (LCDs) was the LCD watch. It was rather bulky, but it was cool.

As LCD elements got smaller, the detail of the patterns became greater, until one day someone thought to make a computer screen out of several of these elements. This screen was very light compared to computer monitors of the day, and it consumed little power. It could easily be added to a portable computer to reduce the weight by as much as 30 pounds. As the components got smaller, so did the computer, and the laptop computer was born.

LCDs are not just limited to laptops; desktop versions of LCD displays are available as well. They use the same technologies as their laptop counterparts but on a much larger scale. Plus, these LCDs are available in either analog or digital interfaces for the desktop computer. The analog interface is exactly the same as the interface used for most monitors. All digital signals from the computer are converted into analog signals by the video card, which are then sent along the same 15-pin connector as a monitor. Digital LCDs, on the other hand, are directly driven by the video card's internal circuitry. They require the video card to be able to support digital output (through the use of a Digital Visual Interface, or DVI, connector). The advantage is that since the video signal never goes from digital to analog, there is no conversion-related quality loss. Digital displays are generally sharper than their analog counterparts.

Two major types of LCD displays are used today: active matrix screen and passive matrix screen. The main differences lie in the quality of the image. However, both types use lighting behind the LCD panel to make the screen easier to view:

Active matrix   An active matrix screen works in a similar manner to the LCD watch. The screen is made up of several individual LCD pixels. A transistor behind each pixel, when switched on, activates two electrodes that align the crystals and turn the pixel dark. This type of display is very crisp and easy to look at. The major disadvantage of an active matrix screen is that it requires large amounts of power to operate all the transistors. Even with the backlight turned off, the screen can still consume battery power at an alarming rate. Most laptops with active matrix screens can't operate on a battery for more than two hours.

Passive matrix   Within the passive matrix screen are two rows of transistors: one at the top, another at the side. When the computer's video circuit wants to turn on a particular pixel (turn it black), it sends a signal to the x- and y-coordinate transistors for that pixel, thus turning them on. This then causes voltage lines from each axis to intersect at the desired coordinates, turning the desired pixel black. Figure 1.47 illustrates this concept.

FIGURE 1.47   A passive matrix display

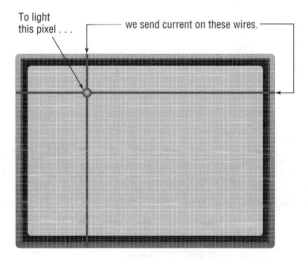

The main difference between active matrix and passive matrix is image quality. Because the computer takes a millisecond or two to light the coordinates for a pixel in passive matrix displays, the response of the screen to rapid changes is poor, causing, for example, an effect known as *submarining*: On a computer with a passive matrix display, if you move the mouse pointer rapidly from one location to another, it will disappear from the first location and reappear in the new location without appearing anywhere in between.

To keep the quality of the image on an LCD the best, the screen must be cleaned often. Liquid crystal displays are typically coated with a clear plastic covering. This covering commonly gets dirtied by fingerprints as well as a generous coating of dust. The best way to clean the LCD lens coating is to wipe it off occasionally with a damp cloth. Doing so will ensure that the images stay crisp and clear.

Ports and Cables

Now that you've learned the various types of items found in a computer, let's discuss the various types of ports and cables used with computers. A *port* is a generic name for any connector on a computer into which a cable can be plugged. A *cable* is simply a way of connecting a peripheral or other device to a computer using multiple copper or fiber optic conductors inside a common wrapping or sheath. Typically, cables connect two ports, one on the computer and one on some other device.

Let's take a quick look at some of the different styles of port connector types as well as peripheral port and cable types. We'll begin by looking at peripheral port connector types.

Peripheral Port Connector Types

Computer ports are interfaces that allow other devices to be connected to a computer. Their appearance varies widely, depending on their function. In this section we'll examine the following types of peripheral ports:

- DB-series
- RJ-series
- Other types

DB-Series

DB connectors, the most common style of connector found on computers today, are typically designated with DB-*n*, where the letter *n* is replaced by the number of connectors. DB connectors are usually shaped like a trapezoid, as you can see in Figure 1.48. The nice part about these connectors is that only one orientation is possible. If you try to connect them upside down or try to connect a male connector to another male connector, they just won't go together, and the connection can't be made. Table 1.5 lists common DB-series ports and connectors as well as their most common uses.

FIGURE 1.48   DB series ports and connectors

On the left is a 15-pin video port, in the center is a 25-pin female printer port, and on the right is a 9-pin male serial port.

TABLE 1.5 Common DB-Series Connectors

Connector	Gender	Use
DB-9	Male	Serial port
DB-9	Female	Connector on a serial cable
DB-25	Male	Serial port
DB-25	Female	Parallel port, or connector on a serial cable
DB-15	Female	Game port
DB-15	Male	Connector on a game peripheral cable
DB-15HD	Female	Video port (HD has three rows of 5 pins as opposed to two rows)
DB-15HD	Male	Connector on a monitor cable

RJ-Series

Registered jack (RJ) connectors are most often used in telecommunications. Figure 1.49 shows the two most common examples of RJ ports and connectors: RJ-11 and RJ-45. RJ-11 connectors are used most often in telephone hookups; your home phone jack is probably an RJ-11 jack or port. RJ-45 connectors, on the other hand, are most commonly found on Ethernet networks that use twisted pair cabling.

FIGURE 1.49 RJ ports and connectors

On the left in this picture is an RJ-11 connector and on the right is an RJ-45 connector. Notice the size difference.

As you can see, RJ connectors are typically square with multiple gold contacts on the top (flat) side. A small locking tab on the bottom prevents the connector and cable from falling or being pulled out of the jack accidentally.

Other

A few other ports are used with computers today. These ports include:

- Universal Serial Bus (USB)
- IEEE 1394 (FireWire)
- Infrared
- RCA
- PS/2 (mini DIN)
- Centronics

Let's look at each one and how it is used.

Universal Serial Bus (USB)

Most computers built after 1997 have one or two flat ports in place of one DB-9 serial port. These ports are Universal Serial Bus (USB) ports, and they are used for connecting multiple (up to 128) peripherals to one computer through a single port (and use of multiport peripheral *hubs*). USB version 1.1 supported data rates as high as 12Mbps (1.5MBps). The newest version, USB 2.0, supports data rates as high as 480Mbps (60MBps). Figure 1.50 shows an example of a USB port.

FIGURE 1.50   A USB port

 The newest version of USB, USB 2.0, uses the same physical connection as the original USB, but it is much higher in transfer rates. You can tell if a computer supports USB 2.0 by looking for the red and blue "High Speed USB" graphic somewhere on the computer (or on the box).

Because of USB's higher transfer rate, flexibility, and ease of use, most devices that in the past used serial interfaces now come with USB interfaces. It's rare to see a newly introduced PC accessory with a standard serial interface cable. For example, PC cameras (like the Logitech QuickCam) used to come as standard serial-only interfaces. Now you can only buy them with USB interfaces.

IEEE 1394 (FireWire)

Recently, one port has been slowly creeping into the mainstream and is seen more and more often on desktop PCs. That port is the IEEE 1394 port (shown in Figure 1.51), more commonly known as a *FireWire* port. Its popularity is due to its ease of use and very high (400Mbps) transmission rates. Originally developed by Apple, it was standardized by IEEE in 1995 as IEEE 1394. It is most often used as a way to get digital video into a PC so it can be edited with digital video editing tools. At the time of this writing, many Apple iMac models include a FireWire port. You can see FireWire on many PCs and laptops.

FIGURE 1.51   A FireWire port on a PC

Infrared

Increasing numbers of people are getting fed up with being tethered to their computers by cords. As a result, many computers (especially portable computing devices like laptops and PDAs) are now using infrared ports to send and receive data. An *infrared port* is a small port on the computer that allows data to be sent and received using electromagnetic radiation in the infrared band. The infrared port itself is a small, dark square of plastic (usually a very dark maroon) and can typically be found on the front of a PC or on the side of a laptop or portable. Figure 1.52 shows an example of an infrared port.

FIGURE 1.52   An infrared port

Infrared ports send and receive data at a very slow rate (maximum speed on PC infrared ports is less than 4Mbps). Most infrared ports on PCs that have them support the *Infrared Data Association (IrDA) standard*, which outlines a standard way of transmitting and receiving information via infrared so that devices can communicate with each other.

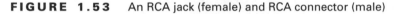

 More information on the IrDA standard can be found at the organization's website: www.irda.org.

Noted that although infrared is a wireless technology, most infrared communications (especially those that conform to the IrDA standards) are line-of-sight only and take place within a short distance (typically less than 4 meters). Infrared is typically used for point-to-point communications like controlling the volume on a device with a handheld remote control.

RCA

The RCA jack (shown in Figure 1.53) was developed by the RCA Victor company in the late 1940s for use with its phonographs. You bought a phonograph, connected the RCA jack on the back of your phonograph to the RCA jack on the back of your radio or television, and used the speaker and amplifier in the radio or television to listen to records. It made phonographs cheaper to produce and had the added bonus of making sure everyone had an RCA Victor radio or television (or at the very least, one with the RCA jack on the back). Either way, RCA made money.

FIGURE 1.53   An RCA jack (female) and RCA connector (male)

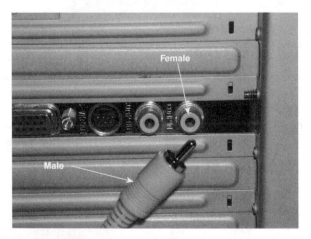

Today, RCA jacks and connectors are used to transmit both audio and video information. Typically, when you see an RCA connector on a PC video card (next to a DB-15HD connector), it's for composite video output (output to a television or VCR).

PS/2 (Keyboard and Mouse)

Another common port, as mentioned earlier, is the PS/2 port. A *PS/2 port* (also known as a *mini-DIN 6* connector) is a mouse and keyboard interface port first found on the IBM PS/2 (hence the name). It is smaller than previous interfaces (the DIN-5 keyboard port and serial mouse connector), and thus its popularity increased quickly. Figure 1.54 shows examples of both PS/2 keyboard and mouse ports. You can tell the difference because usually the keyboard port is purple and the mouse port is green. Also, typically there are small graphics of a keyboard and mouse, respectively, imprinted next to the ports.

FIGURE 1.54   PS/2 keyboard and mouse ports

Centronics

The last type of port connector is the Centronics connector. It has a unique shape, as shown in Figure 1.55. It consists of a central connection bar surrounding by an outer shielding ring. The Centronics connector is primarily used in parallel printer connections and SCSI interfaces. It is most often found on peripherals, not on computers themselves (except in the case of some older SCSI interface cards).

FIGURE 1.55   A Centronics connector

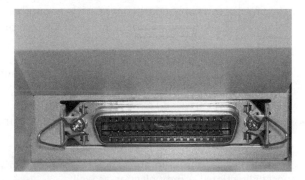

Common Peripheral Interfaces and Cables

An *interface* is a method of connecting two dissimilar items together. A *peripheral interface* is a method of connecting a peripheral or accessory to a computer, including the specification of cabling, connector type, speed, and method of communication used.

The most common interfaces used in PCs today include:

- Parallel
- Serial
- USB
- IEEE 1394 (FireWire)
- Infrared
- RCA
- PS/2

For each type, let's look at the cabling and connector used as well as the type(s) of peripherals that are connected.

Parallel

The most popular type of interface available on computers today is the parallel interface. Parallel communications take the interstate approach to data communications. Normally, interstate travel is faster than driving on city roads. This is the case mainly because you can fit multiple cars going the same direction on the same highway by using multiple lanes. On the return trip, you take a similar path, but on a completely separate road. The *parallel interface* transfers data eight bits at a time over eight separate transmit wires inside a parallel cable (one bit per wire). Normal parallel interfaces use a DB-25 female connector on the computer to transfer data to peripherals.

The most common use of the parallel interface is printer communication. There are three major types: standard, bidirectional, and enhanced parallel ports. Let's look at the differences between the three.

Standard Parallel Ports

The standard parallel port only transmits data *out* of the computer. It cannot receive data (except for a single wire carrying a Ready signal). This parallel port came with the original IBM PC, XT, and AT. It can transmit data at 150KBps and is commonly used to transmit data to printers. This technology also has a maximum transmission distance of 10 feet.

Bidirectional Parallel Ports

As its name suggests, the bidirectional parallel port has one important advantage over a standard parallel port: It can both transmit and receive data. These parallel ports are capable of interfacing with devices like external CD-ROM drives and external parallel port backup drives (Zip, Jaz, and tape drives). Most computers made since 1994 have a bidirectional parallel port.

 In order for bidirectional communication to occur properly, the cable must support bidirectional communication as well.

Enhanced Parallel Ports

As more people began using parallel ports to interface with devices other than printers, they started to notice that the available speed wasn't good enough. Double-speed CD-ROM drives had a transfer rate of 300KBps, but the parallel port could transfer data at only 150KBps, thus limiting the speed at which a computer could retrieve data from an external device. To solve that problem, the Institute of Electrical and Electronics Engineers (IEEE) came up with a standard for enhanced parallel ports called IEEE 1284. The IEEE 1284 standard provides for greater data transfer speeds and the ability to send memory addresses as well as data through a parallel port. This standard allows the parallel port to theoretically act as an extension to the main bus. In addition, these ports are backward compatible with the standard and bidirectional ports.

There are two implementations of IEEE 1284: ECP parallel ports and EPP parallel ports. An *Enhanced Capabilities Port* (ECP port) is designed to transfer data at high speeds to printers. It uses a DMA channel and a buffer to increase printing performance. An *Enhanced Parallel Port* (EPP port) increases bidirectional throughput from 150KBps to anywhere from 600KBps to 1.5MBps.

The cable must also have full support for IEEE 1284 in order for proper communications to occur in both directions and at rated speeds.

Parallel Interfaces and Cables

Most parallel interfaces use a DB-25 female connector as shown earlier in this chapter. Most parallel cables use a DB-25 male connector on one end and either a DB-25 male connector or Centronics-36 connector on the other. Printer cables typically used the DB-25M to Centronics-36 configuration. Inside a parallel cable, eight wires are used for transmitting data, so one byte can be transmitted at a time. Figure 1.56 shows an example of a typical parallel cable (in this case, a printer cable).

FIGURE 1.56   A typical parallel cable

Serial

If parallel communications are similar to taking the interstate, then serial communications are similar to taking a country road. In serial communications, bits of data are sent one after another (single file, if you will) down one wire, and they return on a different wire in the same cable. Three main types of serial interfaces are available today: standard serial, Universal Serial Bus (USB), and FireWire.

Standard Serial

Almost every computer made since the original IBM PC has at least one serial port. They are easily identified because they have either a DB-9 male (shown in Figure 1.57) or DB-25 male port. Standard serial ports have a maximum data transmission speed of 57Kbps and a maximum cable length of 50 feet.

FIGURE 1.57 Standard DB-9 male serial ports

Serial cables come in two common wiring configurations, *standard serial cable* and *null modem serial cable*. A standard serial cable is used to hook various peripherals like modems and printers to a computer. A null modem serial cable is used to hook two computers together without a modem. The transmit wires on one end are wired to the receive pins on the other side, so it's as if a modem connection existed between the two computers, but without the need for a modem. Figures 1.58 and 1.59 show the wiring differences (the *pinouts*) between a standard serial cable and a null modem cable. In the null modem diagram, notice how the transmit (tx) pins on one end are wired to the receive (rx) pins on the other.

FIGURE 1.58 A standard serial cable wiring diagram

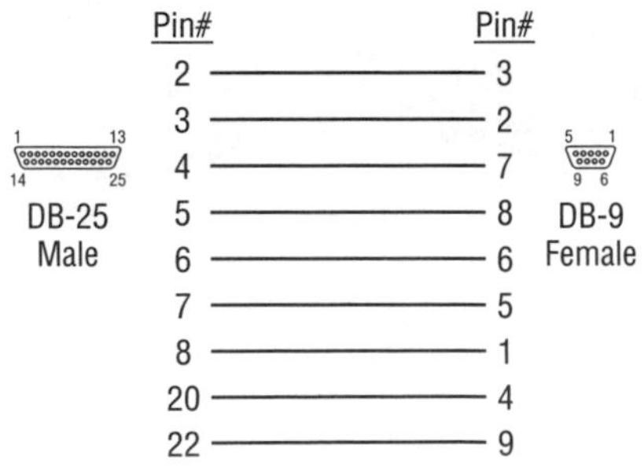

Pin#		Pin#
2	————	3
3	————	2
4	————	7
5	————	8
6	————	6
7	————	5
8	————	1
20	————	4
22	————	9

DB-25 Male / DB-9 Female

Finally, because of the two different device connectors (DB-9 male and DB-25 male), serial cables have a few different configurations. Table 1.6 shows the most common serial cable configurations.

FIGURE 1.59 A null modem serial cable wiring diagram

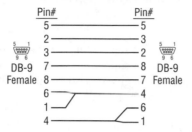

TABLE 1.6 Common Serial Cable Configurations

1st Connector	2nd Connector	Description
DB-9 female	DB-25 male	Standard modem cable
DB-9 female	DB-9 male	Standard serial extension cable
DB-9 female	DB-9 female	Null modem cable
DB-25 female	DB-25 female	Null modem cable
DB-25 female	DB-25 male	Standard serial cable or standard serial extension cable

Universal Serial Bus (USB)

The USB interface is very straightforward. Essentially, it was designed to be plug and play—just plug in the peripheral, and it should work (providing the software is installed to support it). The USB cable is simple: a USB male connector on each end (as shown in Figure 1.60). Sometimes manufacturers put a mini connector on one end to make it fit the form factor of the device that needs a USB connection. These connectors vary widely, and we won't cover them here.

FIGURE 1.60 A USB cable

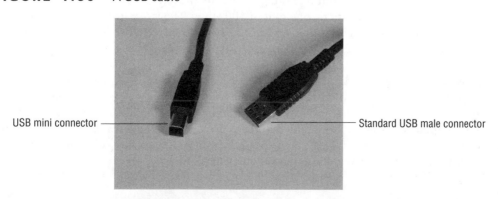

USB mini connector —   — Standard USB male connector

A USB cable will go into a USB port only one way. If the cable is not going into the port properly, try flipping it over.

One part of the USB interface specification that makes it so appealing is the fact that if your computer runs out of USB ports, you can simply plug a device known as a *USB hub* in to one of your computer's USB ports, which will give you several more USB ports from one USB port. Figure 1.61 shows an example of a USB hub.

FIGURE 1.61   A USB hub

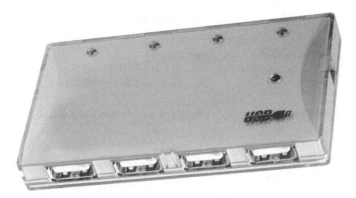

USB cables are used to connect a wide variety of peripherals to computers, including mice, digital cameras, printers, and scanners. USB's simplicity of use and ease of expansion make it an excellent interface for just about any kind of peripheral.

For more information on USB, check out www.usb.org.

IEEE 1394 (FireWire)

The IEEE 1394 interface is about one thing: speed. Its first iteration, now known as Fire-Wire 400, has a maximum data throughput of 400Mbps. The latest iteration, FireWire 800, has a maximum data throughput of 800Mbps. It caries data at that speed over a maximum cable length of 4.5 meters (FireWire 400) and 100 meters (FireWire 800 over fiber optic cables).

FireWire (also known as i.Link in Sony's parlance) uses a very special type of cable, as shown in Figure 1.62. It is difficult to mistake this cable for anything but a FireWire cable.

Although most people think of FireWire as a tool for connecting their digital camcorders to their computers, it's much more than that. Because of its high data transfer rate, it is being used more and more as a universal, high-speed data interface for things like hard drives, CD-ROM drives, and digital video editing equipment.

FIGURE 1.62   A FireWire (IEEE 1394) cable

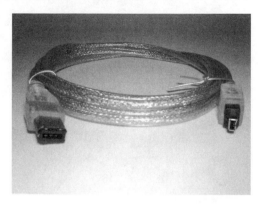

RCA

The RCA cable is simple. There are two connectors, usually male, one on each end of the cable. The male connector connects to the female connector on the equipment. Figure 1.63 shows an example of an RCA cable. An RCA male to RCA female connector is also available; it's used to extend the reach of audio or video signals.

FIGURE 1.63   An RCA cable

The RCA male connectors on a connection cable are sometimes plated in gold to increase their corrosion resistance and to improve longevity.

PS/2 (Keyboard and Mouse)

The final interface we'll discuss is the PS/2 interface for mice and keyboards. Essentially, it is the same connector for the cables from both items: a male mini-Din 6 connector. Most keyboards today still use the PS/2 interface, whereas most mice are gravitating toward the USB interface (especially optical mice). However, mice that have USB cables still may include a special USB-to-PS/2 adapter so they can be used with the PS/2 interface. Figure 1.64 shows an example of a PS/2 keyboard cable.

FIGURE 1.64   A PS/2 keyboard cable

Most often, PS/2 cables have only one connector, because the other end is connected directly to the device being plugged in. The only exception is PS/2 extension cables used to extend the length of a PS/2 device's cable.

Summary

In this chapter, we took a brief tour of the components of a PC. You learned about the different components that make up a PC, including the case, motherboard, drives and storage, expansion cards, and display devices. In addition, we discussed common peripheral ports and cables and their appearance. You learned what each of these items looks like and how they function. In the next chapter, we'll go into more depth about the inner workings of a PC.

Key Terms

Before you take the exam, be certain you are familiar with the following terms:

Accelerated Graphics Port (AGP)	baby AT
adapter card	Berg connector
AT system connector	cable
ATX motherboard	CD-Recordable (CD-R) and CD-Rewriteable (CD-RW) drives
ATX system connector	Central Processing Unit (CPU)

CMOS battery	graphics mode
computer case	hard disk interface
DB connector	Industry Standard Architecture (ISA) expansion slot
desktop case	Infrared Data Association (IrDA) standard
device bay	infrared port
direct-solder method	integrated system board
diskette	interface
dongle	interlaced
dongle connection	joystick port
dot pitch	mid tower case
drive interface	midi tower case
Dual Inline Memory Modules (DIMMs)	mini tower case
electron gun	modem
Enhanced Capabilities Port	Molex connector
Enhanced Parallel Port	monochrome
Ethernet port	motherboard
expansion card	network interface card (NIC)
expansion slot	nonintegrated system board
FireWire	null modem serial cable
Firmware	parallel interface
floppy disk	parallel port
floppy drive	peripheral interface
floppy drive interface	personal computer (PC)
floppy drive power connector	pin
full AT	pixel
full tower case	planar board
game port	port

power supply	Single Inline Memory Module (SIMM)
proprietary case	standard peripheral power connector
proprietary design	standard serial cable
PS/2 port	system board
refresh rate	text mode
registered jack (RJ)	Universal Serial Bus (USB)
riser card	Video (SVGA) port
serial port	watt

Review Questions

1. Which computer component contains all the circuitry necessary for *all* components or devices to communicate with each other?

   A. Motherboard

   B. Adapter card

   C. Hard drive

   D. Expansion bus

2. Which case type is typically used for servers?

   A. Mini tower

   B. Mid tower

   C. Full tower

   D. Desktop

3. What was the original name for a monitor?

   A. Video Display Unit

   B. CRT

   C. LCD

   D. Optical Display Unit

4. Which motherboard design style is the most popular?

   A. ATX

   B. AT

   C. Baby AT

   D. NLX

5. Which motherboard socket type is used on the Pentium IV chip?

   A. Slot 1

   B. Socket A

   C. Socket 370

   D. Socket 478

6. What is the maximum amount of data that can be stored on a 5$\frac{1}{4}$-inch floppy disk?

   A. 360KB

   B. 1.2MB

   C. 320KB

   D. 720KB

7. Which is another term for the motherboard?

    A. A fiberglass board

    B. A planar board

    C. A bus system

    D. An IBM system board XR125

8. Which of the following is used to store data and programs for repeated use? Information can be added and deleted at will, and it does *not* lose its data when power is removed.

    A. Hard drive

    B. RAM

    C. Internal cache memory

    D. ROM

9. Which motherboard socket type is used with the AMD Athlon XP?

    A. Slot 1

    B. Socket A

    C. Socket 370

    D. Socket 478

10. You want to plug a keyboard in to the back of a computer. You know that you need to plug the keyboard cable into a PS/2 port. Which style of port is the PS/2?

    A. RJ-11

    B. DB-9

    C. Din 5

    D. Mini-DIN 6

11. What are the five voltages produced by a common PCs power supply? (Select all that apply.)

    A. +3.3VDC

    B. −3.3VDC

    C. +5VDC

    D. −5VDC

    E. +12VDC

    F. −12VDC

    G. +110VAC

    H. −110VAC

12. What is the maximum speed of USB 2.0 in Mbps?

   A. 1.5

   B. 12

   C. 60

   D. 480

13. If you wanted to connect a LapLink cable (a parallel data transfer cable) so that you could upload and download files from a computer, which type of parallel port(s) does your computer need to have? (Select all that apply.)

   A. Standard

   B. Bidirectional

   C. EPP

   D. ECP

14. What peripheral port type was originally developed by Apple and is currently primarily used for digital video transfers?

   A. DVD

   B. USB

   C. IEEE 1394

   D. IEEE 1284

15. What peripheral port type is expandable using a hub, operates at 1.5MBps, and is used to connect various devices (from printers to cameras) to PCs?

   A. DVD 1.0

   B. USB 1.0

   C. IEEE 1394

   D. IEEE 1284

16. Which peripheral port type was designed to transfer data at high speeds to printers only?

   A. DVD

   B. USB

   C. IEEE 1394

   D. IEEE 1284

17. Which motherboard form factor places expansion slots on a special riser card and is used in low-profile PCs?

   A. AT

   B. Baby AT

   C. ATX

   D. NLX

18. Which Intel processor type(s) use the SEC when installed into a motherboard? (Select all that apply.)

  A. AMD Athlon

  B. 486

  C. Pentium

  D. Pentium II

19. Which of the following can a DVD-ROM store in addition to movies? (Select all that apply.)

  A. Audio files

  B. Word documents

  C. Digital photos

  D. All of the above

20. What type of expansion slot is almost always used for high-speed, 3D graphics video cards?

  A. USB

  B. AGP

  C. PCI

  D. ISA

Answers to Review Questions

1. A.   The spine of the computer is the system board, otherwise known as the motherboard. On the motherboard you will find the CPU, underlying circuitry, expansion slots, video components, RAM slots, and various other chips.

2. C.   Because they have the most expansion room and room for disk drives, full tower cases are used for most servers. In some cases (such as small offices) the other case styles can be used, but they are less common.

3. B.   The first display systems were nothing more than fancy black-and-white TV monitors called CRTs.

4. A.   Although all the motherboard design styles listed are in use today, the ATX motherboard style (and its derivatives) is the most popular design style.

5. D.   Most Pentium IV chips use the Socket 478 motherboard CPU socket.

6. B.   Today, drives that offer anything less than 1.2MB are increasingly rare, because most computers do not carry the 5¼-inch size.

7. B.   The spine of the computer is the system board, otherwise known as the motherboard and less commonly referred to as the planar board.

8. A.   A hard drive stores data on a magnetic medium, which does not lose its information after the power is removed, and which can be repeatedly written to and erased.

9. B.   The Socket A motherboard socket is used primarily with AMD processors, including the Athlon XP.

10. D.   A PS/2 port is also known as a Mini-DIN 6 connector.

11. A, C, D, E, F.   A PC's power supply produces +3.3VDC, +5VDC, –5VDC, +12VDC, and –12VDC from 110VAC.

12. D.   The USB 2.0 spec provides for a maximum speed of 480 megabits per second (Mbps—not megabytes per second, or MBps).

13. B, C, D.   Bidirectional parallel port can both transmit and receive data. An ECP was designed to transfer data at high speeds. EPP parallel ports provide for greater transfer speeds and the ability to send memory addresses as well as data through a parallel port.

14. C.   The 1394 standard provides for greater data transfer speeds and the ability to send memory addresses as well as data through a serial port.

15. B.   USBs are used to connect multiple peripherals to one computer through a single port. They support data transfer rates as high as 1.5MBps (for USB 1.0, which is the option listed here).

16. D.   IEEE 1284 standard defines the ECP parallel port to use a DMA channel and the buffer to be able to transfer data at high speeds to printers.

17. D.   The NLX form factor places expansion slots on a special riser card and is used in low-profile PCs.

18. D.   The unique thing about the Pentium II is that it uses a Single Edge Connector (SEC) to attach to the motherboard instead of the standard PGA package.

19. D.   The DVD-ROM can store many types of data as well as movies. In the computer world, data can be audio files, Word documents, digital photos, and many other things.

20. B.   Although technically PCI and ISA could be used for video adapters, AGP was specifically designed for the use of high-speed, 3D graphic video cards.

Motherboards, CPUs, and RAM

THE FOLLOWING OBJECTIVES ARE COVERED IN THIS CHAPTER:

- ✓ 4.1 Distinguish between the popular CPU chips in terms of their basic characteristics.

- ✓ 4.2 Identify the types of RAM (Random Access Memory), form factors, and operational characteristics. Determine banking and speed requirements under given scenarios.

- ✓ 4.3 Identify the most popular types of motherboards, their components, and their architecture (bus structures).

In the previous chapter, you learned about the basic components that make up a PC, and we provided a brief overview of each component. In this chapter, we'll delve into a select few of the components and teach you more about them. Beginning with motherboard architecture, you will learn about the intricate workings of a motherboard, what they look like, and what each of the items does. You will also learn about the various CPUs used in PCs today and their specifications. Finally, you will learn about the different memory types. These three components most affect performance in a system, so we will discuss them together.

Motherboard Architecture

As discussed in Chapter 1, "PC Architecture," the motherboard is the largest component of a computer. All parts of a computer attach to the motherboard, so you can think of it as being like the computer's "spine." The motherboard is responsible not only for physically connecting the various parts of a computer together, but also for making the data and electrical connections.

In this section, you will learn about the components that make each motherboard different, as well as the functions those components perform. These components are as follows:

- Chipset
- Memory slot types
- Communication ports
- Processor sockets
- Cache memory
- Bus architecture
- BIOS

Chipsets

A *chipset* is a collection of chips or circuits that perform interface and peripheral functions for the processor. This collection of chips is usually the circuitry that provides interfaces for memory, expansion cards, and onboard peripherals, and generally dictates how a motherboard talks to the installed peripherals.

Chipsets are usually given a name and model number by the original manufacturer. For example, if a motherboard has a VIA KT7 chipset, you know that the circuitry for controlling peripherals was designed by VIA and given the designation KT7. Typically, this information also tells you that a particular chipset has a certain set of features (such as onboard video of a certain type or brand, onboard audio of a particular type, and so on).

Chipsets can be made up of one or several integrated circuit chips. Intel-based motherboards typically use two chips, whereas SiS chipsets typically use one. To know for sure, you must check the manufacturer's documentation.

The functions of chipsets can be divided into two major functional groups: *Northbridge* and *Southbridge*. Figure 2.1 shows a diagram of typical motherboard chipsets (both Northbridge and Southbridge) and the components with which they interface; notice which components interface with which parts of the chipset.

FIGURE 2.1   A typical motherboard chipset illustration

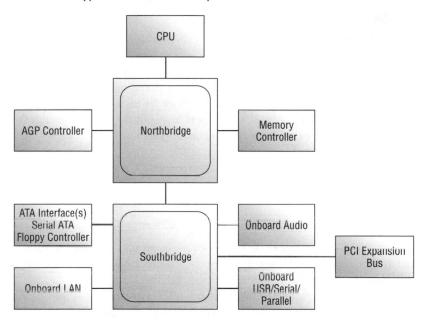

Northbridge

The Northbridge subset of motherboard chipsets includes circuitry or chips that perform one very important function: management of high-speed peripheral communications. The Northbridge subset is primarily responsible for AGP communications and processor-to-memory communications. Therefore, much of the true performance of a PC relies on the performance of the Northbridge chipset and its communication with the peripherals it controls.

The term Northbridge chipset doesn't refer to an actual chipset by that name. We are referring to the set of chips or circuits that make up the Northbridge subset of a motherboard's chipset.

Communication between the CPU and memory occurs over what is known as the *frontside bus*, which is a set of *signal pathways* between the CPU and main memory. The *backside bus*, on the other hand, is a set of signal pathways between the CPU and level 2 *cache memory* (if present).

Northbridge chipsets also manage communication between the Southbridge chipset (discussed next) and the rest of the computer. In addition, if a motherboard has onboard video circuitry (especially if it needs direct access to main memory), that circuitry is found within the Northbridge chipset.

It might help you to remember that the Northbridge plays traffic cop with the computer's data, to ensure the data gets where it needs to go in a timely fashion.

Southbridge

The Southbridge chipset, as mentioned earlier, is responsible for providing support to the myriad of onboard peripherals (PS/2, parallel, IDE, and so on), managing their communications with the rest of the computer and the resources given to them. Most motherboards today have integrated PS/2, USB, parallel, and serial ports. Some of the optional features handled by the Southbridge include LAN, audio, infrared, and FireWire (IEEE 1394). When first integrated, the audio quality of onboard audio was marginal at best; but the latest offerings (such as the AC '97 audio chipset) rival Creative Labs in sound quality and number of features (even including Dolby Digital Theater Surround technology).

The Southbridge chipset is also responsible for managing communications with the other expansion buses, such as PCI, USB, and legacy buses.

Memory

As mentioned in Chapter 1, memory is the part of the computer that stores information as it is being used and manipulated. Generally, memory is temporary storage, because when the power is removed, the information the memory was holding disappears.

We'll discuss the types of memory later in this chapter. However, it is important that you know how motherboards differ based on the types of memory they support.

Each motherboard supports memory based on the speed of the frontside bus and the memory's form factor. For example, if the motherboard's frontside bus is rated at a maximum speed of 133MHz, and you install memory that is rated at 100MHz, the memory will operate at only 100MHz, thus making the computer operate more slowly than it could. In their specifications, most motherboards list the type(s) of memory they support as well as their maximum speeds.

The memory slots on a motherboard are designed for particular chip form factors or styles. The most popular form factors are as follows:

- SIMM
- DIMM

- RIMM
- SoDIMM
- MicroDIMM

SIMM

The first type of RAM packaging that is commonly seen in computers is called the *Single Inline Memory Module (SIMM)*. SIMMs were developed because DIP chips took up too much real estate on the logic board. Someone got the idea to put several DIP chips on a small circuit board and then make that board easily removable. Figure 2.2 shows several versions (there are many configurations).

FIGURE 2.2 Single Inline Memory Modules (SIMMs)

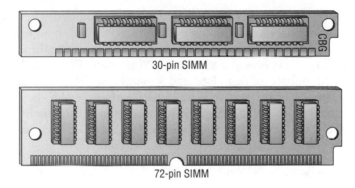

30-pin SIMM

72-pin SIMM

The first SIMMs had nine small DIP chips on them and took up less room than the older DIP memory chips, because four SIMMs could be installed in the same space as one row of DIP chips. In order to accomplish this, the SIMMs were installed very close to each other at approximately a 45° angle. This design was also meant to prevent chip creep, which happens when the chips that have been placed in sockets on the board begin to slowly move out of their sockets (due to the repeated heating and cooling of the system board).

Here's an old technician's trick: If an older computer (PC or XT) is having strange, irreproducible problems, open the case and reseat all socketed chips by pressing them down securely in their sockets. Most of the time, that will solve the problem. If it does, then the problem was caused by chip creep.

Most memory chips are 32-bit; so are several of the processors. You have a problem, however, when you have 32-bit memory chips and a 64-bit processor. To solve it, you must either install the SIMMs in pairs (always installing multiples of two—this is especially true for Pentium computers) or change to a DIMM installation (discussed next).

DIMM

Another type of memory package is known as a *Dual Inline Memory Module (DIMM)*. DIMMs are 64-bit memory modules, as opposed to 32-bit SIMMs. Generally, the DIMMs you'll run into will have 168 pins (as shown in Figure 2.3).

FIGURE 2.3   A Dual Inline Memory Module (DIMM)

RIMM

When the Intel 850 chipset for the Pentium 4 chip was first introduced, a new type of memory technology was also introduced, called Rambus DRAM (RDRAM). It multiplies the number of parallel signal pathways from processor to memory, thus increasing the capacity. It uses a special type of memory slot known as a *RIMM slot*. You would think that this is an acronym, like SIMM or DIMM, but according to Intel and Rambus (the company that developed this technology), *RIMM* is a trademarked word that indicates the type of memory module.

The memory module contains 184 pins, and the corresponding motherboard memory slot contains 184 contacts. The module has two aluminum sheaths called *heat spreaders* that cover the chips on the module to help prevent overheating (see Figure 2.4).

FIGURE 2.4   A Rambus RIMM module

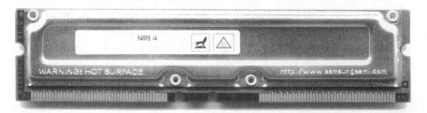

Because of their higher cost, RIMMs aren't as popular as other types of memory modules. Many people who use Pentium 4s use chipsets (like the Apollo Pro 133A) that support other types of memory that don't use RIMMs.

SoDIMM

Notebook computers and other computers that require much smaller components don't use standard RAM packages like the SIMM or the DIMM. Instead, they use a much smaller memory form factor called a *Small Outline DIMM (SoDIMM)*. SoDIMMs are available in both 32-bit (72-pin) and 64-bit (144-pin) configurations. Figure 2.5 shows an example of the 144-pin variety.

FIGURE 2.5   144-pin SoDIMM

MicroDIMM

The newest, and smallest, RAM form factor is the *MicroDIMM*. The MicroDIMM is an extremely small RAM form factor. In fact, it is over 50 percent smaller than a SoDIMM—only 45.5 millimeters (about 1.75 inches) long and 30 millimeters (about 1.2 inches, a bit bigger than a quarter) wide. It was designed for the ultralight and portable subnotebook style of computer (like those based on the Transmeta Crusoe processor). The module has 144 pins and is similar to a DIMM in that it uses 64-bit memory modules.

Communication Ports

Most motherboards have different kinds of expansion ports, as detailed in Chapter 1, so we won't go into much detail here. Be aware that many motherboards differ based on the kinds of communication and expansion ports found on board. Examples include:

- Serial
- USB
- Parallel

- IEEE 1394/FireWire
- Infrared
- LAN
- Video

For a more detailed explanation of these ports, refer to Chapter 1.

Processor Sockets

Motherboards are also differentiated from each other by the type(s) of processor(s) they support. This is designated by the type of *processor socket* or slot on the motherboard. The Central Processing Unit (CPU, also called the processor) must make physical and electrical contact with the motherboard in order to be used. It does so by using a processor socket (or slot). The processor socket serves two purposes: It physically holds the processor in place through the use of clips and/or friction, and it allows the motherboard to electrically connect to the processor.

Processor sockets and slots differ widely. They are primarily differentiated by the number of pins on the processor they connect to (or the number of contacts they make), the physical layout of the socket or slot, and the type of processor they support. In this section, you will learn the most common type of processor sockets and slots and the key differences between them. The most common include:

- Socket 7
- Socket 8
- Slot 1
- Slot A
- Socket 370
- Slot 2
- Socket A
- Socket 423
- Socket 478

Although there were earlier sockets (Sockets 1 through 6), the most current are Socket 7 and above; so, we will focus on them.

Socket 7

The *Socket 7* processor socket is a motherboard processor socket that supports Intel Pentium processors and AMD processors with 321 pins in a *Zero Insertion Force (ZIF)* socket. A Zero

Insertion Force socket is just that—it takes no effort to insert the processor into the socket. The processor drops into place and is held there by the friction of two sliding plates. Figure 2.6 shows an example of a Socket 7 processor socket.

FIGURE 2.6   A Socket 7 processor socket

Supported processors for the Socket 7 include all 2.5V to 3.3V Pentiums at 75 to 233MHz, AMD K5 through K6, and Cyrix 6×86 P120 through P233.

After the Socket 7, a new Super 7 processor socket was released that gave an approximate 10 percent performance boost over the Socket 7 (due to faster access to L2 cache and memory). The Super 7 supports all Socket 7 processors.

Socket 8

The *Socket 8* processor socket is the physical and electrical specification for the 387-pin ZIF socket used by various Intel Pentium Pro and Pentium II overdrive processors. The pins are arranged in a 24×26 matrix that is more rectangular than the Socket 7. Voltages used with the Socket 8 fall in the range of 3.1 to 3.3V. Figure 2.7 shows an example of a Socket 8 processor socket.

FIGURE 2.7   A Socket 8 processor socket

The Intel Pentium Pro 150 to 200MHz and Pentium II Overdrive 300 to 333MHz use this socket.

Slot 1

Until the development of this processor slot, all processors were ether directly soldered to the motherboard or used a socket with holes for the pins on the processor. However, with the development of the Pentium II, all that changed. Intel designed the *Single Edge Processor Package (SEPP)* and the *Single Edge Contact Cartridge (SECC)* to contain its processors. The SECC is very similar to an SEPP; the SECC is essentially an SEPP encased in a plastic cartridge. Figure 2.8 shows examples of both an SEPP and SECC; note the plastic covering on the SECC.

FIGURE 2.8   An SEPP and an SECC

SEPP

SECC

The SEPP has the processor on a small circuit board (called a daughterboard) with 242 small fingers, or leads. This daughterboard is then inserted into a special slot on the motherboard called a *Slot 1 connector*. The functionality is similar to that of a processor socket, but the connector is similar to an expansion slot.

Intel went to this Slot 1 design initially because it allowed for higher bus rates than its predecessor, the Socket 7. However, the large form factor tended to limit airflow and make overheating more of an issue. Figure 2.9 shows an example of a Slot 1 connector on a motherboard.

FIGURE 2.9 A Slot 1 connector on a motherboard

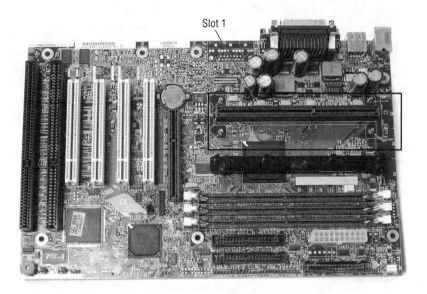

Slot 1

The Slot 1 connector supports SEPP and SECC processors including the Intel Celeron, Pentium II, and some Pentium IIIs.

Slot A

About the same time the Slot 1 connector began to gain use, AMD developed its own card and slot processor interface: the *Slot A*. The Slot A looks the same as a Slot 1, and they are physically the same size, so the two are compatible mechanically (the processor from one can fit into the other). However, electronically they are completely different, so they are ultimately incompatible.

The Slot A allows for a higher bus rate than a Socket 7 or Super 7 and is used primarily with the AMD K7 processor family.

Socket 370

Once Intel changed designs from sockets to slots, there was an uproar. People were used to the socket design's ease of use and didn't want to use a slot. So, Intel developed the *Socket 370* (named for the fact that it uses 370 pins). People could then buy a version of the CPU that worked in a socket. Plus, it cost less. Figure 2.10 shows an example of a Socket 370.

FIGURE 2.10   An example of a Socket 370

The Socket 370 socket type supports Intel Pentium II and III as well as several Celeron processors. Intel then announced that it was going to develop most new processors on the Socket 370 platform, instead of the developing them on the slot 1 platform.

One problem arose, however. A few people had bought Slot 1 motherboards, but wanted to use the new processors. So, a device called a *slocket* was developed. It's basically a circuit board that plugs into a Slot 1, but it has a socket (typically a Socket 370) on it. This device allows Socket 370-based chips to be plugged into Slot 1 motherboards.

During the time the Socket 370 was released, many motherboard manufacturers released motherboards with both a Slot 1 and Socket 370 to satisfy demand for both socket types with a single motherboard.

Slot 2

After the Slot 1 configuration, another Intel processor slot specification was developed. This Slot 2 specification specified a 330-lead edge connector for the processor card. It functions similarly to the Slot 1 setup, but has more leads on the connector between the card and the motherboard slot; it also allows the CPU to communicate with the L2 cache at the CPU's full clock speed, thus enhancing performance. Slot 2 was primarily designed for use in high-end workstations and servers and is used with SECC Pentium III and Xeon processors.

Socket A

One of the most popular socket interfaces today is the *Socket A*. This socket style consists of 462 pins and looks similar to other socket types; however, the Socket A primarily supports AMD Athlon, Duron, and Athlon XP processors. Figure 2.11 shows an example of a Socket A motherboard socket.

FIGURE 2.11 A Socket A motherboard CPU socket

Socket 423

With the introduction of the Pentium 4 came (you guessed it) another motherboard CPU socket style. The *Socket 423* is for Intel processors with 423 pins; it was introduced alongside the Intel 850 motherboard chipset. It is currently used with the first releases of the Pentium 4 from 1.3 to 2GHz. Figure 2.12 shows an example of a Socket 423 socket.

FIGURE 2.12 A Socket 423 socket

Socket 478

The latest development as of this writing is the *Socket 478*, which is used with Pentium 4 processors. Intel has announced that it will use this platform for this processor until it's retired. The Socket 478 is similar in appearance to the Socket 423, but it supports more pins for extra capabilities. Figure 2.13 shows an example of the Socket 478.

FIGURE 2.13   A Socket 478 socket

External Cache Memory (Level 2)

In addition to the CPU type, motherboards can be differentiated by the availability of cache memory. When a CPU goes to get either its program instructions or data, it always has to get them from main memory. However, some systems have a small amount of very fast SRAM memory called cache memory between the processor and main memory, which is used to store the most frequently accessed information. Because it's faster than main memory and contains the most frequently used information, cache memory increases the performance of any system.

There are two types of cache memory: on-chip (also called internal or *L1 cache*) and off-chip (also called external or *L2 cache*). Internal cache memory is found on Intel Pentium, Pentium Pro, and Pentium II processors, as well as on other manufacturers' chips. The original Pentium contains two 8KB on-chip caches: one for program instructions and the other for data. External cache memory is typically either a SIMM of SRAM or a separate expansion board that installs in a special processor-direct bus.

To get the most out of cache memory, if you have the option of installing an external cache card onto your motherboard, do it. It can give you as much as a 25 percent boost in speed.

Bus Architectures

A bus is a set of signal pathways that, as we have already alluded to, allow information and signals to travel between components inside or outside of a computer. There are three types of buses inside a computer: the *external bus*, the *address bus*, and the *data bus*.

The external bus allows the CPU to talk to the other devices in the computer and vice versa. It is called that because it's external to the CPU. When the CPU wants to talk to a device, it uses the address bus to do so. It selects the particular memory address the device is using and uses the address bus to write to that address. When the device wants to send information back to the microprocessor, it uses the data bus.

In this chapter, we'll focus primarily on the most common type of external bus—the expansion bus.

Expansion Bus Features

The *expansion bus* lets you expand a computer using a modular approach. Whenever you need to add something to the computer, you plug specially made circuit boards into the connectors (also known as *expansion slots*) on the expansion bus. The devices on these circuit boards can then communicate with the CPU and are semipermanently part of the computer.

The Connector, or Slot

The connector slots are made up of several tiny copper finger slots, the row of very narrow channels that grab the fingers on the expansion circuit boards. These finger slots connect to copper pathways on the motherboard. Each set of pathways has a specific function. One set of pathways provides the voltages needed to power the expansion card (Typically +3.3V, +5, +12, and ground). Another set of pathways makes up the data bus, transmitting data back to the processor. A third set makes up the address bus, allowing the device to be addressed through a set of I/O addresses. Finally, there are other lines for different functions like interrupts, *Direct Memory Access (DMA)* channels, and clock signals.

Interrupt Lines

Interrupts are special lines connected directly to the processor. A device uses an interrupt to get the attention of the CPU when it needs to. It's rather like the cord you use to signal the driver when you need to get off at the next stop when you're a passenger on an actual bus. Just as you would use the "stop requested" cord to send a signal when you need the bus driver's attention, a computer device uses the *interrupt request (IRQ)* line to get the attention of the CPU.

Each type of bus includes several interrupt request lines. Lines 0 and 1 (corresponding to IRQ 0 and IRQ 1, respectively) are used by the processor for special purposes. The other lines are allocated to the various pieces of hardware installed in the computer. Not every line is used; an average PC usually has at least one free IRQ line. When you configure a device for a computer, you must tell it which IRQ to use to get the attention of the processor. If two devices use the same IRQ line, the processor will get confused and neither device will work. This is true with older expansion cards (for example, 8 bit, ISA), but PCI expansion cards can share IRQs.

DMA Channels

The bus also allows devices to bypass the processor and write their information directly into main memory. This feature is known as *Direct Memory Access (DMA)*. Each type of bus has a different number of channels that can be used for DMA. If two devices are set to the same DMA channel, neither device will write information to memory correctly; thus, neither device will work.

I/O Addresses

Each bus type has a set of lines that are used to allow the CPU to send instructions to the devices installed in the bus's slots. Each device is given its own unique communication line to the CPU. These lines are called *input/output (I/O) addresses* and they function a lot like unidirectional mailboxes. If you want to send an invitation for people to come to a party, you write a message and address it to the mailbox of the person you want to invite. When the person receives the message, they read it and return some information, perhaps via another method (such as a phone call). The I/O addresses (also called *I/O ports* or *hardware ports*) work in a similar fashion. When the CPU wants a device to do something, it sends a signal to a particular I/O address telling the device what to do. The device then responds via the data bus or DMA channels.

Clock Signals

Each computer has a built-in *clock signal*. There are two types: the *CPU clock* and the *bus clock*. The former dictates how fast the CPU can run; the latter indicates how fast the bus can transmit information. (In the first PCs, the CPU clock was also the clock for the bus.) The speed of the clocks is measured by how fast they "tick" and is given in millions of cycles per second (megahertz [MHz]) or billions of cycles per second (gigahertz [GHz]). The bus or the CPU can perform an operation only on the occurrence of a tick signal. Think of the clock signal as a type of metronome that keeps the processor in time.

Bus Mastering

With DMA channels, a device can write directly to memory. But what if a device needs to read or write directly to another device, such as the hard disk? For this purpose, bus designers came up with *bus mastering*. This feature allows a device to distract the CPU for a moment, take control of the bus, and read from or write information to the device. This feature can greatly improve performance of the device. Some buses can use several bus-mastering devices. The more bus-mastering devices, the faster the bus can operate.

Now that we have discussed the basic expansion bus concepts, we'll use these concepts to describe each of the different types of buses.

ISA

The design of the IBM AT processor specified a processor with a 16-bit data path. A new bus was needed for this processor because the old bus caused the traffic jam scenario described earlier. The new bus design was a 16-bit bus, and it was given the same name as the computer it was designed for: the *AT bus*. It was also known as the *Industry Standard Architecture (ISA) bus*.

The ISA bus is easily identifiable by the presence of the small bus connector behind the 8-bit connector, as shown in Figure 2.14. This additional connector adds several signal lines to make the bus a full 16-bit bus. The other connector is a regular 8-bit bus connector. The ISA bus has eight more interrupts than the 8-bit bus and four additional DMA channels. This bus can also operate at nearly twice the speed of the older, 8-bit bus (ISA can run at 8MHz, and Turbo models can run as fast as 10MHz reliably). In addition, this bus can use one bus-mastering device, if necessary.

FIGURE 2.14 An ISA bus connector

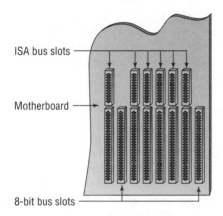

ISA expansion cards use a connector similar to the 8-bit bus but with the additional connector for the 16-bit data and address lines (see Figure 2.15).

FIGURE 2.15 An ISA bus expansion card

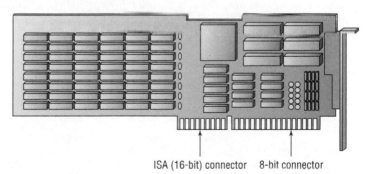

One interesting thing about the ISA bus is that it is backward compatible with the older, 8-bit bus. ISA bus slots are basically 8-bit slots with the extra signal lines required to make them 16-bit on a second connector. Expansion cards made for the PC's 8-bit bus can be inserted into ISA slots, and they will function properly. There is one exception, however. Some 8-bit cards have a "skirt" extending below the bus slot. This skirt will not allow the 8-bit card to be inserted all the way into the ISA slot. For this reason, 8-bit slots are sometimes mixed in with ISA slots on the same motherboard.

A major problem cropped up when CPU speed outpaced the 8MHz bus speed (like the early Compaq with its 12MHz 286 processor). The computer could not use the ISA bus, because that bus ran at 8MHz and the processor ran faster. Putting a 12MHz processor in this type of system would limit it to running at 8MHz, thus negating any benefits received from the faster processor.

The solution was to dissociate the CPU clock from the bus clock. Doing so allowed the 12MHz processor to run at its rated speed and allowed the 8MHz ISA bus to run at its rated speed. When information needed to be transferred to a component on the ISA bus, it was transferred at the 8MHz clock speed—but all other operations inside the processor happened at 12MHz.

This process works well, with one exception: Some boards (like memory expansion boards) need to run at the processor's speed. If you put memory in an ISA board and place it in an ISA bus along with a 33MHz processor, information will be transferred from memory to the processor at 8MHz instead of 33MHz! This is a serious performance degradation. Granted, you don't find many ISA memory boards, but the potential is there. Take heart, though—this problem has been solved in a few of the other bus types (those that are considered local buses).

 You may also hear of one kind of expansion bus that is based on ISA-VL-Bus. VL-Bus was an expansion technology that added a 32-bit connector to the standard ISA connector. This 32-bit connector was connected directly to the processor and was used primarily with video cards and expansion cards where high speed was a requirement.

ISA Bus Configuration

Configuring expansion cards for use in ISA buses is a little less complex than configuring 8-bit buses, mainly because more choices are available for interrupts and DMA channels. Tables 2.1 and 2.2 list the interrupts and DMA channels available in an ISA system.

TABLE 2.1   ISA Bus IRQ Defaults

IRQ	Default Assignment
IRQ 0	System timer
IRQ 1	Keyboard
IRQ 2	Cascade to IRQ 9
IRQ 3	COM 2 and 4
IRQ 4	COM 1 and 3

TABLE 2.1   ISA Bus IRQ Defaults *(continued)*

IRQ	Default Assignment
IRQ 5	LPT2 (usually available)
IRQ 6	Floppy controller
IRQ 7	LPT1
IRQ 8	Real Time Clock (RTC)
IRQ 9	Cascade to IRQ 2
IRQ 10	Available (often used for a sound card or NIC)
IRQ 11	Available
IRQ 12	PS/2 mouse port (available if not used)
IRQ 13	Math coprocessor
IRQ 14	Primary hard disk controller board
IRQ 15	Secondary hard disk controller

TABLE 2.2   ISA Bus DMA Channel Defaults

DMA Channel	Default Assignment
DMA 0	Available
DMA 1	Available
DMA 2	Floppy controller
DMA 3	Available
DMA 4	Second DMA controller
DMA 5	Available
DMA 6	Available
DMA 7	Available

Note that COM 1 and COM 3 share the same interrupt, as do COM 2 and COM 4. The pairs are differentiated by using different I/O addresses for the different COM ports. This arrangement can work without conflict. The only problem is if you connect two devices that need to use an interrupt to the COM ports that use the same interrupt (for example, a mouse on COM 1 and a modem on COM 3). When this happens, the devices will work separately—but if you try to use both at the same time (for example, use the mouse while downloading a file with the modem), they will conflict and problems will occur.

To configure ISA cards, you use the same procedures that are used to configure the 8-bit expansion cards. You need to configure the card for interrupts, memory addresses, DMA channels, and I/O ports. Again, you do so using jumpers and DIP switches.

One special case exists when configuring interrupts. You will notice that some interrupts are cascaded to each other. This means that in an ISA system, when the computer needs to access an interrupt higher than 9, it uses IRQ 2 to get to it. This method ensures backward compatibility with 8-bit buses.

As the ISA bus and its expansion cards evolved, people got tired of setting all those jumpers and DIP switches. As the saying goes, "Build a better mousetrap, and the world will beat a path to your door." Well, someone found a better way to configure ISA devices: They found that if they put the jumper positions into an EEPROM chip on the device, they could set them using a special software configuration program. Because it's so easy, this method is used to configure the settings of most ISA cards today.

 There is a special case with regard to configuring ISA buses: the ISA Plug-and-Play bus. This bus consists of a standard ISA bus and a special set of BIOS extensions. The extensions examine the installed Plug-and-Play–compatible cards at startup and set them to available settings. (At least, that's the theory.)

PCI Bus

With the introduction of the Pentium-generation processors, all existing buses instantly became obsolete. Because the Pentiums were 64-bit processors and most buses were of the 16-bit or 32-bit variety, using existing buses would have severely limited the performance of the new technology. Primarily for this reason, the Peripheral Component Interconnect (PCI) bus was developed.

PCI has many benefits over other bus types. First, it supports both 64-bit and 32-bit data paths, so it can be used in both 486 and Pentium-based systems. In addition, it is processor independent. The bus communicates with a special bridge circuit that communicates with both the CPU and the bus. This has the benefit of making the bus almost universal. You can find PCI buses in PCs, Mac OS–based computers, and RISC computers. The same expansion card will work for all of them; you just need a different configuration program for each.

Another advantage of PCI over other buses is its higher clock speed. PCI (in its current revision) can run up to 66MHz. The bus can also support multiple bus-mastering expansion cards. These two features give PCI a maximum bus throughput of up to 265Mbps (with 64-bit cards). With the newest revision of PCI, PCI-Extended (PCI-X), the PCI bus is taking on new life. With bus speeds of 133MHz and throughput rates of more than 1GBps, PCI-X adds much to the performance of the PCI bus.

The final aspect of PCI that we'll mention is its backward compatibility. The PCI bus uses a chipset that works with PCI, ISA, and Extended Industry Standard Architecture (EISA). If you haven't seen EISA before, it's probably because EISA wasn't used much in desktop computers. It was essentially a 32-bit extension of the ISA bus with a connector that allowed 16-bit ISA cards to be installed into the EISA bus.

It is possible to have a PC that contains all these buses on the same motherboard. In addition, PCI cards are mostly Plug and Play. The cards automatically configure themselves for IRQ, DMA, and I/O port addresses.

In some systems that are a combination of PCI and ISA, each PCI slot is located next to an ISA slot. When you put a card in that PCI slot, you disable the ISA slot, and vice versa. Only one card will fit in a combination slot at a time.

Information and Identification

Identification of PCI bus slots is simple. The finger slots in the bus (Figure 2.16) are packed together tightly. This connector is usually white and contains two sections.

FIGURE 2.16   PCI bus connectors

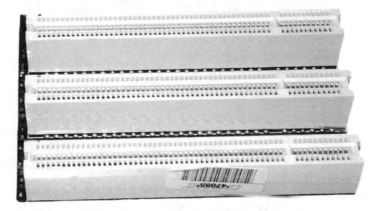

Two versions of the PCI bus are found in today's systems; these versions are differentiated by the voltages that they use. One uses +5.5VDC to power the expansion cards, and the other uses +3.3VDC. When you look at the connectors for these buses, the only difference you'll see is the placement of the *blocker* (called a key) in each connector—a +3.3VDC card can't be plugged into a +5.5VDC bus slot or vice versa.

AGP Bus

As Pentium systems became faster, PC game players acquired games that had better graphics, more realism, and more speed. However, as the computers got faster, the video technology couldn't seem to keep up, as was the case with the VL-Bus discussed earlier. VL-Bus could only run at 33MHz, and with 100 and 200MHz processors, there was a need for a faster, processor-direct, video expansion bus. The bus that was developed to meet this need was the *Accelerated Graphics Port (AGP)* bus.

Information and Identification

The AGP connector is similar in physical size and appearance to a PCI connector (as shown in Figure 2.17), but it's usually darker in color and offset from the other PCI slots to avoid confusion. The reason for the similarities is that Intel started with PCI 2.1 interface specifications to develop AGP. The bus is 32 bits wide, just like one version of PCI. However, the similarities end there. AGP is able to transfer multiple blocks of data per clock cycle (all AGP cards run at 66Mhz, but they can sometimes transfer more than one block of data per clock cycle). AGP is designed to be managed by the Northbridge chipset; thus it gets much higher priority than the PCI bus.

FIGURE 2.17   An AGP slot on a motherboard

AGP slot

Configuration of an AGP expansion card is simplicity itself. Motherboards that support AGP have Plug-and-Play BIOSs that automatically configure the card. To add an AGP card, power down the system, install the card in the AGP slot, and power the system back up. Once the system comes back up, the BIOS will configure the card automatically. Then, you can install the drivers for your operating system.

There are four main types of AGP, all of which are based on their multiplier of the memory bus speed. Table 2.3 describes the four types.

TABLE 2.3   AGP Types

Type	Maximum Speed	Max Throughput	Details
1x	66MHz	266MBps	Specified in AGP 1.0
2X	132MHz	532MBps	Specified in AGP 1.0
4X	264MHz	1064MBps	Specified in AGP 2.0
8X (Pro)	528MHz	2128MBps	Specified in AGP 3.0

USB (Universal Serial Bus)

As discussed in Chapter 1, the Universal Serial Bus (USB) is an expansion bus that allows up to 128 peripherals to be chained together off a single port. This technology uses serial communications. For the purposes of this chapter, you only need know that it is a very popular option that distinguishes one motherboard model over another.

AMR (Audio Modem Riser) Slots

Intel and other manufacturers are constantly looking for ways to improve the production process. One lengthy process that often slowed the production of motherboards with integrated analog I/O functions was FCC certification. So, the manufacturers developed a way to separate the analog circuitry (the modem and analog audio) onto its own card. Doing so allowed the analog circuitry to be separately certified (it was its own expansion card), thus reducing time for FCC certification. This slot and riser card technology is known as the Audio Modem Riser (AMR). AMR slots are fairly common on many Intel motherboards. Figure 2.18 shows an example of an AMR slot.

FIGURE 2.18   An AMR slot

CNR (Communication Network Riser) Slots

The *Communication Network Riser (CNR)* slots that are appearing on Intel motherboards are a neat idea. Essentially, they allow a motherboard designer (in this case, Intel) to design a motherboard chipset with certain integrated features. Then, if the built-in features of that chipset need to be enhanced (for example, by adding Dolby Digital Surround to a standard sound chipset), a CNR riser card can be added to enhance the onboard capabilities. Figure 2.19 shows an example of a CNR slot.

FIGURE 2.19   A CNR slot

Disk Interfaces

These days, most motherboards include onboard *disk interfaces*. A disk interface is the port or connector on the motherboard that allows a disk subsystem to be connected to and work with a particular motherboard. Most motherboards today include support for either some type of IDE/ATA disk drives (typically there are two interfaces: one high-speed bus, like UltraDMA or similar, and one standard EIDE) or SCSI drives. In addition, most motherboards include support for at least two floppy drives. You can identify the connectors by their pin count: 34 pins for a floppy connector, 40 for IDE/EIDE/UltraDMA, and either 50 or 68 for SCSI.

Motherboards differ based on the number and type of disk interfaces included onboard. Figure 2.20 shows an example of the onboard disk interfaces found on a motherboard.

BIOS

In addition to these other hardware components, a computer contains a special chip known as a BIOS chip. The BIOS chip contains built-in software that determines how the computer interacts with its own hardware, as well as what devices it can support. Different motherboards have different BIOS chips, but most often the motherboard manufacturer either makes its own BIOS or uses one from another manufacturer.

FIGURE 2.20   Onboard IDE and floppy disk interfaces

CPUs

The brain of the computer is the Central Processing Unit (CPU), also known as the processor. It is responsible for doing all the computational calculations within the computer.

In this section, you will learn about the different types of CPUs and their operational characteristics. But first, let's examine the functional differences between processors.

Architecture Differences

There's more to a chip than meets the eye. Several factors affect the performance of a processor, including clock speed, internal/external cache memory, supporting circuitry, voltages and form factors.

Clock Speed

The *clock speed* is the frequency with which a processor executes instructions. This frequency is measured in millions of cycles per second (megahertz [MHz]) or billions of cycles per second (gigahertz [GHz]). Generally speaking, the higher the MHz value, the faster the PC.

As we mentioned earlier, there is a clock of sorts within the CPU. This clock signal is generated by a quartz crystal, which vibrates as electricity passes through it, thereby generating a steady pulse to every component synchronized with the signal. A system cycle is generated by this pulse (called a clock tick), which sends a signal through the processor telling it to perform another operation.

To transfer data to and from memory, an 8086 computer needed four cycles plus wait states. Wait states allowed the processor to wait for the slower-speed RAM that was used in 8086-based computers.

Cache Memory

Cache memory is a storage area for frequently used data and instructions. It requires a small amount of physical RAM that can keep up with the processor; it uses this RAM for storage. The processor contains an internal cache controller that integrates the cache with the CPU. The controller stores frequently accessed RAM locations to provide faster execution of data and instructions. This type of cache is known as a level 1(L1) cache.

It is also possible to have a cache external to the CPU, called a level 2 (L2) cache (although it may reside in the same CPU package, it is outside of the CPU circuitry). This type of cache performs the same functions as an L1 cache, but it is usually much larger and can speed up the perceived performance.

Finally, the level 3 (L3) cache is cache memory over and above the L1 and L2 caches, and is typically off-chip and off-package. This type was first seen in early 1999 on AMD's K6-III CPU. Basically, a larger cache leads to the perception of a faster computer.

The Bus

The processor's ability to communicate with the rest of the system's components relies on the supporting circuitry. The system board's underlying circuitry is called the bus. The computer's bus moves information into and out of the processor and other devices, allowing all the devices to communicate with each other. The bus consists of several components, including the external bus, the data bus, and the address bus.

The External Bus (System Bus)

As we already learned, the external bus is also referred to as the *system bus* or expansion bus. The expansion bus is a bus system that allows the processor to talk to another device. It is known as an external bus system because it is outside the processor. The devices are connected through expansion cards and slots. (An expansion card is a removable circuit board that expands the capability of the computer.)

The Data Bus

The data bus is used to send and receive data. The larger the bus width, the more data that can be transmitted (and, therefore, the faster the bus).

The data bus and address bus are independent of each other, but for better performance, larger data buses require larger address buses. The data bus width indicates how much data the chip can move through at one time, and the size of the address bus indicates how much memory a chip can handle.

Data in a computer is transferred digitally. A single wire carries +3.3V or +5V to indicate a 1 data bit; it carries 0 volts to indicate a 0 data bit. (Remember, computers use the binary system to transmit information.) The greater number of wires allows more bits to be transmitted simultaneously. For example, a 16-bit data bus width has 16 wires to transmit data, and a 32-bit data chip can transmit twice the amount of data as a 16-bit chip. A good comparison is the highway system. A single traffic lane allows only one car through at a time, whereas two lanes allow twice the amount of traffic to pass.

Be careful not to assume that data flows at the same speed within the processor as it does outside the processor. Some Intel processors have an internal data bus whose speed is greater than that of the external data bus. The 8088 and 80386SX are good examples; they are designed with an internal bus that has twice the width of the external bus. This design provides for backward compatibility with other processors that do not support a wider bus.

The Address Bus

The address bus also contains a set of wires to carry information into and out of the processor, but the information the address bus sends is addressing information used to describe memory locations. These locations are used for data being sent or retrieved. The address bus carries a single bit of information, representing a digit in the address, along each wire. The size of the address bus corresponds to the number of address locations. The larger the address bus, the more memory address locations can be supported. The more memory address locations a processor can address, the more RAM a processor can use.

As an analogy, we can compare the address bus to the address of a house. If the house numbers for a street were limited to two digits, then the street could have only 100 addresses (00 to 99). For an address bus, which communicates in binary language, a limit of two digits would give four addresses (00, 01, 10, and 11). Thus, the larger the address bus, the more combinations of 0 and 1 are permitted to pass through at one time. A 286 processor has a 24-bit address bus width. Using binary theory, this translates to a little over 16 million locations, which means it allows access to as much as 16MB of RAM. Using similar calculations, a 386DX with a 32-bit address bus allows access to up to 4GB of RAM.

Bus Speed

Motherboards are designed to be more or less universal. They have a processor socket or slot that can support many different processor types and speeds. The speed at which a processor can run is set via jumper or the CMOS, as is the speed at which the expansion bus transfers data to and from the processor. The speed of the bus and the speed of the processor are directly related.

When installing a processor into a motherboard, you must set both the processor speed and the bus speed with a jumper. Typically, the bus speed is set to 66MHz, 100MHz, or 133MHz plus a multiplier. For example, if you have a 450MHz processor, you set the processor speed jumper to 450MHz, the expansion bus speed to 100MHz, and the multiplier to 4.5 (4.5 × 100MHz = 450MHz). Speeds for processors below 200MHz are generally set without a multiplier.

> Some motherboards have either processor speed jumpers or bus speed/
> multiplier jumpers, or both. To see which your motherboard uses, check the
> documentation that comes with your motherboard.

Voltages

As discussed in Chapter 1, power supplies provide most of the voltages a computer needs directly, including +5VDC and +3.3VDC. However, processors often run at different voltages than the standard power supplies provide. Therefore, you need a small module known as a *Voltage Regulator Module (VRM)*. The VRM regulates the voltage fed to the processor. For example, if a processor requires 1.5VDC, the VRM steps down the voltage so the processor has the correct voltage.

To make it easier on system builders (and, to some degree, the end user), some VRMs are *voltage ID (VID) programmable*. This means that on power up, the processor tells the VRM what voltage it needs, and the VRM supplies that voltage.

Form Factors

A *processor form factor* is the way the package of the processor is laid out, including how many pins it has, and the composition and size of the processor itself. Some of the most common Intel processor form factors include:

- PGA
- SECC
- SEP
- SECC2
- PPGA
- FC-PGA
- FC-PGA2
- OOI

PGA Package Type

PGA stands for *Pin Grid Array*, which is the way the pins on the processor are laid out. These pins interface with the small wafer of silicon inside the processor package and are inserted into a motherboard socket. The PGA package has a nickel-plated copper heatsink on top to help with thermal conductivity. The pins on the bottom of the processor are laid out such that the processor can be inserted only one way (to prevent accidental damage by incorrect installation). The PGA package is primarily used by the Intel Xeon processor, which has 603 pins.

SECC Package Type

The Single Edge Contact Cartridge (SECC) is a style of processor package in which the CPU is soldered directly to a small circuitboard that has many gold finger contacts. These fingers on this circuitboard make a connection with the contacts in a motherboard slot connector (discussed earlier). The SECC is covered with a metal shell to protect the processor and to provide heat dissipation. This cartridge may also have an integrated L2 cache.

The SECC package was used in the Intel Pentium II processors (with 242 contacts) and the Pentium II Xeon and Pentium III Xeon processors (with 330 contacts).

SEP Package Type

The Single Edge Processor (SEP) package is very similar to an SECC package, but it does not have the plastic housing covering the circuit board. The early Intel Celeron processors used the SEP package, which has 242 contacts.

SECC2 Package Type

The SECC2 package type is similar to the SECC package type, but the SECC2 plugs into the Slot 1 connector and does not use the metal heatsink. SECC2 was used with later model Pentium II and early model Pentium III processors.

PPGA Package Type

The *Plastic Pin Grid Array (PPGA)* package is similar to the PGA package type; however, the pins are staggered a bit differently. The pins are arranged so that the processor can be inserted only one way into its socket. PPGA also has the nickel-plated copper heatsink on top. This package type was used primarily by early Intel Celeron processors with 370 pins that fit into a Socket 370.

FC-PGA Package Type

The *Flip Chip-PGA (FC-PGA) package* is just what its name describes: The internal processor die in the package is put in with the die toward the top, so the heatsink and thermal grease that are normally applied to the insulation of a package can be used directly on the part that puts out the heat. This arrangement makes for much more efficient cooling of the processor. As with other PGA types, the pins are arranged in such a way that the processor can only go into its socket one way. The FC-PGA package type is found in Pentium III and Celeron processors with 370 pins that fit into a Socket 370.

FC-PGA2 Package Type

The *FC-PGA2 package* type is almost identical to the FC-PGA package type, with one important difference: The FC-PGA2 package includes what is known as an *Integrated Heat Sink (IHS)*. This heatsink is attached directly to the processor during manufacturing. You can't mistake the FC-PGA2 for FC-PGA, because of the large copper or metal block on the top of the processor. Because it is directly attached to the die, it is a more efficient heatsink and can better conduct heat away from the processor.

This package is used primarily with the Intel Celeron and Pentium III with 370 pins and the Pentium 4 with 478 pins.

OOI Package Type

The *OLGA on Interposer (OOI)* package type is the type most often found on Pentium 4 processors with 423 pins. OLGA stands for *Organic Land Grid Array*, which is the way the pins are laid out on this type of package. The OOI package has an IHS, similar to FC-PGA2.

CPU Manufacturers

The computer industry is very profitable, so many companies make CPUs for PCs. The market leader in the manufacture of chips is Intel Corporation. Intel's competition includes Motorola, Advanced Micro Devices (AMD), Cyrix, and IBM. When it first began making CPUs for the IBM PC, Intel shared its designs with other manufacturers; but with the introduction of the 80386 model in 1985, Intel ceased licensing its designs.

In this section, we'll look at Intel and its competitors. Together, the Intel processors (and their compatibles) make up the bulk of the IBM-compatible personal computer processor market, so our coverage of Intel will take up most of this section.

Intel Processors

When the first PC was introduced, IBM decided to go to the chip manufacturer Intel for a CPU. Since then, Intel has been the CPU supplier for almost all IBM-compatible computers.

The Intel family of PC processors started with the 8088, which found only limited use in the computer industry. The 8088 was rectangular, using a DIP array of its 40 pins. It originally ran at 4.77MHz with 29,000 transistors. It was used primarily in the IBM PC.

Next to be released was the 8086 (it was actually developed before the 8088), which had a 16-bit external data bus; however, the processor used an 8-bit bus for compatibility with older systems.

After the 808x series came the 80x86 series, otherwise known simply as Intel's *x86 series*. The 80286 was the first to implement the Pin Grid Array (PGA), as described earlier in this section. It ran hotter than the 8088, with speeds from 6MHz to 20MHz. Both internal and external bus structures were 16 bits wide, and it could physically address up to 16MB of RAM.

80386

Intel introduced the 80386 in 1985. With 275,000 transistors, the 80386 represented a new generation of processors, because it was the first Intel x86 processor that used both a 32-bit data bus and a 32-bit address bus. The situation with the 386 was unique, because up until this point Intel licensed its technology to other manufacturers. As we mentioned earlier, with the 386, Intel decided to stop licensing. Not to be outdone, other manufacturers like AMD and Cyrix came up with a chip they called the 386SX. This chip still operated internally at 32 bits (just like the full-blown 386), but it had only a 16-bit external data path and a 16-bit address bus. In order to compete on the same ground, Intel renamed its 386 to 386DX and introduced its own version of the 386SX with similar specifications.

The 386SX had a 24-bit data path, whereas the 386DX had a 32-bit data path. Overall, the 386 ranged in speed from 16MHz to 33MHz, used up to 4GB of memory (except the SX, which could only support 16MB of memory), supported multitasking, and was significantly faster than the 286.

80486

Intel introduced the 486DX in 1989. This processor boasted 1.25 million transistors, 32-bit internal and external data paths, a 32-bit address bus, an 8KB on-chip cache, and an integrated math coprocessor. In 1991, Intel introduced the 486SX (a cheaper version of the

486 processor). The only difference between the 486DX and the 486SX was that the internal math coprocessor was disabled on the SX. To add the math coprocessor to the chip, it was necessary to purchase a 487SX chip and insert it into the math coprocessor slot. Interestingly, this was basically a 486DX chip that, once installed, disabled the onboard 486SX chip and took over all processing functions from the SX chip. Figure 2.21 shows a 486 processor.

FIGURE 2.21   An Intel 486 processor

The 80486 operated at a maximum speed of 33MHz. To overcome this limitation, Intel came up with a technology known as *clock doubling*. It worked by allowing a chip to run at the bus's rated speed externally, but running the processor's internal clock at twice the speed of the bus. For example, Intel designed a chip that ran at 33MHz externally and 66MHz internally. This chip was known as the 486DX2.

Then, someone came up with idea that if you could double the clock speed, why not triple it? So, the clock-tripled 486DX became available not long after the 486DX2 came into production. These chips were called DX4 chips (don't ask me why Intel used the number 4 to indicate a clock tripled chip).

The Pentium and Pentium Pro

Intel introduced the Pentium processor (Figure 2.22) in 1993. This processor had 3.3 million transistors using a 64-bit data path, a 32-bit address bus, and a 16KB on-chip cache, and came in speeds from 60MHz to 200MHz. It was basically a combination of two 486DX chips in one larger chip. The benefit to this two-chips-in-one architecture was that each chip could execute instructions independently of the other. This was a form of *parallel processing* that Intel called *superscalar*. Pentiums require special motherboards, because they run significantly hotter than previous processors. They also require the use of a heatsink on top of the processor to absorb and ventilate the heat. (The designers said the processor typically generates heat to the tune of 185° Fahrenheit!)

Interestingly, when Intel first introduced the Pentium, it came in two versions: 60MHz and 66MHz. They were essentially the same chip; the only difference was that the 60MHz version didn't quite pass the 66MHz quality-control cut. Although these chips were not rated for 66MHz, the designers found that if they slowed them down a bit (to 60MHz), they ran just fine.

FIGURE 2.22 An Intel Pentium processor

After the initial introduction of the Pentium came the Pentium Pro, designed to meet the needs of today's server. Released in 1995, it runs at speeds around 200MHz in a 32-bit operating system environment using dynamic execution. Dynamic execution performs out-of-order guesses to execute program codes, so they can run more efficiently. The processor runs the program code in the order that makes the most sense.

Overdrive and MMX: The Need for Speed

Intel's 486 Overdrive processor was designed for 486 users who wanted to give their machines Pentium performance without having to pay the price for a full Pentium chip. Installing an Overdrive chip is simply a matter of replacing the existing CPU with the Overdrive CPU. Once installed, the Overdrive runs at approximately two and a half times the motherboard's bus speed. For example, if you have a motherboard with a bus speed of 33MHz, the Overdrive processor will run at approximately 83MHz.

Of course, there are tradeoffs to taking the Overdrive approach as opposed to making the step up to a conventional Pentium chip. First, Overdrive processors are only 32-bit processors, whereas Pentiums are completely 64-bit. Second, the Overdrive runs at least as hot as a conventional Pentium, so you must make sure the system's ventilation can withstand the additional heat.

Another major change was the introduction of MMX technology. This version of the Pentium processor added three new features:

- It includes 57 new instructions for better video, audio, and graphic capabilities.

- It features Single Instruction Multiple Data (SIMD) technology, which enables one instruction to give instructions to several pieces of data rather than a single instruction per piece of data.

- Its cache was doubled to 32KB.

For more information about MMX technology, check out Intel's website, www.intel.com.

Pentium II

After the Pentium, the fastest Intel processor available was the Pentium II. Speeds for this processor ranged from 233MHz to over 400MHz. It was introduced in 1997 amid much hoopla and some rather annoying commercials from Intel (remember the dancing clean-room technicians in their multicolored outfits?). It was designed to be a multimedia chip with special on-chip multimedia instructions and high-speed cache memory.

The most unique thing about the Pentium II, compared to earlier Intel processors, was that it used an SECC package type to attach to the motherboard instead of the standard PGA package used with the earlier processor types. The processor was a card that could easily be replaced—you simply shut off the computer, pulled out the old processor card, and inserted a new one.

When released, the Pentium II was designed to be used by itself in a computer. For multiprocessor servers and workstations, Intel also released a separate processor, the Pentium II Xeon, based on the same Pentium II circuitry. Generally speaking, multiprocessor Pentium II servers with between four and eight processors used the Pentium II Xeon.

Celeron

When the Pentium II came out, consumers loved it. The only problem was that it was a bit too expensive for use in low-buck machines. To meet that market need, Intel came out with the Celeron processor. Its computing power was roughly equivalent to that of the Pentium II, but it cost less.

Pentium III

The Pentium III was released in 1999 and used the same SECC connector as its predecessor, the Pentium II. It included 70 new instructions and was optimized for voice recognition and multimedia. Aside from faster speeds, one of the more significant features of the Pentium III was the processor serial number (PSN), a unique number electronically encoded into the processor. This number can be used to uniquely identify a system during Internet transactions. As you can imagine, Internet privacy advocates had a field day with this feature. Some Pentium IIIs and all Pentium 4s have gone back to the PGA package.

 Like the Pentium II, the Pentium III has a multiprocessor Xeon version.

Pentium 4

The Pentium 4 was the next logical step in the Intel Pentium line of processors. Introduced in November 2000, it supports a system bus of up to 533MHz and is Intel's highest performing PC processor as of the writing of this book. It has 512KB of what Intel calls advanced transfer cache, which is essentially an L2 Cache. Its core speed is a maximum of 3.06GHz, which makes it a real screamer.

The Future of Intel Processors

Intel is constantly innovating. It always has at least two processors in development. These processors are given code names until the official marketing name is announced. No one knows all the features of an Intel processor until it's released (except Intel, of course). Table 2.4 lists the code names of some of the upcoming processors in development as this book is being written.

TABLE 2.4 Upcoming Intel Processor Code Names and Descriptions

Code Name	Description
Prescott	Available Q4 2003. Adds support for Rambus as well as DDR memory.
Nocona	Available Q4 2003. Xeon version of Prescott.
Potomac	Available 2nd half of 2004. MP Xeon version of Prescott.
Tejas	Available 2005. To contain some 64-bit support for IA-64 instructions and support for DDR-II memory.
Nehalem	Available 2005. Possibly a low-power version.

Summary of Intel Processors

Table 2.5 provides a summary of the history of the Intel processors. Table 2.6 shows the physical characteristics of Pentium (and higher) class processors.

TABLE 2.5 The Intel Family of Processors

Chip	Year Added	Data Bus Width (in Bits)	Address Bus Width (in Bits)	Speed (in MHz)	Transistors	Other Specifications
Pentium	1993	64	32	60–200	3.3 million	Superscalar
Pentium Pro	1995	64	32	150–200	5.5 million	Dynamic execution
Pentium II	1997	64	32	233–450	7.5 million	32KB of L1 cache, dynamic execution, and MMX technology
Pentium II Xeon	1998	64	32	400–600	7.5 million	Multiprocessor version of Pentium II

TABLE 2.5 The Intel Family of Processors *(continued)*

Chip	Year Added	Data Bus Width (in Bits)	Address Bus Width (in Bits)	Speed (in MHz)	Transistors	Other Specifications
Celeron	1999	64	32	400–600	7.5 million	Value version of Pentium II
Pentium III	1999	64	32	350–1000	9.5–28 million	SECC2 package
Pentium III Xeon	1999	64	32	350–1000	9.5–28 million	Multiprocessor version of Pentium III
Pentium 4	2002	64	32	1200–3100	42 million	20KB L1, 256–512KB L2 on chip

TABLE 2.6 Physical Characteristics of Pentium-Class Processors

Processor	Speed (in MHz)	Socket	Pins	Voltage	Cache
Pentium-P5	60–66	4	273	5V	16KB
Pentium-P54C	75–200	5 or 7	320 or 321	3.3V	16KB
Pentium-P55C	166–333	7	321	3.3V	32KB
Pentium Pro	150–200	8	307	2.5V	32KB
Pentium II	233–450	SECC	N/A	3.3V	32KB
Pentium III	450–1130	SECCII or 370	N/A	3.3V	32KB
Pentium 4	1300–3400+	423 or 478	423 or 478	1.3–1.7	20KB

AMD

Options other than just Intel processors are available for PCs. Among the so-called Intel "clones" are chips made by Advanced Micro Devices (AMD). AMD has made a very profitable business out of being Intel's main competitor in the PC CPU market. Generally speaking, AMD's CPUs are roughly comparable in speed to Intel's chips. However, they end up being about 10 percent cheaper on average. Many individuals who build their own systems love AMD's chips because they seem to have a better "bang for the buck" factor. Table 2.7 lists some of the processors made by AMD.

TABLE 2.7 AMD Processors and Their Intel Equivalents

Chip	Socket	Speed (in MHz)	Transistors	Intel Equivalent
K6	7	166–300	8.8 million	Pentium MMX–Pentium II
K6-II	7/Super 7	266–550	9.3 million	Pentium II
K6-III	Super 7	400–600	21.3 million	Pentium II
Athlon Classic	Slot A	500–1000	22 million	Pentium III
Athlon Thunderbird	Socket A	650–1400	37 million	Pentium III
Athlon XP Palomino	Socket A	1333–1733	37.5 million	Pentium III–4
Athlon XP Thoroughbred	Socket A	1467–2250	37.2–37.6 million	Pentium 4

RAM

Random access memory (RAM) is a type of temporary storage medium that uses the presence or absence of a magnetic or electrical charge to store information in binary format. Most often, RAM is just called memory, because a PC uses RAM for its main system memory. In this section, you will learn about the different types of memory as well as the various operational characteristics of RAM.

Types

There are as many types of memory as there are IC types. Let's look at each type in detail.

SRAM (Static RAM)

Static random access memory (SRAM) is called static because the information doesn't need a constant update (refresh). SRAM stores information as patterns of transistor ons and offs to represent binary digits. This type of memory is physically bulky and somewhat limited in its capacity. It can generally store only 256Kb (kilobits) per IC. The original PC and XT, as well as some notebook computer systems, use SRAM chips for their memory.

Most new computers are moving away from SRAM to the newer, more efficient type of memory known as DRAM.

DRAM (Dynamic Random Access Memory)

Dynamic RAM (DRAM) stores information in capacitors. This storage method is much more efficient than SRAM and, therefore, has gained widespread popularity. As the name dynamic implies, it requires a constant recharge (called a refresh signal) to maintain information.

Fast Page Mode (FPM)

Fast Page Mode (FPM) DRAM, at the time of the 486/Pentium transition, was the most common type of DRAM. Although its technical designation is FPM DRAM, because it was the most common type of DRAM, everyone just started calling it "DRAM." It allows data to be paged (swapped) into memory faster than earlier versions, thus providing better performance.

Extended Data Out (EDO)

In 1995, a new type of RAM became popular. *Extended Data Out (EDO) RAM* increases performance by 10 to 15 percent over FPM DRAM by eliminating memory wait states; this means it eliminates a few steps to access memory, thus decreasing the time it takes to get information and thus increasing the overall performance of the computer. It's usually a bit more expensive than regular DRAM. In order to realize the performance gain, EDO memory must be used in a motherboard designed for EDO memory; otherwise, there will be no significant performance increases.

Synchronous DRAM (SDRAM)

In the final quarter of 1996, a new type of memory, *Synchronous DRAM (SDRAM)* was introduced. SDRAM was developed to match the ever-increasing processing speeds of the Pentium systems. SDRAM, as its name suggests, is synchronized to the speed of the systems in which it will be used (PC66 SDRAM runs at 66MHz, PC100 runs at 100MHZ, PC133 runs at 133MHz, and so on). Synchronizing the speed of the systems prevents the address bus from having to wait for the memory because of different clock speeds.

If you happen to install PC133 SDRAM in a 100MHz bus, the system will function. However, the 133MHz memory will only operate at the 100MHz bus speed, thus reducing overall system performance.

Double Data Rate SDRAM (DDR SDRAM)

Essentially, *Double Data Rate SDRAM (DDR SDRAM)* is clock-doubled SDRAM. The memory chip can perform reads and writes on both sides of any clock cycle (the up or start and the down or ending), thus doubling the effective memory executions per second. So, if you are using DDR SDRAM with a 100MHz memory bus, the memory will execute reads and writes at 200MHz and transfer the data to the processor at 100MHz. The advantage of DDR over regular SDRAM is increased throughput, and thus increased overall system speed.

There is one thing to keep in mind, however. With SDRAM, you know the speed at which PC133 memory operates. With DDR SDRAM, the chips are described slightly differently. For example, a DDR SDRAM chip at 100MHz DDR (200MHz, essentially) isn't known as PC200;

instead, it is called PC1600, for the peak data transfer rate (64 bit × 2 × 100 MHz = 12,800Mbps or 1600MBps). Table 2.8 shows the standard bus speeds, what they would be called under SDRAM naming, and the DDR name.

TABLE 2.8   DDR Naming of Standard Memory

Standard FSB Speed	DDR Speed	SDRAM Name (in Theory)	DDR Name
100MHz	200MHz	PC200	PC1600
133MHz	266MHz	PC266	PC2100
166MHz	333MHz	PC333	PC2700
200MHz	400MHz	PC400	PC3200

Direct Rambus

Direct Rambus is a relatively new and extremely fast (up to 800MHz) technology that uses, for the most part, a new methodology in memory system design. Direct Rambus is a memory bus that transfers data at 800MHz over a 16-bit memory bus. Direct Rambus memory models (often called RIMMs), like DDR SDRAM, can transfer data on both the rising and falling edges of a clock cycle. That feature, combined with the 16-bit bus for efficient transfer of data, results in the ultra-high memory transfer rate (800MHz) and the high bandwidth of up to 1.6GB/second (more than twice that of 100MHz SDRAM).

VRAM (Video RAM)

Video memory (also called video RAM or *VRAM*) is used to store image data for processing by the video adapter. The more video memory an adapter has, the better the image quality it can display. More VRAM also allows the adapter to display higher-resolution images. VRAM may or may not be expandable and is almost always proprietary.

In the case of some chipsets that have integrated, onboard video, a portion of main system memory is carved out for use as VRAM.

Operational Characteristics

The various types of memory can be described in terms of their operational characteristics, including the following:

- Bit size of chip
- Parity vs. non-parity

- ECC vs. non-ECC
- CAS latency

Let's take a quick look at some of the operational characteristics of the various types of memory.

Bit Size of Chip

Most individual memory chips can be identified by their bit size—the number of bits (1 or 0) they can move at any one time. Today's computer chips can be 8-bit, 16-bit, 32-bit, or 64-bit, and are labeled as such, although the form factor of the chip will give you a clue to its bit width. For example, most 168-pin SDRAM DIMMs are 64-bit. Therefore, in systems that have a 64-bit address bus, you can install SDRAM DIMMs singly to add memory to your system. However, if you had an older system that supported 72-pin DIMMs (which are 32-bit), and you had a system with a 64-bit address bus, you would have to install them in pairs. Table 2.9 shows this relationship.

TABLE 2.9   Bit Size to Form Factor Relationship

Form Factor	Bit Size
30-pin SIMM	8-bit
72-pin SIMM	32-bit
168-pin DIMM	64-bit

Parity vs. Non-Parity

Memory is also often classified as either parity or non-parity. Parity is a simple form of error checking used in computers and telecommunications. It works by adding an additional bit to a binary number and using it to indicate any changes in that number during transmission. There are two types of parity: even and odd.

Even parity works by counting the number of 1s in a binary number and, if that number is odd, adding an additional 1 to guarantee that the total number of 1s is even. For example, the number 11101011 has an even number of 1s, so the sending computer assigns a 0 to the parity bit. On the other hand, the number 01101101 has five 1s; it will have a 1 in the parity bit position to make the total number of 1s even. In the second case, if the computer checked the parity position after transmission and found a 0 instead, it would ask the processor to resend the last bit.

Odd parity works in a similar manner. But, instead of guaranteeing that the total number of 1s is even, it guarantees that the total is an odd number.

Parity works well for detecting single-bit errors (where one bit has changed its value during transmission). But if the transmission is extremely garbled, two bits might be switched at the same time. If that is the case, the value for parity is still valid; as a consequence, the sender will not be asked to retransmit. However, because of its speed, memory often uses parity bits for error correction.

It is easy to identify parity memory, because instead of eight chips, it has nine (the extra chip is dedicated to the parity bit).

ECC vs. Non-ECC

Because memory can sometimes have multiple-bit errors, which parity may not detect, *Error Correcting Code (ECC)* memory was developed. It uses a special algorithm that can detect and correct single-bit errors. Essentially, it provides more stability than systems with non-ECC memory.

This type of memory is more expensive than non-ECC memory, and the system must be able to support it properly. Most servers and high-end workstations can use ECC memory. However, it is not necessary for the average user.

Latency

The term *Column Address Strobe (CAS) latency*, as it applies to memory, specifies the time (in clock cycles) from when the request is made for information from memory to when the information is received. The most common markings for *CAS latency* are CL3 and CL2. CL2 is a lower latency (meaning a faster access time) than CL3. There are also some memory chips labeled CL2.5.

Summary

In this chapter, you learned about three of the main components in a PC: the motherboard, the CPU, and RAM. First we discussed the architecture of a motherboard, including chipsets, memory, communication ports, processor sockets, external cache memory, bus architectures, and the BIOS. You also learned about the differences between different types of CPUs, as well as the specifics of the processors from the two major brands: Intel and AMD. Finally, we looked at the different types of memory available for PCs, as well as the operational characteristics that differentiate them.

Key Terms

Before you take the exam, be certain you are familiar with the following terms:

Accelerated Graphics Port (AGP)	bus clock
address bus	bus mastering
AT bus	cache memory
backside bus	CAS latency
blocker	chipset

clock doubling

clock signal

clock speed

Column Address Strobe (CAS) latency

Communication Network Riser (CNR)

CPU clock

data bus

Direct Memory Access (DMA)

Direct Rambus

disk interface

Double Data Rate SDRAM (DDR SDRAM)

Dual Inline Memory Module (DIMM)

Dynamic RAM (DRAM)

Error Correcting Code (ECC)

Even parity

expansion bus

expansion slot

Extended Data Out (EDO) RAM

external bus

Fast Page Mode (FPM)

FC-PGA2 package

Flip Chip-PGA (FC-PGA) package

frontside bus

hardware port

heat spreader

I/O port

Industry Standard Architecture (ISA) bus

input/output (I/O) addresses

Integrated Heat Sink (IHS)

interrupt

interrupt request (IRQ)

L1 cache

L2 cache

MicroDIMM

Northbridge

OLGA on Interposer (OOI)

Organic Land Grid Array

parallel processing

Pin Grid Array

Plastic Pin Grid Array (PPGA)

processor form factor

processor socket

Random access memory (RAM)

RIMM

RIMM slot

signal pathways

Single Edge Contact Cartridge (SECC)

Single Edge Processor Package (SEPP)

Single Inline Memory Module (SIMM)

slocket

Slot 1 connector

Slot A

Small Outline DIMM (SoDIMM)

Socket 370

Socket 423

Socket 478

Socket 7

Socket 8

Socket A

Southbridge

Static random access memory (SRAM)

superscalar

Synchronous DRAM (SDRAM)

system bus

voltage ID (VID) programmable

Voltage Regulator Module (VRM)

VRAM

x86 series

Zero Insertion Force (ZIF)

Review Questions

1. RAM is short for _____.

   A. Readily accessible memory

   B. Recently affected memory

   C. Random access memory

   D. Read and modify

2. What type of memory stores information as patterns of transistor ons and offs to represent binary digits, is physically bulky, and is somewhat limited in capacity?

   A. SRAM

   B. DRAM

   C. EDORAM

   D. ROM

   E. PROM

   F. EPROM

3. Which type of memory found in desktop computers stores information as charges in very small capacitors and needs a constant refresh signal to keep the information in memory?

   A. SRAM

   B. DRAM

   C. EDORAM

   D. ROM

   E. PROM

   F. EPROM

4. Which processor(s) can access as much as 4GB of RAM? (Select all that apply.)

   A. 8088

   B. 8086

   C. 80286

   D. 80386

   E. 80486

   F. Pentium

5. If you are transmitting the 8-bit binary number 11010010 and are using even parity, what will the parity bit be?

   A. 1

   B. 0

   C. None

6. What is meant by a wait state of zero?

   A. The processor is faster than memory in terms of speed.

   B. The processor is slower than memory in terms of speed.

   C. The memory is faster than the processor in terms of speed.

   D. The processor and the memory are equally matched in terms of speed.

7. What type of memory has several chips on a small circuit board that is easily removable?

   A. Dual Inline Package

   B. Single Inline Memory Module

   C. Memory Package Grid Array

   D. Single Inline Package

8. ISA is an acronym for _____.

   A. InSide Architecture

   B. Industry Standard Architecture

   C. Industry Simple Architecture

   D. Internal Systems Architecture

9. PCI has a bus width of _____ bits. (Select all that apply.)

   A. 32

   B. 16

   C. 64

   D. 8

10. ISA has a bus width of _____ bits.

    A. 32

    B. 16

    C. 64

    D. 8

11. Which bus signal line allows a device to request the processor's attention?

    A. I/O address lines

    B. DMA address lines

    C. Clock address lines

    D. Interrupt request (IRQ) address lines

12. Which bus signal line allows a device to send data directly to a computer's memory, bypassing the CPU?

    A. I/O addresses

    B. DMA address

    C. Clock addresses

    D. Interrupt request (IRQ) addresses

13. Which bus signal line allows the CPU to send requests to the device to send data?

    A. I/O addresses

    B. DMA address

    C. Clock addresses

    D. Interrupt request (IRQ) addresses

14. PCI buses were developed mainly because _____.

    A. Pentiums were 8-bit processors

    B. Pentiums were 16-bit processors

    C. Pentiums were 32-bit processors

    D. Pentiums were 64-bit processors

15. The first released version of the Pentium 4 used which type of processor socket?

    A. Socket A

    B. Slot 1

    C. Socket 370

    D. Socket 423

16. Which processor package type is the same as the SECC, but without the plastic covering?

    A. Socket A

    B. Slot A

    C. SEP

    D. SECC2

17. Which AMD processor was the first to use the Socket A?

    A. K6-II

    B. Athlon Classic

    C. Athlon Thunderbird

    D. Athlon XP

18. How many transistors does the Pentium 4 have?

   A. 1 million

   B. 9.5 million

   C. 22 million

   D. 42 million

19. Which of the following memory types is the most reliable?

   A. ECC memory

   B. Non-ECC memory

   C. Both are sufficiently reliable

   D. Neither is sufficiently reliable

20. What is the maximum throughput of AGP 8x (Pro)?

   A. 532MBps

   B. 1064MBps

   C. 2128MBps

   D. 4056Mbps

Answers to Review Questions

1. C.   As it applies to memory, RAM stands for random access memory.

2. A.   Of these choices, SRAM would be the one to choose, because its storage method uses a pattern of transistor ons and offs to represent the data. Because it's bulky and its storage method is inefficient, SRAM is not as popular anymore.

3. B.   DRAM (Dynamic RAM) stores information in capacitors. This storage method is much more efficient than SRAM and, therefore, has gained widespread popularity. As dynamic implies, it requires a constant recharge to maintain the information.

4. D, E, F.   As address buses expanded beyond the 24-bit capability of the 80286, they could access more memory. With a 32-bit address bus width, the 80386, 80486, and Pentium processors can access as much as 4GB of RAM.

5. B.   Because even parity works around the concept that there must be an even number of bits set to 1 (and in this question 4 bits are set to 1), the parity bit must equal 0 to maintain that even number. However, if the number in the question had only 3 bits set to 1, then the parity bit would be set to 1, so the number of 1s would be even.

6. D.   If the memory and the processor do not run at the same speed, then wait states must be used to make sure one does not send more information than the other can handle. If they run at the same speed, a wait state of zero is used.

7. B.   The Single Inline Memory Module (SIMM) is a small circuit board with multiple DIPs soldered to it. Because of this arrangement, SIMMs are very easy to install and remove.

8. B.   ISA stands for Industry Standard Architecture.

9. A, C.   PCI supports both 32-bit and 64-bit bus widths.

10. B.   The ISA bus is a full 16-bit bus.

11. D.   Interrupts are special lines that go directly to the processor; a device uses them to get the attention of the CPU when it needs to.

12. B.   DMA channels allow a device to send data directly to computer memory, bypassing the CPU.

13. A.   The I/O address bus signal line allows the CPU to send requests to the device to send data.

14. D.   PCI buses were developed mainly to support the 64-bit capability of the Pentium processors.

15. D.   Some later Pentium 4 chips were designed to use the Socket 470; however, the first Pentium 4 chips were designed to use the Socket 423.

16. C.   Although the SECC2 is similar to the SECC, it still has a plastic covering—just no heatsink. The SEP package type is basically a bare circuit board with no plastic covering.

17. C.   The Athlon Thunderbird was the first to use the Socket A processor socket. The Athlon XP uses it as well, but it wasn't the first. The K6-II uses the Socket 7 (or Super 7), and the Athlon Classic uses a Slot A.

18. D.   The Pentium 4 (at the time of this writing) has 42 million transistors.

19. A.   ECC memory contains advanced error correction circuitry and therefore increases reliability significantly over non-ECC memory.

20. C.   The maximum throughput of AGP 8x (Pro) is 2128MBps.

Chapter

3

Disk Drive Storage

THE FOLLOWING OBJECTIVES ARE COVERED IN THIS CHAPTER:

✓ 1.6 Identify proper procedures for installing and configuring common IDE devices. Choose the appropriate installation or configuration sequences in given scenarios. Recognize the associated cables.

✓ 1.7 Identify proper procedures for installing and configuring common SCSI devices. Choose the appropriate installation or configuration sequences in given scenarios. Recognize the associated cables.

All information needs to be stored somewhere. It's a simple fact of life. At your office, you may have letters, contracts, and so on that need to be stored somewhere to make them easily accessible and retrievable. This storage space needs to be large enough to hold as much information as possible, but it should also be organized for easy access to that information. Although some people simply use the top of the desk and store documents in piles, the best solution for storing paper documents at most offices is a filing cabinet.

With computers, you have various types of electronic information to store, including data files, application files, and configuration files. In this chapter, we will explain the following A+ exam topics related to information storage:

- Storage types
- Floppy disk systems
- IDE disk systems
- Small Computer System Interface (SCSI)
- Disk system fault tolerance

Storage Types

In this section, we'll give a detailed description of each type of disk storage, starting with a brief overview of punch card and tape storage and moving into the different types of disks. Then we'll give you some tips on how to configure them and discuss their different troubleshooting techniques.

Punch Cards and Tape

Originally, computer information was contained in memory and printed to punch cards. When you wanted to retrieve the data, you ran the punch cards into a special reader; the information was read back into memory and could then be used. This proved to be a very limited storage medium in terms of capacity and ease of retrieval. A single page of data could take several pages of punch cards. Also, the punch card order was very important; the cards had to be put into the reader in the correct order or the program wouldn't run correctly. You did your best to keep the cards in their correct order—God forbid you dropped them on the floor or some jokester shuffled them.

Then, someone discovered that computer signals could be recorded with a tape recorder. When the tape was played back into the computer, the information was retrieved. This was a much more efficient storage system than punch cards. Because the tape moved in only one direction and was a single, long tape (rather than several punch cards), it reduced the possibility of getting the information out of sequence and made the information easier to access. You've probably seen movies where the computer room has massive cabinets with reels of tape moving back and forth. What you might not know is that several early personal computer systems (such as the TRS-80, the Tandy Color Computer, and the Apple II) came with cassette tape storage devices to load and store programs and data.

The major limitations of tape were its speed and precision. Tape was slow to store programs and data, and it was slow to access information because of its linear nature. Tape devices are described as *sequential storage* devices. With these types of devices, if a piece of information is located at the end of a tape, you have to fast-forward through all the other information to get to the data you need. The early tape mechanisms also didn't have good position locators or stepper motors. It was possible to begin reading a tape after the information you needed had already begun, causing you to miss the start of the program or data and making it unusable.

Despite its drawbacks for most tasks you might want to undertake with a computer, magnetic tape in various forms is still a great medium for *backing up* your system—that is, recording some or all of the information stored on your hard disk and putting the recording away in case of hard disk catastrophe. Why is tape, which is not recommended for other types of information storage, recommended so often for backups? In part because of the sheer amount of data it can store. Some types of inexpensive tape media available today can hold more than 4GB and are easily movable, removable, and insertable into their respective recorder/playback drives. Moreover, the relatively low speed of recording or playing back a backup tape is not a significant consideration for most users, as it would be with other computer tasks. Most users know that they are simply performing a safety measure when they utilize a backup, so they schedule their backups to be carried out automatically when no one is using the computer.

Disk Drives

Magnetic disk systems were developed to overcome the limitations of magnetic tape. Rotating stacks of disks are coated with a special substance that is sensitive to magnetism. As the disk rotates, the particles in the substance can be polarized (magnetized), indicating a 1. The unpolarized areas indicate 0s. (We will discuss the way information is stored on a disk in the next section.) This technology is the cornerstone of most current disk storage types and hasn't changed much since its inception. These types of disk systems store data in nonlinear format and are called *random access* storage devices, in contrast to tape's sequential access storage methods. The data can be accessed no matter where it is located on the disk, because the read/write head can be positioned exactly over the requested data—you don't have to fast-forward through the data stored before it.

There are two major types of disk systems: fixed and removable. Let's discuss fixed disks first.

Fixed Disk Drives

Also known as *hard disks* and *hard drives*, *fixed disks* actually contain several disks called *platters*, stacked together and mounted through their centers on a small rod called a *spindle* (see Figure 3.1). The disks are rotated about this rod at a speed between 2,000 and 10,000 revolutions per minute (RPM). As the disks rotate, one or more *read/write heads* float approximately 10 microinches (about one-tenth the width of a human hair) above the disk surfaces and make, modify, or sense changes in the magnetic positions of the coatings on the disks. Several heads are moved together as one unit by an *actuator arm*. There is usually one head for each side of a platter.

FIGURE 3.1   A fixed disk

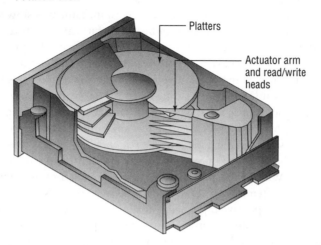

This entire mechanism is enclosed in a hard disk case. These disks are called fixed disks because the mechanism is not designed to be removed. The disk platters, though perfectly free to revolve at high RPM, are otherwise fixed in place.

Disk Organization

We must have a way to organize the disk into usable sections. This is done by first dividing the platters into sections as you would a pie and then further dividing this area into concentric circles called *tracks* (see Figure 3.2). Tracks are numbered from the outside (track 0) to the inside (track 902 on a 903-track hard disk). A *disk sector* is the part of a track that falls in a particular section of the pie slice on the disk.

FIGURE 3.2   Disk organization

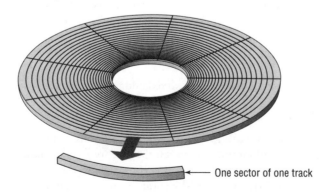

If you can visualize several tracks stacked together vertically (the same tracks on each disk), you might describe that collection of tracks as a *cylinder*. In fact, that's how tracks are referred to in a discussion of the organization of disk information; when information is read from or written to a disk, the heads read or write a sector-sized division of a track a whole stack at a time, from top to bottom (see Figure 3.3). In other words, the disks' tracks aren't treated as individual tracks on single disks; they're treated as cylinders. This amounts to quite a bit of information read or written at one time. The precise amount of information that is read at once depends on the number of cylinders, heads, and sectors, or what is called *drive geometry*.

FIGURE 3.3   Hard drive geometry

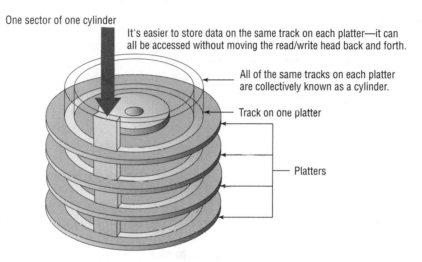

One sector of one cylinder

It's easier to store data on the same track on each platter—it can all be accessed without moving the read/write head back and forth.

All of the same tracks on each platter are collectively known as a cylinder.

Track on one platter

Platters

Disk Specifications

When a fixed disk is rated, several qualities are given as specifications. *Size*, or *capacity*, is just one of the properties. Size is determined by drive geometry. Let's quantify this by giving some values to each variable. Let's say we have 903 cylinders, 12 heads (6 platters—1 head per side, 2 sides to each platter), and 63 sectors per track. A typical fixed disk has 512 bytes per sector (that's 0.5KB/sector). The capacity of the hard disk is 341,334KB, or 333MB (903 cyl × 12 heads × 63 sectors/track × 0.5KB/sector). These values are commonly given on the outside of a fixed disk.

Another quality that is used to gauge the performance of an individual drive is *seek time*. This value, commonly given in milliseconds (ms), is how long the actuator arm takes to move from rest to the position where the read/write head accesses information. Additionally, because the platters rotate, once the read/write head is in position it may take a few milliseconds for the target sector to move under it. This delay is known as the *latency factor*. Latency values are given in milliseconds.

The faster a drive spins, the lower the average latency values; so drives are also rated with a *spin speed*. The spin speed indicates how fast the platters are spinning. It's stated in revolutions per minute (RPM); higher RPM values mean faster speeds and lower latency values. For example, if a disk has a spin speed of 5,000 RPM, it rotates at 83.34 revolutions per second. One rotation takes 1/83.34 seconds, or 11.9 ms. This value represents the largest possible delay (the disk head is in position just after the required sector moved past it). However, disk latency values are only *average latency* values, because the values are not constant. The target sector could be close, or it could be far away. So, in our example, we take the largest possible latency (11.9 ms) and smallest possible latency (0 ms) and average them to get the average latency: (11.9 ms + 0)/2 = 5.95 ms.

The seek time and latency factors together make up the drive's *access time*. The average seek time plus the average latency equals the drive's access time. The smaller the access time value, the faster the drive.

Read/Write Processes

Now that you know how drives function and they are rated, let's discuss the most important topic: how drives store information. At the most basic level, the disk works by making flux transitions with an electromagnet in the read/write head to store information on the disk surface. A *flux transition* is the presence or absence of a magnetic field in a particle of the coating on the disk. As the read/write head passes over an area, the electromagnet is energized to cause the material to be magnetized in a small area. The process by which binary information is changed into flux transition patterns is called *encoding*.

There are many ways of converting 1s and 0s to flux transitions. The simplest way is to interpret the presence of a flux transition as a 1 and the absence as a 0. Because this was the most obvious choice, the first hard disks (either ST-506 or ESDI types) used this method of encoding, known as Frequency Modulation (FM), and its cousin Modified FM (MFM). This method worked well until techniques for increasing the track/cylinder density became almost too successful: Tracks were placed so tightly together that at higher speeds, the read/write heads affected not only the track immediately under the head, but the adjacent ones as well.

To solve this problem, a technology known as *Run Length Limited (RLL)* was developed; it spaced the 1s farther apart using a special code for each byte. This method turned out to be more efficient for large drives than for small ones. RLL encoding also introduced *data compression*, a set of technologies that increased the amount of data that could be stored on the drive. Most of today's drives (IDE, SCSI, and so on) use a form of RLL encoding.

With this new type of encoding, much more data could be transferred to the computer at once; but this ability created a new problem. The interface sometimes got bogged down and stopped reading in order to catch up. This was a problem because during the pause, the platters were still rotating and the read/write heads might skip sectors. To solve this problem, disk designers developed a technology known as *interleaving*.

A Question of Interleaves

Although interleaving may come up on the A+ Certification exam, the topic is almost irrelevant for hard drives available in the last few years, because the hardware technology has improved so much. Here's what you need to know for the test.

Interleaving involves skipping sectors to write the data instead of writing sequentially to every sector. This process evens out the data flow and allows the drive to keep pace with the rest of the system. Interleaving is given in ratios. If the interleave is 2:1, the disk skips 2 minus 1, or 1 sector, between each sector it writes (it writes to one sector, skips one sector, and then writes to the next sector). Most drives today use a 1:1 interleave, because today's drives are very efficient at transferring information. A 1:1 ratio means the drive writes to one sector and then simply goes to the immediate next sector (skipping 1 minus 1 sectors, or 0 sectors). A 1:1 interleave ratio really means the drive has no interleave at all.

To make it easier for the operating system to manage the storage space, the information encoded on the drive is written to groups of sectors known as *clusters*. A cluster is made up of up to 64 sectors grouped together (the actual number of sectors included in a cluster varies with the size of the hard disk). When the operating system stores information, it writes it to a particular cluster instead of to a sector, because it's more efficient for the operating system to keep track of clusters than sectors. The *file allocation table (FAT)* is a file that contains the information about where the tracks and sectors on the disk are located. It is contained in the outermost track (track 0) of the disk.

Why Is the FAT on Track 0?

Advances in disk technology are constantly increasing the number of tracks, even on disks of the same size (the designers are always striving to increase the track density); so, if the FAT were located on the inside track, it might be in a slightly different position on one disk than on another. In addition, because the outside track (track 0) is easily accessible, the FAT is placed there so the computer can use a simple routine to locate its operating system and disk information. Moreover, this routine never needs to change.

Formatting the Disks to Prepare Them for Use

To create the FAT, a machine at the factory performs a procedure known as a *low-level format*. This procedure organizes the disk into sectors and tracks. Once the sectors and tracks have been created, the low-level format procedure makes the FAT file and records in it the positions of the new sectors and tracks. Additionally, during this procedure, the low-level format procedure meticulously checks the disk's surface for defects. If any are found, the locations of these bad spots are entered into the FAT as well, so the operating system knows not to store any information in those locations.

When an operating system is installed, it performs a *high-level format* (or operating system format) and creates its own separate FAT that keeps track of where clusters are located and which files are located in which clusters. These two FAT technologies are applicable to all types of drives.

Removable Media Drives

Another type of drive system is the *removable media* drive. Removable drives use technologies similar to fixed disk (fixed media) drives, except the storage medium is removable. The obvious advantage is that removable media multiplies the usefulness of the drive. With a hard disk, when the disk is full, the only two things you can do to increase space are to delete some information or to get a larger drive. With removable media drives, you can remove the full disk and insert a blank one. Other than the Zip and Jaz drives discussed in Chapter 1 (and other than removable hard drives), the test covers numerous categories of removable media drives, as discussed in the rest of this section.

Floppy Disk Drives

The type of removable media drive that is the most often described is the floppy disk drive. It is called that because the original medium was flexible. Floppy disks are like fixed disks, but they have only one platter encased in a plastic shell. Several types of floppy disk drives are available in many different capacities (Figure 3.4 shows a 1.44MB 3½-inch drive), and we will discuss them in the sections to come.

FIGURE 3.4 A floppy disk drive

A floppy drive has either one or two read/write heads. Each head moves in a straight line on a track over the disk rather than on an angular path as with fixed disk systems. When the disk is placed into the drive, a motor engages the center of the disk and rotates it. This action moves the tracks past the read/write heads.

CD-ROM Drives

Another type of removable media drive is the CD-ROM drive (see Figure 3.5). These drives are slightly different from other storage media in several ways. First, they read information differently than magnetic media disk drives do. Because CD-ROM drives use laser light to read the information from the media, they are described as *optical drives*.

FIGURE 3.5 A CD-ROM drive

When reading information from a CD, the drive basically reads a lot of *pits* and *lands* (lands are the spaces between the pits) in the disc surface. The pits are etched into the CD at production time. The laser reflects off the CD's surface and onto a sensor. The sensor detects the pattern of pits and lands as the disc rotates and translates them into patterns of 1s and 0s. This binary information is fed to the computer that is retrieving the data.

Another difference between magnetic media and CD-ROM drives is that CD-ROM drives are read-only devices (CD-ROM stands for Compact Disc–*Read-Only* Memory). The only way to write to a CD-ROM is during manufacture time, when the pits are burned into the substrate of the disc. Once written, they cannot be erased.

CD-ROMs are so popular because even though they can't be written to, they provide large capacity (greater than 500MB) and easy access. They are a great choice for archival storage. Most often used for software distribution, they have taken off in the past few years as the speed of CD-ROM drives has increased.

Recordable and rewritable CD devices are becoming popular; but strictly speaking, they are not CD-ROMs. Technically, these devices are called *rewritable compact discs*.

A CD-ROM disc has a single track that runs from the center to the outside edge, exactly the reverse of the groove on a record. A CD-ROM uses basically the same technology as the audio compact discs used in most homes today. When a CD-ROM is placed into a CD-ROM drive, a motor spins the CD at a specific rate. A laser that reads the CD is then activated. Because of these basic similarities, several compatibilities exist between the different compact disc technologies. For example, it is possible to play audio CDs in a computer's CD-ROM drive. Also, some computer CDs have audio tracks on them and are made to be used in either type of CD drive (home audio or computer).

This compatibility is possible because of *standards*. Standards are put together by committee (*de jure* standards) or documented simply to recognize a standard that's already in practice (*de facto* standards). CD-ROM standards are put together by several groups, the largest of which is the International Standards Organization (ISO), which has defined several standards. Table 3.1 shows the most popular CD standards and their respective applications. The compact disc standards are given as colors of books (we don't know why—they just are).

TABLE 3.1 Compact Disc Standards

CD Standard	Application	ISO Name
Red Book	Audio CDs	CD-Audio
Yellow Book	Data storage (CD-ROM)	ISO 9660
Green Book	CD-I (Interactive CD)	N/A
Orange Book	Write-once CD and magneto-optical	N/A
White Book	CD-I bridge	N/A

Optical Disk Drives

An optical disk is much like a CD-ROM except that it can be read from and written to (like fixed disks, except a laser is used). The upside is that optical disks are removable and can hold lots of information. The downside is that they are expensive and slower than fixed disks.

Tape Drives

The final type of removable media drive is a tape drive (see Figure 3.6). The tape cartridge uses a long polyester ribbon coated with magnetic oxide wrapped around two spools. As the tape unwinds from one spool, it passes by a read/write head in the drive that retrieves or saves the information. It then proceeds to the other spool where it is kept until needed again.

FIGURE 3.6 A tape drive

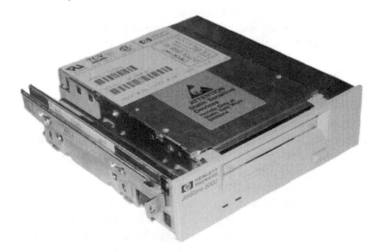

Tape media is great for large-capacity storage, but it is agonizingly slow. The best application for tape media is making backups. Current tape technology uses 4mm or 8mm Digital Audio Tape (DAT) or Digital Linear Tape (DLT) for its storage medium. With these technologies, it is possible to store up to 70GB of data on a single tape cartridge.

Disk Theory

With all of these storage technologies available, there are many to choose from. Which one is the best? The answer is, "It depends." Each type of storage has benefits and drawbacks. Each type of storage is ideally suited to a different application. To help understand these issues, a model has been developed to define the different types of storage. This model is called the *storage pyramid*; it shows the relationship between the types of storage and their benefits (see Figure 3.7).

FIGURE 3.7   The storage pyramid

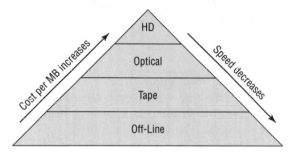

As you can see, at the bottom of the pyramid the storage types have the largest capacity but the slowest access times. Additionally, those types have the least expensive cost per megabyte.

Floppy Disk Systems

Two major types of floppy disk drives are in use today. They are usually identified by the size of the media they use and the capacity of that media. We'll cover each one and its associated configuration and troubleshooting issues. But before we do, let's discuss the four components of a floppy drive subsystem: the disk (also called the medium), the drive, the controller, and the cable.

The Medium

The floppy disk, as we have already mentioned, is the removable medium on which information is stored in a floppy disk system. Two types are in use today: the 5¼-inch *floppy disk* and the 3½-inch *diskette* (sometimes incorrectly called a *hard floppy* or even a *hard disk*). Both are shown in Figure 3.8.

The 5¹/₄-inch disks have almost completely disappeared in the last few years, replaced by the 3¹/₂-inch format. Most newer computers no longer include 5¹/₄-inch drives. As such, you won't be tested on this topic in the A+ exam. We have included coverage in this chapter to provide you with background information.

FIGURE 3.8   A 5¹/₄-inch floppy disk and a 3¹/₂-inch diskette

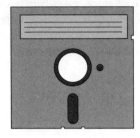 

5¹/₄-Inch Floppy Disk

The 5¹/₄-inch floppy disks are made from a polyester disk coated with iron oxide and a flexible outer covering. The disk has a large hole in the center, called the *drive hole*, which the motor in the disk drive uses to spin the disk. In addition, a 1¹/₂-inch oval window is cut into the case to allow the read/write heads access to the disk media. A small round hole cut into the disk shell next to the drive hole lines up with an even smaller hole cut into the disk media. When this smaller hole spins past the slightly larger hole in the shell, it allows a light to shine all the way through the disk system. In this way, the floppy drive can tell how fast the disk is rotating by how many times per second that hole appears.

Finally, a notch is cut in one side of the disk. This notch is called the *write-protect tab*. When a disk is inserted into a floppy drive, a small lever places itself into this notch. When the lever is in the notch, the disk can be written to. You can *write-protect* the disk (which prevents it from being written to) by covering this hole.

3¹/₂-Inch Diskette

The other type of floppy disk media is not really "floppy" at all. Some people mistakenly call it a hard disk. Its real name is a 3¹/₂-inch *diskette* (to differentiate it from a full-grown disk, I suppose). The 3¹/₂-inch diskettes are also made from a polyester disk coated with a layer of iron oxide. This disk is enclosed in a durable, plastic case. This case is an improvement over the 5¹/₄-inch variety, because the 5¹/₄-inch floppies are easily creased or damaged. The 3¹/₂-inch diskettes also have a metal shutter over the media access window. Again, this is an improvement over 5¹/₄-inch media—people often grasp the disks inadvertently by this edge of the disk, pressing their fingers onto the media and thus contaminating the disk, making it difficult to read.

A notch with a sliding plastic tab over it write-protects the 3 1/2-inch disk. This is also better than 5 1/4-inch disks, because the write-protect notch in the other disks is covered with a type of tape that can come loose in the drive and cause gum-ups.

The Drives

Next we'll discuss the floppy disk drives. We need to discuss three items regarding the drives: media size, form factors, and capacity.

Media Size

Because we covered media size in our discussion of the media, we'll refer you to the previous paragraphs and continue on. We do want to make one note, however: You can't put a 5 1/4-inch diskette into a 3 1/2-inch drive, or vice versa. I know some of you are saying, "Thank you, Captain Obvious, for that enlightening bit of minutia." However, not everyone seems to know this fundamental rule; I always used to constantly pull folded-up 5 1/4-inch disks out of 3 1/2-inch drives on a regular basis.

Form Factors

Three main types of *form factors*, or drive styles, are available: full-height, half-height, and combo form. A form factor usually means the physical dimensions and characteristics of the drive. *Full-height* drives were the only ones available for the first PCs. The drives were large (about 1.63" high) and bulky and usually lower in capacity than today's drives. *Half-height* drives (about 1" high) take up only about half the space (vertically) of full-height drives.

The final form factor is becoming more popular as space is increasingly at a premium in computer cases. The *combination form factor* (or *combo*, for short) contains both 1.2MB 5 1/4-inch and 1.44MB 3 1/2-inch drives in a half-height enclosure. This form factor has the obvious advantage of including both drives in the space for one.

Capacity

Disk capacities range from 360KB to 1.44MB in various form factors. Table 3.2 details the range of capacities available today, their associated form factors, the density of the disk, and the number of sides used. Some disks use only one side of the media, whereas others use both sides. The density of a disk determines how closely the sectors and tracks can be packed. Notice how the combination of all three items relates to the capacity.

TABLE 3.2   Disk Capacities

Capacity	Form Factor	Density	Sides
360KB	5 1/4" FH	Double	Double
720KB	3 1/2" HH	Double	Double

TABLE 3.2 Disk Capacities *(continued)*

Capacity	Form Factor	Density	Sides
1.2MB	5¼" FH or HH	High	Double
1.44MB	3½" HH	High	Double

You may have heard that even though some floppy disks and diskettes are rated as *single-sided*, in fact both sides of a disk are always coated with media. Some people have taken this bit of industry knowledge and decided that it means you can store information on both sides of a single-sided disk. *Don't do it!* Even though the disk *might* be able to be formatted, that doesn't mean the data will stay on the disk. If the disk was rated as single-sided at the factory, you can be assured that the testing process determined there were problems on the other side of the disk. Spend the extra 20 cents and get a disk that's rated for the drive you are using. The same holds true for formatting a low-density disk in a high-density drive and then using it in a low-density drive. Low-density disks aren't designed to have the information packed as tightly as the high-density drives save it.

The Controller

The floppy disk controller (Figure 3.9) is a circuit board installed in a computer that translates signals from the CPU into signals that the floppy disk drive can understand. Often, the floppy controller is integrated into the same circuit board that houses the hard disk controller. Or, even better, the controller can be integrated into the motherboard in the PC. Some people like this approach, but from a technician's standpoint, it's a nightmare. Imagine having to tell the customer that their floppy drive doesn't work because their motherboard needs to be replaced at a cost of $1,100! Wouldn't it be nicer to tell them that you need to replace the $22 floppy disk controller board?

FIGURE 3.9 A floppy controller with cable

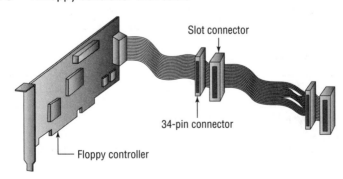

A floppy controller is not a complicated device. The early controllers were large expansion boards that usually contained an Intel 8272 or Zilog 765 controller chip. You can buy a card that contains the floppy controller, two serial interfaces, parallel and game interface ports, and disk interface for about $35.

The Cable

The last topic on our list of prerequisites is the floppy drive cable (shown in Figure 3.9). This cable is made up of a 34-wire ribbon cable and three connectors. One of these connectors attaches to the controller. The other two connect to the drives (one for drive A:, the other for drive B:). You can attach up to two floppy drives to a single controller. These connectors are specially made so that they can be attached to the drives in only one way.

You might think that with 34 wires, the data would be transmitted in a parallel manner (8 bits at a time), but it isn't. Data is transmitted 1 bit at a time, serially. This makes floppy transfers slow, but usually the serial data transfer isn't the bottleneck.

The cable also has a red stripe running down one side, as shown in the detailed version in Figure 3.10. This stripe indicates which wire is for pin #1 on the controller and on the drive(s). This pin is usually marked with a small 1 or a white dot on the controller. When connecting the drives to the controller, you need to make sure the red stripe is oriented so the wire it represents is connected to pin #1 on the drive and pin #1 on the controller. You also connect the drive that will be drive A: *after* the twist in the floppy cable for most floppy systems (very important).

FIGURE 3.10   A typical floppy cable

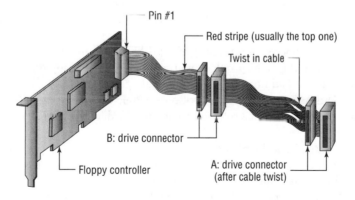

A common technician's trick to remember how to connect floppy drives is to say, "Point the red stripe toward the power cable." The problem is that this trick doesn't work with every brand of floppy drive. It could be considered a general rule of thumb, but not a rule to live by.

Floppy Drive Installation and Configuration

Now that we've covered the basics, let's talk about installation, configuration, and trouble-shooting. Installing floppy drives is no big trick. The first step is to connect the cable to the drive as per the instructions in the previous section. Then, install the drive in the computer by physically mounting it in the computer case and connecting the power cable. Finally, you connect the cable from the drive to the controller, as we discussed already.

With regular diskette drives, when connecting the cable to the drives, you connect the B: drive to the connector before the twist in the cable and the A: drive to the connector after the twist.

One unique situation crops up if you have a Compaq Deskpro. These computers have twists before each of the drives, and the drives are reversed. The first drive on the cable for Deskpros is the A: drive, and the second drive is B:. Deskpros also sometimes have a tape drive connected to the last connector on the cable, after the B: drive and on the same cable. This tape drive must be one specially made for a Deskpro.

Troubleshooting the floppy drive is also relatively simple. The most common problem after installation is a drive light that refuses to go out. This happens if the floppy drive cable is upside down on one side. As you already know, most floppy cables are keyed so they go on in only one direction. However, in some systems, the floppy cable might not be keyed, so you must understand the consequences of not having the cable on in the right direction. Just remember which way the red stripe goes!

In addition to the cable position, you must also set the drive type and size of the floppy drive in the CMOS setup. You do this so the computer knows what drives are attached. If this information is wrong, most computers detect that the wrong drive type is selected, and an error occurs during bootup.

You can also troubleshoot sporadic read/write problems. More often than not, these are caused by a dirty drive. If this is the problem, you can fix it with a floppy-disk head-cleaning kit. Another cause might be a bad floppy disk. Floppies are good for a finite number of uses, and they *can* go bad. (This may come as a shock to some people who think their data is safe forever on a floppy disk.) You can fix this problem by copying the data (if possible) from the old disk to a new one.

Also, don't forget to check the obvious things like a disconnected floppy cable, power not plugged in, or disks not inserted properly. Any one of these can cause problems that most people just assume can't be the difficulty because it's too obvious.

Enough about floppies. Let's talk about disks that have a little more backbone: the hard disks.

IDE/ATA Disk Systems

By the time the IBM AT computer came out, drive sizes were increasing beyond the capabilities of existing technologies to utilize them. The only way out was to use a technology called Small Computer System Interface (SCSI, pronounced *scuzzy*, which we discuss in the next section).

Although it was technologically superior, it was also, at the time, quite expensive. Two companies, Compaq and Western Digital, saw this problem and developed an alternative to SCSI.

They thought that if they could develop a cheap, flexible drive system, people would buy it. They were more right than they realized. That solution, known as *Integrated Drive Electronics (IDE)* because its major feature was a controller located right on the disk, is one of the most popular drive interfaces on the market today. In this section, we'll discuss the theory behind IDE drive systems, as well as configuration and installation issues.

IDE/ATA Technologies

The idea for IDE (more commonly known as *AT Attachment interface*, or *ATA*) was simple: Put the controller on the drive and use a relatively short cable to connect the drive/controller to the system (Figure 3.11). This arrangement has the benefits of decreasing signal loss (thus increasing reliability) and making the drive easier to install.

FIGURE 3.11   An IDE drive and interface

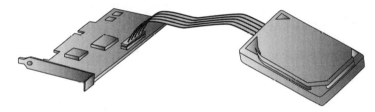

In addition, because the controller is integrated into the same assembly as the drive, the only board that needs to be installed in the computer is an adapter that converted signals between the motherboard and the drive/controller. The board is normally called a *pass-through* or *paddle board*. (This board is often incorrectly called a *controller*. The term is incorrect because the paddle board is often integrated with a floppy controller, two serial ports, a game port, and a parallel port. This combination is normally called a *multifunction interface board*.) With most of today's systems, the IDE adapter is integrated into the motherboard.

In this section, you will learn about the different types of IDE technologies and how they differ from each other. But first, let's go over some terminology.

ATA Terminology

ATA devices are some of the most widely used devices in computers today. We'll discuss some of the common types of ATA standards you can find in computers. However, we need to use some common language to describe them, so let's begin with some of the terms used with IDE/ATA devices.

PIO

When IDE/ATA devices were first introduced, they transferred data using the *Programmed I/O (PIO)* method. In this method, the computer's CPU and supporting hardware directly control the transfer of data between the hard disk and the rest of the computer. This method used several different speeds, which became known as *PIO modes*.

The important thing to note about PIO is that the system CPU is responsible for retrieving the data from the drive, block by block. As drives became faster and had greater transfer abilities, the CPU quickly got bogged down. For this reason, Direct Memory Access (DMA) modes became more popular. Table 3.3 lists the common PIO modes and their *theoretical* maximum transfer rates. Drives are usually slower than their PIO mode's maximum. Also note in this table that the transfer speeds of PIO levels 3 and above are above ISA's maximum transfer rate, so most often PIO modes are not used in favor of DMA (especially on PCI-based systems).

TABLE 3.3 PIO Modes

PIO Mode	Maximum Transfer Rate (MBps)	Defining Standard
Mode 0	3.3	ATA
Mode 1	5.2	ATA
Mode 2	8.3	ATA
Mode 3	11.1	ATA-2
Mode 4	16.6	ATA-2
Mode 5	22.2	None; proposed but not implemented

IDE/ATA interfaces today contain support for several of these modes but may not implement them by default.

DMA Modes

As was suggested with PIO modes, it quickly became unfeasible to have the processor manage the disk transfer process. Therefore, *Direct Memory Access (DMA) transfer modes* were developed. In a DMA transfer, the ATA interface manages the data transfer directly to the rest of the system (typically direct to memory). Note that in addition to being DMA, any disk device using DMA is usually also bus-mastering, which means it takes control of the entire expansion bus.

Several different DMA modes have been developed for the ATA interface, and they can be grouped into two categories: *single word DMA modes* and *multiword DMA modes*. Single word DMA modes transfer data one word at a time (a *word* is two bytes of data, or 16 bits). Multiword DMA transfers transfer several words at a time in a kind of burst. Multiword is used more with later ATA specifications because of the inefficiency of setting up a connection to transfer a single word each time. Multiword transfers set up the connection, transfer multiple words of data, and then close the connection.

Table 3.4 shows examples of the different DMA modes and their theoretical maximum transfer rates.

TABLE 3.4   DMA Transfer Modes

DMA Mode	Transfer Rate (MBps)	Defining Standard
Single Word Mode 0	2.1	ATA
Single Word Mode 1	4.2	ATA
Single Word Mode 2	8.3	ATA
Multiword Mode 0	4.2	ATA
Multiword Mode 1	13.3	ATA-2
Multiword Mode 2	16.7	ATA-2

UltraDMA Mode

Just as the performance of DMA transfers was becoming usable, drive makers began making even faster drives. The designers went to work trying to increase the speed of DMA transfers, but they ran into a snag: They were transferring 16.7MBps of data over an interface and cable designed to handle only 5MBps. Rather than just ramping up the speed, the engineers worked on increasing the efficiency of the interface; and they came up UltraDMA transfer modes. In UltraDMA, data is transmitted on both the rising and falling edges of a clock cycle (similar to the way the DDR memory works). Plus, data integrity is maintained with *Cyclical Redundancy Checking (CRC)*, an error-checking routine that runs a mathematical formula against the data being transmitted. A result is computed and sent with the data. When the data arrives at its destination, the same formula is run against the data. If the results are the same, the transmission is considered successful.

Table 3.5 shows the UltraDMA modes as well as their maximum throughput.

TABLE 3.5   UltraDMA Transfer Modes

UltraDMA Mode	Transfer Rate (MBps)	Specification
Mode 0	16.7	ATA/ATAPI 4
Mode 1	25	ATA/ATAPI 4
Mode 2	33.3	ATA/ATAPI 4
Mode 3	44.4	ATA/ATAPI 5
Mode 4	66.7	ATA/ATAPI 5
Mode 5	100	ATA/ATAPI 6
Mode 6	133	ATA/ATAPI 7; proposed but not official

Now let's take a look at the ATA standards that are used today, starting with the original specification, ATA-1.

ATA-1

The ATA interface was first used with the IBM AT computer. AT Attachment (ATA) was proposed to ANSI as a standard in 1990, but the standard wasn't approved until 1994.

The ATA specification specifies several things. First, the standard allows for the connection of two hard drives (no other kind of device) configured as *master* and *slave* for addressing purposes (they could just as easily have been called drives 1 and 2). The master is designated as the first drive and the slave as the second.

The ATA-1 standard (it was originally called ATA; the 1 differentiates it from the others that came later) also specifies support for PIO modes 0, 1, and 2; DMA single word support for modes 0, 1, and 2; and multiword mode 0 support.

Because drives that support ATA-1 are no longer made and because the standard is hopelessly out of date, the ANSI standard was retired in 1999.

ATA-2

The original ATA standard (also known as ATA-1, as mentioned earlier) was fine for the first IDE hard disks, but it was never meant to grow as a standard. These first disks had limited capacity and a limited throughput. However, ATA wasn't originally developed as a standard. Rather, several companies, in anticipation of the new standard, came up with their own extensions (incompatible with each other, of course) to the original ATA, such as Enhanced IDE (EIDE) and Fast ATA. So, the ANSI standards body had to work backward and essentially combine features of the different manufacturers' ideas into the new standard for ATA-2.

ATA-2 was a new standard for ATA-type drives, and it made several major improvements over the original ATA specification. The most significant addition was *Logical Block Addressing (LBA)*, which provided a method of overcoming the 528MB maximum drive size design limitation of the combination of ATA and the BIOSs of the time. Rather than accessing each block of data by its cylinder, head, and sector address (known as *Cylinder, Head, Sector [CHS] addressing*), LBA specifies that each block on the disk be given its own unique ID number, which is 28 bits long (a maximum of 137GB worth of addresses). Much larger hard drives can therefore be used.

ATA-2 adds support for the much faster PIO modes 3 and 4, in addition to the earlier modes supported by ATA-1. In addition, ATA-2 also supports multiword DMA modes 1 and 2, as well as the modes used in ATA-1. Finally, much to the relief of PC technicians, ATA-2 drives respond well to the Identify Drive command through the BIOS, which allows the BIOS to recognize the various characteristics (including the number of cylinders, heads, and sectors) of the drive(s) being installed.

Many people still call this and all ATA-2 and above specification drives *EIDE drives,* even though that was a marketing term for certain ATA drives developed before the ATA-2 standard was ratified.

ATA-3

ANSI published the *AT Attachment 3 Interface* standard in 1997 as a minor revision of the ATA specification. It specifies only a few new features. Of these, the one that many ATA-3 drives implement and most people don't even know they have is the Self-Monitoring and Analysis Tool (SMART). SMART comprises several circuits within the hard disk's controller that keep track of error conditions and general drive statistics. These circuits try to predict when a hard disk failure will occur. For example, if the number of seek errors increases gradually at first and then suddenly, the SMART controller knows a hard disk failure is imminent and notifies the BIOS and operating system (and, we hope, the user takes notice).

Some marketing pieces claim that PIO Mode 5 was introduced with ATA-3. This is not true. It is true that some BIOSs have PIO Mode 5 as an option in their configuration, but it was never implemented.

Also introduced in the ATA-3 specification was increased reliability for higher speed transfer modes. ATA-2 allowed for higher speeds, but the cable(s) were designed for lower speed ATA-1 drives and interfaces. Finally, ATA-3 introduced a security mode that allows devices to be protected with passwords.

ATA-3 also never defined any of the UltraDMA modes (they were first defined in ATA/ATAPI-4).

ATAPI

As the ATA-standardized hard drives became more popular, people began to wonder if it was possible to put CD-ROM drives on the same bus as the hard drive. It seemed like a natural fit, it would eliminate another expansion card, and it would be much faster than the standard CD-ROM interface. However, there was a problem: The very nature and design of the IDE/ATA bus made it impossible to support any device but a hard disk on the ATA interface.

Engineers in the Small Form Factor group (an ad hoc disk drive industry committee) went to work on solving this problem. The result was the *AT Attachment Packet Interface (ATAPI)*. It allows devices like CD-ROMs, tape drives, and other storage devices to plug in to a standard IDE/ATA cable and be accessed via the standard operating system interface. ATAPI uses the same cable and physical interface, but it requires a special ATAPI driver. The ATAPI driver groups the data to be sent to the CD-ROM or other device into small chunks, called *packets*. These packets can be sent to ATAPI devices via normal PIO or UltraDMA transfer modes.

This is a simplified explanation of how ATAPI works and is sufficient for the A+ exam. The actual process of data encoding is much more complex. If you would like to know more about ATAPI, visit www.ata-atapi.com.

ATAPI CD-ROM drives are often called IDE CD-ROM drives.

ATA/ATAPI-4

With the release of the next revision of the ATA standard, ATA/ATAPI-4, the functions of ATAPI were integrated into the standard. The correct name for this group is *AT Attachment interface with Packet Interface Extension*, but most people just call it *ATA/ATAPI-4* to keep it inline with the other releases.

In addition to the integration of ATAPI, ATA/ATAPI-4 includes several other new features. Some of these include:

New cable design As mentioned earlier, the original 40-pin IDE cable could not support the new, higher throughput rates. In order to avoid transmission problems, a new 80-conductor ATA cable was defined within ATA/ATAPI-4 that interleaves shielding lines between the data lines. Use of this cable is optional, but recommended.

UltraDMA modes UltraDMA modes 0, 1, and 2 were specified that include transfer rates of 16.7, 25, and 33.3MBps, respectively. UltraDMA mode 2 was redubbed UltraDMA/33 by the marketing professionals, and most drives that use the interface are known as UltraDMA/33 drives (even though there is no such standard).

Cyclical Redundancy Checking (CRC) As mentioned earlier, this method of error checking ensures reliable data transmission at the new higher speeds.

ATA/ATAPI-5

As you would expect, computer hardware manufacturers are always looking to make their hardware better and faster (especially faster). Toward that end, the T13 committee that develops these standards for ANSI developed the ATA/ATAPI-5 standard. It was ratified as *AT Attachment with Packet Interface-5* in 2000.

 If you are interested in more information about the T13 committee and its work on the ATA interface, visit www.t13.org/.

Some of the changes in the new revision of the standard include:

ATA command update Several of the old, outdated commands in the ATA command set were removed because they are no longer needed, and several new commands were added.

New UltraDMA modes Even higher-speed UltraDMA modes were added: UltraDMA Mode 3 (44.4MBps) and UltraDMA Mode 4 (66.7MBps). UltraDMA Mode 4 is also known as UltraDMA/66.

Mandatory 80-conductor cable use The new, higher-speed UltraDMA modes required that the ATA/ATAPI-5 interface require the use of the specialized 80-conductor cable.

ATA/ATAPI-6

If there's one thing you can count on, it's that hardware standards will continue to develop. Ratified in September 2002, *AT Attachment with Packet Interface (ATA/ATAPI-6)* is the latest official standard as of this writing. Several new features were added with this version of ATA, including:

New UltraDMA mode The new *UltraDMA Mode 5* transfer mode specifies a transfer rate of 100MBps. This particular transfer mode is one of the most popular interfaces as of this writing (Spring 2003). UltraDMA Mode 5 is also known as UltraDMA/100 (another marketing term).

LBA address size expansion As this standard was being developed, engineers realized that hard drive sizes were rapidly approaching the 28-bit address limit of LBA (refer back to the discussion of LBA). A 28-bit address limit means the largest hard drive can have 268,435,456 (28 in binary) separate 512-byte blocks. If you multiply these two numbers, you get 137,438,953,472 bytes, or 128GB (137,438,953,472 bytes divided by 1,024 bytes per megabyte, and 1,024 megabytes per gigabyte). In ATA/ATAPI-6, the LBA address size has increased to 48 bits, which means a maximum of 281,474,976,710,656 separate blocks. A 48-bit address length means a maximum drive size of 144,115,188,075,855,360 bytes, or 137,438,953,472GB (which is 128 *exabytes*!).

ATA/ATAPI-7

At the time of this writing of this book (Spring 2003), *ATA/ATAPI-7* has yet to be ratified. The development work has been done by T13, and the standard is likely to be ratified by ANSI. But, until it is ratified, it is a proposed standard.

This proposed standard includes some very interesting items. For example, it includes a new type of ATA physical and logical interface: *Serial ATA*. Serial ATA is an implementation of the ATA interface that works over much smaller cables and operates serially (as opposed to the current implementation, which operates via parallel signal lines). In addition, this interface has a proposed speed of 150MBps. Currently it is possible to buy Serial ATA controllers and drives, but they are not necessarily an implementation of ATA/ATAPI-7. ATA/ATAPI-7 may also include UltraDMA mode 6 also known as UltraDMA 133.

Summary of ATA standards

Table 3.6 summarizes the ATA standards and their details.

TABLE 3.6 ATA Standards

Standard	Speed(s) (MBps)	PIO Modes	DMA Modes	UltraDMA Modes	ANSI Standard?	ATAPI Support?
ATA	3.3–8.3	0, 1, 2	Single Word 0, 1, 2 Multiword 0	N/A	Yes	No
ATA-2	11.1–16.7	3, 4	Multiword 1, 2	N/A	Yes	No

TABLE 3.6 ATA Standards *(continued)*

Standard	Speed(s) (MBps)	PIO Modes	DMA Modes	UltraDMA Modes	ANSI Standard?	ATAPI Support?
ATA-3	11.–16.7	All	All	N/A	Yes	No
ATA-4	16.7–33.3	All	All	0, 1, 2	Yes	Yes
ATA-5	44.4–66.7	All	All	3, 4	Yes	Yes
ATA-6	100	All	All	5	Yes	Yes
ATA-7	133?	All	All	6?	No	Yes
Serial ATA	150+	All	All	All	Not yet	Yes (it will have)

Generally speaking, each ATA standard is backward compatible with the standard before it, so each row in Table 3.6 has the features of the rows above it.

IDE/EIDE Installation and Configuration

Installation and configuration of IDE and EIDE devices is much easier than it is with ST-506 and ESDI systems. The basic steps for installing them are the same: Mount the drive in the carrier, connect the cable to the drive, install the drive in the computer, and configure the drive. However, IDE's cabling and configuration issues are less complex. For example, you have only a single 40-pin or 80-pin cable to connect the drives to the computer. (And no, there aren't any twists in this cable.) Cabling is just a matter of connecting the drive(s) to the cable and plugging the cable in to the paddle board or motherboard (see Figure 3.12). This process is made easier because the majority of IDE cables today are keyed so they plug in only one way. If you happen to have a cable that isn't keyed, use the red stripe trick (as discussed earlier in this chapter).

Also note that some IDE drives come with only a two-connector cable, as shown at the top of Figure 3.12. If you need three connectors (for installing a second drive, as in the bottom of the figure), you may have to go to your local electronics supplier and get a three connector cable.

One situation does complicate matters: two (or more) drives in an IDE/EIDE system. Remember that an IDE drive has the controller *mounted on the drive*. If you had two drives connected, which controller would be talking to the computer and sending data back and forth? The answer is, "Only one of them." When you install a second drive, you need to configure it so the controller on one drive is active and the other drives use the controller on this drive for their instructions. You do this by setting the first drive to be the *master drive* and the others to be *slave drives*. As you might suspect, the master is the drive whose controller is used by the other drives (the slaves).

FIGURE 3.12   IDE cable installation

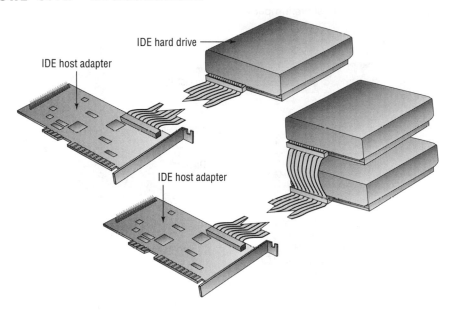

IDE hard drive

IDE host adapter

IDE host adapter

In addition, most computer systems currently use ATA-2 technologies or above, which means they can support four IDE drives. There is a primary and a secondary IDE bus, and each has its own master and slave drives. In these systems, you can have a primary master, a primary slave, a secondary master, and a secondary slave drive. Which bus (primary or secondary) a device is shown as depends on the bus to which you connect the drive. From there, you can designate each drive as master or slave as described in the next section.

Most CMOS setup programs display all the IDE buses and which devices are connected in which positions. You can check the bus and designation (master or slave) for which a device is configured by using View Drive Setup (or a similar command) in your computer's setup program.

Setting Drive Master/Slave Configuration

You implement the master/slave setting by jumpering a set of pins. These pins have several different configurations, so we'll detail just the most common ones. As always, check your documentation to determine which method your drive uses.

The first type of configuration is the simplest. There are two sets of pins: one labeled Master/Single, the other labeled Slave (see Figure 3.13). If you have one drive, you jumper the master side and leave the slave side jumper off. If you have two drives, you jumper the master side only on the first drive (at the end of the cable) and jumper the slave side only on the other drive(s). A variant of this type uses no jumpers on either to indicate just one drive on the bus.

FIGURE 3.13   Master/slave jumpers

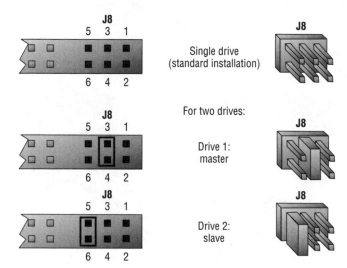

The other type of configuration commonly in use has three sets of pins labeled 1 through 6. These six pins are arranged in three rows of two, with one set labeled Master, another set labeled Slave, and the third set unlabeled. With one drive installed, you leave all jumpers off. With two drives installed, you set the first drive (usually located at the end of the cable) to *master* by jumpering the two pins labeled Master, and then set the second drive to *slave* by jumpering the two pins labeled Slave.

If you have two drives on a bus and both are set to *master* or both are set to *slave*, neither drive will work. In the first case (two masters), they will fight each other for control of the disks. In the latter case (two slaves), the disks won't know where to get their instructions. However, if you have an EIDE interface system, you can have two masters as long as the drives are on two separate IDE buses.

CMOS Drive Configuration

If you have an older computer (one without an IDE auto-detect BIOS), once you have the cable installed and the drives configured as either master or slave, you must tell the computer that the drives exist and what their drive geometry is. You do this by entering the BIOS's *CMOS setup program* (or the disk-based BIOS setup program for older computers). This setup program modifies the computer settings in the CMOS memory that stores the configuration information for the computer. It is accessed by a special key or key combination at startup. Some BIOSs use Del, Esc, or one of the function keys (often F1 or F2); others use Ctrl+Alt+Esc. Note that some of the newer BIOSs auto-detect the type of drive installed in the system and automatically configure these parameters. With this type of system, you only need to accept these parameters and reboot.

Because each machine is different, we'll talk in general terms. Once you have the disks installed, you enter the setup program, go to the Fixed Disk area, and enter the appropriate numbers for the number of cylinders, heads, and sectors the drives have. You then save these values and reboot the machine. At this point, the system should recognize that it includes at least one drive.

There is one problem: Standard BIOS configuration of Cylinder, Head, and Sector (CHS) information is limited to 1,024 cylinders. If you are installing a drive with more than 1,024 cylinders, somehow you must get the BIOS to recognize the drive's full capacity. To enable drive sizes larger than 1,024 cylinders (approximately 600MB), BIOS manufacturers use a technology called is *sector translation*. Sector translation involves remapping the standard CHS layout of a drive in favor of a matrix that allows the full capacity to be used. The most popular method is *Logical Block Addressing* (LBA). In LBA, each sector of the drive is numbered sequentially from the first usable sector to the last. With LBA enabled, the BIOS translates the LBA number of the data being requested into the CHS data for the drive. If you have a drive larger than 1,024 cylinders, you must have a BIOS that supports LBA, and it must be enabled.

Keep in mind that the previous paragraphs regarding setting geometry and LBA apply only to older computers. Most newer computers require little, if any, BIOS configuration in order to recognize a new drive. Most often, the only configuration necessary is the installation of the cable as well as changing the jumper settings.

You do not low-level format IDE (or SCSI) drives! IDE drives are low-leveled at the factory and should never be redone. They use a special utility to perform this delicate procedure. Performing a low-level format on an IDE or SCSI drive will render your drive unreliable, at the least (and will thus compound any problems you may already have). At the worst, it will make the drive completely useless by overwriting sector translation information. Once the drive is installed and recognized by the computer, low-leveling is not necessary.

Now that your drive is installed, you can proceed to format it for the operating system you have chosen. Then, finally, you can install your operating system of choice.

🌐 **Real World Scenario**

The Mystery of Cable Select

In addition to Master and Slave, some drives have a Cable Select jumper option. Cable select is a unique technology that allows the drive's position on the cable to determine whether that drive is a master or slave. This technology is available on most drives in use today. However, it is not compatible with standard 40-wire IDE/ATA cables. You must use either a special cable known as a *Y cable* (because the system board connector is in the middle) or a special 40-pin ATA cable designed for cable select. Thankfully, that special cable is not needed with UDMA ATA drives, because the 80-wire cable used with these technologies includes support for cable select.

In order to use cable select, jumper both devices so they are both cable select and connect them to the cable (which is then connected to the motherboard's IDE bus). In the case of the earlier cable select cables, the drive connected to the middle connector designates itself as master, and the drive at the end designates itself as slave. The opposite is true of UDMA cabling with cable select: The device at the end is the master, and the device connected to the middle connector on the cable is the slave.

Small Computer System Interface (SCSI)

The last type of disk subsystem is probably the most flexible and the most robust. Conversely, it's probably also the most complex. In this section we'll discuss the theory behind the Small Computer System Interface (SCSI), the different types of SCSI, and configuration and installation issues.

SCSI (pronounced *scuzzy*) is a technology developed in the early '80s and standardized by the American National Standards Institute (ANSI) in 1986. The standard, which is known as ANSI document X3.131-1986, specifies a universal, parallel, system-level interface for connecting up to eight devices (including the controller) on a single, shared cable (called the *SCSI bus*). One of the many benefits of SCSI is that it is a very fast, flexible interface. You can buy a SCSI disk and install it in a Mac, a PC, a Sun workstation, or a Whizbang 2000, assuming they make a SCSI host adapter for it. SCSI systems are also known for their speed. At its introduction, SCSI supported a throughput of 5MBps (5 to 10 times faster than previous buses).

SCSI devices can be either internal or external to the computer. If they are internal, they use a 50-pin ribbon cable (similar to the 40-pin IDE drive cable). If the devices are external, they use a thick, shielded cable with Centronics-50 or male DB-25 connectors. These devices aren't always disk drives. Scanners and some printers also use SCSI, because it has a *very* high data throughput.

To configure SCSI, you must assign a unique device number (often called a *SCSI address*) to each device on the SCSI bus (sometimes called the *SCSI chain*). These numbers are configured through either jumpers or DIP switches. When the computer needs to send data to the device, it sends a signal on the wire addressed to that number. A device called a *terminator* (technically a *terminating resistor pack*) must be installed at both ends of the bus to keep the signals from reflecting and causing interference. The device then responds with a signal that contains the device number that sent the information and the data itself.

This information is sent back to the *SCSI adapter*, which operates somewhat like a controller and somewhat like a paddle board. The adapter is used to manage all the devices on the bus as well as to send and retrieve data from the devices.

The adapter doesn't have to do as much work as a true controller because the SCSI devices are *smart* devices; they contain a circuit board that can control the read/write movement. They can also receive signals like "Get this information and give it to me." When a device receives a command like that, it is smart enough to interpret the signal and return the correct information.

Types of SCSI

There are many different types of SCSI devices, but they can all be divided into categories based on the ANSI standard on which they are based. The three main categories are SCSI-1, SCSI-2, and SCSI-3. Let's look at each of these types and the differences between them.

SCSI-1

The original implementation of SCSI was just called *SCSI* at its inception. However, as new implementations came out, the original was referred to as *SCSI-1*. It has been standardized, but this standard is very old and has been withdrawn by ANSI. This implementation is characterized by its 5MBps transfer rate, its Centronics-50 or DB-25 female connectors, and its 8-bit bus width (SCSI-1 is known as *narrow SCSI* because of its smaller bus width). SCSI-1 also had some problems. Some devices wouldn't operate correctly when they were on the same SCSI bus as other devices. The primary issue was that the ANSI SCSI standard was so new that vendors chose to implement it differently.

One important distinction about SCSI-1 devices is that they are *single-ended*, which means they use *single-ended (SE) signaling*. This means these devices use a simple method of communicating with each other. One voltage is used to represent a binary 1, and another is used to represent a binary 0. These voltages are sent over a single wire for each bit in the signal path (for example, eight wires for an 8-bit SCSI bus). Later SCSI technologies use what is known as *differential signaling*. Two wires each are used, each carrying the electrical opposite of the other. The receiving device takes the difference (subtracts one from the other) and uses the resulting value. For example, if the wires are electrically opposite (+5V and −5V), the difference is zero, which represents a binary 0. However, if one wire is +10V and the other is +1V, the difference is a positive voltage, which represents a binary 1. Differential signaling is much more tolerant of cable distances, whereas single-ended signaling has more cable length restrictions.

SCSI-2

After a time, the first major improvement to SCSI-1 was introduced. Known as SCSI-2 (ANSI Standard document X3.131-1994), it enhanced SCSI-1 by allowing for more options. These options produced several subsets of SCSI-2, each having its own name and characteristics. But the most obvious change from SCSI-1 is that SCSI-2 now uses a higher-density connector (see Figure 3.14). SCSI-2 is also backward-compatible with SCSI-1 devices.

FIGURE 3.14 A SCSI-2 connector

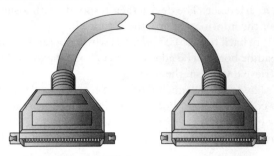

The first improvement designed into SCSI-2 was a wider bus. The new specification specified 8-bit, 16-bit, and (in some cases) 32-bit buses. The larger of the specifications is known as Wide SCSI-2 because it has a wider bus width. It also increased the number of devices per channel (16 as opposed to 8). It basically improved data throughput for large data transfers.

Another important change was to improve on the now-limiting 5MBps transfer rate. The Fast SCSI-2 specification allowed for a 10MBps transfer rate, thus allowing transfers twice as fast as SCSI-1. So, Wide SCSI-2 transfers data 16 bits at a time, and Fast SCSI transfers data 8 bits at a time, but twice as fast (at 10MBps).

Another option combined both specifications into a blazingly fast technology known as SCSI-2 Fast-Wide. It combined the speed of Fast SCSI-2 with the bus width of Wide SCSI-2 to produce a transfer rate of 40MBps.

Finally, SCSI-2 added support for differential signaling. This was later renamed *High Voltage Differential (HVD)* to differentiate it from the *Low Voltage Differential (LVD)* signaling introduced in SCSI-3.

SCSI-3

The newest standard for SCSI is SCSI-3. One of its feature sets is known as Fast-20 SCSI (also known to some as Ultra SCSI). Basically, this is a faster version of Fast SCSI-2 operating at 20MBps for narrow SCSI and 40MBps for Wide SCSI. Another feature set is the Ultra2 Low Voltage Differential (LVD), which increases the maximum SCSI bus length to 25 meters (82 feet) (with HVD devices) and increases the maximum possible throughput up to 80MBps (on Ultra3 Wide LVD).

In theory, LVD is essentially the same as High Voltage Differential (HVD). The major difference between them is the voltage level used: LVD uses a lower voltage than HVD.

Be careful when mixing SE, LVD, and HVD devices. *Never* put either SE or LVD devices on the same channel with HVD. Actual physical damage may result. Also, although SE and LVD devices are electrically compatible, any SE devices on a chain with LVD devices will cause all devices to run at the SE device's slower rated speed. For best results, make sure all SCSI devices are the same type (SE, LVD, or HVD) on a single chain.

Other Proposed Implementations

There are other proposed SCSI implementations, such as Apple's FireWire, Fibre Channel, and IBM's SSA, all offering speeds in the hundreds of MBps range. Fibre Channel, specifically, is gaining support in the LAN arena because of its high-speed storage access and shared-media capability. (The name *Fibre Channel* is somewhat of a misnomer, because the technology will run over fiber optic cable, STP, or coaxial cable.)

SCSI Device Installation and Configuration

Installing SCSI devices is rather complex, but you follow the same basic steps mentioned for the other types of drives (refer back to the previous discussed of hard disk interfaces if you're unclear). The main issues when installing SCSI devices are cabling, termination, and addressing.

Termination and Cabling

We'll discuss termination and cabling together because they are closely tied. There are two types of cabling:

- *Internal cabling* uses a 50-wire or 68-wire ribbon cable with several keyed connectors. These connectors are attached to the devices in the computer (the order is unimportant), with one connector connecting to the adapter.

- *External cabling* uses thick, shielded cables run from adapter to device to device in a fashion known as *daisy-chaining* (see Figure 3.15). Each device has two ports on it (most of the time). When hooking up external SCSI devices, you run a cable from the adapter to the first device. Then you run a cable from the first device to the second device, from the second to the third, and so on.

FIGURE 3.15   A daisy chain

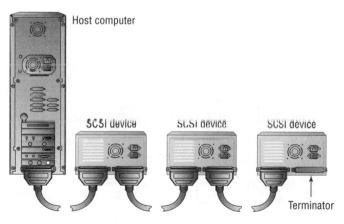

Host computer

SCSI device   SCSI device   SCSI device

Terminator

Because there are two types of cabling devices, you have three ways to connect them. The methods differ by where the devices are located and whether the adapter has the terminator installed. The guide to remember is that *both ends* of the bus must be terminated:

Internal devices only   When you have only internal SCSI devices (Figure 3.16), you connect the cable to the adapter and to every SCSI device in the computer. You then install the terminating resistors on the adapter and on the last drive in the chain only. All other terminating resistors are removed.

FIGURE 3.16 Cabling internal SCSI devices only

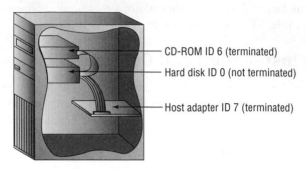

CD-ROM ID 6 (terminated)

Hard disk ID 0 (not terminated)

Host adapter ID 7 (terminated)

Some devices and adapters don't use terminating resistor packs; instead you use a jumper or DIP switch to activate or deactivate SCSI termination on such devices. (Where do you find out what type your device uses? In the documentation, of course.)

External devices only In the next situation, you have external devices only (Figure 3.17). By *external* devices, we mean that each has its own power supply. You connect the devices in the same manner you connect internal devices, but you use several very short (less than 0.5 meters) stub cables to run between the devices in a daisy chain (rather than one, long cable with several connectors). The effect is the same. The adapter and the last device in the chain (which has only one stub cable attached to it) must be terminated.

FIGURE 3.17 Cabling external SCSI devices only

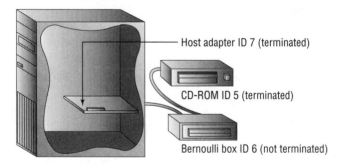

Host adapter ID 7 (terminated)

CD-ROM ID 5 (terminated)

Bernoulli box ID 6 (not terminated)

Both internal and external devices There's also the hybrid situation in which you have both internal and external devices (Figure 3.18). Most adapters have connectors for both internal and external SCSI devices—if yours doesn't have both, you'll need to see if anybody makes one that will work with your devices. For adapters that have both types of connectors, you connect your internal devices to the ribbon cable and attach the cable to the adapter. Then, daisy-chain your external devices off the external port. Finally, terminate the last device on each chain, leaving the adapter *unterminated*.

FIGURE 3.18   Cabling internal and external SCSI devices together

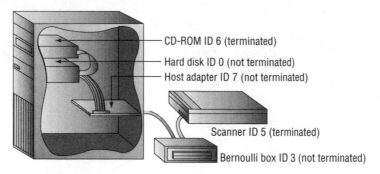

- CD-ROM ID 6 (terminated)
- Hard disk ID 0 (not terminated)
- Host adapter ID 7 (not terminated)
- Scanner ID 5 (terminated)
- Bernoulli box ID 3 (not terminated)

Even though the third technique described is the technically correct way to install termination for the hybrid situation (in which you have both internal and external devices), some adapter cards still need to have terminators installed (for instance, Adaptec AHA-1542s). If you set up both internal and external devices and none of them work, you might have one of these adapters. Try enabling termination on it to see if that fixes the problem.

Types of Termination

No discussion of termination would be complete without mentioning the types of termination methods used. The first type, and the type most people relate to, is *passive termination*. In passive termination, you must install terminating resistor packs on the ends of the SCSI buses. Compare this with *active termination*, where the terminator contains (in addition to terminating resistors) voltage regulators that actively take terminator power from the SCSI bus and use it for powering the termination of the bus.

Maximum Bus Length

In addition to running the cable(s) correctly, it is important to realize that the number of devices you can have on the SCSI channel is limited, as is the maximum length of the SCSI bus. Generally speaking, the faster the SCSI, the shorter the total length of the bus. Table 3.7 shows some of the different types of SCSI and the differences between them, including the maximum length of the bus.

TABLE 3.7   SCSI Differences

SCSI Type	Bus Width (Bits)	Max Devices	Transfer Rate (MBps)	SE (Length in Meters)	LVD (Length in Meters)	HVD (Length in Meters)	Pins
SCSI-1	8	8	5	6	12*	25	25
Fast SCSI	8	8	10	3	12*	25	50

TABLE 3.7 SCSI Differences *(continued)*

SCSI Type	Bus Width (Bits)	Max Devices	Transfer Rate (MBps)	SE (Length in Meters)	LVD (Length in Meters)	HVD (Length in Meters)	Pins
Wide SCSI, a.k.a. Fast-Wide SCSI	16	16	20	3	12*	25	68
Ultra SCSI	8	8	20	1.5	12*	25	50
Ultra SCSI	8	4	20	3	-	-	50
Wide Ultra SCSI	16	16	40	-	12*	25	68
Wide Ultra SCSI	16	8	40	1.5	-	-	68
Wide Ultra SCSI	16	4	40	3	-	-	68
Ultra2 SCSI	8	8	40	N/A	12	25	68
Wide Ultra2 SCSI	16	16	80	N/A	12	25	68
Ultra3 SCSI, a.k.a. Ultra160	16	16	160	N/A	12	-	68
Ultra4 SCSI, a.k.a. Ultra320	16	16	320	N/A	12	-	68

*NOTE: LVD was not part of these specs; however, if all devices are LVD, 12 meters applies. If any device is single ended, then the length in the SE column applies.

Information for this chart was obtained from the SCSI Trade Association (STA), San Francisco, CA (www.scsita.org).

Device Addressing

Now that you have the devices correctly connected, you need to assign each device a unique SCSI ID number. This number can be assigned by jumper (with internal devices) or with a rotary switch (on external devices). You begin by assigning your adapter an address. This number can be any number from 0 to 7 on an 8-bit bus, 0 to 15 on a 16-bit bus, and 0 to 31 on a 32-bit bus, as long as no other device is using that ID.

We have an 8-bit bus at our office, so we normally set our adapter to 7 if we're using regular PC SCSI. We do so because on PC SCSI, the higher the number, the higher the priority. If two devices request the bus at the same time, the device with the higher priority wins. However, if we were running PS/2 SCSI (also known as IBM SCSI), the opposite would hold true (lower numbers, higher priority). So, on PS/2s, we would set our adapter to 0.

Every other device can be set to any number that isn't in use. However, some recommendations are commonly accepted by the PC community. Remember that these are guidelines, not rules:

- Generally speaking, give slower devices higher priority so they can access the bus whenever they need it.

- Set the bootable (or first) hard disk to ID 0.

- Set the CD-ROM to ID 3.

If you accidentally set two devices to the same SCSI ID, you will have a *SCSI ID conflict*. In that case, neither device will work properly, if at all. The best way to solve SCSI ID conflicts is not to have them in the first place. Whenever you are going to install a new SCSI device, check to see which IDs are already in use by devices in your system. To do this, you can either physically examine each device's ID jumpers (discussed next) or use the built-in diagnostics on the SCSI controller in your system (which can be accessed at boot using a key combination like Ctrl+A). These diagnostics display a list of all devices connected to a particular SCSI controller and their IDs.

One other note regarding setting the SCSI ID on internal devices: Most internal devices use three sets of jumpers to set the SCSI ID. These three sets of jumpers represent three binary digits. The highest three-digit binary number is 111, the decimal equivalent of which is 7, or eight discrete positions (0–7). The presence of a jumper on one of these jumper sets represents a binary 1 in that position. The absence of the same indicates a binary 0. You set the decimal SCSI ID of a device by placing or removing jumpers on the three sets of pins so that the binary number indicated represents the SCSI ID for the device. For example, suppose you want to set a device to SCSI ID 3. Remember from Chapter 1 that 011 is the binary representation of the decimal number 3. Therefore, you jumper the rightmost two pins (although you should check which pins in your drive's documentation).

Now that the devices are cabled together and terminated correctly, you have to get the PC to recognize the SCSI adapter and its devices. The good news is that you don't have to modify the PC's CMOS settings. Because SCSI devices are intelligent, you tell the PC that no disk is installed, and let the adapter handle controlling the devices. You have two other ways to get the PC to recognize the SCSI devices:

- If the device is bootable, then you must set the card to be *BIOS enabled*, meaning it has its own BIOS extension that allows the PC to recognize the device without a software driver. The downside to this method is that the adapter must be configured to use an area in reserved memory for its BIOS. However, in a machine with only SCSI devices, it's the most efficient method.

- Load a driver for the adapter into the operating system. This method only works if you are booting from some other, non-SCSI device. If you have to boot from the SCSI drive, you must use the preceding method. This method is commonly used when the only SCSI device attached to the computer is a scanner or CD-ROM drive.

Now that you have the drive installed and talking to the computer, you're almost done. At this point you can high-level format the media and install the operating system.

WARNING Remember the earlier note about low-level formatting IDE and SCSI drives—
don't do it!

> If you have problems, double-check the termination and ID numbers. If everything looks correct, try changing ID numbers one at a time. SCSI addressing is one of those areas that is a voodoo art. Some things that should work don't, and some things that shouldn't work do.

Disk System Fault Tolerance

A hard disk is a temporary storage device, and every hard disk will eventually fail. The most common problem is a complete hard disk failure (also known as a hard disk *crash*). When this happens, all stored data is irretrievable. Therefore, if you want your data to be accessible 90 to 100 percent of the time, you need to use some method of disk fault tolerance. Typically, disk fault tolerance is achieved through disk management technologies such as mirroring, striping, and duplexing drives, and provides a level of data protection. As with other methods of fault tolerance, disk fault tolerance means a disk system is able to recover from an error condition. These technologies are available for both ATA and SCSI drive technologies but require controller support (especially in the case of RAID).

The methods that provide fault tolerance for hard disk systems include:

- Mirroring
- Duplexing
- Data striping
- Redundant array of independent (or inexpensive) disks (RAID)

Understanding Disk Volumes

Before we can discuss the various methods of providing fault tolerance for disk systems, we must mention an important concept: *volumes.* When you install a new hard disk into a computer and prepare it for use, the NOS uses a process known as *formatting* to set up the disk so that you can store data on it. Once this has been achieved, the OS can access the disk. Before it can store data on the disk, it must set up a *volume.* A *volume,* for all practical purposes, is a named chunk of disk space. This chunk can exist on part of a disk, can exist on all of a disk, or can span multiple disks. Volumes provide a way of organizing disk storage, as you can see in this illustration:

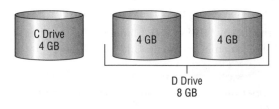

Disk Mirroring

Mirroring a drive means designating a hard disk drive in the computer as a mirror or duplicate of another specified drive. The two drives are attached to a single disk controller. This disk fault tolerance feature is provided by most network operating systems. When the OS writes data to the specified drive, the same data is also written to the drive designated as the mirror. If the first drive fails, the mirror drive is already online, and because it has a duplicate of the information contained on the specified drive, the users won't know that a disk drive in the server has failed. The NOS notifies the administrator that the failure has occurred. The downside is that if the disk controller fails, neither drive is available. Figure 3.19 shows how disk mirroring works.

FIGURE 3.19   Disk mirroring

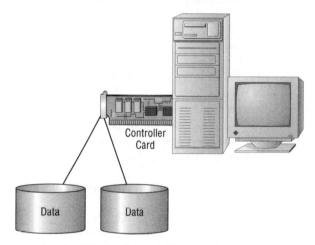

Controller
Card

Data   Data

The drives do not need to be identical, but it helps if they are. Both drives must have the same amount of free space to allow a mirror to be formed. For example, suppose you have two 4GB drives; one has 3GB free, and the other has 2GB free. You can create one 2GB mirrored system.

NOTE   Mirroring is an implementation of RAID Level 1, which is discussed in more detail later in this chapter.

Disk Duplexing

Like mirroring, *duplexing* saves data to a mirror drive. The only major difference between duplexing and mirroring is that duplexing uses two separate disk controllers (one for each disk). Thus, duplexing provides not only a redundant disk, but a redundant controller as well. Duplexing provides fault tolerance even if one of the controllers fails. Figure 3.20 shows a duplexed disk system. Compare this figure with Figure 3.19; notice that the system includes an extra disk controller.

FIGURE 3.20 Disk duplexing

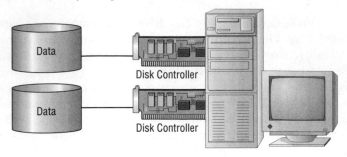

 Duplexing is also an implementation of RAID level 1.

Disk Striping

From a performance point of view, writing data to a single drive is slow. When three drives are configured as a single volume, information must fill the first drive before it can go to the second, and fill the second before filling the third. If you configure that volume to use *disk striping*, you will see a definite performance gain. Disk striping breaks up the data to be saved to disk into small portions and sequentially writes the portions to all disks simultaneously in small areas called *stripes*. These stripes maximize performance because all the read/write heads are working constantly. Figure 3.21 shows an example of striping data across multiple disks. Notice that the data is broken into sections and that each section is sequentially written to a separate disk.

FIGURE 3.21 Disk striping

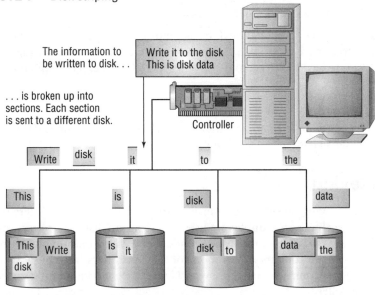

Each disk holds a piece of the original information.

Striping data across multiple disks improves only performance; it does not provide a level of fault tolerance. To add fault tolerance to disk striping, you need to use parity.

Parity Information

Parity, as it relates to disk fault tolerance, is a general term for the fault tolerance information computed for each chunk of data written to a disk. This parity information can be used to reconstruct missing data, should a disk fail. Striping can use parity or not, but if the striping technology doesn't use parity, you won't gain any fault tolerance. When you use striping with parity, the parity information is computed for each block and written to the drive.

The advantage of using parity with striping is gaining fault tolerance. If any part of the data is lost or destroyed, the information can be rebuilt from the parity information. The downside to using parity is that computing and writing parity information reduces the total performance of a disk system that uses striping. The parity information also reduces the total amount of free disk space.

Redundant Array of Inexpensive (or Independent) Disks (RAID)

RAID is a technology that uses an array of less-expensive hard disks instead of one enormous hard disk and that provides several methods for writing to those disks to ensure redundancy. Those methods are described as *levels*, and each level is designed for a specific purpose:

RAID 0 (Commonly used.) This RAID method is the fastest because all read/write heads are constantly being used without the burden of parity or duplicate data being written. A system using this method has multiple disks, and the information to be stored is striped across the disks in blocks without parity. This RAID level only improves performance; it does not provide fault tolerance. It requires a minimum of two drives.

RAID 1 (Commonly used.) This level uses pairs of hard disks, one mirrored to the other (commonly known as *mirroring*; duplexing is also an implementation of RAID 1). This is the most basic level of disk fault tolerance. If the first hard disk fails, the second automatically takes over. No parity or error-checking information is stored. Rather, each drive has duplicate information of the other. If both drives fail, a new drive must be installed and configured, and the data must be restored from a backup. This setup requires a minimum of two drives.

RAID 2 Individual bits are striped across multiple disks. One drive (designated as the *parity drive*) in this configuration is dedicated to storing parity data. If any data drive (a drive in this configuration that is not the parity drive) fails, the data on that drive can be rebuilt from parity data stored on the parity drive. At least three disk drives are required in this configuration. This is not a commonly used implementation.

RAID 3 (Commonly used.) Data is striped across multiple hard drives using a parity drive (similar to RAID 2). The main difference is that the data is striped in bytes, not bits, as in RAID 2. This configuration is popular because more data is written and read in one operation, increasing overall disk performance.

RAID 4   This method is similar to RAID 2 and RAID 3 (striping with parity drive), except data is striped in blocks, which facilitates fast reads from one drive. RAID 4 is the same as RAID 0, with the addition of a parity drive. This is not a popular implementation. So, at least three drives are required in this configuration.

RAID 5   (Commonly used.) The data and parity are striped across several drives, allowing for fast writes and reads. The parity information for data on one disk is stored with the data on another disk; so, if any one disk fails, the drive can be replaced, and its data can be rebuilt from the parity data stored on the other drives. A minimum of three disks is required. Five or more disks are most often used.

There are other levels of RAID, including RAID 53, 6, 7, and 10. However, because they aren't covered on the exam, we won't discuss them here.

Summary

Storage systems for PCs store data until it is called for by the process. In this chapter, you learned about the various types of disk and storage systems available on PCs today, how they work, and the various capacities and access times for each.

First you learned to differentiate among the various types of storage. We discussed storage types used on older computer systems (punch cards and magnetic tape). These storage systems were the grandparents of the magnetic disks of today. You also learned how the basic types of storage work, as well as how they are laid out. You learned terms like FAT, cylinders, sectors, encoding, and interleaving.

Next we explained how floppy disk storage works, the basic components of a floppy disk subsystem, and how to install and configure a floppy disk system. You learned about the different types of floppy disks available ($3\frac{1}{2}$-inch and $5\frac{1}{4}$-inch), as well as the different types of drives associated with each type. You also learned about the controller and cable used to hook the floppy disk drive to the system so that data can be stored on it.

IDE disk drives are the most popular type of disk subsystem used by home PCs today. We discussed the differences between the various types of IDE drives; how to properly configure a multiple-IDE disk system, including the concepts of multiple IDE buses and master and slave drives; and how to properly install and configure the different types of IDE disks.

You also learned about Small Computer System Interface (SCSI) drives. SCSI drives aren't normally found in desktop PCs; they are more commonly used in servers because of their increased performance (and corresponding increased price). They are the preferred drives for servers because they are able to multitask much better than IDE. We discussed the different types of SCSI buses, how to properly install and configure a SCSI disk, how to properly terminate a SCSI bus, and how to set a device's SCSI ID.

Finally, we presented the different methods of disk system fault tolerance, including mirroring, striping, and RAID. It is important to note that both ATA/IDE and SCSI technologies can use these methods, provided the host PC supports them.

Key Terms

Before you take the exam, be certain you are familiar with the following terms:

access time	encoding
active termination	file allocation table (FAT)
actuator arm	fixed disks
AT Attachment 3 Interface	flux transition
AT Attachment interface	hard disks
AT Attachment interface with Packet Interface Extension	hard drives
AT Attachment Packet Interface (ATAPI)	High Voltage Differential (HVD)
AT Attachment with Packet Interface-5	high-level format
AT Attachment with Packet Interface (ATA/ATAPI-6)	Integrated Drive Electronics (IDE)
ATA	interleaving
ATA/ATAPI-4	latency factor
ATA/ATAPI-7	levels
ATA-2	Logical Block Addressing (LBA)
clusters	Low Voltage Differential (LVD)
CMOS setup program	low-level format
Cyclical Redundancy Checking (CRC)	master
cylinder	master drive
Cylinder, Head, Sector (CHS) addressing	multiword DMA modes
daisy-chaining	optical drives
data compression	packets
Direct Memory Access (DMA) transfer modes	passive termination
disk sector	PIO modes
drive geometry	platters
drive hole	Programmed I/O (PIO)

read/write heads

removable media

Run Length Limited (RLL)

SCSI adapter

SCSI address

SCSI bus

SCSI chain

SCSI ID conflict

seek time

Serial ATA

single word DMA modes

single-ended

single-ended (SE) signaling

slave

slave drives

spin speed

spindle

terminating resistor pack

tracks

UltraDMA Mode 5

volume

word

write-protect tab

Review Questions

1. Which IDE-related standard is able to transfer data at 33MBps?

    A. IDE

    B. ATA

    C. ATA-2

    D. UltraDMA/33

2. What are the most common sizes for floppy drives? (Select all that apply.)

    A. $3\frac{1}{4}$ inch

    B. $3\frac{1}{2}$ inch

    C. $5\frac{1}{4}$ inch

    D. $5\frac{1}{2}$ inch

3. How many devices can SCSI-1 support (including the controller)?

    A. 8

    B. 7

    C. 1

    D. 9

4. How many devices can be used by a single IDE controller channel?

    A. 1

    B. 2

    C. 3

    D. 7

5. Which device converts signals from an IDE drive into signals the CPU can understand?

    A. Controller

    B. Host bus adapter

    C. Bus

    D. Paddle board

6. Which implementation of SCSI has a transfer rate of 20MBps?

    A. Fast SCSI-2

    B. Fast-Wide SCSI-2

    C. Wide SCSI-2

    D. Ultra SCSI

7. Suppose you have an internal SCSI hard drive and two external devices: a scanner and a CD-ROM drive. The scanner is the last device on the chain. Which device(s) should be terminated? (Select all that apply.)

   A. Hard disk

   B. Scanner

   C. CD-ROM drive

   D. Host bus adapter

8. Which process converts binary information into patterns of magnetic flux on a hard disk's surface?

   A. Fluxing

   B. Warping

   C. Encoding

   D. Decoding

9. What is the name for the areas into which a typical hard disk is divided (they look like the wedges in a pie)?

   A. Tracks

   B. Sectors

   C. Clusters

   D. Spindles

10. How do you low-level format an IDE drive?

    A. Enter the DEBUG.EXE program and enter **g=c800:5** at the – prompt.

    B. Run LOWLEVEL.COM.

    C. Execute FORMAT.COM.

    D. You don't; it's done at the factory.

11. Which SCSI implementation can transfer data at up to 10MBps?

    A. SCSI-1

    B. Fast SCSI-2

    C. Ultra SCSI

    D. Wide Ultra2 SCSI

12. How do you low-level format a SCSI drive?

    A. Enter the DEBUG.EXE program and enter **g=c800:5** at the – prompt.

    B. Run LOWLEVEL.COM.

    C. Execute FORMAT.COM.

    D. You don't; it's done at the factory.

13. Which of the following must be done when installing SCSI devices? (Select all that apply.)

    A. Terminate the first and last devices in the chain.

    B. Set unique SCSI ID numbers.

    C. Connect the first device to the connector before the twist.

    D. Set every device on the same SCSI channel to the same SCSI ID number.

14. Low-leveling a disk drive means doing which of the following?

    A. Installing the drive in the bottom of the computer

    B. Getting a disk drive ready for the installation of an operating system

    C. Organizing the disk into sectors and tracks

    D. Organizing the disk into clusters and FATs

15. You have just replaced the floppy drive in a PC. When you turn on the computer, you discover you can't boot to the floppy drive. The drive light turns on during power-up and stays lit until you turn the computer off. What should you do to solve this problem? (Select all that apply.)

    A. Change the drive type in the CMOS setup.

    B. Reverse the floppy drive cable.

    C. Remove the terminating resistor on the floppy drive.

    D. Move the floppy drive to the end of the floppy cable.

16. Which of the following is *not* a feature of disk drives?

    A. Rotating disks are coated with a special substance sensitive to magnetism.

    B. As the disk rotates, the particles of the substance become polarized or magnetized, indicating a 1.

    C. The unpolarized areas indicate a 0.

    D. These disk systems store data in linear format and access it sequentially.

17. Which of the following is *not* a disk specification?

    A. Size or capacity

    B. Individual seek time

    C. Access time to perform read/write requests

    D. Spin speed

18. A typical hard drive has how many bytes per sector?

    A. 512

    B. 501

    C. 515

    D. 520

19. Which of the following is *not* a means of disk organization?

    A. Tracks

    B. Heads

    C. Sectors

    D. Cylinders

20. If a typical hard disk has 903 cylinders, 12 heads, 63 sectors per track, and 512 bytes per sector, what is its capacity?

    A. 333MB

    B. 350MB

    C. 323MB

    D. 373MB

Answers to Review Questions

1. D. UDMA can transfer data at 33MBps. IDE and ATA are essentially the same technology and can transfer data at 3.3MBps. ATA-2 can transfer data at 11.1MBps.

2. B, C. The two sizes of drives that can be found are $3\frac{1}{2}$ inch and $5\frac{1}{4}$ inch, but $3\frac{1}{2}$ inch is more common now.

3. A. Including the controller card, SCSI-1 can support up to 8 devices, with address IDs ranging from 0 to 7.

4. B. Each IDE controller can have a single master and a single slave device. Up to two IDE controllers are supported in most PCs.

5. D. The paddle board is the device responsible for converting signals from an IDE drive into signals the CPU can understand. It is commonly (and erroneously) called the controller card.

6. D. The Ultra SCSI, or SCSI-3, standard supports a transfer rate of 20MBps. This is twice as fast as the Fast SCSI-2 implementation.

7. A, B. In this example, you terminate the internal hard drive, not the adapter. You also terminate the scanner, because it is the last device of the external chain.

8. C. Encoding converts binary information into patterns of magnetic flux on a hard disk's surface. This is how the data is written to the surface.

9. B. Although all the options are terms that describe characteristics of the hard drive, sectors most closely resemble pie-shaped wedges.

10. D. Low-level formatting should *never* be performed, because it is done before the drive leaves the factory. If you attempt to do this, you can render your drive unusable.

11. B. SCSI transfers data at 5MBps, Fast SCSI-2 at 10MBps, Ultra SCSI at 20MBps, and Wide Ultra2 SCSI at 80MBps.

12. D. Just as with IDE drives, you should *never* low-level format a SCSI drive. Doing so can render your disk unusable.

13. A, B. To properly configure SCSI devices, the ends of the chain(s) must be properly terminated and each device must have a unique ID.

14. C. Low-leveling is a formatting process done at the factory that arranges the disk into the correct number of sectors and tracks. You should not do this to IDE or SCSI drives because it will render them unusable.

15. A, B. One or both of two things need to be changed. More than likely, pin #1 is not properly connected to the ribbon cable on either the controller or the drive side of the cable. It is also possible that in the CMOS setup, the drive is set to the wrong type and needs to be corrected.

16. D. Fixed disk drives store data randomly. Therefore, option D is not a feature of disk drives.

17. C. Generally, disk specifications are given as the capacity, the seek time, and the spin speed of the drive.

18. A. A typical hard drive has 512 bytes per sector.

19. B. Heads are a physical part of the drive system responsible for reading/writing the data, whereas all the other options are means of organizing the disk.

20. A. To solve this problem, you must understand how the math works. Take (903 × 12 × 63 × 512 bytes) ÷ 1,024 bytes per kilobyte ÷ 1,024 kilobytes per megabyte. The answer is 333MB. The division by 1,024 twice is necessary to convert bytes to megabytes.

Chapter

4

Printers

THE FOLLOWING OBJECTIVES ARE COVERED IN THIS CHAPTER:

✓ 5.1 Identify printer technologies, interfaces, and options/upgrades.

✓ 5.2 Recognize common printer problems and techniques used to resolve them.

Let's face it. Our society is dependent on paper. When we conduct business, we use different types of paper documents. Contracts, letters, and, of course, money are all used to conduct business. As more and more of those documents are created on computers, printers will become increasingly important.

Printers are electromechanical output devices that are used to put information from the computer onto paper. They have been around since the introduction of the computer. Other than the display monitor, the printer is the most popular peripheral purchased for a computer, because most people need to have paper copies of the documents they create.

In this chapter, we will discuss the details of each major type of printer, including impact printers, ink printers, and laser (page) printers. We'll also talk about printer interfaces and the supplies used for printers. Finally, we'll go over some of the problems that arise during printer use and how to troubleshoot them.

Take special note of the section on laser and page printers. The A+ exams test these subjects in detail, so we'll cover them in just as much depth.

Impact Printers

There are several categories of printers, but the most basic type is the category known as *impact printers*. Impact printers, as their name suggests, use some form of impact and an inked ribbon to make an imprint on the paper. In a manner of speaking, typewriters are like impact printers. Both use an inked ribbon and an impact head to make letters on the paper. The major difference is that the printer can accept input from a computer.

There are two major types of impact printers: daisy wheel and dot matrix. Each type has its own service and maintenance issues.

Daisy-Wheel Printers

Although they aren't really covered on the A+ exam, the first type of impact printer we're going to discuss is the *daisy-wheel printer*. These printers contain a wheel (called the *daisy wheel* because it looks like a daisy) with raised letters and symbols on each "petal" (see Figure 4.1). When the printer needs to print a character, it sends a signal to the mechanism that contains the wheel. This mechanism is called the *printhead*. The printhead rotates the daisy wheel until the required character is in place. An electromechanical hammer (called a *solenoid*) then strikes the back of the petal containing the character. The character pushes up against an inked ribbon that ultimately strikes the paper, making the impression of the requested character.

FIGURE 4.1   A daisy-wheel printer mechanism

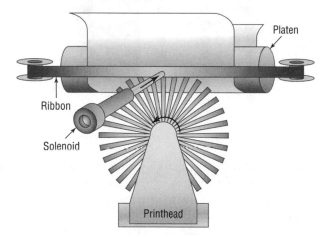

Daisy-wheel printers were one of the first types of impact printer developed. Their speed is rated by the number of *characters per second (cps)* they can print. The early printers could only print between two and four characters per second. Aside from their poor speed, the main disadvantage to this type of printer is that it makes a lot of noise when printing—so much, in fact, that special enclosures were developed to contain the noise.

The daisy-wheel printer has a few advantages, of course. First, because it is an impact printer, you can print on multipart forms (like carbonless receipts), assuming they can be fed into the printer properly. Second, it is relatively inexpensive compared to the price of a laser printer of the same vintage. Finally, the print quality is comparable to a typewriter because it uses a very similar technology. This typewriter level of quality was given a name: *letter quality (LQ)*.

Dot-Matrix Printers

The other type of impact printer we'll discuss is the *dot-matrix printer*. These printers work in a manner similar to daisy-wheel printers, but instead of a spinning, character-imprinted wheel, the printhead contains a row of *pins* (short, sturdy stalks of hard wire). These pins are triggered in patterns that form letters and numbers as the printhead moves across the paper (see Figure 4.2).

The pins in the printhead are wrapped with coils of wire to create a solenoid and are held in the rest position by a combination of a small magnet and a spring. To trigger a particular pin, the printer controller sends a signal to the printhead, which energizes the wires around the appropriate print wire. This turns the print wire into an electromagnet, which repels the print pin, forcing it against the ink ribbon and making a dot on the paper. The arrangement of the dots in columns and rows creates the letters and numbers you see on the page. Figure 4.2 shows this process.

FIGURE 4.2 Formation of images in a dot-matrix printer

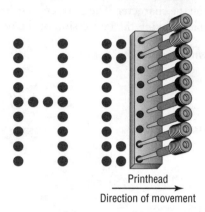

Printhead

Direction of movement

The main disadvantage of dot-matrix printers is their image quality, which can be quite poor compared to the quality produced with a daisy wheel. Dot-matrix printers use patterns of dots to make letters and images, and the early dot-matrix printers used only nine pins to make those patterns. The output quality of such printers is referred to as *draft quality*—good mainly for providing your initial text to a correspondent or reviser. Each letter looked fuzzy because the dots were spaced as far as they could be and still be perceived as a letter or image. As more pins were crammed into the printhead (17-pin and 24-pin models were eventually developed), the quality increased because the dots were closer together. Dot-matrix technology ultimately improved to the point that a letter printed on a dot-matrix printer was *almost* indistinguishable from typewriter output. This level of quality is known as *near letter quality (NLQ)*.

Dot-matrix printers are noisy, but the print wires and printhead are covered by a plastic dust cover, making them quieter than daisy-wheel printers. They also use a more efficient printing technology, so the print speed is faster (typically in the range of 36 to 72cps). Some dot-matrix printers (like the Epson DFX series) can print at close to a page per second! Finally, because dot-matrix printers are also impact printers, they can use multipart forms. Because of these advantages, dot-matrix printers quickly made daisy-wheel printers obsolete.

Bubble-Jet Printers

The next category of printer technology is one of the most popular in use today. This category is actually an advanced form of an older technology known as *ink-jet printers*. Both types of printers spray ink on the page, but ink-jet printers use a reservoir of ink, a pump, and an ink nozzle to accomplish this. They were messy, noisy, and inefficient. Bubble-jet printers work much more efficiently and are much cheaper.

In a *bubble-jet printer*, bubbles of ink are sprayed onto a page and form patterns that resemble the items being printed. In this section, you will learn the parts of a bubble-jet printer, as well as how bubble-jet printers work.

Parts of a Typical Bubble-Jet Printer

Bubble-jet printers are simple devices. They contain very few parts (even fewer than dot-matrix printers) and, as such, are inexpensive to manufacture. It's common today to have a $99 bubble-jet printer with print quality that rivals that of basic laser printers.

In this section, you will learn the parts of a typical bubble-jet printer and what they do. The printer parts can be divided into the following categories:

- Printhead/ink cartridge
- Head carriage, belt, and stepper motor
- Paper feed mechanism
- Control, interface, and power circuitry

Printhead/Ink Cartridge

The first part of an bubble-jet printer is the one people see the most: the *printhead*. This part of a printer contains many small nozzles (usually 100–200) that spray the ink in small dots onto the page. Many times the printhead is part of the *ink cartridge*, which contains a reservoir of ink and the printhead in a removable package. Color bubble-jet printers include multiple printheads, one for each of the *CMYK* print inks (cyan, magenta, yellow, and black).

Every bubble-jet printer works in a similar fashion. As we just mentioned, each bubble-jet printer contains a special part called an ink cartridge (see Figure 4.3) that contains the printhead and ink supply (although some printers separate them so they can be replaced separately). The print cartridge must be replaced as the ink supply runs out.

FIGURE 4.3   A typical ink cartridge (size: approximately 3 inches by 1 1/2 inches)

Inside the ink cartridge are several small chambers. At the top of each chamber is a metal plate and a tube leading to the ink supply. At the bottom of each chamber is a small pinhole. These pinholes are used to spray ink on the page to form characters and images as patterns of dots (similar to the way a dot-matrix printer works, but with much higher resolution).

There are two methods of spraying the ink out of the cartridge. The first was developed by Hewlett-Packard (HP): When a particular chamber needs to spray ink, an electric signal is sent to the heating element, energizing it. The elements heat up quickly, causing the ink to vaporize. Because of the expanding ink vapor, the ink is pushed out the pinhole and forms a bubble.

As the vapor expands, the bubble eventually gets large enough to break off into a droplet. The rest of the ink is pulled back into the chamber by the surface tension of the ink. When another drop needs to be sprayed, the process begins again. The second method, developed by Epson, uses a piezoelectric element that flexes when energized. The outward flex pushes the ink from the nozzle; on the return, it sucks more ink from the reservoir.

When the printer is done printing, the printhead moves back to its maintenance station. The *maintenance station* contains a small suction pump and ink-absorbing pad. To keep the ink flowing freely, before each print cycle, the maintenance station pulls ink through the ink nozzles using vacuum suction. This expelled ink is absorbed by the pad. The station serves two functions: to provide a place for the printhead to rest when the printer isn't printing, and to keep the printhead in working order.

Head Carriage, Belt, and Stepper Motor

Another major component of the bubble-jet printer is the head carriage and the associated parts that make it move. The *printhead carriage* is the component of a bubble-jet printer that moves back and forth during printing. It contains the physical as well as electronic connections for the printhead and (in some cases) the ink reservoir. Figure 4.4 shows an example of a head carriage. Note the clips that keep the ink cartridge in place and the electronic connections for the ink cartridge. These connections cause the nozzles to fire, and if they aren't kept clean, you may have printing problems.

FIGURE 4.4   A printhead carriage in a bubble-jet printer

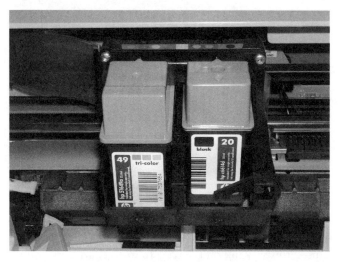

The stepper motor and belt make the printhead carriage move. A *stepper motor* is a precisely made electric motor that can move in the same very small increments each time it is activated. That way, it can move to the same position(s) time after time. The motor that makes the printhead carriage move is most often called the *carriage motor* or *carriage stepper motor*. Figure 4.5 shows an example of a stepper motor.

FIGURE 4.5 A carriage stepper motor

In addition to the motor, a belt is placed around two small wheels or pulleys and attached to the printhead carriage. This belt, called the *carriage belt*, is driven by the carriage motor and moves the printhead back and forth across the page while it prints. To keep the printhead carriage aligned and stable while it traverses the page, the carriage rests on a small metal *stabilizer bar*. Figure 4.6 shows the stabilizer bar, carriage belt, and pulleys.

FIGURE 4.6 Stabilizer bar, carriage belt, and pulleys in a bubble-jet printer

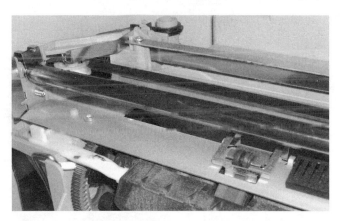

Paper-Feed Mechanism

In addition to getting the ink onto the paper, the printer must have a way to get the paper into the printer. That's where the paper-feed mechanism comes in. The *paper-feed mechanism* picks up paper from the paper drawer and feeds it into the printer. This assembly consists of several smaller assemblies. First you have the *pickup rollers* (Figure 4.7), which are several rubber rollers with a slightly flat spot; they rub against the paper as they rotate, and feed the paper into the printer. They work against small cork or rubber patches known as *separator pads* (Figure 4.8), which help keep the rest of the paper in place (so only one sheet goes into the printer). The pickup rollers are turned on a shaft by the *pickup stepper motor*.

FIGURE 4.7   Bubble-jet pickup rollers

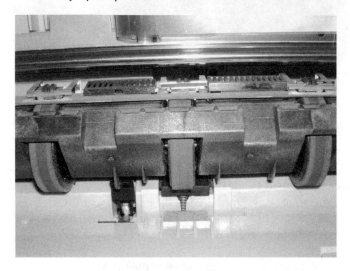

FIGURE 4.8   Bubble-jet separator pads

Sometimes the paper that is fed into a bubble-jet printer is placed into a *paper tray*, which is simply a small plastic tray in the front of the printer that holds the paper until it is fed into the printer by the paper-feed mechanism. On smaller printers, the paper is placed vertically into a *paper feeder* at the back of the printer; it uses gravity, in combination with feed rollers and separator pads, to get the paper into the printer. No real rhyme or reason dictates which manufacturers use these different parts; some models use them, some don't. Generally, more expensive printers use paper trays, because they hold more paper. Figure 4.9 shows an example of a paper tray on a bubble-jet printer.

FIGURE 4.9   A paper tray on a bubble-jet printer

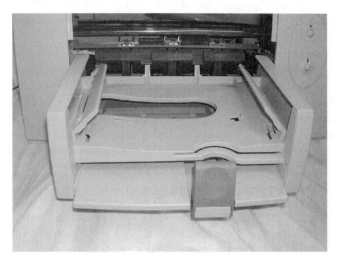

The final part of the paper-feed mechanism is the *paper-feed sensors*. These components tell the printer when it is out of paper, as well as when a paper jam has occurred during the paper-feed process. Figure 4.10 shows an example of a paper-feed sensor.

FIGURE 4.10   A paper-feed sensor on a bubble-jet printer

Control, Interface, and Power Circuitry

The final component group is the electronic circuitry for printer control, printer interfaces, and printer power. The *printer control circuits* are usually on a small circuit board that contains all the circuitry to run the stepper motors the way the printer needs them to work (back and forth, load paper and then stop, and so on). These circuits are also responsible for monitoring the health of the printer and reporting that information back to the PC.

Next, the *interface circuitry* not only makes the physical connection to whatever signal is coming from the computer (parallel, serial, SCSI, network, infrared, and so on), but also connects the interface to the control circuitry. The interface circuitry converts the signals from the interface into the datastream that the printer uses.

The last set of circuits the printer uses are the *power circuits*. Essentially, these conductive pathways convert 110V or 220V house current into the voltages the bubble-jet printer uses (usually 12V and 5V) and distribute those voltages to the other printer circuits and devices that need it. This is accomplished through the use of a transformer. A transformer, in this case, takes the 110VAC current and changes it to 12VDC (among others). This transformer can be either internal (incorporated into the body of the printer) or external. Today's bubble-jets can use either design, although the integrated design is preferred because it is simpler and doesn't show the bulky transformer.

The Bubble-Jet Printing Process

Just as with other types of printing, the bubble-jet printing process consists of a set of steps the printer must follow in order to put the data onto the page being printed. The following steps happen whenever you click the Print button in your favorite software (like Microsoft Word or Internet Explorer):

1. You click the Print button (or similar) that initiates the printing process.

2. The software you are printing from sends the data to be printed to the printer driver you have selected.

 The function and use of the printer driver is discussed later in this chapter.

3. The printer driver uses a page-description language to convert the data being printed into the proper format that the printer can understand. The driver also ensures that the printer is ready to print.

4. The printer driver sends the information to the printer via whatever connection method is being used (parallel, USB, network, and so on).

5. The printer stores the received data in its onboard *print buffer* memory. A print buffer is a small amount of memory (typically 512KB to 16MB) used to store print jobs as they are received from the printing computer. This buffer allows several jobs to be printed at once and helps printing to be completed quickly.

6. If the printer has not printed in a while, the printer's control circuits activate a cleaning cycle. A *cleaning cycle* is a set of steps the bubble-jet printer goes through in order to purge

the printheads of any dried ink. It uses a special suction cup and sucking action to pull ink through the printhead, dislodging any dried ink or clearing stuck passageways.

7. Once the printer is ready to print, the control circuitry activates the paper-feed motor. This causes a sheet of paper to be fed into the printer until the paper activates the paper-feed sensor, which stops the feed until the printhead is in the right position and the leading edge of the paper is under the printhead. If the paper doesn't reach the paper-feed sensor in a specified amount of time after the stepper motor has been activated, the Out of Paper light is turned on and a message is sent to the computer.

8. Once the paper is positioned properly, the printhead stepper motor uses the printhead belt and carriage to move the printhead across the page, little by little. The motor is moved one small step, and the printhead sprays the dots of ink on the paper in the pattern dictated by the control circuitry. Typically, this pattern is either a pattern of black dots, or a pattern of *cyan, magenta, yellow, and black (CMYK)* inks that are mixed to make colors. Then the stepper motor moves the printhead another small step; the process repeats all the way across the page. This process is so quick, however, that the entire motion of starts and stops across the page looks like one smooth motion.

9. At the end of a pass across the page, the paper-feed stepper motor advances the page a small amount. Then, the printhead repeats step 8. Depending on the model, the printhead either returns to the beginning of the line and prints again in the same direction only, or it moves backward across the page so that printing occurs in both directions. This process continues until the page is finished.

10. Once the page is finished, the feed-stepper motor is actuated and ejects the page from the printer into the output tray. If more pages need to print, printing the next page begins again at step 7.

11. Once printing is complete and the final page has been ejected from the printer, the printhead is *parked* (locked into rest position) and the print process is finished.

Laser Printers (Page Printers)

Laser printers are referred to as *page printers* because they receive their print job instructions one page at a time (rather than receiving instructions one line at a time). There are two major types of page printers: those that use the Electrophotographic (EP) print process and those that use the light-emitting diode (LED) print process. Each works in basically the same way, with slight differences.

Electrophotographic (EP) Laser Printers

When Xerox and Canon developed the first laser printers in the late 1980s, they were designed around the Electrophotographic (EP) process (a technology developed by scientists at Xerox). This technology uses a combination of static electric charges, laser light, and a black powdery substance called *toner*. Printers that use this technology are called EP process laser printers, or just *laser printers*. Every laser printer technology has its foundations in the EP printer process.

Let's discuss the basic components of the EP laser printer and how they operate so you can understand the way an EP laser printer works.

Basic Components

Any printer that uses the EP process contains nine standard assemblies: the toner cartridge, laser scanner, high-voltage power supply, DC power supply, paper-transport assembly (including paper-pickup rollers and paper-registration rollers), corona, fusing assembly, printer controller circuitry, and ozone filter. Let's discuss each of the components individually before we examine how they all work together to make the printer function.

The Toner Cartridge

The EP toner cartridge (Figure 4.11), as its name suggests, holds the toner. Toner is a black, carbon substance mixed with polyester resins (to make it flow better) and iron oxide particles (to make the toner sensitive to electrical charges). These two components make the toner capable of being attracted to the photosensitive drum and of melting into the paper. In addition to these components, toner contains a medium called the *developer* (also called the *carrier*), which carries the toner until it is used by the EP process. The toner cartridge also contains the EP print drum. This drum is coated with a photosensitive material that can hold a static charge when not exposed to light (but *cannot* hold a charge when it *is* exposed to light—a curious phenomenon, and one that EP printers exploit for the purpose of making images). Finally, the drum contains a cleaning blade that continuously scrapes the used toner off the photosensitive drum to keep it clean.

FIGURE 4.11   An EP toner cartridge

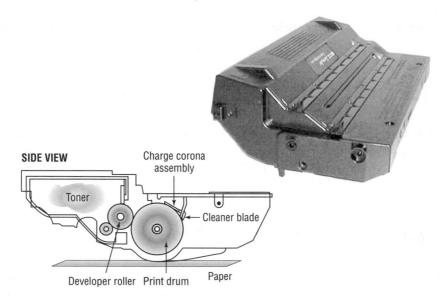

In most laser printers, *toner cartridge* means an EP toner cartridge that contains toner and a photosensitive drum in one plastic case. In some laser printers, however, the toner and photosensitive drum can be replaced separately instead of as a single unit. If you ask for a toner cartridge for one of these printers, all you will receive is a cylinder full of toner. Consult the printer's manual to find out which kind of toner cartridge your laser printer uses.

The Laser Scanning Assembly

As we mentioned earlier, the EP photosensitive drum can hold a charge if it's not exposed to light. It is dark inside an EP printer, except when the laser scanning assembly shines on particular areas of the photosensitive drum. When it does that, the drum discharges, but only in that area. As the drum rotates, the laser scanning assembly scans the laser across the photosensitive drum. Figure 4.12 shows the laser scanning assembly.

FIGURE 4.12   The EP laser scanning assembly (side view and simplified top view)

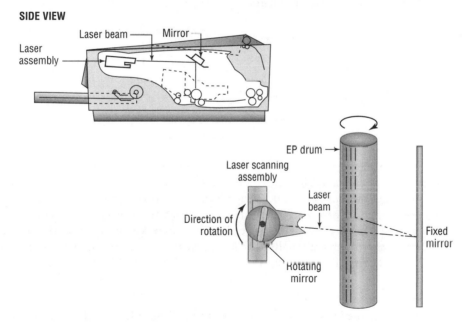

Laser light is damaging to human eyes. Therefore, it is kept in an enclosure and will operate only when the laser printer's cover is closed.

High-Voltage Power Supply (HVPS)

The EP process requires high-voltage electricity. The high-voltage power supply (HVPS) provides the high voltages used during the EP process. This component converts house AC current (120 volts, 60 Hertz) into higher voltages that the printer can use. This high voltage is used to energize both the corona wire and the transfer corona wire.

DC Power Supply (DCPS)

The high voltages used in the EP process can't power the other components in the printer (the logic circuitry and motors). These components require low voltages, between +5 and +24VDC. The DC power supply (DCPS) converts house current into three voltages: +5VDC and –5VDC for the logic circuitry and +24VDC for the paper transport motors. This component also runs the fan that cools the internal components of the printer.

Paper Transport Assembly

The paper transport assembly is responsible for moving the paper through the printer. It consists of a motor and several rubberized rollers that each perform a different function.

The first type of roller found in most laser printers is the *feed roller*, or *paper pickup roller* (Figure 4.13). This D-shaped roller, when activated, rotates against the paper and pushes one sheet into the printer. This roller works in conjunction with a special rubber separator pad to prevent more than one sheet from being fed into the printer at a time.

FIGURE 4.13   Paper transport rollers

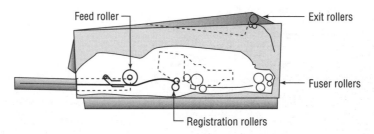

Another type of roller that is used in the printer is the *registration roller* (also shown in Figure 4.13). There are actually two registration rollers, which work together. These rollers synchronize the paper movement with the image-formation process in the EP cartridge. The rollers don't feed the paper past the EP cartridge until the cartridge is ready for it.

Both of these rollers are operated with a special electric motor known as an *electronic stepper motor*. This type of motor can accurately move in very small increments. It powers all the paper transport rollers as well as the fuser rollers.

The Transfer Corona Assembly

When the laser writes the images on the photosensitive drum, the toner then sticks to the exposed areas; we'll cover this in the next section, "Electrophotographic (EP) Print Process." How does the toner get from the photosensitive drum onto the paper? The *transfer corona assembly* (Figure 4.14) is charged with a high-voltage electrical charge. This assembly charges the paper, which pulls the toner from the photosensitive drum.

Included in the corona assembly is a *static-charge eliminator strip* that drains away the charge imparted to the paper by the corona. If you didn't drain away the charge, the paper would stick to the EP cartridge and jam the printer.

FIGURE 4.14   The transfer corona assembly

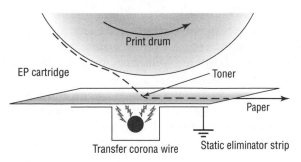

Print drum

EP cartridge   Toner

Paper

Transfer corona wire   Static eliminator strip

There are two types of corona assemblies: those that contain a *corona wire* and those that contain a *corona roller*. The corona wire is a small-diameter wire that is charged by the HVPS. The wire is located in a special notch in the floor of the laser printer (under the EP print cartridge). The corona roller performs the same function as the corona wire, but it's a roller rather than a wire. Because the corona roller is directly in contact with the paper, it supports higher speeds. For this reason, the corona wire is no longer used much in laser printers.

Fusing Assembly

The toner in the EP toner cartridge will stick to just about anything, including paper. This is true because the toner has a negative static charge and most objects have a net positive charge. However, these toner particles can be removed by brushing any object across the page. This could be a problem if you want the images and letters to stay on the paper permanently!

To solve this problem, EP laser printers incorporate a device known as a *fuser* (Figure 4.15), which uses two rollers that apply pressure and heat to fuse the plastic toner particles to the paper. You may have noticed that pages from either a laser printer or a copier (which uses a similar device) come out warm. This is because of the fuser.

FIGURE 4.15   The fuser

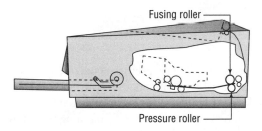

Fusing roller

Pressure roller

The fuser is made up of three main parts: a halogen heating lamp, a Teflon-coated aluminum fusing roller, and a rubberized pressure roller. The fuser uses the halogen lamp to heat the fusing roller to between 165°C and 180°C. As the paper passes between the two rollers, the pressure roller pushes the paper against the fusing roller, which melts the toner into the paper.

Printer Controller Circuitry

The final component in the laser printer we need to discuss is the *printer controller assembly*. This large circuit board converts signals from the computer into signals for the various assemblies in the laser printer, using a process known as *rasterizing*. This circuit board is usually mounted under the printer. The board has connectors for each type of interface and cables to each assembly.

When a computer prints to a laser printer, it sends a signal through a cable to the printer controller assembly. The controller assembly formats the information into a page's worth of line-by-line commands for the laser scanner. The controller sends commands to each of the components, telling them to wake up and begin the EP print process.

Ozone Filter

Your laser printer uses various high-voltage biases inside the case. As anyone who has been outside during a lightning storm can tell you, high voltages create ozone. Ozone is a chemically reactive gas that is created by the high-voltage coronas (charging and transfer) inside the printer. Because ozone is chemically reactive and can severely reduce the life of laser printer components, most laser printers contain a filter to remove ozone gas from inside the printer as it is produced. This filter must be removed and cleaned with compressed air periodically (cleaning it whenever the toner cartridge is replaced is usually sufficient).

Electrophotographic (EP) Print Process

The *EP print process* is the process by which an EP laser printer forms images on paper. It consists of six major steps, each for a specific goal. Although many different manufacturers call these steps different things or place them in a different order, the basic process is still the same. Here are the steps in the order you will see them on the exam:

1. Cleaning
2. Charging
3. Writing
4. Developing
5. Transferring
6. Fusing

Before any of these steps can begin, however, the controller must sense that the printer is ready to start printing (toner cartridge installed, fuser warmed to temperature, and all covers in place). Printing cannot take place until the printer is in its ready state, usually indicated by an illuminated Ready LED light or a display that says something like 00 READY (on HP printers).

Step 1: Cleaning

In the first part of the laser print process, a rubber blade inside the EP cartridge scrapes any toner left on the drum into a used toner receptacle inside the EP cartridge, and a fluorescent lamp discharges any remaining charge on the photosensitive drum (remember that the drum, being photosensitive, loses its charge when exposed to light). This step is called the *cleaning step* (Figure 4.16).

FIGURE 4.16   The cleaning step of the EP process

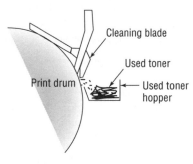

The EP cartridge is constantly cleaning the drum. It may take more than one rotation of the photosensitive drum to make an image on the paper. The cleaning step keeps the drum fresh for each use. If you didn't clean the drum, you would see ghosts of previous pages printed along with your image.

 The amount of toner removed in the cleaning process is quite small. The cartridge will run out of toner before the used toner receptacle fills up.

Step 2: Charging

The next step in the EP process is the *charging step* (Figure 4.17). In this step, a special wire (called a *charging corona*) within the EP toner cartridge (above the photosensitive drum) gets a high voltage from the HVPS. It uses this high voltage to apply a strong, uniform negative charge (around –600VDC) to the surface of the photosensitive drum.

FIGURE 4.17   The charging step of the EP process

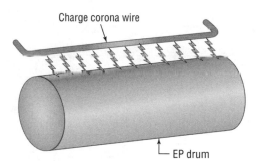

Step 3: Writing

Next is the *writing step*. In this step, the laser is turned on and scans the drum from side to side, flashing on and off according to the bits of information the printer controller sends it as it communicates the individual bits of the image. Wherever the laser touches, the photosensitive drum's charge is severely reduced from –600VDC to a slight negative charge (around –100VDC).

As the drum rotates, a pattern of exposed areas is formed, representing the images to be printed. Figure 4.18 shows this process.

FIGURE 4.18   The writing step of the EP process

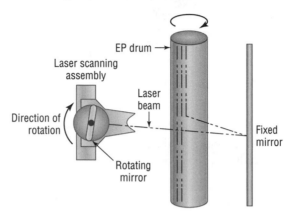

At this point, the controller sends a signal to the pickup roller to feed a piece of paper into the printer, where it stops at the registration rollers.

Step 4: Developing

Now that the surface of the drum holds an electrical representation of the image being printed, its discrete electrical charges need to be converted into something that can be transferred to a piece of paper. The EP process step that accomplishes this is the *developing step* (Figure 4.19). In this step, toner is transferred to the areas that were exposed in the writing step.

FIGURE 4.19   The developing step of the EP process

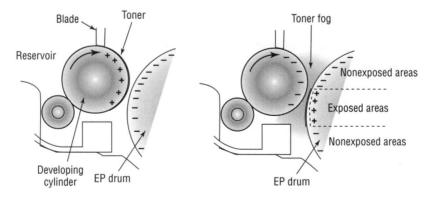

A metallic roller called the *developing roller* inside an EP cartridge acquires a –600VDC charge (called a *bias voltage*) from the HVPS. The toner sticks to this roller because there is a magnet located inside the roller and because of the electrostatic charges between the toner and the developing roller. While the developing roller rotates toward the photosensitive drum, the toner acquires the charge of the roller (–600VDC). When the toner comes between the developing roller and the photosensitive drum, the toner is attracted to the areas that have been exposed by the laser (because these areas have a lesser charge, of –100VDC). The toner also is repelled from the unexposed areas (because they are at the same –600VDC charge, and like charges repel). This toner transfer creates a fog of toner between the EP drum and the developing roller.

The photosensitive drum now has toner stuck to it where the laser has written. The photosensitive drum continues to rotate until the developed image is ready to be transferred to paper in the next step.

Step 5: Transferring

At this point in the EP process, the developed image is rotating into position. The controller notifies the registration rollers that the paper should be fed through. The registration rollers move the paper underneath the photosensitive drum, and the process of transferring the image can begin, with the *transferring step*.

The controller sends a signal to the corona wire or corona roller (depending on which one the printer has) and tells it to turn on. The corona wire/roller then acquires a strong *positive* charge (+600VDC) and applies that charge to the paper. The paper, thus charged, pulls the toner from the photosensitive drum at the line of contact between the roller and the paper, because the paper and toner have opposite charges. Once the registration rollers move the paper past the corona wire, the static-eliminator strip removes all charge from that line of the paper. Figure 4.20 details this step. If the strip didn't bleed this charge away, the paper would attract itself to the toner cartridge and cause a paper jam.

FIGURE 4.20   The transferring step of the EP process

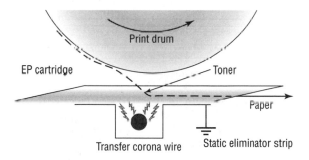

The toner is now held in place by weak electrostatic charges and gravity. It will not stay there, however, unless it is made permanent, which is the reason for the fusing step.

Step 6: Fusing

In the final step, the *fusing step*, the toner image is made permanent. The registration rollers push the paper toward the fuser rollers. Once the fuser grabs the paper, the registration rollers push for only a short time more. The fuser is now in control of moving the paper.

As the paper passes through the fuser, the 180°C fuser roller melts the polyester resin of the toner, and the rubberized pressure roller presses it permanently into the paper (Figure 4.21). The paper continues on through the fuser and eventually exits the printer.

FIGURE 4.21 The fusing step of the EP process

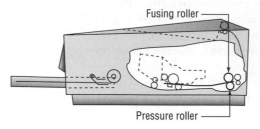

Once the paper completely exits the fuser, it trips a sensor that tells the printer to finish the EP process with the cleaning step. At this point, the printer can print another page, and the EP process can begin again.

Summary of the EP Print Process

Figure 4.22 summarizes all the EP process printing steps. First, the printer uses a rubber scraper to clean the photosensitive drum. Then the printer places a uniform, negative, –600VDC charge on the photosensitive drum by means of a charging corona. The laser "paints" an image onto the photosensitive drum, discharging the image areas to a much lower voltage (–100VDC). The developing roller in the toner cartridge has charged (–600VDC) toner stuck to it. As it rolls the toner toward the photosensitive drum, the toner is attracted to (and sticks to) the areas of the photosensitive drum that the laser has discharged. The image is then transferred from the drum to the paper at its line of contact by means of the corona wire (or corona roller) with a +600VDC charge. The static-eliminator strip removes the high, positive charge from the paper, and the paper, now holding the image, moves on. The paper then enters the fuser, where a fuser roller and the pressure roller make the image permanent. The paper exits the printer, and the printer begins printing the next page or returns to its ready state.

FIGURE 4.22 The EP print process

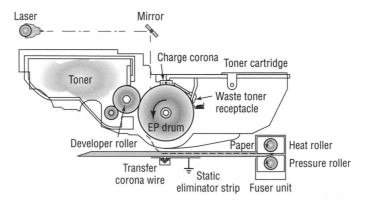

To help you remember the steps of the EP print process in order, learn the first letter of each step: CCWDTF. The most often used mnemonic sentence for this combination of letters is "Charlie Can Walk, Dance, and Talk French."

LED Page Printers

Now we'll discuss another laser printer: the light-emitting diode (LED) page printer. This technology is primarily developed and used by Okidata and Panasonic. Because the A+ exam does not currently cover LED page printers, we will discuss only the differences between them and laser printers.

The two main differences between a LED page printer and a laser printer are the toner cartridges and the print process.

LED Page Printer Toner Cartridges

One problem with laser printers is that the toner usually runs out before the photosensitive drum needs to be replaced. But because they're usually both housed in the same replaceable unit, every time you replace the toner, you're also replacing the drum, whether it needs replacing or not. So, the designers of LED page printers made the photosensitive drum and toner separate, replaceable items.

 The main parts of the LED page printer toner cartridge are integrated into the printer. The charging corona (or roller) and erasing lamps are also integrated into the printer. These items cannot be replaced by the average user; an authorized service technician must remove them.

When replacing the photosensitive drum, you swing the photosensitive drum/toner cartridge out of the printer first. Then you remove the drum from its carrier and install the new one (this also replaces the waste toner receptacle).

Filling the toner hopper is fairly easy. On most LED page printers, you place the new toner cartridge over the toner hopper and lock it in place. Between the new toner cartridge and the toner hopper are a lever and door. When you slide the lever over, it opens the door and allows the toner to fall through the opening. Once all the toner is out of the cartridge and hopper, you slide the lever back, closing the door. You can then remove the cartridge and throw it away.

The LED Page Printer Process

The LED page printer uses the same process as any other laser printer, with one major exception. It uses a row of small light-emitting diodes held very close to the photosensitive drum to expose it. Each LED is about the same size as the diameter of the laser beam used in laser printers. These printers are basically the same as EP process printers, except that in the exposure step, they use LEDs instead of a laser.

LED page printers offer several benefits over laser printers. First, because they use LEDs instead of lasers, LED page printers are much cheaper than similar laser printers—they're about half the cost. Also, because the LEDs are close to the drum, the whole printer is smaller—about two-thirds the size of a comparable laser printer. Finally, LEDs aren't as dangerous to the eye as lasers (you could probably damage your eyes if you stared at one long enough, but it's unlikely you'd do such a thing).

If they have so many advantages, why isn't everyone using them? Mainly because LED technology isn't as advanced as laser technology. The resolutions of LED page printers have yet to break the 800 dots-per-inch (dpi) mark. Another reason is that the toner system in an LED printer, although more efficient, is also messier. Because of its slight static charge, toner isn't easy to remove from surfaces.

WARNING Never ship a printer anywhere with a toner cartridge installed! If the printer is a laser printer, remove the toner cartridge first. If it's an LED page printer, there is a method to remove the photosensitive drum and toner hopper (check your manual for details).

Other Printers

The types of printers you have learned about so far in this chapter account for 90 percent of all printers used with home or office computers and that you will see as a repair technician. The other 10 percent consist of other types of printers that primarily differ by the method they use to put colored material on the paper to represent what is being printed.

The three other major types of printers in use today are as follows:

- Solid ink
- Thermal
- Dye sublimation

Keep in mind throughout this section that for the most part, these printers operate like other printers in many ways: They all have a paper-feed mechanism (sheet-fed or roll); they all require consumables; they all use the same interfaces, for the most part, as other types of printers; and they are usually about the same size.

Solid-Ink Printers

Solid-ink printers work much like bubble-jet and dot-matrix printers: A printhead moves across the paper that's being printed on. However, in a solid-ink printer, the ink is in a waxy solid form, rather than in liquid form, which allows it to stay fresh and not cause problems like spillage. In addition, solid-ink printers usually print an entire line at one time, which makes them faster than bubble-jet printers. Because of the type of ink used, solid-ink printers are better for graphics companies that need true color at a price lower than a color laser printer.

Thermal Printers

You almost surely have seen a thermal printer. They can be found in many older fax machines (most newer ones use either ink-jet or laser printing). They print on a kind of special, waxy paper that comes on a roll; the paper turns black when heat passes over it. *Thermal printers* work by using a printhead the width of the paper. When it needs to print, the printhead heats and cools spots on the printhead. The paper below the heated printhead turns black in those spots. As the paper moves through the printer, the pattern of blackened spots forms an image on the page of what is being printed.

Thermal printers typically have long lives because they have few moving parts. However, the paper is somewhat expensive, doesn't last long (especially if it is left in a very warm place, like a closed car in summer), and produces poorer image quality than most of the other printing technologies.

Dye-Sublimation Printers

The last type of printer you will learn about in this chapter is the *dye-sublimation printer*. These printers use sheets of solid ink that *sublimate*, or go from the solid phase directly to gas. During printing, a printhead passes over these sheets (one each of cyan, magenta, yellow, and gray for tonal change) inside the printer. As it passes over the page, spots on the printhead heat up, causing the ink under those spots to sublimate into gas. This gas then passes through the paper being printed, where the ink turns back into solid, embedded into the paper. The printhead in most printers make four passes, one for each color.

Dye-sublimation printers are used most often in the graphics or printing industries, because they really do only one thing well: photo-quality images. They take time to produce their images, but those images are of extremely high quality. It would expensive and impractical to use a dye-sublimation printer for word-processing.

Printer Interfaces and Supplies

Besides understanding the printer's operation, for the A+ exam you need to understand how the printer talks to a computer and all the items involved in that process. You must also understand how the different types of print media affect the print process.

Interface Components

A printer's *interface* is the collection of hardware and software that allows the printer to communicate with a computer. Each printer has at least one interface, but some printers have several, in order to make them more flexible in a multiplatform environment. If a printer has several interfaces, it can usually switch between them on the fly so that several computers can print at the same time.

An interface incorporates several components, including its communication type as well as the *interface software*. Each aspect must be matched on both the printer and the computer. For example, an HP LaserJet 4L has only a parallel port. Therefore, you must use a parallel cable as well as the correct software for the platform being used (for example, a Macintosh HP LaserJet 4L driver if you connect it to a Macintosh computer).

Communication Types

When we say *communication types*, we're talking about the hardware technologies involved in getting the printed information from the computer to the printer. There are eight major types: serial, parallel, Universal Serial Bus (USB), network, infrared, SCSI, IEEE 1394, and wireless. You've learned about these connections in earlier chapters, but now you will learn how they apply to printers.

Serial

When computers send data serially, they send it one bit at a time, one after another. The bits stand in line like people at a movie theater, waiting to get in. Just as with modems, you must set the communication parameters (baud, parity, start and stop bits) on both entities—in this case, the computer and its printer(s)—before communication can take place.

Parallel

When a printer uses parallel communication, it is receiving data eight bits at a time over eight separate wires (one for each bit). Parallel communication is the most popular way of communicating from computer to printer, mainly because it's faster than serial.

A parallel cable consists of a male DB-25 connector that connects to the computer and a male 36-pin Centronics connector that connects to the printer. Most of the cables are less than 10 feet long.

WARNING Keep printer cable lengths to less than 10 feet. Some people try to run printer cables more than 50 feet. If the length is greater than 10 feet, communications can become unreliable due to cross talk (stray signals from adjacent wires cause electrical interference).

Universal Serial Bus (USB)

The most popular type of printer interface as this book is being written is the Universal Serial Bus (USB). In fact, it is the most popular interface for just about every peripheral. The convenience for printers is that it has a higher transfer rate than either serial or parallel and it automatically recognizes new devices.

Network

Some of the newer printers (primarily laser and LED printers) have a special interface that allows them to be hooked directly to a network. These printers have a *network interface card (NIC)* and ROM-based software that allow them to communicate with networks, servers, and workstations.

The type of network interface used on the printer depends on the type of network the printer is being attached to. For example, if you're using a Token Ring network, the printer should have a Token Ring interface.

Infrared

With the explosion of Personal Digital Assistants (PDAs), the need grew for printing under the constraints they provide. The biggest hurdle faced by PDA owners who need to print is the lack of any kind of universal interface. Most interfaces are too big and bulky to be used on handheld computers like PDAs. The solution was to incorporate the standardized technology used on some remote controls: infrared transmissions. *Infrared transmissions* are simply wireless transmissions that use radiation in the infrared range of the electromagnetic spectrum. Many laser printers (and some computers) come with infrared transmitter/receivers (transceivers) so that they can communicate with the infrared ports on many handhelds. This allows the user of a PDA, handheld, or laptop to print to that printer by pointing the device at the printer and initiating the print process.

As far as configuring the interface is concerned, very little needs to be done. The infrared interfaces are enabled by default on most computers, handhelds, and printers equipped with them. The only additional item that must be configured is the print driver on the PDA, handheld, or computer. The driver must be the correct one for the printer to which you are printing.

SCSI

Only a few types of printers use SCSI interfaces to the PC, and most of them are laser printers, dye-sublimation printers, or typesetters. When these printers were introduced, they all came with an option for a SCSI interface. The benefits in these situations were:

- There could be more than one device on a single SCSI connection through daisy chaining.

- It was fairly simple to implement.

- It had relatively large throughput compared to other interfaces of the time.

Because of the advent of higher-speed peripheral connection methods, like IEEE 1394/FireWire and USB 2.0, SCSI interfaces for printers are rapidly becoming obsolete.

IEEE 1394 FireWire

The IEEE 1394 interface (also known as *FireWire*—an Apple trademark) has had an explosion of popularity recently. As discussed in Chapter 1, this interface has a maximum throughput of 800MBps, so more and more devices that need to send a lot of data in a short period of time will use this interface. Printers used for tasks such as graphics and typesetting that need to receive hundreds of megabytes of camera-ready art and graphics have IEEE 1394 ports. Not many home printers use IEEE 1394, however, because it is an extra feature most people wouldn't use (and thus don't want to pay for). In addition, not every computer has an IEEE 1394 port (except for most Macintosh computers sold today).

Wireless

The latest boom in printer interface technology is wireless (of many different kinds). With the advent of IEEE 802.11b wireless networking (discussed in Chapter 5, "Networking Fundamentals"), it is possible for people to roam around an office and still remain connected to each other and to their corporate network. So, someone had the idea that it would be nice if printers could be that mobile as well (after all, many are on carts with wheels). Some printers either have built-in 802.11b interfaces or are hooked to 802.11b bridges with their built-in network cards.

Another wireless technology that has been gaining acceptance rapidly, especially among peripheral manufacturers, is *Bluetooth*. Bluetooth is a wireless technology that is used to replace the myriad of interface cables that run between your computer and all its peripherals. It's not meant to work over long distances (its absolute maximum range is 100 meters, and most devices are specified to work within 10 meters). Printers like the HP 955c have Bluetooth capability.

When printing with a Bluetooth-enabled device (like a PDA or cell phone) and a Bluetooth-enabled printer, all you need to do is get within range of the device (i.e. move closer), select the print driver from the device, and select "print". The information is transmitted wirelessly, through the air using radio waves, and is received by the device.

For more information about the Bluetooth specification and its details, visit www.bluetooth.org.

Interface Software

Computers and printers can't talk to each other by themselves. They need interface software to translate software commands into commands the printer can understand.

There are two factors to consider with interface software: the page-description language and the driver software. The page-description language determines how efficient the printer is at converting the information to be printed into signals the printer can understand. The driver software understands and controls the printer. It is very important that you use the correct interface software for your printer. If you use either the wrong page-description language or the wrong driver software, the printer will print garbage, or possibly nothing at all.

Page-Description Languages

A *page-description language* works just as its name says it does. It describes the whole page being printed by sending commands that describe the text as well as the margins and other settings. The controller in the printer interprets these commands and turns them into laser pulses (or pin strikes).

Life without a Page-Description Language

The most basic page-description language is no page-description language. The computer sends all the instructions the printer needs in a serial stream, like so: Position 1, print nothing; Position 2, strike pins 1 and 3; Position 3, print nothing. This type of description language works great for dot-matrix printers, but it can be very inefficient for laser printers. For example, if you wanted to print a page using a standard page-description language and there was only one character on the page, there would be a lot of wasted signal for the "print nothing" commands.

With graphics, the commands to draw a shape on the page are relatively complex. For example, to draw a square, the computer (or printer) has to calculate the size of the square and convert that into lots of "strike pin *x*" (or "turn on laser") and "print nothing" commands. This is where the other types of page-description languages come into the picture.

The first page-description language was PostScript. Developed by Adobe, it was first used in the Apple LaserWriter printer. It made printing graphics fast and simple. Here's how PostScript works: The PostScript printer driver describes the page in terms of "draw" and "position" commands. The page is divided into a very fine grid (as fine as the resolution of the printer). When you want to print a square, a communication like the following takes place:

```
POSITION 1,42%DRAW 10%POSITION 1,64%DRAW10D% . . .
```

These commands tell the printer to draw a line on the page from line 42 to line 64 (vertically). In other words, a page-description language tells the printer to draw a line on the page, gives it the starting and ending points, and that's that. Rather than send the printer the location of each and every dot in the line and an instruction at each and every location to print that location's individual dot, PostScript can get the line drawn with fewer than five instructions. As you can see, PostScript uses commands that are more or less in English. The commands are interpreted by the processor on the printer's controller and converted into the print-control signals.

Another page-description language is the Printer Control Language (PCL). Currently in revision 6 (PCL 6), it was developed by Hewlett-Packard for its LaserJet series of printers as a competitor to PostScript. PCL works in much the same manner as PostScript, but it's found mainly in HP printers (including the DeskJet bubble-jet printers). Other manufacturers use PCL, however. In fact, some printers support both page-description languages and will automatically switch between them.

The main advantage of page-description languages is that they move some of the processing from the computer to the printer. With text-only documents, they don't offer much benefit. However, with documents that have large amounts of graphics or that use numerous fonts, page-description languages make the processing of those print jobs happen much faster. This makes them an ideal choice for laser printers. However, other printers can use them as well (the aforementioned DeskJets, as well as some dot-matrix printers).

Driver Software

The *driver software* controls how the printer processes the print job. When you install a printer driver for the printer you are using, it allows the computer to print to that printer correctly (assuming you have the correct interface configured between the computer and printer).

Installation and configuration of printer drivers will be covered in the second part of this book, "Operating Systems Technologies Exam."

When you need to print, you select the printer driver for your printer from a preconfigured list. The driver you select has been configured for the type, brand, and model of printer as well as the computer port to which it is connected. You can also select which paper tray the printer should use, as well as any other features the printer has (if applicable). Also, each printer driver is configured to use a particular page-description language.

If the wrong printer driver is selected, the computer will send commands in the wrong language. If that occurs, the printer will print several pages full of garbage (even if only one page of information was sent). This "garbage" isn't garbage at all, but the printer page-description language commands printed literally as text instead of being interpreted as control commands.

Printer Supplies

Just as it is important to use the correct printer interface and printer software, you must use the correct printer supplies. These supplies include the print media (what you print on) and the consumables (what you print with). The quality of the final print job has a great deal to do with the print supplies.

Print Media

The *print media* is what you put through the printer to print on. There are two major types of print media: paper and transparencies. Of the two types, paper is by far the most commonly used.

Paper

Most people don't give much thought to the kind of paper they use in their printers. It's a factor that can have tremendous effect on the quality of the hard-copy printout, however, and the topic is more complex than people think. For example, if the wrong paper is used, it can cause the paper to jam frequently and possibly even damage components.

Several aspects of paper can be measured; each gives an indication as to the paper's quality. The first factor is *composition*. Paper is made from a variety of substances. Paper used to be made from cotton and was called *rag stock*. It can also be made from wood pulp, which is cheaper. Most paper today is made from the latter or a combination of the two.

Another aspect of paper is the property known as *basis weight* (or simply *weight* for short). The weight of a particular type of paper is the actual weight, in pounds (lb), of 500 sheets of the standard (basic) size of that paper made of that material. For regular bond paper, that size is 17×22. The most common paper used in printers is 20lb bond paper.

The final paper property we'll discuss is the *caliper* (or thickness) of an individual sheet of paper. If the paper is too thick, it may jam in feed mechanisms that have several curves in the paper path. (On the other hand, a paper that's too thin may not feed at all.)

These are just three of the categories we use to judge the quality of paper. Because there are so many different types and brands of printers as well as paper, it would be impossible to give the specifications for the "perfect" paper. However, the documentation for any printer will give specifications for the paper that should be used in that printer.

For best results with any printer, buy the paper that has been designated specifically for that printer by the manufacturer. It will be more expensive, but you'll have fewer problems related to having the wrong type of paper for the printer. The print quality will also be the best it can possibly be.

Transparencies

Transparencies are still used for presentations made with overhead projectors, even with the explosion of programs like PowerPoint (from Microsoft) and peripherals like LCD computer displays, both of which let you show a whole roomful of people exactly what's on your computer screen. PowerPoint has an option to print slides, and you can also use any program to print to a transparent sheet of plastic or vinyl for use with an overhead projector. The problem is, these "papers" are *exceedingly* difficult for printers to work with. That's why special transparencies were developed for use with laser and bubble-jet printers.

Each type of transparency was designed for a particular brand and model of printer. Again, check the printer's documentation to find out which type of transparency works in that printer. Don't use any other type of transparency!

Never run transparencies through a laser printer without first checking to see if it's the type recommended by the printer manufacturer. The heat from the fuser will melt most other transparencies, and they will wrap themselves around it. It is impossible to clean a fuser after this has happened. The fuser will have to be replaced. *Use only the transparencies that are recommended by the printer manufacturer.*

Print Consumables

Besides print media, other things in the printer run out and need to be replenished. These items are the *print consumables*. Most consumables are used to form the images on the print media. There are two main types of consumables in printers today: ink and toner. Toner is used primarily in laser printers; most other printers use ink.

Ink

Ink is a liquid that is used to stain the paper. Printers use several different colors of ink, but the majority use some shade of black or blue. Both dot-matrix printers and bubble-jet printers use ink, but with different methods.

Dot-matrix printers use a cloth or polyester ribbon soaked in ink and coiled up inside a plastic case. This assembly is called a *printer ribbon* (or *ribbon cartridge*). It's very similar to a typewriter ribbon, but instead of being coiled into the two rolls you'd see on a typewriter, the ribbon is continuously coiled inside the plastic case. Once the ribbon has run out of ink, it must be discarded and replaced. Ribbon cartridges are developed closely with their respective printers. For this reason, ribbons should be purchased from the same manufacturer as the printer. The wrong ribbon could jam in the printer as well as cause quality problems.

It is possible to reink a ribbon. Some vendors sell a bottle of ink solution that can be poured into the plastic casing, where the cloth ribbon will soak up the solution.

Bubble-jet cartridges have a liquid ink reservoir. The ink in these cartridges is sealed inside. Once the ink runs out, the cartridge must be removed and discarded. A new, full one is installed in its place. Because the ink cartridge contains ink as well as the printing mechanism, it's like getting a new printer every time you replace the ink cartridge.

In some bubble-jet printers, the ink cartridge and the printhead are in separate assemblies. This way, the ink can be replaced when it runs out, and the printhead can be used several times. This works fine if the printer is designed to work this way. However, some people think they can do this on their integrated cartridge/printhead system, using special ink cartridge refill kits. These kits consist of a syringe filled with ink and a long needle. The needle is used to puncture the top of an empty ink cartridge, and the syringe is then used to refill the reservoir. Don't use these kits! See the warning about using them for more information.

Do not use ink cartridge refill kits! These kits (the ones you see advertised with a syringe and a needle) have several problems. First, the kits don't use the same kind of ink that was originally in the ink cartridges. The new ink may be thinner, causing the ink to run out or not print properly. Also, the printhead is supposed to be *replaced* around this same time. Refilling the cartridge doesn't replace the printhead, so you'll have print-quality problems. Finally, the hole the syringe leaves cannot be plugged and may allow ink to leak out. The bottom line: *Buy new ink cartridges from the printer manufacturer.* Yes, they are a bit more expensive, but you will actually save money because you won't have any of the problems described here.

Toner

The final type of consumable is toner. Each model of laser printer uses a specific toner cartridge. We covered the types of toner cartridges in the discussions of the different types of printers. You should check the printer's manual to see which toner cartridge it needs.

Just as with ink cartridges, you should always buy the exact model recommended by the manufacturer. The toner cartridges have been designed specifically for a particular model. Additionally, *never* refill toner cartridges, for most of the same reasons we don't recommend refilling ink cartridges. The printout quality will be poor, and the fact that you're just refilling the toner means you're *not* replacing the photosensitive drum (which is usually inside the cartridge), and the drum might *need* to be replaced. Simply replacing refilled toner cartridges with proper, name-brand toner cartridges has solved most laser printer quality problems we have run across. We keep recommending the right ones, but clients keep coming back with the refilled ones. The result is that we take our clients' money to solve their print-quality problems when all it involves is a toner cartridge, our (usually repeat) advice to buy the proper cartridge next time, and the obligatory minimum charge for a half hour of labor (even though the job of replacing the cartridge takes all of five minutes!).

Options/Upgrades

Most printers (especially laser printers) can be upgraded with different capabilities. This is done to add functions or to increase the printing capacity of a printer. As the complexity of laser printers increases, they are often becoming what are known as *mopiers* (short for multiple original copiers). Rather than your having to print one copy of a document and then copy it with double-sided and stapling or hole-punch options, the laser printer manufacturer has included those functions in the printer, so each printed "copy" is essentially an original.

Each manufacturer, with the documentation for each printer, includes a list of all the accessories, options, and upgrades available for that printer. Some of these options include:

- Memory
- Hard drives
- NICs
- Trays and feeders
- Finishers
- Scanners, fax modems, and copiers
- Firmware

Memory

One of the most common options for a printer is to add memory to it to increase its buffer size. The larger the buffer, the larger a print job it can handle. So, by adding memory, you can increase the performance of a printer.

For the most part, printer memory is specific to the make and model of printer being upgraded. You can check with the manufacturer of your printer to see what kind of memory it takes and how best to upgrade it. The procedures are slightly different for each make and model of printer.

Hard Drives

In order to print properly, the typestyle or *font* being printed must be downloaded to the printer along with the job being printed. Desktop-publishing and graphic-design businesses that print color pages on slower color printers are always looking for ways to speed up their print jobs. So, they install multiple fonts into the onboard memory of the printer to make them *printer-resident fonts*.

But, there's a problem: Most printers have a limited amount of storage space for these fonts. To solve this problem, printer manufacturers made it possible for hard drives to be added to many printers. These hard drives can be used to store many fonts used during the print process, and are also used to store the large document file while it is being processed for printing.

NICs

Networks are everywhere. Almost every business has one, as do some homes. They are used to share information and resources between computers. In the past, you could share your printer with your neighbor over the network through software installed on your computer. But doing so had two drawbacks: It was slow, because your computer does other things in addition to sharing the printer; and it was cumbersome, because your computer had to be on in order for someone to print to your printer. Thus, the network interface card (NIC) option for a printer became popular as more and more people needed their printers to be on the network without the need for a host computer.

The NIC in a printer is similar to the NIC in a computer, with a couple of important differences. First, the NIC in a printer has a small processor on it to perform the management of the NIC interface (functions that the software on a host computer would do). Second, the NIC in a printer is proprietary, for the most part. It is made by the same manufacturer as the printer.

When a person on the network prints to a printer with a NIC, they are printing right to the printer and not going through any third-party device (although in some situations, that is desirable and possible with NICs). Because of its dedicated nature, the NIC option installed in a printer makes printing to that printer faster and more efficient—that NIC is dedicated to receiving print jobs and sending printer status to clients.

 Some printer NICs have small web servers installed that allow clients to check their print jobs' status as well as toner levels from any computer on the network.

Trays and Feeders

One option that is popular in office environments is the addition of paper trays. Most laser and bubble-jet printers come with at least one paper tray (usually 250 sheets or less). The addition of a paper tray allows a printer to print more sheets between paper refills, thus reducing its operating cost. In addition, some printers can accommodate multiple paper trays, which can be loaded with different types of paper, stationery, and envelopes. The benefit is that you can print a letter and an envelope from the same printer without having to leave your desk or change the paper in the printer.

Related to trays is the option of *feeders*. Some types of paper products need to be watched as they are printed, to make sure the printing happens properly. One example is envelopes: You usually can't put a stack of envelopes in a printer, because they won't line up straight or may get jammed. An accessory that you might add for this purpose is the *envelope feeder*. An envelope feeder typically attaches to the front of a laser printer and feeds in envelopes, one at a time. It can hold usually between 100 and 200 envelopes.

 If you're curious about the procedure for installing an envelope feeder, go to www.hp.com and search on "Envelope Feeder Install".

Finishers

A printer's *finisher* does just what it says: It finishes the document being printed. It does this by folding, stapling, hole punching, sorting, or collating the sets of documents being printed into their final form. So, rather than your printing out a bunch of paper sheets and then having to collate and staple them, the finisher can do the same thing for you.

This particular option, while not cheap, is becoming more popular on laser printers in order to turn them into the aforementioned mopiers. As a matter of fact, many copiers are now digital and can do all the same things a laser printer can, but much faster and for a much cheaper cost per page.

Scanners, Fax Modems, and Copiers

The last few options are a bit of a stretch for laser printers, but they do somewhat fit. First, It is possible to add a scanner to a laser printer. A *scanner* is an accessory that takes a document and puts it into digital form. From there it can be edited or printed. If you use the scanner and print directly from the scanned-in image, you have just made a copy and turned the laser printer into a digital version of a copier. You can also add a device known as a *fax modem* to a printer configured with a scanner to turn the printer into a fax machine. A fax modem is a device you install into a computer or other device that takes the signals from that device and turn them into signals a fax machine can understand over a phone line.

By adding these two accessories, you can turn your simple printer into a home office copier capable of sending faxes as well. In this age of home offices, such devices are becoming commonplace. Several printer companies manufacture *multifunction printers*. These peripherals are essentially a printer, copier, scanner, and fax machine all in one. They're perfect for the home office without a lot of desk space.

Firmware

Many higher-end printers (including most laser printers) include their own upgradable firmware. It is possible to download newer firmware from the manufacturer to solve certain problems. For example, if a printer doesn't render a particular character correctly or doesn't recognize a certain brand or type of memory, even though the memory was designed for that printer, a firmware update may solve the problem.

Upgrading the firmware is printer- and manufacturer-specific; however, generally speaking, you download a special file from the printer's manufacturer then run a special installation utility. The utility will communicate with the printer and install the new firmware update. Some printer manufacturers require that you buy the actual chip the firmware comes on and have an authorized dealer install it.

Printer Troubleshooting

As we mentioned, other than the monitor, the most popular peripheral purchased for computers today is the printer. Printers are also the most complex peripheral, as far as troubleshooting is concerned. In this section, we will cover the most common types of printer problems you will run into. We will break the section into three areas, for the three major types of printers.

Dot-Matrix Printer Problems

Dot-matrix printers are relatively simple devices. Therefore, only a few problems usually arise. We will cover the most common problems and their solutions here.

Low Print Quality

Problems with print quality are easy to identify. When the printed page comes out of the printer, the characters are too light or have dots missing from them. Table 4.1 details some of the most common print quality problems, their causes, and their solutions.

Printout Jams Inside the Printer

Printer jams are very frustrating because they always seem to happen more than halfway through your 50-page print job, requiring you to take time to remove the jam before the rest of your pages can print. A paper jam happens when something prevents the paper from advancing through the printer evenly. Print jobs jam for two major reasons: an obstructed paper path and stripped drive gears.

Obstructed paper paths are often difficult to find. Usually it means disassembling the printer to find the bit of crumpled-up paper or other foreign substance that's blocking the paper path. A common obstruction is a piece of the *perf*—the perforated sides of tractor-feed paper—that has torn off and gotten crumpled up and then lodged in the paper path. It may be necessary to remove the platen roller and feed mechanism to get at the obstruction.

TABLE 4.1   Common Dot-Matrix Print Quality Problems

Characteristics	Cause	Solution
Consistently faded or light characters	Worn-out printer ribbon	Replace the ribbon with a new, vendor-recommended ribbon.
Print lines that go from dark to light as the printhead moves across the page	Printer ribbon-advance gear slipping	Replace the ribbon-advance gear or mechanism.
A small, blank line running through a line of print (consistently)	Printhead pin stuck inside the printhead	Replace the printhead.
A small, blank line running through a line of print (intermittently)	A broken, loose, or shorting printhead cable	Secure or replace the printhead cable.
A small, dark line running through a line of print	Printhead pin stuck in the out position	Replace the printhead. (Pushing the pin in may damage the printhead.)
Printer makes a printing noise, but no print appears on the page	Worn, missing, or improperly installed ribbon cartridge	Replace the ribbon cartridge correctly.
Printer prints garbage	Cable partially unhooked, wrong driver selected, or bad printer control board (PCB)	Hook up the cable correctly, select the correct driver, or replace the PCB (respectively).
Print appears "wavy" or out of alignment	Printhead not aligned	Use alignment procedure from owners manual to calibrate printing.

Use extra caution when printing peel-off labels in dot-matrix printers. If a label or even a whole sheet of labels becomes misaligned or jammed, *do not* roll the roller backward to realign the sheet. If a label is misaligned, try realigning the whole sheet of labels *slowly* using the *feed roller*, with the power off, moving it in very small increments.

Stepper Motor Problems

Printers use stepper motors to move the printhead back and forth as well as to advance the paper (these are called the *carriage motor* and *main motor*, respectively). These motors get damaged when they are forced in any direction while the power is on. This includes moving the printhead over to install a printer ribbon as well as moving the paper-feed roller to align paper. These motors are very sensitive to stray voltages. If you are rotating one of these motors by hand, you are essentially turning it into a small generator, and thus damaging it.

A damaged stepper motor is easy to detect. Damage to the stepper motor will cause it to lose precision and move farther with each step. Lines of print will be unevenly spaced if the main motor is damaged (which is more likely). Characters will be scrunched together if the printhead motor goes bad. If the motor is bad enough, it won't move at all in any direction; it may even make high-pitched squealing noises. If any of these symptoms show themselves, it's time to replace one of these motors.

Stepper motors are usually expensive to replace—about half the cost of a new printer! Damage to them is easy to avoid, using common sense.

Bubble-Jet Printer Problems

Bubble-jet printers are the most commonly sold printers for home use. For this reason, you need to understand the most common problems with these printers so your company can service them effectively. Let's take a look at some of the most common problems with bubble-jet printers and their solutions.

Print Quality

The majority of bubble-jet printer problems are quality problems. Ninety-nine percent of these can be traced to a faulty ink cartridge. With most bubble-jet printers, the ink cartridge contains the printhead and the ink. The major problem with this assembly can be described by "If you don't use it, you lose it." The ink will dry out in the small nozzles and block them if they are not used at least once a week.

An example of a quality problem is when you have thin, blank lines present in every line of text on the page. This is caused by a plugged hole in at least one of the small, pinhole ink nozzles in the print cartridge. Replacing the ink cartridge solves this problem easily.

As we warned earlier, some people try to save a buck by refilling their ink cartridge when they need to replace it. If you are one of them, *stop it*! Don't refill your ink cartridges! Almost all ink cartridges are designed *not* to be refilled. They are designed to be used once and thrown away! By refilling them, you make a hole in them—ink can leak out, and the printer will need to be cleaned. The ink will probably also be of the wrong type, and print quality can suffer. Finally, a refilled cartridge may void the printer's warranty.

If an ink cartridge becomes damaged or develops a hole, it can put too much ink on the page and the letters will smear. Again, the solution is to replace the ink cartridge. (You should be aware, however, that a very small amount of smearing is normal if the pages are laid on top of each other immediately after printing.)

One final print quality problem that does not directly involve the ink cartridge occurs when the print goes from dark to light quickly, and then prints nothing. As we already mentioned, ink cartridges dry out if not used. That's why the manufacturers include a small suction pump inside the printer that primes the ink cartridge before each print cycle. If this priming pump is broken or malfunctioning, this problem will manifest itself and the pump will need to be replaced.

If the problem of the ink going from dark to light quickly and then disappearing ever happens to you, and you really need to print a couple of pages, try this trick I learned from a fellow technician: Take the ink cartridge out of the printer. Squirt some window cleaner on a paper towel and gently tap the printhead against the wet paper towel. The force of the tap plus the solvents in the window cleaner should dislodge any dried ink, and the ink will flow freely again.

If you need to install a new cartridge, the printheads in that cartridge must be aligned. *Printhead alignment* is the process by which the printhead is calibrated for use. A special utility that comes with the printer software is used to do this. You run the alignment utility, and the printer prints several vertical and horizontal lines with numbers next to them. It then shows you a screen and asks you to choose the horizontal and vertical lines that are the most "in line". Once you enter the numbers, the software realizes whether the printhead(s) are out of alignment, which direction, and by how much. The software then makes slight modifications to the print driver software to tell it how much to offset when printing. Sometimes, alignment must be done several times to get the images to align properly.

Paper Jams

Bubble-jet printers usually have simple paper paths. Therefore, paper jams due to obstructions are less likely. They are still possible, however, so an obstruction shouldn't be overlooked as a possible cause of jamming.

Paper jams in bubble-jet printers are usually due to one of two things:

- A worn pickup roller
- The wrong type of paper

The pickup roller usually has one or two D-shaped rollers mounted on a rotating shaft. When the shaft rotates, one edge of the D rubs against the paper, pushing it into the printer. When the roller gets worn, it gets smooth and doesn't exert enough friction against the paper to push it into the printer.

If the paper used in the printer is too smooth, it causes the same problem. Pickup rollers use friction, and smooth paper doesn't offer much friction. If the paper is too rough, on the other hand, it acts like sandpaper on the rollers, wearing them smooth. Here's a rule of thumb for paper smoothness: Paper slightly smoother than a new one-dollar bill will work fine.

Laser and Page Printer Problems

I've got good news and bad news. The bad news is that laser printer problems are the most complex, because the printer is the most complex. The good news is that most problems are easily identifiable and have specific fixes. Most of the problems can be diagnosed with knowledge of the inner workings of the printer and a little common sense. Let's discuss the most common laser and page printer problems and their solutions.

Paper Jams

Laser printers today run at copier speeds. Because of this, their most common problem is paper jams. Paper can get jammed in a printer for several reasons. First, feed jams happen when the paper-feed rollers get worn (similar to feed jams in bubble-jet printers). The solution to this problem is easy: Replace the worn rollers.

 If your paper-feed jams are caused by worn pickup rollers, there is something you can do to get your printer working while you're waiting for the replacement pickup rollers. Scuff the feed roller(s) with a Scotch-Brite pot-scrubber pad (or something similar) to roughen up the feed rollers. This trick only works once. After that, the rollers aren't thick enough to touch the paper.

Another cause of feed jams is related to the drive gear of the pickup roller. The drive gear (or clutch) may be broken or have teeth missing. Again, the solution is to replace it. To determine if the problem is a broken gear or worn rollers, print a test page, but leave the paper tray out. Look into the paper-feed opening with a flashlight and see if the paper pickup roller(s) are turning evenly and don't skip. If they turn evenly, the problem is probably worn rollers.

Worn exit rollers can also cause paper jams. These rollers guide the paper out of the printer into the paper-receiving tray. If they are worn or damaged, the paper may catch on its way out of the printer. These types of jams are characterized by a paper jam that occurs just as the paper is getting to the exit rollers. If the paper jams, open the rear door and see where the paper is. If the paper is very close to the exit roller, the exit rollers are probably the problem.

The solution is to replace all the exit rollers. You must replace all of them at the same time because even one worn exit roller can cause the paper to jam. Besides, they're inexpensive. Don't be cheap and skimp on these parts if you need to have them replaced.

🌐 Real World Scenario

Printer Triage

I was in our local hospital ER a while ago having my hand looked at (I had cut it pretty badly on some glass). The receptionist who examined me asked me a few questions and filled out a report in the medical database on her computer. When she had finished asking me questions, she got up to get the printout from her laser printer.

I was shocked to see what she did next. When the paper starting coming out of the laser printer, she grabbed it and "ripped" it from the printer as you might do if the paper were in an old typewriter! The printer's exit rollers complained bitterly and made a noise that made me cringe. I don't know what hurt worse, my hand or my ears. She did this for every sheet of paper she printed. I didn't say anything, because my health was of primary concern at the time.

The following week, I noticed a familiar laser printer come in for service from that same hospital. As the technician started to work on it, I sauntered over and said, "I bet you 20 dollars it's the exit rollers." He said, "You're on!" Needless to say, I had a really good steak dinner that night with my wife.

I had a word with the person in charge of computer repair at that hospital the next day. They were surprised at what I told them, but glad that I pointed it out. I saved them from many future repairs, and they were grateful. As far as I know, the ER receptionist doesn't rip the pages from the printer anymore, because we haven't seen that printer back in for service in a while.

Paper jams can also be the fault of the paper. If your printer consistently tries to feed multiple pages into the printer, the paper isn't dry enough. If you live in an area with high humidity, this could be a problem. I've heard some solutions that are pretty far out, but that work (like keeping the paper in a Tupperware-type airtight container or microwaving it to remove moisture). The best all-around solution, however, is humidity control and to keep the paper wrapped until it's needed. Keep the humidity around 50 percent or lower (but above 25 percent if you can, in order to avoid problems with electrostatic discharge).

Finally, a metal, grounded strip called the static eliminator strip inside the printer drains the corona charge away from the paper after it has been used to transfer toner from the EP cartridge. If that strip is missing, broken, or damaged, the charge will remain on the paper and may cause it to stick to the EP cartridge, causing a jam. If the paper jams after reaching the corona assembly, this may be the cause.

Blank Pages

There's nothing more annoying than printing a 10-page contract and receiving 10 pages of blank paper from the printer. Blank pages are a somewhat common occurrence in laser and page printers. Somehow, the toner isn't being put on the paper. There are three major causes of blank pages:

- The toner cartridge

- The corona assembly
- The high-voltage power supply (HVPS)

Toner Cartridge

As we have already discussed, the toner cartridge is the source of most quality problems, because it contains most of the image-formation pieces for laser and page printers. Let's start with the obvious. A blank page will come out of the printer if there is no toner in the toner cartridge. I know it sounds simple, but some people think these things last forever. It's easy to check: Just open the printer, remove the toner cartridge, and shake it. You will be able to hear if there's toner inside the cartridge. If it's empty, replace it with a known, good, manufacturer-recommended toner cartridge.

Another issue that crops up rather often is the problem of using refilled or reconditioned toner cartridges. During their recycling process, these cartridges may be filled with the wrong kind of toner (for example, one with an incorrect charge). This can cause toner to be repelled from the EP drum instead of attracted to it. Thus, there's no toner on the page because there was no toner on the EP drum to begin with. The solution once again is to replace the toner cartridge with the type recommended by the manufacturer.

A third problem related to toner cartridges happens when someone installs a new toner cartridge and forgets to remove the sealing tape that is present to keep the toner in the cartridge during shipping. The solution to this problem is as easy as it is obvious: Remove the toner cartridge from the printer, remove the sealing tape, and reinstall the cartridge.

Corona Assembly

The second cause of the blank-page problem is a damaged or missing corona wire. If a wire is lost or damaged, the developed image won't transfer from the EP drum to the paper. Thus, no image appears on the printout. To determine if this is causing your problem, do the first half of the self-test (described later in this chapter). If there is an image on the drum, but not on the paper, you know that the corona assembly isn't doing its job.

To check if the corona assembly is causing the problem, open the cover and examine the wire (or roller, if your printer uses one). The corona wire is hard to see, so you may need a flashlight. You will know if it's broken or missing just by looking (it will either be in pieces or just not there). If it's not broken or missing, the problem may be related to the HVPS.

The corona wire (or roller) is a relatively inexpensive part and can be easily replaced with the removal of two screws and some patience.

High-Voltage Power Supply (HVPS)

The HVPS supplies high-voltage, low-current power to both the charging and transfer corona assemblies in laser and page printers. If it's broken, neither will work properly. If the self-test shows an image on the drum but none on the paper, and the corona assembly is present and not damaged, then the HVPS is at fault.

All-Black Pages

Only slightly more annoying than 10 blank pages are 10 black pages. This happens when the charging unit (the charging corona wire or charging corona roller) in the toner cartridge malfunctions and fails to place a charge on the EP drum. Because the drum is grounded, it has no charge. Anything with a charge (like toner) will stick to it. As the drum rotates, all the toner is transferred to the page and a black page is formed.

This problem wastes quite a bit of toner but can be fixed easily. The solution (again) is to replace the toner cartridge with a known, good, manufacturer-recommended one. If that doesn't solve the problem, then the HVPS is at fault (it's not providing the high voltage that the charging corona needs to function).

Repetitive Small Marks or Defects

Repetitive marks occur frequently in heavily used (as well as older) laser printers. The problem may be caused by toner spilled inside the printer. It can also be caused by a crack or chip in the EP drum (this mainly happens with recycled cartridges), which can accumulate toner. In both cases, some of the toner gets stuck onto one of the rollers. Once this happens, every time the roller rotates and touches a piece of paper, it leaves toner smudges spaced a roller circumference apart.

The solution is relatively simple: Clean or replace the offending roller. To help you figure out which roller is causing the problem, the service manuals contain a chart like the one in Figure 4.23. To use the chart, place the printed page next to it. Align the first occurrence of the smudge with the top arrow. The next smudge will line up with one of the other arrows. The arrow it lines up with tells you which roller is causing the problem.

Remember that the chart in Figure 4.23 is only an example. Your printer may have different-sized rollers (and thus need a different chart). Check your printer's service documentation for a chart like this. It is valuable in determining which roller is causing a smudge.

FIGURE 4.23 Laser printer roller circumference chart

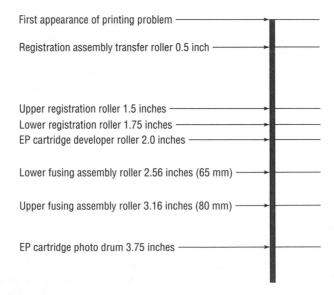

Vertical Black Lines on the Page

A groove or scratch in the EP drum can cause the problem of vertical black lines running down all or part of the page. Because a scratch is lower than the surface, it doesn't receive as much (if any) of a charge as the other areas. The result is that toner sticks to it as though it were discharged. The groove may go around the circumference of the drum, so the line may go all the way down the page.

Another possible cause of vertical black lines is a dirty charge corona wire. A dirty charge corona prevents a sufficient charge from being placed on the EP drum. Because the EP drum is almost zero, toner sticks to the areas that correspond to the dirty areas on the charge corona.

The solution to the first problem is, as always, to replace the toner cartridge (or EP drum, if your printer uses a separate EP drum and toner). You can also solve the second problem with a new toner cartridge, but in this case that would be an extreme solution. It's easier to clean the charge corona with the brush supplied with the cartridge.

Vertical White Lines on the Page

Vertical white lines running down all or part of the page are a relatively common problem on older printers, especially ones that don't see much maintenance. They are caused by foreign matter (more than likely toner) caught on the transfer corona wire. The dirty spots keep the toner from being transmitted to the paper (at those locations, that is), with the result that streaks form as the paper progresses past the transfer corona wire.

The solution is to clean the corona wires. LaserJet Series II printers contain a small corona wire brush to help in this procedure. It's usually a small, green-handled brush located near the transfer corona wire. To use it, remove the toner cartridge and run the brush in the charge corona groove on top of the toner cartridge. Replace the cartridge and use the brush to brush away any foreign deposits on the transfer corona. Be sure to put it back in its holder when you're finished.

Image Smudging

If you can pick up a sheet from a laser printer, run your thumb across it, and have the image come off on your thumb, you have a fuser problem. The fuser isn't heating the toner and fusing it into the paper. This could be caused by a number of things—but all of them can be taken care of with a fuser replacement. For example, if the halogen light inside the heating roller has burned out, that would cause the problem. The solution is to replace the fuser. The fuser can be replaced with a rebuilt unit, if you prefer. Rebuilt fusers are almost as good as new ones, and some even come with guarantees. Plus, they cost less.

 The whole fuser may not need to be replaced. Fuser components can be ordered from parts suppliers and can be rebuilt by you. For example, if the fuser has a bad lamp, you can order a lamp and replace it in the fuser.

Another problem similar to this occurs when small areas of smudging repeat themselves down the page. Dents or cold spots in the fuser heat roller cause this problem. The only solution is to replace either the fuser assembly or the heat roller.

Ghosting

Ghosting is what you have when you can see light images of previously printed pages on the current page. This is caused by one of two things: bad erasure lamps or a broken cleaning blade. If the erasure lamps are bad, the previous electrostatic discharges aren't completely wiped away. When the EP drum rotates toward the developing roller, some toner sticks to the slightly discharged areas. A broken cleaning blade, on the other hand, causes old toner to build up on the EP drum and consequently present itself in the next printed image.

Replacing the toner cartridge solves the second problem. Solving the first problem involves replacing the erasure lamps in the printer. Because the toner cartridge is the least expensive cure, you should try that first. Usually, replacing the toner cartridge will solve the problem. If it doesn't, you will have to replace the erasure lamps.

Printer Prints Pages of Garbage

This has happened to everyone at least once. You print a one-page letter, and 10 pages of what looks like garbage come out of the printer. This problem comes from one of two different sources: the print driver software or the formatter board.

Printer Driver

The correct printer driver needs to be installed for the printer you have. For example, if you have an HP LaserJet III, then that is the driver you need to install. Once the driver has been installed, it must be configured for the correct page-description language: PCL or PostScript. Most HP LaserJet printers use PCL (but can be configured for PostScript). Determine what page-description your printer has been configured for and set the print driver to the same setting. If this is not done, you will get garbage out of the printer.

> Most printers that have LCD displays will indicate that they are in PostScript mode with a *PS* or *PostScript* somewhere in the display.

If the problem is the wrong driver setting, the garbage the printer prints will look like English. That is, the words will be readable, but they won't make any sense.

Formatter Board

The other cause of several pages of garbage being printed is a bad formatter board. This circuit board takes the information the printer receives from the computer and turns it into commands for the various components in the printer. Usually, problems with the formatter board produce wavy lines of print or random patterns of dots on the page.

It's relatively easy to replace the formatter board in a laser printer. Usually this board is installed under the printer and can be removed by loosening two screws and pulling the board out. Typically, replacing the formatter board also replaces the printer interface, which is another possible source of garbage printouts.

Example Printer Testing: HP LaserJet

Now that we've defined some of the possible sources of problems with laser printers, let's discuss a few of the testing procedures you use with them. We'll discuss HP LaserJet laser printers because they are the most popular type of laser printer, but the topics covered here can be applied to other types of laser printers as well.

When you troubleshoot laser printers, you can perform three tests to narrow down which assembly is causing the problem: the engine self-test, the engine half self-test, and the secret self-test. (These tests are internal diagnostics for the printers and are included with most laser printers.). In addition to these tests, laser printers with LCD displays can display error codes that help in the diagnosing of laser printer problems.

Self-Tests

As we mentioned, there are three significant printer self-tests—tests the printer runs on its own (albeit when directed by the user). These are the engine self-test, the print engine half self-test, and the secret self-test:

Engine Self-Test   The engine self-test tests the print engine of the LaserJet, bypassing the formatter board. This test causes the printer to print a single page with vertical lines running its length. If an engine self-test can be performed, you know the laser print engine can print successfully. To perform an engine self-test, you must press the printer's self-test button, which is hidden behind a small cover on the side of the printer (see Figure 4.24). The location of the button varies from printer to printer, so you may have to refer to the printer manual. Using a pencil or probe, press the button, and the print engine will start printing the test page.

FIGURE 4.24   Print engine self-test button location. (The location may vary on different printers.)

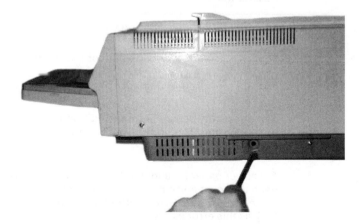

Half Self-Test   A print engine half self-test is performed the same as the self-test, but you interrupt it halfway through the print cycle by opening the cover. This test is useful in determining which part of the print process is causing the printer to malfunction. If you stop the print process and part of a developed image is on the EP drum and part has been transferred to the paper, you know that the pickup rollers, registration rollers, laser scanner, charging roller, EP drum, and transfer roller are all working correctly. You can stop the half self-test at various points in the print process to determine the source of a malfunction.

Secret Self-Test   To activate this test, you must first put the printer into service mode. To accomplish this, turn on the printer while simultaneously holding down the On Line, Continue, and Enter buttons (that's the first secret part, because nobody knows it unless somebody tells them). When the screen comes up blank, release the keys and press, in order, Continue and then Enter. The printer will perform an internal self-test, and then display 00 READY. At this point you are ready to initiate the rest of the secret self-test: Take the printer offline, press the Test button on the front panel, and hold the button until you see the 04 Self Test message. Then, release the Test button. This will cause the printer to print one self-test page. (If you want a continuous printout, instead of releasing the Test button at the 04 Self Test message, keep holding the Test button until the message 04 Self Test is displayed. The printer will print continuous self-test pages until you power off the printer or press On Line, or until the printer runs out of paper.)

Error Codes

In addition to the self-tests, you have another tool for troubleshooting HP laser printers. Error codes are a way for the LaserJet to tell the user (and a service technician) what's wrong. Table 4.2 details some of the most common codes displayed on an HP LaserJet.

TABLE 4.2   HP LaserJet Error Messages

Message	Description
00 Ready	The printer is in standby mode and ready to print.
02 Warming Up	The fuser is being warmed up before the 00 Ready state.
05 Self-Test	Full self-test has been initiated from the front panel.
11 Paper Out	The paper tray sensor is reporting that there is no paper in the paper tray. The printer will not print as long as this error exists.
13 Paper Jam	A piece of paper is caught in the paper path. To fix this problem, open the cover and clear the jam (including all pieces of the jam). Close the cover to resume printing. The printer will not print as long as this error exists.
14 No EP Cart	There is no EP cartridge (toner cartridge) installed in the printer. The printer will not print as long as this error exists.

TABLE 4.2 HP LaserJet Error Messages *(continued)*

Message	Description
15 Engine Test	An engine self-test is in progress.
16 Toner Low	The toner cartridge is almost out of toner. Replacement will be necessary soon.
50 Service	A fuser error has occurred. This problem is most commonly caused by fuser lamp failure. Power off the printer and replace the fuser to solve. The printer will not print as long as this error exists.
51 Error	Laser-scanning assembly problem. Test and replace, if necessary. The printer will not print as long as this error exists.
52 Error	The scanner motor in the laser-scanning assembly is malfunctioning. Test and replace as per the service manual. The printer will not print as long as this error exists.
55 Error	Communication problem between the formatter and the DC controller. Test and replace as per the service manual. The printer will not print as long as this error exists.

Troubleshooting Tips for HP LaserJet Printers

Printer technicians usually use a set of troubleshooting steps to help them solve HP LaserJet printing problems. Let's detail each of them to bring our discussion of laser printer trouble-shooting to a close:

1. **Is the exhaust fan operational?** This is the first component to receive power when the printer is turned on. If you can feel air coming out of the exhaust fan, this confirms that AC voltage is present and power is turned on, that +5VDC and +24VDC are being generated by the AC power supply (ACPS), and that the DC controller is functional. If there is no power to the printer (no lights, fan not operating), the ACPS is at fault. Replacement involves removing all printer covers and removing four screws. You can purchase a new ACPS module, but it is usually cheaper to replace it with a rebuilt unit.

If you are into electronics, you can probably rebuild the ACPS yourself simply and cheaply. The main rectifier is usually the part that fails in these units; it can easily be replaced if you know what you're doing.

2. **Do the control panel LEDs work?** If so, the formatter board can communicate with control panel. If the LEDs do not light, it could mean the formatter board is bad, the control panel is bad, or the wires connecting the two are broken or shorting out.

3. **Does the main motor rotate at power up?** Turn the power off. Remove the covers from the side of the printer. Turn the printer back on and carefully watch and listen for main motor rotation. If you see and hear the main motor rotating, this indicates that a toner cartridge is installed, all photosensors are functional, all motors are functional, and the printer can move paper (assuming there are no obstructions).

4. **Does the fuser heat lamp light after the main motor finishes its rotation?** You will need to remove the covers to notice. The heat lamp should light after the main motor rotation and stay lit until the control panel says 00 Ready.

5. **Can the printer perform an engine test print?** A sheet of vertical lines indicates that the print engine works. This test print bypasses the formatter board and indicates whether the print problem resides in the engine. If the test print is successful, you can rule out the engine as a source of the problem. If the test print fails, you will have to further troubleshoot the printer to determine which engine component is causing the problem.

6. **Can the printer perform a control panel self-test?** This is the final test to ensure printer operation. If you can press the Test Page control panel button and receive a test printout, this means the entire printer is working properly. The only possibilities for problems are outside the printer (interfaces, cables, and software problems).

Summary

In this chapter, we discussed how the different types of printers work as well as the most common methods of connecting them to computers. You learned how computers use page-description languages to format data before they send it to printers. You also learned about the various types of consumable supplies and how they relate to each type of printer.

The most basic category of printer currently in use is the impact printer. Impact printers form images by striking something against a ribbon, which in turn makes a mark on the paper. You learned how these printers work and the service concepts associated with them.

One of the most popular types of printer today is the bubble-jet printer, so named because of the mechanism used to put ink on the paper.

The most complex type of printer is the laser printer. The A+ exam covers this type of printer more than any other. You learned about the steps in the Electrophotographic (EP) process, the process that explains how laser printers print. We also explained the various components that make up this printer and how they work together.

You then learned about the interfaces used to connect printers to PCs and the consumable supplies printers use. We discussed various interfaces and how they are used, and how printer supplies can affect print output quality.

Finally, you learned about the various methods used to troubleshoot printing and print quality for both bubble-jet and laser printers. We also explained what causes failures and the best way to fix them.

Key Terms

Before you take the exam, be certain you are familiar with the following terms:

corona wire

cyan, magenta, yellow, and black (CMYK)

daisy-wheel printer

developing roller

developing step

dot matrix

dot-matrix printer

driver software

dye-sublimation printer

electronic stepper motor

envelope feeder

fax modem

feed roller

feeder

finisher

FireWire

font

fuser

fusing step

impact printer

infrared transmission

ink cartridge

interface

interface circuitry

interface software

laser printer

letter quality (LQ)

main motor

print consumables

print media

printer control circuits

printer controller assembly

printer ribbon

printer-resident fonts

printhead

printhead alignment

printhead carriage

rag stock

rasterizing

ribbon cartridge

scanner

separator pads

solenoid

solid-ink printer

stabilizer bar

static-charge eliminator strip

stepper motor

sublimate

thermal printer

toner

transfer corona assembly

transferring step

writing step

Review Questions

1. Which step in the EP print process uses a laser to discharge selected areas of the photosensitive drum, thus forming an image on the drum?

   A. Writing

   B. Transferring

   C. Developing

   D. Cleaning

2. What is the correct order of the steps in the EP print process?

   A. Developing, writing, transferring, fusing, charging, cleaning

   B. Charging, writing, developing, transferring, fusing, cleaning

   C. Transferring, writing, developing, charging, cleaning, fusing

   D. Cleaning, charging, writing, developing, transferring, fusing

3. What is the most basic printer type?

   A. Impact printer

   B. Bubble-jet printer

   C. Laser printer

   D. Interfaces and print media

4. Which voltage is used to transfer the toner to the paper in an EP process laser printer?

   A. +600VDC

   B. −600VDC

   C. +6000VDC

   D. −6000VDC

5. If the static-eliminator strip is absent (or broken) in either an EP process or HP LaserJet laser printer, what will happen?

   A. Nothing. Both printers will continue to function normally.

   B. Nothing will happen in EP process printers, but HP LaserJet printers will flash a "−671 error" message.

   C. Paper jams may occur in both types of printers because the paper may curl around the photosensitive drum.

   D. Nothing will happen in HP LaserJet printers, but EP process printers will flash a "−671 error" message.

6. Which type of printers are referred to as page printers, because they receive their print job instructions one page at a time?

   A. Daisy wheel

   B. Dot matrix

   C. Bubble jet

   D. Laser

7. Which of the following are possible interfaces for printers? (Select all that apply.)

   A. Parallel

   B. Mouse port

   C. Serial

   D. Network

8. Which laser printer component formats the print job for the type of printer being used?

   A. Corona assembly

   B. DC power supply

   C. Printer controller assembly

   D. Formatter software

9. Which of the following are page-description languages? (Select all that apply.)

   A. Page Description Language (PDL)

   B. PostScript

   C. PageScript

   D. Printer Control Language (PCL)

10. The basis weight is the weight in pounds of 500 sheets of bond paper for what size of paper?

    A. 8 1/2 × 11 inch

    B. 11 × 17 inch

    C. 17 × 22 inch

    D. 8 1/2 × 17 inch

11. Any printer that uses the electrophotographic process contains how many standard assemblies?

    A. Five

    B. Six

    C. Four

    D. Eight

12. Which type(s) of printers can be used with multipart forms?

    A. Bubble-jet printers

    B. EP process laser printers

    C. HP process laser printers

    D. Dot-matrix printers

13. LED page printers differ from EP process laser printers in which step?

    A. Writing

    B. Charging

    C. Fusing

    D. Cleaning

    E. Developing

    F. Transferring

14. What part of both EP process and HP LaserJet process printers supplies the voltages for the charge and transfer corona assemblies?

    A. High-voltage power supply (HVPS)

    B. DC power supply (DCPS)

    C. Controller circuitry

    D. Transfer corona

15. With EP process laser printers, the laser discharges the charged photosensitive drum to _____ VDC.

    A. +600

    B. 0

    C. −100

    D. −600

16. Which impact printer has a printhead that contains a row of pins that are triggered in patterns that form letters and numbers as the printhead moves across the paper?

    A. Laser printer

    B. Daisy-wheel printer

    C. Dot-matrix printer

    D. Bubble-jet printer

17. Which printer contains a wheel that looks like a flower with raised letters and symbols on each petal?

A. Bubble-jet printers

B. Daisy-wheel printer

C. Dot-matrix printer

D. Laser printer

18. Which of the following is *not* an advantage of the daisy-wheel printer?

A. Can print multipart forms

B. Relatively inexpensive

C. Print quality is comparable to a typewriter

D. Speed

19. Which printer part gets the toner from the photosensitive drum onto the paper?

A. Laser scanner assembly

B. Fusing assembly

C. Corona assembly

D. Drum

20. Which of the following is *not* an advantage of a Universal Serial Bus (USB) printer interface?

A. It has a higher transfer rate than a serial connection.

B. It has a higher transfer rate than a parallel connection.

C. It automatically recognizes new devices.

D. It allows the printer to communicate with networks, servers, and workstations.

Answers to Review Questions

1. A.   The writing step uses a laser to discharge selected areas of the photosensitive drum, thus forming an image on the drum.

2. D.   The correct sequence in the EP print process is cleaning, charging, writing, developing, transferring, fusing.

3. A.   Of the types listed here, the impact printer is the most basic.

4. A.   Because the toner on the drum has a slight negative charge (–100VDC), it requires a positive charge to transfer it to the paper. +600VDC is the voltage used in an EP process laser printer.

5. C.   If the static-eliminator strip is absent (or broken) in either an EP process or HP LaserJet laser printer, the paper will maintain its positive charge. Should this occur, paper jams may result due to the paper curling around the photosensitive drum.

6. D.   Laser printers receive their print job instructions one page at a time.

7. A, C, D.   Printers can communicate via parallel, serial, and network connections.

8. C.   The printer controller assembly is responsible for formatting the print job for the type of printer being used.

9. B, D.   Of those listed, only PostScript and PCL are page-description languages.

10. C.   The basis weight is the weight in pounds of 500 sheets of bond 17×22 inch paper.

11. D.   There are eight standard assemblies in an electrophotographic process printer.

12. D.   Of the choices listed, only dot-matrix printers are impact printers and therefore can be used with multipart forms.

13. A.   LED page printers differ from EP process laser printers in the writing step. They use a different process to write the image on the EP drum.

14. A.   The high-voltage power supply is the part of both EP process and HP LaserJet process printers that supplies the voltages for the charge and transfer corona assemblies.

15. C.   With EP process laser printers, the laser discharges the charged photosensitive drum to –100VDC.

16. C.   The dot-matrix impact printer's printhead contains a row of pins that are triggered in patterns that form letters and numbers as the printhead moves across the paper.

17. B.   The daisy-wheel printer gets its name because it contains a wheel with raised letters and symbols on each petal.

18. D.   The daisy-wheel printer is much slower when compared to the dot-matrix printer and therefore speed is a *disadvantage*.

19. C.   The corona assembly gets the toner from the photosensitive drum onto the paper. For some printers, this is a corona wire, and for others, it is a corona roller.

20. D.   The rate of transfer and the ability to automatically recognize new devices are two of the major advantages that make USB the current most popular type of printer interface. However, it is the network printer interface that allows the printer to communicate with networks, servers, and workstations.

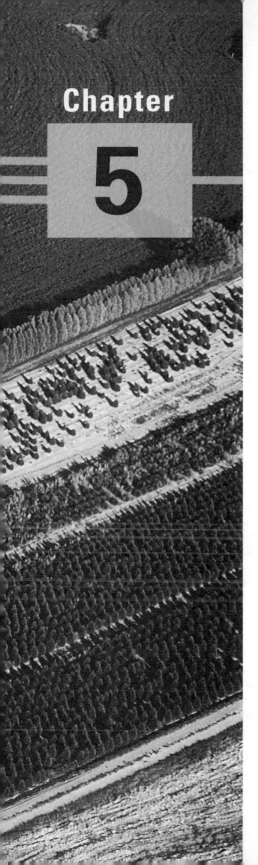

Chapter

5

Networking Fundamentals

THE FOLLOWING OBJECTIVES ARE COVERED IN THIS CHAPTER:

✓ 6.1 Identify the common types of network cables, their characteristics and connectors.

✓ 6.2 Identify basic networking concepts including how a network works.

✓ 6.3 Identify common technologies available for establishing Internet connectivity and their characteristics.

Imagine working in an office 20 years ago with little or no computer equipment. It's hard to envision now, isn't it? We take for granted a lot of what we have gained in technology the past few decades. Now, imagine having to send a memo to everyone in the company. Back then we used interoffice mail; today we use e-mail. This is an example of one form of communication that only became available due to the introduction and growth of networks.

This chapter focuses on the basic concepts surrounding how a network works, including the way it sends information and what tools it uses to send information. This information is covered only to a minor degree by the A+ certification exam. However, if you're interested in becoming a service technician, this information will prove to be very useful, because you will in all likelihood be asked to troubleshoot both hardware and software problems on existing networks. Included in this chapter is information on the following topics:

- What a network is
- Network types
- Media types
- Connectivity devices

If the material in this chapter interests you, you might consider studying for, and eventually taking, CompTIA's Network+ exam. It is a generic networking certification (similar to A+, but for network-related topics). You can study for it using Sybex's *Network+ Study Guide* materials, available at www.sybex.com.

What Is a Network?

Stand-alone personal computers, first introduced in the late 1970s, gave users the ability to create documents, spreadsheets, and other types of data and save them for future use. For the small-business user or home-computer enthusiast, this was great. For larger companies, however, it was not enough. The larger the company, the greater the need to share information between offices, and sometimes over great distances. Stand-alone computers were insufficient for the following reasons:

- Their small hard drive capacities were inefficient.
- To print, each computer required a printer attached locally.
- Sharing documents was cumbersome. People grew tired of having to save to a diskette and then take that diskette to the recipient. (This procedure was called *sneakernet*.)

- There was no e-mail. Instead, there was interoffice mail, which was not reliable and frequently was not delivered in a timely manner.

To address these problems, *networks* were born. A network links two or more computers together to communicate and share resources. Their success was a revelation to the computer industry as well as businesses. Now, departments could be linked internally to offer better performance and increase efficiency.

You have heard the term *networking* in the business context, where people come together and exchange names for future contact and to give them access to more resources. The same is true with a computer network. A computer network allows computers to link to each other's resources. For example, in a network, every computer does not need a printer connected locally in order to print. Instead, one computer has a printer connected to it and allows the other computers to access this resource. Because they allow users to share resources, networks offer an increase in performance as well as a decrease in the outlay for new hardware and software.

LANs vs. WANs

Local area networks (LANs) were introduced to connect computers in a single office. *Wide area networks (WANs)* expanded the LANs to include networks outside the local environment and also to distribute resources across distances. Today, LANs exist in many businesses, from small to large. WANs are becoming more widely accepted as businesses become more mobile and as more of them span greater distances. It is important to understand LANs and WANs as a service professional, because when you're repairing computers you are likely to come in contact with problems that are associated with the computer's connection to a network.

Local Area Networks (LANs)

The 1970s brought us the minicomputer, which was a smaller version of the mainframe. Whereas the mainframe used *centralized processing* (all programs ran on the same computer), the minicomputer used *distributed processing* to access programs across other computers. As depicted in Figure 5.1, distributed processing allows a user at one computer to use a program on another computer as a *back end* to process and store the information. The user's computer is the *front end*, performing the data entry. This arrangement allowed programs to be distributed across computers rather than centralized. This was also the first time computers used cable to connect rather than phone lines.

FIGURE 5.1   Distributed processing

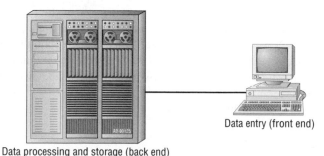

Data entry (front end)

Data processing and storage (back end)

By the 1980s, offices were beginning to buy PCs in large numbers. Portables were also introduced, allowing computing to become mobile. Neither PCs nor portables, however, were efficient in sharing information. As timeliness and security became more important, diskettes were just not cutting it. Offices needed to find a way to implement a better means to share and access resources. This led to the introduction of the first type of PC LAN: ShareNet by Novell. LANs are simply the linking of computers to share resources within a closed environment. The first simple LANs were constructed a lot like Figure 5.2.

FIGURE 5.2   A simple LAN

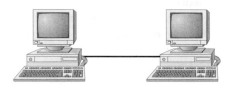

After the introduction of ShareNet, more LANs sprouted. The earliest LANs could not cover a great distance. Most of them could only stretch across a single floor of the office and could support no more than 30 users. Further, they were still simple, and only a few software programs supported them. The first software programs that ran on a LAN were not capable of permitting more than one user at a time to use a program (this constraint was known as *file locking*). Nowadays, we can see multiple users accessing a program at one time, limited only by restrictions at the record level.

Wide Area Networks (WANs)

By the late 1980s, networks were expanding to cover ranges considered geographical in size and were supporting thousands of users. WANs, first implemented with mainframes at massive government expense, started attracting PC users as networks went to this new level. Businesses with offices across the country communicated as if they were only desks apart. Soon the whole world saw a change in its way of doing business, across not only a few miles but across countries. Whereas LANs are limited to single buildings, WANs can span buildings, states, countries, and even continental boundaries. Figure 5.3 gives an example of a simple WAN.

Networks of today and tomorrow are no longer limited by the inability of LANs to cover distance and handle mobility. WANs play an important role in the future development of corporate networks worldwide. Although the primary focus of this chapter is LANs, we will feature a section on WAN connectivity. This section will briefly explain the current technologies and what you should expect to see in the future. If you are interested in more information about LANs or WANs, or if you plan to become a networking technician, check your local library resources or the Internet.

FIGURE 5.3   A simple WAN

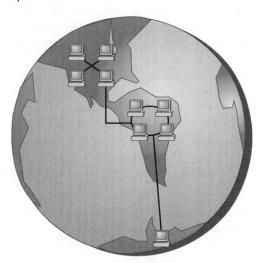

Primary Network Components

Putting together a network is not as simple as it was with the first PC network. You can no longer consider two computers cabled together a fully functional network. Today, networks consist of three primary components:

- Servers
- Clients or workstations
- Resources

Every network requires two more items to tie these three components together. A network operating system (NOS) and some kind of shared medium. These components are covered later in their own sections.

No network would be complete without these three components working together.

Servers

Servers come in many shapes and sizes. They are a core component of the network, providing a link to the resources necessary to perform any task. The link the server provides could be to a resource existing on the server itself or a resource on a client computer. The server is the "leader of the pack," offering directions to the client computers regarding where to go to get what they need.

Servers offer networks the capability of centralizing the control of resources and can thus reduce administrative difficulties. They can be used to distribute processes for balancing the load on computers and can thus increase speed and performance. They can also departmentalize files for improved reliability. That way, if one server goes down, not all of the files are lost.

Servers perform several tasks. For example, servers that provide files to the users on the network are called *file servers*. Likewise, servers that host printing services for users are called *print servers*. (There are other tasks, as well, such as remote-access services, administration, mail, and so on) Servers can be *multipurpose* or *single-purpose*. If they are multipurpose, they can be, for example, both a file server and a print server at the same time. If the server is a single-purpose server, it is a file server only or a print server only.

Another distinction we use in categorizing servers is whether they are *dedicated* or *nondedicated*:

Dedicated Servers   Assigned to provide specific applications or services for the network, and nothing else. Because a *dedicated server* specializes in only a few tasks, it requires fewer resources from the computer that is hosting it than a nondedicated server might require. This savings in overhead may translate to a certain efficiency and can thus be considered as having a beneficial impact on network performance. A web server is an example of a dedicated server: It is dedicated to the task of serving up web pages.

Nondedicated Servers   Assigned to provide one or more network services *and* local access. A *nondedicated server* is expected to be slightly more flexible in its day-to-day use than a dedicated server. Nondedicated servers can be used not only to direct network traffic and perform administrative actions, but also often to serve as a front end for the administrator to work with other applications or services. The nondedicated server is not really what some would consider a true server, because it can act as a workstation as well as a server. The workgroup server at your office is an example of a nondedicated server. It might be a combination file, print, and e-mail server. Plus, because of its nature, a nondedicated server could also function well in a peer-to-peer environment. It could be used as a workstation, in addition to being a file, print, and e-mail server.

Many networks use both dedicated and nondedicated servers in order to incorporate the best of both worlds, offering improved network performance with the dedicated servers and flexibility with the nondedicated servers.

Workstations or Client Computers

Workstations are the computers on which the network users do their work, performing activities such as word processing, database design, graphic design, e-mail, and other office or personal tasks. Workstations are basically everyday computers, except for the fact that they are connected to a network that offers additional resources. Workstations can range from diskless computer systems to desktop systems. In network terms, workstations are also known as *client computers*. As clients, they are allowed to communicate with the servers in the network in order to use the network's resources.

It takes several items to make a workstation into a client. You must install a *network interface card (NIC)*, a special expansion card that allows the PC to talk on a network. You must connect it to a cabling system that connects to another computer (or several other computers). And you must install special software, called *client software*, which allows the computer to talk to the servers and request resources from them. Once all this has been accomplished, the computer is "on the network."

To the client, the server may be nothing more than just another drive letter. However, because it is in a network environment, the client can use the server as a doorway to more storage or more applications, or through which it may communicate with other computers or other networks. To users, being on a network changes a few things:

- They can store more information, because they can store data on other computers on the network.

- They can share and receive information from other users, perhaps even collaborating on the same document.

- They can use programs that would be too large or complex for their computer to use by itself.

Network Resources

We now have the server to share the resources and the workstation to use them, but what about the resources themselves? A *resource* (as far as the network is concerned) is any item that can be used on a network. Resources can include a broad range of items, but the most important ones include the following:

- Printers and other peripherals
- Files
- Applications
- Disk storage

When an office can purchase paper, ribbons, toner, or other consumables for only one, two, or maybe three printers for the entire office, the costs are dramatically lower than the costs for supplying printers at every workstation. Networks also give more storage space to files. Client computers can't always handle the overhead involved in storing large files (for example, database files) because they are already heavily involved in users' day-to-day work activities. Because servers in a network can be dedicated to only certain functions, a server can be allocated to store all the larger files that are worked with every day, freeing up disk space on client computers. Similarly, applications (programs) no longer need to be on every computer in the office. If the server is capable of handling the overhead an application requires, the application can reside on the server and be used by workstations through a network connection.

The sharing of applications over a network requires a special arrangement with the application vendor, which may wish to set the price of the application according to the number of users who will be using it. The arrangement allowing multiple users to use a single installation of an application is called a *site license*.

🌐 Real World Scenario

Being on a Network Brings Responsibilities

You are part of a community when you are on a network, which means you need to take responsibility for your actions. First, a network is only as secure as the users who use it. You cannot randomly delete files or move documents from server to server. You do not own your e-mail, so anyone in your company's management can choose to read it. Additionally, printing does not mean that if you send something to print that it will print immediately—your document may not be the first in line to be printed at the shared printer. Plus, if your workstation has also been set up as a nondedicated server, you cannot turn it off.

Network Operating Systems (NOSs)

PCs use a disk operating system that controls the filesystem and how the applications communicate with the hard disk. Networks use a network operating system (NOS) to control the communication with resources and the flow of data across the network. The NOS runs on the server. Many companies offer software to start a network. Some of the more popular NOSs at this time include Unix; Novell's NetWare; and Microsoft's Windows NT Server, Windows 2000 Server, Windows XP, and Windows 2003 (not yet released as of early 2003). Although several other NOSs exist, these are the most popular.

Back in the early days of mainframes, it took a full staff of people working around the clock to keep the machines going. With today's NOSs, servers are able to monitor memory, CPU time, disk space, and peripherals, without a baby-sitter. Each of these operating systems allows processes to respond in a certain way with the processor.

With the new functionality of LANs and WANs, you can be sitting in your office in Milwaukee and carry on a real-time electronic chat with a coworker in France, or maybe print an invoice at the home office in California, or manage someone else's computer from your own while they are on vacation. Gone are the days of disk-passing, phone messages left but not received, or having to wait a month to receive a letter from someone in Hong Kong. NOSs provide this functionality on a network.

Network Resource Access

Now that we have discussed the makeup of a typical network, let's examine the way resources are accessed on a network. There are generally two resource access models: peer-to-peer and client-server. It is important to choose the appropriate model. How do you decide what type of resource model is needed? You must first think about the following questions:

- What is the size of the organization?
- How much security does the company require?
- What software or hardware does the resource require?
- How much administration does it need?

- How much will it cost?
- Will this resource meet the needs of the organization today and in the future?
- Will additional training be needed?

Networks cannot just be put together at the drop of a hat. A lot of planning is required before implementation of a network to ensure that whatever design is chosen will be effective and efficient, and not just for today but for the future as well. The forethought of the designer will create the best network with the least amount of administrative overhead. In each network, it is important that a plan be developed to answer the previous questions. The answers will help the designer choose the type of resource model to use.

Peer-to-Peer Networks

In a peer-to-peer network, the computers act as both service providers and service requestors. An example of a peer-to-peer resource model is shown in Figure 5.4.

FIGURE 5.4   The peer-to-peer resource model

Peer-to-peer networks are great for small, simple, inexpensive networks. This model can be set up almost immediately, with little extra hardware required. Windows 3.11, Windows 9x, Windows NT, Windows 2000, and Windows XP are popular operating system environments that support a peer-to-peer resource model.

Generally speaking, there is no centralized administration or control in the peer-to-peer resource model. Every station has unique control over the resources the computer owns, and each station must be administrated separately. However, this very lack of centralized control can make it difficult to administer the network; for the same reason, the network isn't very secure. Moreover, because each computer is acting as both a workstation and server, it may not be easy to locate resources. The person who is in charge of a file may have moved it without anyone's knowledge. Also, the users who work under this arrangement need more training, because they are not only users but also administrators.

Will this type of network meet the needs of the organization today and in the future? Peer-to-peer resource models are generally considered the right choice for companies that don't expect future growth. For example, the business might be small, possibly an independent subsidiary of a specialty company, and has no plans to increase its market size or number of employees. Companies that expect growth, on the other hand, should not choose this type of model. Although it could very well meet the company's needs today, the growth of the company will necessitate making major changes over time. Choosing to set up a peer-to-peer resource model simply because it is cheap and easy to install could be a costly mistake. A company's management may find that it costs them more in the long run than if they had chosen a server-based resource model.

Client-Server Resource Model

The client-server (also known as server-based) model is better than the peer-to-peer model for large networks (say, 25 users or more) that need a more secure environment and centralized control. Server-based networks use a dedicated, centralized server. All administrative functions and resource sharing are performed from this point. This makes it easier to share resources, perform backups, and support an almost unlimited number of users. This model also offers better security. However, the server needs more hardware than a typical workstation/server computer in a peer-to-peer resource model. Additionally, it requires specialized software (the NOS) to manage the server's role in the environment. With the addition of a server and the NOS, server-based networks can easily cost more than peer-to-peer resource models. However, for large networks, it's the only choice. An example of a client-server resource model is shown in Figure 5.5.

FIGURE 5.5 The client-server resource model

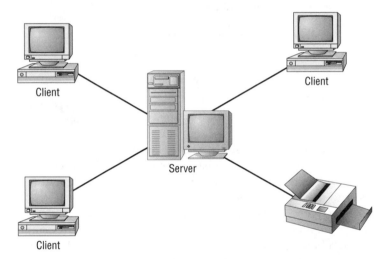

Will this type of network meet the needs of the organization today and in the future? Client-server resource models are the desired models for companies that are continually growing or that need to initially support a large environment. Server-based networks offer the flexibility to add more resources and clients almost indefinitely into the future. Hardware costs may be more, but, with the centralized administration, managing resources becomes less time-consuming. Also, only a few administrators need to be trained, and users are only responsible for their own work environment.

If you are looking for an inexpensive, simple network with little setup required, and there is no need for the company to grow in the future, then the peer-to-peer network is the way to go. If you are looking for a network to support many users (more than 25), strong security, and centralized administration, consider the server-based network your only choice.

Whatever you decide, be sure to take the time to plan. A network is not something you can just throw together. You don't want to find out a few months down the road that the type of network you chose does not meet the needs of the company—this could be a time-intensive and costly mistake.

Network Topologies

A *topology* is a way of laying out the network. Topologies can be either physical or logical. *Physical topologies* describe how the cables are run. *Logical topologies* describe how the network messages travel. Deciding which type of topology to use is the next step when designing your network.

You must choose the appropriate topology in which to arrange your network. Each type differs by its cost, ease of installation, fault tolerance (how the topology handles problems like cable breaks), and ease of reconfiguration (like adding a new workstation to the existing network).

There are five primary topologies (some of which can be both logical and physical):

- Bus (can be both logical and physical)

- Star (physical only)

- Ring (can be both logical and physical)

- Mesh (can be both logical and physical)

- Hybrid (usually physical)

Each topology has advantages and disadvantages. At the end of this section, check out Table 5.1, which summarizes the advantages and disadvantages of each topology.

Bus Topology

A bus is the simplest physical topology. It consists of a single cable that runs to every workstation, as shown in Figure 5.6. This topology uses the least amount of cabling, but also covers the shortest distance. Each computer shares the same data and address path. With a logical bus topology, messages pass through the trunk, and each workstation checks to see if the message is addressed to itself. If the address of the message matches the workstation's address, the network adapter copies the message to the card's onboard memory.

FIGURE 5.6 The bus topology

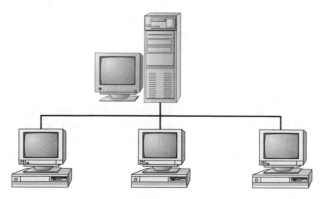

Cable systems that use the bus topology are easy to install. You run a cable from the first computer to the last computer. All the remaining computers attach to the cable somewhere in between. Because of the simplicity of installation, and because of the low cost of the cable, bus topology cabling systems (such as Ethernet) are the cheapest to install.

Although the bus topology uses the least amount of cabling, it is difficult to add a workstation. If you want to add another workstation, you have to completely reroute the cable and possibly run two additional lengths of it. Also, if any one of the cables breaks, the entire network is disrupted. Therefore, such a system is very expensive to maintain.

Star Topology

A physical star topology branches each network device off a central device called a *hub*, making it very easy to add a new workstation. Also, if any workstation goes down, it does not affect the entire network. (But, as you might expect, if the central device goes down, the entire network goes down.) Some types of Ethernet, ARCNet, and Token Ring use a physical star topology. Figure 5.7 gives an example of the organization of the star network.

FIGURE 5.7 The star topology

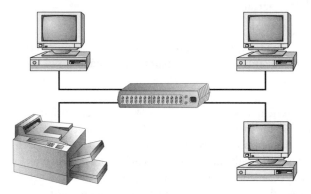

Star topologies are easy to install. A cable is run from each workstation to the hub. The hub is placed in a central location in the office (for example, a utility closet). Star topologies are more expensive to install than bus networks, because several more cables need to be installed, plus the hubs. But, the ease of reconfiguration and fault tolerance (one cable failing does not bring down the entire network) far outweighs the drawbacks.

Although the hub is the central portion of a star topology, many networks use a device known as a switch *instead* of a hub. The primary difference between them is that the switch makes a virtual connection between sender and receiver instead of simply sending each message to every port. Thus, a switch provides better performance over a hub for only a small price increase.

Ring Topology

A physical ring topology is a unique topology. Each computer connects to two other computers, joining them in a circle and creating a unidirectional path where messages move from workstation to workstation. Each entity participating in the ring reads a message, and then regenerates it and hands it to its neighbor on a different network cable. See Figure 5.8 for an example of a ring topology.

FIGURE 5.8   The ring topology

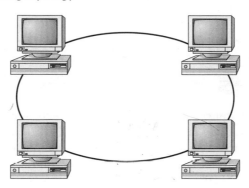

The ring makes it difficult to add new computers. Unlike a star topology network, the ring topology network will go down if one entity is removed from the ring. Physical ring topology systems don't exist much anymore, mainly because the hardware involved was fairly expensive and the fault tolerance was very low. However, one type of logical ring still exists: IBM's Token Ring technology. We'll discuss this technology later in the "Network Architectures" section.

Token Ring does *not* use a physical ring. It actually uses a physical star topology. Remember that physical topologies describe how the cables are connected, and logical topologies describe information flow.

Mesh Topology

The *mesh topology* is the simplest logical topology in terms of data flow, but it is the most complex in terms of physical design. In this physical topology, each device is connected to every other device (Figure 5.9). This topology is rarely found in LANs, mainly because of the complexity of the cabling. If there are x computers, there will be $(x \times (x - 1)) \div 2$ cables in the network. For example, if you have five computers in a mesh network, it will use $5 \times (5 - 1) \div 2 = 10$ cables. This complexity is compounded when you add another workstation. For example, your 5-computer, 10-cable network will jump to 15 cables if you add just one more computer. Imagine how the person doing the cabling would feel if you told them they had to cable 50 computers in a mesh network—they'd have to come up with $50 \times (50 - 1) \div 2 = 1225$ cables!

FIGURE 5.9   The mesh topology

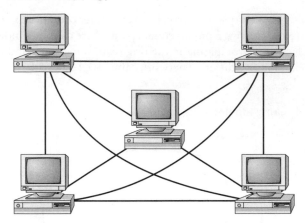

Because of its design, the physical mesh topology is very expensive to install and maintain. Cables must be run from each device to every other device. The advantage you gain is high fault tolerance. With a logical mesh topology, there will always be a way to get the data from source to destination. The data may not be able to take the direct route, but it can take an alternate, indirect route. For this reason, the mesh topology is found in WANs to connect multiple sites across WAN links. It uses devices called *routers* to search multiple routes through the mesh and determine the best path. However, the mesh topology does become inefficient with five or more entities.

Hybrid Topology

The hybrid topology is simply a mix of the other topologies. It would be impossible to illustrate it, because there are many combinations. In fact, *most* networks today are not only hybrid, but heterogeneous (they include a mix of components of different types and brands). The hybrid network may be more expensive than some types of network topologies, but it takes the best features of all the other topologies and exploits them.

Summary of Topologies

Table 5.1 summarizes the advantages and disadvantages of each type of network topology. This table is a good study aid for the A+ exam. (In other words, memorize it!)

TABLE 5.1   Topologies—Advantages and Disadvantages

Topology	Advantages	Disadvantages
Bus	Cheap. Easy to install.	Difficult to reconfigure. Break in the bus disables the entire network.
Star	Cheap. Easy to install. Easy to reconfigure. Fault tolerant.	More expensive than bus.

TABLE 5.1   Topologies—Advantages and Disadvantages *(continued)*

Topology	Advantages	Disadvantages
Ring	Efficient. Easy to install.	Reconfiguration is difficult. Very expensive.
Mesh	Simplest for data flow. Most fault tolerant.	Reconfiguration is extremely difficult. Extremely expensive. Very complex.
Hybrid	Gives a combination of the best features of each topology used.	Complex (less so than mesh, however).

Network Communications

You have chosen the type of network and arrangement (topology). Now the computers need to understand how to communicate. Network communications use protocols. A *protocol* is a set of rules that govern communications. Protocols detail what "language" the computers are speaking when they talk over a network. If two computers are going to communicate, they both must be using the same protocol.

Different methods are used to describe the different protocols. We will discuss two of the most common: the OSI model and the IEEE 802 standards.

OSI Model

The International Standards Organization (ISO) introduced the *Open Systems Interconnection (OSI)* model to provide a common way of describing network protocols. The ISO put together a seven-layer model providing a relationship between the stages of communication, with each layer adding to the layer above or below it.

 This OSI model is just that: a model. It can't be implemented. You will never find a network that is running the "OSI protocol."

The theory with the OSI model is that as transmission takes place, the higher layers pass data through the lower layers. As the data passes through a layer, the layer tacks its information (also called a *header*) onto the beginning of the information being transmitted until it reaches the bottom layer. At this point, the bottom layer sends the information out on the wire.

At the receiving end, the bottom layer receives the information, reads its information from its header and removes its header from the information, and then passes the remainder to the next highest layer. This procedure continues until the topmost layer receives the data that the sending computer sent.

The OSI model layers from top to bottom are listed here. We'll *describe* each of these layers from bottom to top, however. After the descriptions, we'll summarize the entire model:

- Application layer

- Presentation layer
- Session layer
- Transport layer
- Network layer
- Data Link layer
- Physical layer

Physical Layer   Describes how the data gets transmitted over a physical medium. This layer defines how long each piece of data is and the translation of each into the electrical pulses that are sent over the wires. It decides whether data travels unidirectionally or bidirectionally across the hardware. It also relates electrical, optical, mechanical, and functional interfaces to the cable.

Data Link Layer   Arranges data into chunks called *frames*. Included in these chunks is control information indicating the beginning and end of the data stream. This layer is very important because it makes transmission easier and more manageable and allows for error checking within the data frames. The Data Link layer also describes the unique physical address (also known as the *MAC address*) for each NIC.

Network Layer   Addresses messages and translates logical addresses and names into physical addresses. At this layer, the data is organized into chunks called *datagrams*. The Network layer is something like the traffic cop. It is able to judge the best network path for the data based on network conditions, priority, and other variables. This layer manages traffic through packet switching, routing, and controlling congestion of data.

Transport Layer   Signals "all clear" by making sure the data frames are error-free. This layer also controls the data flow and troubleshoots any problems with transmitting or receiving datagrams. This layer's most important job is to provide error checking and reliable, end-to-end communications. It can also take several smaller messages and combine them into a single, larger message.

Session Layer   Allows applications on different computers to establish, use, and end a session. A session is one virtual conversation. For example, all the procedures needed to transfer a single file make up one session. Once the session is over, a new process has begun. This layer enables network procedures such as identifying passwords, logons, and network monitoring. It can also handle recovery from a network failure.

Presentation Layer   Determines the "look," or format, of the data, network security, and file transfers. This layer performs protocol conversion and manages data compression, data translation, and encryption. The character set information also is determined at this level. (The character set determines which numbers represent which alphanumeric characters.)

Application Layer   Allows access to network services. This is the layer at which file services and print services operate. It also is the layer that workstations interact with, and it controls data flow and, if there are errors, recovery.

Summary of the OSI Model

Figure 5.10 shows the complete OSI model. Note the relation of each layer to the others and the function of each layer.

FIGURE 5.10   OSI model and characteristics

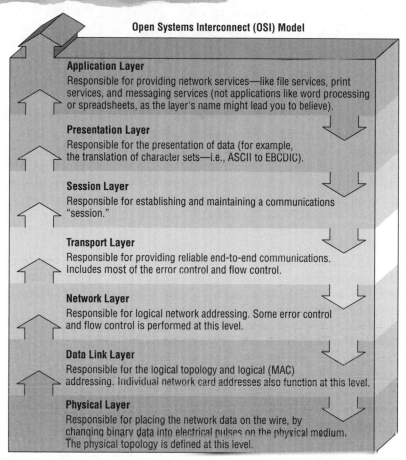

Open Systems Interconnect (OSI) Model

Application Layer
Responsible for providing network services—like file services, print services, and messaging services (not applications like word processing or spreadsheets, as the layer's name might lead you to believe).

Presentation Layer
Responsible for the presentation of data (for example, the translation of character sets—i.e., ASCII to EBCDIC).

Session Layer
Responsible for establishing and maintaining a communications "session."

Transport Layer
Responsible for providing reliable end-to-end communications. Includes most of the error control and flow control.

Network Layer
Responsible for logical network addressing. Some error control and flow control is performed at this level.

Data Link Layer
Responsible for the logical topology and logical (MAC) addressing. Individual network card addresses also function at this level.

Physical Layer
Responsible for placing the network data on the wire, by changing binary data into electrical pulses on the physical medium. The physical topology is defined at this level.

IEEE 802 Project Models

The Institute of Electrical and Electronics Engineers (IEEE) formed a subcommittee to create the 802 standards for networks. These standards specify certain types of networks, although not every network protocol is covered by the IEEE 802 committee specifications. This model breaks down into the following 12 categories:

- 802.1 Internetworking
- 802.2 Logic Link Control
- 802.3 CSMA/CD LAN
- 802.4 Token Bus LAN
- 802.5 Token Ring LAN
- 802.6 Metropolitan Area Network

- 802.7 Broadband Technical Advisory Group
- 802.8 Fiber Optic Technical Advisory Group
- 802.9 Integrated Voice/Data Networks
- 802.10 Network Security
- 802.11 Wireless Networks
- 802.12 Demand Priority Access LAN

The IEEE 802 standards were designed primarily for enhancements to the bottom three layers of the OSI model. The IEEE 802 model breaks the Data Link layer into two sublayers: a Logical Link Control (LLC) sublayer and a Media Access Control (MAC) sublayer. In the Logical Link Control sublayer, data link communications are managed. The Media Access Control sublayer watches out for data collisions, as well as assigning physical addresses.

We will focus on the two predominant 802 models on which existing network architectures have been based on: 802.3 CSMA/CD and 802.5 Token Ring.

IEEE 802.3 CSMA/CD

The *802.3* CSMA/CD model defines a bus topology network that uses a 50-ohm coaxial baseband cable and carries transmissions at 10Mbps. This standard groups data bits into frames and uses the Carrier Sense Multiple Access with Collision Detection (CSMA/CD) cable access method to put data on the cable.

CSMA/CD specifies that every computer can transmit at any time. When two machines transmit at the same time, a *collision* takes place, and no data can be transmitted for either machine. The machines then back off for a random period of time and try to transmit again. This process repeats until transmission takes place successfully. The CSMA/CD technology is also called *contention*.

The only major downside to 802.3 is that with large networks (more than 100 computers on the same cable), the number of collisions increases to the point where more collisions than transmissions are taking place.

Ethernet is an example of a protocol based on the IEEE 802.3 CSMA/CD standard.

 CSMA/CD and Ethernet are discussed in more detail later in this chapter.

IEEE 802.5 Token Ring

The IEEE *802.5* standard specifies a physical star, logical ring topology that uses a token-passing technology to put the data on the cable. IBM developed this technology for its mainframe and minicomputer networks. IBM's name for it was Token Ring. The name stuck, and any network using this type of technology is called a Token Ring network.

In *token passing*, a special chunk of data called a *token* circulates through the ring from computer to computer. Any computer that has data to transmit must wait for the token. A transmitting computer that has data to transmit waits for a free token and takes it off the ring. Once it has the token, this computer modifies it in a way that tells the computers who has the token. The transmitting computer then places the token (along with the data it needs to transmit) on the ring, and the token travels around the ring until it gets to the destination computer. The destination computer takes the token and data off the wire, modifies the token (indicating it has received the data), and places the token back on the wire. When the original sender receives the token back and sees that the destination computer has received the data, the sender modifies the token to set it free. It then sends the token back on the ring and waits until it has more data to transmit.

The main advantage of the token-passing access method over contention (the 802.3 model) is that it eliminates collisions. Only workstations that have the token can transmit. It would seem that this technology has a lot of overhead and would be slow. But remember that this whole procedure takes place in a few milliseconds.

This technology scales very well. It is not uncommon for Token Ring networks based on the IEEE 802.5 standard to reach hundreds of workstations on a single ring.

 The story of the IEEE 802.5 standard is rather interesting. It's a story of the tail wagging the dog. With all the other IEEE 802 standards, the committee either saw a need for a new protocol on its own or got a request for one. They would then sit down and hammer out the new standard. A standard created by this process is known as a *de jure* ("by law") standard. With the IEEE 802.5, however, everyone was already using this technology, so the IEEE 802 committee got involved and simply declared it a standard. This type of standard is known as a *de facto* ("from the fact") standard—a standard that was being followed without having been formally recognized.

Network Communication Protocols

As already discussed, a communications protocol is a standard set of rules governing communications. Protocols cover everything from the order of transmission to how to address the stations on a network. Without network protocols, no communication could take place on a network.

Four major protocols are in use today:

- TCP/IP
- IPX/SPX
- NetBEUI/NetBIOS
- AppleTalk

TCP/IP

The *Transmission Control Protocol/Internet Protocol (TCP/IP) suite* is called a suite because it's a collection of protocols. The two most important protocols are used to name the suite (TCP and IP). Although the name represents a collection of multiple protocols, the suite is usually referred to as simply TCP/IP.

TCP/IP is the only protocol suite used on the Internet. In order for any workstation or server to communicate with the Internet, it must have TCP/IP installed. TCP/IP was designed to get information delivered to its destination, even in the event of a failure of part of the network. It uses various routing protocols to discover the network it is traveling on and keep apprised of network changes.

The TCP/IP suite includes many protocols. A few of the more important include:

Internet Protocol (IP)   Handles the movement of data between computers as well as network node addressing

Transmission Control Protocol (TCP)   Handles the reliable delivery of data

Internet Control Message Protocol (ICMP)   Transmits error messages and network statistics

User Datagram Protocol (UDP)   Performs a similar function to TCP, with less overhead and more speed, but with lower reliability

IPX/SPX

The *Internetwork Packet Exchange/Sequenced Packet Exchange (IPX/SPX)* is the default communications protocol for versions of the Novell NetWare operating system before NetWare 5. It is often used with Windows networks as well, but in Windows networks, the implementation of the IPX/SPX protocol is known as *NWLINK*.

IPX/SPX is a communications protocol similar to TCP/IP, but it's used primarily in LANs. It has features for use in WAN environments as well; before the mid 1990s, most corporate networks ran IPX/SPX because it was easy to configure and could be routed across WANs.

The two main protocols in IPX/SPX, IPX and SPX, provide the same functions that TCP and UDP do in TCP/IP. For information about IPX/SPX, search Novell's knowledgebase at `support.novell.com/search/kb_index.jsp`.

NetBEUI/NetBIOS

NetBIOS (pronounced "net-bye-os") is an acronym formed from *network basic input/output system*. It's a Session-layer network protocol originally developed by IBM and Sytek to manage data exchange and network access. NetBIOS provides an interface with a consistent set of commands for requesting lower-level network services to transmit information from node to node, thus separating the applications from the underlying NOS. Many vendors provide either their own version of NetBIOS or an emulation of its communications services in their products.

NetBEUI (pronounced "net-boo-ee") is an acronym formed from *NetBIOS Extended User Interface*. It's an implementation and extension of IBM's NetBIOS transport protocol from Microsoft. NetBEUI communicates with the network through Microsoft's Network Driver Interface Specification (NDIS). NetBEUI also has no networking layer and therefore no routing capability, which means it is only suitable for small networks; you cannot build internetworks with NetBEUI, so it is often replaced with TCP/IP. Microsoft has added extensions to NetBEUI in Windows NT to remove the limitation of 254 sessions per node; this extended version of NetBEUI is called the NetBIOS Frame (NBF).

Together, these protocols make up a very fast protocol suite that most people call NetBEUI/NetBIOS. It is a very good protocol for LANs because it's simple and requires little or no setup (apart from giving each workstation a name). It allows users to find and use the network services they need easily, by simply browsing for them. However, because it contains no

Network-layer protocol, it cannot be routed and thus cannot be used on a WAN. It also would make a poor choice for a WAN protocol because of the protocol overhead involved.

 NetBIOS can be used over other protocols in addition to NetBEUI. Many Windows computers use NetBIOS over TCP/IP. This allows them to have NetBIOS functionality over a routed network.

AppleTalk

AppleTalk is not just a protocol, it is a proprietary network architecture for Macintosh computers. It uses a bus and typically either shielded or unshielded cable.

AppleTalk uses a Carrier Sense-Multiple Access with Collision Avoidance (CSMA/CA) technology to put data on the cable. Unlike Ethernet, which uses a CSMA/CD method (where the CD stands for *collision detection*), this technology uses smart interface cards to detect traffic *before* it tries to send data. A CSMA/CA card listens to the wire. If there is no traffic, it sends a small amount of data. If no collisions occur, it follows that amount of data with the data it wants to transmit. In either case, if a collision happens, it backs off for a random amount of time and tries to transmit again.

A common analogy is used to describe the difference between CSMA/CD and CSMA/CA. Sending data is like walking across the street. With CSMA/CD, you just cross the street. If you get run over, you go back and try again. With CSMA/CA, you look both ways and send your little brother across the street. If he makes it, you can follow him. If either of you gets run over, you both go back and try again.

Another interesting point about AppleTalk is that it's fairly simple. Most Macintosh computers already include AppleTalk, so it is relatively inexpensive. It assigns itself an address. In its first revision (Phase I), it allowed a maximum of 32 devices on a network. With its second revision (Phase II), it supports faster speeds and multiple networks with EtherTalk and TokenTalk. EtherTalk allows AppleTalk network protocols to run on Ethernet coaxial cable (used for Mac II and above). TokenTalk allows the AppleTalk protocol to run on a Token Ring network.

Protocol Addressing

Every network address in either TCP/IP or IPX has both a network portion and a node portion. The network portion is the number that is assigned to the network segment to which the station is connected. The node portion is the unique number that identifies that station on the segment. Together, the network portion and the node portion of an address ensure that a network address is unique across the entire network.

IPX addresses use an eight-digit hexadecimal number for the network portion. This number, called the *IPX network address*, can be assigned randomly by the installation program or manually by the network administrator. The node portion is the 12-digit hexadecimal MAC address assigned by the manufacturer. A colon separates the two portions. Here is a sample IPX address:

Network Address   Node Address

00004567:006A7C11FB56

TCP/IP addresses, on the other hand, use a dotted decimal notation in the format xxx.xxx.xxx.xxx, as shown here:

199.217.67.34 IP Address

255.255.255.0 Subnet Mask

The address consists of four collections of eight-digit binary numbers (or up to three decimal digits) called *octets*, separated by periods. Each decimal number in an IP address is typically a number in the range 1 through 254. Which portion is the network and which portion is the node depends on the class of the address and the *subnet mask* assigned with the address. A subnet mask is also a dotted-decimal number with numbers in the range 0 through 255. If a subnet mask contains 255 in a position (corresponding to a binary number of all ones), the corresponding part of the IP address is the network address. For example, if you have the mask 255.255.255.0, the first three octets are the network portion, and the last portion is the node.

Network Architectures

Network architectures define the structure of the network, including hardware, software, and layout. We differentiate each architecture by the hardware and software required to maintain optimum performance levels. A network architecture's performance is usually discussed in terms of *bandwidth*, or how much data a particular network technology can handle in a period of time. The major architectures in use today are Ethernet, Token Ring, and ARCNet.

Ethernet

The original definition of the 802.3 model included a bus topology using a baseband coaxial cable. From this model came the first Ethernet architecture. *Ethernet* was originally codeveloped by Digital, Intel, and Xerox and was known as *DIX Ethernet*.

Ethernet has several specifications, each one specifying the speed, communication method, and cable. The original Ethernet was given a designation of 10Base5. The *10* in Ethernet 10Base5 stands for the 10Mbps transmission rate, *Base* stands for the baseband communications used, and *5* stands for the maximum distance of 500 meters to carry transmissions. This method of identification soon caught on, and as vendors changed the specifications of the Ethernet architecture, they followed the same pattern in the way they identified these specifications.

After 10Base5 came 10Base2 and 10BaseT. These quickly became standards in Ethernet technology. Many other standards (including 100BaseF, 10BaseF, and 100BaseT) developed since then, but those three are the most popular.

Ethernet 10Base2 uses thin coaxial cables and bus topology, and transmits at 10Mbps with a maximum distance of 185 meters. Ethernet 10BaseT uses twisted-pair cabling, transmitting at 10Mbps with a maximum distance of 100 meters, and a physical star topology with a logical bus topology.

Token Ring

Token Ring networks are exactly like the IEEE 802.5 specification because the specification is based on IBM's Token Ring technology. Token Ring uses a physical star, logical ring topology.

All workstations are cabled to a central device called a *multistation access unit (MAU)*. The ring is created within the MAU by connecting every port together with special circuitry in the MAU. Token Ring can use shielded or unshielded cable and can transmit data at either 4Mbps or 16Mbps.

ARCNet (Attached Resource Computing Network)

A special type of network architecture that deserves mention is the *Attached Resource Computer Network (ARCNet)*. Developed in 1977, it was not based on any existing IEEE 802 model. However, ARCNet is important to mention because of its ties to IBM mainframe networks and also because of its popularity. Its popularity came from its flexibility and price. It was flexible because its cabling used large trunks and physical star configurations, so if a cable came loose or is disconnected, the network did not fail. Additionally, because it used cheap, coaxial cable, networks could be installed fairly cheaply.

Even though ARCNet enjoyed an initial success, it died out as other network architectures became more popular. The main reason was its slow transfer rate of only 2.5Mbps. Thomas-Conrad (a major developer of ARCNet products) developed a version of ARCNet that runs at 100Mbps, but most people have abandoned ARCNet for other architectures. ARCNet is also not based on any standard, which makes it difficult to find compatible hardware from multiple vendors.

Fiber-optic networks use fiber-optic cabling, which does not suffer from the *electromagnetic interference (EMI)* problems that traditional copper-based cabling does. This is primarily because the technology doesn't use electricity to transmit data. Instead, light pulses (which aren't affected by EMI) are sent through the cable.

Network Media

We have looked at the types of networks, network architectures, and the way a network communicates. To bring networks together, we use several types of media. A *medium* is the material on which data is transferred from one point to another. There are two parts to the medium: the network interface card and the cabling. The type of network card you use depends on the type of cable you are using, so let's discuss cabling first.

Cabling

When the data is passing through the OSI model and reaches the Physical layer, it must find its way onto the medium that is used to physically transfer data from computer to computer. This medium is *cable*. It is the network interface card's role to prepare the data for transmission, but it is the cable's role to properly move the data to its intended destination. It is not as simple as just plugging it into the computer. The cabling you choose must support both the network architecture and topology. There are five main types of cabling methods: coaxial cable, twisted-pair cable, fiber-optic cable, RS-232 Serial, and wireless. We'll summarize all four cabling methods after the brief descriptions that follow.

Coaxial

Coaxial cable (or coax) contains a center conductor made of copper, surrounded by a plastic jacket, with a braided shield over the jacket (as shown in Figure 5.11). Either Teflon or a plastic such as PVC covers this metal shield. The Teflon-type covering is frequently referred to as a *plenum-rated* coating. That simply means that the coating does not produce toxic gas when burned (as PVC does) and is rated for use in air plenums that carry breathable air. This type of cable is more expensive but may be mandated by electrical code whenever cable is hidden in walls or ceilings. Plenum rating applies to all types of cabling.

 Other types of cabling (namely twisted pair) can be rated for plenum use.

FIGURE 5.11   Coaxial cable

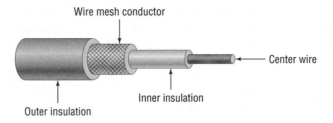

Coaxial cable is available in different specifications that are rated according to the *RG* Type system. Different cables have different specifications and, therefore, different RG grading designations (according to the U.S. military specification MIL-C-17). Distance and cost are considerations when selecting coax cable. The thicker the copper, the farther a signal can travel—and with that comes a higher cost and a less flexible cable.

Coaxial cable comes in many thicknesses and types. The most common use for this type of cable is Ethernet 10Base2 cabling. It is known as Thinnet or Cheapernet. Table 5.2 shows the different types of RG cabling and their uses.

TABLE 5.2   Coax RG Types

RG #	Popular Name	Ethernet Implementation	Type of Cable
RG-6	Cable TV cable	N/A	Solid copper
RG-8	Thicknet	10Base5	Solid copper
RG-58 U	N/A	None	Solid copper
RG-58 AU	Thinnet	10Base2	Stranded copper

TABLE 5.2   Coax RG Types *(continued)*

RG #	Popular Name	Ethernet Implementation	Type of Cable
RG-59	Cable TV cable	N/A	Solid copper
RG-62	ARCNet	N/A	Solid/stranded copper

Coax Connector Types

With coax cable used in networking, generally you use *BNC* connectors (see Figure 5.12) to attach stations to a Thinnet network. It is beyond our province to settle the long-standing argument over the meaning of the abbreviation BNC. We have heard BayoNet Connector, Bayonet Nut Connector, and British Navel Connector. What is relevant is that the BNC connector locks securely with a quarter-twist motion.

FIGURE 5.12   Male and female BNC connectors

Male

Female

With Thick Ethernet, a station attaches to the main cable via a vampire tap, which clamps onto the cable. A *vampire tap* is so named because a metal tooth sinks into the cable, thus making the connection with the inner conductor. The tap is connected to an external transceiver that in turn has a 15-pin AUI connector (also called *DIX* or DB 15 connector) to which you attach a cable that connects to the station (shown in Figure 5.13). DIX got its name from the companies that worked on this format—Digital, Intel, and Xerox.

FIGURE 5.13   Thicknet and vampire taps

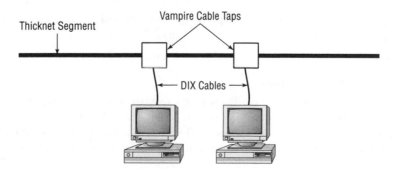

Thicknet Segment

Vampire Cable Taps

DIX Cables

Twisted-Pair

Twisted-pair is one of the most popular methods of cabling because of its flexibility and low cost. It consists of several pairs of wire twisted around each other within an insulated jacket, as shown in Figure 5.14. Twisted-pair is most often found in 10BaseT Ethernet networks, although other systems can use it.

FIGURE 5.14 Twisted-pair cable

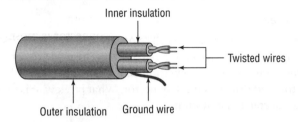

Twisted-pair cabling is usually classified in two types: unshielded twisted-pair (UTP) and shielded twisted-pair (STP). UTP is simply twisted-pair cabling that is unshielded. STP is the same as UTP, but it has a braided foil shield around the twisted wires (to decrease electrical interference).

UTP comes in seven grades to offer different levels of protection against electrical interference:

- Category 1 is for voice-only transmissions and is in most phone systems today. It contains two twisted pairs.

- Category 2 is able to transmit data at speeds up to 4Mbps. It contains four twisted pairs of wires.

- Category 3 is able to transmit data at speeds up to 10Mbps. It contains four twisted pairs of wires with three twists per foot.

- Category 4 is able to transmit data at speeds up to 16Mbps. It contains four twisted pairs of wires.

- Category 5 is able to transmit data at speeds up to 100Mbps. It contains four twisted pairs of copper wire to give the most protection.

- Category 5e is able to transmit data at speeds up to 1Gbps. It also contains four twisted pairs of copper wire, but they are physically separated and contain more twists per foot than Category 5 to provide maximum interference protection.

- Category 6 is able to transmit data at speeds up to 1Gbps and beyond. It also contains four twisted pairs of copper wire, and they are oriented differently than in Category 5 or 5e.

Each of these levels has a maximum transmission distance of 100 meters.

Twisted-Pair Connector Types

Clearly, a BNC connector won't fit easily on UTP cable, so you need to use an *RJ (registered jack)* connector. You are probably familiar with RJ connectors. Most telephones connect with an RJ-11 connector. The connector used with UTP cable is called RJ-45. The RJ-11 has four wires, or two pairs, and the network connector RJ-45 has four pairs, or eight wires.

In almost every case, UTP uses RJ connectors. Even the now-extinct ARCnet used RJ connectors. You use a crimper to attach an RJ connector to a cable, just as you use a crimper with the BNC connector. The only difference is that the die that holds the connector is a different shape. Higher quality crimping tools have interchangeable dies for both types of cables.

In addition to the RJ-series used on UTP, STP (when used with Token Ring) often uses a special connector known as the *IBM data connector (IDC)*, *universal data connector (UDC)*, or *hermaphroditic data connector*. An example of this type of connector is shown in Figure 5.15. The IDC is unique in many ways. First, it isn't as universal as the other types of network connectors. Second, there aren't male and female versions, as with the others—the IDC is both male and female, so any two data connectors can connect. This connector is most commonly used with IBM's Token Ring technology and Type 1 or 2 STP cable.

FIGURE 5.15   An IDC/UDC

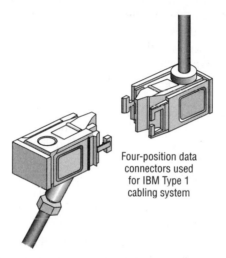

Four-position data connectors used for IBM Type 1 cabling system

The IDC also uses a tab to hold the connectors together, but this tab is a little more rigid than the tab on the RJ-series connectors and doesn't move as much. Therefore, breakage is not much of an issue.

Fiber-Optic

Fiber-optic cabling has been called one of the best advances in cabling. It consists of a thin, flexible glass or plastic fiber surrounded by a rubberized outer coating (see Figure 5.16). It provides transmission speeds from 100Mbps to 1Gbps and a maximum distance of several miles. Because it uses pulses of light instead of electric voltages to transmit data, it is immune from electric interference and from wiretapping.

Fiber-optic cable has not become a standard in networks, however, because of its high cost of installation. Networks that need extremely fast transmission rates, transmissions over long distances, or have had problems with electrical interference in the past often use fiber-optic cabling.

Fiber-optic cable is referred to as either single-mode or multimode fiber. The term *mode* refers to the bundles of light that enter the fiber-optic cable. Single-mode fiber-optic cable uses only a single mode of light to propagate through the fiber cable, whereas multimode fiber allows multiple modes of light to propagate. In multimode fiber-optic cable, the light bounces off the cable walls as it travels through the cable, which causes the signal to weaken more quickly.

FIGURE 5.16 Fiber-optic cable

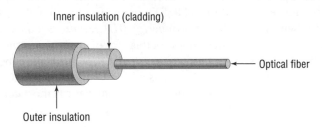

Multimode fiber-optic is most often used as horizontal cable. It permits multiple modes of light to propagate through the cable and this lowers cable distances and has a lower available bandwidth. Devices that use multimode fiber-optic cable typically use light-emitting diodes (LEDs) to generate the light that travels through the cable; however, higher bandwidth network devices such as Gigabit Ethernet are now using lasers with multimode fiber-optic cable. TIA/EIA-568-A recognizes two-fiber (duplex) 62.5/125-micron multimode fiber; TIA/EIA-568-A also recognizes 50/125-micron multimode fiber-optic cable.

Single-mode optical fiber cable is commonly used as backbone cabling; it is also usually the cable type used in phone systems. Light travels through single-mode fiber-optic cable using only a single mode, meaning it travels straight down the fiber and does not bounce off the cable walls. Because only a single mode of light travels through the cable, single-mode fiber-optic cable supports higher bandwidth and longer distances than multimode fiber-optic cable. Devices that use single-mode fiber-optic cable typically use lasers to generate the light that travels through the cable.

TIA/EIA-568-A recognizes 62.5/125-micron, 50/125-micron, and 8.3/125-micron single-mode optical fiber cables. TIA/EIA-568-A states that the maximum backbone distance using single-mode fiber-optic cable is 3,000 meters (9,840 feet), and the maximum backbone distance using multimode fiber is 2,000 meters (6,560 feet).

Fiber-Optic Connector Types

The *subscriber connector* (SC; also sometimes known as a *square connector*) is a type of fiber-optic connector, as shown in Figure 5.17. As you can see, SC connectors are latched connectors. This makes it impossible for you to pull out the connector without releasing the connector's latch, usually by pressing a button or release.

SC connectors work with either single- or multimode optical fibers and last for around 1,000 matings. They are currently seeing increased use but they still aren't as popular as ST connectors for LAN connections.

The *straight tip (ST)* fiber-optic connector, developed by AT&T, is probably the most widely used fiber-optic connector. It uses a BNC attachment mechanism, similar to the Thinnet Ethernet connection mechanism, which makes connections and disconnections fairly easy. The ease of use of the ST is one of the attributes that makes this connector so popular. Figure 5.18 shows some examples of ST connectors. Notice the BNC attachment mechanism.

Because it is so widely available, adapters to other fiber connector types are available for this connector type. The ST connector type also has a maximum mating cycle of around 1,000 matings.

FIGURE 5.17   A sample SC connector

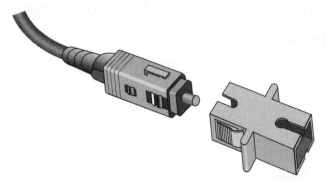

FIGURE 5.18   Examples of ST connectors

RS-232 (Serial Cables)

Occasionally, networks use *RS-232 cables* (also known as *serial cables*) to carry data. The classic example is in older mainframe and minicomputer terminal connections. Connections from the individual terminals go to a device known as a *multiplexer* that combines the serial connections into one connection and connects all the terminals to the host computer. This cabling system is seen less and less as a viable LAN cabling method, however, because LAN connections like twisted-pair Ethernet are faster, more reliable, and easier to maintain.

Wireless Networks

One of the most fascinating cabling technologies today—actually, it doesn't really *use* cable—is wireless. Wireless networks offer the ability to extend a LAN without the use of traditional cabling methods. Wireless transmissions are made through the air by infrared light, laser light, narrow-band radio, microwave, or spread-spectrum radio.

Wireless LANs are becoming increasingly popular as businesses become more mobile and less centralized. You can see them most often in environments where standard cabling methods are not possible or wanted. However, they are still not as fast or efficient as standard cabling methods. They are also more susceptible to eavesdropping and interference than standard cabling methods.

Summary of Cabling Types

Each type of cabling has its own benefits and drawbacks. Table 5.3 details the most common types of cabling in use today. As you look at this table, pay particular attention to the cost, length, and maximum transmission rates of each cabling type.

TABLE 5.3   Cable Types

Characteristics	Twisted-Pair	Coaxial	Fiber-Optic	Wireless
Cost	Least expensive	More than twisted-pair	Expensive	Most expensive
Maximum length	100 meters (328 feet)	185 meters (607 feet) to 500 meters (1640 feet)	>10 Miles	Up to 2 miles
Transmission rate	10Mbps to 100Mbps	10Mbps	100Mbps or more	2Mbps to 54Mbps
Flexibility	Most flexible	Fair	Fair	Limited
Ease of installation	Very easy	Easy	Difficult	Depends on the implementation
Interference	Susceptible	Better than UTP; more susceptible than STP	Not susceptible	Susceptible
Special features	Often pre-installed; similar to the wiring used in telephone systems	Easiest installation	Supports voice, data, and video at the highest transmission speeds	Very flexible

TABLE 5.3   Cable Types *(continued)*

Characteristics	Twisted-Pair	Coaxial	Fiber-Optic	Wireless
Preferred uses	Networks	Medium-size networks with high security needs	Networks of any size requiring high speed and data security	WANs and radio/TV communications
Connector	RJ-45	BNC-T and AUI	Special (SC and ST, and others)	Dish, transceiver, or access point
Physical topology	Star	Bus	Star (typically)	Bus or star
Other information	Five categories of quality	RG-58 and RG-59 family; also called Thinnet and Thicknet, respectively	Requires special training to configure	Most must comply with FCC regulations

The Network Interface Card (NIC)

The network interface card (NIC) provides the physical interface between computer and cabling. It prepares data, sends data, and controls the flow of data. It can also receive and translate data into bytes for the CPU to understand. It communicates at the Physical layer of the OSI model and comes in many shapes and sizes.

Different NICs are distinguished by the PC bus type and the network for which they are used. This section describes the role of the NIC and how to choose the appropriate one. The following factors should be taken into consideration when choosing a NIC:

- Preparing data
- Sending and controlling data
- Configuration
- Drivers
- Compatibility
- Performance

Preparing Data

In the computer, data moves along buses in parallel, as on a four-lane interstate highway. But on a network cable, data travels in a single stream, as on a one-lane highway. This difference can cause problems when you're transmitting and receiving data, because the paths traveled are not the same. It is the NIC's job to translate the data from the computer into signals that can flow easily along the cable. It does this by translating digital signals into electrical signals (and in the case of fiber-optic NICs, to optical signals).

Sending and Controlling Data

For two computers to send and receive data, the cards must agree on several things. These include the following:

- The maximum size of the data frames
- The amount of data sent before giving confirmation
- The time needed between transmissions
- The amount of time to wait before sending confirmation
- The amount of data a card can hold
- The speed at which data transmits

If the cards can agree, then the sending of the data is successful. If the cards cannot agree, the sending of data does not occur.

In order to successfully send data on the network, you need to make sure the network cards are the same type (such as all Ethernet, all Token Ring, all ARCNet, and so on) and they are connected to the same piece of cable. If you use cards of different types (for example, one Ethernet and one Token Ring), neither of them will be able to communicate with the other (unless you use a gateway device, such as a router).

Additionally, network cards can send data using either full-duplex or half-duplex mode. *Half-duplex communication* means that between the sender and receiver, only one of them can transmit at any one time. In *full-duplex communication*, a computer can send and receive data simultaneously. The main advantage of full-duplex over half-duplex communication is performance. Network cards (specifically Fast Ethernet network cards) can operate twice as fast (200Mbps) in full-duplex mode as they do normally in half-duplex mode (100Mbps).

NIC Configuration

The NIC's configuration includes things like a manufacturer's hardware address, IRQ address, base I/O port address, and base memory address. Some may also use Direct Memory Access (DMA) channels to offer better performance.

Each card must have a unique hardware address. If two cards have the same hardware addresses, neither one will be able to communicate. For this reason, the IEEE committee has established a standard for hardware addresses, and assigns blocks of these addresses to NIC manufacturers, which then hard-wire the addresses into the cards.

Configuring a NIC is similar to configuring any other type of expansion card. The NIC usually needs a unique IRQ channel and I/O address, and possibly a DMA channel. Token Ring cards often have two memory addresses that must be excluded in reserved memory to work properly.

 You will learn more about installing and configuring expansion cards in later chapters (primarily Chapter 6, "Building a PC").

One item to note: You have installed and configured a NIC properly if the LED next to the port on the NIC (usually a green LED labeled LINK) glows solid when plugged into the network. The *link light* indicates when a basic electrical connection to the network has been made.

NIC Drivers

For the computer to use the network interface card, it is very important to install the proper device drivers. These drivers communicate directly with the network redirector and adapter. They operate in the Media Access Control sublayer of the Data Link layer of the OSI model.

PC Bus Type

When you're choosing a NIC, use one that fits the bus type of your PC. If you have more than one type of bus in your PC (for example, a combination ISA/PCI), use a NIC that fits into the fastest type (the PCI, in this case). This is especially important in servers, because the NIC can quickly become a bottleneck if this guideline isn't followed.

Refer back to Chapter 2, "Motherboards, CPUs, and RAM," to refresh your memory about the bus architectures mentioned in this discussion.

Network Card Performance

The most important goal of the network adapter card is to optimize network performance and minimize the amount of time needed to transfer data packets across the network. There are several ways of doing this, including assigning a DMA channel, using a shared memory adapter, and deciding to allow bus mastering.

If the network card can use DMA channels, then data can move directly from the card's buffer to the computer's memory, bypassing the CPU. A shared memory adapter is a NIC that has its own RAM. This feature allows transfers to and from the computer to happen much more quickly, increasing the performance of the NIC. Shared system memory allows the NIC to use a section of the computer's RAM to process data. Bus mastering lets the card take temporary control of the computer's bus to bypass the CPU and move directly to RAM. This process is more expensive, but it can improve performance by 20 to 70 percent. However, EISA, MCA, VLB, and PCI buses all support bus mastering.

Each of these features can enhance the performance of a NIC. Most cards today have at least one, if not several, of these features.

Installing a Network Card

Before you can begin configuring your network, you must have a network card installed in the machine. Installing a network card is a fairly simple task if you have installed any expansion card before; a NIC is just a special type of expansion card. To install a NIC, follow these steps:

1. Move jumpers or flip DIP switches on the expansion card to set it to the correct IRQ/ DMA/IO port settings, as per the factory instructions. If the card uses a software-set program, you can ignore this step. Most newer NICs do not have jumpers and are entirely software configured.

2. Power off the PC, remove the case and the metal or plastic blank covering the expansion slot opening, and insert the expansion card into an open slot.

3. Secure the expansion card with the screw provided.

 These first three steps may not be necessary if you have an onboard NIC.

4. Put the case back on the computer and power it up (you can run software configuration at this step, if necessary). If there are conflicts, change any parameters so that the NIC doesn't conflict with any existing hardware.

5. Install a driver for the NIC for the type of operating system that you have. Windows should auto-detect the NIC and install the driver automatically. It may also ask you to provide a copy of the necessary driver if it does not recognize the type of NIC you have installed. If the card is not detected at all, run the Add New Hardware Wizard by double-clicking Add New Hardware in the Control Panel.

6. After installing a NIC, you must hook the card to the network using the cable supplied by your network administrator. Attach this patch cable to the connector on the NIC and to a port in the wall, thus connecting your PC to the rest of the network.

 Sometimes older NICs conflict with newer Plug-and-Play (PnP) hardware. Additionally, some newer NICs with PnP capability don't like some kinds of networking software. To resolve a PnP conflict of the latter type, disable PnP on the NIC either with a jumper or with the software setup program. In this chapter, we will assume that your NIC is installed and the drivers are loaded.

Media Access Methods

You have put the network together in a topology. You have told the network how to communicate and send the data, and you have told it how to send the data to another computer. You also have the communications medium in place. The next problem you need to solve is how to put the data on the cable. What you need now are the *cable access methods*, which define a set of rules for how computers put data on and retrieve it from a network cable. We've mentioned a few of these earlier in this chapter, but now let's take a closer look at the four methods of data access:

Carrier Sense Multiple Access with Collision Detection (CSMA/CD)   As we've already discussed, NICs that use CSMA/CD listen to or "sense" the cable to check for traffic. They compete for a chance to transmit. Usually, if access to the network is slow, too many computers are trying to transmit, causing traffic jams.

Carrier Sense Multiple Access with Collision Avoidance (CSMA/CA)   Instead of monitoring traffic and moving in when there is a break, CSMA/CA allows the computer to send a signal that it is ready to transmit data. If the ready signal transmits without a problem, the computer then transmits its data. If the ready signal is not transmitted successfully, the computer waits and tries again. This method is slower and less popular than CSMA/CD.

Token Passing   As previously discussed, token passing is a way of giving every NIC equal access to the cable. A special packet of data is passed from computer to computer. Any computer that wants to transmit has to wait until it has the token. It can then transmit its data.

Polling   Polling is an old method of media access that is still in use. Not many topologies support polling anymore, mainly because it has special hardware requirements. This method requires a central, intelligent device (meaning the device contains either hardware or software intelligence to enable it to make decisions) that asks each workstation in turn if it has any data to transmit. If the workstation answers "yes," the controller allows the workstation to transmit its data.

The polling process doesn't scale well. That is, you can't take this method and simply apply it to any number of workstations. Additionally, the high cost of the intelligent controllers and cards has made the polling method all but obsolete.

Connectivity Devices

The cabling links computer to computer. Most cabling allows networks to be hundreds of feet long. But what if your network needs to be bigger than that? What if you need to connect your LANs to other LANs to make a WAN? What if the architecture you've picked for your network is limiting the growth of your network along with the growth of your company? The answer to these questions is found in a special class of networking devices known as *connectivity devices*. These devices allow communications to break the boundaries of local networks and let your computers talk to other computers in the next building, the next city, or the next country.

There are several categories of connectivity devices, but we are going to discuss the six most important and frequently used:

- Repeaters
- Hubs/Switches
- Bridges
- Routers
- Brouters
- Gateways

These connectivity devices have made it possible to lengthen networks to almost unlimited distances.

Repeaters

Repeaters are simple devices. They allow a cabling system to extend beyond its maximum allowed length by amplifying the network voltages so they travel farther. Repeaters are nothing more than amplifiers and, as such, are very inexpensive.

Repeaters operate at the Physical layer of the OSI model. Because of this, repeaters can only be used to regenerate signals between similar network segments. For example, you can extend an Ethernet 10Base2 network to 400 meters with a repeater. But you can't connect an Ethernet network and a Token Ring network together with one.

The main disadvantage of repeaters is that they just amplify signals. These signals not only include the network signals, but any noise on the wire as well. Eventually, if you use enough repeaters, you could possibly drown out the signal with the amplified noise. For this reason, repeaters are used only as a temporary fix.

Hubs/Switches

Hubs are devices used to link several computers together. They are most often used in 10BaseT Ethernet networks. They are also simple devices. In fact, they are just multiport repeaters: They repeat any signal that comes in on one port and copy it to the other ports (a process that is also called *broadcasting*).

There are two types of hubs: active and passive. *Passive hubs* connect all ports together electrically and are usually not powered. *Active hubs* use electronics to amplify and clean up the signal before it is broadcast to the other ports. In the category of active hubs, there is also a class called *intelligent* hubs, which are hubs that can be remotely managed on the network.

Switches operate very similarly to hubs because they connect several computers (usually twisted-pair Ethernet networks). However, switches don't repeat everything they receive on one port to every other port as hubs do. Rather, switches examine the header of the incoming packet and forward it properly to the right port and only that port. This greatly reduces overhead and thus performance as there is essentially a virtual connection between sender and receiver.

 If it helps you to remember their functions: a hub is essentially a multiport repeater, whereas a switch functions like a multiport bridge (and in some cases, a multiport router).

Bridges

Bridges operate in the Data Link layer of the OSI model. They join similar topologies and are used to divide network segments. Bridges keep traffic on one side from crossing to the other. For this reason, they are often used to increase performance on a high-traffic segment.

For example, with 200 people on one Ethernet segment, performance will be mediocre, because of the design of Ethernet and the number of workstations that are fighting to transmit. If you divide the segment into two segments of 100 workstations each, the traffic will be much lower on either side and performance will increase.

Bridges are not able to distinguish one protocol from another, because higher levels of the OSI model are not available to them. If a bridge is aware of the destination address, it can forward packets; otherwise it forwards the packets to all segments.

Bridges are more intelligent than repeaters but are unable to move data across multiple networks simultaneously. Unlike repeaters, bridges *can* filter out noise.

The main disadvantage of bridges is that they can't connect dissimilar network types or perform intelligent path selection. For that function, you need a router.

Routers

Routers are highly intelligent devices that connect multiple network types and determine the best path for sending data. They can route packets across multiple networks and use routing tables to store network addresses to determine the best destination. Routers operate at the Network layer of the OSI model.

The advantage of using a router over a bridge is that routers can determine the best path for data to take to get to its destination. Like bridges, they can segment large networks and can filter out noise. However, they are slower than bridges because they are more intelligent devices; as such, they analyze every packet, causing packet-forwarding delays. Because of this intelligence, they are also more expensive.

Routers are normally used to connect one LAN to another. Typically, when a WAN is set up, at least two routers are used.

Brouters

Brouters are truly an ingenious idea, because they combine the best of both worlds—bridges and routers. They are used to connect dissimilar network segments and also to route only one specific protocol. The other protocols are bridged instead of being dropped. Brouters are used when only one protocol needs to be routed or where a router is not cost-effective (as in a branch office).

Gateways

Gateways connect dissimilar network environments and architectures. Some gateways can use all levels of the OSI model, but frequently they are found in the Application layer. There, gateways convert data and repackage it to meet the requirements of the destination address. This makes gateways slower than other connectivity devices and more costly. An example of a gateway is the NT Gateway Service for NetWare, which, when running on a Windows NT Server, can connect a Microsoft Windows NT network with a Novell NetWare network.

Networking and the Internet

One of the procedures performed most often by today's technicians is setting up a computer to connect to the Internet. The Internet is no longer just a buzzword, it's a reality. It has been estimated that over 50 percent of the homes in America have computers and that over 50 percent of those computers are connected to the Internet. It's no wonder that most computers come with software to connect them to the Internet.

Before we can discuss connecting Windows to the Internet, we need to discuss the Internet itself. There are some common terms and concepts every technician must understand about the Internet. First, the Internet is really just a bunch of private networks connected using public telephone lines. These private networks are the access points to the Internet and are run by companies called *Internet Service Providers (ISPs)*. They sell you a connection to the Internet for a monthly service charge (kind of like your cable bill or phone bill). Your computer talks to the ISP using public phone lines, or even using new technologies such as cable or wireless.

Types of Connections

Your computer might use several designations and types of Internet connections to talk to an ISP, ranging in speeds from 56Kbps to several megabits per second (Mbps). Remember that these same types of phone lines connect the ISPs to each other to form the Internet.

Dial-Up/POTS

The most common of Internet access still seen in most parts of the United States is dial-up. In a *dial-up* Internet connection, the computer connecting to the Internet uses a modem to connect to the ISP over a standard telephone line. The telephone company technicians usually call the phone line that goes into your house a *POTS line* (short for *Plain Old Telephone Service*).

Dial-up Internet connections are relatively slow, when compared to the other methods listed here. At the most, dial-up connections are theoretically limited to 56Kbps, and practically limited to 53Kbps by FCC rules. In reality, the 53Kbps speed is for downloads only (from the Internet to your computer) and only under ideal conditions. In the real world, you are most likely to get speeds around 40Kbps. The maximum upload speed (from your computer to the Internet) for this connection is around 33.6Kbps.

To make a connection with POTS, you must have a modem installed in your computer. You also must connect your home phone line to the line port on your modem. Then, you must configure some software on your computer known as a *dialer*. A *dialer* is a special program that initiates the connection with the ISP, takes the phone off hook, dials the ISP's access number, and establishes the connection. Most versions of Windows have a built-in dialer known as dial-up networking.

Other ISPs may have their own dialer program that they give you on disk or CD-ROM when you sign up for their service. ISPs like AOL and AT&T Worldcom have their own dialer software (AOL is its own program, which encompasses dialer, browser, and other functions in one software, but can also function as an Internet dialer).

Dial-up networking is basic Internet access. Most people use the Internet so much that they are moving on to higher-speed methods of Internet access. These higher-speed methods are generally lumped together and called *broadband Internet access*.

Digital Subscriber Line (DSL)

One of the first methods of broadband Internet access to become popular was a technology called *Digital Subscriber Line (DSL)*. DSL uses the existing phone line from your home to the phone company to carry digital signals at higher speeds. Essentially, DSL piggybacks a digital signal on the line used for analog communication (your voice). So, with DSL it is possible to have high-speed Internet access and use your phone at the same time.

However, DSL has some drawbacks. It's more expensive than dial-up; in some areas, DSL can run $30 to $100 per month more than dial-up connections. Plus, there are distance limitations.

You must be within a certain distance of the phone company's central office (usually less than 1 mile, but it varies on the type of DSL being used). Also, because the phone line is carrying digital signals, many phone lines in older homes and neighborhoods may not be up to par.

When connecting to DSL, you need a special device, most often called a DSL modem. This is actually a misnomer, because modems change digital to analog and back again. Because DSL is digital, the signals are never changed into analog. The proper term for the device used to access DSL is a *DSL endpoint*. Endpoints often have the functions of network bridges or routers.

Endpoints can be either internal or external. Internal endpoints go inside a computer as an expansion card, but that means only that computer can access the Internet directly. External endpoints can be hooked to a hub, switch, or router, which can share the Internet connection with multiple computers.

To see if DSL is available in your area, go to www.dslreports.com. You can also talk to your local telephone provider.

Cable

One of the most popular broadband Internet access methods these days is *cable Internet*. Cable Internet provides broadband Internet access via the television cable that runs to your home via a specification known as *Data Over Cable Service Interface Specification (DOCSIS)*. It is relatively cheap (usually less than $50 per month) and provides fast Internet download speeds (typically between 256Kbps and 1000Kbps). It is theoretically available to anyone with a cable TV connection and a cable provider that provides the service.

Although cable sounds great, it has a few drawbacks. If you have a cable Internet connection, because of the way it is designed, essentially you are on a LAN with all the neighbors in your cable segment. Thus, if you (or your cable company) don't protect your connection, theoretically you could see your neighbors' computers and they could see yours. So, security might be a problem.

Also, in some markets, the cable itself may not be in the best condition to provide the higher-speed data services. It may need to be replaced (at cost to the cable provider), so cable may not be available in some markets.

For detailed information about cable Internet availability and performance, check out www.cablemodemhelp.com.

Integrated Services Digital Network (ISDN)

Integrated Services Digital Network (ISDN) is a digital, point-to-point network capable of maximum transmission speeds of about 2Mbps, although speeds of 128Kbps are more common. Because it is capable of much higher data rates at a fairly low cost, ISDN is becoming a viable remote user connection method, especially for those who work out of their homes. ISDN uses the same UTP wiring as POTS, but it can transmit data at much higher speeds. That's where the similarity ends. What makes ISDN different from a regular POTS line is how it uses the copper wiring. Instead of carrying an analog (voice) signal, it carries digital signals.

A computer connects to an ISDN line via an *ISDN terminal adapter* (often incorrectly referred to as an ISDN modem). An ISDN terminal adapter is not a modem because it does not convert a digital signal to an analog signal; ISDN signals are digital.

An ISDN line has two types of channels. The data is carried on special *Bearer, or B, channels*, each of which can carry 64Kbps of data. A typical *Basic Rate Interface (BRI)* ISDN line has two B channels. One channel can be used for a voice call while the other is being used for data transmissions, and this occurs on one pair of copper wires. The second type of channel is used for call setup and link management and is known as the *signal*, or D channel (also referred to as the *Delta channel*). This channel has only 16Kbps of bandwidth. BRI ISDN is also known as 2B+D because of the number and type of channels used.

You can also obtain a *Primary Rate Interface (PRI)* known as 23B+D, which means it has 23 B channels and one D channel. The total bandwidth of a 23B+D ISDN line is 1472Kbps (23 B channels × 64Kbps per channel).

In many cases, to maximize throughput, the two Bearer channels are combined into one data connection for a total bandwidth of 128Kbps. This is known as *bonding* or *inverse multiplexing*. This still leaves the Delta channel free for signaling purposes. In rare cases, you may see user data, such as e-mail, on the D line. This was introduced as an additional feature of ISDN, but it hasn't caught on.

The main advantages of ISDN are:

- Fast connection
- Higher bandwidth than POTS; bonding yields 128Kb bandwidth
- No conversion from digital to analog

However, ISDN does have a few disadvantages:

- It's more expensive than POTS.
- Specialized equipment is required at the phone company and at the remote computer.
- Not all ISDN equipment can connect to every other type of equipment.
- ISDN is a type of dial-up connection and therefore the connection must be initiated.

Satellite

One type of Internet connection that does not get much fanfare is satellite Internet. *Satellite Internet* is not much like any other type of broadband connection. Instead of a cabled connection, it uses a satellite dish to receive data from a satellite and relay station that is connected to the Internet.

There are two types of satellite connection: *unidirectional* and *bidirectional*. In unidirectional satellite Internet, the satellite connection is used for only one part of the connection: the download of information from the Internet. The request for information is made via some other transmission method (usually a phone line). The request goes to a relay station, where it is made on behalf of the user. The response is then transmitted back to the user via the satellite. The benefit is that because you use your Internet connection for much more downloading than uploading, downloads happen at a much higher speed (usually 128Kbps or better). The downside is you still need to use a phone line for part of the connection.

In bidirectional satellite Internet, the satellite is used for both uploads and downloads. However, uploads are still slower than downloads. This type relieves you of needing a phone line for part of the Internet connection. But, you still need a satellite dish.

The need for a satellite dish and the reliance upon its technology is one of the major drawbacks to satellite Internet. People who own satellite dishes will tell you that there are occasional problems due to weather and satellite alignment. You must keep the satellite dish aimed precisely at the satellite, or your signal strength (and thus your connection reliability and speed) will suffer. Plus, cloudy or stormy days can cause interference with the signal, especially if there are high winds that could blow the satellite dish out of alignment.

Another drawback to satellite technology is the delay (also called *propagation delay*). The delay occurs because of the length of time required to transmit the data and receive a response via the satellite. This delay (between 250 and 350 milliseconds) comes from the time it takes to transmit data the approximately 35,000 kilometers into space and return. To compare it with other types of broadband signals, cable and DSL have a delay between customer and ISP of 10 to 30 milliseconds. With standard web and e-mail traffic, this delay, while slightly annoying, is acceptable. However, with technologies like Voice over IP and live Internet gaming, this delay is intolerable.

Online gamers are especially sensitive to propagation delay. They often refer to it as *ping time*. The higher the ping time (in milliseconds), the worse the response time in the game is. It sometimes means the difference between winning and losing an online game.

Satellite Internet is best used in remote rural areas where other types of Internet may not be practical or available and speeds higher than dial-up are required. In most other cases, land-based Internet is preferable.

Wireless

The final type of Internet access technology you will learn about is wireless. There are many different types of wireless access technology, but all of them have one thing in common: no physical cable between the computer and the ISP. *Wireless Internet* is an Internet access technology that uses radio frequency signals to communicate between ISP and user. It allows the user to roam about a particular area while remaining connected to the Internet. Speeds typically range from 128Kbps to 1.544Mbps (and in some cases, higher).

Wireless Internet comes in two forms: local and wide area. Local wireless is usually available within a particular room or building only. Once you leave that area, it is no longer available. Local wireless has an operating range of around 100 meters outdoors and about 30 meters indoors. It usually conforms to either the 802.11b or 802.11g standard and has speeds of 1Mbps, 11Mbps, and 54Mbps maximum. However, note that this is not an Internet access technology in itself unless the wireless host device (known as an *access point [AP]*) is connected in some way to the Internet (usually via a cabled connection).

Intel has recently released its Centrino technology, which integrates local area wireless access cards into laptops.

Wide-area wireless, on the other hand, is typically used to cover an entire metropolitan area from a few, strategically placed towers. Speeds range from 64Kbps to 784Kbps (higher for point-to-point connections between two towers).

The biggest advantage of wireless is that you can be anywhere in the vicinity of the wireless devices and get Internet access. You don't need to be near an outlet or jack. This technology is catching on quickly with PDA and laptop users because they can get their e-mail and browse the Web from just about anywhere (as long as there is an AP within range).

There are a few downsides to wireless Internet as well. The first is cost. Typically, wireless Internet costs more than an equivalent cabled service. This will change as wireless becomes more widespread (and it is rapidly becoming so). Another limitation is availability. At the time of this writing, wireless Internet is still not available everywhere; it doesn't have the availability of other, wired technologies, like cable or DSL.

Finally, most wide-area wireless Internet technologies that allow you to be anywhere don't have the same speed as wired broadband technologies, although as the standards mature that too is changing.

Summary of Connection Types

Table 5.4 details a few of the more common connection types and speeds.

TABLE 5.4 Common Connection Types and Speeds

Designation	Download Speed Range	Description
POTS	2400bps to 53Kbps	Plain Old Telephone System. Your regular analog phone line.
ISDN	64Kbps to 1.544Mbps	Integrated Services Digital Network. Popular for home office Internet connections.
DSL	256Kbps to 10Mbps	Digital Subscriber Line. Shares existing phone wires with voice service.
Cable	128Kbps to 1.544Mbps	Inexpensive broadband Internet access method with wide availability.
Satellite	128Kbps to 784Kbps	Great for rural areas without cabled broadband methods.
Wireless (local)	1Mbps to 54Mbps	Allows a user to roam around a small area like an office or building while remaining connected to the access point and the Internet.
Wireless (wide area)	64Kbps to 784Kbps	Allows a user to roam around a metropolitan area while remaining connected to a broadband-level Internet service.

Connection Protocols

Whichever connection type you use, there must be a plan for how to transmit data across a network's lines. Network connection types use different protocols to communicate, just as computers do, so we also need to mention these connection protocols. For instance, TCP/IP Internet traffic runs over two different analog connection protocols: Serial Line Internet Protocol (SLIP) and Point-to-Point Protocol (PPP). Both work to get you on the Internet, but PPP is more commonly used because it is more easily configured; it's also more stable because it includes enhanced error-checking capabilities. Other common connection protocols include X.25, Frame Relay, and ATM (the name is used for both the network and the connection protocol controlling traffic across it).

Summary

In this chapter, you learned about the various network hardware topics that you will be tested on in the A+ exam. A few years ago, you wouldn't have seen many computers with network cards come in for service; networks were found only in offices and large companies. Now, networks can be found in many homes. For this reason, the A+ exam requires that you have at least a basic understanding of network hardware.

In the first section, you learned to define exactly what a network is. You also learned what components make up a network, what the network resource models are, and what a network topology is. We discussed the OSI model and the IEEE 802 committee and their impact on networks. Finally, we examined the various network architectures in use today.

In the next section, you learned about the different kinds of network media used to connect computers to a network. Some of these media include copper cable, fiber-optic cable, and wireless media. You also learned about the different kinds of network interface cards (NICs) used to connect computers to the network media. Finally, we discussed the methods of network access (contention, token passing, and so on) each major network technology uses to gain access to the network media.

Next, you learned to differentiate between the types of devices that connect to networks. These network connectivity devices are very important to facilitating communications on a network. We explained how each device (including hubs, routers, bridges, brouters, and so forth) works and how it relates to network communications.

Finally, you learned about the different methods of connecting to the Internet: POTS, ISDN, DSL, cable, satellite and wireless Internet connections. We discussed how each of these methods differs in terms of speed and method of connection.

Key Terms

Before you take the exam, be certain you are familiar with the following terms:

802.3	Data Over Cable Service Internet Specification (DOCSIS)
802.5	datagram
access point (AP)	de facto
active hub	de jure
AppleTalk	dedicated server
Attached Resource Computer Network (ARCNet)	Delta channel
bandwidth	dialer
Basic Rate Interface (BRI)	dial-up
Bearer, or B, channel	Digital Subscriber Line (DSL)
bidirectional	distributed processing
BNC	DIX Ethernet
bonding	DSL endpoint
bridge	electromagnetic interference (EMI)
broadband Internet access	Ethernet
broadcasting	file locking
brouter	frames
cable access method	full-duplex communication
cable Internet	gateway
centralized processing	half-duplex communication
client computer	header
client software	hermaphroditic data connector
coaxial cable	hub
collision	IBM data connector (IDC)
connectivity device	Integrated Services Digital Network (ISDN)
contention	Internet Control Message Protocol (ICMP)

Internet Protocol (IP)

Internet Service Provider (ISP)

Internetwork

inverse multiplexing

IPX network address

ISDN terminal adapter

link light

local area network (LAN)

logical topology

MAC address

mesh topology

multiplexer

multipurpose

multistation access unit (MAU)

NetBEUI

NetBIOS

NetBIOS Extended User Interface

network

network basic input/output system

network interface card (NIC)

nondedicated server

NWLINK

Open Systems Interconnection (OSI)

Packet Exchange/Sequenced Packet Exchange (IPX/SPX)

passive hub

physical topology

plenum-rated

POTS line

Primary Rate Interface (PRI)

propagation delay

protocol

resource

router

RS-232 cable

Satellite Internet

serial cable

signal

single-purpose

site license

straight tip (ST)

subnet mask

switch

token passing

Token Ring

topology

Transmission Control Protocol (TCP)

Transmission Control Protocol/Internet Protocol (TCP/IP) suite

unidirectional

universal data connector (UDC)

User Datagram Protocol (UDP)

wide area network (WAN)

Wireless Internet

workstation

Review Questions

1. Which device is most efficient at moving packets between similar network topologies?
   A. Gateway
   B. Router
   C. Brouter
   D. Bridge

2. Which IEEE 802 standard uses a bus topology and coaxial baseband cable and is able to transmit at 10Mbps?
   A. 802.4
   B. 802.3
   C. 802.2
   D. 802.1

3. _____ is immune to electromagnetic or radio-frequency interference.
   A. Broadband coaxial cabling
   B. Fiber-optic cabling
   C. Twisted-pair cabling
   D. CSMA/CD

4. Printers, files, e-mail, and groupware can all be categorized as _____.
   A. Office equipment
   B. Peer-to-peer networking
   C. Resources
   D. Protocols

5. Which OSI layer signals "all clear" by making sure the data frames are error-free?
   A. Application layer
   B. Session layer
   C. Transport layer
   D. Network layer

6. Which topology is the easiest to modify?
   A. Star
   B. Bus
   C. Ring
   D. Token Ring

7. The _____ layer is responsible for logical addressing.

   A. Physical

   B. Data Link

   C. Network

   D. Transport

8. Which layer of the OSI model has the important role of providing error checking?

   A. Session layer

   B. Presentation layer

   C. Application layer

   D. Transport layer

9. Which type of cabling is easiest to install?

   A. Twisted-pair

   B. Coaxial

   C. Fiber-optic

   D. Wireless

10. _____ is the type of media access method used by NICs that listen to or sense the cable to check for traffic and send only when they hear that no one else is transmitting.

   A. Token passing

   B. CSMA/CD

   C. CSMA/CA

   D. Demand priority

11. A physical star topology consists of several workstations that branch off a central device called a _____.

   A. Repeater

   B. Brouter

   C. Router

   D. Hub

12. A _____ links two or more computers together to communicate and share resources.

   A. Server

   B. Resource

   C. Network

   D. Client

13. Which access method asks the other workstations for permission to transmit before transmitting?

    A. CSMA/CD

    B. CSMA/CA

    C. Token passing

    D. Demand priority

14. _____ offers the longest possible segment length.

    A. Unshielded twisted-pair cabling

    B. Coaxial cable

    C. Fiber-optic cabling

    D. Shielded twisted-pair cabling

15. _____ uses a thin baseband coaxial cable and bus topology, transmits at 10Mbps, with a distance up to 185 meters.

    A. Token Ring

    B. Ethernet 10BaseT

    C. Ethernet 10Base5

    D. Ethernet 10Base2

16. Which topology uses the least amount of cabling, but also covers the shortest distance?

    A. Bus

    B. Star

    C. Mesh

    D. Hybrid

17. Which layer describes how the data is transmitted over a physical medium?

    A. Session layer

    B. Data Link layer

    C. Physical layer

    D. Application layer

18. What is another name for IEEE 802.3?

    A. Logic link control

    B. Token passing

    C. CSMA/CD LAN

    D. Token Ring LAN

19. What type of cabling looks similar to the cable used to connect cable television?

   A. Twisted-pair

   B. Coaxial

   C. Fiber-optic

   D. Wireless

20. What devices transfer packets across multiple networks and use tables to store network addresses to determine the best destination?

   A. Brouters

   B. Routers

   C. Gateways

   D. Bridges

Answers to Review Questions

1. D.   Bridges keep traffic on one side from crossing to the other. For this reason they are often used to increase performance on a high-traffic segment.

2. B.   The IEEE 802.3 standard specifies the use of a bus topology, typically using coaxial baseband cable, and can transmit data up to 10Mbps.

3. B.   Companies that wish to ensure the safety and integrity of their data should use fiber-optic cable, because it cannot be affected by electromagnetic or radio-frequency interference.

4. C.   Resources are any items that can be used on a network by multiple people. Therefore, printers, files, and e-mail are all considered resources when they are available on a network.

5. C.   It is the responsibility of the Transport layer to signal an "all clear" by making sure the data frames are error-free. It also controls the data flow and troubleshoots any problems with transmitting or receiving data frames.

6. A.   The star topology is the easiest to modify. A physical star topology branches each network device off a central device called a hub, making it easy to add a new workstation.

7. C.   The Network layer is responsible for logical network addressing as well as route determination.

8. D.   The most important role of the Transport layer is to provide error checking. The Transport layer also provides functions such as: reliable end-to-end communications, segmentation and reassembly of larger messages, and combination of smaller messages into a single larger message.

9. A.   Of the choices listed here, twisted-pair cabling is generally considered the easiest to install. It is lighter than coaxial and doesn't require a lot of special tools or knowledge like fiber-optic cable.

10. B.   CSMA/CD (Carrier Sense Multiple Access with Collision Detection) specifies that the NIC pause before transmitting a packet to ensure that the line is not being used. If no activity is detected, then it transmits the packet. If activity is detected, it waits until it is clear. In the case of two NICs transmitting at the same time (a collision), both NICs pause to detect, and then retransmit the data.

11. D.   The hub provides the central connecting device in a star topology. All workstations must therefore connect to the hub in order to gain access to each other or any other resources present on the network. The one disadvantage is that the hub becomes a single point of failure. If the hub stops working, no one connected to the hub has network connectivity.

12. C.   The purpose of a network is to link computers together so that they can communicate and share available resources such as printers, data, and applications.

13. B.   CSMA/CA (Carrier Sense Multiple Access with Collision Avoidance) is slightly more sophisticated than CSMA/CD. It transmits a very small packet on the network. If it is successful, then the NIC transmits the actual data. This initial transmission can be viewed as an "Is it OK for me to send?" message. Therefore, it is said to avoid causing collisions.

14. C.   Fiber-optic cable can span distances of several kilometers, because it has higher bandwidth and much lower crosstalk and interference in comparison to copper cables.

15. D.   The name of each option tells you exactly what it is. In the case of Ethernet 10Base2, the *Ethernet* part states that it uses Ethernet architecture, *10* means it can transmit up to 10Mbps, *Base* signifies baseband transmission, and *2* is the distance (in this case, it equates to the 185-meter limitation of coaxial Thinnet cable).

16. A.   Due to its design, which includes a central trunk that runs the distance between the two most distant computers (as long as it does not exceed the maximum distance allowed for the cabling), a bus topology requires the least amount of cable.

17. C.   The Physical layer is responsible for formatting the final packet of data for transmission (length being the most important format property, because the upper layers are not concerned with the fact that Ethernet and Token Ring packets are not the same size). Once it has done this, it is responsible for taking this digital data and transforming it into electrical impulse representations and, finally, the actual transmission of the data. The Physical layer on the receiving side then has to do this in reverse: remove the signal from the wire, convert the electrical impulses to digital data, reconstruct the packet based on the proper size of that network (Ethernet or Token Ring, for example), and then pass the packet up to the Data Link layer.

18. C.   As a part of the IEEE 802.3 specification, it states that CSMA/CD is the standard access method for Ethernet networks.

19. B.   Coaxial cable and television cable are very similar in appearance. Because of this, you need to make sure you have the proper RG rating (RG-58 for Thinnet, RG-59 for Thicknet), so that you can ensure proper data transmission.

20. B.   Routers are designed to route (transfer) packets across networks. They are able to do this routing, and determine the best path to take, based on internal routing tables they maintain.

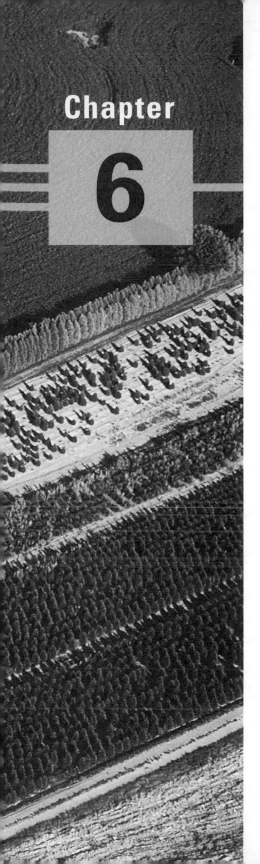

Chapter

6

Building a PC

THE FOLLOWING EXAM OBJECTIVES ARE COVERED IN THIS CHAPTER:

✓ **1.2 Identify basic procedures for adding and removing field-replaceable modules for desktop systems. Given a replacement scenario, choose the appropriate sequences.**

✓ **1.4 Identify typical IRQs, DMAs, and I/O addresses, and procedures for altering these settings when installing and configuring devices. Choose the appropriate installation or configuration steps in a given scenario.**

✓ **4.4 Identify the purpose of CMOS (Complementary Metal-Oxide Semiconductor) memory, what it contains, and how and when to change its parameters. Given a scenario involving CMOS, choose the appropriate course of action.**

Every A+ certified technician will at some time be called upon to add components to a computer, remove and replace a component, or build a computer from scratch. As a technician, these are some of the most fun things you get to do (especially if the components are going into a computer of yours).

Throughout this chapter, keep in mind that while the procedures listed are correct, new hardware is being released on a weekly basis. Each new piece of hardware may have its own method of installation and caveats for doing so. So, the lesson is, always read the manual or instructions that come with a piece of hardware before installing it! You may think you know exactly how to install something, only to find out later that you made a mistake that could have been avoided had you only read the instructions first.

It has been several years since I last bought a computer from a major computer manufacturer such as Dell, HP, or Gateway. As long as I've been in the computer repair business, I have built my own computers. Not only can you build a computer yourself, but you can usually build it more cheaply than you could buy a similar computer from a PC manufacturer. Plus, you can usually get more "bang for your buck" by building it yourself. Finally, there is nothing like the satisfaction of creating something yourself. (As a matter of fact, my old computer was not quite fast enough to do all the things I needed it to do for writing, so I just built the one I am using to write the book you are reading.)

In this chapter, you will learn the skills necessary to assemble your own computer from selected parts, configure them into a working computer, and upgrade some of the parts within the computer to increase its functionality.

Before You Begin

Keep in mind that although these steps will work when applied correctly, each step is a generalization that applies to most situations; the newest hardware may have special steps that need to be followed before the item you are installing will work correctly. Always check the documentation that comes with the item you are installing for its proper installation procedures.

In this first section, you will learn what you need to know before you even touch a computer component, so that you are prepared for the process ahead.

Background Information

There are a few basic computer service concepts you must understand before you begin assembling the computer. You must also be familiar with the specialized concepts that are used during the assembly of a computer. These include *jumpers*, *DIP switches*, and configuration settings.

Jumpers

Jumpers were developed as a way of allowing a particular device option (such as which interrupt is being used) to be both user-settable and semipermanent without requiring the user to own a chip burner. Jumpers consist of a row of pins and a small plastic cap with metal inserts. The user can move the cap to cover different pairs of pins. The cap completes a circuit between those two pins, thus selecting one of the possible configuration options for that device (see Figure 6.1).

FIGURE 6.1   Jumpers and their use

A jumper (above left) can be used to make a connection between various pairs of pins in an array of pins. On some devices you may need to jumper multiple pairs, using several jumpers. This arrangement of six pins offers eight different jumper settings.

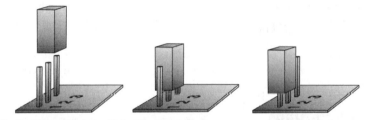

You'll often see devices with just three pins. These are common for devices that require only two settings, like on and off, or enabled and disabled.

Some cards or circuit boards have several jumpers, so you will need to select the appropriate jumpering option to configure the device. To find out which pins have to be jumpered in order to select different configuration options, consult the device's documentation.

If you don't have the documentation, you may have to try all the different jumpering combinations to see if you can get the device configured properly:

- With a six-pin device (as shown in the top part of Figure 6.1), you have eight possible settings: all unjumpered, left pair jumpered, middle pair jumpered, right pair jumpered, left and middle pairs jumpered, left and right pairs jumpered, middle and right pairs jumpered, and all jumpered. This arrangement is common for setting the ID number or other configuration setting of a SCSI device.

- With a three-pin device (as shown in the bottom part of the figure), you are usually only concerned with setting the device to an active or inactive status. Any one of the options shown in the bottom of Figure 6.1 may mean "on"; one of the others would then be the "off" setting. (The third, perhaps in this case represented by the all-unjumpered configuration on the left, might mean "let Plug and Play determine the setting.")

Dual Inline Package (DIP) Switches

Jumpers are fine for single settings, but what if you have a number of settings that have to be user-settable and semipermanent? You could use several jumpers, but in larger numbers, they are difficult to work with. Someone came up with the idea of using several *really* small switches and having the pattern of their ons and offs represent the different settings. These switches are known as DIP switches, and they can be either rocker type or slide type (see Figure 6.2).

FIGURE 6.2   DIP switches

"Rocker-type" DIP switch   "Slide-type" DIP switch

If you look carefully at Figure 6.2, you will notice that there is a little 1 imprinted on one side of the switches. When a rocker switch is depressed on that side, it is considered *on*. By comparison, when the nub of a sliding switch is sticking *up* on the side with the 1 marking, *that* indicates *on*. (Some DIP switches are marked with a 0 to indicate the side that is the *off* position for the switch.)

Because these switches are so small, it is often easier to set them with a pen, probe, or small screwdriver than it is to set them with your fingers. If you do use your fingers, you may notice that you move more than just the switch you were intending to move.

Configuration Settings

As you assemble the computer or add a component to a computer, the instructions will tell you how to configure the device properly. This usually means changing some setting so that the setting does not conflict with any other device in the computer.

These configuration settings are becoming less necessary because computer components today are almost self-configuring. However, when the self-configuration method does not work, you must know which setting is wrong or conflicting and how to configure the device(s) so that they work properly.

For each item you are going to install in this chapter, you will learn its optional configuration settings and how to configure it in the most common situations. However, four configuration settings are used that apply to many different devices:

- IRQ address
- Memory address
- DMA address
- I/O address

Let's take a quick look at each of these and how they apply to configuring components for a computer.

Interrupt Request (IRQ) Lines

IRQs, or *interrupt requests*, are appropriately named. Interrupts are used by peripherals to interrupt or stop the CPU and demand attention. When the CPU receives an interrupt alert, it stops whatever it is doing and handles the request. This is one of the techniques used to make it appear as if the computer is actually doing multiple things simultaneously (also known as *multitasking*). In reality, the CPU does one thing at a time; it just does it (and moves to the next task) so quickly that it appears to be handling multiple tasks simultaneously.

Each device is given its own interrupt to use when alerting the CPU. AT-based PCs have 16 interrupts available. (You wouldn't want too many things to interrupt the CPU or it would never get anything done.) Given the limited number of available interrupts, it is critical that you assign them wisely! For each of the 16 interrupts available on a PC, Table 6.1 lists the standard use and other uses associated with it.

TABLE 6.1   Common Interrupts

Interrupt	Most Common Use	Other Common Uses
0	System timer	Nothing else uses (or should use) interrupt 0.
1	Keyboard	Nothing else uses (or should use) interrupt 1.
2	None; this interrupt is used to cascade to the higher 7 interrupts (see note following this table)	Modems; COM 3, COM 4.
3	COM 2	COM 4, network interface cards, sound cards, and just about anything else.
4	COM 1	COM 3, network interface cards, sound cards, and just about anything else.
5	Sound card	LPT2, LPT3, COM 3, COM 4, and disk controllers on older XT-based computers.
6	Floppy disk controller	Tape controllers.
7	LPT1	LPT2, COM 3, COM 4, network interface cards, sound cards, and just about anything else.
8	Real-time clock	Nothing else uses (or should use) interrupt 8.
9		SCSI controllers, PCI cards, and just about anything else.
10		Secondary IDE channel, SCSI controllers, PCI cards, and just about anything else.

TABLE 6.1 Common Interrupts *(continued)*

Interrupt	Most Common Use	Other Common Uses
11		Third or fourth IDE channel, SCSI controllers, PCI cards, and just about anything else.
12	PS/2-style mouse	Just about anything.
13	Floating-point coprocessor	None.
14	Primary IDE channel	SCSI controllers.
15	Secondary IDE channel	SCSI controllers and network adapters.

 Interrupt 2 is a special case. Earlier (XT-based) PCs had only eight interrupts because those computers used an 8-bit bus. With the development of the AT, eight more interrupts were created (to match the 16-bit bus), but no mechanism was available to use them. Rather than redesign the entire interrupt process, AT designers decided to use interrupt 2 as a gateway, or *cascade*, to interrupts 9–15. In reality, interrupt 2 is the same as interrupt 9. You should never configure your system so that both interrupt 2 and 9 are used.

Configuring interrupts is so common that most experienced field technicians have the standards (as listed in Table 6.1) memorized.

Memory Addresses

Many components use blocks of memory as part of their normal functioning. Network interface cards, for instance, often buffer incoming data in a block of memory until they can be processed. Doing so prevents the card from being overloaded if a burst of data is received from the network.

When the device driver loads, it lets the CPU know which block of memory should be set aside for the exclusive use of the component. This prevents other devices from overwriting the information stored there. (Of course, it also sets you up for hardware conflicts, because two components cannot be assigned the same address space.) Certain system components also need a *memory address*. Some of the more common default assignments are listed in Table 6.2.

TABLE 6.2 Common Memory Address Assignments

Address	Assignment
F0000–FFFFF	System BIOS
E0000–EFFFF	In use on true IBM compatibles

TABLE 6.2   Common Memory Address Assignments *(continued)*

Address	Assignment
CA000–DFFFF	Available on most PCs
C8000–C87FF	Hard-disk controller on an XT system
C0000–C7FFF	EGA/VGA display
B8000–BFFFF	CGA/EGA/VGA display
B0000–B7FFF	Monochrome display
A0000–AFFFF	EGA/VGA display
00000–9FFFF	System memory

Direct Memory Access (DMA)

When a device stores information in a memory address, this process is controlled by the CPU. In other words, if a network card needs to buffer data, it requests that the CPU write that data to its assigned memory address. Because the CPU knows which area of memory is dedicated to each device, it can help prevent any other process from overwriting the information in memory (the CPU denies any request to write to that area of memory except those that come from the proper device). Using memory addresses is a safe, stable way to for a peripheral to store data in memory; it is also rather processor intensive and inefficient.

Direct Memory Access (DMA) is a method used by peripherals to place data in memory without utilizing (or bothering) the CPU. As an example, a sound card can buffer music in memory while the CPU is busy recalculating a spreadsheet. The DMA peripheral has its own processor to move the data. It uses dead time on the ISA bus to perform the transfer. At the hardware level, DMA is quite complex, but the important feature to remember is that the transfer of data is accomplished without intervention from the CPU.

All DMA transfers use a special area of memory known as a *buffer*, which is set aside to receive data from the expansion card (or CPU, if the transfer is going in the other direction). The basic architecture of the PC DMA buffers is limited in size and memory location.

DMA transfers are made using a predefined DMA channel. The PC supports up to eight DMA channels, although not all are compatible with all expansion cards. Each channel is dedicated to a specific device—no DMA channel can be used by more than one device. If you accidentally choose a DMA channel that another card is using, the usual symptom is that no DMA transfers will take place (in other words, for our example, no sound would play).

Certain DMA channels are assigned to standard AT devices. Table 6.3 lists the eight DMA channels and their default assignments.

TABLE 6.3   DMA Assignments

DMA Channel	Default Assignment
0	Dynamic RAM refresh
1	Hard-disk controller
2	Floppy-disk controller
3	Available on all PCs
4–7	Available on AT and Micro Channel PS/2 computers

I/O Addresses

I/O (input/output) addresses, also known as *port addresses*, are a specific area of memory that a component uses to communicate with the system. As such, they sound quite a bit like the memory addresses we just discussed. The major difference is that memory addresses are used to store information that will be used by the device itself, whereas I/O addresses are used to store information that will be used by the system. In other words, it is information waiting to be processed rather than information waiting to be prepared for processing.

The keyboard is a perfect example of how I/O addresses are used. When you type, the information (such as which letters you typed and in which order) is stored in a specific area of memory (an I/O address). The CPU knows to look at this address to find information from the keyboard. Each I/O address acts as a mail stop for information being exchanged between the CPU and a device and also acts as a reserved place to drop off data to be picked up (by either the device or the CPU, depending on which way the transfer is going). Because I/O addresses are reserved for a particular device, no two devices can share an I/O address.

Certain system devices are automatically assigned an I/O address. Table 6.4 lists some of the common default assignments.

TABLE 6.4   Common I/O Address Assignments

Address	Assignment
000–0FF	Reserved for the system itself
1F0–1F7	Primary hard-disk controller
170–177	Secondary hard-disk controller
200–207	Game port
278–27F	Second parallel port (LPT2)
2F8–2FF	Second serial port (COM 2)

TABLE 6.4   Common I/O Address Assignments *(continued)*

Address	Assignment
378–37F	First parallel port (LPT1)
3F0–3F7	Floppy-disk controller
3F8–3FF	First serial port (COM 1)

Clearing a Workspace

Now that you understand the basics of device configuration, you must find a place to build the computer. You should find a level, flat surface about 4 feet wide by 4 feet deep and standing about waist height. Most people who don't work professionally as computer techs just use the kitchen table (provided you finish your work before the next meal).

For any work you do on a computer, you must have an adequate workspace. This could mean any number of things. First, the work area must be flat. If it's not, small parts could roll around and possibly get lost or damaged. Second, the area must be sturdy. A typical computer weighs about 25 pounds. Printers and other peripherals will add to that weight. Make sure the work surface you are using can support the weight. In addition, the area must be well lit, clean, and large enough to hold all pieces (assembled and disassembled) and all necessary tools. Figure 6.3 shows an adequate workspace for most computers.

FIGURE 6.3   A typical computer workspace

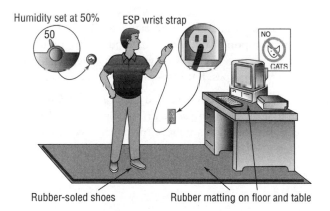

Before you begin, make sure all necessary tools are available and in working order (as we'll discuss next). It may help to lay out some of the more commonly used disassembly tools such as screwdrivers and nut drivers so you can find them easily. You should also lay out the parts you will be using (ideally, on a separate table or work surface). Make sure the documentation for the system you are working on is available (including owner's manuals, service manuals, and Internet resources). Three tools in particular that will be very handy aren't tools in the traditional sense but are, rather, timesavers: an egg carton, a pen, and a notepad. An egg carton is perfect for organizing screws and small parts that might otherwise end up in the "extra parts" pile. You should use a pen and notepad to record anything that may easily be forgotten, such as cable positions, DIP-switch settings, and the locations from which you remove the components.

The final guideline to preparing your work area is to set aside plenty of time to complete the task. To do this, estimate the time required to complete the entire task (disassembly, installation, reassembly, and testing) and then *double it*. Too often, a technician will start a "simple" job and underestimate the time needed to complete it. When you run out of time, you must come back later to complete the job. Because of this interruption, you may forget exactly where you left off—which can lead to the "extra parts" syndrome.

Gathering Tools

Behind every great technician is an even greater set of tools. Your troubleshooting skills alone can get you only so far in diagnosing a problem; you also need some troubleshooting tools. And once the problem has been identified, you need a different set of tools—to fix the problem.

There are two major types of tools: hardware and software. We'll cover the hardware category first. (Note that there are very few questions on the test about this material; we're only including it for background and reference information.)

Hardware Tools

Hardware tools are those tools that are "hard," meaning you can touch them, as opposed to software tools, which cannot be touched. Several different kinds of hardware tools are used in PC service today. We will discuss the most commonly used tools in this section.

Screwdrivers

The tool that can most often be found in a technician's toolkit is a set of nonmagnetic screwdrivers. Most of the larger components in today's computers are mounted in the case with screws. If these components need to be removed, you must have the correct type of screwdriver available. There are three major types: flat blade, Phillips, and Torx.

Flat-Blade Screwdriver The first type is often called a *flat-blade* or *flathead screwdriver*, although most people simply refer to it as a *standard screwdriver* (Figure 6.4). The type of screw that this screwdriver removes is not used much anymore (primarily because the screw head is easily damaged).

FIGURE 6.4 A flat-blade screwdriver and screw

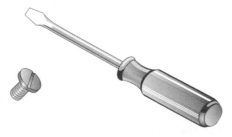

WARNING We strongly advise against using a flathead screwdriver to *pry* anything open on a computer. Computers are usually put together very well, and if it seems that you need to pry something apart, it's probably because a screw or fastener is still holding it together somewhere.

Phillips Screwdriver   The most commonly used type of screwdriver for computers today is the *Phillips screwdriver* (Figure 6.5). Phillips-head screws are used because they have more surfaces to turn against, reducing the risk of damaging the head of the screw. More than 90 percent of the screws in most computers today are Phillips-head screws.

FIGURE 6.5   A Phillips screwdriver and screws

NOTE Phillips screwdrivers come in different sizes, identified by numbers. The most common size is a #2 Phillips. It is important to have a few different-sized screwdrivers available. If you use the wrong size (for example, a Phillips driver that is too pointed or too small), it can damage the head of the screw.

Torx Screwdriver   Finally, there is the type of screwdriver you use when you're working with those maddening little screws found on Compaq and Apple computers (as well as on dashboards of later-model GM cars). Of course, we're referring to the *Torx screwdriver* (Figure 6.6). The Torx type of screw has the most surfaces to turn against and therefore has the greatest resistance to screw-head damage. It is becoming more popular because people like its clean, technical look.

FIGURE 6.6   A Torx screwdriver and screw

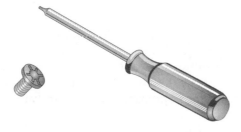

The sizes of Torx drivers are given with the designation T-*xx*, where the *xx* is replaced with a number from 1 through 20. The most common sizes are T-10 and T-15, but for some note-book computers, you will need to have much smaller Torx drivers on hand.

Several screwdrivers are available with changeable tips, like bits for a drill. The advantage is that you can easily change these screwdrivers from a flat blade to a Phillips to a Torx just by changing the bits in the driver. The bits are usually stored in the handle of this type of screwdriver.

Although it may seem convenient, don't use a multiple-bit driver that is magnetized. Magnetism and computers don't make good friends. The magnetism can induce currents in conductors and burn out components without your knowledge. It could also erase magnetic disk storage media.

Needle-Nose Pliers

Another great tool to have in your toolkit is a set or two of needle-nose pliers (Figure 6.7). They are great for grasping connectors or small screws when your hands are too big. If a needle-nose is still too large for the job, a standard pair of tweezers will work as well.

FIGURE 6.7   A pair of needle-nose pliers

Flashlight

Another handy tool to have is a small flashlight. You'll know how especially handy it is when you're crawling around under a desk looking for a dropped screw or trying to find a particular component in a dark computer case. Maglite makes a powerful small flashlight that runs on two AA batteries. It also fits well into a toolkit.

Compressed Air

When you work on a computer, typically you'll first remove the case. While the cover is off, it is a good idea to clean the computer and remove the accumulated dust bunnies. These clumps of dust and loose fibers obstruct airflow and cause the computer to run hotter, thus shortening its life. The best way to clean out the dust is with clean, dry, compressed air. If you work for a large company, it will probably have a central air compressor as a source for compressed air. If an air compressor is not available, you can use cans of compressed air, but they can be expensive—especially if several are needed. In any case, be sure to take the computer outside before squirting it with compressed air.

Soldering Iron

One tool that is used less and less in the computer service industry is the soldering iron. You might use one occasionally to splice a broken wire; otherwise you won't have much need for it.

 The soldering iron isn't used much anymore because most components have been designed to use quick-disconnect connectors to facilitate easy replacement.

Traditionally, the soldering iron was used to connect electronic components to circuit boards. The most common iron used in electronic applications has a narrow tip rated at 15 to 20 watts. Generally, the component was heated with the iron, and then rosin-core solder (*not* acid-core) was applied to the component. The solder melted and, flowing into the joint, joined the component to the circuit board.

Wire Strippers

When you're soldering, it is a good idea to have a combination wire cutter/stripper available to prepare wires for connection. Stripping a wire simply means to remove the insulation from the portion that will be involved in the connection. The tool shown in Figure 6.8 is a good example of one that does both. However, you must be careful not to cut the wire when stripping it.

FIGURE 6.8   A combination wire cutter/stripper

Multimeters

The final hardware device we will discuss is the *multimeter* (see Figure 6.9). It gets its name from the fact that it is a combination of several different kinds of testing meters, including an ohmmeter, ammeter, and voltmeter. In trained hands, it can help detect the correct operation or failure of several different types of components.

FIGURE 6.9 A common multimeter

Meter

Function
Selector Switch

Red (+)
Probe

Black (−)
Probe

The multimeter consists of a digital or analog display, two probes, and a function selector switch. This rotary switch not only selects the function being tested, it also selects the range to which the meter is set. If you're measuring a battery using an older meter, you may have to set the range selector manually (to a range close to, but greater than, 1.5 volts). Newer meters, especially digital ones, automatically set their ranges appropriately.

WARNING

Never connect a non–auto-ranging meter to an AC power outlet to measure voltage. This action will almost surely result in permanent damage to the meter mechanism, the meter itself, or both.

When you're measuring circuits, it is very important to have the meter hooked up correctly so that the readings are accurate. Each type of measurement may require that the meter be connected in a different way. In the following paragraphs, we will detail the most commonly used functions of the multimeter and how to make measurements correctly with them:

Measuring Resistance with a Multimeter *Resistance* is the electrical property most commonly measured in troubleshooting components. Measured in ohms, resistance is most often represented by the Greek symbol omega (Ω). A measurement of infinite resistance indicates that electricity cannot flow from one probe to the other. If you use a multimeter to measure the resistance in a segment of wire and the result is an infinite reading, there is a very good chance that the wire has a break in it somewhere between the probes.

To measure resistance, you must first set the multimeter to measure ohms. You do so either through a button on the front or through the selector dial. (Assume for the rest of this book that we are using newer *auto-ranging multimeters*.) Then you must properly connect the component to be measured between the probes (see the warning and Figure 6.10). The meter will then display the resistance value of the component being measured.

Do not test resistance on components while they are mounted on a circuit board! The multimeter applies a current to the component being tested. That current may also flow to other components on the board, thus damaging them.

FIGURE 6.10   Connecting a multimeter to measure resistance

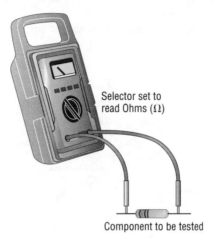

Selector set to read Ohms (Ω)

Component to be tested

Measuring Voltage with a Multimeter   You follow a similar procedure when measuring voltage, but with two major differences. First, when measuring voltage, you must be sure you connect the probes to the power source correctly: With DC voltage, the + must connect to the positive side and the – to the negative. (The position doesn't matter with AC voltage.) Second, you must change the selector to VDC (Volts DC) or VAC (Volts AC), whichever is appropriate, to tell the meter what you are measuring (see Figure 6.11). Note that these settings protect the meter from overload. If you plug a meter into a power supply while it's still set to measure resistance, you may blow the meter.

FIGURE 6.11   Connecting a multimeter to measure voltage

Selector set to read DC or AC volts

Red probe (+)   Black probe (−)

Connect directly to terminals of power source

Battery

Measuring Current with a Multimeter The final measurement that is commonly made is that of current, in amperes (amps). Again, the procedure is similar to those used for the other measurements. A major difference here is that when you connect an ammeter to measure the current a circuit is drawing, you must connect the ammeter in series with the circuit being measured. Figure 6.12 illustrates the proper connection of a multimeter to measure current.

FIGURE 6.12 Connecting a multimeter to measure current

Selector set to Amps (current)

Connect meter in series with the circuit being tested

Positive lead

Red probe (+)

Black probe (−)

Power Source (unplugged)

Negative lead

Component being tested

 Real World Scenario

Tweaker: A Computer Geek's Answer to Duct Tape

If you ask farmers which tool in their toolbox is most valuable, the answer is almost always "duct tape." It is said that anything can be fixed with enough duct tape. Unfortunately, computers generally are not easily fixed with duct tape.

There *is* a tool that is invaluable when working on a computer. It can be bought from different tool vendors and is often given away at trade shows. That tool is commonly known as a *tweaker*. It is a screwdriver that is shaped like a pen and is about the same size. It has a Phillips screwdriver on one end and a flat-blade screwdriver on the other and will clip easily into a shirt pocket:

I have been able to fix several computers in a pinch with nothing more than a tweaker. I recommend that you run out and buy or find one immediately.

Collecting Software Tools

Hardware tools are used when major failures have occurred. However, a great portion of problems aren't related to a failing component but are due to malfunctioning or incorrectly configured hardware. You can use software diagnostics programs to troubleshoot some hardware problems. There are also programs available (usually from the component manufacturers) for configuring hardware, which relieves some or all of the task of setting jumpers or DIP switches. Finally, there are programs for testing the operation of other programs. In this section, we'll look briefly at two of the most important types of software tools.

Bootable Disks

The very best software diagnostic tool for DOS machines is a *bootable floppy disk*: a disk that has been formatted with a version of DOS and made bootable. It belongs in every technician's bag of essentials. You create a bootable disk by typing **FORMAT A: /S** with a blank floppy in the A: drive. Diagnostic and configuration programs can also be copied onto this disk and run without the possibility of software conflicts.

The advantage to this approach is that when the computer boots from a DOS bootable floppy disk, it doesn't have any drivers loaded that might conflict with your diagnostics. You can thus get real information. Also, if the machine boots successfully with a bootable disk but won't boot normally without it, this tells you that the motherboard, RAM, and major components are probably okay—which means that the problem may be the hard disk, a corrupt operating system (OS), or a device-driver conflict. From this point, you can narrow down the problem.

Software Diagnostics

Several software tools examine the hardware, report its configuration, and identify any errors they find. Programs like CheckIt Pro, QAPlus, and Microsoft's MSD (Microsoft Diagnostics) work in this manner. Other programs serve mainly as reference materials. For example, some manufacturers distribute CD-ROMs that contain all the reference material concerning their brand of computer equipment. (Toshiba, for instance, distributes a set of CD-ROMs to authorized service centers on a quarterly basis, with parts-ordering information, troubleshooting flowcharts, exploded diagrams, and FRU replacement information. All of the information is searchable. A very handy tool, indeed.)

Gathering Parts

Once you have prepared your workspace sufficiently, you need to make sure you have all the right parts. Many stores in larger communities sell computer parts so you can build your own computer system. Each one is slightly different and carries different brands of components. However, this trend is so popular that many larger chain stores such as Best Buy and CompUSA are starting to carry components so that individuals can "do it themselves."

In order to build a computer, you will need several parts. The shopping list of parts you need should look something like this:

PC Case The most important component to some people is the case. It is the part you see most often and reflects most on the aesthetics of the PC. Buy one that you don't mind looking at and that has enough space for the number of drives you are going to add. The case should also contain at least two fans or space to add more cooling equipment if necessary. If it doesn't, you will have to buy some case fans. As you put together your computer, make sure the cooling fans are oriented so air enters the front of the case and travels over the processor and expansion cards to exit at the back of the computer.

As mentioned in earlier chapters, the case is designed around the type of motherboard used, typically AT or ATX. Most cases today use the ATX form factor (or some derivation). Make sure the case type matches the motherboard you are buying.

Power Supply The power supply provides power to the components inside the PC. Power supplies are rated in watts. A *watt* is a unit of power. To calculate the number of watts your system needs, you need the formula $P = IE$, where P is the power in watts, I is the amps drawn by a device, and E is the voltage required by a device. If you want to know exactly how much power your system requires, calculate P for every device in your system and add up the numbers. An easier method is to just get a power supply bigger than you think you might need. Typically, power supplies greater than 300 watts are sufficient for most home PCs.

Motherboard One of the most complicated purchases you will ever make is the motherboard for your computer. You must buy a motherboard that supports the type of processor you plan to use (AMD or Intel). It must fit the case you want to use, and it must have the feature set you want (including on-board items). Generally speaking, this component may require the most research. Make sure you ask lots of questions of the salesperson regarding the features of a particular motherboard (including which processors it supports, features, on-board functions, and so on).

CPU/Processor You can group CPUs/processors into three categories, based on price and performance:

- Low-end processors (like the Celeron and entry-level AMD Athlons) provide decent performance at a minimal price and can be used for basic computing.

- Mid-level processors (like the slower Pentium 4 and AMD Athlon XP) provide a good balance of speed without costing a lot. Most processors for home computers come from this range.

- The high-end processors (like the newest Pentium 4 and AMD Athlon XP) are the highest performance processors, but you must be prepared to pay a premium for their speed. Most gamers and graphics professionals use these processors in their computers.

Memory You must have enough memory to run the programs you are going to use as well as to keep the OS in memory. This amount varies depending on the requirements of the programs installed. Every program has a list of how much memory you should have in order to run the program properly. At this time of this writing (early 2003), most computers sold come with between 256MB and 512MB of memory.

> As a rule of thumb, I always tell people to buy as much memory as you can fit into the budget. You won't regret it.

Hard Disk(s)   Most computers only need one hard disk. The question is how big a hard disk to get and what features it should have. You should buy a hard drive that has enough capacity to store all of your programs, data, and OS. Most computers today have between 20 and 120 giga-bytes (GB) of storage capacity. Whatever hard drive you get, make sure the disk interface tech-nology it uses matches the interface you have on your motherboard (such as UltraDMA 100 or UDMA 133) and that it is the fastest possible drive (higher spin speeds, onboard cache, and so on).

Floppy Drive   This component is quickly becoming less of a necessity. Although many people still use floppy disks for data transport between computers, CD-ROMs have almost completely replaced the floppy since the advent of the CD-ROM burner. Brand almost doesn't matter, because the specs are the same across manufacturers (as long as you get a 3 1/2-inch floppy drive). Buy one (if you even want it) and move on.

CD-ROM Drive(s)   Most computers today either already have, or need, a CD-ROM drive. Many computers have two (typically a CD-RW as well as a DVD drive). There are many different types (as discussed in Chapter 3). Buy one of each type, if you want, or buy a combo drive. Just make sure you have at least one in your computer, because most software (including operating systems) comes on CD-ROMs.

Expansion Cards   This category is also very dependent upon the specifications of your mother-board. Many motherboards have almost everything you might need built right into the motherboard's chipset, including video, sound, and a network. If your motherboard doesn't have one of these three, you will have to buy a separate expansion card to add that capability (unless you didn't want it). Or, you can buy an expansion card if you want to upgrade the capabilities of the on-board video (which I recommend, because most on-board video is only good for basic use). Remember that your motherboard must have enough slots for all the expansion devices you want to add.

Keyboard   There are many different styles, but they all do the same job. Make sure to get one that uses a keyboard connector that fits into the keyboard connector on your motherboard (usually PS/2).

Mouse   People have a lot of personal opinions about this particular peripheral, because it has to fit their hand just right or they won't like using it. Make sure that when you buy one, it will plug into your motherboard, either via the PS/2 mouse port or via USB.

> I recommend that you purchase an optical mouse. Most mice today are *optical* (no ball on the bottom of the mouse). They don't need to be cleaned and generally run much more smoothly.

Monitor The last component you need is a monitor. You can buy either CRT or LCD. LCDs don't take up as much space, but if you buy one, make sure you either have a video card capable of connecting to it, or that you have an adapter so that it will plug into your on-board video.

 By and large, make sure every part you buy will interoperate with everything else. You can ask the salesperson to help you with this, but you can also do the research yourself. The Web has literally tons of compatibility information available. In addition, you can post messages on public hardware forums like those at www.tomshardware.com to get answers to your questions from people who have done it before.

Software You will need software to run on your computer. At the very least, you need an OS. You can choose from the many flavors of Linux, or Windows, or some other OS if you wish (although Windows is the most popular by far). Typically, discounts are available if you buy your OS at the time you buy your components. You also should have available any other software (like a word-processing/spreadsheet package such as Microsoft Office) that you are going to install.

Now that you have purchased all your components, bring them home and lay them out near your workspace.

Preparing the Motherboard

The first step in building a computer is to prepare the motherboard for installation. As part of this process, you will install several hardware components—it will be easier to do so now, while the board is out of the computer (although you can do it later, if you prefer). To prepare the motherboard, you must do the following:

- Remove the motherboard from its box.
- Install the CPU/processor and its cooling mechanism.
- Install the memory.

This step of the installation process goes fairly quickly, although it can be a bit nerve-wracking—accidental damage to any of these components can be expensive.

Removing the Motherboard from Its Box

The first part is somewhat obvious: You must remove the motherboard from its box. Several items come in a motherboard box besides the motherboard itself. Typically, you will get the following:

- A motherboard in an antistatic bag
- A manual for the motherboard

- Multiple cables (IDE, floppy, serial ATA, and so on)
- Dongles for on-board USB, sound, and so on
- Registration card

For now, remove the motherboard from the box and set it on your work surface inside its antistatic bag. Ground yourself using an antistatic wrist strap (see Chapter 9, "Optimizing PC Performance, Preventative Maintenance, and Safety"). Then, carefully remove the motherboard from its antistatic bag (be careful not to touch any exposed conductors) and set it on top of the bag.

Installing the CPU/Processor and Its Cooling Mechanism

Now that the motherboard is out of the box and out of its antistatic bag, you are ready to install the processor. Most processors today use a *Zero Insertion Force (ZIF) processor socket*. So, installing the processor is easy.

For the purposes of this chapter, you will learn how to install an AMD processor. The steps for installing a Pentium 4 processor are very similar.

Installing the Processor

First, locate the processor socket. It's a large plastic square with a square hole in the middle, it's usually white or light brown, and it's surrounded by lots of small pinholes (an example is shown in Figure 6.13). On one side of the socket is a small lever. Lift the lever into the complete vertical position (as shown in Figure 6.14). You may have to push the lever gently to one side to release it from its locking tabs.

FIGURE 6.13   The processor socket on a motherboard

FIGURE 6.14 The lever on a processor socket

 Most processors come with instructions for doing this procedure. For an example, check out www.amd.com/us-en/assets/content_type/white_papers_and_tech_docs/23986.pdf.

Once you have opened the socket, remove the processor from its packaging. *Be very careful not to bend any pins on the processor.* In fact, don't even touch the pins, because you may damage them. They are almost impossible to straighten properly, and if they're bent or damaged, the processor may not fit properly into the socket.

The processor has two sides: the side with many small pins and the top side. On the top side, notice that there is a small dot. Also notice that on the pin side, the pins are arranged in a square with two corners cut off. These cut-off corners match up with a similar pattern in the socket. Figure 6.15 shows an example of the pins and how they line up properly with the socket.

FIGURE 6.15 Processor pin alignment with processor socket

You will know if you line up the processor properly because it will simply drop into place flush with the socket. If the processor is raised above the socket at all, the processor is oriented improperly.

 Above all, do not force the insertion of the processor. You will break something.

When the processor slips into place, it should look like Figure 6.16. To secure the processor, simply push the retaining lever back down into its original position, as shown in Figure 6.17.

FIGURE 6.16   Processor in place, not yet locked into place

FIGURE 6.17   Processor locked in place

Cooling Mechanisms

Once the processor is locked in place, you must then install whatever cooling mechanism you are going to use to cool the CPU. There are two main types: air cooled and water cooled. The most popular type of CPU cooling method is the air-cooled method. Air-cooled processors use a large block of copper or aluminum, called a *heatsink*, that is shaped into fins. A small fan is usually mounted on top of these fins to provide the moving air to cool them (similar to the way most motorcycle engines are cooled). Figure 6.18 shows an example of a processor heatsink and fan. Note the fins and the fan on top, as well as the small clip used to hold the assembly to the processor socket.

FIGURE 6.18   Processor heatsink and fan

Water cooling, on the other hand, involves the use of a smaller block of aluminum (called a *water block*) mounted to the processor. Instead of fins, the block has two small connectors for a water inlet and outlet. These are connected to a small pump and a radiator. Cool water is pumped into the water block. It flows through a series of back-and-forth channels, where it absorbs heat from the processor. The heated water travels to a radiator, where it is cooled by air blown over the fins of the radiator. The cooled water then returns to the pump and is ready to do it again.

WARNING   Water cooling systems are somewhat dangerous. If water were ever to leak out of the system or spill, it could cause major damage to your computer. I recommend that only a person who has built a few computers should install a water cooling system. Even then, you should double- and triple-check your connections and run the system for a day or two *without* a motherboard to see if leaks develop.

Whichever method you use, you need to use a special substance that allows the heatsink or water block to make the best contact with the processor. This compound is known as *thermal interface material (TIM)* and comes in two styles: a tube of grease (a.k.a. *thermal grease*) or a special *thermal contact patch* (looks like double-sided tape stuck to the heatsink). The most popular method is to use thermal grease, although the heatsink combos that come boxed with many AMD processors include a thermal contact patch already on the heatsink.

If you have one of these heatsinks, it is best to use the thermal contact patch already attached to the heatsink. It may be difficult to remove, and if you don't completely remove it and clean the surface before you use thermal grease, it can cause overheating problems.

The thermal interface material works by eliminating the very small air gaps that occur between the processor and heatsink due to the uneven metal surface of the heatsink, thus creating the largest possible surface area for the greatest heat transfer efficiency. Some of these imperfections can be removed through *lapping*. Lapping is a process by which the heatsink or water block surface is sanded using a very flat surface (like a sheet of glass) and progressively finer grits of sandpaper until the surface is as flat as it can get.

Lapping your heatsink, if done improperly, can cause an even larger air gap between processor and heatsink. So, if you're going to do it, be forewarned that it can be costly if done wrong.

Because most computers today use heatsinks, you'll learn the proper way to install a processor heatsink and fan.

If you have a water block, instead of a heatsink and fan, the procedures are similar—you just won't have a fan. Instead, you'll have a water reservoir, a pump, hoses, and a radiator that must be installed.

Installing the Heatsink and Fan

The heatsink and fan are typically one unit and are installed together. When installing this unit, you must first put some kind of thermal compound on the processor *die* (the small chip in the center of the big CPU chip package) or use the thermal contact patch that comes with the heatsink, if it has one. But don't use both—if the heatsink has a thermal contact patch, just use that and no thermal grease.

Never operate the computer without a heatsink installed. You can permanently damage the processor in a manner of seconds.

Cut the tip off the tube of thermal grease that comes with the processor. Spread an amount equal to about one-half grain to one full grain of rice onto the processor die. Figure 6.19 shows the proper amount.

The amount of compound is *critical*. Too much, and you won't get good heat transfer. Too little, and you won't get good heat transfer. There should be just enough to cover the die with a *very* thin layer of material. To see if you have the proper amount, gently set the heatsink onto the processor. The weight of the heatsink will spread out the grease. Remove the heatsink and examine the grease that remains on the processor die. You should still be able to see the die through the thermal grease after the heatsink has been removed.

FIGURE 6.19   Proper amount of thermal grease on a processor die

Once the thermal compound is on the processor, you can permanently install the heatsink. Set the heatsink on the processor and make sure that the step in the bottom of the heatsink is located over the processor socket's raised portion. Do *not* hook up any of the heatsink's clamps at this time. To make sure you have the correct orientation, examine Figures 6.20 and 6.21. Figure 6.20 shows the *incorrect* way of installing the heatsink. Notice how the heatsink is riding on the processor socket. This will cause undue pressure on the processor and possibly break the processor when you install the fastening clamp. The proper way is to ensure that the heatsink completely "floats" on the processor and doesn't touch any part of the socket (as shown in Figure 6.21).

FIGURE 6.20   The *wrong* way of installing a heatsink

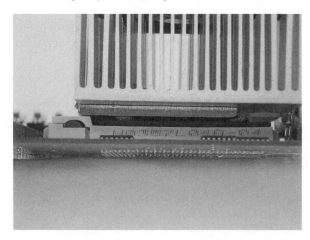

FIGURE 6.21   The correct way of installing a CPU heatsink

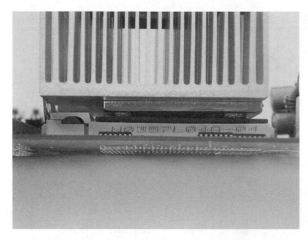

When the heatsink is properly located, you can proceed to fasten it permanently to the processor socket with the included spring-loaded clamp. The clamp has two sides: One side has a small clip on it (in some cases, three small clips) and the other has a clip about the same size, but with a tab that allows you to fit a screwdriver into it. For the purposes of our discussion we'll call the former the short-side clip (because it's attached to the shorter portion of the spring); it is shown in Figure 6.22. We'll call the latter (with the slot for the screwdriver) the long-side clip; it is shown in Figure 6.23.

FIGURE 6.22   Short-side heatsink retainer clip

Right now, your heatsink is just resting on the processor. The clamp will hold it in place permanently (or at least until you need to remove it). The heatsink is already properly positioned, so you simply push the short-side clip down and hook it under the tabs on the processor socket, as shown in Figure 6.24.

FIGURE 6.23 Long-side heatsink retainer clip

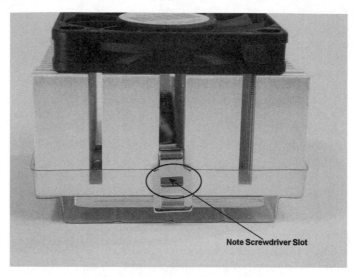

Note Screwdriver Slot

FIGURE 6.24 Installing the short-side heatsink clip

WARNING   If the clip doesn't slide into place easily, *do not* tip the processor. You may end up putting undue stress on the processor and cracking it. The spring clamp has significant tension.

Once you have installed the short side, you must install the long side. Some heatsink clamps can be put on with finger pressure, but more often, a tool is required (in most cases, a flat-bladed screwdriver). Insert the blade into the slot made for it in the long-side clamp, and then push it down until it slides over the tab on the processor socket and locks into place (Figure 6.25). You will have to push with a bit of effort, because this is in fact a spring. If you must, move the screwdriver slightly from angled to vertical to cause the clamp to bow out away from the heatsink so it can slip past the tab.

FIGURE 6.25   Installing the long-side heatsink clip

 Be careful that the heatsink doesn't move while you are doing this step. If you install the clamp and the heatsink shifts until part of it is resting on the socket, you may crack the processor package or processor die.

   Once the heatsink is installed, you only need to hook up the heatsink fan to the motherboard.

 Again, this procedure is a generalization that will work for most CPUs (Intel and other CPUs may use a slightly different retainer, but the procedure is roughly the same). Check the documentation that comes with your processor for any differences in procedure.

Installing the CPU Heatsink Fan

Most motherboards today have a special connector known as the *CPU_FAN connector* (an example is shown in Figure 6.26). This connector powers the fan for the CPU and also monitors its speed. The connector is usually what is known as a *three-pin fan connector*. PC fans can use either two or three wires. The first two wires are for power and ground, and the third wire (usually a yellow wire) is for speed sensing. That way, the fan can report its speed to the motherboard or other sensing device. This is very important for CPU fans, because if the CPU fan isn't spinning at the proper speed, the CPU won't get adequate cooling. By using a three-wire fan, the motherboard can constantly tell if the fan is spinning properly and can shut down the computer (or not let it boot up) if the fan doesn't spin up properly.

FIGURE 6.26 A motherboard CPU_FAN connector

To hook the CPU fan to the motherboard, first find the CPU_FAN connector. It is usually white or brown and is labeled on the motherboard next to it as CPU_FAN. Consult the motherboard's documentation to be sure. Then, push the fan's connector onto the motherboard connector (it will only go on one way, because it is a keyed plug-socket combination). Figure 6.27 shows how this is done.

FIGURE 6.27 Hooking the CPU heatsink fan to the motherboard

 Don't force it. The connectors will join only one way.

There are usually at least two fan connectors on a typical motherboard today: one for the CPU's fan and the others for other case fans, chipset fans, and so on. Some motherboards will refuse to boot unless they can detect that a CPU fan is attached and spinning at the proper speed.

Before you proceed, make sure that the heatsink is seated firmly on the processor and that it is not in any way resting on the processor socket. If so, you are ready to proceed to the next step: installing memory onto the motherboard.

You Spin Me Right 'Round...

Once, when building a system for a friend, I experienced what I thought was the oddest thing. After I put the system together completely, the system would power up, and then immediately power down and refuse to turn back on until I unplugged the computer, waited 15 seconds, and then plugged it back in. The motherboard was a SOYO Dragon Ultra KT400, and upon searching the manual and the Internet support sites, I found the answer. Apparently, the motherboard will turn off if it senses that the CPU fan isn't turning at 3000 RPM. I checked and saw that the fan was plugged into the right connector, so that wasn't the problem. However, after looking up the specs for the CPU fan (it was the heatsink combo that came in the retail AMD processor), I found out that that particular fan spins at a maximum speed of 2700 RPM. So, I went back to PCHertz.com, where I had bought the processor, and purchased a different heatsink (a ThermalTake heat pipe heatsink) with a much better fan. I brought it home, installed it, plugged it in, and voilà! It worked fine.

Installing Memory

The next step in preparing the motherboard for installation is to install the memory chip(s) that you purchased for your computer. This is a fairly simple procedure. If you have DIMMs or RIMMs (which most motherboards today use), the process is the same.

You may need to install memory in particular sockets for the system to work properly. For example, you may need to install the memory in pairs in sockets 1 and 3 on a particular motherboard, and singly on a different motherboard. Before proceeding, consult your motherboard's documentation to find out which sockets should be used.

Locate the memory slots (an example is shown in Figure 6.28). Note the small levers. Flip down the two white or brown levers (known as *retaining clips*) on the sides of the socket in which you will be installing memory. Line up the memory so that it will fit into the socket. In order to do this, you must notice where the notches are on the bottom of the *stick of memory* (another term for a memory module). The stick should be oriented so that these notches (as shown in Figure 6.29) line up with the small bumps in the bottom of the memory slot (as shown in Figure 6.30) and so that the copper or gold fingers are down (toward the motherboard).

FIGURE 6.28 Memory slot location

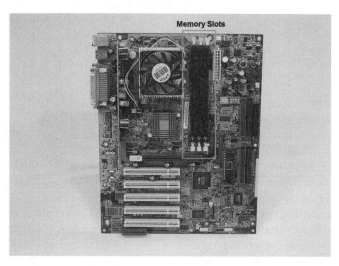

FIGURE 6.29 Notch in a memory stick

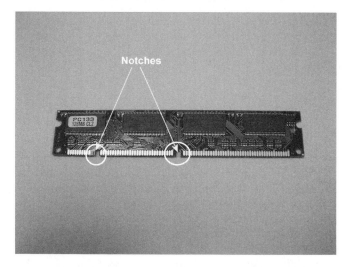

Next, slip the memory stick into the slot and push it down until it makes contact with the slot's retaining clips. Once the memory makes contact with these clips, it will be increasingly difficult to push on the memory stick. However, you must continue to push until the memory seats into the bottom of the slot and the memory retainer clips fold over and latch into the sides of the memory stick, thus holding it in place (Figure 6.31).

FIGURE 6.30 Bumps in a memory slot

FIGURE 6.31 Memory installed

Now that you have installed the memory into the motherboard, the motherboard can be installed into the computer case.

Installing the Motherboard

The next step in building the computer is to install the motherboard into the computer case. Before you do, however, make sure you have completed all the steps to prepare the motherboard. Also, review the following section and make sure you have all the parts, tools, and pieces you will need to complete the installation.

Set the motherboard you have been working on aside for a moment. Throw away any trash and clean up your work area. Then, open the box containing the computer's case and place the case on your work area.

Removing the Case Cover

To begin installing the motherboard, you must remove the side (or top, if you are installing into a desktop case) cover of the case so you can access the mounting holes inside the computer case. Typically, in order to remove the case, you must either remove some screws, slide a latch, or release some other fastening mechanism that is holding the case cover in place. Figure 6.32 shows the location of the case-cover fasteners for the case we are using to build our computer. These can be removed and the case cover removed, exposing the interior of the case.

There are almost as many different ways to hold the case cover on as there are case types. It should be fairly obvious how to remove the case cover. When in doubt, check with the case manufacturer or the case documentation (if there is any).

FIGURE 6.32   The location of the case cover fasteners

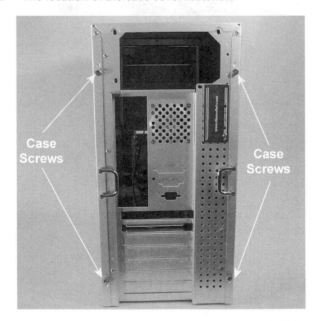

Once you've removed the case cover, locate the motherboard mounting plate (an example is illustrated in Figure 6.33). Position the case so that the mounting plate is at the bottom of the case. The case in Figure 6.33 is already in this position.

FIGURE 6.33   Location of the motherboard mounting plate

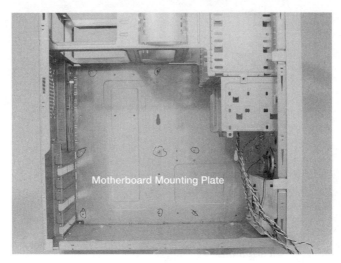

Motherboard Mounting Plate

Installing Mounting Standoffs

A motherboard is made up of a circuit board to which many components are soldered. The connection pins and soldered joints often stick out the back of the motherboard. If you were to just lay the motherboard in the computer and power it up, the metal case would cause electrical shorts between these components and damage the motherboard.

For this reason, you must mount the motherboard on small metal or plastic spacers, known as *standoffs*. These small items hold the motherboard away from the motherboard mounting plate in the case and prevent the components of the motherboard from touching the mounting plate and shorting out.

There are two types of standoffs: push in and screw in (see Figure 6.34). *Push-in standoffs* are typically made of nylon plastic and have a small one-way barb that fits into any of the mounting holes in the motherboard. To install them, you push the barb into the motherboard and slide the small tab on the bottom into a precut hole in the mounting plate (you can also install the standoff into the mounting plate and push the motherboard onto it—whichever way is easier). *Screw-in standoffs* are usually made of brass. They simply screw into the mounting plate into a predrilled, pretapped hole.

These standoffs must be installed first, before you can install the motherboard. You will notice several threaded holes and cutouts in the mounting plate. These holes are where you place the standoffs and mount the motherboard. There are also several mounting holes in the motherboard, each with a silver-colored ring around it (as shown in Figure 6.35). These holes are used to connect the motherboard to the standoffs.

There are different layouts for the holes in the mounting plate. Actually, the mounting plate is drilled, tapped, and cut to accept multiple motherboard configurations. You can tell which mounting points to use by test-fitting the motherboard and noting which holes in the motherboard line up with holes in the mounting plate.

FIGURE 6.34 Push-in and screw-in standoffs

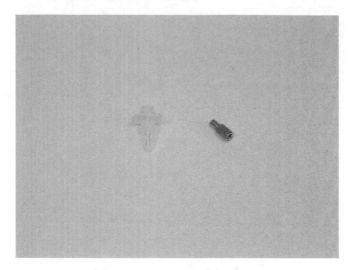

FIGURE 6.35 Motherboard mounting hole locations

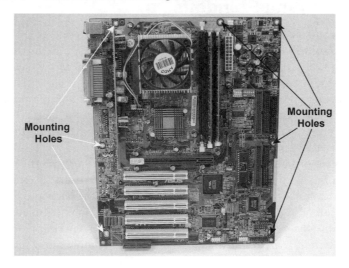

 Not all holes in the motherboard will necessarily line up with holes/slots in the mounting plate. However, the motherboard must be supported at least on its four corners and at one spot near the middle of the board, to minimize flexing of the motherboard during device installation (which may cause cracks).

Once you have determined which locations will work for your motherboard, mark them with a marker. Then, install the standoffs in those marked locations, using the appropriate type for the kind of hole or slot (small brass screw-in standoffs for the tapped holes, plastic push-ins for the slots).

Do *not* install the motherboard just yet. You still need to take care of a couple of items before you can secure the motherboard to the inside of the case.

Removing the Back-Panel Punchouts

Most cases come with a back panel that has standard *cutouts* (also known as *punchouts*) for the standard on-board ports (keyboard, mouse, serial, and parallel). There are also cutouts that have metal covers on them for the other on-board ports your motherboard might have (LAN, video, sound, and so on). However, in order for your motherboard to fit properly and the ports to be exposed, you must remove these metal covers from the cutouts.

To remove the metal covers, take your flat-head screwdriver, place the tip against the cover you wish to remove, and push against it (inward, toward the inside of the case). The small metal cover should push inward, and you can remove it with pliers by bending it back and forth several times until it breaks off. Make sure to remove these metal pieces from the case before you proceed, because they can cause shorts.

On several cheaper case designs, the expansion slot covers are covered with the same kind of cutouts, as opposed to stamped slot covers secured with a screw. If you have this kind of case, now would also be a good time to remove any expansion slot covers for the expansion cards you need to install.

Most ATX cases today have a cutout panel that you can remove in order to punch out these metal covers. Also, motherboards often come with precut cutout panels you can use to replace the one that comes with the case. It will save you from having to punch out any metal covers.

Connecting the Front-Panel Connectors

The last step before you secure the motherboard to the inside of the case is to install the front-panel connectors. As previously mentioned, most cases today come with front-panel switches and lights for things like the power button and light, reset button, hard-drive light, and so on. Additionally, many cases come with front-panel USB ports and microphone/headphone ports. These all have cables that must be run to pins on the motherboard.

To do this, start with one connector at a time from the bundle of cables and, using your motherboard's manual, locate the pin(s) on which they should be installed. Typically, the pins are in groups on the motherboard and labeled as to their function. Once you have located the proper pins, slip the connector over the pins, making sure to orient the connectors properly as per the motherboard's documentation (+ to +, – to –, and so on).

It's easiest to do this while holding the motherboard in one hand and installing the connectors with the other. You can also try balancing the motherboard on the side of the case, but be careful not to damage the CPU/heatsink or memory that's already been installed.

Figure 6.36 shows an example of these connectors and the labeling on the motherboard.

FIGURE 6.36 Connecting the cables

Installing Front-Panel Connectors

When you're installing the front-panel connectors to a motherboard, often you will have to act as a kind of translator between the motherboard manufacturer and the case manufacturer. For example, once I was connecting my new computer's SkyHawk case front-panel USB header to my Abit motherboard. As it turns out, Abit likes to number things starting at zero, and SkyHawk likes to start numbering as one. So, when I went to install my case's #1 USB port connector, I had to install it to the #0 USB port pins on the motherboard, and the case's #2 USB port connector went to the #1 connector on the motherboard. It might seem weird, but it just meant that each company was using a different numbering system. You need to use your head a bit and interpret what each company is trying to accomplish when you use parts from two different companies.

This step could also be done with the board inside the case, but it is much easier to see the small writing on the board with the motherboard out of the case. However, sometimes you have no choice, because the cables may not be long enough to let you work outside the case.

Installing and Securing the Motherboard

Finally, you can install the motherboard into the case. Just slip the motherboard into the case. You may have to push the motherboard against the back-panel cutouts to make it line up with its mounting standoffs. Then, put one screw in to secure the motherboard. You can use two hands to push the motherboard down onto any plastic push-in standoffs. Finally, put screws through the motherboard holes into any remaining standoffs. Figure 6.37 shows the completed installation.

The screws are included with the standoffs (both usually come in the box of hardware that comes with the case).

FIGURE 6.37   Motherboard installed with screws and standoffs

Now you can install the computer's other components.

Installing the Power Supply

At this point, you have the motherboard installed. You can now install the power supply (assuming the case didn't come with it already installed) and provide power to components. To install the power supply, hold the power supply in position as shown in Figure 6.38, and install the four mounting screws from the back of the computer.

FIGURE 6.38   Installing a power supply

Note the small red switch with the label 110V on it in Figure 6.38. That is the input voltage selector switch. It sets the power supply to use 110V (in the U.S. and as is the case here) or 220V (European standard). Before you continue, make sure the power supply is set to the correct input voltage, or you could have major problems!

You'll connect power connectors to the various devices as you install them. However, because the motherboard is already installed, you must install the power to the motherboard. The motherboard power connector is the largest of the many power connectors coming out of the power supply. The ATX motherboard power connector is shown in Figure 6.39.

FIGURE 6.39 The ATX motherboard power connector

To install the motherboard power connector, push the power connector onto the special power connector on the motherboard, as shown in Figure 6.40, until it latches. The power connector cannot be installed the wrong way. If the connectors aren't mating properly, turn the connector around and try again.

FIGURE 6.40 Installing the motherboard power connector onto the motherboard

This procedure works for most motherboards in use today. However, old AT-based power supplies have two connectors labeled P8 and P9 for power to an AT motherboard. To install those connectors, hold the two connectors together (oriented so the black wires from each connector are together) and push them together onto the proper motherboard connector.

Installing Storage Devices

The next step in assembling the computer is to install the disk drives. For the most part, installing any kind of storage device involves the same procedures: set the drive to the appropriate setting(s), mount the drive in the case, connect the data cable(s), and then connect the power to the device. Notice the repetition of these general steps and the specifics for each type of device as you read this section.

Before installing the storage devices, you may want to go back and read Chapter 3, "Disk Drive Storage," to remind yourself of the different types of disks and ways they can be connected.

Installing Floppy Disk Drives

Although floppy disk drives are not often used anymore, most computers today are built with at least one such drive. Typically, that drive is a 3 1/2-inch disk drive.

Mounting the Drive in the Case

To install the floppy disk drive, locate a 3 1/2-inch mounting bay (or use a 5 1/4-inch bay with an adapter bezel and frame) inside the case with a corresponding front panel blank (a *blank* is a piece of plastic that is removed when a removable media drive is installed). Remove the blank according the case directions (usually just push out the blank from inside the case).

You may need to remove a metal blank behind the front plastic blank. To do this, grasp the top of the blank with needle-nose pliers and work it back and forth until it snaps out.

Once you have removed the blank, slide the drive into the drive bay and secure it from both sides (as shown in Figure 6.41) with the mounting screws that came with either the drive or the case.

FIGURE 6.41   Mounting a floppy drive

 Some cases (like the very popular Antec SX series) have removable 3 1/2-inch drive bays. They are secured either by a lever or by a single screw. You can remove the entire bay, mount the drive(s) first, and then remove the blanks and install the drives. Some cases include special drive rails that can be attached to the drives. You can then slide the drives in and out of the case on preformed tracks, making it much easier to change drives.

Connecting the Data Cable

Now that you have the drive physically mounted in the case, it's time to connect it to the drive controller. Almost all motherboards since the Pentium have the floppy controller integrated into the motherboard. Find the 34-wire floppy cable (it should be the gray ribbon cable with a twisted section in the middle, as shown in Figure 6.42) that comes either with the floppy drive or in the motherboard box.

FIGURE 6.42   A floppy-drive cable

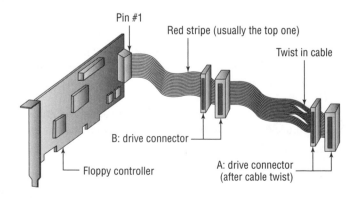

Connect the end of floppy-drive cable after the twist to the floppy drive. Make sure that the red stripe on the cable is oriented so that it connects with pin #1 on the floppy drive's data connector (the pins are usually labeled with pin numbers or with a dot to denote pin #1). Then, connect the opposite end to the floppy connector on the motherboard. The resulting setup should look like Figure 6.43.

FIGURE 6.43   A complete floppy-drive data connection

Connecting the Power

The final step in installing the floppy drive is connecting the power. Find a small-form-factor power connector (also known as a *floppy power connector*) on one of the power connectors coming from the power supply and connect it to the power pins on the floppy drive, as shown in Figure 6.44.

FIGURE 6.44   A proper floppy-drive power connection

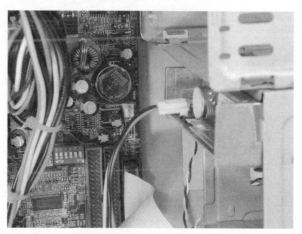

That's it. The floppy drive is installed. You can now install the other storage devices.

If you boot the computer and the floppy-drive light comes on and stays on, the floppy cable is on backward. Power down the computer and flip over one end of the cable.

Installing Hard Disk(s)

Installing your computer's hard drive is just as straightforward as installing the floppy drive. There's a bit more configuration and you use a different cable and drive, but the basics are the same.

 For the purposes of this section, we assume you are installing an ATA hard disk. For SCSI disks, the procedure is almost identical, but you use a different set of disk settings, cables, and interfaces.

Configuring Jumpers

Before you install the computer's hard drive, take the drive out of its antistatic bag and find the configuration jumpers (Figure 6.45). They should be located between the data connector and the power connector. As you may recall from Chapter 3, if there's only one drive in the system, it should be set to Master or Single, *not* Slave.

 For most drives, Master or Single is the default setting, so you shouldn't have to move the jumpers.

FIGURE 6.45 Configuration jumpers

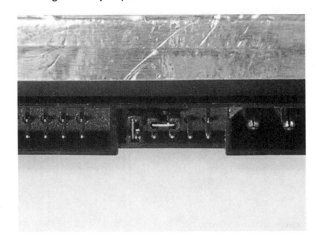

Mounting the Drive in the Case

Once the jumpers are set appropriately, you are ready to mount the drive in the case. Find a 3 1/2-inch drive bay *without* a front blank. Typically, most cases have at least two 3 1/2-inch bays with front access and two without, unless the case has a smaller form factor. Your hard drive should be mounted in one of the bays without a front blank. That way, you can save the remaining bays for other removable media drives. If you don't have any 3 1/2-inch bays without front blanks, you can install the hard drive in a bay that does have a blank; just don't remove the blank from the front cover.

When you've chosen the bay for the hard drive, slide the hard drive into the bay and secure it with the mounting screws (or drive rails) that come either with it or with the case (as shown in Figure 6.46).

FIGURE 6.46   Mounting the hard drive

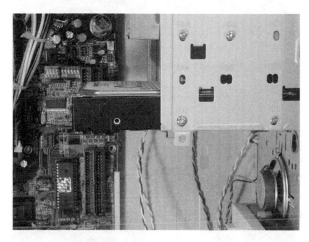

Connecting the Data Cables

Now that the drive is physically mounted in the case, you are ready to connect the data cable. Find the 80-wire (for UltraDMA/33 and faster drives) or 40-wire (EIDE) cable that usually comes with the motherboard, drive, or other interface. Figure 6.47 shows examples of ATA cables (both EIDE and UltraDMA/33). Note that there are three connectors on the cable: two located toward one end of the cable for drives, and a third at the other end for the connection to the motherboard.

Connect one end of the data cable to the hard disk (as shown in Figure 6.48) and the other end to the proper connector on the motherboard. The cable is keyed so it will only go into the drive and motherboard one way. If it doesn't fit, flip the connector over.

Usually, the first hard disk should go to the connector labeled Primary ATA/IDE (or something similar) on the motherboard. Check your motherboard's manual to be sure which connector to use.

FIGURE 6.47   EIDE and UltraDMA/33 cables

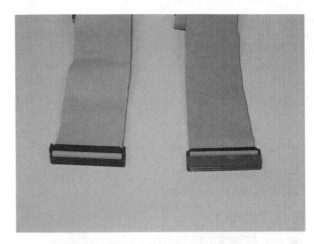

FIGURE 6.48   Connecting a hard-drive data cable

 Never put a CD-ROM (especially a burner) on the same IDE channel as your hard drive, because doing so will decrease performance.

Connecting the Power Cable

Now that the data cable is connected to the hard drive, all that's left is to connect the power to the drive. Find a standard peripheral power connector (as shown in Figure 6.49) and plug it into the drive power connector (an example of which is shown in Figure 6.50). You may have to push firmly to ensure that the power cable makes good contact with the power connector.

Figure 6.51 shows how the drive should look once the power is connected. Your hard disk is now installed.

FIGURE 6.49   Standard peripheral power connector

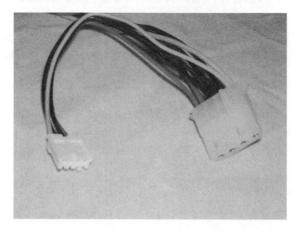

FIGURE 6.50   A disk-drive power connector on a hard disk

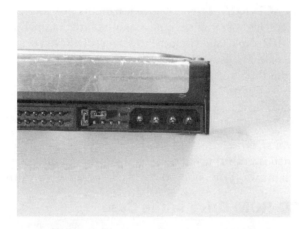

FIGURE 6.51   Disk-drive power connected

Installing a CD-ROM//CD-RW/DVD/DVDRW

The procedure for installing a CD-ROM drive is very similar to that for installing a hard drive. However, the CD-ROM drive uses a 5 1/4-inch bay with a blank, and the CD-ROM drive is usually set to Slave from the factory (assuming the drive is an ATAPI drive).

 The process for installing a CD-RW, CD-R, DVD-ROM, or any other removable media drive that uses CD-ROM technology is exactly the same as that detailed for installing a CD-ROM.

 For this section, we will assume that the CD-ROM drive being installed is an ATAPI drive.

Configuring Jumpers

To begin to install your CD-ROM drive, remove it from its box and packaging and locate the Master/Slave jumpers. Because you're going to put it on the motherboard's secondary IDE bus, you need a second IDE cable, and you need to set the CD-ROM drive to Master (because it will be the only drive on that bus). Most CD-ROM drives come from the factory set to Slave, so move the jumper from the Slave pins to the pins labeled Master (or similar), as shown in Figure 6.52.

Preparing the Case

Just as with the floppy disk drive, you must select a bay with a blank. However, in the case of a CD-ROM drive (which is a 5 1/4-inch device), you must select an empty 5 1/4-inch bay and remove its blank, the same way you removed the blank for the floppy drive.

Mounting the CD-ROM Drive in the Case

Mounting a CD-ROM drive is just like mounting the other drives. First, slide the CD-ROM drive into place. Then, secure it on both sides using the provided screws. Figure 6.53 illustrates a properly secured CD-ROM drive.

Connecting the Data Cables

Similar to the way you connected the hard-disk data cable, once you have the CD-ROM drive mounted in the case, you can connect it to the motherboard's secondary IDE channel. In order to do this, you must use either the 40- or 80-pin IDE cable that comes with the CD-ROM drive or motherboard that matches the type of ATA technology the drive and motherboard secondary IDE channel use (40-pin for standard IDE and EIDE, 80-pin for UltraDMA/33 and above).

The connectors on the cable can only be installed one way on the CD-ROM drive and the motherboard. Match the key on the cable connectors to the slots on the CD-ROM and motherboard connectors and push the cable connector onto the device.

FIGURE 6.52   Setting the CD-ROM drive to Master

FIGURE 6.53   A properly mounted CD-ROM drive

If for some reason the CD-ROM doesn't have a keyed connector, follow the same rule as for floppy cables: Orient the connector so that the red stripe on the cable matches up with pin #1 on the connector.

Connecting the Sound Pass-through Cable

The one unique CD-ROM installation step is the installation of the sound pass-through cable. This cable allows sound from DVDs and audio CDs to be passed directly (either in digital or analog form) to either the on-board sound or the sound expansion card. Figure 6.54 shows an example of this cable.

FIGURE 6.54   A CD-ROM sound pass-through cable

To install this cable, find the four-pin connector (for analog) or the two-pin connector (for digital) on the CD-ROM drive and the matching connector on the motherboard (as shown in Figure 6.55). Then, push the cable into the connectors until it clicks and locks into place.

FIGURE 6.55   CD-ROM audio connectors (analog and digital)

Connecting the Power Cable

Once the CD-ROM is mounted and the data and sound cables are connected, you are ready for the final step: connecting the power cable. Just as with the hard drive, find a peripheral power connector that is not used and plug it into the power connector on the back of the CD-ROM drive.

The CD-ROM drive is now installed.

The process for installing other removable media drives, such as tape backup drives, is exactly the same (only there is no sound cable on a tape backup drive, obviously).

Installing Expansion Cards

After the floppy drive, hard disk drive, and CD-ROM drive are installed, you need only install the various adapter cards your computer requires in order to complete the assembly of your new computer. If your computer has all its features on board, you can skip this step.

By and large, the process for installing different expansion cards is very similar. There are only a few minor differences, and they are noted here.

Installing a Video Card

Most computers today use a separate video card because it can provide better performance than the on-board video circuitry. This is especially true if you play lots of video games that require more advanced graphics.

In this section, you will learn the steps necessary to install a video card. Let's begin by preparing the case to accept the video card.

Preparing the Case

Today, most video cards are AGP devices (although a few are PCI for those computers that don't have an AGP slot). To begin installing a video card, locate an open AGP or PCI slot in the motherboard. If it's a PCI slot, try to find a slot that is spaced at least one slot away from any other PCI device (for better airflow and cooling).

Then, if the place you are installing the device has a *blank* (a piece of plastic or metal that covers that space where the device is going to go), remove it by either taking out the screw holding it in place or using a pair of pliers to bend it back and forth until it breaks. Don't throw these blanks away. If you ever want to remove a component, you will need to replace the blank so that dirt, dust, and other contaminants can be kept out. I have a small box of blanks that I keep handy, just in case I need them when removing components. Figure 6.56 shows an example of a slot with the blank removed.

FIGURE 6.56   An expansion slot with the blank removed

    Many technicians ignore the need for a blank when they remove a component—do not make this mistake! The most important function of a blank is to promote proper airflow over the internal components of your PC. PC manufacturers have spent hours determining the proper placement of fans and air holes for their computers. Adding a new hole in the back of your computer will often result in *less* airflow rather than more, as you might assume. The end result is often a computer that overheats and burns out components.

Inserting the Card

Now that you have chosen a slot and removed the blank that was covering the opening on the outside of the case, you are ready to insert the card. Align the connector on the bottom of the card with the connector on the motherboard and insert the card into its connector. You should feel a slight amount of resistance. Push the card firmly into place with an even pressure on the front and back of the card. Stop pushing when all of the card's connectors are making contact with the fingers in the expansion slot. Figure 6.57 shows a properly installed expansion card.

FIGURE 6.57   A properly installed video expansion card

WARNING If the card doesn't go in easily, don't force it. You could break the card or the connector.

Securing the Card

Install the mounting screws through the tab in the expansion card to secure the video card in place. In this case, you only have one screw to install, and it's located at the back of the computer. This screw holds the metal tab on the expansion card to the computer's case.

That's it; the video card is now installed. When it's installed properly, the tab on the AGP card should be locked under the lever behind the AGP slot. This lever holds the AGP card in place. If you need to remove the card, you will first have to move this lever to the side.

NOTE Video cards should automatically configure themselves in either an AGP or PCI slot. ISA cards may require manual configuration of the card's resources (IRQ, DMA, and so on, as discussed earlier in this chapter).

Installing Other Expansion Cards or Devices

For the most part, installing other expansion cards follows the same procedure. The only differences are what the cards look like and whether they need to be configured (and that depends on the bus).

You should observe one special note, however. With today's computers, it is best to install only the video card before the first power-up. After you have powered up the computer for the first time and configured its CMOS settings, shut down the computer, remove the power from the computer completely, wait 30 seconds for all power to discharge, and then install the next expansion card. Power up the computer so that the BIOS can configure the resources of the card. Then, shut down the computer and remove power as before. Repeat this procedure until all cards have been installed. This process will minimize the chances of resource conflicts, because the BIOS has the opportunity to configure the cards one by one, and it's less likely to make a mistake configuring them all at once.

NOTE This process assumes that you are using a Plug-and-Play BIOS with a PCI bus (which most computers today are using). You may have to configure resources manually if this is not the case.

Some of the expansion cards you may have to install in your computer (depending on the motherboard's configuration) include:

- Network interface card (NIC)
- Sound card
- Video card
- Modem
- SCSI

- IEEE 1394/FireWire
- USB
- Wireless

 Pictures of these expansion cards and their functions can be found in Chapter 1, "PC Architecture."

Installing Dongles

If your computer case comes with dongles for USB, IEEE 1394, or digital sound, you may have to mount them in a spare expansion slot in the case and connect their cable to the appropriate pins on the motherboard (similar to connecting the front panel connectors as discussed earlier in this chapter). Mount the dongle into a free expansion slot (preferably one that doesn't match up with a motherboard expansion slot) and secure it with a screw. Then, connect the cable(s) to the motherboard onto the appropriate pins (refer to your motherboard's manual for details on which pins to match up and where they are located).

Installing Case Fans

You also may have to install case fans (if your case has any). A *case fan* is just a small fan that is used to bring air into, or take air out of, the computer's case. Case fans should be mounted so as to provide airflow that's as close to ideal as possible, as shown in Figure 6.58 (refer to the fan's documentation to see which way the fan should be mounted for the proper airflow).

FIGURE 6.58   Ideal computer case airflow for cooling

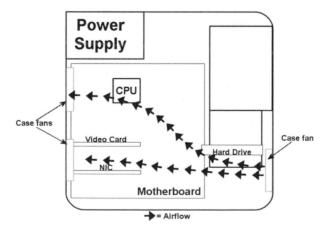

The case fans can be connected to the motherboard (there are usually multiple motherboard fan locations), or there are adapters that allow fans to be directly connected to the power supply. Check your motherboard's manual to see where case fans can be connected.

Connecting External Peripherals

Now that you have installed all the components into the computer, you are almost ready to power it up and test it. However, before you can do that, you must connect a few external peripherals. The three important peripherals you must connect are as follows:

- Keyboard
- Mouse
- Monitor or LCD display

This is a very easy task, and you may have to do it many times during the course of testing your computer. To connect the keyboard, take the PS/2 connector of the keyboard's cable and connect it to the motherboard's PS/2 connector that is labeled with a keyboard (as shown in Figure 6.59). The same is true for the mouse (if you are using a PS/2 mouse); connect the PS/2 connector on the mouse to the PS/2 connector on the motherboard that is labeled with a mouse icon (as shown in Figure 6.60).

FIGURE 6.59   Installing a PS/2 keyboard

If you have a USB mouse, the process is similar. Insert the USB connector on the mouse's cable into an open USB slot in the computer (Figure 6.61 shows how).

 A few USB keyboards are in use as well. Just like a USB mouse, connect the keyboard to an open USB port.

Once the keyboard and mouse are connected, you must connect either the standard CRT monitor (analog) or the liquid crystal display (LCD; either analog or digital). Figure 6.62 shows how a standard analog CRT or analog LCD is connected to a computer. Notice that these cables can go on only one way. If the cable doesn't fit properly, flip it over and try again.

FIGURE 6.60 Installing a PS/2 mouse

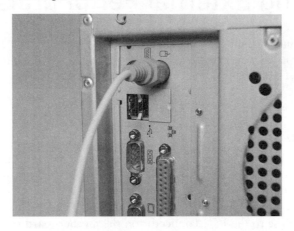

FIGURE 6.61 Installing a USB mouse

FIGURE 6.62 Installing a standard analog monitor or an analog LCD display

Double-Checking Everything

You are essentially finished installing components into or onto the computer. Most people would begin to reassemble the computer at this point. However, you don't want to do that just yet. I've found that Murphy's Law applies quite often when installing computer components. So, leave off the case while you perform the next steps. If something goes wrong, you won't have to remove the case again to get at the components.

At this stage, you should double-check all your connections, both data and power. Remember that every cable has two ends, and both should be connected to something (although in the case of IDE, floppy, and power cables, you may have extra connectors in the middle).

Also make sure all devices are firmly secured to the inside of the case with the appropriate number of screws (friction isn't enough, and the cards or devices may work themselves loose if the computer is accidentally jarred).

Finally, go back through these sections and make sure you haven't forgotten anything.

Connecting the Power, and Testing

You are now ready to connect power to everything and test the computer for the first time. Plug the monitor and the computer's power supply into wall power using the cables that come with the monitor and power supply, respectively.

When you feel you are ready for the moment of truth, turn on the monitor with its power switch and push the PC's power button. If everything has been connected properly, you should hear the computer's fans turn on, and the computer should display an image on the monitor (usually it will start counting up memory and go through its own self diagnostics). Finally, it should say something like *Please insert boot diskette*. If it says this, *congratulations*! You have built a working PC, and you are almost finished.

If the computer doesn't do all of these things, don't panic. Here is list of some of the most common errors that occur on first boot-up:

No Power When You Push the Power Button   Most often the power cord isn't pushed in all the way, you forgot to connect the front panel power switch connector to the motherboard (or it fell off), or the power supply has its own power switch that might be turned off.

If you are having problems turning the computer on and it is emitting several beeps, check with the motherboard manufacturer's website to see what the beeps mean and what the possible fix(es) are.

***CMOS Configuration Has Changed* (or Similar) Error**   Believe it or not, this is normal. Your computer is telling you that a bunch of new devices, memory, and so on are attached to the motherboard. Well, *duh*! It's a new computer.

One Long Beep, Three Short Beeps, and No Video   This is typically a memory failure. It means you don't have memory installed, the memory is not seated properly, or the memory is installed in the wrong banks.

Computer Powers Up for a Moment, and Then Powers Down and Won't Turn Back On Until You Unplug It   This is usually caused by a CPU fan that won't turn on, isn't turning at the right speed, or is the kind that can't send speed information to the motherboard (that is, it isn't a three-wire fan).

A Loud Bang, Smoke, or Both at the Back of the Case   More than likely, the power supply was set to the wrong input voltage. If you have this problem, you may have to replace the power supply.

The Computer Is On, But No Video on the Monitor and You Hear One Beep   Chances are, the video card isn't inserted correctly, is inserted only half way, or is faulty.

No Video, and You Smell Burning Silicon   Don't panic! Chances are, the manufacturer has installed the BIOS chip improperly, causing a short. The chip has burned up on power-up. Immediately shut down the computer. You will have to replace the motherboard, but it should be under warranty from the manufacturer (after all, they installed it wrong).

Several other less common problems can occur on first power-up, but these are the most common. If the problem you have isn't listed, check your motherboard's manual and the manufacturer's website for a possible cure.

Configuring CMOS

Once you have turned on the computer for the first time and fixed any minor issues, you must configure the computer's BIOS CMOS (*Complementary Metal Oxide Semiconductor*) memory. CMOS contains settings that determine how the computer is configured. These settings are user-configurable and can be accessed through the CMOS setup program by pressing some key combination at startup (such as Shift+F1, the Delete key, F2 on Dell computers, or Ctrl+Shift+Esc). For example, one setting in CMOS controls the boot sequence. The parameter is usually called boot sequence and can be set to many different settings that tell the computer in what order to search the internal disk drives for boot information.

Every CMOS setup program is different and uses different commands for configuration. Usually, though, the CMOS setup program is menu driven and will present you with a list of settings that you can configure, as well as the possible settings for them. When you're done configuring, you can press Esc, and the CMOS setup program will ask you to press Enter to save the changes and reboot. After rebooting, the computer will operate with the modified settings.

 During the system boot, the computer checks the hardware settings in the CMOS versus what is actually installed in the computer. If they are different, the BIOS will issue a warning and usually bring you to the CMOS setup screen.

CMOS is used for more than just configuring hard-drive information. It also contains the following:

- The physical resources used by parallel and serial ports, as well as any other configuration information needed for those components.

- A description of the floppy drive—its speed, density, and so on.

- Memory configuration.

- The date and time.

- Any passwords that have been assigned to the hardware. Many computers require a password to complete the boot sequence.

- A list of the resources that have been reserved for use by Plug-and-Play components (and those that have been set aside for legacy equipment).

- BIOS shadowing configuration information.

In the following subsections, you will learn where to find the most common settings for the CMOS and how to change them.

For the purposes of our discussion, you will learn what these settings are and how they are used. Because each BIOS and vendor is slightly different, you should look in your motherboard's manual to find out where these settings are in your motherboard's CMOS setup program and how exactly to change them.

If you're not willing to play on your only home computer, or you are afraid of messing up, try the CMOS setup simulator at www.grs-software.de/sims/.

CMOS-Related Problems

Many obscure settings in the CMOS control how your computer operates. As such, occasionally problems occur that aren't really "problems" but rather "features." That is, the computer is doing what it's supposed to but isn't producing the desired result. For example, the link http://support.microsoft.com/default.aspx?scid=kb;en-us;q125480 details a problem where the virus detection built into some BIOSes prevents Windows 98 from installing correctly. Basically, the antivirus routine built into the computer, when active, prevents any program from writing to the boot sector of the hard disk. While that's what the program was designed to do, this causes the Windows installation program to have issues, whereby it promptly hangs.

In addition, most computers today have built-in power management. The computers can go into low-power consumption states when not being used and can even eventually go to "sleep." This can cause problems for programs that like to run at full speed all the time (like game programs); they might not come back from this hibernation properly and might lock up the computer. Both of the features described here can be disabled in the CMOS.

Returning to Default Settings

Before we examine the other settings, it is important to know that every CMOS setup program stores the *default CMOS settings* (the settings programmed by the factory that allow the computer to become functional, at a basic level anyway). Most often, you can restore the CMOS settings back to their factory defaults by pressing a particular key (usually F6, F9, or something similar). Some CMOS setup utilities call them *fail-safe defaults*. At any rate, they are the factory settings that should allow you to get your system running properly in the event you make a change that causes your computer not to work.

Changing the Date/Time

One of the most basic settings you may need to make is to change your computer's internal clock. Your computer has a built-in timer that doesn't keep the best time. It occasionally needs to be set. You can change the computer's time (usually under General Settings or something similar) in the CMOS setup utility.

Changing CPU Settings

This particular category of settings gets a lot of attention. When you install a CPU, most of the newer computers automatically detect the speed of the CPU that is installed and adjust three main parameters for its proper function: *CPU clock speed*, *clock multiplier*, and *core voltage*:

- The CPU clock speed is the setting, in MHz, of how fast the CPU's clock ticks. The faster it ticks, the faster the CPU works.

- The clock multiplier is the number used to change the working speed of the processor relative to the speed of the external clock. For example, if the CPU external clock speed was set to 166 and the clock multiplier was set to 12.5, the CPU would be running at 2075MHz internally.

- The core voltage is the voltage a processor uses internally while running at a separate voltage externally. The external voltage is usually known as the *I/O voltage*.

Most motherboards today will detect which processor you've installed and set these parameters accordingly. However, it is possible to modify them yourself for better performance. This process is known as *overclocking*, and it can very easily damage your CPU, your motherboard, or both.

> **WARNING**   This practice, while possible, is very dangerous and can cause major damage to system components, especially if adequate cooling is unavailable.

These settings can usually be found in a CMOS section titled something like Processor/CPU Settings or Advanced Settings.

Changing the Parallel and Serial Port Configuration

With integrated motherboards, the parallel and serial ports, as well as their controlling circuitry, are located right on the motherboard rather than on expansion cards. So, most parameters that control how these ports are configured can be found in the CMOS setup program.

Parallel ports require little configuration. About the only items that ever need changing are the disabling of a port, or changing a port's type. If you'll remember from Chapter 1, there are several different types of parallel port, including unidirectional, bidirectional, EPP, and ECC. You can usually change the parallel port's configuration from within the On-board Peripherals section (or something similar).

Similarly, you can change which resources the on-board serial ports are using as well as enable or disable a specific port. The latter comes in handy especially when you're trying to install an internal modem and you have a resource conflict.

Changing Floppy-Drive Configurations

Other on-board peripherals that sometimes need changing are the settings for the floppy-drive controller. These settings indicate what types of floppy drives are connected (if any), their type (3 1/2-inch or 5 1/4-inch), and their capacity. You can specify all these settings within the CMOS setup program's floppy device settings.

These settings are usually auto-discovered by the BIOS at first boot-up.

Changing Hard-Drive Configurations

In addition to auto-detecting the type of processor installed in the motherboard, most BIOSs today can auto-detect the configurations of their attached hard drives (cylinders, heads, sectors, and so on). In the General Configuration section of most CMOS setup utilities, you can view the configurations of attached hard drives as well as the on-board IDE channel devices to which they are attached. These utilities usually also tell you the model and brand of the attached device.

In most CMOS setup utilities, you have the option of staying with the detected settings or entering the configuration manually. It is generally recommended that you stay with the detected settings.

This area is a good place to check to see if your hard drives and CD-ROM drives are connected to the proper IDE channels (primary or secondary) and if they are configured for master or slave.

Changing the Boot Sequence

In most CMOS setup utilities today, you are able to check what is known as the *boot sequence* (discussed earlier). This is the order in which the BIOS searches devices during boot-up, looking for a bootable OS. Most often, you want it to search the floppy drive first, then the CD-ROM drive, then the hard disk, and finally (if you have an on-board NIC) the network. That way, when you are installing the OS or doing other diagnostic work, you can bypass the hard-disk OS and boot to a floppy disk.

CMOS setup utilities usually have this setting either under General Settings or Boot Settings.

Finishing Up

Once you have double-checked everything and the system comes up with no errors or beep codes, you are ready to finish building the PC. These are the last steps before you will be able to use your computer. Most of these tasks fall into the category of connecting peripheral devices.

Installing Network/Modem Connections

If you have a NIC or modem in your computer (either as an expansion card or as an on-board device), you must connect it appropriately before you can use the computer.

Connect the NIC to your network using the appropriate type of network cable. Most often, if your network is 10BaseT or 100BaseT, you'll connect it with a twisted-pair cable to the RJ-45 connector on your computer. If you use another type of network, you'll use a different cable and a different type of NIC.

If you are going to use a modem, on the other hand, simply connect a phone cable from the wall jack to the RJ-11 jack on your modem labeled Line, as shown in Figure 6.63.

Installing Speakers/Headphones

If your computer has a sound card (as most do these days), you're probably going to want to hear what your computer is using that sound card for. In that case, you can connect either headphones or speakers to your computer.

FIGURE 6.63   Connecting a phone line to a modem

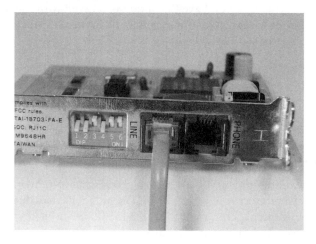

Most sound-card ports and multimedia peripherals are color-coded to make hookup easier. Standard speaker 1/8-inch phono cables (as shown in Figure 6.64) that plug into a sound card are color-coded green. The port they plug into is green as well. Microphone connections are typically color-coded pink. Figure 6.65 shows the sound inputs and outputs on a typical computer. Notice that they are all 1/8-inch phono jacks.

Typically, headphones can use the same jack as the speakers. As always, check your sound card's documentation and manual to verify which connections go where.

FIGURE 6.64   A 1/8-inch phono cable from a set of speakers

FIGURE 6.65   1/8-inch phono jacks

Installing the Operating System

Finally, you are ready to install the operating system into your computer and get it fully functional. You've installed all the components, and you know the computer works because the BIOS tells you so (no errors, no beep codes). If you are having any problems at this point, you should fix them before installing the OS, because that will only make the problems worse (and you'll be wasting effort).

Ensure that your computer is set to boot to the CD-ROM drive. Insert your OS's boot CD into the drive and begin the installation.

You will learn more about Windows OS installation in the second half of this book.

Congratulations! You've successfully built your own computer! Once you have installed the OS and everything is working fine, replace the case cover and secure it with screws (or whatever locking mechanism is present).

Removal and Replacement Procedures

In this chapter so far, you have learned a great deal about installing components into computers. During your employment as a PC service technician, you will troubleshoot many computers. Occasionally, you will find a bad part that needs to be replaced. Thankfully, service technicians don't desolder individual chips anymore. Service practices have advanced to the point where we think in terms of *Field Replaceable Units (FRUs)*. An FRU is a computer subassembly (motherboard, expansion card, and so on) that can be easily replaced by removing and replacing some screws and cables. Although the components are individually more expensive, there is a much greater savings to the consumer in terms of time. With labor rates always on the rise, FRUs make PC service much more economical.

If you need to remove a part and replace it, the procedures aren't much different than those you've already learned. To remove a component, simply reverse the process for installation (for the most part). To replace a component, remove the broken or damaged unit, and then follow the installation procedures for the specific component. You may have to remove a few other components to get at the component you are trying to replace, but that just means you must reinstall them when you are finished replacing the FRU. You may then have to return the damaged component to the manufacturer for a warranty credit.

You should always safely dispose of any components removed from a computer, because they are considered hazardous waste. In Chapter 9 you will learn about the various environmental concerns involved when you're working on computers.

Summary

In this chapter, you learned all the information necessary to build your own PC, including much of the background information needed to understand the procedures involved. You first learned about the various service concepts involved in PC service and repair as well as the background needed for building a PC. These concepts include PC device configuration, necessary tools, and workspace. You also learned about the parts you need to buy to build a PC.

Then, we explained how to build the PC, starting with the motherboard, CPU, and memory, and moving on to the case, disk drives, and expansion cards. You learned what procedures to follow when first booting the computer, as well as common problems people have when doing this.

You also learned what to do to finalize the build of a computer, including changing CMOS settings, installing peripherals, and installing the OS. Finally, we went over the differences between building a PC and replacing components during service work.

Key Terms

Before you take the exam, be certain you are familiar with the following terms:

auto-ranging multimeters	buffer
blank	case fan
bootable floppy disk	clock multiplier
Complementary Metal Oxide Semiconductor	optical
core voltage	overclocking
CPU clock speed	Phillips screwdriver
CPU_FAN connector	push-in standoffs
default CMOS settings	retaining clips
die	screw-in standoffs
DIP switches	standoffs
Direct Memory Access	stick of memory
Field Replaceable Units (FRUs)	thermal contact patch
floppy power connector	thermal grease
heatsink	thermal interface material (TIM)
I/O (input/output) addresses	three-pin fan connector
I/O voltage	Torx screwdriver
interrupt requests	water block
jumpers	water cooling
lapping	watt
memory address	Zero Insertion Force (ZIF) processor socket
multimeter	

Review Questions

1. A _____ is installed to help keep the CPU cool.

   A. Motherboard

   B. Heatsink

   C. Processor

   D. Floppy drive

2. A _____ connects a CD-ROM to a sound card so audio can be heard from a music CD.

   A. Audio pass-through cable

   B. CD-ROM data cable

   C. IDE cable

   D. Ethernet cable

3. A large bang followed by a puff of smoke at the back of the computer indicates what problem?

   A. Processor explosion

   B. Single-bit memory error

   C. Wrong power supply voltage setting

   D. Improper cable connecting the power supply and motherboard

4. How much thermal compound is needed when installing a processor?

   A. Doesn't matter

   B. A dollop as big as the processor die

   C. None; the processor will operate fine without it

   D. A small ribbon about the size of one-half to a full grain of rice

5. _____ is used to fill in the microscopic imperfections in a heatsink, thus increasing the contact area and thermal efficiency.

   A. Sanding

   B. Buffing

   C. Lapping

   D. Thermal compound

6. Water-cooling systems use a _____ on the CPU instead of a heatsink.

   A. Cooling tube

   B. Water block

   C. Block of ice

   D. Fan

7. You have just installed a new floppy drive. Upon powering up the computer, you discover that the floppy drive isn't working properly. The floppy-drive light remains on as long as the computer is powered up. What should you check first?

   A. Whether the floppy drive is in the wrong position on the floppy cable

   B. Whether the floppy cable is installed upside down

   C. Whether an incorrect ribbon cable is installed

   D. Whether the floppy cable is defective

8. _____ is another name for a part that is designed to be replaced as a unit in a computer (you don't have to desolder and resolder individual components).

   A. Field Replaceable Unit

   B. Field Restorable Unit

   C. Field Recognizable Unit

   D. Field Raster Unit

9. You need to change the boot sequence of the computer. What would you use to change the order in which the computer searches for an operating system?

   A. Boot disk

   B. DIP switches on the motherboard

   C. CMOS setup

   D. Jumpers on the hard drive

10. When preparing the work area, which of the following should you *not* consider?

    A. Having a small workspace available to do all the work that has to be done.

    B. That the work area must be flat.

    C. That the area must be sturdy.

    D. That the area must be well lit and clean.

11. When building a computer, what is the first step to perform?

    A. Install the motherboard

    B. Install the disk drives

    C. Configure the CMOS

    D. Install the power supply

12. Which of the following is *not* a good assembly aid?

    A. Read the directions.

    B. Take your time.

    C. Check cables for proper orientation.

    D. Don't worry about the connections—once you plug them in, they're secure.

13. CD-ROM drives normally come set to _____ out of the box. When installing one in a computer and making it the only device on a secondary IDE bus, you often have to set it to _____.

    A. Primary, Secondary

    B. Secondary, Primary

    C. Master, Slave

    D. Slave, Master

14. A downward pressure of _____ pounds per square inch (PSI) is required to install a Pentium 4 processor.

    A. 0

    B. 1

    C. 3

    D. 5

15. _____ are used to mount the motherboard into the case.

    A. Pins

    B. Standoffs

    C. Tie wraps

    D. Zip ties

16. Put the following PC build steps in order:

    1. Mount the motherboard inside the case.

    2. Remove the case cover.

    3. Install the floppy drive.

    4. Install memory.

    A. 4, 3, 2, 1

    B. 1, 2, 3, 4

    C. 4, 2, 1, 3

    D. 4, 3, 1, 2

17. _____ is the practice of increasing the clock multiplier to force the processor to run faster, thus increasing performance.

   A. Speeding

   B. Overclocking

   C. CMOS editing

   D. Hacking

18. Which of the following is the best method for cooling a PC's case and components?

   A. To have the front fan blowing in and the rear fan(s) blowing out

   B. To have the rear fan(s) blowing in and the front fan blowing out

   C. To have all fans blowing into the case

   D. To have all fans blowing air out of the case

19. Where would *not* be a good place to find out which front panel connectors go to which pins on the motherboard?

   A. Motherboard

   B. Manual

   C. Manufacturer's website

   D. The panel connectors themselves

20. When installing speakers for a PC, you connect the speaker's cable to (one of) the _____ jack(s) on the back of the PC.

   A. RJ-11

   B. RJ-45

   C. 1/8-inch phono

   D. RCA

Answers to Review Questions

1. B. A heatsink conducts heat away from the processor where it is dissipated by moving air, thus helping the CPU keep cool.

2. A. The audio pass-through cable allows CD audio to be transferred from a CD-ROM directly to the sound card so it can be played.

3. C. Most often, if this symptom occurs, the red switch on the power supply that determine the input voltage (either 110VAC or 220VAC) is set incorrectly.

4. D. A very small amount of thermal compound is needed to ensure the best contact with the processor. A small ribbon of compound (about the size of one-half to one full grain of rice) is sufficient.

5. D. Although lapping is a method by which the microscopic imperfections are leveled off to produce the greatest possible contact with the processor, the correct answer is thermal compound because it *fills in* the microscopic imperfections, rather than removes them (as lapping does).

6. B. Instead of a heatsink, water-cooled systems use a device known as a water block that transfers the heat generated by the processor to the water being pumped through the cooling system (which is then cooled by a radiator).

7. B. When the floppy cable is installed with one end installed correctly and the other end upside down, the system will exhibit the behavior noted. Simply turn over one end of the floppy cable, and the system will work properly.

8. A. A Field Replaceable Unit (FRU) is a system module that is designed to be replaced as a unit.

9. C. The CMOS setup utility has an area that lets you specify the order in which the system searches internal bootable devices for operating systems.

10. A. The work area should be as large as possible, not small, as answer A suggests.

11. A. Of the items listed, one of the first things you do when building a computer is install the motherboard.

12. D. You should always double-check your cable connections to make sure they are secure. Although a cable may seem secure upon visual inspection, it could in fact be loose.

13. D. Typically, a CD-ROM drive comes in the box set to Slave. You must set it to Master when making it the only device on a secondary IDE bus.

14. A. No pressure is required to insert a processor. The processor simply drops into place. If pressure is required, the processor is not aligned properly.

15. B. Plastic or metal standoffs are used to mount the motherboard to the inside of the case.

16. C.   Based on the standard method of building a PC, the proper sequence is to install memory, remove the case cover, mount the motherboard inside the case, and then install the floppy drive. Although it is possible to remove the case cover, install the motherboard, and *then* install memory, and so on, it is easier to install the memory with the motherboard out of the case.

17. B.   The term for running the clock multiplier faster is *overclocking*.

18. A.   According to heat patterns inside a computer's case, it is best to have cool air enter at the front of the case and move over the processor to exit at the upper rear of the case.

19. D.   Although the front-panel connectors are labeled as to their function, they don't tell you where to connect them on the motherboard. However, you can tell from the motherboard (as well as the motherboard's manual and manufacturer's website) where to put those connectors.

20. C.   Speaker and headphone connections most often use 1/8-inch phono plugs, which connect to one of the 1/8-inch phono jacks at the back of the computer.

Chapter

7

Portable Systems

THE FOLLOWING OBJECTIVES ARE COVERED IN THIS CHAPTER:

✓ 1.3 Identify basic procedures for adding and removing field-replaceable modules for portable systems. Given a replacement scenario, choose the appropriate sequences.

If miniaturization trends continue, soon we will all be able to have a computer with the power of a current mainframe contained in a wristwatch or other piece of jewelry. Toward that end, many people have embraced the current crop of portable systems. A *portable computer* is any computer that contains all the functionality of a desktop computer system but is portable. Most people define *portable* in terms of weight and size. So we can discuss things on the same level, let's define *portable* as less than 20 pounds and smaller than an average desktop computer.

Most portable computers fall into one of three categories: luggable, laptop, or PDA. Luggable computers were the first truly portable computers, but they were the size of sewing machines the term portable didn't really describe them. So the term "luggable" was coined. Compaq, Kaypro, and Osborne made some of the first luggable computers.

Laptops were the next type of portable computer. They contain a built-in keyboard, pointing device, and LCD screen in a clamshell design. They are also called *notebook* computers because they resemble large notebooks. Most portable computers in use today are laptop computers.

The final type of portable computer, which has really taken off recently, is the palmtop computer (also known as a Personal Digital Assistant, or PDA). These computers are designed to keep the information you need close to you so you have access to it whenever you need it. There are two different approaches to the PDA. Pen-based assistants are basically small digital notepads that use a stylus and handwriting-interpretation software to perform operations. The Palm Pilot and Compaq Ipaq are two examples of this type of PDA.

The other type of PDA is known as a *handheld PC (HPC)*. These are basically shrunken laptops. HPCs run an operating system known as Windows CE, from (whom else?) Microsoft. Windows CE is basically Windows $9x$, shrunk to fit into the limited RAM of the HPC. Instead of using a mouse to point to the icons and menus in Windows CE, you use a stylus on the HPC's touch-sensitive screen.

In this chapter, you will learn primarily about the architecture of laptop computers as well as the methods used to service laptop computers.

Laptop Architecture

Laptops are similar to desktop computers in architecture in that they contain many parts that perform similar functions. However, the parts that make up a laptop are completely different from those in desktop computers. They are physically much smaller and lighter, and they must fit into the compact space of a laptop's case. Also, laptop parts are designed to consume less power and to shut themselves off when not being used (although many desktops have some components that go into a low-power state when not active, such as video circuitry). Finally, most laptop components (especially the motherboard) are proprietary—the LCD screen from one laptop will not necessarily fit on another.

In this section, you will learn about the various components that make up laptops and how they differ from desktop computer components. It may help you to refer back to Chapters 1 and 2 occasionally as you read this chapter.

Comparing Laptops to Desktops

If you've ever shopped for a laptop, you have no doubt noticed that the prices of desktop PCs keep dropping, whereas the prices of notebook computers stay about the same. If you've ever wondered what makes a laptop so much different than a PC, here are the primary differences between laptops and desktops:

Portability   This is probably the most obvious difference. Laptops are designed to be portable. They run on batteries, so you aren't tied to one spot at home or at the office. Networking options are now available that allow you to connect to a network wirelessly and do work from just about anywhere, including malls, airports, and so on. As anyone who's tried to bring their full-tower PC to a LAN party can tell you, desktops just aren't that portable.

Cost   Laptops cost more—sometimes as much as 60 to 80 percent more—than similar desktop computers with similar features. The primary reason is that portability requires small components and unique (proprietary) designs for those components so they fit into the small size necessary. Miniature versions of components cost more money than standard size (desktop) versions.

Building Your Own   You can't build your own laptop. Because laptop components are designed to fit exacting specifications to fit properly inside the notebook, there generally are no universal motherboards, video boards, and so on for laptops. Memory and hard drives are the exception. You can get different brands of memory and hard drives for laptops, but you can't buy a motherboard from one company and the video circuitry from another. Even things as mundane as floppy drives are designed to work only with a specific model.

Performance   By and large, laptops are always going to loose out somewhere in the performance department. Because compromises have to be made between performance and portability, performance is what usually suffers. While it is possible to have laptops with comparable performance to a desktop, the amount of money one would have to spend for a "desktop replacement" laptop is considerable. This is not to say that a laptop can't outperform a desktop, it's just that the "bang for the buck" factor is higher in a desktop.

Expandability   Because desktop computers were designed to be modular, their capabilities can be upgraded quite easily. It is next to impossible to upgrade the processor or motherboard on most laptops.

Quality of Construction   Considering how much abuse laptops get, it is much more important that the materials construction of the laptop case and other components be extremely durable. Not that it isn't important in a desktop—but it's more important in a laptop.

Now that we've illustrated the primary differences between laptops and desktops, let's examine the parts of the laptop and what they do.

Laptop Case

A typical laptop case is made up of three main parts: the *display* (usually an LCD display), the *case frame* (the metal reinforcing structure inside the laptop that provides rigidity and strength and that most components mount to), and the laptop's *case* itself (the plastic cover that surrounds the components and provides protection from the elements). The cases are typically made of some type of plastic (usually ABS plastic or ABS composite) to provide for light weight as well as strength.

 A few notebooks have cases made of a strong, lightweight metal, like aluminum or titanium. However, the majority of laptop cases are made of plastic.

Laptop cases are made in what is known as a *clamshell design*. In a clamshell design, the laptop has two halves, hinged together at the back. Usually, the display is the top half and everything else is in the bottom half.

Occasionally, part of the laptop's case will crack and need to be replaced. However, you can't simply replace the cracked section (usually). Most often, you must remove every component from inside the laptop's case and swap the components over to the new case. This is a labor-intensive process, because the screws in laptops are often very small and hard to reach. Often, repairing a cracked case may cost several hundred dollars in labor alone. Most times, people who have cracked laptop cases wait until something else needs to be repaired before having the case fixed. I have a crack on my laptop that I haven't bothered to fix for this very reason.

Motherboard and Supporting Circuitry

As with desktop computers, the motherboard of a laptop is the backbone structure to which all internal components connect. However, with a laptop, almost all components are integrated onto the motherboard, including onboard circuitry for the serial, parallel, USB, IEEE 1394, video, expansion, and network ports of the laptop.

The primary differences between a laptop motherboard and a desktop motherboard are the lack of standards and the much smaller form factor. As mentioned earlier, most motherboards are designed along with the laptop case so that all the components will fit inside. Therefore, the motherboard is mostly proprietary. Figure 7.1 shows an example of a laptop motherboard.

 Occasionally, to save space, components of the video circuitry (and possibly other circuits as well) are placed on a thin circuit board that connects directly to the motherboard. This circuit board is often known as a *daughterboard*.

FIGURE 7.1 A laptop motherboard

Memory

As discussed in Chapter 2, notebooks don't use standard desktop computer memory chips. In fact, until fairly recently, there were no standard types of memory chips. If you wanted to add memory to your laptop, you had to order it from the laptop manufacturer (and usually pay a premium over and above a similar-sized desktop memory chip).

However, there are now two main types of laptop memory package: The Small Outline DIMM (SoDIMM) and the MicroDIMM (these form factors were discussed in Chapter 2). To see what kind of memory your laptop uses, check either the manual or the manufacturer's website. You can also check third-party memory producers' websites (such as www.crucial.com).

Interestingly, the Apple iMac desktop uses SoDIMMs.

Storage

Just like desktop computers, most laptops have a hard drive. However, not all laptops have both a floppy drive and a CD-ROM drive. Many times there just isn't room for both. So, often there is a *drive bay* that can be used to hold either drive. If this drive bay exists, users generally keep the CD-ROM drive installed most of the time and leave out the floppy drive. In some cases, the floppy drive is an external device that you connect with a special cable to a proprietary connector. Figure 7.2 shows an example of one of these connectors, and Figure 7.3 shows an example of a laptop floppy drive. Notice how thin the floppy drive is and how compact the electronics are.

FIGURE 7.2   A proprietary floppy connector

FIGURE 7.3   A laptop floppy drive

Laptops don't have the room for the full-size 3¹/₂-inch hard drives that desktop computers use. Instead, they use a small-form-factor hard drive that's only 2¹/₂-inches wide and less than ¹/₂-inch thick! These drives share the same interface technologies (usually ATA and UDMA) as desktop computers. Figure 7.4 shows an example of a standard hard drive compared to a laptop hard drive.

Laptop CD-ROM drives come in many different kinds, just like desktop CD-ROM drives. You can get standard CD-ROM, CD-R, CD-RW, DVD, DVD-RAM, and (probably the most popular option) CD-RW/DVD-ROM drives that can both burn CDs and play DVD movies. It is also possible to get CD-ROM drives that manage to cram a floppy drive into the same drive bay along with the CD-ROM.

Often, these drives are very small in form factor (usually less than ¹/₂-inch high). Figure 7.5 shows an example of a desktop CD-ROM drive compared to a laptop CD-ROM drive. Note that the laptop drive is very small, but it has all the functionality of a desktop unit. The drive mechanism and circuits have all been miniaturized to save space. The functionality is basically the same, but the cost is higher. Any time a component's functionality remains the same while its size decreases, you will notice an increase in price over the standard-sized item.

FIGURE 7.4 A desktop hard drive compared to a laptop hard drive

FIGURE 7.5 A desktop CD-ROM drive compared to a laptop CD-ROM drive

Displays

As discussed in Chapter 1, laptops normally use liquid crystal displays (LCDs) that are integrated into the case. These LCD displays are designed to consume less power and be more portable than other display types.

 For a full discussion of the different types of LCD displays used in laptops, refer to Chapter 1.

A laptop's display takes the most power to run. It is also the device that drains the battery the fastest when the laptop is running on batteries only.

Because the technology behind LCD displays is complex, there are almost no service procedures for the display in a laptop. Most often, when the display is broken, it can be removed by a service technician (usually the display is only held in with a few screws and a plastic bezel) and exchanged with the manufacturer for a new one. This procedure may be under warranty (depending on the length of the manufacturer's warranty).

One particular sore spot with laptop owners and manufacturers is the phenomenon known as *bad pixels*. As you learned in Chapter 1, most higher-end laptops use active matrix displays (they have a transistor for each pixel on the screen). With these types of displays, small defects sometimes occur during the manufacturing process that cause a few transistors in the display to not function. The corresponding pixels on the screen are completely black. To put this in perspective, a 15-inch laptop display (at a resolution of 1028×768 pixels) has 789,504 pixels. If one of them is black, you may not notice it (unless it's right in the center of your field of vision).

Manufacturers have warranty stipulations that indicate they will replace the display only if a certain number of pixels go bad. Manufacturers usually consider a display to be fully operational if 99.999 percent of its pixels are operating. On the previously mentioned 1028×768 display, that would mean the manufacturer would replace the screen only if eight of the pixels were bad. This figure is actually pretty good—some manufacturers indicate in their warranties that 99.99 percent is good enough (meaning approximately 79 pixels would have to be bad before they would replace the display).

Many people seem to think that if one pixel is bad, the display should be replaced. However, the pixels are so small that you might hardly notice the problem. Bad pixels are part of the manufacturing process; if you buy a laptop, you will most likely have a couple of bad pixels. Be aware of your laptop manufacturer's warranty policy.

Input Devices

Because of laptops' small size, getting data into them presents unique challenges to designers. They must design a keyboard that fits within the case of the laptop. They must also design some sort of pointing device that users can use in graphical interfaces like Windows. The primary challenge in both cases is to design these peripherals so they fit within the design constraints of the laptop (low power and small form factor) while remaining usable.

Keyboards

A standard-size desktop keyboard wasn't designed to be portable. It wouldn't fit well with the portable nature of a laptop. That usually means laptop keys are not normal size; they must be smaller and packed together more tightly. People who learned to type on a typewriter or regular computer often have a difficult time adjusting to a laptop keyboard because the keys are smaller and closer together.

Laptop keyboards are built into the lower portion of the clamshell. Sometimes, they can be removed easily to access peripherals below them (like memory and hard drives, as in the IBM Thinkpad series).

Because of the much smaller space available for keys, some laptop keys (like the number pad, Home, Insert, PgUp, and PgDn keys) are consolidated into special multifunction keys. These keys are accessed through the standard keys by using a special function key (usually labeled Fn).

To use a multifunction key, you press the function key and the key that contains the function you want (for example, press <Function>+? for the slash [/] normally found on a numeric keypad on a regular keyboard).

Mice and Pointing Devices

In addition to the keyboard, you must have a method of controlling the on-screen pointer in the Windows interface. There are many methods of doing this, but the most common are as follows:

- Trackball
- Touchpad
- Touchpoint
- Touch screen

> Some laptops use multiple pointing devices, to appeal to a wider variety of people who have different pointing-device preferences.

Most laptops today include a mouse/keyboard port, a USB port, or both. Either of these ports can be used to add an input device like a mouse or a standard-sized keyboard.

Trackball

Many early laptops used trackballs as pointing devices. A *trackball* is essentially the same as a mouse turned upside down. When you move the ball with your thumb or fingers, the on-screen pointer moves in the same direction and at the same speed you move the trackball.

Trackballs were cheap to produce. However, the primary problem with trackballs was that they did not last as long as other types of pointing devices; a trackball picks up dirt and oil from operators' fingers, and those substances clog the rollers on the trackball and prevent it from functioning properly.

Touchpad

To overcome the problems of trackballs, a new technology that has become known as the touchpad was developed. *Touchpad* is actually the trade name of a product. But, like Kleenex, the trade name is now used to describe an entire genre of products that are similar in function.

A *touchpad* is a device that has a pad of touch-sensitive material. The user draws with their finger on the touchpad, and the on-screen pointer follows the finger motions. Included with the touchpad are two buttons for left- or right-clicking (although with some touchpads, you can perform the functions of the left-click by tapping on the touchpad).

Touchpoint

With the introduction of the Thinkpad series of laptops, IBM introduced a new feature known as the *Touchpoint*. The Touchpoint is a pointing device that uses a small rubber-tipped stick (see Figure 7.6 for an example). When you push the Touchpoint in a particular direction, the on-screen pointer goes in same direction. The harder you push, the faster the on-screen pointer moves. The Touchpoint allows the fingertip control of the on-screen pointer, without the reliability problems associated with trackballs.

This type of pointing device is also known as a *finger mouse*.

FIGURE 7.6 A Touchpoint pointing device

 Touchpoints have their own problems. Often, the stick does not return to center properly, causing the pointer to drift when not in use.

Touch Screen

The last type of pointing device we'll discuss can be found in use at many department stores: the little informational *kiosks* with screens that respond to your touch and give you information about product specials or bridal registries. Instead of a keyboard and mouse, these computer screens have a film over them that is sensitive to touch. This technology is known as a *touch screen* (see Figure 7.7). With most of the interfaces in use on touch screens, touching a box drawn on the monitor does the same thing as double-clicking that box with a mouse. These screens are most commonly found on monitors; however, with the advent of the *tablet PC* (a laptop designed to be held like a pad of paper), the touch screen is becoming more popular as an input device for a laptop.

FIGURE 7.7 A typical touch screen

Cleaning a touch screen is usually just as easy as cleaning a regular monitor. With optical touch screens, the monitor *is* a regular monitor, so it can be cleaned with glass cleaner. However, if the screen has a capacitive coating, glass cleaner may damage it. Instead, use a cloth dampened with water to clean the dirt, dust, and fingerprints from the screen.

Expansion Bus and Ports

Although laptop computers are less expandable than their desktop counterparts, they can be expanded to some extent. Laptops have expansion ports similar to those found on desktop computers, as well as a couple that are found only on laptops.

PCMCIA (PC Card) Expansion Bus

The tongue-twister *PCMCIA* stands for Personal Computer Memory Card International Association. The PCMCIA was organized to provide a standard way of expanding portable computers. The PCMCIA bus was originally designed to provide a way of expanding the memory in a small, handheld computer. The PCMCIA bus has been renamed *PC Card* to make it easier to pronounce. It uses a small expansion card (about the size of a credit card). Although it is primarily used in portable computers, PC Card bus adapters are available for desktop PCs. The PCMCIA bus now serves as a universal expansion bus that can accommodate any device.

The first release of the PCMCIA standard (PCMCIA 1, the same used in the original handheld computer) defined only the bus to be used for memory expansion. The second release (PCMCIA 2) is the most common; it is used throughout the computer industry and has remained relatively unchanged. PCMCIA 2 was designed to be backward compatible with version 1, so memory cards can be used in the version 2 specification. It was then modified to version 2.1 so card and socket services could be used as a standard driver platform. Finally, PCMCIA version 3 increased the bus width to 32-bit and the bus speed from 8MHz to a maximum of 33MHz. In addition, the new CardBus adapters used PCI-like access methods, and the throughput speeds increased dramatically (speeds of 80Mbps and higher are possible).

Information and Identification

PCMCIA's bus width is either 16-bit or 32-bit, as discussed. Also, PC Cards support only one IRQ (a problem if you need to install in a PC Card bus two devices that both need interrupts). PC Cards also do not support bus mastering or Direct Memory Access (DMA). However, because of its flexibility, PCMCIA has quickly become a very popular bus for all types of computers (not just laptops).

Three major types of PC Cards (and slots) are in use today. Each has different uses and physical characteristics (see Figure 7.8). Coincidentally, they are called Type I, Type II, and Type III:

- Type I cards are 3.3mm thick and are most commonly used for memory cards.

- Type II cards are 5mm thick and are mostly used for modems and LAN adapters. This is the most common PC Card type found today, and most systems have at least two Type II slots (or one Type III slot).

- The Type III slot is 10.5mm thick. Its most common application is PC Card hard disks. Developers have been slowly introducing these devices to the market.

FIGURE 7.8   PC Card types, by thickness

In addition to the card, the PC Card architecture includes two other components:

▪ *Socket Services software* is a BIOS-level interface to the PCMCIA bus slot. When loaded, it hides the details of the PC Card hardware from the computer. This software can detect when a card has been inserted and what type of card it is.

▪ *Card Services software* is the interface between the application and Socket Services. It tells the applications which interrupts and I/O ports the card is using. Applications that need to access the PC Card don't access the hardware directly; instead, they tell Card Services that they need access to a particular feature, and Card Services gets the appropriate feature from the PC Card.

This dual-component architecture allows the PCMCIA architecture to be used in different types of computer systems (that is, not just Intel's). For example, Apple laptop computers currently use PC Cards for modems and LAN interface cards and are based on Motorola processors.

USB Ports

Just as desktops do, laptops use USB ports for expansion. However, because of the lack of internal expansion in laptops, most peripherals for laptops are either found as PC Cards or USB expansion devices.

For more information about USB ports and their function, refer to Chapters 1 and 2.

Mouse/Keyboard Port

Just in case you don't like using your laptop's built-in keyboard or pointing device, most laptops come with a combination *keyboard/mouse port* that allows you to connect either an external keyboard or an external mouse to the laptop. On laptops that don't have USB ports, this port is most often used for a standard PS/2 mouse. On those laptops that do have USB ports, this port is used for an external keypad or keyboard (because the USB port can accommodate an external mouse).

Infrared Port

Laptops were the first computers to use infrared ports regularly. Handheld computers had them before that (including the Palm Pilot and HPC platforms). This port is used for many things, although one of the most common uses is to send information to another device (like a Palm Pilot).

For more information about infrared ports, see Chapter 2.

Networking

In addition to expansion buses and ports, most laptops today include support for some kind of network. Because it is the most common, the majority of laptops include support for 10BaseT or 100BaseT (usually both) in the form of an RJ-45 connector. The circuitry for the network is included in the motherboard (similar to the way it is included in desktop motherboards, as discussed in Chapter 2).

Some of the newest laptops include support for wireless network connections (typically 802.11b or 802.11g) built into the laptop. The laptop can then connect to a network wirelessly, without the need for a PC Card or a built-in NIC.

Docking Stations

Some laptops are designed to be *desktop replacement laptops*. That is, they will replace a standard desktop computer for day-to-day use and are thus more full-featured than other laptops. These laptops often have a proprietary docking port. A *docking port* (as shown in Figure 7.9) is used to connect the laptop to a special laptop-only peripheral known as a *docking station*. A docking station is basically an extension of the motherboard of a laptop. Because a docking station is designed to stay behind when the laptop is removed, it can contain things like a full-size drive bay and expansion bus slots. Also, the docking station can function as a port replicator. A *port replicator* either is a separate type of dock, or is integrated into the docking station itself. It reproduces the functions of the ports on the back of a laptop, so that peripherals such as monitors, keyboards, printers, and so on that don't travel with the laptop can remain connected to the dock and don't have to all be physically unplugged each time the laptop is taken away.

These docking ports and docking stations are *proprietary*. That is, the port only works with docking stations designed by the laptop's manufacturer and vice versa.

FIGURE 7.9   A docking port

Power Systems

Because portable computers have unique characteristics as a result of their portability, they have unique power systems as well. Portable computers can use either of two power sources: batteries or AC power. There are many different sizes and shapes of batteries, but most of them are Nickel-Cadmium (NiCad), Lithium Ion (LiIon), or Nickel Metal Hydride (NiMH). All of these perform equally well, but NiCad batteries can only be recharged a finite number of times. After a time, they develop a memory and must be recharged on a special deep-charging machine. NiMH and LiIon batteries don't usually develop a memory and can be recharged many times, but they're a little more expensive. Some of the much smaller handheld or palmtop computers can use any of these types of battery, but a few vendors like Hewlett-Packard took a more common-sense approach: They designed their handhelds to use standard AA batteries.

Most notebook computers can also use AC power with a special adapter (called an *AC adapter*) that converts AC power into DC power. The adapter either is integrated into the notebook (as on some Compaq notebooks) or is a separate "brick" with a cord that plugs into the back of the laptop.

Another power accessory that is often used is a *DC adapter*, which allows a user to plug the laptop into the power source (usually a cigarette lighter) inside a car or on an airplane. These adapters allow people who travel frequently to use their laptops while on the road (literally).

Laptop Component Installation

The maintenance of portable computers has its own set of rules to follow. Due to the complexity of laptop design, most manufacturers insist that all upgrades be performed at an authorized service center. Equipment such as LCD display screens, DC controllers, video boards, and processors is often unreachable in a laptop. Most field service will involve replacing hard drives or other storage, adding memory, configuring PCMCIA cards, or adding a battery to extend useable time.

Installing Storage Devices

Many portable computers have an open bay that can be used to install one of the following (what can be installed depends on the model of laptop and the manufacturer):

- Battery
- Floppy drive
- CD-ROM drive
- CD-RW drive
- DVD-ROM drive
- CD-RW/DVD-ROM combo drive
- Hard disk
- Memory card reader

Read the documentation to determine the exact installation process for your brand of portable computer.

The basic installation process for devices that go into an accessory storage bay is the same:

1. Remove any bay-cover blank or existing device to open the bay.

2. Slide the new device into place, using any guides that may be present.

3. Ensure that the connections are lined up properly and will make good contact.

4. Secure the device in place with either a screw or a latch lever.

The removal process is the same, but the steps are reversed.

Installing Power Systems

Installing the various power-related accessories should be a no-brainer. For AC adapters, plug the two- or three-pronged end into the wall outlet and the other end into the laptop (check the laptop's manual if you're not sure which end is which). The DC adapter's procedure is almost the same: Plug the barrel-shaped connector into the accessory power plug (also known as the cigarette lighter) in your car, and then plug the other end into the laptop.

Batteries, on the other hand, can be installed in different ways. As mentioned earlier, they can be installed in an accessory device bay (if your laptop has one and supports installing a battery in this manner). Most laptops have the battery installed from the bottom of the computer. The battery is secured by either a single screw or (more often) a simple slide latch that lets you remove the battery without using tools. The laptop's manual will dictate exactly how to remove a battery on that specific model.

Replacing or Adding Memory

To replace or add memory to a portable computer, you follow the same rules you do when adding memory to any other computer. However, you may need to read the manual for directions. There are as many ways to access memory on portable computers as there are manufacturers.

Most often, you install memory by removing a cover that is fastened with a screw. On some notebooks, the memory is located under the keyboard.

Adding Input Devices

Many people, myself included, dislike the touchpad for controlling mouse actions. Luckily, most of today's portable computers have a PS/2 mouse port available. Plugging a PS/2 mouse into the keyboard/mouse port usually causes the system to automatically configure the mouse. If a system does not have a PS/2 port, you can add a standard serial or USB mouse and load the appropriate drivers.

Installing Expansion Devices

PC Cards are one of the most common expansion methods for laptops because of their ease of use and flexibility. Many different types of PC Cards are available for laptops, including:

- Network interface cards (NICs)
- Modems
- SCSI adapters
- IEEE 1394/FireWire cards
- USB cards
- Sound cards

The process for installing a PC Card is different than that for any of the other bus types, mainly because this type was designed to allow the cards to be *hot swapped*—inserted or removed while the computer is powered up. The only other bus that can do this is the USB. However, see the following warning before taking advantage of this feature.

 WARNING Even though you can remove a PC Card while the power is on, *you shouldn't!* If you remove a PCMCIA card while the system is up, realize that some software may not like having its hardware ripped out from underneath it. That software will then have no hardware to talk to, and it may crash the system. (As for other expansion cards, *never* remove them without first shutting off the power to the computer! If the power is on, you will certainly damage the card, the computer, or both.)

The process for installing a PC Card is straightforward. Just slip the card into an available slot, making sure the card type matches the slot type. Also, make sure the card is pushed in all the way to ensure that the connection to the bus is good. Once the card is installed, you must install the software to use the card (Windows should do this automatically, although you sometimes must run an installation program before installing the card).

 WARNING If you are installing newer PCMCIA cards, note whether the card and your laptop use standard PC Card (16-bit) or CardBus (32-bit) technology. They use different voltages, and damage can result from inserting the wrong card in the wrong type of slot.

You need to note a few items when installing and configuring PC Cards:

- You must have the Card and Socket Services software installed before you try to physically install the card, so the computer can manage the card's resources.
- You may have a PC Card bus that supports two Type II cards or one Type III. If you have one of these buses, you can have only one or the other situation. If you have a Type II card installed, you can't install a Type III card without removing the existing Type II.

- PC Cards are too small to have jumpers or DIP switches, so you must configure the hardware through a software configuration program. This program can be a separate program, or it can be built into the BIOS.

Card and Socket Services software is normally part of all Windows operating systems since Windows 98 SE.

 Real World Scenario

Old World, New World

Sometimes there is not enough memory to load all the files for Card and Socket Services. In the DOS world, the software for Card and Socket Services loads in conventional memory (or in UMBs, if you choose). With many such DOS drivers being loaded, you may run out of conventional memory and not be able to run some DOS programs.

To solve this, PC Card manufacturers have come up with a piece of software called a PC Card *shim* that allows the card to be used as any other expansion card is used. In addition, it takes up less conventional memory. The only downside is that the shim may not be completely compatible with the system. Windows 9*x* incorporates this software as virtual device drivers, (VXDs).

Replacing Displays

Most often, the cost of replacing the display on your laptop is prohibitive to the point that it would be almost as much as buying a new laptop (or an excellent used model). Replacing an LCD screen is not that difficult, in terms of the service procedure, but the part is very expensive. Although every laptop is different, the procedure for replacing the LCD display follows this generalization fairly closely. Basically, most times to replace the display a technician must completely disassemble the laptop, exposing the mounting screws for the display as well as the data connection to the motherboard (usually a ribbon cable). To replace the display, you must remove the display from its mounting mechanism, although some displays are actually orderable only as a complete top-half, including hinge, case, and support frame. Once you have removed the old display, simply install the new display in the reverse order you removed the old display.

Enabling Wireless Networking

As previously mentioned, wireless networking is a popular option these days. Most corporate networks are starting to use it for public areas and meeting spaces. In addition, many public spaces (like airports and malls) are incorporating it into their businesses so that traveling professionals can access the Internet from their wireless-equipped laptops.

There are different standards for Wireless networking, but the two most common are IEEE standards *802.11b* and *802.11g*. The 802.11b standard operates at either 1Mbps or 11Mbps over the 2.4GHz radio frequency band. The 802.11g standard operates on the same frequency band, but operates at 1Mbps, 11Mbps, and 54MBps (and is interoperable with the 802.11b equipment).

Essentially, wireless networking is a way to connect your laptop to a LAN without a wire. If your LAN is connected to the Internet, you can get Internet access within a small area like your home or office. In order to accomplish this, you need two pieces of equipment: a *wireless access point (AP)* and a wireless NIC (usually a PC Card, unless it's integrated into the laptop itself). You can also use a device known as a *wireless gateway* (also known as a *wireless router*) instead of a wireless access point. This device includes a simple router in addition to the wireless access point in a single enclosure. Typically, there are also a few (usually four or five) hub or switch ports. The benefit is that with one device, you can connect both wired and wireless computers together into a home network while at the same time connecting them all to the Internet.

The wireless AP is usually connected to your LAN with an Ethernet connection. Then, you install the wireless NIC's driver on your computer and plug in the PC Card. The NIC should connect automatically.

If you have security set up (such as Wired Equivalency Protocol [WEP]), then you need to make sure the settings on your access point and your wireless NIC match.

If the reception range on your PC Card isn't good, you can increase it by adding an external antenna. These are available from the PC Card's manufacturer (although not all PC Cards can use external antennae—check with the manufacturer to be sure).

Summary

In this chapter, you learned about the various laptop architecture and service issues that are on the A+ core exam. We discussed the primary differences between laptops and desktops, including the various components that make up a laptop and how they differ in appearance and function from those on a desktop.

You also learned how to install the components and peripherals that are found in laptops today, including storage, power systems, memory, input devices, expansion devices, displays, and wireless networking components. For each of these items, you learned a general method for installing the component. We also explained that because each brand of laptop is different, it is important to refer to the service manual for the proper procedure for replacing each item.

Key Terms

Before you take the exam, be certain you are familiar with the following terms:

802.11b	handheld PC (HPC)
802.11g	keyboard/mouse port
AC adapter	PC Card
case	PCMCIA
case frame	port replicator
clamshell design	portable computer
daughterboard	proprietary
DC adapter	tablet PC
desktop replacement laptops	touch screen
display	touchpad
docking port	Touchpoint
docking station	trackball
finger mouse	wireless access point (AP)

Review Questions

1. Which of the following is *not* a benefit of laptop design?

    A. Portability

    B. Increased performance

    C. Desktop replacement

    D. Higher-quality construction

2. Which laptop input device was released with the IBM Thinkpad series of laptops?

    A. Touchpad

    B. Touchball

    C. Touchpoint

    D. Touchway

3. Which laptop input device is a flat surface that you can draw on with your finger to control the mouse pointer?

    A. Touchpad

    B. Touchball

    C. Touchpoint

    D. Touchway

4. Which laptop accessory allows you to power your laptop from a car or airplane?

    A. AC adapter

    B. DC adapter

    C. Battery converter

    D. Automotive Wizard

5. _____ is used as an expansion method for external peripherals like mice, web cams, scanners, printers, and so on, and is popular on laptops and desktops alike.

    A. Parallel

    B. PS/2

    C. USB

    D. ATA

6. Which kind of laptop was designed to look and function like a paper notebook?

   A. Clamshell PC

   B. Tablet PC

   C. Paper PC

   D. Notebook PC

7. Which type of PC Card is used most often for expansion devices like NICs, sound cards, and so on?

   A. Type I

   B. Type II

   C. Type III

   D. Type IV

8. Which wireless IEEE standard operates on the 2.4GHz radio frequency and transmits data at a maximum of 11Mbps?

   A. 802.11b

   B. 802.11c

   C. 802.11e

   D. 802.11g

9. Which items are required in order to make a wireless 802.11b connection to a LAN? (Select all that apply.)

   A. Access point

   B. Wireless-approved computer

   C. Wireless NIC

   D. Wireless TCP/IP

10. PCMCIA expansion cards need which software in order to operate? (Select all that apply.)

   A. Cardmember Services

   B. PC Card Services

   C. Modem Services

   D. Socket Services

Answers to Review Questions

1. B. By and large, compromises always must be made when comparing laptops to desktops. Although laptops can be used as desktop replacements, their performance is almost always lower than comparably priced desktops.

2. C. The Touchpoint (a.k.a. finger mouse) was released with the IBM Thinkpad series of laptops.

3. A. The touchpad is a mousing surface built into the laptop. It allows you to use your finger to control the mouse pointer by drawing on the surface.

4. B. A DC adapter converts the DC output from a car or airplane accessory power plug into the voltages required by your laptop.

5. C. USB is used most often in laptops as an expansion bus for external peripherals. Although parallel and PS/2 allow for connection of external peripherals, they are not as flexible or widely used for expansion as USB.

6. B. The tablet PC is a notebook with a flip-around screen that allows a user to hold it like a large notebook and write notes directly on the screen with a special stylus.

7. B. A Type II PC Card is the type used most often for expansion devices like NICs, sound cards, SCSI controllers, modems, and so on.

8. A. The IEEE standard for 11Mbps wireless transmission over 2.4GHz radio is the 802.11b standard. The 802.11g standard has a maximum transmission speed of 54Mbps.

9. A, C. The wireless AP and wireless NIC are all that are required. You must have a computer, but there is no such thing as "wireless approved" (if there is, it's just a marketing term).

10. B, D. The PC Card architecture has two components. The first is the Socket Services software, and the second is the Card Services software.

Chapter

8

Upgrading PC Components

THE FOLLOWING OBJECTIVES ARE COVERED IN THIS CHAPTER:

- ✓ 1.8 Identify proper procedures for installing and configuring common peripheral devices. Choose the appropriate installation or configuration sequences in given scenarios.

- ✓ 1.10 Determine the issues that must be considered when upgrading a PC. In a given scenario, determine when and how to upgrade system components.

A home PC is not a static device. It is an ever-changing, ever-evolving electronic assistant. People are always expanding its capabilities and making it better than it was. There are two ways this is done: by performing upgrades and by adding peripherals. Upgrading a PC involves replacing components already found in the computer with newer, updated versions of those components (with new features). Adding peripherals simply involves adding new devices to a computer. Upgrading a PC by adding components causes the PC to grow beyond its original design limitations.

In this chapter, you will learn the types of items added to a PC to expand its capabilities and the methods used to add them. Let's start by learning about upgrades.

PC Upgrade Background

Soon after the first IBM PC was released, various manufacturers decided to get in on the PC's market success by releasing components that were better (and cheaper) than IBM's. These items could be installed by qualified technicians, although gradually, through the years, it has been conceded that the average user with basic mechanical skills can handle the procedures if the steps are simple enough.

The idea of an upgrade is simple: to replace a component in your computer with a better, faster, more reliable component that performs the same function. However, several things affect this process. Before you can upgrade, you must consider the three most important questions about upgrading:

- Why upgrade?

- Is an upgrade possible?

- What can be upgraded?

Let's ask these three questions of ourselves and find out why they are important.

Why Upgrade?

First, you must ask yourself, "Is an upgrade really necessary?" This question isn't as simple as it sounds. You may *want* an upgrade so that you can play the latest video game; however, you may not *need* an upgrade. Your computer will play the game, just not as well as you want it to.

Also, the answer to this question may be "No" if the cost of the new component you must buy to replace the old one is close to or more than the cost of a new computer with similar speeds and abilities. As your computer gets older, it doesn't necessarily get any slower (unless you have problems related to disks that are full or fragmented), but the new software you install requires more and more relative power to operate correctly. And, your computer may not be as fast as the computers the application was designed to run on, so you perceive that your computer is getting slower.

So, the longer you wait before trying to upgrade, the less likely it is that an upgrade is the right thing to do—primarily because you may have to upgrade more than one thing to get the new, upgraded component to work. At that point, the upgrade can quickly become expensive. Which brings us to the next question.

Is an Upgrade Possible?

When you're deciding whether to upgrade, this is a major question you must ask yourself before proceeding. Many times, the newer hardware and software you want to run aren't compatible with your existing hardware. For example, if you want to install a new, AGP-based video card to replace the older PCI card in your system that doesn't support the newest game you want to run, the prerequisites state that you must have an AGP port in your system that will support that card. If you don't have the proper AGP port on your system, you may have to upgrade your motherboard. If you do that, and your processor isn't supported by the newer motherboard, you have to replace it. This could go on until you essentially have a whole new computer. In this case, the upgrade is possible, but you may be back to the first question: Why upgrade?

Some issues that affect the possibility of an upgrade include:

Power Supply Output Capacity   Whenever you add a newer device to an older system, you must keep in mind the power requirements of the newer device and the output level of your power supply. If your system is already drawing the maximum power output from the power supply and you try to add a component that draws more power than the component it replaces, you could have major problems. At the very least, the new component won't function. But, more possibly, you could blow a fuse on the power supply or cause damage to the other components in the computer. Always calculate the power requirements of your system before you add a new component (especially components that draw more power, like video cards and disk drives). You can do this by adding the power requirements (in watts) of each component (they either are printed on the devices or can be obtained from the manufacturer). Make sure the power supply is able to put out at least 10 percent more than your existing system requires. Otherwise, you may have to buy a new power supply before you upgrade.

Memory Capacity and Characteristics   This particular requirement is necessary when you're upgrading to a new operating system (OS) or adding new memory to a system. First, you must ensure that you have enough memory to meet the requirements of any OS upgrade (the requirements are usually listed on the operating system's packaging or promotional materials). On the other hand, if you are upgrading the memory to more capacity or a different kind of memory, you must make sure the memory you are installing matches the motherboard. For example, if your motherboard uses RIMMs, you must make sure you are buying and installing RIMMs. Also, if you have a non-DDR motherboard and install DDR memory, don't expect it to work properly.

Processor Speed and Compatibility   If you need to upgrade the processor in your computer, you must make sure the processor you are adding is compatible with the motherboard. Processors and motherboards are designed together, and after some time, the processor and motherboard architectures change. Although it may be possible to change from, say, a Pentium III 450MHz to a Pentium III 550MHz (assuming the processor type is the same), it may not be possible to upgrade to a Pentium 4, because that processor uses a completely different processor socket and supporting motherboard circuitry.

Hard-Drive Capacity and Characteristics   If you are installing new software, you must ensure that you have enough hard disk space available for the new software. As mentioned earlier, the requirements for installation are located on the packaging of the software you want to install. However, if you are installing a new hard drive, make sure it is compatible with the hard-drive controller in your PC. For example, if you are installing a new ATA/133 hard drive, make sure the controller in your PC will support it. Otherwise, your system may not perform at optimum efficiency.

System/Firmware Limitations   These are the hardest things to check and predict. As you know, the BIOS controls which hardware is supported by the motherboard. Most times, the BIOS is forgiving about what can be installed. However, as new features are released, you may need to upgrade the software in your BIOS in order to support newer hardware. So, make sure your motherboard supports the component you are installing before you purchase it.

Bus Types and Characteristics   This particular requirement is fairly easy to meet. If you need to install an expansion card of any type, you must make sure the expansion card and the bus are compatible. For example, if you're installing an AGP video card to replace your old AGP video, be sure the new video is supported by the motherboard. Remember that there is more than one speed of AGP; newer motherboards might support 4x and 8x AGP, whereas older ones will not. The same is true with PCI and ISA. Whenever you are upgrading an expansion card, be sure your motherboard supports the expansion card you are installing.

See Chapter 2 for a detailed explanation of these bus types.

Drivers for Legacy Devices   If you are upgrading your OS, the most crucial thing to check is that new drivers are available for your older devices (often known as *legacy devices*). For example, Windows XP has support for some older hardware, like certain ISA expansion cards, but it has little or no support for 8-bit expansion cards—the motherboards that support them are too old to handle Windows XP, so the driver support was removed from the Windows XP CD-ROM. You must check with Microsoft to see if all your hardware is supported before upgrading the OS.

You can check the compatibility of Microsoft operating systems and hardware at the Windows Logo Program website: winqual.microsoft.com/download/default.asp. From this website, you can access the individual Hardware Compatibility Lists (HCLs) for each OS under the Browse list.

Cache in Relationship to Motherboards   With some motherboards, it may be possible to add or upgrade the cache memory on the board. However, the memory for these cache cards is very specialized and proprietary. Most often, the only cache memory that works on a motherboard is the cache from the motherboard's manufacturer. So, you must order the cache upgrade directly from the manufacturer (or one of its dealers).

What Can Be Upgraded?

Now that you understand most of the issues involved in upgrading, you must understand one more item: not everything in a computer can be upgraded. Some components are designed to *not* be upgraded, because they rely heavily on other components in the system and would cause problems if they were upgraded.

The following is a list of the most commonly upgraded items on a computer:

- Memory
- Hard disk
- CD-ROM (including DVD, CD-RW, and so on)
- Video card
- Motherboard
- CPU
- Power supply
- BIOS

This is by no means a comprehensive list, but you will notice a trend: All of these items are Field Replaceable Units (FRUs). That is, they are modules that are designed to be replaced at some point. So, the connections used to secure them to the computer and other components are temporary in nature.

On the other hand, some components are not designed to be upgraded. These components are usually subcomponents of the FRUs, and although many people would like to upgrade them, they aren't upgradeable without replacing the entire FRU:

- Chipset
- Onboard video circuits
- Onboard ports (parallel, LAN, mouse, and so on)
- Anything proprietary (designed only for that brand and model of computer)

The main thing to notice is that a component is upgradeable when:

- It can be removed and replaced
- A replacement is available that is better than the old component
- The new component is supported by the supporting hardware already in the computer
- The new component is supported by the current OS

Upgrading PC Components

Now that you have some background in upgrading PC components, it is time to begin discussing the methods of upgrading the various components of the PC. If you haven't already done so, please read Chapter 6, "Building a PC," before you continue. It is important to keep one thing in mind while reading this section: Essentially, an upgrade follows the same path as installing a component for the first time. The only difference is that you usually must remove an existing component first.

> Note that before you upgrade anything in your computer, you should do two things: document the current configuration (including cable positions, expansion-card locations, and so on) and power-down the system and unplug it. Documenting your system provides a reference for upgrading the component. Powering down the computer properly ensures that it won't be damaged when you install a new component.

In this section, you will learn about the various types of components that are typically upgraded within a PC as well as the methods used to upgrade them.

Upgrading the Motherboard

Although this is not done often, upgrading the motherboard is relatively easy. However, before you can begin, you must make sure the new motherboard and the other components in the system are compatible (as mentioned in the previous section). Also, make sure any peripheral in the system has a place to connect to the new motherboard. If it doesn't, you either need to choose a different motherboard or purchase an adapter card for that component. For example, if the motherboard you are upgrading has onboard video, then either the new board must have onboard video, or you must purchase a video card for the new motherboard.

To upgrade the motherboard, follow these steps:

1. Power down the system, unplug it, and remove any components or cables attached to it (be sure you document cable locations, expansion-card positions, and so on before removing them so you can put them back in the same location).

2. Remove any expansion cards from the system, cables connected to other peripherals, and the front panel button and light connectors. You can remove the processor, heatsink, and memory if you wish, but it will probably be easiest to remove them after the motherboard is removed from the computer case. Make sure anything that connects the motherboard to any other part of the computer has been disconnected.

3. You are ready to remove the motherboard from its mounting plate. The motherboard is held away from the metal case using plastic or brass spacers and is secured and grounded using mounting screws. To remove the motherboard, remove the screws holding the motherboard to the mounting brackets. Then, slide the motherboard to the side to release the spacers from their mounting holes in the case (see Figure 8.1).

FIGURE 8.1   Removing the motherboard

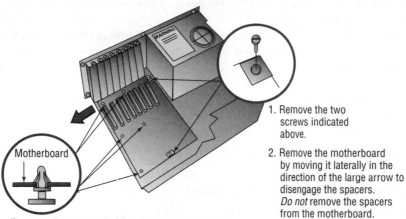

1. Remove the two screws indicated above.

2. Remove the motherboard by moving it laterally in the direction of the large arrow to disengage the spacers. *Do not* remove the spacers from the motherboard.

Motherboard

There are five spacers holding the motherboard off the case. A spacer is shown above, viewed from its side.

4.   Remove the new motherboard from its packaging and transfer the memory, CPU, and CPU heatsink from the old motherboard to the new motherboard (again, assuming they are compatible—if they aren't, you must purchase a compatible CPU and memory and install them).

> **NOTE**   While doing this, make sure you remove the old thermal compound from the heatsink and processor with isopropyl alcohol, and then install new thermal compound as discussed in Chapter 6. Thermal compound can't be reused.

5.   Check the motherboard mounting (standoff) locations and make sure they match up with the holes in the new motherboard. If necessary, you may have to change the positioning of the standoffs so the new motherboard can mount firmly in the case.

6.   Install the motherboard with the screws provided and the plastic standoffs.

7.   Reconnect all cables (including the power connector) and peripherals. You may have to check the motherboard for the locations of the connections for existing peripheral ports.

Upgrading the CPU

Occasionally, there may come a time when you need to upgrade your computer's CPU. You may want just a bit more performance, or you may want to go all out and get the latest possible processor. You need to understand one major issue before you upgrade your CPU: Generally speaking, you can't just remove your old processor and replace it with a different one. You must use a processor that matches the socket type and chipset speed, as mentioned in Chapter 2. This is the case because as processor architectures change, so do motherboard architectures, so that the new CPU will have the proper amount and type of supporting circuitry.

So, if you want to upgrade from a 1.8GHz Pentium 4 to a 1.9GHz Pentium 4, chances are good that it will work with no problems. However, if you want to upgrade from an AMD Thunderbird to a Pentium 4, you will have to replace the motherboard (and possibly the RAM as well) in order to make the upgrade successful—the AMD and the Pentium 4 use completely different architectures and require different motherboards and supporting circuitry.

To upgrade a processor, you simply need to remove the old CPU and heatsink and replace them with the new processor and heatsink. A new heatsink isn't absolutely necessary, but your new, faster processor will put out more heat than the one being replaced, so it's a good idea to upgrade them both at the same time. Besides, most CPUs come with a heatsink (assuming you're buying the processor in retail packaging). Follow these steps:

1. Shut down the computer and unplug it from the wall.

2. Remove the heatsink clamps holding the heatsink onto the processor. Then, disconnect the heatsink fan from the motherboard and gently remove the heatsink.

3. Lift up on the CPU retaining lever and lift out the processor.

4. Gently place the new CPU in the socket (making sure to orient the processor properly, as discussed in Chapter 6). Do NOT force the CPU into the socket. If aligned and placed properly, the CPU should simply drop into place.

5. Push down on the CPU retaining lever to secure the CPU.

6. Install the new heatsink according to manufacturer directions, including installing thermal compound (illustrated in Chapter 6).

7. Reconnect the heatsink fan and power up the system.

Upgrading Memory

There are two types of memory upgrades: more memory and faster memory. Adding more memory increases the performance of the computer because more of the OS and other files being worked on can be loaded at once. Replacing the existing memory with faster memory accomplishes the same goal. However, you must replace *all* the existing memory with faster memory, because one piece of slower memory will slow all the memory to the speed of the slowest chip.

Also, like the CPU, you need to make sure you first check the type of memory your motherboard supports and then use only that memory. Most often, stores that sell memory have a book or chart that can help you choose the right kind of memory to install. Or, you can go to the website of your motherboard's manufacturer, which should have a reference for the type of memory that goes in the system as well as how much memory can be installed into the system. Finally, you can look at the website of a major memory manufacturer, like Crucial (`www.crucial .com`) or Kingston (`www.kingston.com`). Their websites tell which of their products work with which motherboards or systems.

To replace memory with faster memory, you need to first order and receive the faster memory (memory speeds are discussed in Chapter 2). Then, shut down your computer and remove the existing memory by releasing the memory retainer clips (most often, you simply push down on them, and the memory stick will pop out). Finally, install the new memory as discussed in Chapter 6.

Upgrading Hard Drives/Storage

Adding storage to a computer is a popular upgrade, because people are always running out of storage in their computers. However, just as with the other items you are upgrading, it is extremely important that you check to see if your computer can use the type of drive you are installing and that the new storage device's interface is compatible with the disk interface on your motherboard (or on the expansion card). Remember that if you install a hard disk or other storage device (CD-ROM, DVD, tape drive, and so on) and it is faster than the interface it is connecting to, the new, faster device will only operate as fast as the slowest link in the chain (the onboard interface).

You must also ensure that you have enough space in the computer's case (an available drive bay) for the new storage device you are adding. If you are replacing an existing drive (which you won't do often, unless the drive completely fails), you must remove the drive from its mounting (see Figure 8.2).

FIGURE 8.2   Removing the hard drive

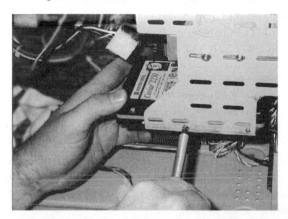

Many CD-ROM and other drives are installed in IBM-compatible computers with *rails* that are attached to the drives with screws. These rails allow you to slide the drives into the computer's drive bays like drawers. The drives are then secured with at least two screws on the sides. Many desktop computers (such as Compaqs, IBM PS/2s, and Hewlett-Packards) use a special drive carrier that holds the drive in place and can be easily removed without tools, thus eliminating the need for special rails. With most drives, however, you can just remove the mounting screws and slide the drive out. Consult the computer's (or case's) documentation to see exactly how to remove your specific type of drive.

To remove drives from higher-end computers, you should also consult the documentation. It is possible on many higher-end machines to swap drives while the computer is still running (this is known as a *hot-swap*); to prevent damage to the drive (or other components), you should know the correct procedure.

If you are adding a new drive, start by unplugging the computer. Then, locate an empty drive bay, set the Master/Slave/CS jumper accordingly (more than likely, set it to either Slave or CS if you have only one drive in the computer), mount the drive in the unused bay, connect the data cable to the drive and (if necessary) the motherboard, and connect the power. If you are installing a device like a CD-ROM, DVD, or other non-hard-disk drive, you may have to install OS drivers once you've got the drive physically installed.

> This procedure is also the second half of the drive-replacement procedure (except you set the new drive's jumpers the same as those on the drive you are replacing).

Upgrading the BIOS

The system *BIOS (basic input/output system)* is software (usually stored on a ROM chip) that contains all the code required to control the keyboard, display screen, disk drives, serial ports, and various other PC components. Basically, the BIOS determines what a computer can do without accessing any outside software.

Storing the BIOS on a ROM chip ensures that it will always be available and will not be damaged by disk failure. The problem is that ROM is usually much slower than RAM, so many systems copy the BIOS to RAM each time the computer boots (this is known as *shadowing*).

Because the BIOS determines what devices a computer can utilize before the OS loads, there might be times when you need to update the BIOS to support a new component. The most common reason to upgrade the BIOS is to support hard drives that are larger than the limit imposed by BIOS code. There are two ways to upgrade system BIOS: the old way and the new way.

The old way involves ordering a replacement BIOS chip, opening the computer, removing the old chip, and inserting the new one. In some ways, this is the least nerve-wracking method of upgrading, but you must be careful not to bend or break the connectors on the BIOS chip. You should also ensure that the chip isn't installed backward, because that can short out the chip (and possibly the motherboard).

Most modern computers store their BIOS on an *EEPROM (Electrically Erasable Programmable Read Only Memory)*. An EEPROM can be updated the new way: using flash software. In many ways, this method is more dangerous than the old-fashioned method of replacing a chip. Because the flash software overwrites the information on the chip, if you make a mistake, your computer can become unbootable. You need to follow the instructions very carefully!

> *Be careful when flashing the BIOS!* Most flash software packages include the ability to back up the current BIOS before flashing the chip. *Always* take advantage of this step before performing the flash process, *even if you have used the software before!* Also, do not assume that because two computers are the same make and model and were purchased at the same time, you can use the same backup as protection against errors for both machines. Manufacturers are constantly revising BIOS software. Perform the backup for every computer you update!

To update, or flash, your BIOS, you must perform the following steps:

1. Determine the current version of your BIOS. Most computers with nonproprietary motherboards display their BIOS type and version (and occasionally the date of the BIOS) during boot. The information may only display for a moment, so you must pay attention. You can also enter the BIOS setup utility and find it.

2. Download the latest version. Most motherboard manufacturers have a support website. Go to the support website for your motherboard and look for Downloads or BIOS Updates or something similar. Find the most current BIOS revision (usually they are listed by date and revision number) and download it. You may also have to download a BIOS update utility (like AFLASH.EXE) if it is not included in the BIOS download.

3. Create a boot floppy. Using your operating system's utility, create a boot floppy (as discussed in Chapter 13). Then, unzip both the BIOS update and the update utility to this floppy disk.

4. Boot to the floppy and back up your BIOS. Power down your computer, insert the boot floppy, and boot up to the floppy. Your screen should show an A:\> prompt. Type in the name of your flash utility executable (such as AFLASH.EXE) and press Enter to start the utility. The utility should prompt you to save a copy of your existing BIOS. You should do this in case the new BIOS is incompatible with some hardware, so you can always go back to an earlier version.

5. Flash the BIOS. Follow the instructions in the utility to start the flashing process. *Do not turn off the computer during this process!* The computer may appear to not respond (for example, it may just show a flashing cursor or similar), but it is really flashing the BIOS. If you turn off your computer during the process, you won't be able to boot the computer. If anything goes wrong during this process, you won't be able to boot the computer. The only way to fix a failed flash is to send the motherboard to the manufacturer to have the BIOS chip replaced (manufacturers generally won't send out the chip as a replacement part). Let the utility flash the BIOS until it says the flash is complete. Then, follow the instructions it gives you (this usually means rebooting).

6. Verify the new BIOS. Once the utility has completed, remove the floppy disk from the disk drive and reboot. You should see a new revision of the BIOS number on the boot screen. To be sure the flash was successful, enter the BIOS setup utility and double-check your settings.

7. Boot the computer. If all was successful, you should now be able to boot your computer.

Upgrading Expansion Cards

As mentioned in previous chapters, expansion cards add to the capabilities of the computer and are installed in expansion slots on the motherboard. The process for upgrading using expansion cards is basically the same for all types of slots (AGP, PCI, and so on). In this section, you will learn the procedures for upgrading an expansion card.

Just as with other types of components, it is critical to ensure that your motherboard will support the upgraded component. However, because expansion buses are designed to have some flexibility, this is less of a problem; their standards don't change nearly as fast as those for CPUs, chipsets, and memory.

If you are upgrading an expansion card, you must remove the old one first. To do this, power down the system, unplug it, and remove the computer's case cover. Once you have the case off, you will be able to see the inside of the computer. The next step in disassembly is to put on an antistatic wrist strap, plugging one end into the ground plug of an outlet. Removing expansion cards involves four major steps; to do this correctly, you need to follow these steps in order:

1. Remove any internal or external cables or connectors. (You should already have removed the external ones in the prerequisite steps.) When you are removing a cable or connector, use your pen and notepad to diagram their installed positions. Also, use the pen to make identifying marks on the cables to make sure they align correctly when reinstalled.

2. Remove any mounting screws that are holding the boards in place, and place the screws somewhere where they won't be lost. If you don't have an egg carton, you can put each screw back into its mounting hole as you remove each expansion board. Just be sure to screw them in all the way, not just a couple of turns.

3. Grasp the board by the top edge with both hands and *gently* rock it front to back (*not* side to side). Figure 8.3 clarifies this procedure. If the expansion board doesn't come out easily, don't force it. You may damage it. Check to see that the board is not being obstructed.

4. Once the board is out, place it in an antistatic bag to help prevent ESD damage while the board is out of the computer. Place the board aside and out of the way before you continue.

Be sure to note which slot the board came out of, because some bus types (EISA, MCA, and PCI) keep track of the slots in which expansion boards are installed.

FIGURE 8.3   Removing an expansion board

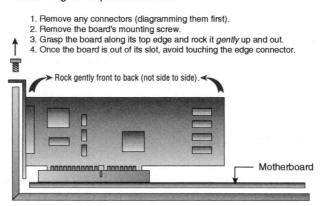

1. Remove any connectors (diagramming them first).
2. Remove the board's mounting screw.
3. Grasp the board along its top edge and rock it *gently* up and out.
4. Once the board is out of its slot, avoid touching the edge connector.

Rock gently front to back (not side to side).

Motherboard

Once again, many manufacturers have moved to a screwless design. IBM high-end servers, for instance, use a plastic tab to hold boards in place. This prevents a metal screw from falling into the case and shorting out the motherboard. If your computer still uses screws to secure expansion boards, keep a running count of the number of screws you have removed—and be sure you can account for every screw before you plug the power cord back in!

Once you have removed the old card, you can install the new card. Remove the new expansion card from its antistatic bag and install it as described in Chapter 6. Because there was a card in place already, all you need to do is insert the card into the slot the old card came out of. Push down on the card firmly until it seats in the bottom of the slot, and install the mounting screw. Then, you can replace the computer's case cover, reattach any cables, boot the computer, and install any updated drivers, if necessary.

Laptop Upgrades

As mentioned in Chapter 7, there aren't as many laptop upgrades as there are upgrades for desktop PCs. This is mainly due to the closed-design nature of laptops. However, you can change a few things on a laptop, like power sources, memory, hard drives, and PCMCIA cards. Let's take a look at these laptop upgrade items.

Laptop Power Sources

Laptops are designed to run on batteries. Even though they can run on wall-outlet power, the quality and run time of a battery is a key factor in deciding which laptop to buy. Essentially, to upgrade a battery you must first determine which kind of battery you have and whether your laptop will support a battery that either uses newer technology or has a higher capacity (longer run time). Then, simply remove the old battery and slide in the new one (this step usually involves moving a locking lever to release the old battery; the new battery will snap in). Currently, three main types of batteries are used in laptops:

Nickel Cadmium (NiCad)   Probably the most popular batteries for laptops today. They last approximately 700 charge cycles (a *charge cycle* is one cycle from full charge to complete discharge). These batteries hold a charge well, but they don't function well when overcharged or undercharged. They suffer from a problem known as the *memory effect*, which happens when a laptop battery is discharged partially, and then charged. The next time the battery is discharged, it doesn't last as long. Eventually, the battery gets so bad that it is unusable. Thankfully, NiCad batteries are relatively cheap to replace.

Nickel Metal Hydride (NiMH)   Much better than NiCad batteries for several reasons. They don't suffer from the memory effect, so they can be discharged partially many times without that problem. They are also made from nontoxic metals, so they are more environmentally friendly. NiMH batteries do provide about 10 percent more power than their NiCad counterparts, but they only last for about 400 charge cycles and they cost more as well.

Lithium Ion (LiON)   The latest technology in laptop batteries. They can't be overcharged, have a longer life than either of the other two types (about twice that of an equal-sized NiMH), and provide more power than the other two types. However, these batteries require that the laptop have special support circuitry, and they are more expensive than the other two. LiON batteries last for approximately 400 charge cycles.

Do not use LiON batteries in a laptop that isn't designed for them. Electrical shorts and possibly fire may result.

Fuel Cells

One topic that deserves special mention is the proposed use of fuel cells for laptop batteries. A *fuel cell* is a device that produces power from the electrochemical or catalytic breakdown of some chemical substance (usually hydrogen or a hydrocarbon), with water vapor as the only emission. Fuel cells have been used in the space program since the 1960s and are currently being researched for use in automobiles.

In laptop applications, their primary benefit is long runtime in a small package. Many hours are possible with fuel cells. Although they are a bit bulkier and costly to produce, the technology shows promise.

  Refer to www.smartfuelcell.de/en/index.html for more information on this topic.

Memory

Upgrading laptop memory is easy, as long as you get the proper memory for the your laptop. Your best bet for getting the right type of memory is to try the laptop manufacturer's support website first, because these sites usually have a list of upgrade options for particular laptops. Among them will be lists of compatible memory chip. You can also try memory manufacturers' websites (like www.crucial.com). They will have a utility that lists memory part numbers that are compatible with specific laptops.

The upgrade procedure is quite simple, but it varies slightly among laptop models and manufacturers. Usually, you must remove a small cover on the bottom of the laptop to expose the memory expansion slots (although sometimes they are accessed through other means—for example, they may be under the keyboard). Once the expansion slot(s) are exposed, release the locking tabs on the memory and remove the existing memory module. Then, insert the new module. If there is no module already in place, just insert the memory module.

Hard Drives

Upgrading a hard drive in a laptop isn't as easy as it is in a desktop computer. The concepts are basically the same: Remove the old hard drive and replace it with a new hard drive. The main difference is that laptop hard drives are much smaller than desktop hard drives. And, the laptop's hard drive usually is encased in a special carrier that allows the drive to slide in and out of the laptop, although this differs from model to model and manufacturer to manufacturer. Sometimes, this carrier is only a frame that is mounted to the inside of the laptop.

To upgrade the hard drive, follow these steps:

1. Power down the laptop, remove the battery, and unplug the AC adapter (if present).

2. Remove the hard-drive carrier from the laptop, using whatever means are necessary (it may be as simple a procedure as releasing a lever, or it may involve completely disassembling the laptop). In removing the carrier, you may have to disconnect the data/power cable. In some laptops, the hard drive is connected to the laptop by a small ribbon cable; in others, the

hard drive is cabled to the carrier, which uses its own proprietary cable. Remove the small screws holding the hard drive to the carrier and disconnect any cables holding it to the carrier.

3. Replace the hard drive and reconnect any cables. Secure the hard drive into the carrier and replace the carrier back into the laptop.

 You may have to format the hard drive after replacement. You may also need to reinstall an OS and replace the data.

PCMCIA Cards

In addition to replacing the battery, it is possible to upgrade the functions of a laptop by adding PCMCIA cards. As you learned in Chapter 7, these cards can be used to expand a laptop's capabilities. PCMCIA cards can be used to add a modem, NIC, video input/output, sound card, and many other capabilities to a laptop.

 Because PCMCIA cards were covered in detail in Chapter 7, we won't duplicate the information here.

Installing PCMCIA cards is a simple matter. Most often, you must install the card's software first, and then insert the card into an open PCMCIA expansion slot. If you need to upgrade, remove the card and insert the upgraded version. The PCMCIA standard hasn't changed much since its introduction, and most laptops support it by default.

Installing PC Peripherals

The other method of increasing the capabilities of a PC involves installing peripherals. A *peripheral* is a device that is not part of a PC, but is connected to the outside of the PC and increases its functionality. Examples of peripherals include modems, scanners, printers, digital cameras, PDAs, and so on. In this section, you will learn about the most common types of PC peripherals and how to connect them to a PC.

Installing Modems and Transceivers

Modems are devices used by computers to communicate over long distances. The word *modem* is a partial acronym; it stands for MOdulator-DEModulator. It got this name from the way it works. When a computer wants to send data, it uses a digital signal (fluctuations in voltage, representing 1s and 0s). The problem is that these signals can attenuate (decrease in strength) over long distances. For example, if you want to transmit the binary number 10110101 as a series of voltages, you might say to both computers, "A 1 is represented by a voltage of +5.0 volts; a 0 is any voltage less than that." If you try to transmit that number over a distance of only a few feet, +5.0 volts (representing the 1s) will still be +5.0 volts when it comes out the other end of the wire. However, if you try to transmit that same number over a distance of a mile or more, after the first few hundred feet, the +5.0 voltages might drop to 4.5 volts, which of course is below +5.0 volts. This voltage will get lower as the distance gets longer. When the signals get to the other end, the number will be 00000000, because *all* the voltages will be less than +5.0 volts.

Analog signals, on the other hand, don't suffer from this problem, because analog values are typically many values in a range, like sound waves. As a matter of fact, sound waves travel *very* well over long distances in wires. The sound waves are converted to pulses of voltages. Over long distances, the pulses get weaker, but the sound remains the same. It can be said, then, that analog signals are more reliable over longer distances.

Wouldn't it be great to have the best of both worlds? You can—with a modem. Modems convert digital signals into analog signals by using variations of tones to represent 1s and 0s (this is the MOdulation). The modem then sends these sounds over a phone line. At the other end, the tones are converted back into 1s and 0s (this is the DEModulation). Using two modems and a phone line, you transmit digital data through an analog medium.

The only downside to modems is that this process is relatively inefficient. Because modem communications are so sporadic, they use asynchronous communications, which have their overhead of start and stop bits. Also, today's phone lines are limited to a maximum throughput of 56Kbps.

Bits vs. Baud

The most confusing terms used to describe modem speed are *bits per second* (or *bps*) and *baud*. Actually, it's an easy distinction. The bps value of a modem is how much data is transmitted in one second. Baud is how many signal (tone) changes happen in one second. Through a process known as *encoding*, several bits can be transmitted using only a few signal changes. Modern phone lines are limited to 9600 baud. If you make the baud rate any higher, the modem on the other end starts to have difficulty distinguishing the individual tonal changes. However, with modern encoding techniques, it is possible to transmit up to 56Kbps with 9600 baud.

Many different types of modems are used today. Some of these devices, although called modems, are actually all-digital devices (they transmit information digitally, so the information is never translated into analog form). We'll make note of these devices as we talk about them.

Regular (a.k.a. Dial-Up) Modem

Many devices today are called modems, but the original is still just known as a *modem* (although for our purposes, we've designated it as the regular dial-up modem to differentiate it from the others we'll discuss). There are two types of regular dial-up modems: internal and external. Internal modems are installed as expansion cards inside a computer. External modems have their own power supplies and connect to an external COM port with an RS-232 cable. There are advantages and disadvantages to each.

Internal modems are usually smaller and cheaper than their external counterparts. They are expansion cards that can be installed into any open slot. However, they are more difficult to configure. You need to configure them to use an unused COM port (either through Windows, software, or other methods like jumpers). Table 8.1 lists the IRQ and I/O port addresses of the standard COM ports installed.

External modems use an existing serial port, so they don't have the configuration problem with IRQs and I/O addresses. However, they don't interface directly with the computer's expansion bus, so data transfers may be slowed (especially if the modem is faster than 9600bps). If this is the case, the serial port must use a higher-speed Universal Asynchronous Receiver/Transmitter (UART). The UART is the chip that manages the serial data that's moving in and out through the serial port. If the modem is 9600bps or faster, you need to use a 16-bit UART (for example, the 16450 or 16550 model). Most computers come with 16550 UARTs, so you don't have to worry about this. However, some older computers came with the 8-bit 8550 UART and may need to be upgraded.

TABLE 8.1   Standard COM Port and IRQ Addresses

COM Port	IRQ Address	I/O Address
COM 1	4	3F8-3FF
COM 2	3	2F8-2FF
COM 3	4	3E8-3EF
COM 4	3	2E8-2EF

 Real World Scenario

The Blinking Lights on the Modem...

An additional benefit of an external modem is that the status lights on the modem are visible. It's sometimes helpful to know when the modem has hung up or is transmitting data. Here's a quick guide to the common abbreviations found next to the lights on a modem:

OH   Off Hook. The modem is dialing or otherwise has the phone off the hook.

SD(TX)   Transmit Data. The modem is sending data.

RD(RX)   Receive Data. The modem is receiving data.

AA   Auto Answer. The modem is set to automatically pick up after a few rings.

Cable Modem

Another device that is known as a type of modem is the cable modem. A *cable modem* is used to connect computers and other devices to a cable television data network. Cable modem technology is one example of high-speed Internet access, also known as *broadband Internet access* (a.k.a. *broadband*). Because the cable company already has a cabled infrastructure in most cities, cable was a natural choice to bring high-speed Internet connections to homes. The cable television companies got together and developed the *Data Over Cable Service Interface Specification (DOCSIS)* that, among other things, specifies how to allow data services over a cable system. Most cable modems adhere to this standard.

Cable modems are simply small boxes that have a cable connection and a connection to the computer (as shown in Figure 8.4). There are two ways to connect a cable modem to a computer: USB and Ethernet (usually 10BaseT). Most cable modems can use either of these methods, and some modems have both types (as shown in Figure 8.4).

FIGURE 8.4   A cable modem's connections

If you are going to connect the cable modem via USB, simply install the software driver for the cable modem into the computer, and then plug in the cable modem. The computer will detect the modem and configure it automatically.

If you are using Ethernet to connect, you must have an Ethernet NIC in your computer that is properly installed and configured. Once the NIC is installed, all you need to do is connect the cable modem to the NIC with an appropriate 10BaseT Patch cable (RJ-45 connector on both ends—usually supplied with the cable modem).

 For more information on the DOCSIS specification and cable modem technology, visit www.cablemodem.com/.

DSL Modem

Another example of broadband communication is the *Digital Subscriber Line (DSL)*. DSL uses the existing phone wires between you and the phone company to deliver digital data services. Because the communications are all digital, the speed of the connection is significant. In addition, the digital signal and your voice signal from the telephone can co-exist (you can be on the Internet and still make and receive phone calls). However, this technology has limitations: You must be within a certain distance from the phone company central office, and the service is not available everywhere.

In the case of the DSL modem, the term *modem* is somewhat incorrect. Because the communications between computer and modem, and modem and central office, are all digital, no modulation/demodulation takes place—just simple signal translation. But, because it looks like a modem and functions somewhat like modem, most people call it a modem.

DSL modems are available in either internal or external versions. Both versions connect directly to a phone line (similar to the way a standard POTS modem connects). The modem then is connected to the PC via the internal expansion bus (if the modem is an internal DSL modem expansion card) or externally via either USB or Ethernet (the latter requires a NIC).

ISDN Modem

Integrated Services Digital Network (ISDN) was one of the first high-speed Internet connection methods that found its way into homes. In most cases, a connection of only 128Kbps was used, so the modem connected primarily through a serial port (although there were a few internal ISDN modems). However, because the speeds were slower than DSL or cable and the cost was much greater (for the basic service rates), ISDN has quickly become the follower rather than the leader in the broadband market.

Adding External Storage

As mentioned in previous chapters, there are methods of connecting storage to a computer that do not involve removing the case cover. In fact, many popular storage devices that connect (usually via USB or SCSI) to a computer can be moved from PC to PC. *External storage* means that the storage drive and media are outside the computer and that the drive is physically attached to the computer.

Many types of external drives can be used, including external hard drives, CD-ROM/DVD/CD-RW drives, tape backup devices, and storage arrays. Essentially, they all connect to an interface, either SCSI or USB. For the most part, the process is the same: connect the cable to the device and the computer, and then install the software on the host computer.

Connecting Scanners and Digital Cameras

In addition to using keyboards and pointing devices, there is another common method of getting data into a computer. The *charge-coupled device (CCD)* converts light (and shades of light) into electrical pulses. This technology opened the arena to allow a new breed of devices to input data to a computer. The largest classes of these devices are scanners and digital cameras.

Optical Scanners

Optical scanners (their full name) use CCDs and a light source to convert pictures into a stream of data. Figure 8.5 shows an example of a scanner.

FIGURE 8.5   A flatbed scanner

Scanners can be connected to the computer in several ways, but the three most commonly used are SCSI, parallel, and USB. SCSI scanners require a SCSI interface in the computer and connect to the PC using a SCSI cable. This connection must follow all the rules regarding SCSI bus connections, bus lengths, and termination. (Chapter 3 discusses SCSI connections, so we won't reiterate the information here.)

Scanners that connect to the parallel port use a special bidirectional parallel cable that comes with the scanner. These scanners usually require that the parallel port and cable support bidirectional communications in order to function properly.

Most scanners today connect to a PC using a USB cable. This method is the easiest connection, because it follows the same connection procedure as other USB peripherals. Simply install the scanner software that comes with the scanner. Then, with the computer on, plug the scanner's USB cable into an available USB port on the host PC. The PC will recognize the scanner and automatically install and configure it.

Digital Cameras

Digital cameras use CCDs, lenses, and natural light sources to take pictures of objects, much as a standard camera works. However, in a digital camera, the CCD replaces the film and records the picture as a pattern of bits. Figure 8.6 shows an example of a digital camera.

Most digital cameras use a USB connection and are connected in almost the same way as scanners and other USB peripherals. However, most digital cameras include software that allows you to pick which pictures you would like to download, so you only download the pictures you want to keep.

FIGURE 8.6   A digital camera

PDAs

Personal Digital Assistants (PDAs) such as the Palm handheld, Compaq iPAQ, and other pocket PCs can be considered computing devices by themselves and not so much peripherals. However, they are peripherals for a PC to the extent that they allow PC data to be transferred to them and carried with the owner. As such, PDAs require proper installation and configuration to the PC.

The PDA must have a method of connecting to the host PC. Most often, this is done with either serial or USB (although, as previously mentioned, some use infrared).

Software or a driver must also be installed on the host PC to facilitate the transfer of information between PDA and host PC. In the case of the Palm, a piece of software known as the *Palm Desktop* functions as a repository for the Palm data on the PC. Additionally, pieces of software known as *conduits* facilitate the communication between software on the PC (like Microsoft Outlook) and the applications on a PDA. Conduits direct information from the host PC's application to the PDA and vise versa.

Installing Wireless Access Points

If you are going to use wireless networking with your computer, you will need to install a wireless access point (an example of which is shown in Figure 8.7). The *wireless access point (AP)* is the device that allows wireless devices to talk to each other and the network. It provides the functions of network access as well as security monitoring.

The AP is a simple device. It forms a bridge between the wireless devices and the wired network. It provides the central point from which the wireless devices gain access to the physical network. The AP can also provide security, through the use of encryption and other wireless security methods.

FIGURE 8.7   A wireless access point

In order to connect an AP, you connect the antennas to the AP, connect the AP to the LAN with a network cable, and power up the AP. At this point, wireless devices can connect. You may need to configure the AP further in order to set up authentication and security. However, each AP uses a different method for this, so check the documentation for your AP.

Using Infrared Devices

As you learned in previous chapters, infrared devices are wireless devices that communicate using the infrared radiation spectrum. Most infrared devices require little installation. Because there is no cable, these devices may only need software. For example, if you want to configure your computer to talk to your Palm handheld (assuming that your computer already has an infrared interface installed and configured properly), all you need to do is tell the Palm Desktop software that instead of communicating via a cabled method like serial or USB, you'd like to communicate with your Palm via an infrared connection.

Connecting Printers

Almost every computer today has a printer. Most people consider a printer a necessity in order to be able to see the work they are doing on the computer put onto paper.

Whether you are using a dot matrix, ink-jet, laser, or other type of printer, the connection process is usually the same: Connect the printer using the supplied cable, and then install the printer driver on the computer. That is true with serial- and parallel-based printers (however, you must have the appropriate cable for the printer to work properly).

With printers that use USB interfaces, however, it is best to perform those steps in the opposite order. First install the printer software that comes with the printer. Then, with both the printer and the PC powered up, connect the cable. The PC will recognize that the printer has been attached and automatically configure the USB connection.

Printers with network interfaces are just plugged into the network. The only thing you need to do on the individual PCs is to configure the printer driver with the network address of the printer and make sure the PC can connect to the network (and thus, the printer).

UPSs (Uninterruptible Power Supplies) and Suppressors

Unfortunately, it's rare for the power that comes out of the wall (what we normally call *line power*) to be consistently 110V, 60Hz. It may be of a slightly higher or lower voltage, it may cycle faster or slower, there may occasionally be no power, or (the worst) a 5000V spike may come down the power line from a lightning strike and fry the expensive electronic components of your computer and its peripherals. That is why there are specialized devices like the uninterruptible power supply (UPS) and surge suppressors. Before we discuss them, you must learn about the power problems these devices were designed to solve.

Technicians have to deal with three main classes of power problems: power quality problems, problems where too much power is coming out of the wall, and problems where there is not enough power. Almost every outlet has at least one of these problems. Let's examine each of these problems in detail.

Power Quality Problems and Solutions

The first type of power problem exists when the power coming out of the wall has a different frequency than normal (60Hz is considered "normal"). This type of problem manifests itself when stray electromagnetic signals are introduced into the line. This *electromagnetic interference (EMI)* is usually caused by the electromagnetic waves emitted by the electric motors in appliances. Additionally, televisions and other electronic devices (including computers) can produce a different type of interference, called *radio frequency interference (RFI)*, which is really just a higher-frequency version of EMI. If your power lines run near a powerful radio broadcast antenna or factory, it can also introduce noise into your power.

To solve these problems, companies like BEST Power Systems and APC make accessories called *line conditioners*. The function of these devices is to produce "perfect" power of 110V/60Hz. Line conditioners remove most of the stray EMI and RFI signals from the incoming power. They also reduce any power overages to 110V.

Power Overage Problems and Solutions

The most common type of power problem that causes computer damage is power overages. As the name suggests, these problems happen when too much power comes down the power lines. There are two main types of overage problems: spikes and surges. The primary difference between the two is the length of time the events last. A *spike* is a power overage condition that exists for an extremely short period of time (a few milliseconds at most). *Surges*, on the other hand, last much longer (up to several seconds). Spikes are usually the result of faulty power transformer equipment at power substations. Surges can come from both power equipment and lightning strikes.

A common misconception is that a power strip can protect your computer from power overage problems. Most power strips (the ones that cost less than $15.00) are nothing more than multiple outlets with a circuit breaker. There are real surge protectors, but they usually cost upward of $25.00. These devices have MOSFET (Metal Oxide Semiconductor Field Effect Transistor) semiconductors that sacrifice themselves in the case of a power overage. But even these aren't perfect. They are rated in terms of clamping speed (how long it takes to go from the overvoltage to zero volts) and clamping voltage (at what voltage the MOSFET shorts out). The problem is that by the time the clamping voltage is reached, some of the overvoltage has gotten through to the power supply and damaged it. After a time, the power supply will be damaged permanently.

Realistically, having a surge protector is better than not having one, but not much. It's better to use a line conditioner that can absorb the overvoltage than to use a circuit breaker.

Undervoltage Power Problems and Solutions

Undervoltage problems usually don't damage hardware. More often, they cause the computer to shut down completely (or at the very least, to reboot), thus losing any unsaved data in memory. There are three major types of undervoltage problems: sags, brownouts, and blackouts.

A *sag* is a momentary drop in voltage, lasting only a few milliseconds. Usually, you can't even tell one has occurred. Your house lights won't dim or flicker (actually, they will, but it's too fast for you to notice). But your computer will react strangely to this sudden drop in power. Have you ever been on the up side of a seesaw and had someone jump off the other end? You were surprised at the sudden drop, weren't you? Your computer experiences the same kind of disorientation when the power drops suddenly to a lower voltage. A computer's normal response to this kind of disorientation is to reboot itself.

You've probably experienced one of the other two power undervoltage problems: brownouts and blackouts. A *brownout* occurs when voltage drops below 110V for a second or more. Brownouts are typically caused by an immediate increase in power consumption in your area and the lag time it takes for your power provider to respond by increasing production. You might notice when brownouts occur, because the lights in your home will dim, but not go out, and then go back to full brightness a second or two later. You might also notice because your computer will reboot or the screen will flicker. (While writing this section, I have counted two brownouts. Luckily, my computer hasn't rebooted, so the voltage drop probably wasn't too bad.)

Everyone has experienced a blackout. A *blackout* occurs when the power drops from 110V to 0V in a very short period of time. It is a complete loss of power for anywhere from a few seconds to several minutes (or more). Blackouts are typically caused by a power failure somewhere in your area. Sometimes backup systems are available, but it may take anywhere from a couple of seconds to several hours to get power available in your area again.

There are two different hardware solutions to power undervoltage conditions: the SPS and the UPS. Each takes a different approach to keeping the power at 110V. In both cases, you plug the units into the wall, and then plug your computer equipment into the SPS or UPS. Let's look at the SPS first. SPS stands for *standby power supply*. It's called that because a battery is waiting to take over power production in case of a loss of line voltage. The SPS contains sensors that constantly monitor the line voltage and a battery with a step-up transformer. While conditions are normal, the line voltage charges the internal battery. When the line voltage drops below a preset threshold (also called the *cutover* threshold—for example, 105V), the sensors detect it and switch the power from the wall to the internal battery. When the power comes back above the threshold, the sensors detect the restoration of power and switch the power source back to the line voltage.

The main problem with SPSs is that they take a few milliseconds to switch to the battery. During those few milliseconds, there is *no* voltage to the computer. This lack of voltage can cause reboots or crashes (rather like a brownout). An SPS is great for preventing blackouts, but it does little for brownouts and sags.

The better choice for undervoltage problems is the *uninterruptible power supply* (UPS). The UPS works similarly to an SPS, but with one important difference: The computer equipment is always running off the battery. While the line voltage is normal, the battery gets charged. When power fluctuates, only the charging circuit is affected. The battery continues to provide power to the equipment uninterrupted. Because the equipment is constantly operating off the battery, the UPS also acts as a kind of line conditioner.

There is one primary problem with UPSs: the quality of power they provide. Batteries provide DC power, and computer power supplies run on AC power. Inside the UPS is a power inverter that converts the DC into AC. It isn't perfect. AC power produces a 60Hz sine waveform, whereas the inverter produces a square wave. A computer's power supply will accept these square waveforms, but it doesn't like them (see Figure 8.8). To help with this problem, UPS manufacturers are using more sensitive inverters that can more closely approximate the sine wave. So, a UPS should be put on every piece of computer equipment where data loss would be a problem (in other words, almost every piece of computer equipment).

FIGURE 8.8   A comparison between line power and UPS-supplied power

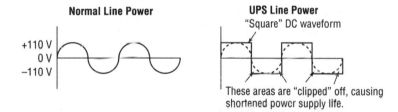

 Never plug a laser printer or copier into a UPS! The large surge of power they draw when they are first turned on (close to 15 amps) can burn out the inverter and battery.

Power System Testing

Since your computer needs power to function, and you are taking steps to provide consistent, clean power to your computer, it is imperative from a preventative maintenance standpoint to test those power systems (e.g., UPSes and surge suppressors) once a month. Most UPSes include a Test button, which will test the power-failure detection circuitry. If your UPS doesn't include one of these buttons, you could pull the power cord out of the wall, simulating a blackout, but that could be dangerous (sparks and other dangers).

Surge suppressors aren't as easily tested, although some suppressors have built-in circuit breakers that can be tested. You'll know if you have one of these because there will be both a Test and a Reset button, similar to GFCI outlets you might have in your kitchen and bathroom. To test, press the Test button. If successful, the circuit breaker will trip. Reset it by pushing the Reset button.

It is best not to do these tests on a system performing critical tasks. Perform tests at night or during low-usage periods. In a UPS test, power might be interrupted, but in a surge suppressor test, if successful, power will be interrupted and the computer might lose data.

Upgrading Monitors

As we have already mentioned, a monitor contains a CRT. But how does it work? Basically, a device called an *electron gun* shoots electrons toward the back side of the monitor screen (see Figure 8.9). The back of the screen is coated with special chemicals (called *phosphors*) that glow when electrons strike them. This beam of electrons scans across the monitor from left to right and top to bottom to create the image.

There are two ways to measure a monitor's image quality: dot pitch and refresh (scan) rate. A monitor's *dot pitch* is the shortest distance between two dots of the same color on the monitor. Usually given in fractions of a millimeter (mm), it tells how sharp the picture is. The lower the number, the closer together the pixels are, and thus the sharper the image. An average dot pitch is 0.28mm. Anything smaller than 0.28mm is considered great.

FIGURE 8.9   How a monitor works

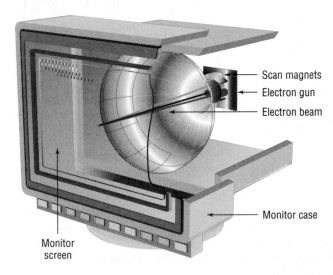

A monitor's *refresh rate* (technically called the *vertical scan frequency*) specifies how many times in one second the scanning beam of electrons redraws the screen. The phosphors stay bright for only a fraction of a second, so they must constantly be hit with electrons to stay lit. Given in draws per second, or Hertz, the refresh rate specifies how much energy is being put into keeping the screen lit. The standard refresh rate is 60Hz for VGA. However, some monitors have a refresh rate of 72Hz, which is much easier on the eyes (less flicker is perceived).

One note about monitors that may seem rather obvious: When you're upgrading from one monitor to another, or buying a new monitor, you must use a video card that supports the type of monitor you are using. For example, you can't use a CGA monitor on a VGA adapter. This includes LCD technologies, because not all LCD displays are supported by some video cards. Also, some LCD displays use a digital connection, which requires a video card that supports a digital LCD output.

To use a 72Hz monitor, your video card must support the 72Hz refresh rate. Most video cards sold today support this faster 72Hz refresh rate but are configured as 60Hz out of the box. If you intend to use the 72Hz rate (or higher rates), you must configure the card to do so. Check the documentation that came with the card for details on how to configure it. If you are running Windows, this is usually accomplished through the Advanced tab of the Display control panel.

If you are using a video switchbox to switch between two monitors of differing refresh rates, you may have problems with the signal quality. Be careful, and make sure your switchbox supports switching between different resolutions and qualities.

Summary

In this chapter, you learned about the various types of upgrades available for a PC. You also learned how to install those upgrades. Where appropriate, we explained what you need to check for compatibility before doing an upgrade.

You also learned about the different kinds of peripherals available for computers today and the various methods used to install them. We described what these peripherals do and how they enhance the functionality of the average PC.

Key Terms

Before you take the exam, be certain you are familiar with the following terms:

BIOS (basic input/output system)

blackout

broadband Internet access (a.k.a. broadband)

brownout

cable modem

charge-coupled device (CCD)

conduits

cutover

Data Over Cable Service Interface Specification (DOCSIS)

digital camera

Digital Subscriber Line (DSL)

dot pitch

electromagnetic interference (EMI)

electron gun

fuel cell

Integrated Services Digital Network (ISDN)

line conditioner

line power

memory effect

optical scanner

peripheral

Personal Digital Assistants (PDAs)

refresh rate

sag

spike

standby power supply

surge

uninterruptible power supply

wireless access point (AP)

Review Questions

1. Which of the following are the most important to consider when installing new expansion cards? (Select all that apply.)

A. ESD effects

B. Capacity of the hard disk

C. Position of expansion cards

D. Removing the cover

2. Which of the following is *not* a factor to consider when upgrading an expansion card

A. Available expansion slot

B. Compatibility with system memory

C. Updated drivers

D. Motherboard slot type

3. Which type of laptop battery type lasts the longest (can withstand the most charge cycles)?

A. NiCad

B. LiON

C. NiMH

D. Alkaline

4. The _____ is the distance between two pixels in a monitor.

A. Line pitch

B. Dot resolution

C. Dot pitch

D. Dot size

5. _____ is the specification used by cable providers to provide Internet services over cable television cable.

A. TCP/IP

B. OPENGL

C. CABLEMODEM

D. DOCSIS

6. At this time, *legacy* could correctly be used to refer to which types of expansion cards? (Select all that apply.)

A. 8-bit

B. ISA

C. MCA

D. All of the above

7. _____ indicates how fast the monitor redraws the screen.

A. Dot pitch

B. Refresh rate

C. Refresh signal

D. Hertz

8. Which of the following statements about flashing the BIOS is *false*?

A. You cannot recover from a failed BIOS flash.

B. Some kind of flashing utility is required.

C. A BIOS backup is not necessary.

D. The BIOS can be downloaded from the motherboard's support website.

9. Where can you find the type of memory that can be installed into your motherboard? (Select all that apply.)

A. Written on the motherboard

B. Motherboard manual

C. Motherboard manufacturer's support website

D. Memory manufacturer's website

10. Place the following options in order. The correct sequence in removing expansion cards is:

1. Once the board is out, place it in an antistatic bag to help prevent ESD damage.

2. Grasp the board by the top edge with both hands and rock it front to back.

3. Remove any mounting screws that are holding the board in place and place the screws somewhere where they won't be lost.

4. Remove any internal or external cables or connectors.

A. 4, 3, 2, 1

B. 1, 2, 3, 4

C. 2, 4, 3, 1

D. 2, 3, 1, 4

11. What was the original name for a monitor?

    A. Video Display Unit

    B. CRT

    C. LCD

    D. Optical Display Unit

12. Which power device would be best to attach to your computer if you were having undervoltage power problems?

    A. Surge protector

    B. UPS

    C. Line conditioner

    D. SPS

13. Which of the following steps are *not* required when removing the motherboard? (Select all that apply.)

    A. After removing the screws, remove the motherboard from the case because of ESD discharge.

    B. Remove the screws holding the motherboard to the mounting brackets.

    C. Slide the motherboard to the side to release the spacers from their mounting holes in the case.

    D. Ensuring that you are properly grounded, remove the motherboard and place in a static-free environment.

14. Which of the following is *not* a prerequisite to disassembling a computer?

    A. Disconnecting the power cable

    B. Shutting down the computer

    C. Disconnecting the monitor and keyboard cables

    D. Disassembling the power supply

16. The installation of a new replacement component follows all of these steps except
_____.

    A. Determining the available resources

    B. Configuring the new device

    C. Installing the component and its supporting software

    D. Turning on the computer and letting it run

16. What two connections must be made when installing a wireless AP?

    A. Power

    B. LAN

    C. Wireless

    D. WAN

17. Which of the following can be upgraded by replacing only those components? (Select all that apply.)

    A. Chipset

    B. Video card

    C. Video circuits on the motherboard

    D. Hard disk

18. What is the voltage of line voltage?

    A. 110V

    B. 12V

    C. 5V

    D. 3.3V

19. Which power problem is an overvoltage condition that lasts for up to several seconds?

    A. Spike

    B. Surge

    C. Sag

    D. Blackout

20. Which power problem is an undervoltage condition that results in the complete loss of power?

    A. Spike

    B. Surge

    C. Sag

    D. Blackout

Answers to Review Questions

1. A, C.   Whenever you remove expansion cards, ESD effects should be foremost in your mind. Therefore, always remember your ESD wrist strap. Some buses will remember the slot a particular card was in. Therefore, if you will be replacing it (either with itself or a new card), you should write down which slot it came out of so you can put the replacement in the same slot.

2. B.   Although most cards interact with memory at some level, the replacement card's compatibility with memory is not an issue.

3. A.   Nickel Cadmium (NiCad) batteries last the longest in terms of the number of charge cycles they can withstand (700, versus 400 for the other types).

4. C.   The dot pitch is a measurement of the quality of a monitor and is indicated by the distance between two pixels.

5. D.   The Data Over Cable System Interface Specification (DOCSIS) specifies how cable modems are used to connect home computers to the cable television network.

6. D.   *Legacy* is generally used as a term to describe older technology. Therefore, it could correctly be used to refer to 8-bit, ISA, and MCA expansion cards.

7. B.   The refresh rate is the number of times per second the screen is redrawn by the monitor.

8. C.   You should always perform a BIOS backup so that in case of an incompatibility, you can roll back the BIOS to its previous version.

9. B, C, D.   These methods are proper ways of determining which kind of memory can be installed in your computer.

10. A.   The correct sequence for removing the expansion cards is:

1. Remove any internal or external cables or connectors.

2. Remove any mounting screws that are holding the board in place and place the screws somewhere where they won't be lost.

3. Grasp the board by the top edge with both hands and rock it front to back.

4. Once the board is out, place it in an antistatic bag to help prevent ESD damage.

11. B.   Cathode ray tube (CRT) was the original name for a monitor.

12. B.   The best choice for undervoltage problems is the UPS. The computer equipment is always running off the battery. While the line voltage is normal, the battery gets charged. When power fluctuates, only the charging circuit is affected.

13. A.   After removing the screws, you should never remove the motherboard from the case because of ESD discharge. If you need to remove the motherboard (due to a replacement or upgrade situation), it will be necessary to remove the original motherboard so the new one may be installed.

14. D. The step that is *not* a prerequisite to disassembling a computer is disassembling the power supply. Only a service technician who has been specially trained to operate on power supplies should attempt to disassemble one. This is due to the fact that many components can be fatally dangerous to an unknowing technician.

15. D. You will have to turn on the computer and use it sooner or later, but once you get to this point you have completed the installation process (and have moved to the testing and maintenance process).

16. A, B. Wireless APs require connections to the LAN and to power. Connections to a WAN are optional and are usually done through a router first.

17. B, D. Even though you could replace the chipset and the video circuits on the motherboard by replacing the motherboard, we are talking about upgrading by replacing *only* those components listed. The only Field Replaceable Units (FRUs) are the video card and the hard disk, because each can be removed and replaced as a whole unit.

18. A. Line voltage is the power that comes out of the wall, or house current: 110 volts AC.

19. B. A surge is a momentary increase in power level that lasts for several seconds (a spike lasts only for a millisecond or two, up to a second).

20. D. A blackout happens when all power is completely lost for a significant amount of time.

Chapter

9

Optimizing PC Performance, Preventative Maintenance, and Safety

---

THE FOLLOWING OBJECTIVES ARE COVERED IN THIS CHAPTER:

- ✓ 1.9 Identify procedures to optimize PC operations in specific situations. Predict the effects of specific procedures under given scenarios.

- ✓ 3.1 Identify the various types of preventive maintenance measures, products and procedures and when and how to use them.

- ✓ 3.2 Identify various safety measures and procedures, and when/how to use them.

- ✓ 3.3 Identify environmental protection measures and procedures, and when/how to use them.

We've all experienced it. You buy a new computer, and it runs great. Then, after nine months to a year, you buy and install a new piece of software, and your computer won't run it properly. Or, your computer just seems to keep getting slower and slower. You begin to get frustrated and wonder why this computer, which is supposed to be so intelligent, can't seem to run right.

Over time, most computers experience degraded performance. The problem is not usually the fault of the computer, but of the basic nature of the computer industry. When a new piece of hardware comes out, it runs current software very quickly. Then, software vendors write newer software that runs better with the newer hardware. People with older hardware want to run the newer, better software, so they try it on their older hardware and it doesn't work properly. So, they must either buy a new computer or upgrade their older computer so that it can run the newer software.

In this chapter, you will learn about the various methods to optimize PC performance. You will also learn about the methods used to prevent problems before they occur as well as how to keep your PC's existing configuration running properly. Finally, you will learn about the methods used to maintain safety.

Optimizing PC Performance

Optimizing a PC's performance means making it operate as efficiently as it can. It can also mean making the PC run faster, making it more stable, or both; or enhancing the performance of the PC by adding updated components.

People have become obsessed with computer performance. They are always trying to squeeze the last possible megahertz out of their processor or make the entire system run as fast as possible. This pursuit has become like hot-rodding for the geek generation. In this section, you will learn about some of the common methods used to optimize PC performance.

Cooling System Optimization

PCs turn electrical energy into work and heat. The more performance we try to squeeze out of PCs today, the more transistors must be used in the same space, and thus the more heat that is generated. All this heat must go somewhere. Usually, the ambient air inside the case is cooler than the components, so some heat transfer occurs. For quite some time, PCs have had heatsinks to cool the hottest components (usually the CPU, chipset, and video processor on the video card).

In this section, you will learn about the various methods of improving a PC's cooling performance. There are two primary methods of improving cooling system performance: air cooling and water cooling. Let's take a brief look at each of these.

Air Cooling

There are two main ways to improve a PC's air cooling performance: increase airflow over a heatsink by adding more or bigger fans, or increase heat transfer by boosting the performance of the heatsinks. The first method is the easiest for people to implement. By adding more fans (using the ideal airflow diagram found in Chapter 6, "Building a PC"), you can bring more cool air to the heatsinks that need it.

Fans are rated by the amount of air they can move in a minute (cubic feet per minute [CFM]). If you want to increase the cooling performance of your system, either add more fans to bring air in and out of the case, or replace the existing fans with fans rated at a higher CFM. Be warned, however, that fans with higher CFM rates tend to be noisier. People say that some extremely cooled systems sound like jet engines!

The other alternative is to increase the efficiency of the heatsinks in the system. You can do this by getting a bigger heatsink, or one with more surface area (more fins or larger fins). You can also install a heatsink made of a better heat-conducting material, such as a copper-aluminum combination.

 For information about high-performance heatsinks, check out Zalman Tech cooling products at http://www.zalman.co.kr/english/intro.htm.

Another way of increasing the efficiency (even if only slightly) is to use a different thermal compound. As you learned in Chapter 6, a thermal compound increases the efficiency of heat transfer by increasing the contact area between the CPU and the heatsink. By using a different thermal compound, you can decrease the temperature by as much as 5°C. Arctic Silver thermal compound (www.arcticsilver.com) is one brand of such compounds. The company's newest product, Arctic Silver 3, is made of ultrafine silver particles suspended in a mix of polysynthetic oils. It does seem to work better than standard thermal compounds.

Liquid Cooling

Liquid cooling is a new trend in PC cooling. As discussed in earlier chapters, liquid cooling is a technology whereby a water block is used to conduct heat away from the processor (as well as chipsets). Water is circulated through this block to a radiator, where it is cooled.

The theory is that you can achieve better cooling performance through the use of this technology. For the most part, this is true. However, with traditional cooling methods (air and water), the lowest temperature you can achieve is room temperature. Plus, with liquid cooling, the pump is submerged in the coolant (generally speaking), so as it works it produces heat—which adds to the overall system temperature.

The main benefit of liquid cooling is silence. Only one fan is needed: the fan on the radiator to cool the water. So, a liquid-cooled system can run extremely quietly.

Liquid cooling, while more efficient than air cooling and much quieter, has its drawbacks. Most liquid cooling systems start at around $100 (although the price is always coming down); that price includes reservoir, pump, water block(s), hose, and radiator. Air cooling systems are usually cheaper, although if you are really into cooling performance, the total price of all your fans and heatsinks could easily add up to more than $100. In addition to the price, the other drawback is the possibility of a leak. Water and electronic components don't mix. Thankfully, most water cooling systems use quality hose and clamps and leaks are extremely rare.

Phase Change Cooling

A new type of PC cooling is just beginning to be used: *phase change cooling*. The cooling effect from a liquid changing to a gas is used to cool the inside of a PC. This cooling method is very expensive, but it works. Most often, external air conditioner–like pumps, coils, and evaporators cool the coolant, which is sent—ice cold—to the heatsinks on the processor and chipset. Think of it as a water cooling system that chills the water below room temperature. Using this technology, it is possible to get CPU temperatures in the range of –20°C (normal CPU temps hover between 40°C and 50°C).

Disk Subsystem Enhancements

Disk subsystem enhancements can also be used to increase your PC's overall performance. By increasing the speed at which information is obtained for the storage disks, you can increase your overall performance—usually the disk system is the performance bottleneck, not the other items in the system.

One thing you can do to increase overall speed is to increase the number of hard drives in the system and connect them in a RAID 0 configuration (see Chapter 3, "Disk Drive Storage," for an explanation of the different RAID levels). Doing so will increases raw performance only, not reliability. You may want to use RAID 5 instead, to provide a measure of redundancy.

Another thing you can do is to change your disk system to a higher performance interface. If you are using ATA-66 as your hard drive interface, upgrade your interface to ATA-100, ATA-133, or Serial ATA by installing a new interface expansion card and drives that support the new standard. Doing so will increase your overall system throughput significantly.

 If you change from ATA-1, ATA-2, or ATA-3 to ATA-4 and above, you also have to change the cable you are using.

Using *rounded cables* can also increase system performance (although this is not a speed-related enhancement). Most disk interface cables are flat ribbon cables; when they are inside a case, they impede airflow. Many systems part manufacturers now sell rounded cables that don't impeded airflow as much. (Plus, they look nicer.)

NIC Performance

In many cases, the network interface card (NIC) is not a system performance bottleneck. Ethernet network cards on most systems are combination 10/100 cards, which means they can run at either 10Mbps or 100Mbps. For most network workstations, that level of performance is more than sufficient.

However, some applications, especially on computers functioning as servers, can use increased NIC performance. There are only two primary methods of increasing network performance: upgrading the NIC to a higher performance model with dedicated DMA channels and onboard buffers; or upgrading to a completely new, faster network technology like Gigabit Ethernet (which runs at 1000Mbps). The former method is simple, because it just requires replacing the NIC in the computer. The latter method requires not only the replacement of the NIC, but also the upgrading of switches, cabling, and any other network hardware that does not support the new technology.

Specialized Video Cards

A popular performance option you can add to a PC is a specialized video card. This option is popular with individuals for whom quality and performance of the image on the screen is extremely important. Most video cards released today have at least 32MB of RAM on the card (although some video circuitry can be built in to the motherboard's chipset, which performs about as well).

Most video cards that have increased performance use the Accelerated Graphics Port (AGP) bus (discussed in Chapter 2, "Motherboards, CPUs, and RAM"). The higher performance graphics cards use specialized, dedicated, high-speed circuitry for drawing pixels and can draw at a higher rate than regular video cards. They also have other specialized circuits for doing such graphical work as shading and motion control. Most of these circuits in the video card increase performance by taking the processing load off the computer's CPU, thus increasing overall system performance.

Memory Performance

Memory is much like closet space: You can never have enough. When most people consider memory performance, they think about expanding the amount of memory in a system. Doing so increases overall system performance because the system is able to get the entire operating system, programs, and data into memory, where they can be manipulated faster—the system doesn't have to rely on swapping the information back and forth to the hard disk.

You can also increase memory performance by using memory matched for your system. For example, if your system is capable of supporting PC3200 memory, make sure the memory installed in the system is PC3200 memory and not the slower PC2700 memory. If you are running memory that is operating at a slower speed than your system can handle, you are not taking full advantage of the performance features of that system.

Additional Performance Enhancements

You can do other things to increase the performance of your computer. Many of them aren't so much performance increasers as simple upgrades that make your computer function better— like a better sound card that has a higher signal-to-noise ratio (meaning the sound is cleaner).

In addition to these items, you can replace your motherboard with one that has a faster front-side bus. The same peripherals will seem to operate faster (at least, the data can be exchanged more quickly with those peripherals).

Speaking of peripherals, if you have older peripherals that connect via a serial bus, exchange them for newer versions that can use the USB ports on your computer. They will be able to exchange data faster with the computer and will generally be less troublesome.

Finally, you can try overclocking your system so it will run faster. Although doing so increases performance, it can also decrease reliability (possibly to the point of complete system failure). When you *overclock* your computer, you usually increase the front side bus (FSB) clock multiplier in the CMOS setup utility to force the processor to run faster. This produces more heat because the processor has to work harder.

Overclocking your system can damage components. Make sure you know what you are doing before you begin. At the very least, overclocking voids almost every warranty for every component in the computer.

Preventing Electrostatic Discharge (ESD)

ESD charges can cause problems such as making a computer hang or reboot. Electrostatic discharge (ESD) happens when two objects of dissimilar charge come in contact with one another. The two objects exchange electrons in order to standardize the electrostatic charge between them. This charge can, and often does, damage electronic components.

The likelihood that a component will be damaged grows with the increasing use of Complementary Metal Oxide Semiconductor (CMOS) chips, because these chips contain a thin metal oxide layer that is hypersensitive to ESD. The previous generation's Transistor-Transistor Logic (TTL) chips are more robust than the newer CMOS chips because they don't contain this metal oxide layer. Most of today's ICs are CMOS chips, so ESD is more of a concern.

CPU chips and memory chips are particularly sensitive to ESD. Be extremely cautious when handling these chips.

When you shuffle your feet across the floor and shock your best friend on the ear, you are discharging static electricity into the ear of your friend. The lowest static voltage transfer you can feel is around 3,000 volts (it doesn't electrocute you because there is extremely little current). A static transfer that you can *see* is at least 10,000 volts! Just by sitting in a chair, you can generate around 100 volts of static electricity. Walking around wearing synthetic materials can generate around 1,000 volts. You can easily generate around 20,000 volts simply by dragging your smooth-soled shoes across a shag carpet in the winter. (Actually, it doesn't have to be winter to run this danger. This voltage can occur in any room with very low humidity—like a heated room in wintertime.)

It makes sense that these thousands of volts can damage computer components. However, a component can be damaged with as little as 80 volts! That means if a small charge is built up in your body, you could damage a component without realizing it.

Symptoms of ESD damage may be subtle, but they can be detected. One of the authors, David Groth, relates this experience:

"When I think of ESD, I always think of the same instance. A few years ago, I was working on an Apple Macintosh. This computer seemed to have a mind of its own. I would troubleshoot it, find the defective component, and replace it. The problem was that as soon as I replaced the component, it failed. I thought maybe the power supply was frying the boards, so I replaced both at the same time, but to no avail.

"I was about to send the computer off to Apple when I realized that it was winter. Normally this would not be a factor, but winters where I live (North Dakota) are extremely dry. Dry air promotes static electricity. At first I thought my problem couldn't be that simple, but I was at the end of my rope. So, when I received my next set of new parts, I grounded myself with an antistatic strap for the time it took to install the components, and prayed while I turned on the power. Success! The components worked as they should, and a new advocate of ESD prevention was born."

Antistatic Wrist Strap

The silver lining to the cloud described in David's story is that there are measures you can implement to help contain the effects of ESD. The first and easiest item to implement is the antistatic wrist strap, also referred to as an ESD strap. To use the ESD strap, you attach one end to an earth ground (typically the ground pin on an extension cord) and wrap the other end around your wrist. This strap grounds your body and keeps it at a zero charge. Figure 9.1 shows the proper way to attach an antistatic strap.

FIGURE 9.1   Proper ESD strap connection

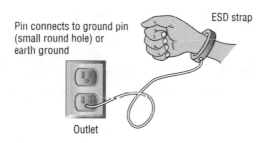

Pin connects to ground pin (small round hole) or earth ground

ESD strap

Outlet

WARNING   An ESD strap is a specially designed device to bleed electrical charges away *safely*. It uses a 1-megaohm resistor to bleed the charge away slowly. A simple wire wrapped around your wrist will not work correctly and could electrocute you!

WARNING   There is only one situation in which you should not wear an ESD strap. If you wear one while working on the inside of a monitor, you increase the chance of getting a lethal shock.

Antistatic Bags for Parts

Antistatic bags are important tools to have at your disposal when servicing electronic components, because they protect the sensitive electronic devices from stray static charges. These silver or pink bags are designed so that the static charges collect on the outside of the bags rather than on the electronic components.

You can obtain the bags from several sources. The most direct way to acquire antistatic bags is to go to an electronics supply store and purchase them in bulk. Most supply stores have several sizes available. Perhaps the easiest way to obtain them, however, is simply to hold on to the ones that come your way. That is, when you purchase any new component, it usually comes in an antistatic bag. Once you have installed the component, keep the bag. It may take you a while to gather a collection of bags if you take this approach, but eventually you will have a fairly large assortment.

ESD Antistatic Mats

It is possible to damage a device by simply laying it on a bench top. For this reason, you should have an ESD mat in addition to an ESD strap. This mat drains excess charge away from any item coming in contact with it (see Figure 9.2). ESD mats are also sold as mouse/keyboard pads to prevent ESD charges from interfering with the operation of the computer. Many wrist straps can be connected to the mat, thus causing the technician and any equipment in contact with the mat to be at the same electrical potential and eliminating ESD. There are even ESD bootstraps and ESD floor mats, which are used to keep the technician's entire body at the same potential.

FIGURE 9.2 Proper use of an ESD antistatic mat

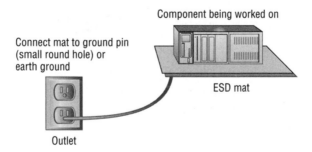

Component being worked on

Connect mat to ground pin
(small round hole) or
earth ground

ESD mat

Outlet

Other Protection Methods

Another preventive measure you can take is to maintain the relative humidity at around 50 percent. Be careful not to increase the humidity too far—to the point where moisture begins to condense on the equipment. Also, make use of antistatic spray, which is available commercially, to reduce static buildup on clothing and carpets. In a pinch, a solution of dilute fabric softener sprayed on these items will have the same effect.

Vendors have methods of protecting components in transit from manufacture to installation. They press the pins of ICs into antistatic foam to keep all the pins at the same potential. In addition, circuit boards are shipped in antistatic bags, as discussed earlier. However, keep in mind that unlike antistatic mats, antistatic bags do not "drain" the charges away, and they should never be used in place of an antistatic mat.

At the very least, you can be mindful of the dangers of ESD and take steps to reduce its effects. Beyond that, you should educate yourself about those effects so you know when ESD is becoming a major problem.

 If an ESD strap or mat is not available, you can discharge excess static voltage by touching the metal case of the power supply. However, the power supply *must be plugged into a properly grounded outlet* for this technique to work as intended. Because the power supply is plugged in, you should be extra cautious so you don't get electrocuted. Also, maintain continuous contact to continuously drain excess charge away. As you can see, it would be easier to have an antistatic wrist strap.

Maintaining Safety

As a provider of a hands-on service (repairing, maintaining, or upgrading someone's computer), you need to be aware of some general safety tips, because if you are not careful, you could harm yourself or the equipment. First, let's talk about playing it safe. Computers, display monitors, and printers can be dangerous if not handled properly.

Perhaps the most important aspect of computers that you should be aware of is the fact that they not only *use* electricity, they *store* electrical charge after they're turned off. This makes the power supply and the monitor pretty much off-limits to anyone but a trained electrical repair person. In addition, the computer's processor and various parts of the printer run at extremely high temperatures, and you can get burned if you try to handle them immediately after they've been in operation.

Those are just two general safety measures that should concern you. There are plenty more. When discussing safety issues with regard to repairing and upgrading PCs, it is best to break them down into five general areas:

- The computer
- The power supply
- The printer
- The monitor
- The keyboard and mouse

The Computer

If you have to open the computer to inspect or replace parts (as you will with most repairs), be sure to turn off the machine before you begin. Also be sure to read the next section, which covers safety issues with the power supply.

Some of the cheaper computer cases have metal with sharp edges, so be careful when handling them. You can, for example, cut yourself by jamming your fingers between the case and the frame when you try to force the case back on. The more well-built models use rounded edges and are safer.

The Power Supply

Do not take the issue of safety and electricity lightly. If you were to remove the power supply from its case (and we don't recommend doing so), you would be taking a great risk. The current flowing through the power supply normally follows a complete circuit; when your body breaks that circuit, your body becomes part of the circuit.

The two biggest dangers with power supplies are burning yourself and electrocuting yourself. These risks usually go hand in hand. If you touch a bare wire that is carrying current, you may get electrocuted. A large enough current passing through the wire (and you) can cause severe burns. (It can also cause your heart to stop, your muscles to seize, and your brain to stop functioning. In short, it can kill you.) Electricity always finds the best path to ground. And because we are basically bags of salt water (an excellent conductor of electricity), electricity will use us as a conductor if we are grounded.

Because of the way electricity conducts itself (get it?), electrical burn victims usually have two kinds of wounds: the entry wound and the exit wound. The entry wound happens at the point of contact between the conductor and the person. It's rather gruesome. The current flowing through you has enough power to boil the water in the tissues it comes in contact with, essentially cooking you from the inside out. The electricity sears the tissue on its way toward whatever part of the body is closest to a ground. Then, at the point closest to a ground, the electricity bolts from the body, producing an exit wound. We hope this description will encourage you to learn proper electrical safety so you may never experience the pain of electrical burns.

Fire Safety

Repairing a computer isn't often the cause of an electrical fire. However, you should know how to extinguish such a fire properly. Four major classes of fire extinguishers are available, one for each type of flammable substance: A (water-based extinguishing material) for wood and paper fires, B (carbon dioxide) for flammable liquids, C for electrical fires, and D (metal powder or NaCl [salt]) for flammable metals like phosphorus and sodium. The most popular type of fire extinguisher today is the multipurpose, or ABC-rated, extinguisher. It contains a dry chemical powder that smothers the fire and cools it at the same time. For electrical fires (which may be related to a shorted-out wire in a power supply), make sure the fire extinguisher will work for class C fires. If you don't have an extinguisher that is specifically rated for electrical fires (type C), you can use an ABC-rated extinguisher.

Although it is possible to work on a power supply, doing so is *not* recommended. Power supplies contain several capacitors that can hold *lethal* charges *long after they have been unplugged!* It is extremely dangerous to open the case of a power supply. Besides, power supplies are inexpensive, so it would probably cost less to replace one than to try to fix it, and this approach would be much safer.

Current vs. Voltage—Which Is More Dangerous?

When talking about power and safety, you will almost always hear the saying, "It's not the volts that kill you, it's the amps." That's mostly true. However, an explanation is in order.

The number of volts in a power source represents its potential to do work. But volts don't do anything by themselves. Current (amperage, or amps) is the force behind the work done by electricity. Here's an analogy to help explain this concept. Say you have two boulders; one weighs 10lbs, the other 100lbs, and each is 100 feet off the ground. If you drop them, which one will do more work? The obvious answer is the 100lb boulder. They both have the same potential to do work (100 feet of travel), but the 100lb boulder has more mass, and thus more force. Voltage is analogous to the distance the boulder is from the ground, and amperage is analogous to the mass of the boulder.

This is why you can produce static electricity on the order of 50,000 volts and not electrocute yourself. Even though this electricity has a great *potential* for work, it does very little work because the amperage is so low. This also explains why you can weld metal with 110 volts. Welders use only 110 (sometimes 220) volts, but they also use anywhere from 50 to 200 amps!

If you ever have to work on a power supply, for safety's sake you should discharge all capacitors within it. To do this, connect a resistor across the leads of the capacitor with a rating of three watts or more and a resistance of 100 ohms (Ω) per volt. For example, to discharge a 225-volt capacitor, you would use a 22.5kΩ resistor (225 volts times 100Ω = 22500Ω or 22.5kΩ).

The Printer

If you've ever attempted to repair a printer, have you sometimes thought there was a little monster in there hiding all the screws from you? Besides missing screws, here are some things to watch out for when repairing printers:

- When handling a toner cartridge from a laser printer or page printer, do not shake the cartridge or turn it upside down. You will find yourself spending more time cleaning the printer and the surrounding area than fixing the printer.

- Do not put any objects into the feeding system (in an attempt to clear the path) when the printer is running.

- Laser printers generate a laser that is hazardous to your eyes. Do not look directly into the source of the laser.

- If it's an ink-jet printer, do not try to blow in the ink cartridge to clear a clogged opening—that is, unless you like the taste of ink.

- Some parts of a laser printer (like the EP cartridge) will be damaged if you touch them. Your skin produces oils and has a small surface layer of dead skin cells. These substances can collect on the delicate surface of the EP cartridge and cause malfunctions. Bottom line: Keep your fingers out of where they don't belong!

The Monitor

Other than the power supply, one of the most dangerous components to try to repair is the monitor, or cathode ray tube (CRT). In fact, we recommend that you *do not* try to repair monitors. To avoid the extremely hazardous environment contained inside the monitor—it can retain a high-voltage charge for hours after it's been turned off—take it to a certified monitor technician or television repair shop. The repair shop or certified technician will know and understand the proper procedures to discharge the monitor, which involve attaching a resistor to the flyback transformer's charging capacitor to release the high-voltage electrical charge that builds up during use. They will also be able to determine whether the monitor can be repaired or needs to be replaced. Remember, the monitor works in its own extremely protective environment (the monitor case) and may not respond well to your desire to try to open it.

WARNING   The CRT is vacuum sealed. Be extremely careful when handling the CRT. If you break the glass, it will implode, which can send glass in any direction.

Even though we recommend not repairing monitors, the A+ exam tests your knowledge of the safety practices to use when you need to do so. If you have to open a monitor, you must first discharge the high-voltage charge on it using a *high-voltage probe*. This probe has a very large needle, a gauge that indicates volts, and a wire with an alligator clip. Attach the alligator clip to a ground (usually the round pin on the power cord). Slip the probe needle underneath the high-voltage cup on the monitor. You will see the gauge spike to around 15,000 volts and slowly reduce to zero. When it reaches zero, you may remove the high-voltage probe and service the high-voltage components of the monitor.

WARNING   Do *not* use an ESD strap when discharging the monitor; doing so can lead to a fatal electric shock.

The Keyboard and Mouse

Okay, we know you're thinking, "What danger could a keyboard or mouse cause?" We admit that not much danger is associated with these components, but there are a couple of safety concerns you should always keep in mind.

First, the mouse usually has a cord, and you can trip over it, so make sure it's safely out of the way. Second, you could short-circuit your keyboard if you accidentally spill liquid on it. Keyboards don't function well with half a can of cola in their innards!

⊕ **Real World Scenario**

Play It Safe with Common Sense

When you're repairing a PC, do not leave it unattended. Someone could walk into the room and inadvertently bump the machine, causing failure. Worse, they could step on pieces that may be lying around and get hurt. It is also not a good idea to work on the PC alone. If you're injured, someone should be around to help if you need it. Finally, if you're fatigued, you may find it difficult to concentrate and focus on what you are doing. There are real safety measures related to repairing PCs, so the most important thing to remember is to pay close attention to what you are doing.

Environmental Concerns

It is estimated that more than 25 percent of all the lead (a poisonous substance) in landfills today is a result of consumer electronics components. Because consumer electronics (televisions, VCRs, stereos) contain hazardous substances, many states require that they be disposed of as hazardous waste. Computers are no exception. Monitors contain several carcinogens and phosphors, as well as mercury and lead. The computer itself may contain several lubricants and chemicals as well as lead. Printers contain plastics and chemicals like toners and inks that are also hazardous. All of these items should be disposed of properly.

Remember all those 386 and 486 computers that came out in the late 1980s and are now considered antiques? Where did they all go? Is there an Old Computers Home somewhere that is using these computer systems for good purposes, or are they lying in a junkyard somewhere? Or could it be that some folks just cannot let go, and have a stash of old computer systems and computer parts in the dark depths of their basements?

Although it is relatively easy to put old machines away, thinking you might be able to put them to good use again someday, doing so is not realistic. Most computers are obsolete as soon as you buy them. And if you have not used them recently, your old computer components will more than likely never be used again.

We recycle cans, plastic, and newspaper, so why not recycle computer equipment? The problem, as we mentioned, is that most computers contain small amounts of hazardous substances. Some countries are exploring the option of recycling electrical machines, but most have still not enacted appropriate measures to enforce their proper disposal. However, we can do a few things as consumers and caretakers of our environment to promote the proper disposal of computer equipment:

- Check with the manufacturer. Some manufacturers will take back outdated equipment for parts (and may even pay you for them).

- Properly dispose of solvents or cleaners used with computers, as well as their containers, at a local hazardous waste disposal facility.

- Disassemble the machine and reuse the parts that are good.

- Check out businesses that can melt down the components for the lead or gold plating.

- Contact the Environmental Protection Agency (EPA) for a list of local or regional waste disposal sites that accept used computer equipment. The EPA's web address is www.epa.gov.

- Check with local nonprofit or education organizations interested in using the equipment.

- Check out the Internet for possible waste disposal sites. Table 9.1 lists a few websites we came across that deal with disposal of used computer equipment.

- Check with the EPA to see if what you are disposing of has an MSDS (Material Safety Data Sheet). These sheets contain information about the toxicity of a product and whether it can be disposed of in the trash. They also contain lethal dose information.

TABLE 9.1   Computer Recycling Websites

Site Name	Web Address
Computer Recycle Center	www.recycles.com/
Recompute	www.recompute.co.uk
RE-PC	www.repc.com/

In addition to hardware recycling, there are businesses that offer to recycle consumables, like ink cartridges or printer ribbons. However, although these businesses are doing us a favor in our quest to recycle, it might not be the best way to keep up with the recycle agenda. Why? Well, we don't recommend the use of recycled ink cartridges; they may clog, the ink quality is not as good, and the small circuit board on the cartridge may be damaged. Similarly, recycled printer ribbons will lose their ability to hold ink after a while and don't last as long as new ribbons. And, recycled toner cartridges don't operate properly after refilling. However, when you are through with the old cartridges, give them to organizations that do recycle so they can have some fresh cores. That way, you can safely dispose of your cartridge and benefit the environment at the same time.

Remember that recycling is a way to keep our environment clean and our landfills empty. If we can take one step to recycle or redistribute outdated computer equipment, we are one step closer to having a healthier environment. However, we should not have to sacrifice quality in the process.

In particular, you should make a special effort to recycle batteries. Batteries contain several chemicals that are harmful to the environment and won't degrade safely. Batteries should not be thrown away; they should be recycled according to your local laws. Check with your local authorities to find out how batteries should be recycled.

Cleaning Systems

The cleanliness of a computer is extremely important. Buildup of dust, dirt, and oils can prevent various mechanical parts of a computer from operating. Because this topic is important, the

A+ exam will test your knowledge of the proper way to use various cleaning products on computer systems.

Computer components get dirty. Dirt reduces their operating efficiency and, ultimately, their life. Cleaning them is definitely important. But cleaning them with the right cleaning compounds is equally important. Using the wrong compounds can leave residue behind that is more harmful than the dirt you are trying to remove.

Most computer cases and monitor cases can be cleaned using mild soapy water on a clean, lint-free cloth. Do *not* use any kind of solvent-based cleaner on either monitor or LCD screens, because doing so can cause discoloration and damage to the screen surface. Most often, a simple dusting with a damp cloth (moistened with water) will suffice. Make sure the power is off before you put anything wet near a computer. Dampen (don't soak) a cloth in mild soap solution and wipe the dirt and dust from the case. Then wipe the moisture from the case with a dry, lint-free cloth. Anything with a plastic or metal case can be cleaned in this manner.

Additionally, if you spill anything on a keyboard, you can clean it by soaking it in distilled, demineralized water and drying it off. The extra minerals and impurities have been removed from this type of water, so it will not leave any traces of residue that might interfere with the proper operation of the keyboard after cleaning. The same holds true for the keyboard's cable and its connector.

The electronic connectors of computer equipment, on the other hand, should never touch water. Instead, use a swab moistened in distilled, denatured isopropyl alcohol (also known as electronics or contact cleaner and found in electronics stores) to clean contacts. Doing so will take oxidation off of the copper contacts.

> **WARNING** Some technicians say you can use a pencil eraser to clean the oxidation from contacts. You should *never* do this, because erasers contain trace amounts of acids from their manufacturing process that can damage the contacts after cleaning.

Finally, the best way to remove dust and dirt from the inside of the computer is to use compressed air instead of vacuuming. Compressed air can be more easily directed and doesn't easily produce ESD damage (like vacuuming could). Simply blow the dust from inside the computer using a stream of compressed air. However, make sure to do this outside, so you don't blow dust all over your work area or yourself. Nonstatic vacuum cleaners are available that are specially made for cleaning computer components (like keyboards and case fans). Their nozzles are grounded to prevent ESD from damaging the components of the computer. However, compressed air is usually a better method, as long as it's done outside.

> **NOTE** One unique challenge when cleaning computers is spilled toner. It sticks to everything. There are two methods to deal with this. First, blow all the loose toner out of the printer using compressed air, being careful not to blow the toner into any of the printing mechanisms. Then, using a cool, damp cloth, wipe any remaining particles out of the printer.

Summary

In this chapter, you learned about ways to optimize your PC, as well as preventative maintenance and system maintenance techniques. You also learned about different safety measures: for you, your computer, and the environment.

First, you learned about the different methods and products you can use to enhance your PC's performance. We examined the hardware components, such as cooling components, hard disk technologies, and memory, that can increase overall system performance.

We then discussed electrostatic discharge (ESD) and its effects on computers and electronics. You learned what ESD is and the various methods used to prevent it from damaging components.

We talked about the various safety procedures you should follow when working on computers and their peripherals. You learned which components can cause injury as well as how to avoid injury during service work.

After that, you learned about the various environmental concerns that computers cause. We explained the methods used to properly dispose of computer components without harming the environment.

Finally, you learned the best ways to clean computer components, including the best tools and methods to use.

Key Terms

Before you take the exam, be certain you are familiar with the following terms:

high-voltage probe	phase change cooling
liquid cooling	rounded cables

Review Questions

1. Which proper method of CPU cooling is the cheapest?

   A. Fan/heatsink

   B. Water cooling

   C. Phase change cooling

   D. Alpha cooling

2. The amount of air a case fan can move is measured in _____.

   A. BTU

   B. CFM

   C. AMU

   D. PCS

3. Your PC is running an AMD Athlon XP 2100+ processor with a Soyo Dragon Ultra Platinum motherboard. It currently has PC2700 memory but is capable of supporting PC3200. The motherboard supports ATA-133, and you have a single 20GB ATA-100 drive. What can you do to increase this system's performance that would have the largest effect? (Select all that apply.)

   A. Replace the motherboard

   B. Replace memory

   C. Replace the hard disk

   D. Replace the system fan

4. What should you use to clean the contacts of a video card?

   A. Water

   B. Soap and water

   C. A dry cloth

   D. An alcohol swab

5. You smell smoke and notice that a fire has started inside your computer. The fire extinguisher you reach for should have what rating?

   A. Class A

   B. Class B

   C. Class C

   D. Class D

6. What does ESD stand for?

   A. Every single day

   B. Electric system degradation

   C. Electrosilicon diode

   D. Electrostatic discharge

   E. None of the above

7. When connecting an ESD strap to an extension cord, you must connect it to _____.

   A. The hot pin

   B. The negative pin

   C. The ground pin

   D. All of the above

8. Before servicing the inside of a monitor, you should do which of the following?

   A. Discharge the capacitor

   B. Clean the outside with a non-detergent cloth

   C. Make note of the knob positions

   D. Look for any loose screws

9. Liquid-cooled computers use a _____ on the CPU to keep it cool.

   A. Heat pipe

   B. Water pipe

   C. Water block

   D. Water cylinder

10. _____ are chemicals used to increase the surface area in contact with a heatsink.

    A. Metaloids

    B. Silver solids

    C. Polysynthetics

    D. Thermal compounds

11. Antistatic wrist straps should be connected to which hole in an outlet?

    A. Short slot

    B. Long slot

    C. Round hole

    D. They shouldn't be connected to an outlet

12. _____ contain information about harmful chemicals, their properties, and safety information.

   A. ESD

   B. MSDS

   C. CFM

   D. EPA

13. What is the best method for preventing ESD damage?

   A. Antistatic mat

   B. Antistatic spray

   C. Antistatic wrist strap

   D. Antistatic thinking

14. An _____ provides for ESD protection while a component is in transit between producer and consumer.

   A. Antistatic wrist strap

   B. Antistatic spray

   C. Antistatic mat

   D. Antistatic bag

15. How many volts does it take to damage a CMOS-based IC?

   A. 1

   B. 100

   C. 1,000

   D. 10,000

16. True or False. It is possible to brush clean the surface of a laser printer's EP cartridge imaging drum with the palm of your hand.

   A. True

   B. False

17. If you wanted to increase performance in your computer by replacing your hard disk subsystem with the highest possible performer, which of the following technologies would you replace it with?

   A. ATA-2

   B. Serial ATA

   C. ATA-100

   D. ATA-133

18. What effect will increasing the number of fins on a heatsink have on the cooling efficiency of that heatsink?

    A. None

    B. Little

    C. Some

    D. Great

19. _____ uses the effect of liquid changing to a gas and back again to cool a processor.

    A. Heatsink

    B. Water cooling

    C. Phase change cooling

    D. Gaseous phase cooling

20. _____ is the most efficient method of cleaning dust from inside a computer.

    A. Vacuuming the dust out

    B. Dusting with a cloth

    C. Blowing the dust out with compressed air

    D. Washing the dust out with soap and water

Answers to Review Questions

1. A. A traditional fan with heatsink air cooling is cheaper than other methods of cooling a CPU.

2. B. The number of cubic feet per minute (CFM) is the measure of how much air a fan can move at any one time.

3. B, C. By replacing the memory with PC3200 memory and replacing the hard drive with one that has an ATA-133 interface, you can increase the system's performance significantly. Replacing the motherboard may not have much effect (unless you are replacing the processor and all other components along with it). Replacing the system fan will have little effect on total system performance.

4. D. The connectors of a video card lead to delicate circuitry. A dry cloth would almost certainly introduce ESD. Water should never touch electrical contacts, because it may corrode them. The correct answer is to swab them with denatured isopropyl alcohol.

5. C. Because your computer uses electronic circuits, you would reach for a class C (or in a pinch, a class ABC) fire extinguisher. The other classes may cause severe damage to the components or may cause electrocution.

6. D. ESD is a very common computer acronym. It stands for electrostatic discharge.

7. C. When connecting an ESD strap to an extension cord, you must connect it to the ground pin to ensure both your safety and the proper discharge of ESD.

8. A. Before working on any components of the monitor, you should discharge the flyback transformer's capacitor to prevent injury to yourself.

9. C. Liquid-cooled computers use a special piece of equipment known as a water block to replace the heatsink.

10. D. Thermal compounds fill in the microscopic voids in a heatsink's surface to provide the greatest contact area possible for the processor.

11. C. An antistatic wrist strap should be connected to ground on either an outlet or an extension cord or power plug. The ground is usually indicated by a round hole below the long and short slots.

12. B. Material Safety Data Sheets (MSDS) contain information about harmful chemicals, the properties of those chemicals, and what kinds of safety precautions should be taken around the chemicals.

13. C. Of all the options listed, an antistatic wrist strap will provide you with the most ESD protection.

14. D. An antistatic bag protects a component from static charge damage while a component is not installed in a computer. Charges will collect on the outside of the bag, preventing them from damaging the component.

15. B. Because CMOS chips use a thin metal oxide layer that is hypersensitive to ESD, it takes only 100 volts to damage them.

16. B. You should never touch the surface of an EP cartridge's imaging drum. The oil in your hands that would be transferred to the imaging drum may cause imperfections in the developed images.

17. B. Serial ATA currently has the highest possible throughput (150MBps).

18. D. By increasing the number of fins on a heatsink, you increase the overall area of the heatsink exposed to the cool air, thus greatly increasing the heatsink's efficiency.

19. C. Phase change cooling uses the cooling effect of liquid changing to a gas to cool the CPU.

20. C. Taking the computer outside and blowing the dust out with compressed air is the quickest and easiest way to clean dust out of a computer.

Chapter 10

Hardware Troubleshooting

THE FOLLOWING OBJECTIVES ARE COVERED IN THIS CHAPTER:

✓ 2.1 Recognize common problems associated with each module and their symptoms, and identify steps to isolate and troubleshoot the problems. Given a problem situation, interpret the symptoms and infer the most likely cause.

✓ 2.2 Identify basic troubleshooting procedures and tools, and how to elicit problem symptoms from customers. Justify asking particular questions in a given scenario.

Troubleshooting is the process of identifying a computer problem so that it can be fixed. Until you've had the opportunity to troubleshoot several computers with several different types of customers, the only way to gain the troubleshooting skills you will rely on as a certified technician is to learn from other people's experiences. In this chapter, I'll summarize for you some of the experience that my colleagues and I have gained over the course of our careers as service technicians, and I'll attempt to organize these experiences by providing you with guidelines and general tips for approaching the task of troubleshooting.

Printer troubleshooting is covered in Chapter 4, "Printers." Go back and review the section on printer troubleshooting, because it is tested heavily on the exam.

Troubleshooting Resources

Just as an artist has paintbrushes, paints, and a vision of how things should work together, a great troubleshooter has several tools to make their job easier. And, like the artist's brushes, palette, and vision, a technician's resources can be put into service to accomplish a complex goal: the identification of a problem.

Intellectual Resources

Most technicians actually relish a computer problem, because they know it's a chance to find a solution and maybe to brag to their colleagues. Solving the problem can feel almost like being the first to discover a star or a comet, although very seldom do you get to name a problem or its solution (like "The Roger Smith General Protection Fault Solution" or "The Dan Jones AUTOEXEC.BAT Conundrum"). Each time a technician solves a new problem, they know that if they ever run into that problem again, they'll be able to fix it easily (or at least have a starting point for troubleshooting).

The first major resource you can use for troubleshooting a problem is your own brain. Your brain can hold a lot of information. We remember almost everything we're exposed to. For this reason, the best troubleshooters are usually the people who have been exposed to the most problems. They have seen several different types of problems and their solutions. If they run into a particular problem, they may have seen it before and can quickly fix the problem.

Service documentation is another important intellectual resource, and we might point out that it's not used as often as it should be. As soon as a new product is released, several resources are released at the same time (or shortly thereafter). These include items like the owner's manual, the buyer's guide, and (most importantly) the service and replacement parts manuals. These books can be a valuable source of troubleshooting information. They can also contain replacement-parts information, such as which part(s) should be replaced when a particular component is found to be bad. In addition, they usually contain exploded diagrams of the model being repaired.

The Internet, of course, has become an extremely valuable resource for troubleshooting guidance. Almost every technology company now has a website. One feature of most companies' websites is the *knowledge base* (many have a different name for this feature), an area that contains several pieces of information that can be very valuable to technicians working with its products. First, the knowledge base usually contains one or more *Frequently Asked Questions (FAQ)* files. These files are summaries of the questions technical support technicians are asked, and their answers. Second, this is a good place to look for reports of bugs that have been discovered or suspected in the company's products. You may have to go to the company's support page (or some similarly purposed section of the website) to ask your question directly or perform a search on the knowledge base or FAQ to determine if a specific question or problem relates to your situation, but in many cases, a problem you're spending time trying to solve has already been solved by someone else and reported.

Yet another intellectual resource that is seldom used, except in the most difficult cases, is a coworker. If you don't have the knowledge to troubleshoot or repair the component, a coworker might. (This resource is the most seldom used because people hate to admit that they don't know something. But as the saying goes, "The beginning of wisdom is 'I don't know.'")

Hardware and Software Resources

In addition to intellectual resources, you have other items you can use to troubleshoot the computer. These items fall into two categories: hardware and software.

You can use several hardware resources in the troubleshooting process. First, you have your computer toolkit. When you're troubleshooting, though, the only tools you should need from the toolkit are those for removing the case, because most troubleshooting is done with the computer on and as is. After all, you need to see what's happening before you start making changes.

 See Chapter 6, "Building a PC," for more information about the tools used to service a computer.

Another example of a hardware resource is a *resource discovery expansion card*. These cards, when installed into any expansion slot, will tell you what resources are being used in the computer and will indicate any possible conflicts. Several different companies make these cards.

Software resources are any software tools that are used to help troubleshoot a computer problem. We will discuss these resources (like boot disks, diagnostic utilities, and so on) in Chapter 18, "Windows Diagnostics and Troubleshooting."

Top 10 Troubleshooting Steps

Just as every artist has their own style, every technician has their own way to troubleshoot. Some people use their instincts; others use advice from other people. I have condensed the most common troubleshooting tips into a 10-step process. You try each step, in order. If that step doesn't narrow the problem down, you move on to the next step.

Step 1: Define the Problem

If you can't define the problem, you can't begin to solve it. You can define the problem by asking questions of the user. Here are a few questions to ask the user to aid you in determining exactly what the problem *is*:

Can you show me the problem?   This question is one of the best. It allows the user to show you exactly where and when they experience the problem.

How often does this happen?   This question establishes whether this problem is a one-time occurrence (usually indicating a soft memory error or the like) that can be solved with a reboot, or whether a specific sequence of events causes the problem to happen (usually indicating a more serious problem that may require software installation or hardware replacement).

Has any new software been installed recently?   New software can mean incompatibility problems with existing programs. This is especially true for Windows programs. A new Windows program can overwrite a required DLL file with a newer version of the same name, which an older program may not find useful. Windows XP now has a feature called *restore points*. Each time Windows XP boots successfully, it notes its configuration. If you install new software and it overwrites a DLL, causing major functionality problems, you can reboot in Safe mode back to the last logged restore point and roll back the configuration to when the computer last worked properly.

Have any other changes been made to the computer recently?   If the answer is "Yes," ask if the user can remember approximately when the change was made. Then ask them approximately when the problem started. If the two dates seem related, there's a good chance the problem is related to the change. If the change involved a new hardware component, check to see that the hardware component was installed correctly.

Step 2: Check the Simple Stuff First

This step is the one that most experienced technicians overlook. Often, computer problems are the result of something simple. Technicians overlook these problems because they're so simple that the technicians assume they *couldn't* be the problem. Some examples of simple problems are shown here:

Is it plugged in?   And plugged in on both ends? Cables must be plugged in on *both ends* in order to function correctly. Cables can be easily tripped over and inadvertently pulled from their sockets.

Is it turned on?   This one seems the most obvious, but we've all fallen victim to it at one point or another. Computers and their peripherals must be turned on in order to function. Most have power switches that have LEDs that glow when the power is turned on.

Is the system ready?   Computers must be ready before they can be used. *Ready* means the system is ready to accept commands from the user. An indication that a computer is ready is when the operating system screens come up and the computer presents you with a menu or a command prompt. If that computer uses a graphical interface, the computer is ready when the mouse pointer appears. Printers are ready when the On Line or Ready light on the front panel is lit.

Reseat chips and cables.   You can solve some of the strangest problems (random hang-ups or errors) by opening the case and pressing down on each socketed chip. This remedies the chip creep problem mentioned earlier in the book. In addition, you should also reseat any cables to make sure that they are making good contact.

Step 3: Check to See If It's User Error

One of the more common errors that technicians run into is the *EEOC error* (Equipment Exceeds Operator Capability). This error is common, but preventable. The indication that a problem is due to user error is when a user says they can't perform some very common computer task—"I can't print," "I can't save my file," "I can't run my favorite application," and so on. As soon you hear these words, you should start asking questions of the user to determine if it is EEOC or a real problem. A good question to ask following their statement of the problem would be, "Were you *ever* able to perform that task?" If they answer "No" to this question, it means they are probably doing the procedure wrong—EEOC. If they answer "Yes," you must move on to another set of questions.

This doesn't mean you should assume the user is always wrong. An attitude like that can come across on the phone, and in person, as arrogance.

The Social Side of Troubleshooting

A few years ago, I attended troubleshooting courses from two different major vendors (who shall remain nameless) in two back-to-back weeks. In the first course, the instructor opened by saying, "I'm now going to give you the secret to successful troubleshooting. Users lie!" Of course, we were all shocked to hear this from a representative of a major software vendor, but he was right. Consider the typical answers to the following questions:

1. Question: So, what were you doing when it broke?

    Answer: Nothing.

2. Question: What have you changed recently?

    Answer: Nothing.

3.   When was the last time it worked?

Answer: The last time I touched anything.

The truth is, users *do* lie—not intentionally, but the result is the same. As troubleshooters, our job is to drag the truth out of them.

The second class opened with the instructor saying, "I'm going to clue you in to the secret of successful troubleshooting. Troubleshooting is more social than technical." All the computer geeks in the room gasped to hear someone belittle the value of their technical knowledge. Bottom line, though, the instructor was right. A problem isn't fixed until the user believes it is fixed!

When you combine those two "secrets," you get to the heart of troubleshooting. As technicians, we need to be able to communicate clearly, use less intimidating questioning techniques (notice that the previous questions all seem to imply that the user was at fault), and reassure the user that the problem has been corrected.

When you're looking for clues to the nature of a problem, no one can give you more information than the person who was there when it happened. The user can tell you what led up to the problem, what software was running, and the exact nature of the problem ("It happened when I tried to print"), and can help you re-create the problem, if possible.

Use questioning techniques that are neutral in nature. Instead of "What were you doing when it broke?" be more compassionate and say, "What was going on when the computer decided not to work?" It sounds silly, but these types of changes can make your job a lot easier!

Step 4: Reboot the Computer

It is amazing how often a simple computer reboot can solve a problem. Rebooting the computer clears the memory and starts the computer with a clean slate. Whenever I perform phone support, I always ask the customer to reboot the computer and try again. If rebooting doesn't work, try powering down the system completely, and then powering it up again. More often than not, that will solve the problem.

Step 5: Determine If the Problem Is Hardware Related or Software Related

This step is important because it determines what part of the computer you should focus your troubleshooting skills on. Each part requires different skills and different tools.

To determine if a problem is hardware- or software related, you can do a few things to narrow down the issue. For instance, does the problem manifest itself when you use a particular piece of hardware (a modem, for example)? If it does, the problem is more than likely hardware related.

This step relies on personal experience more than any of the other steps do. You will without a doubt run into strange software problems. Each one has a particular solution. Some may even require reinstallation of the software or the entire operating system.

Step 6: If the Problem Is Hardware Related, Determine Which Component Is Failing

Hardware problems are pretty easy to figure out. If the modem doesn't work, and you know it isn't a software problem, the modem is probably the piece of hardware that needs to be replaced.

With some of the newer computers, several components are integrated onto the motherboard. If you troubleshoot the computer and find a hardware component to be bad, there's a good chance that the bad component is integrated into the motherboard (for example, the parallel port circuitry) and the whole motherboard must be replaced—an expensive proposition, to be sure.

 Some specifics of hardware and software troubleshooting will be covered in later sections.

Step 7: If the Problem Is Software Related, Boot Clean

If you are experiencing software problems, a common troubleshooting technique with DOS-based computers is to *boot clean*. This means starting the computer with a bootable diskette that uses a CONFIG.SYS and AUTOEXEC.BAT with no third-party drivers (for example, no drivers for sound card, CD-ROM, or network). If the software that's experiencing the problem is incompatible with something in these clean CONFIG.SYS and AUTOEXEC.BAT files, this will indicate the problem. Once you have determined that there's an incompatibility, you can further determine what your chances are for fixing the problem by using the REM techniques presented later in this chapter. Restarting the computer in Safe mode is a clean boot for Windows 9x and Windows 2000. Only Windows default drivers will be loaded.

 For more on this topic, see the section "Software Troubleshooting" later in this chapter.

Step 8: Check Service Information Sources

As you may have figured out by now, I'm fond of old sayings. There's another one that applies here: "If all else fails, read the instructions." The service manuals are your instructions for troubleshooting and service information. Almost every computer and peripheral made today has a set of service documentation in the form of books, service CD-ROMs, and websites. The latter of the three is growing in popularity as more service centers get connections to the Internet.

Step 9: If It Ain't Broke...

When doctors take the Hippocratic oath, they promise to not make their patients any sicker than they already were. Technicians should take a similar oath. It all boils down to, "If it ain't broke, don't fix it." When you troubleshoot, make one change at a time. If the change doesn't solve the problem, change the computer back to its original state before making a different change.

Step 10: Ask for Help

If you don't know the answer, ask one of your fellow technicians. They may have run across the problem you are having and know the solution.

This solution does involve a little humility. You must admit that you don't know the answer. If you ask questions, you will get answers, and you will learn from the answers. Making mistakes is valuable as well, as long as you learn from them.

Software Troubleshooting

This section deals with a canvas the troubleshooting artist may have to paint often: software problems. More than half of all computer problems are software related. The problems usually don't stem from the software itself, but rather from the interaction of that software with other software that may be running on the machine. However, before you can start troubleshooting, you must determine if the problem is hardware related or software related. In order to determine the source of a problem (hardware or software), you can do a few things to narrow it down:

1. **In DOS/Windows computers, boot the computer clean.** Booting *clean* means starting the computer with no software drivers loading. The only things that should be in the AUTOEXEC.BAT and CONFIG.SYS (the two DOS configuration files) are the necessary memory managers and settings to get the computer up and running. Leave out sound card, CD-ROM, network, and other device drivers. You can also boot clean by using a bootable floppy disk (see the sidebar "Making a Bootable Diskette"). If the computer functions normally, then the problem is usually software related (although it could be a hardware problem, and the device driver just enabled the device, causing the conflict to show itself).

2. **Check the operating system error messages.** Every operating system has built-in error-detection routines. These routines are designed to intercept problems and notify the user. If there is a major problem, these routines display an error message for the software or hardware component that caused the problem. For example, when you try to print to a printer connected to your primary parallel port (LPT1) and the system returns an error like "Error writing to device LPT1," the problem is more than likely hardware related because a hardware device was mentioned (or alluded to) in the error message.

3. **Uninstall and then reinstall the application that's having problems.** This step ensures that you have the correct version of all the application's components and that no files are missing that may be required by the application. (For example, many applications today are intelligent enough to tell you when they're missing a necessary file to complete an operation—perhaps a spell-checker's dictionary files, or a library of programming objects, or even a file created by a coworker but stored in the wrong place on the network. The solution to this problem is simple: If the missing file is a program file, reinstall that program from the original disks. If the file is a data file, restore the data file from a backup.)

If you are using Windows 2000, you can take advantage of a new set of features known as Intellimirror. Intellimirror and its associated tools can maintain applications—replacing missing files, updating INI or Registry files, or doing a complete installation—automatically.

4. **Look for ways to repeat the problem.** If it is a phantom problem, ask the user to help you by finding a way to repeat the problem or looking for some type of pattern to the problem.

5. **Make sure you are using the latest patches.** This is especially important with machines that are on a network; having a buggy *network client* (the software that communicates with the network server and network resources) can cause a host of strange application problems. Also, make sure all the machines running on the network are using the latest bug fixes to the application. You should be able to obtain these by looking on the application company's website.

6. **Check the Internet.** This is related to the previous point. Often, software publishers post FAQs and have a searchable knowledge base on the Internet with useful resources for troubleshooting problems with their products. For example, check out Microsoft's support website at www.microsoft.com/support.

7. **Compare and isolate.** It can be difficult to determine whether an application problem is caused by the software or hardware. The best troubleshooting tools in this case are the twins, comparison and isolation. Try comparing how the application behaves on the problem machine and on a machine that you know is working fine; then remove and/or replace hardware components from the two machines to eliminate possible causes and isolate the solution.

These indicators, along with your experience, should help you narrow the problem to either a hardware or software problem.

Making a Bootable DOS Diskette

A DOS *bootable diskette* is a valuable tool for troubleshooting. The creation process is simple. Insert a blank 1.44MB or 720KB diskette into your floppy drive and type the following at a DOS prompt:

FORMAT A: /S

(You can replace A: with the drive letter that represents your floppy drive.) The /S parameter instructs DOS to include the DOS system files on the floppy after formatting it. If the disk is already formatted, you can add the system files to a disk and make it bootable by typing the following at a DOS prompt:

SYS A:

> When the computer is done, the "System Transferred" message will appear, telling you that the computer has finished making the disk bootable. This disk, when inserted before turning the computer on, allows the computer to be booted because it contains the smallest portion of DOS necessary to start the computer.
>
> Windows offers several other ways of creating a bootable diskette using graphical tools.

DOS Troubleshooting

Troubleshooting DOS problems is a fundamental skill that most technicians get several chances to practice. Understanding and being able to modify the two main DOS configuration files—AUTOEXEC.BAT and CONFIG.SYS—can solve most DOS problems.

 These topics apply to both MS-DOS and PC-DOS versions.

The DOS Configuration Files: *CONFIG.SYS* and *AUTOEXEC.BAT*

DOS is a simple operating system. It requires very few system resources to operate. It is also simple to operate. Unless you've damaged or misplaced part of DOS itself, you just type the command you want the computer to execute, and the computer does it. Despite the fact that it can take a lot of study to familiarize yourself with *all* the commands DOS has to offer, you don't need to know very many of them to take advantage of its most useful capabilities. For these reasons, it stands as the most popular operating system of all time.

DOS uses two main configuration files, CONFIG.SYS and AUTOEXEC.BAT. Each file is a simple ASCII text file that contains commands and variables that set up the user environment in DOS:

CONFIG.SYS   The main configuration file that DOS uses. As such, it can be the source of several problems with DOS. The problems that are normally experienced are things like insufficient conventional memory, incorrect drivers loading, and not enough file handles. CONFIG.SYS also has a detailed role in the logical mapping of the PC's memory. It loads memory drivers (like EMM386 .EXE and HIMEM.SYS) as well as specifying the location of the DOS files (with statements like DOS=HIGH, UMB). It can also load device drivers by using lines that start with a DEVICE= statement.

AUTOEXEC.BAT   A special batch file that executes automatically at system startup. This configuration file establishes the user environment and loads system drivers. Because it's a batch file, you can add statements to it that can automatically start other programs.

If either file becomes damaged or corrupt (with incorrect entries), the best two tools you have are the REM statement and backup files.

REM Statements

Let's say the PC you're working on is inconsistently locking up. Further, let's say you have already determined that the problem is software related, because when you boot clean with a boot diskette, the computer functions normally. This means that one of the statements in CONFIG.SYS or AUTOEXEC.BAT is causing the problem.

In order to solve the problem, you must remove (or change) the line that is causing the problem. However, first you must find the offending line. You can do so using *REM statements*. The REM command is short for *remark*; by placing it at the beginning of any command line, you ensure that DOS will skip that line when running the file. The initial purpose for the REM command was to insert remarks or comments into batch files, so that the programmer or curious user could annotate what was going on in different sections of the file without requiring the computer to run the comment. However, you can also use it to *remove* suspect commands one at a time in order to test the effect of booting with and without them. By editing both CONFIG.SYS and AUTOEXEC.BAT and *REMming out* one command at a time (and rebooting between each change), you can progressively eliminate statements that might be the cause of the problem.

 There is another way to step through the CONFIG.SYS and AUTOEXEC.BAT files to determine which line is causing the problem. During the boot process, press the F8 key when you see the words, "Starting MS-DOS." Doing so will allow you to choose whether to execute a particular line in either of these files.

Let's take a look at a sample computer problem: The computer is randomly locking up. Listings 10.1 and 10.2 show the CONFIG.SYS and AUTOEXEC.BAT files (the lines are numbered to facilitate our discussion here; the real files would not have the numbers):

Listing 10.1: CONFIG.SYS

```
1.DEVICE=C:\DOS\HIMEM.SYS
2.DEVICE=C:\DOS\EMM386.EXE
3.DOS=HIGH
4.FILES=40
5.BUFFERS=9,256
6.DEVICE=C:\SB16\DRV\CTSB16.SYS /UNIT=0
/BLASTER=A:220 I:5 D:1 H:5
7.DEVICE=C:\SB16\DRV\DRV\SBCD.SYS /D:MSCD001 /P:220
```

Listing 10.2: AUTOEXEC.BAT

```
1.@ECHO OFF
2.SET BLASTER=A220 I5 D1 T4
3.C:\DOS\MSCDEX.EXE /D:MSCD001
4.SET PATH=C:\DOS;C:\;C:\WINDOWS;C:\MOUSE
5.SET TEMP=C:\TEMP
6.C:\WINDOWS\SMARTDRV.EXE
```

When troubleshooting a software problem, the first thing I always check is the non-DOS items in either configuration file. Lines 6 and 7 of the CONFIG.SYS file and line 2 of the AUTOEXEC.BAT file are from a recent sound-card installation. To check if one of these drivers is the problem, always start by REMming out the non-DOS items. So, if you edit both the configuration files and REM out the non-DOS items, CONFIG.SYS and AUTOEXEC.BAT will look as shown in Listings 10.3 and 10.4:

Listing 10.3: CONFIG.SYS

```
1.DEVICE=C:\DOS\HIMEM.SYS
2.DEVICE=C:\DOS\EMM386.EXE
3.DOS=HIGH
4.FILES=40
5.BUFFERS=9,256
6.rem DEVICE=C:\SB16\DRV\CTSB16.SYS /UNIT=0
/BLASTER=A:220 I:5 D:1 H:5
7.rem DEVICE=C:\SB16\DRV\DRV\SBCD.SYS /D:MSCD001 /P:220
```

Listing 10.4: AUTOEXEC.BAT

```
1.@ECHO OFF
2.rem SET BLASTER=A220 I5 D1 T4
3.C:\DOS\MSCDEX.EXE /D:MSCD001
4.SET PATH=C:\DOS;C:\;C:\WINDOWS;C:\MOUSE
5.SET TEMP=C:\TEMP
6.C:\WINDOWS\SMARTDRV.EXE
```

If the computer boots and operates normally with this configuration, you can assume that the problem was related to one of the non-DOS entries—that is, a driver for a peripheral (if not the peripheral itself). Note that REMming out the statements (as we did in this example) will cause the devices that the statements were intended to configure to not function at all. This is not a failure, but simply the way computers work.

Sherlock Holmes said it best: "When you have eliminated the impossible, whatever remains, no matter how improbable, must be the truth." In our example, the only device drivers were for the sound card, so it's probable that the sound card was configured improperly. If you had multiple device drivers in the configuration files, you would have to test each possibility separately to find out the source of the problem. Troubleshooting with REM statements is a process of elimination. Step by step, you must eliminate the impossible, so that you can find the improbable.

Backups

Whenever you install drivers for a hardware device, the installation program will ask if you want it to modify CONFIG.SYS and AUTOEXEC.BAT for you or if you would like to modify the files yourself. When the installation program modifies these files, it makes duplicates, or *backups*, of them just in case the drivers it installs cause problems. That way, if there *is* a problem, you can reboot using the backup files instead of the ones modified during the installation process.

To reboot using the backup files, first you need to rename the new CONFIG.SYS and AUTOEXEC.BAT files (to anything other than those names). A good way to keep track of them is to replace the .SYS and .BAT filename extensions with your initials. Then you need to rename (to CONFIG.SYS and AUTOEXEC.BAT, of course) the backups that the installation process created.

Before you can rename your backups to CONFIG.SYS and AUTOEXEC.BAT as directed, you have to find them. Installation programs usually name the backup file for CONFIG.SYS something like CONFIG.BAK or CONFIG.OLD, or, if you already have files with those names, by providing a numbered filename extension, like CONFIG.001 or CONFIG.002. Similarly, these programs rename the backup file for AUTOEXEC.BAT with a .BAK, .OLD, or numbered filename extension.

> Because it's possible that over a matter of months a system will contain numerous backups from different installations, it can be helpful to view the list of files according to date (in some listings, you do this by clicking the Last Modified option). Such a list makes it easy to find the most recently changed files—that is, the configuration files created and modified by the problem installation.

Windows Troubleshooting

Windows problems are the most troublesome of all software-related issues, mainly because several components work together in Windows. If any of these components develops a problem or corruption, it can bring Windows to a screeching halt. There are three primary areas you can check to find troubleshooting information in Windows: system resources, General Protection Faults, and the Windows configuration files.

> This is just an introduction to Windows troubleshooting. We will cover Windows troubleshooting in much more detail in Part II.

System Resources

When Windows runs out of memory, hard disk space, or both, we say it has run out of *system resources*. Windows 3.1 has an About window (in the Windows Program Manager screen, select Help ➢ About) that you can use to check the amount of available system resources (see Figure 10.1). For optimal Windows performance, the available system resources should be above 80 percent. If they are below 80 percent, you need to add RAM, disk space, or both.

FIGURE 10.1   Windows 3.1 system resources

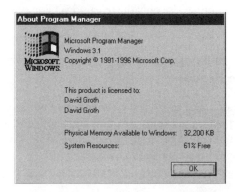

You can check the system resources in Windows 95/98 by using the Resource Meter (select Start ➢ Programs ➢ Accessories ➢ System Tools, if you have installed the Microsoft Plus! pack). The Resource Meter shows up as a small bar graph on your Taskbar at the bottom of the screen. If you double-click the bar graph, it brings up a screen that shows the available system resources (similar to the Windows 3.1 statistics). Figure 10.2 shows this window.

FIGURE 10.2   Checking Windows 95/98 system resources

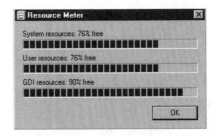

General Protection Faults

A misbehaving Windows program may overstep its bounds and try to take memory from another application. When it does this, Windows halts the misbehaving program and displays an error called a *General Protection Fault (GPF)*. This type of error is one of the most common Windows errors as well as the most frustrating. Such errors are generally the result of nonstandard programming—the programmer took shortcuts and left out the safety nets that would prevent a program from taking memory away from another, running program.

There is no way to make a system 100 percent GPF-free. You can, however, reduce the number of GPFs that occur by taking a couple of precautions. First, monitor your system resources carefully. When Windows starts running out of available memory, it means the programs that are running are tightly packed in memory. In a system with only a little space available, the likelihood is relatively great that a program will use another program's memory when it goes looking for more memory, and thus cause a GPF. (By way of comparison, when a program tries to take more memory in a system that has *plenty* of available memory, the chances are good that it will find memory that is *not* being used by some other program.) This underscores the guideline, "You can never have enough closet space or RAM."

Second, exercise some discipline: Use only the released version of software—the retail version, available commercially.

The Software Release Process

Software goes through three major steps of development: In the *alpha release*, the program is intended only for testing within the software company itself, and it may not include all the features that are intended to be included in the eventual release. Also, software at this stage still has many errors (called *bugs*) that need to be worked out.

The *beta release* includes all the features that will be included in the release version, as well as the installation program (often missing in the alpha version), and is ready for consumer testing. The features may have changed significantly between alpha and beta, based on feedback generated in-house by the alpha testers and management. There may be numerous alpha cycles before the software is ready for outside (beta) testing; and betas themselves frequently undergo numerous builds during a beta cycle, as platform issues and bugs are found and addressed. By the final beta, although some of the loose ends may need to be tightened up, the software is basically ready. When the software is released commercially (*final release*), the developers consider it to be more-or-less bug-free. A few minor bugs may crop up after the initial release, but the software will be stable for use.

WARNING *Never* use alpha or beta software on your computer. These software programs *are* buggy and *will* cause problems, as well as GPFs.

There are two ways to fix bugs that appear after the initial release of the software. You can either use a *patch* (a type of software Band-Aid to fix the problem until the next release) on the software or wait until the next release of the software. Which brings us to our next tip: Try to avoid version 1.0 of any piece of software. Because this version is the first release, it usually contains the most bugs. Wait until the software has been released for a few months and has gone through a few revisions before buying it and installing it on your computer. By revision 1.2, most of the bugs have been worked out and the software can be considered stable.

How to Read the Version Numbers on Software

When you're reading the version number of most software titles, you can deduce a few things. The leftmost digit in a version number indicates the *major release version*. Each major release introduces several new features and may completely change the way the software operates.

The first number to the right of the decimal point is the *revision number*. When a single feature (or small set of features) needs to be introduced, along with several bug fixes, a new revision of the software is released. Revision numbers increment until the software developers decide to release another major release.

Any numbers to the right of the revision number can be considered patch levels. When software is released with a second number to the right of a decimal point, it usually means that it is a bug fix only. No new features are released in such a version.

For example, let's examine the following revision number: FURBLE 1.24. This indicates that the software contains all the features of the first major release of the FURBLE program and is the second revision of that release and the fourth patch at that level. This software should be quite stable by this stage.

Also note that some vendors (mainly Microsoft) have abandoned this convention in favor of naming software with the year it is released (Windows 95, Office 97, and so on.). However, production schedules fall behind, and sometimes software is released the following year.

Windows Configuration

When Windows 3.*x* programs are installed, their files are copied to the hard disk and entries are made into the Windows configuration files: the INI files and the System Registry. The entries that are made into these files control various settings and tell the program (or Windows itself) how to operate. Let's discuss each of them.

INI Files

Primarily used for Windows 3.*x* programs, *INI files* (short for initialization files) are made for each program as well as for Windows. When a new application is installed, the installation program creates an INI file that contains the new application's settings. INI files are text files that can be edited with any text editor if necessary.

The three primary INI files that Windows uses are SYSTEM.INI, WIN.INI, and PROGMAN.INI. You should back up each of them before making changes. SYSTEM.INI has settings for the drivers that Windows uses. It is probably the most critical of the three. Changes made to this file affect Windows' resource usage as well as resource availability.

WIN.INI controls the Windows operating environment. It includes entries for the programs Windows starts automatically, screensaver settings, desktop color schemes, wallpaper, and system compatibility information. Changes made to this file can be critical (your screen might come up in a different color, for example), and you should take care when modifying the [Compatibility] section, because you could cause problems with programs designed to run under older versions of Windows.

Finally, PROGMAN.INI contains settings for the Program Manager. The settings control the number and filenames of the program groups in the Program Manager. Changing these settings modifies which program groups appear in the Program Manager. You can also control Program Manager security (such as what menu options appear or are grayed out) by modifying the [Restriction] section.

 If you delete the INI file of some programs, the program will create a new one with the default settings.

A problem can be tracked to an INI file if a setting was made in a Windows 3.1 program and now the program doesn't function properly or if it GPFs frequently. To solve this type of problem, it is best to rename an old INI file to replace the corrupt one (like WINWORD.OLD to WINWORD.INI).

Just like with DOS installation programs, Windows setup programs make backups of the configuration files they change and name them with `.BAK` or `.OLD` extension or with a number extensions (`.001`, `.002`, and so on). If you have a problem with a new INI file, you can rename one of the backups (preferably the most recent one) to the `.INI` extension to make *it* the active INI file.

The Registry

With the introduction of Windows 95, Microsoft did away with the practice of using several INI files to contain program configuration information. The company introduced a special database called the *Registry* to provide a single common location for all configuration and program setting information. Every Windows 95/98 program, upon installation, will register itself so that Windows 95/98 knows about it. When other programs need information about what printers and devices are available in Windows 95/98, they query the Registry to get this information.

You can view and edit the Registry with `REGEDIT.EXE` (for 32-bit versions of Windows, like NT/2000/XP, you can view it with `regedt32.exe`). When you run this program, it presents the view shown in Figure 10.3. Each folder represents a section or *key* that contains specific information. The settings for Windows programs are kept within these keys.

FIGURE 10.3   Viewing the Registry with `REGEDIT.EXE`

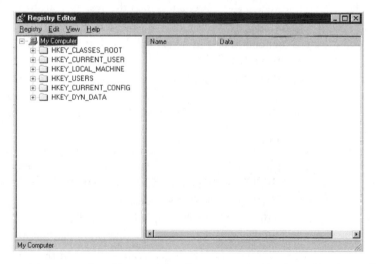

Generally speaking, you should not make changes to the Registry. Registry changes can be exceedingly complex and are not covered on the A+ core exam, so we won't devote any more space to them here.

Hardware Troubleshooting

When you're troubleshooting hardware, there are a few common problems that any experienced technician should know about. These common problems usually have simple solutions. Knowing these problems (and their respective solutions) will make you a more efficient troubleshooter.

POST Routines

The first item we'll discuss isn't really a hardware problem, but a hardware troubleshooting aid. Every computer has a diagnostic program built into its BIOS called the *power on self-test (POST)*. When you turn on the computer, it executes this set of diagnostics. These tests go by pretty quickly, so we'll detail them here:

 The POST described here is typical of IBM-brand PCs; other manufacturers have similar POSTs, but they may differ in certain aspects.

1. **The processor is tested.** POST runs checks on the CPU. If the tests fail, the system stops with no error message (usually).

2. **The ROMs are checked.** POST computes a checksum for the BIOS ROMs. If the checksums do not match, the system halts with no error message.

3. **The DMA controller is tested.** Again, if there are problems, the system halts.

4. **The Interrupt controller is checked.** If there is a problem with this component, the system will give a long beep and then a short beep, and then the system will stop.

5. **The system timing chip is tested.** This is not the chip that tells time, but rather the chip that provides timing signals for the bus and processor. If this chip fails, the system will give a long beep and then a short beep, and then halt.

6. **The BASIC ROMs are tested (if they exist).** Most computers since the IBM AT have not included BASIC, so this step is usually not part of their POST routines. However, on older computers, if the BASIC ROMs fail the POST test, the system gives another long beep and then a short beep, and then halts.

7. **The video card is checked.** At this point the system runs the diagnostics for the video card. If they fail, the system issues one long beep and two short beeps and halts. If they're successful, the video ROM BIOS is copied into RAM, and you will usually see a message about the type of video card the computer is using.

8. **Expansion boards are initialized.** During this part of the POST routine, any expansion boards that need to can initialize and copy their ROMs into upper memory.

9. **RAM is counted and tested.** The system tests and counts all RAM that's installed in the machine by writing a bit to each bit of memory. If a 1 is written and read back successfully, the counter increments. A failure during this portion of the POST will generate a "201— Memory Error" message on the screen. (Here's a free tip for you: Any POST error numbers starting with 2 are memory related.)

10. **The keyboard is tested.** The keyboard controller is contacted and signals are sent to detect the presence of a keyboard. Checks for stuck keys are also made. If this test fails, a "301— Keyboard Failure" error is generated along with a short beep. Some systems halt; others don't. (Some systems also ask you to press the F1 key, which is kind of silly if the keyboard isn't working.)

11. **The cassette interface is checked.** This is another POST routine that's valid only on IBM PCs and XTs. If the cassette interface doesn't work, a "131—Cassette Interface" error is generated. The system does not halt.

12. **The floppy drives are tested.** The floppy disk adapter is contacted and asked to activate the drive motors of any floppy disks, in order (A: and then B:). If there are problems, a "601—Floppy Disk" error is generated and the system tries to load cassette BASIC (if it's present, on an IBM PC or XT).

13. **Resources are checked and the computer is booted.** The POST routine queries any remaining devices (LPT ports, serial ports, and so on.), makes a short beep, and then queries the disk drives looking for an operating system. If one is found on either a floppy drive or hard disk, it is loaded, and the computer is functional. If an operating system can't be found, most systems issue an "Operating system not found" error (or something to that effect).

The POST routines are a great tool for troubleshooting. They usually give English descriptions of any problems they find. Some BIOS POST routines may give suggestions on how to fix the problem (don't expect this kind of friendliness on an IBM AT, though; it only gives cryptic error codes). Tables 10.1 and 10.2 summarize the POST beep and error codes, respectively, that are most often seen on computers today.

TABLE 10.1   Common POST Beep Codes

Beep Code	Problem
No beep, system dead	Power supply bad, system not plugged in, or power not turned on
Continuous beeps	Power supply bad, not plugged into motherboard correctly, or keyboard stuck
Repeating short beep	Power supply problem
One short beep, nothing on screen	Video card failure
One short beep, video present, but system won't boot	Bad floppy drive, cable, or controller
Two short beeps	Configuration error (on most PS/2 systems)
One long beep, one short beep	System board bad
One long beep, two short beeps	Video card failure

TABLE 10.2 Common POST Error Codes

Error Number	Explanation
1**	Any number starting with 1 usually indicates a system board problem.
161	CMOS battery failure.
164	Memory size error. Always happens after memory has been added. Running the BIOS Setup program allows the system to recognize the memory, and the error should go away.
2**	Any number starting with 2 usually indicates a memory-related problem.
201	Memory test failed. One or more portions of RAM were found to be bad. Any numbers following this error code may indicate which RAM chip is bad. See the computer's documentation for information on interpreting those codes.
3**	Any error number starting with 3 usually indicates a problem with the keyboard. Problems include a missing or malfunctioning keyboard, as well as stuck keys.
301	Keyboard error. Usually means a missing or malfunctioning keyboard or a key that has been pressed too long during startup (are you resting your hand on the keyboard? is something leaning against one of the keys?). Also happens if a key remains depressed during the POST keyboard test.
4**	Monochrome video problems.
5**	Color video problems.
6**	Floppy disk system problems.
601	Floppy disk error. Either the floppy adapter or the floppy drive failed. Check to see that the floppy cable isn't on upside down and that the power to the floppy drive(s) is hooked up correctly.
17**	Hard disk problems. The hard disk geometry may not be set correctly, or the disk adapter can't communicate with the hard disk.
1780	Drive 0 (C:) drive failure. The C: drive or controller isn't functioning. The disk might not be configured, or the adapter isn't installed correctly.
1781	Drive 1 (D:) drive failure. The D: drive or controller isn't functioning. The disk might not be configured, or the adapter isn't installed correctly.

Motherboard Problems

The motherboard's (or logic board's) functions are tested, for the most part, by the POST routines. The 1** errors and beep codes during startup indicate the biggest problems. There are very few problems that don't show up in the POST. The occasional phantom problem does happen, however.

One problem becomes visible when the system constantly loses its clock—the time resets to 12:00 on 12/01/83, for example. At the same time, you may begin seeing "1780—Hard Disk Failure" problems. When you try to reset the time, it sets correctly. But as soon as you turn off the computer and turn it back on, the time is lost.

These symptoms indicate that the system's CMOS is losing the time, date, and hard-disk settings (as well as several other system settings). The CMOS is able to keep this information when the system is shut off because a small battery powers this memory. Because it is a battery, it eventually loses power and goes dead.

 Some older systems use a special chip called a *Dallas chip* to provide the same functionality as the CMOS battery. But, like the CMOS battery, it too will die eventually.

When you replace the CMOS battery (or Dallas chip), you must reset the system settings, but they will be retained when the power is shut off. Some people immediately think "system board problem," when the real answer is a cheap battery and 10 minutes of labor. Because of the simplicity of this repair, most service professionals replace these batteries as a courtesy service for their customers. Consider it an outpatient repair.

Hard Disk System Problems

Hard disk system problems usually stem from one of three causes:

- The adapter is bad.
- The disk is bad.
- The adapter and disk are connected incorrectly.

The first and last causes are easy to identify, because in either case the symptom is obvious: the drive won't work. You simply won't be able to get the computer to communicate with the disk drive. (You can further narrow down whether it's a configuration problem by checking to see if the drive is connected correctly. If it is, then the problem is usually a bad or misconfigured disk adapter.)

However, if the problem is a bad disk drive, the symptoms aren't as obvious. As long as the BIOS POST tests can communicate with the disk drive, they are usually satisfied. But the POST tests may not uncover problems related to storing information. For example, even with healthy POST results, you may find that you're permitted to save information to a bad disk—but of course when you try to read it back, you get errors. Or the computer may not boot as quickly as it used to, because the disk drive can't read the boot information successfully every time.

Bad disk drives could be the cause of the problems in both of these examples, but they would not be indicated by a POST test. Keep in mind, then, that a successful POST test doesn't necessarily mean a happy computer.

In some cases, reformatting the drive can solve the problems described in the preceding paragraph. In other cases, reformatting only brings the drive back to life for a short while. The bottom line is that read and write problems usually indicate that the drive is going south and should be replaced soon. Never expect a Band-Aid repair like reformatting to cover a major trauma problem like disk failure.

WARNING Never low-level format IDE or SCSI drives! They are low-leveled from the factory, and you may cause problems by using low-level utilities on these types of drives.

Peripheral Problems

The biggest set of peripheral problems is related to modem communications. The symptoms of these problems include the following:

- The modem won't dial.
- The modem keeps hanging up in the middle of the communications session.
- The modem spits out strange characters to the terminal screen.

If the modem won't dial, first check that it has been configured correctly, including its IRQ setting (as discussed in Chapter 6). If the configuration is correct, then the problem usually has to do with *initialization commands*. These commands are sent to the modem by the communications program to initialize it. These commands tell the modem things like how many rings to wait before answering, how long to wait after the last detected keystroke before disconnecting, and at what speed to communicate.

For a while, each manufacturer had its own set of commands, and every communications program had to have settings for every kind of modem available. In particular, every program had commands for the Hayes line of modems (mainly because Hayes made good modems and their command language was fairly easy to program). Eventually, other modem manufacturers began using the Hayes-compatible command set. This set of modem initialization commands became known as the *Hayes command set*, or the *AT command set*, because each Hayes modem command started with the letters *AT* (presumably calling the modem to ATtention).

Each AT command does something different. The letters *AT* by themselves (when issued as a command) ask the modem if it's ready to receive commands. If it returns *OK*, the modem is ready to communicate. If you receive *error*, there is an internal modem problem that may need to be resolved before communication can take place.

Table 10.3 lists a few of the most common AT commands, their functions, and the problems they can solve. You can send these commands to the modem by opening a terminal program (such as the Windows Terminal or HyperTerminal (supplied with Windows 3.x and Windows 9x/ME/NT/2000/XP, respectively), WINTERM.EXE, or ProCOMM) and typing them in. All commands should return *OK* if they were successful.

If you can't type anything, you either don't have the right COM port selected for the modem or you have half-duplex mode enabled. To address this problem, you must enter **ATF1** and then press Enter. The modem should return the message *OK*, and you will be able to see your commands. It is also possible that you have the flow control set improperly. Some modems only echo to the display if flow control is turned off.

TABLE 10.3   Common AT Commands

Command	Function	Usage
AT	Tells the modem that what follows the letters *AT* is a command that should be interpreted	Used to precede most commands.
ATDT *nnnnnnn*	Dials the number *nnnnnnn* as a tone-dialed number	Used to dial the number of another modem if the phone line is set up for tone dialing.
ATDP *nnnnnnn*	Dials the number *nnnnnnn* as a pulse-dialed number	Used to dial the number of another modem if the phone line is set up for rotary dialing.
ATA	Answers an incoming call manually	Places the line off-hook and starts to negotiate communication with the modem on the other end.
ATH0 (or +++ and then ATH0)	Tells the modem to hang up immediately	Places the line on-hook and stops communication. (Note: The 0 in this command is a zero, not the letter *O*.)
AT&F	Resets the modem to the factory default settings	This setting works as the initialization string when others don't. If you have problems with modems hanging up in the middle of a session or failing to establish connections, use this string by itself to initialize the modem.
ATZ	Resets the modem to the power-up defaults	Almost as good as AT&F, but may not work if the power-up defaults have been changed with S-registers.
ATS0-*n*	Waits *n* rings before answering a call	Sets the default number of rings the modem will detect before taking the modem off-hook and negotiating a connection. (Note: The 0 in this command is a zero, not the letter *O*.)
ATS6-*n*	Waits *n* seconds for a dial tone before dialing	If the phone line is slow to give a dial tone, you may have to set this register to a number higher than 2.

TABLE 10.3 Common AT Commands *(continued)*

Command	Function	Usage
" , "	Pauses briefly	When placed in a string of AT commands, the comma causes a pause to occur. Used to separate the number for an outside line (many businesses use 9 to connect to an outside line) and the real phone number (such as 9,555-1234).
*70 or 1170	Turns off call waiting	The click you hear when you have call waiting (a feature offered by the phone company) will interrupt modem communication and cause the connection to be lost. To disable call waiting for a modem call, place these commands in the dialing string like so: *70,555-1234. Call waiting will resume after you hang up the call.
CONNECT	Displayed when a successful connection has been made	You may have to wait some time before this message is displayed. If this message is not displayed, it means the modem couldn't negotiate a connection with the modem on the other end of the line, possibly due to line noise.
BUSY	Displayed when the number dialed is busy	If this is displayed, some programs wait a certain amount of time and try again to dial.
RING	Displayed when the modem has detected a ringing line	When someone is calling your modem, the modem displays this in the communications program. You type ATA to answer the call.

If two computers can connect, but they both receive garbage to their screens, there's a good chance that the computers aren't agreeing on the communications settings. Settings like data bits, parity, stop bits, and compression must all agree in order for communication to take place. When both computers have different settings, it's a lot like two people from different countries trying to communicate. They can meet and shake hands, but from there they can't communicate, because they are both speaking different languages.

One of the most common settings for serial communications is 8N1. That stands for (8) data bits, (N)o parity, (1) stop bit.

Keyboard and Mouse Problems

Keyboards are simple devices. Therefore, they either work or they don't. There are rarely any phantom problems with keyboards. Usually, keyboard problems are environmental—keyboards get dirty, and the keys start to stick. This problem is easily avoided: *Don't eat or drink near the computer.* It is my personal opinion that anyone who drinks near a computer keyboard should be made to clean one that has had a soft drink spilled in it. That person will never drink near a keyboard again. The liquid works its way into the plungers under the key caps and, instead of drying, turns into a sticky, syrupy substance that doesn't easily wash away.

To clean a keyboard, it's best to use the keyboard cleaner sold by electronics supply stores. This cleaner foams up quickly and doesn't leave a residue behind. Spray it liberally on the keyboard and keys. Work the cleaner in between the keys with a stiff toothbrush. Blow away the excess with a strong blast of compressed air. Repeat until the keyboard functions properly. If you do have to clean a keyboard that's had a soft drink spilled on it, remove the key caps before you perform the cleaning procedure. It makes it easier to reach the sticky plungers.

A friend of mine told me about his way of cleaning a keyboard: Remove the electronics and place the keyboard in a dishwasher in the rinse cycle! Then, let it air dry. I wouldn't recommend this approach for some of the newer, capacitive keyboards. However, it will work for the older keyswitch keyboards (as long as the water isn't hard enough to leave residue inside the key switches or hot enough to melt the keys). Jet-Dry, anyone? My friend had a part-time business—PM PM (Preventative Maintenance at night) and offered keyboard cleanup services for $20 (in the late 1970s, this was easy money).

With mechanical keyboards, you can desolder a broken key switch and replace it. However, most of the time, the labor to replace one key is more expensive than a new keyboard. New keyboards can be had for less than 50 dollars, so keep the one with the single malfunctioning key as a spare and replace it with a new one.

To clean the key caps on a keyboard, spray keyboard cleaner on a soft, lint-free cloth and rub it briskly onto the surface of each key. Be careful not to rub too hard; some of the cheaper keyboards use decals on their keys, and you might rub them right off!

Display System Problems

There are two types of video problems: no video and bad video. *No video* means no image appears on the screen when the computer is powered up. *Bad video* means the quality is substandard for the type of display system being used.

No Video

Any number of things can cause a blank screen. The first two are the most common: either the power is off, or the contrast or brightness is turned down. It's surprising how many people get stuck on that first one. I've gotten panicked phone calls (some from experienced technicians) that go like this: "I can't get the monitor working!" or "I don't get any video on my screen!" Usually the technicians tell me they've even checked the video card's ROM address and changed it a couple of times just to be sure. I love this part:

Me: "Is it turned on?"

Them: (long pause) "Oh. Never mind." <click>

Or, if they verify that it's turned on:

Me: "Are the brightness and contrast turned down?"

Them: "Where do I check that?"

Me: "Can you see the knobs or buttons that have a picture of a sun on one and a picture of a circle with half dark and half light on the other?"

Them: "Found 'em. Now what?"

Me: "Turn them one direction and then the other, and see if the screen gets brighter."

Them: "Okay. Oh! Wow! Cool! Sorry about that."

If they checked the power as well as the brightness and contrast settings, then the problem is either a bad video card or blown monitor. An easy way to determine which is to turn on the computer and monitor, and then touch the monitor screen. The high voltage used to charge the monitor leaves a static charge on a working monitor, and it's a charge you can feel. If there's no charge, then there's a good chance the flyback transformer has blown and the monitor needs to be repaired. If there is a charge, the video card and cable are suspect. This charge drains away fairly quickly, so the test only works immediately after power-up. Also, it's not a conclusive test, but it gives you a good indication.

WARNING — Be *very* careful when working with monitors! Monitors contain capacitors that store a charge used when starting up. The power in the capacitor dissipates fairly quickly, but if the timing is right (or wrong), you could end up with a nasty shock.

Bad Video

You may have seen a monitor that has a bad data cable. This is the monitor nobody wants; everything has a blue (or red, or green) tint to it, and it gives everyone a headache. This monitor could also have a bad gun, but more often than not, the problem goes away if you wiggle the cable (indicating a bad cable).

You may have also seen monitors that are out of adjustment. Their pictures don't fill the screen (size adjustment), the images roll (vertical or horizontal hold), or they are distorted (angle and pincushion adjustments). With most new monitors, these problems are easy to fix. Old monitors had to be partially disassembled to change these settings. New monitors have push-button control panels for changing these settings.

The earth generates a very strong magnetic field. This magnetic field can cause swirls and fuzziness even in high-quality monitors. Most monitors have metal shields that protect against magnetic fields. But eventually these shields can get polluted by taking on the same magnetic field as the earth, and become useless. To solve this problem, these monitors have a built-in *degauss* feature. This feature removes the effects of the magnetic field by creating a stronger magnetic field with opposite polarity that gradually fades to a field of zero. A special Degauss button activates it. You only need to press it when the picture starts to deteriorate. The image will shake momentarily during the degauss cycle, and then return to normal.

> You shouldn't use the degauss feature every day. Once a month is usually sufficient if you are having color or clarity problems that get worse with time. You would only need to degauss every day if you lived in a place where high magnetic fields were a problem (for example, near an electrical substation or high-powered overhead lines). If that's the situation you find yourself in, you might need to purchase a special, heavily shielded monitor for those conditions.

LCD Problems

For the most part, desktop LCD systems can suffer from the same video problems as monitors. However, one problem that LCD systems have that monitors don't have (at least, not to a great extent) is bad pixels. LCD displays can and often do leave the factory with a few pixels that just won't turn on. This pixel is known as a *dead pixel*. This problem is discussed at length in Chapter 7, "Portable Systems."

LCD displays may have to be reconfigured from time to time, if they won't detect the correct resolution. You do this with a special Auto Reconfigure button or an option on the LCD display. Pressing this button causes the display to reconfigure itself to properly show the signal coming from the video card.

Floppy Drive Problems

Today the floppy drive is almost unnecessary—most applications, hardware drivers, and utilities ship on CD-ROMs. Besides, most of the things we want to back up and carry away are too large for the traditional floppy media (thus the proliferation of Zip, Jaz, and other removable media storage devices). Even so, the floppy is still a mainstay of the PC—and when you need it, it had better work.

Most floppy drive problems result from bad media. For some reason, people will not admit that a 10-cent floppy disk can (and will) go bad over time. Personally, I do not use a floppy disk more than twice—once to write to it and once to read from it. (Of course, being a computer geek, I've got other options for long-term storage.) Your first troubleshooting technique with floppy drive issues should be to try a new disk.

One of the most common problems that develops with floppy drives is misaligned read/write heads. The symptoms are fairly easy to recognize—you can read and write to a floppy on one machine but not on any others. This problem is usually caused by the mechanical arm in the floppy drive becoming misaligned so that the format it creates is not properly positioned on the disk (thus preventing other floppy drives from reading it).

Numerous commercial tools are available to realign floppy drive read/write heads. They use a floppy drive that has been preformatted to reposition the mechanical arm. In most cases, though, this fix is temporary—the arm will move out of place again fairly soon. Given the inexpensive nature of the problem, the best solution is to spend a few dollars and replace the drive.

Sound Card Problems

Sound cards are traditionally one of the most problem-ridden components in a PC. They demand a lot of PC resources and are notorious for being very inflexible in their configuration. The most common sound card–related problems involve resource conflicts (IRQ, DMA, or I/O address).

Luckily, most sound card vendors are aware of the problems and ship very good diagnostic utilities to help resolve them. Use your PC troubleshooting skills to determine the conflict, and then reconfigure until you have found an acceptable set of resources that are not in use.

BIOS Issues

Computer BIOSs don't really go bad; they become out of date. This is not necessarily a critical issue—they will continue to support the hardware that came with the box. It *does*, however, become an issue when the BIOS doesn't support a component you would like to install—a larger hard drive, for instance.

Most of today's BIOSs are written to a Flash EEPROM and can be updated using software. Each manufacturer has its own method for accomplishing this. Check out the documentation for complete details.

One warning: If you make a mistake in the upgrade process, the computer can become unbootable. If this happens, often your only option is shipping the box to a manufacturer-approved service center. *Be careful!*

Power Supply Problems

Power supply problems are usually easy to troubleshoot—nothing happens when you flip the switch. When that happens (and it will), first try disconnecting the power from the wall for a few minutes. Doing so will cause the power supply's internal relay to reset. If this doesn't work, open the case, remove the power supply, and replace it with a new one. No one services power supplies anymore; replacement is much cheaper and easier.

Be aware that different cases have different types of on/off switches. The process of replacing a power supply is a lot easier if you purchase a replacement with the same mechanism. Even so, remember to document exactly how the power supply was connected to the on/off switch. (I've spent hours trying various combinations of connections, trying to get the on/off switch to work.)

In addition, newer ATX power supplies have two switches: a main power switch on the back of the computer and the internal on/off switch activated by the motherboard. The switch at the back of the power supply must be turned on and the front case power switch properly connected to the motherboard. If neither is done, the computer won't turn on no matter how many times you hit the power switch.

Miscellaneous Problems

A couple of problems don't fit well into any category but "Miscellaneous." So, we'll cover them here.

Dislodged Chips and Cards

The inside of your computer is a fairly harsh environment. The temperature inside the case of some Pentium computers is well over 100°F! When you turn on your computer, it heats up. Turn it off, and it cools down. After several hundred such cycles, some components can't handle the stress and start to move out of their sockets. This phenomenon is known as *chip creep*, and it can really be frustrating.

Chip creep can affect any socketed device, including ICs, RAM chips, and expansion cards. The solution to chip creep is simple: Open the case and reseat the devices. It's surprising how often this is the solution to phantom problems of all sorts.

Environmental Problems

I'll never forget the time I had to work on a computer that had been used on the manufacturing floor of a large equipment manufacturer. The computer and keyboard were covered with a black substance that would not come off. (I later found out it was a combination of paint mist and molybdenum grease.) There was so much diesel fume residue in the power supply fan that it would barely turn. The insides and components were covered with a thin, greasy layer of muck. To top it all off, the computer *smelled terrible*!

Despite all this, the computer still functioned. However, it was prone to reboot itself every now and again. The solution was (as you may have guessed) to clean every component thoroughly and replace the power supply. The muck on the components was able to conduct a small current. Sometimes that current would go where it wasn't wanted, and zap!—a reboot. In addition, the power supply fan is supposed to partially cool the inside of the computer. In this computer, the fan was detrimental to the computer because it got its cooling air from the shop floor, which contained diesel fumes, paint fumes, and other chemical fumes. Needless to say, those fumes aren't good for computer components.

Computers are like human beings. They have similar tolerances to heat and cold (although computers like the cold better than we do). In general, anything comfortable to us is comfortable to a computer. Computers need lots of clean, moving air to keep them functioning. They don't, however, require food or drink (except maybe a few RAM chips now and again)—keep those away from the computer.

WARNING The worst thing you can do is eat, drink, or smoke around your computer. Smoke particles contain tar that can get inside the computer and cause problems similar to those described earlier.

One way to ensure that the environment has the least possible effect on your computer is to always leave the blanks in the empty slots on the back of your box. These pieces of metal are designed to keep dirt, dust, and other foreign matter out of the inside of the computer. They also maintain proper airflow within the case to ensure that the computer does not overheat.

FRUs

When a component has been deemed to be bad, it needs to be replaced. That's where the FRU comes in. As you learned in Chapter 6, FRU stands for *Field Replaceable Unit*.

FRUs can be individual parts (such as gears, springs, and shafts) or whole assemblies (like monitors, power supplies, and keyboards). In most cases you don't (or can't) replace individual parts. Most companies have gone to the strategy of using whole assemblies for FRUs. For example, you can't order a #2415 capacitor for a Compaq power supply from Compaq anymore. Instead, you order a #A5123G power supply assembly. The individual assembly costs more, but there is less labor involved in replacing a whole power supply than a single capacitor, so it's actually cheaper for the customer as well as the service centers.

When you have determined that a particular component needs to be replaced, you look in a catalog (usually produced by the manufacturer) for the part number of the FRU you need. The catalog may also indicate the FRU's cost and shipping information. Some FRUs require an exchange of the old, broken component (called a *core* or *exchange* FRU). In this case, the catalog will indicate two prices: one for the FRU alone, and another for the FRU with an exchange. The price of the single FRU is usually double (sometimes triple) the price of a core FRU.

Summary

This book can give you the basic knowledge you need to be a good troubleshooter, but not the instinct you need to be a great one. Very few people have mastered the art of troubleshooting. The reason is that troubleshooting *is* an art, and as with any art, excellence comes only through experience. The best way to get experience is through reading, practicing, research, and asking questions.

Although experience is key, there are also basic resources and procedures that can help you troubleshoot while you are gaining that experience. In this chapter we presented a few of those tools.

We started the chapter with a discussion of some of the intellectual resources that are available. Product documentation, the Internet, and other technicians can often be used to answer questions based on your description of a problem. We also went over the basic hardware and software utilities you can use to help you troubleshoot.

In the next section, we presented our top 10 general troubleshooting steps, which guide you through a basic system for any troubleshooting scenario. Following the steps should eventually lead you to a satisfactory conclusion of your troubleshooting process.

We then moved to troubleshooting specific software issues. Starting with DOS and moving to Windows, we discussed common configuration files and techniques that can be used to test their validity.

Finally, we concentrated on specific hardware troubleshooting techniques. We discussed the POST routine (what it is and how it warns you of problems), motherboard problems, hard disk issues, keyboard and mouse problems, display system troubleshooting, BIOS issues, power supply problems, and a few other miscellaneous hardware issues.

Key Terms

Before you take the exam, be certain you are familiar with the following terms:

backup	network client
bootable diskette	power on self-test (POST)
Field Replaceable Unit (FRU)	Registry
Frequently Asked Questions (FAQ)	REM statement
General Protection Fault (GPF)	resource discovery expansion card
INI file	revision number
initialization command	system resources

Review Questions

1. A customer complains that his hard disk is making a lot of noise. After examining the computer and hearing the high-pitched noise for yourself, you notice that the noise seems to be coming from the fan in the power supply. Which component(s) should be replaced? (Select all that apply.)

    A. Hard disk

    B. Power supply

    C. Motherboard

    D. Nothing. This is a software problem.

2. When you try to turn on the computer, you notice that it will not activate. The monitor is blank, and the fan on the power supply is not active. Turning the switch off and then back on makes no difference. What is the most likely cause of this problem?

    A. The computer is unplugged.

    B. The BIOS on the motherboard needs to be upgraded.

    C. The monitor is malfunctioning.

    D. Both the fan on the power supply and the video card are bad.

    E. The power supply is bad.

    F. None of the above.

3. A customer complains that they can't get their computer to work. When they turn it on, they get no video and hear one long beep, followed by two short beeps. You tell the customer to bring in the machine. Upon further examination, you are able to reproduce the problem. What is your next step?

    A. Upgrade the PC's BIOS to the newest version.

    B. Replace the motherboard.

    C. Replace the video card.

    D. Replace the RAM.

    E. Upgrade the BEEP.COM file.

    F. Boot clean to a bootable floppy disk.

4. A 201 error at system startup means what?

    A. Bad floppy drive

    B. Bad system board

    C. Bad hard disk system

    D. Bad memory

    E. Bad keyboard

5. Which Windows error is caused by an application being greedy and taking memory away from other programs?

   A. General System Error

   B. General Protection Fault

   C. System Fault

   D. Memory Protection Fault

6. What two files are used by DOS to configure a computer?

   A. INI files

   B. `AUTOEXEC.BAT`

   C. `CONFIG.BAT`

   D. `CONFIG.SYS`

7. A computer is experiencing random reboots and phantom problems that disappear after reboot. What should you do?

   A. Tell the customer that it's normal for the computer to do that.

   B. Replace the motherboard.

   C. Boot clean.

   D. Replace the power supply.

   E. Open the cover and reseat all cards and chips.

8. What is the largest cause of computer problems?

   A. Hardware failure

   B. Software failure

   C. ESD

   D. Technician inexperience

   E. User error

9. A user is getting a 301 error when they turn on the computer. What is a possible cause?

   A. A virus on the boot sector of the hard disk

   B. User error

   C. Dust and dirt on the power supply fan

   D. A book lying on the keyboard during system startup

10. You install a newly purchased sound card into your computer, but upon rebooting you find that the new device is not recognized by the system. Moreover, your modem, which has always worked perfectly, has stopped functioning. What is probably the problem?

A. The sound card and modem are using the same slot on the motherboard.

B. The drivers for the sound card need to be updated.

C. The sound card is using the same IRQ as the modem.

D. The modem is 16-bit and the sound card is 32-bit, meaning that they cannot both be used in the same system.

Answers to Review Questions

1. B.   Because the noise is coming from the power supply, the first logical choice is to check the power supply.

2. A.   Because turning the switch on and off makes no difference, the first item to check is whether the computer is properly plugged in.

3. C.   When a computer is turned on, there is no video, and you here a series of beeps in the sequence one long beep and then two short beeps, it means something is wrong with the video card. Check first to see that it is seated properly and in the proper slot for its bus type. If this checks out fine, replace it with a known good card and turn the machine back on. If this solves the problem, then the issue was a bad card, and it needs to be permanently replaced.

4. D.   Most error codes that begin with a 2 indicate a memory error of some sort.

5. B.   Although other factors might contribute, most General Protection Fault errors are generated when an application either monopolizes too much memory or attempts to access inappropriate memory addresses.

6. B, D.   The two files that DOS uses to configure a computer are AUTOEXEC.BAT and CONFIG.SYS. In general, the CONFIG.SYS file sets up the operating system environment, and the AUTOEXEC.BAT file sets up the user environment.

7. E.   When a computer is experiencing random reboots and phantom problems that disappear after reboot, you should open the cover and reseat all cards and chips. Most likely, some components have experienced chip creep.

8. E.   Unfortunately, the largest cause of computer problems is user error. These errors have the potential to be the most difficult to troubleshoot. A technician must have very good diplomatic skills to obtain all the answers necessary to fix the problem.

9. D.   Errors that begin with 3 are typically keyboard errors. Common suspects to look for are a keyboard that is not properly connected, or a key stuck in the depressed position—in this case, because a book was lying on the keyboard.

10. C.   When two otherwise healthy devices both are malfunctioning, there is a good chance that they are both trying to use the same system resources. The IRQ and DMA settings are the most common culprits.

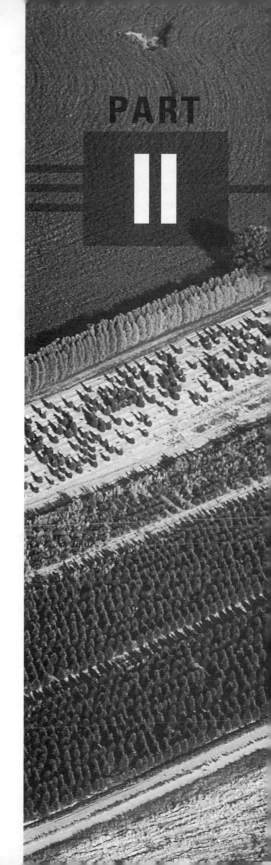

Operating Systems Technologies Exam

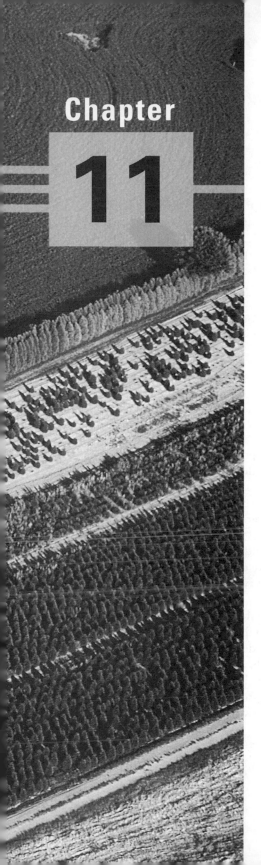

Chapter

11

Introduction to Operating Systems

"I think there is a world market for maybe five computers."

—Thomas Watson
Chairman of IBM, 1943

In previous chapters, we looked at the hardware that composes a personal computer's physical components. Hardware is only half the story, though. When poor Mr. Watson made his prediction 60 years ago, he was looking at a very different machine from the ones we have today. At that time computers were bulky—as in room-sized—slow, and difficult to use. As recently as the 1970s, most machines were still using punch cards as a primary data input tool, and anyone wanting to use a computer had to navigate a complex, uninviting interface with only a keyboard to help them. In such an environment, Watson probably was correct to believe that few people would go through the time, effort, and expense to use computers.

After years of training people to pass the A+ certification exam, we realize how important this material is to passing the test. Even though this chapter doesn't directly cover any objectives, it provides crucial context for working in the field.

As computer technology has evolved toward smaller, more powerful machines, the personal computer has made significant strides toward Microsoft's grandiose stated goal of "a computer in every home." The incredible global computer revolution is not due just to hardware, though. In many ways, the acceleration of computer usage over the last decade has had more to do with the ever-improving operating systems that humans use to interact with these machines. Computers require programmed code (called *software*) to run, and they require an input-output mechanism to allow users to give the machine instructions and to view the results of those commands. The *operating system* (OS) is the primary software used to achieve these ends, and the evolution of more powerful and user-friendly operating systems has made computers less difficult to use and more enjoyable.

In order to understand the emergence of modern personal computer OSs, you should know about the technologies that led to our present systems and about the critical relationship between hardware and software over the course of the PC's development. Graphics, speed, GUI interfaces, and multiple programs running concurrently are all made possible because software designers take full advantage of the hardware for which they are designing their software. As a result, you will see that as computer hardware has improved, software has improved with it. Because the OS is the platform on which all other software builds, it is generally the development of a new OS that drives the development of other software. This chapter is therefore the story of that very special, and crucial, type of software—the personal computer OS. This chapter looks at where operating systems have been, and the rest of the book will concentrate on where they are currently, by focusing on Microsoft's Windows 95/98, Windows NT, Windows 2000, and Windows XP operating systems.

Types of Software

There are a number of different types of personal computer software, and each has a specific role in the operation of the machine. Among these are the following major distinctions:

Operating System (OS)   Provides a consistent environment for other software to execute commands. The OS gives users an interface with the computer so they can send commands (input) and receive feedback or results back (output). To do this, the OS must communicate with the computer hardware to perform the following tasks:

- Disk and file management
- Device access
- Memory management
- Output format

Once the OS has organized these basic resources, users can give the computer instructions through input devices (such as a keyboard or a mouse). Some of these commands are built into the OS, whereas others are issued through the use of applications. The OS becomes the center through which the system hardware, other software, and the user communicate; the rest of the components of the system work together through the OS, which coordinates their communication.

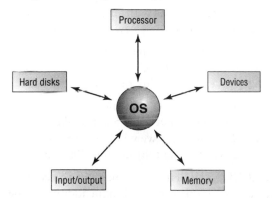

Network Operating System (NOS)   Similar to a standard operating system, except that the NOS is optimized to provide services to other machines on the network. NOS software is examined briefly in Chapter 16, "Windows Networking," but is discussed in depth in David Groth's *Network+ Study Guide* (Sybex, 2003).

Application   Used to accomplish a particular task, an application is software that is written to supplement the commands available to a particular OS. Each application is specifically compiled (configured) for the OS on which it will run. For this reason, the application relies on the OS to do many of its basic tasks. Examples of applications include complex programs, such as Microsoft Word and Netscape Navigator, as well as simple programs, such as a command-line FTP program. Either way, when accessing devices and memory, the programs can simply request that the OS do it for them. This arrangement saves substantially on programming overhead, because much of the executable code is *shared*—it is written into the operating system and can therefore be used by multiple applications running on that OS.

Driver   Extremely specific software written for the purpose of instructing a particular OS on how to access a piece of hardware. Each modem or printer has unique features and configuration settings, and the driver allows the OS to properly understand how the hardware works and what it is able to do.

Operating System Terms and Concepts

Before we get too far into our discussion of PC operating systems, it will be useful to define a few key terms. Following are some terms you will come across as you study this chapter and visit with people in the computer industry:

Version   A particular revision of a piece of software, normally described by a number, which tells you how new the product is in relation to other versions of the product. MS-DOS, for instance, is currently in its sixth major version. Major revisions are distinguished from minor ones in this manner: DOS 5.0 to 6.0 was a major revision, whereas 6.0 to 6.2 was a minor revision. This way of marking changes is now relatively standard for other OS and application software. Very minor revisions are indicated with an additional decimal point. Upgrading from DOS version 6.21 to 6.22 involved only a few new files, but it was still an upgrade.

Source   The actual code that defines how a piece of software works. Computer operating systems can be *open source*, meaning the OS can be examined and modified by users, or they can be *closed source*, meaning users cannot modify or examine the code.

Shell   A program that runs on top of the OS and allows the user to issue commands through a set of menus or some other graphical interface. Shells make using an OS easier to use by changing the user interface. The two shells we will look at most closely are Microsoft's DOS Shell (a menuing system) and Windows (a fully graphical user interface).

Graphical User Interface (GUI)   The method by which a person communicates with a computer. GUIs use a mouse, touch pad, or another mechanism (in addition to the keyboard) to interact with the computer to issue commands.

Network   Any group of computers that have a physical communication link between them. Networks allow computers to share information and resources quickly and securely.

Cooperative Multitasking   A multitasking method that depends on the application itself to be responsible for using and then freeing access to the processor. This is the way Windows 3.1 managed multiple applications. If any application locked up while using the processor, the application was unable to properly free the processor to do other tasks, and the entire system locked, usually forcing a reboot.

Preemptive Multitasking   A multitasking method in which the OS allots each application a certain amount of processor time and then forcibly takes back control and gives another application or task access to the processor. This means that if an application crashes, the OS takes control of the processor away from the locked application and passes it on to the next application, which should be unaffected. Although unstable programs still lock, only the locked application will stall—not the entire system.

Multithreading   The ability of a single application to have multiple requests in to the processor at one time. This results in faster application performance, because it allows a program to do many things at once. Only 32-bit or higher OSs support multithreading.

Types of PC Operating Systems

This chapter introduces a few of the major operating systems of the past 20 years and briefly describes how they work. These are not the only OSs out there, but are simply the ones accepted by a large enough segment of the PC market to become *de facto* standards. As you read about these different software products, try to think about the ways they differ from one another and the reasons they were designed in the fashion they were. The A+ exam focuses only on OS options available on Intel, so those systems are given the most space in this chapter. Although Macintosh, for instance, has a strong following in certain niche markets, it is little-used in corporate settings (except for graphics professionals). Intel/Windows machines dominate the corporate market almost completely. By knowing some of the OS options available to you, it will be easier to decide which OS will work best in a particular situation, and you can be better prepared to recommend a particular OS to your customers.

The following OSs are discussed over the course of this chapter:

- CP/M
- DOS
- Windows (1–3.*x*)
- OS/2
- Windows 95 and later
- Linux
- Macintosh OS

To understand the current operating systems and how they are used, it is helpful to know their lineage and the environment in which they were developed. In this section, you will learn about the various types of PC operating systems and the differences between them.

Classic Operating Systems

The word *classic* sounds so much better than *obsolete*, doesn't it? Still, this isn't exactly the type of heading that makes you want to take notes. That's OK, because the material in this chapter won't be on the A+ exam. Then why, you may ask, is it in the *A+ Complete Study Guide*? Two reasons. First, it is easier to understand the modern OS versions you will be tested on if you understand where they come from. Second, being a technician isn't just about passing a test, and these systems will come up in discussions all through your career, when someone reminisces about the "good old days" of DOS or OS/2.

It is important to know where we have been and how we have gotten where we are. Knowing this background is an essential part of being an informed and effective computer-support person or service technician and certainly is in accordance with the overall goals of certification. Customers and clients will be more confident of your abilities when you can show that you have a solid understanding of your industry.

CP/M

The *Control Program for Microcomputer (CP/M)* is an OS you may never have heard of, because it is not in use on modern PCs. Gary Kildall wrote this OS in 1973, using his PL/M programming language. It initially ran on the Intel 8008. It was later ported to the 8080 chip and was, in many ways, very similar in function to DOS. As a matter of fact, it looks quite similar to DOS, as you can see in Figure 11.1.

FIGURE 11.1 Control Program for Microcomputer (CP/M)

```
Z80 C>SUBMIT AUTOEXEC.Z80
Z80 C>set_bdos min
Z80 C>set_cpmecho off
Z80 C>set_cpmlist lpt1
Z80 C>set_cpmpun com1
Z80 C>set_cpmrdr com1
Z80 C>set_cpu z80
Z80 C>set_fake off
Z80 C>set_illop fault
Z80 C>set_iobase 400
Z80 C>set_mask on
Z80 C>set_source z80
Z80 C>set_term h19
Z80 C>set_vars on
Z80 C>coldboot
Z80 C>
Z80 C>
```

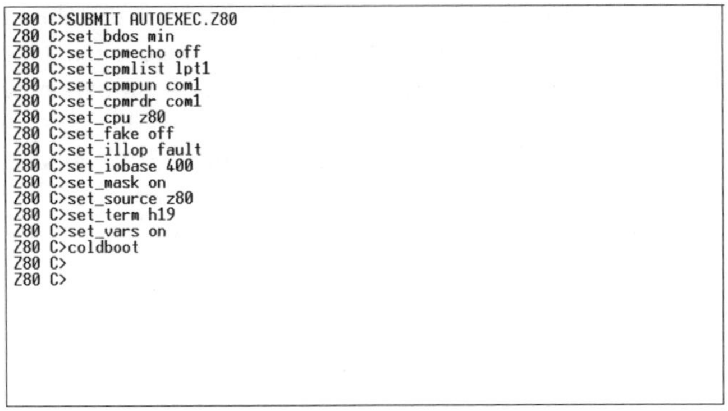

The following bit of computer folklore, which, despite questionable authenticity, has become well known in the industry, underscores the relationship between CP/M and DOS. In 1981, IBM decided to begin marketing machines to home users and small offices. The company decided that, for reasons of time and efficiency, it would simply license an OS rather than develop and support one of its own. Toward that end, IBM scheduled a meeting with Gary Kildall. The IBM representative arrived for the meeting at Kildall's house, but Gary wasn't there; he was out flying his plane. After an unsuccessful meeting with Kildall's wife and lawyer, the IBM representative left without an OS. Not long after, IBM found a different system, entering into a contract with Bill Gates by which Gates' fledgling company Microsoft (you may have heard of them) agreed to license its DOS operating system to IBM. Kildall says that this story is not accurate, and claims that Bill Gates was the first to tell the apocryphal tale. One way or the other, the fact remains that Kildall's OS lost a huge opportunity. At the time that IBM allegedly came calling, CP/M was the industry standard for low-cost computers on the Intel platform. Within a few years of losing the IBM contract, it was nothing but a memory.

A copy of CP/M is as hard to find these days as a baby sauropod, but the good folks at ZDNet have a great emulator called 22Nice available for download if you are interested in digging into computer history. Go to `http://www.cpm.z80.de/download/22nce132.zip` to read more about it. Warning: Downloading and using command-line OSs will quickly earn you the "geek" label.

MS-DOS and PC-DOS

In the 1980s and early 1990s, the OS that shipped with most PCs was a version of the *Disk Operating System (DOS)* created by Microsoft: *MS-DOS.* (A number of companies manufactured DOS, but most of them produced similar versions—they differed only in syntax and a few utilities. The important differences among DOS variants are to be found from one chronological version to the next, not among manufacturers.)

In the next section, you will look at the origins of DOS and the way it has evolved, version by version, over time. After the history lesson, you will examine some of the commands and syntax of the DOS OS, because you need some knowledge of command-line syntax before taking the A+ exam.

The Origins of DOS

The story behind MS-DOS is one of the most often told of all computer fables. But the intrigue goes further than the mystery of why Gary Kildall missed his meeting with IBM. As noted, Microsoft contracted with IBM to write the OS for IBM's new Intel-based microcomputer project. Although Bill Gates and his partner, Paul Allen, were both experienced programmers, they had gained their success through the creation of programming languages, not OSs.

Gates and Allen had created the BASIC language in 1976 and had also released versions of COBOL and Fortran for Intel-based machines. However, they had never created an OS from scratch, which is exactly what they promised to do for IBM. In an interesting twist, just as Seattle-based Microsoft was finishing up a secretive deal with IBM, Tim Patterson of Seattle Computer Products began writing an OS specifically for use with the 8086-based computer Patterson was dissatisfied with how long it was taking for an x86 version of CP/M to be released, so he named his operating system *Quick-and-Dirty Disk Operating System (QDOS),* and showed it to Microsoft, even as Microsoft was in the middle of talks with IBM. Paul Allen soon contracted with Seattle Computer Products to purchase QDOS, to then sell to an unnamed client (IBM, of course). The purchase price of around $50,000 bought Microsoft an OS, and a few months later, Patterson followed his OS—he quit SCP and took a job with Gates and Allen. Microsoft soon acquired all rights to QDOS and renamed it MS-DOS.

From there, MS-DOS was modified for use with the new IBM minicomputer, and in the fall of 1981, IBM announced the IBM 5150 PC Personal Computer. The 5150 had a 4.77MHz Intel 8088 CPU, 64KB RAM, 40KB ROM, one 51/4-inch floppy drive, color graphics capability, and an OS called *PC-DOS 1.0.* PC-DOS was simply IBM's moniker for the MS-DOS that it was licensing from Microsoft.

Before the PC, most computers were sold as kits. This meant that the customer had to assemble the machine, install the OS, and so on. IBM debuted its IBM PC as a machine anyone could use, because it was ready to go right out of the box.

Gates and Allen had contracted to allow IBM to *use* their OS, rather than allow IBM to *buy* it outright. Moreover, IBM had not been granted any type of exclusivity over DOS; hence Microsoft was also able to license versions of DOS to other companies, allowing the creation of what were originally called *IBM clone* machines. These machines ran on the same Intel chip as the IBM PC and used a similar version of the OS. From 1981 on, the future of the PC was largely determined by the increasingly powerful processors created by Intel and the increasingly sophisticated OSs Microsoft wrote to take advantage of Intel's enhancements.

MS-DOS Versions

Over time, MS-DOS evolved into a robust, widely used OS. It was the only OS used on IBM-compatible PCs. Let's look at the evolution of the MS-DOS OS and the major changes in microcomputer architecture and standards that are reflected in each revision. Smaller revisions—1.0 to 1.1, 6.0 to 6.1—are not enumerated, but their changes are included in the overall enhancements made to the overall version.

You will notice as you read about and use DOS that most of the versions of this OS are very similar, because DOS proved to be very stable in its original design. Although various enhancements or features may or may not be available to you, depending on the version you are using, in a general sense you can trust that if you learn one version, you can probably use any of them:

MS-DOS 1.0   The original version of MS-DOS was, to put it mildly, a no-frills OS. It had no provisions for networking, did not include any sort of graphical shell program, and had limited ability to manage system resources. Approximately a year after the release of DOS 1.0, a revision—DOS 1.1—added support for double-sided 320KB floppy drives. Double-sided disks were important, because they effectively doubled the machine's storage and retrieval capacity. It is difficult to grasp this concept today, when a 10- or 20-gigabyte hard drive is standard on most new desktop machines, but in 1981 internal hard drives were neither easily available nor supported by DOS. Users generally had only a single 5 1/4-inch drive, so the OS, any programs that the users wanted to run, and any data that they wanted to retrieve all had to be accessed through the 5 1/4-inch floppies!

MS-DOS 2.0   In early 1983, IBM introduced the IBM PC XT. The XT featured a 10MB hard drive, a serial interface, and three additional expansion slots. It also had 128KB of RAM and a 360KB floppy drive (40KB more capacity than that of single-sided floppies on the previous PC) and could support a 10MB internal hard drive. Users of this new PC needed an OS that would allow them to take advantage of this new hardware, and Microsoft did not disappoint them. MS-DOS 2.0 featured support for more devices and more memory.

MS-DOS 3.0   With DOS 3.0, released in the summer of 1984, Microsoft continued to include additional DOS features and to support more powerful hardware. DOS 3.0 supported hard drives larger than 10MB, as well as enhanced graphics formats. Three revisions—3.1, 3.2, and 3.3—provided additional innovations. The IBM PC AT was the first machine shipped with DOS 3.0. It had 256KB of RAM, an Intel 80286 processor (6MHz!), and a 1.2MB 5 1/4-inch floppy drive. A 20MB hard drive and color video card were also available. Later upgrades to version 3.0 of MS-DOS included support for networking and 32MB partition sizes, as well as 1.44MB floppy drives.

DOS 3.1 Notable because it featured the first DOS support for networking. The IBM PC Network was a simple local area network structure that was similar to today's workgroup networks.

DOS 3.2 Introduced the XCOPY command, enabling the user to identify more than one file at a time to be copied, and made important modifications to other DOS commands. It was also the first version to support IBM's Token Ring network topology and the first to allow for 720KB 3 1/2-inch floppies. Version 3.3, introduced in 1987, offered additional enhancements to numerous existing commands and introduced support for 1.44MB floppy disks. Logical partition sizes could be up to 32MB, and a single machine could support both a primary and a secondary partition on each hard disk.

It is important to note that DOS 3.0 was released in 1984, the same year that Apple's infamous "1984" ad aired during the Super Bowl, marking the release of the Apple Macintosh. IBM had a great thing going with the PC, but the company had gotten lazy and just made occasional improvements to DOS as needed, rather than really trying to make significant changes to it. As the challenge came in from Apple, whose graphical Macintosh OS was clearly superior to DOS, Microsoft and IBM announced the creation of a second PC OS, OS/2. Unfortunately, "announcing" and "delivering" are very different things, and the story of OS/2's production problems is a long one. We will look at both Apple and OS/2 later in this chapter.

MS-DOS 4.0 By 1988, it was apparent that the wave of the future was the graphical interface. DOS 4.0 provided users with the DOS Shell, a utility much like the Windows File Manager. Actually, DOS Shell was simply a scaled down version of Windows (which we will look at in a minute) that allowed users to manage files, run programs, and do routine maintenance, all from a single screen. The DOS Shell even supported a mouse. (That's right, DOS offered no ability to use a mouse before this version. Oh, how Mac lovers must have mocked Microsoftics back in the dark days of 1988!)

MS-DOS 5.0 Several important features were introduced in the 1991 release of DOS 5.0. First, the ability to load drivers into reserved (upper) memory by pooling Expanded Memory Specification (EMS) and Extended Memory Specification (XMS) using EMM386.EXE was a relief to those people who were constantly running out of conventional memory. This feature allowed more complex DOS programs (that took up more conventional memory) to be developed.

In addition to this feature, several software utilities made their debut. The most commonly used utility introduced at this time was EDIT.COM. This ASCII text editor has since become one of the most popular text editors for simple text files (and a welcomed relief from the single-line view of EDLIN.COM—previously the only choice for a text editor). Also added in DOS 5.0 were QBASIC.EXE, DOSKEY, UNFORMAT, and UNDELETE.

MS-DOS 6.0 Released in 1993 to excellent sales (and a lawsuit for patent infringement), DOS 6.0 offered a number of new commands and configuration options. DOS 6.0 has subsequently been revised a number of times—once (DOS 6.2 to 6.21) because of a court order. Microsoft was found to have violated Stac Electronics' patent rights in the creation of the

DoubleSpace utility for 6.0 and 6.1, and the only real difference between 6.2 and 6.21 is that DoubleSpace is removed. Never to be denied, Microsoft soon released DOS 6.22 with a disk-compression program called DriveSpace.

As of this writing, DOS 6.22 is the most current MS-DOS version available as a stand-alone OS. Microsoft has included certain DOS-style command-line utilities for use within Windows 9x, Windows NT, Windows 2000, and Windows XP, but these are really Windows programs that simply mimic the familiar, old command-prompt environment of DOS.

 Windows will be discussed later in its own section.

OS/2

Even as Windows 3.1 was in development, Microsoft was participating in a joint effort with IBM to create a next-generation OS for use with 286 and higher processors. This OS was to be IBM/Microsoft's second-generation OS, or OS/2, intended to replace DOS. Differing goals for the design of the new system caused a number of disagreements, though, and the partnership soon broke up. IBM continued the development of OS/2 on its own, and Microsoft took its part of the technology and began to develop LAN Manager, which would eventually lead to the development of Windows NT.

With the second version, IBM made OS/2 a 32-bit system that required at least a 386 processor to run. Although this made it vastly more stable and powerful than Windows 3.1, both it and Microsoft's NT product had a problem finding a market. The main reason was probably that most users did not have powerful enough computers to properly use the system, and few pieces of software were available that leveraged the new architecture and OS properly.

With version 3 (OS/2 Warp), IBM created a multitasking, 32-bit OS that required a 386 but preferred a 486. Warp also required a ridiculous 4MB of RAM just to load. With a graphical interface and the ability to do a great deal of self-configuration, the Warp OS was a peculiar cross between DOS and a Macintosh. Warp featured true preemptive multitasking, did not suffer from the memory limitations of DOS, and had a desktop similar to the Macintosh.

For all of its tremendous features, OS/2 Warp had a funny name and was badly marketed. It never established a wide user base. Nonetheless, until Windows NT 3.51 was released in 1995, OS/2 was the OS of choice for high-end workstations, and until recently the OS retained a small but faithful following. The last year or so has been harsh on OS/2 fans, though, as IBM has essentially abandoned the high-end desktop market to Windows NT, Windows 2000, and Linux. OS/2 has been largely forgotten, and IBM now ships Windows 2000 Professional with its own desktops. When even the company that makes an OS stops pushing it, it quickly drops into the "obsolete" category. For more info on OS/2, including current support options, go to IBM's OS/2 information page at www.ibm.com/software/os/warp.

Alternative PC Operating Systems

Although most people run some version of Windows on their computers, a few OSs out there aren't Microsoft's. And, people seem to get by just fine. As a matter of fact, there are software releases for these alternative OSs for major productivity software such as word processing, spreadsheets, and so forth.

Mac OS

The Mac OS isn't a PC OS (although many people are trying hard to get it to be one), in that it runs only on a Macintosh computer. The A+ exam doesn't cover Macintosh topics, but the Mac OS is a very important part of PC culture. The long-standing holy war between Macintosh users and Windows users is a topic of legend.

Linux

Over the past couple of years, the *open-source* movement has been rallying around Linus Torvalds and his Linux OS. Linux is a Unix-type OS that has been released into the public domain and is being developed as an OS standard, much as TCP/IP is a protocol standard. A number of computer users are uncomfortable with Microsoft's dominance of the crucial OS market, and, as a result, Linux has been positioned as an excellent alternative to the Microsoft juggernaut. There were suspicions that CompTIA would be adding Linux questions to the A+ exam, but in the end it decided that Linux's time had not yet come.

This was probably the right decision, for two reasons. First, although Linux is making inroads with knowledgeable home users and is even being used as a server in many corporate environments, it has not been able to break into the mass home or corporate desktop markets that the A+ exam objectives prepare you to serve. The second reason follows from the first. Because most Linux users are computer junkies themselves, few of them take in their computers for professional (paid) configuration or support. As an A+-certified tech, you will be working for people who will pay you, and most of them are still running Windows.

That said, Linux is a nifty idea. The theory behind it is to make core OS code available to anyone who wants it, so that the code can then be explored and enhanced by users. Those who choose to can create a full Unix-type OS from the Linux source code, modify it as they see fit, and release it to the world as a Linux *distribution*. Distributions are similar to versions, but where versions are chronological enhancements to a single company's OS, distributions are variations on a single OS theme. For a list of Linux distributions, refer to www.linux.org/dist/english.html.

The architecture of Linux is based on Unix, the OS used in mainframes and other high-end computers, and it is extremely powerful and stable. Linux is also commonly used as a web server or an e-mail server on the Internet, and can function as either a network OS or a desktop OS, just as Windows NT can.

Few creatures are more rabid in defense of their cause than Linux fans, and for good reason. The basic philosophy of Linux is that the people who use an OS are the ones who know best what needs to be improved on it, and that user feedback should be respected and acted upon. Linux has not always been an OS for the masses, because early distributions were complex to install and had little application support. But a small army of users has sent suggestions, so it has improved markedly.

The Linux vs. Microsoft debate is an interesting one in the computer world, because it is a face-off between idealism and corporate power, open-source and proprietary code. It is a battleground where we will eventually see whether users prefer a system that gives them power (but requires a bit more work) or one that makes everything easy (but gives them fewer choices). Should be fun to watch, if nothing else.

For detailed information about the world of Linux, two websites are obvious starting points: www.linux.org and www.linux.com. Linux.org is probably the better of the two for those interested in simply learning about what Linux is, and it has a great online course called "Getting Started with Linux."

Microsoft Windows

Any real understanding of the success of DOS after 1987 requires knowledge of Windows. In the early years of its existence, Microsoft's DOS gained great acceptance and became a standard as a PC OS. Even so, as computers became more powerful and programs more complex, the limitations of the DOS command-line interface became apparent (as well as the aforementioned conventional memory limitation).

The solution to the problem was to make the OS easier to navigate, more uniform, and generally more friendly to the user. IBM understood that the average user did not want to receive their computer in pieces but preferred to have it ready to go out of the box. Oddly, the company did not understand that the same user who wanted their *hardware* to be ready to go also wanted their *software* to be the same way. They also did not want to edit batch files or hunt through directories using CD or DIR commands. As a result, when Microsoft came to IBM with a graphical user interface (GUI) based on groundbreaking work done by Xerox labs, IBM was not interested, preferring to go onward with the development of OS/2 (a project it had already started with Microsoft).

The Xerox Corporation maintains a think-tank of computer designers in Palo Alto, California called the Palo Alto Research Center (PARC). One of the results of its work was the Alto workstation, which is generally thought to be the forerunner of all modern graphical OSs. The Alto had a mouse and a GUI interface, and it communicated with other stations via Ethernet. Oh, and it was finished in 1974! Although it was never promoted commercially, both Microsoft and Apple viewed the Alto and incorporated its technology into their own systems. The accomplishments of the PARC lab in laying the groundwork for modern graphical computing systems cannot be overstated. Check out www.parc.xerox.com for more information on PARC past and present.

Regardless of IBM's interest, Microsoft continued on its own with development of the GUI—which it named *Windows* after its rectangular work areas—and released the first version to the market in 1985. Apple filed a lawsuit soon after, claiming that the Microsoft GUI had been built using Apple technology, but the suit was dismissed. Both Apple's Macintosh and Microsoft's DOS-with-Windows combo have continued to evolve, but until a recent deal between Apple and Microsoft, tensions have always been high. Mac and PC *users*, of course, remain adamantly chauvinistic about their respective platforms.

Oh, the stories that have been told around the glow of a monitor about Gates vs. Jobs. One of the easiest ways to get a bit of the flavor of the struggle is through a movie called *Pirates of Silicon Valley*, in which Anthony Michael Hall of *The Breakfast Club* plays Gates and Noah Wyle of *ER* fame plays Jobs. For more info, visit tnt.turner.com/movies/tntoriginals/pirates.

The Windows interface to MS-DOS is really just a shell program that allows users to issue DOS commands through a graphical interface—a prettier extension of Microsoft's earlier DOS Shell work. The integration of a mouse for nearly all tasks—a legacy of the Xerox Alto computer on which both the Macintosh and Windows GUIs are based—further freed users from DOS by allowing them to issue common commands without using the keyboard. Word processors, spreadsheets, and especially games were revolutionized as software manufacturers happily took advantage of the ease of use and flexibility that Windows added to DOS.

Windows Versions

After the development of Windows, many of the enhancements made to subsequent versions of DOS were designed to help free up and reallocate resources to better run Windows and Windows-based applications. Similarly, PC hardware continued to evolve far past the limits of DOS's ability to effectively use the power available to it, and later versions of Windows were designed to hide and overcome the limitations of the OS. The combination of MS-DOS and its Windows shell made Microsoft the industry leader and spurred the PC movement to new heights in the early 1990s. Following is a brief examination of the development of the Windows shell and a look at its different versions.

Windows 1

Version 1 of Windows featured the tiling windows, mouse support, and menu systems that still drive next-generation OSs such as Windows 98, Windows CE, and Windows 2000. It also offered *cooperative multitasking*, meaning that more than one Windows application could run concurrently. This was something that MS-DOS, up to this point, could not do.

Windows 1 was far from a finished product. For one thing, it didn't use icons, and it had few of the programs we have come to expect as Windows standards. Windows 1 was basically just an updated, more graphical version of the DOSSHELL.EXE program.

Windows 2

Version 2, released in 1987, added icons and allowed application windows to overlap each other, as well as tile. Support was also added for PIFs (program information files), which allowed the user to configure Windows to run their DOS applications more efficiently.

Windows 3.*x*

Windows 3.0 featured a far more flexible memory model, allowing it to access more memory than the 640KB limit normally imposed by DOS. It also featured the addition of the File Manager and Program Manager, allowed for network support, and could operate in *386 Enhanced mode*. 386 Enhanced mode used parts of the hard drive as *virtual memory* and was therefore able to use disk memory to supplement the RAM in the machine. Windows today is still quite similar to the Windows of version 3.0.

In 1992, a revision of Windows 3, known as Windows 3.1, provided for better graphical display capability and multimedia support. It also improved the Windows error-protection system and let applications work together more easily through the use of object linking and embedding (OLE).

After the introduction of version 3.1, Windows took a marked turn for the better, because Microsoft started making a serious effort to change to a full 32-bit application environment. With version 3.11, also known as Windows for Workgroups, Windows offered support for both 16-bit and 32-bit applications. (Windows 3.1 could only support 16-bit applications.) Significant progress on the 32-bit front was not made until very late in 1995, however, when Microsoft introduced Windows 95. Since that time, the venerable DOS/Windows team has been largely replaced by newer, more advanced systems. You may occasionally still run into a Windows 3.1 machine, but it is not a common occurrence.

With the introduction of Windows for Workgroups, people speaking generically about the two *flavors* of Windows—3.1 and 3.11—started referring to them collectively as *Windows 3.x,* as in the heading of this section.

Windows 95

Although it dominated the market with its DOS operating system and its add-on Windows interface, Microsoft found that the constraints of DOS were rapidly making it difficult to take full advantage of rapidly improving hardware and software developments. The future of computing was clearly a 32-bit, preemptively multitasked system such as IBM's OS/2; but many current users had DOS-based software or older hardware that was specifically designed for DOS and would not operate outside of its Windows 3.1, cooperatively multitasked environment.

Because of this problem, in the fall of 1995 Microsoft released a major upgrade to the DOS/Windows environment. Called Windows 95, the new product integrated the OS and the shell. Where previous versions of Windows simply provided a graphic interface to the existing DOS OS, the Windows 95 graphical interface *is* part of the OS. Moreover, Windows 95 was designed to be a hybrid of the features of previous DOS versions and newer 32-bit systems. It also supports both 32-bit and 16-bit drivers as well as DOS drivers, although the 32-bit drivers are strongly recommended over the DOS ones because they are far faster and more stable.

Among the most important of the other enhancements debuted by Microsoft with Windows 95 was support for the Plug-and-Play standard (PnP). This meant that if a device was designed to be plug-and-play, a technician could install the device into the computer, start the machine, and have the device automatically be recognized and configured by Windows 95. This was a major advance; but unfortunately, in order for PnP to work properly, three things had to be true:

- The OS had to be PnP compatible.
- The computer motherboard had to support PnP.
- All devices in the machine had to be PnP compatible.

At the time Windows 95 came out, many manufacturers were creating their hardware for use in DOS/Windows machines, and DOS did not support PnP, so most pre-1995 computer components (sound cards, modems, NICs, and so on) were not PnP compliant. As a result, these components—generally referred to as *legacy* devices—often interfered with the PnP environment. Such devices are not able to dynamically interact with newer systems. They therefore require manual configuration or must be replaced by newer devices, which don't usually need manual configuration. Due to problems managing legacy hardware under Windows 95, many people soured on PnP technology. Worse, they blamed Windows 95 for their problems, not the old hardware. "It worked fine in DOS" was the standard logic! Now, half a decade later, nearly all PC components are PnP compliant, and configuring computer systems is far easier than it was under DOS.

The foibles of PnP aside, to say that the new system was a success would be a major understatement. Within just a few years of its release, the Windows 95–style GUI had won over nearly all Windows users, and the more resilient architecture of 95 had won over network administrators and computer technicians. Although it was far from perfect, Windows 95 was a tremendous advance out of the DOS age. Perhaps the only ones not thrilled were the folks at Apple, who continued to make a cottage industry out of starting lawsuits against Microsoft. This time, Apple contended that the Windows 95 interface itself was stolen from the Macintosh. It is undeniable that the Windows 95 interface is nearly a twin of the Mac interface, it turned out that Apple itself got its GUI from PARC Alto! Xerox not only designed the first computer GUI, but had created an interface that could not be significantly improved upon in over 20 years of OS development—and both Apple and Microsoft settled on it as the basis for their GUIs. All subsequent versions of Windows (98, NT, 2000, and XP) use an interface essentially identical to the Windows 95 GUI.

 Chapter 12, "Using the Microsoft Windows GUI," goes into depth on the nature of the Windows 95/98/NT/2000/XP interface. Overall, the Windows 95 OS is only marginally different from its Windows 98 upgrade, which is one of the OSs you will be tested on during the A+ exam. As such, Windows 95 will be grouped with Windows 98 for the rest of this book, and we will be more concerned with the differences between Windows 9x and Windows 2000 than we will with differences between Windows 95 and Windows 98.

Windows 98/Me/NT/2000/XP

After Windows 95, Windows 98 was introduced as its successor, followed by Windows Me (Millennium Edition). Windows 98/Me is currently the most common PC OS on the market, although XP is poised to replace it quickly. Still, for users who need more power, other options are available. One of these is the Windows NT OS. NT (which unofficially stands for New Technology) is an OS that was designed to be far more powerful than any previous Windows version. It uses an architecture based entirely on 32-bit code and is capable of accessing up to 4GB (4,000MB) of RAM.

After Windows 98 and NT, Windows 2000 was released. It used the same interface as Windows 98 (with a few important enhancements). It came in many versions, but the most popular were Windows 2000 Professional (workstation OS) and Windows 2000 Server (server OS).

Recently came the introduction of Windows XP. It comes in two versions: XP Home and XP Professional. They are close to being the same, but XP Professional contains more corporate and networking features.

We will talk about Windows 98/Me, Windows 2000, and Windows XP in depth throughout the rest of this book, because they are the OSs you need to know for the A+ exam.

Choosing an Operating System

Now that we have sampled the variety of PC OSs, let's briefly look at the systems that dominate the current environment: Windows 95/98, Windows 2000, and Windows XP.

If your users have older hardware, Windows 95 may be the best bet, simply because of its low resource usage. Most other home users will be happiest with Windows 98/Me or Windows XP Home, and corporate users are generally divided between Windows 98/Me, Windows NT Workstation, Windows 2000 Professional, and Windows XP Professional. As you will see, users who need higher performance or strong security should be nudged toward NT, 2000 Professional, or XP Professional. The choices you will probably deal with come down to the OS options described in depth in the following chapters.

Summary

In this chapter, we have looked at the evolution of the personal computer and how it has changed over the past two decades. The PC and especially its ever-improving operating systems have revolutionized the way computing is done. From the Xerox Alto GUI to DOS to Macs and Windows, a number of different solutions have been found for the problem of allowing humans to communicate with machines. For the rest of this book, we will leave behind most of the operating systems, just as CompTIA has done, and focus on the Windows platforms—including Windows 9x, Windows NT, Windows 2000, and Windows XP. The choices that you will probably face come down to the two OS options dealt with in depth in the following chapters.

Key Terms

Before you take the exam, be certain you are familiar with the following terms:

Control Program for Microcomputer (CP/M)	PC-DOS 1.0
cooperative multitasking	preemptive multitasking
Disk Operating System (DOS)	Quick-and-Dirty Disk Operating System (QDOS)
graphical user interface (GUI)	shell
MS-DOS	source
multithreading	version
network	

Review Questions

1. Which of the following is *not* an important development in Intel platform PC operating systems?

   A. CP/M

   B. MS-DOS and PC-DOS

   C. Windows interfaces to DOS

   D. OS/1

2. What does CP/M stand for?

   A. Control Processing Management

   B. Control Program for Microcomputer

   C. Control Power for Microcomputer

   D. Control Processing Microcomputer

3. What was the original version of MS-DOS?

   A. MS-DOS 2.0

   B. MS-DOS 3.0

   C. MS-DOS 1.0

   D. MS-DOS 5.0

4. What major innovation came after MS-DOS 1.0?

   A. 5 1/4-inch disk drive

   B. 3 1/2-inch disk drive

   C. Double-sided 3 1/2-inch disk

   D. Double-sided 320KB floppy drive

5. In early 1983, IBM introduced the IBM PC-XT. The PC-XT featured all of the following except _____.

   A. DOS 1.25 operating system

   B. 10MB hard drive

   C. Serial interface

   D. Three additional expansion slots

   E. 128KB of RAM

6. The XT shipped with which version of DOS?

   A. MS-DOS 3.0

   B. MS-DOS 2.0

   C. MS-DOS 4.0

   D. MS-DOS 1.0

7. Which of the following was *not* a feature of MS-DOS 3.0?

A. Supported hard drives larger than 10MB

B. Enhanced graphics formats

C. Support for networking

D. Supported 1.44MB floppy drives

8. Which of the following was *not* featured on the IBM PC-AT, introduced in 1984?

A. 128KB of RAM

B. Intel processor 80286

C. 1.2MB floppy drive

D. 20MB hard drive

9. What was the first graphical interface that was introduced with MS-DOS 4.0?

A. GUI

B. DOSwin

C. DOS Shell

D. DOSini

10. The XCOPY command was introduced with which DOS version?

A. DOS version 3.2

B. DOS version 3.1

C. DOS version 3.0

D. DOS version 4.0

11. Which of the following features was *not* introduced by MS-DOS 5.0?

A. The ability to load drivers into reserved or upper memory

B. EDIT.COM utility

C. EDLIN.COM

D. QBASIC.EXE

12. In which version of MS-DOS were DOSKEY.COM and UNDELETE.EXE introduced?

A. MS-DOS version 6.0

B. MS-DOS version 5.0

C. MS-DOS version 4.0

D. MS-DOS version 3.0

13. The ability to pool EMS and XMS memory using EMM386.EXE was introduced in which version of DOS?

   A. MS-DOS 5.0

   B. MS-DOS 4.0

   C. MS-DOS 6.0

   D. MS-DOS 3.0

14. Windows featured tiling windows, mouse support, and menu systems in which versions? (Select all that apply.)

   A. Windows 1

   B. Windows 2

   C. Windows 3

   D. Windows 95

   E. All of the above

15. What was the first Windows version that allowed more memory than the 640KB limit normally imposed by DOS?

   A. Windows 1

   B. Windows 2

   C. Windows 3

   D. Windows 95

16. What was the first 32-bit preemptive multitasking system?

   A. Windows 2

   B. Windows 3

   C. Windows 1

   D. Windows 95

17. Which of these Microsoft operating system is best for users who need to deal with large files or complex programs?

   A. Windows NT

   B. Windows 95

   C. Windows 3.11

   D. Windows 2

18. What was the minimum processor required by version 2 of OS/2, a 32-bit system?

    A. 486

    B. 586

    C. 686

    D. 386

19. Which Windows operating system provides high performance and file security?

    A. Windows 95

    B. Windows 98

    C. Windows NT

    D. Windows Me

20. Which of these "classic" operating systems can be viewed as the model on which modern graphical systems such as Windows 2000 and the Apple Macintosh are based?

    A. Windows 1.0

    B. OS/2

    C. CP/M

    D. Alto

Answers to Review Questions

1. **D.** CP/M, MS-DOS and PC-DOS, and Windows interfaces are all important developments in Intel platform PC operating systems.

2. **B.** This OS was written in 1973 by Gary Kildall, using Kildall's PL/M programming language; it initially ran on the Intel 8008. It was later ported to the 8080 chip and was in many ways very similar in function to DOS.

3. **C.** This DOS version had a no-frills operating system. It had no provisions for networking, did not include any sort of graphical shell program, and had limited ability to manage system resources.

4. **D.** Double-sided 320KB floppy drives were the major innovation that came after MS-DOS 1.0. At the time, hard drives were not easily available; therefore, all information was stored on 5 1/4-inch floppy disks.

5. **A.** The XT featured a 10MB hard drive, a serial interface, and three additional expansion slots. It also had 128KB of RAM and a 360KB floppy drive.

6. **B.** The XT shipped with MS-DOS 2.0, a revision of the DOS operating system that had to be redone almost from the ground up. It closely fit the machine it was built for, and it supported 10MB hard drives and the new 360KB floppy disks.

7. **D.** MS-DOS 3.0 could not support 1.44MB floppy drives. MS-DOS used 5 1/4-inch floppy drives.

8. **A.** The IBM PC-AT did not feature 128KB of RAM. It was the first machine shipped with DOS 3.0. It had 256KB of RAM, an Intel 80286 processor, and a 1.2MB, 5 1/4-inch floppy drive. A 20MB hard drive and color video card were also available.

9. **C.** MS-DOS 4.0 introduced the first graphical interface, which was called DOS Shell. The DOS Shell was simply a scaled-down version of Windows that allowed users to manage files, run programs, and do routine maintenance from a single screen. The DOS Shell even supported a mouse.

10. **A.** The XCOPY command was introduced with DOS version 3.2. It enables the user to identify more than one file at a time to be copied. It also copies file attributes.

11. **C.** MS-DOS introduced all of the features listed except the line editor `EDLIN.COM`, which was introduced in MS-DOS 3.0.

12. **B.** `DOSKEY.COM` and `UNDELETE.EXE` were introduced in MS-DOS version 5.0. The `DOSKEY.COM` command loads the `DOSKEY` program into memory. `DOSKEY` runs in the background of other programs. The `UNDELETE.EXE` command makes it possible to recover a deleted file if the space on the disk has not been written over by a new file.

13. **A.** The ability to pool EMS and XMS memory using `EMM386.EXE` was introduced in MS-DOS 5.0. EMS (Expanded Memory Specification) provides access for the microprocessor to the upper memory area. XMS (Extended Memory Specification) is loaded by `HIMEM.SYS`.

14. E.   Windows featured tiling windows, mouse support, and menu systems in all Windows versions from Windows 1 through Windows 95.

15. C.   Windows 3 substantially increased the size and complexity of programs that could be executed under DOS/Windows and was a crucial step in making Windows a viable product.

16. D.   The first 32-bit preemptive multitasking system was Windows 95. Windows 95 can emulate and support cooperative multitasking for programs that require it. It also supports both 32-bit and 16-bit drivers as well as DOS drivers, although the 32-bit drivers are strongly recommended over the DOS ones because they are far more stable and are faster.

17. A.   Support for large files or complex programs was the specialty of Windows NT, and its mantle has now been passed to Windows 2000. These operating systems are designed to support more and faster hardware and to provide greater stability and security.

18. D.   IBM made version 2 of OS/2 a 32-bit system that required at least a 386 processor to run. This made it immensely more stable and powerful.

19. C.   Windows NT is a 32-bit operating system that offers file-level security and support for multiple processors.

20. D.   Although all these systems have had some effect on the composition of modern GUIs, the Xerox Alto was first with many of the innovations that we now consider the basis of a GUI system, including the mouse and windowing capability.

Chapter

12

Using the Microsoft Operating System GUI

THE FOLLOWING OBJECTIVES ARE COVERED IN THIS CHAPTER:

✓ 1.1 Identify the major desktop components and interfaces, and their functions. Differentiate the characteristics of Windows 9*x*/Me, Windows NT 4.0 Workstation, Windows 2000 Professional, and Windows XP.

✓ 1.3 Demonstrate the ability to use command-line functions and utilities to manage the operating system, including the proper syntax and switches.

✓ 1.4 Identify basic concepts and procedures for creating, viewing, and managing disks, directories and files. This includes procedures for changing file attributes and the ramifications of those changes (for example, security issues).

✓ 1.5 Identify the major operating system utilities, their purpose, location, and available switches.

The development of the graphical user interface (GUI) from the Alto to Windows 2000 was discussed in Chapter 11, "Introduction to Operating Systems," and highlighted as a major reason the personal computer industry has taken off in the last decade or two. What exactly is it all about, though? In this chapter, we will look at the Microsoft GUI from the ground up, beginning with a detailed look at its key components and ending with an exploration of basic tasks common across Windows 9x/Me and Windows NT/2000/XP. The following general topics will be covered:

- Windows GUI components
- Using Windows Explorer
- Using Control Panel
- The command prompt
- File and disk management
- The Windows Registry

The Windows GUI has been incredibly successful since its debut. All Microsoft operating system GUIs share features, but they also have differences. For the A+ operating systems exam, you'll need to know various aspects of the GUI interface for the Windows 9x, Me, NT, 2000, and XP operating systems.

The Windows Interface

When you look at the monitor of a machine running Windows 98 and then look at the monitor of a machine running Windows Me/NT/2000, it is difficult to tell them apart. If you look closely, you will notice that the names of some of the icons are different, but for the most part they're identical and look very much like the screen in Figure 12.1. If you look at the monitor of a machine running Windows XP, you'll notice that it looks a bit different than the older interfaces. However, don't despair; things still basically work the same way.

As a technician, you will quickly realize that this overall standardization of Microsoft's graphical interface for all of its OSs is good for you. Most basic tasks are accomplished in almost identical fashion on everything from a Windows 95 workstation computer to a Windows 2000 Advanced Server computer to a Windows XP Professional computer. Also, although the tools that are used often vary between the different OSs, the way you use those tools remains remarkably consistent across *platforms*.

FIGURE 12.1   The Windows interface

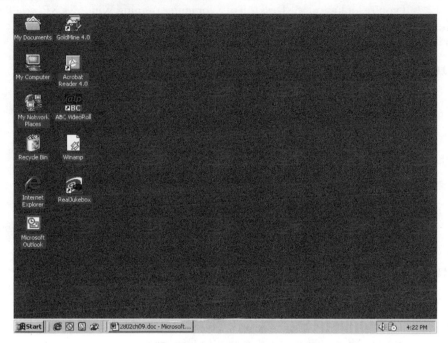

We will begin with an overview of the common elements of the Windows GUI. We will then look at some tasks that are similar across Windows 9*x*/Me and NT/2000/XP. If you have a copy of Windows 9*x*/Me or Windows NT4/2000/XP available, you may want to follow along by exploring each of the elements as they are discussed.

If you are able to follow along, you may notice that there are numerous icons and options we do not mention. Some of them are covered in other chapters. For now, simply ignore them, or browse through them on your own and then return to the text.

The Desktop

The Desktop is the virtual desk on which all of your other programs and utilities run. By default it contains the *Start menu*, the *Taskbar*, and a number of *icons*. The Desktop can also contain additional elements, such as web page content, through the use of the Active Desktop feature. Because it is the base on which everything else sits, the way the Desktop is configured can have a major effect on how the GUI looks and how convenient it is for users.

You can change the Desktop's background patterns, screensaver, color scheme, and size by right-clicking any area of the Desktop that doesn't contain an icon. The menu that appears allows you to do several things, such as creating new Desktop items, changing how your icons are arranged, or selecting a special command called Properties, similar to the one shown in Figure 12.2. If you're looking at the Desktop of a computer running Windows XP, you'll notice that the Active Desktop option is missing from the menu. This feature is still available, but you access it through Properties ≻ Desktop ≻ Customize Desktop ≻ Web.

FIGURE 12.2 The Desktop right-click menu

The Three Clicks in Windows

- *Primary mouse click*—A single click used to select an object or place a cursor.

- *Double-click*—Two primary mouse clicks in quick succession. Used to open a program through an icon or for other application-specific functions.

- *Secondary mouse click (or alternate click)*—Most mice have two buttons. Clicking once on the secondary button (usually the one on the right, although that can be modified) is interpreted differently from a left mouse click. Generally in Windows this click displays a context-sensitive menu from which you can perform tasks or view object properties.

When you right-click the Desktop and choose Properties, you will see the Display Properties screen shown in Figure 12.3. From this screen, you can click the various tabs at the top to move to the different screens of information about the way Windows looks. Tabs are similar to index cards, in that they are staggered across the top so you can see and access large amounts of data within a single small window. Each Properties window has a different set of tabs. Among the tabs in the Display Properties window are the following:

Themes (Windows XP Only) Used to select a theme that enables you to quickly customize the look and feel of your machine. Selecting a theme sets several items at once, such as a picture to display on the Desktop, the look of icons, sounds to use, and so on. All of these options can also be selected individually through the other Desktop Properties tabs. For example, if you're more comfortable with the look and feel of previous versions of Windows, you can select the Windows Classic theme.

Background (Windows 9x/Me/NT/2000)/Desktop (Windows XP) The Background tab in Windows 9x/Me/NT/2000 is used to select an HTML document or a picture to display on the Desktop. In addition to letting you perform this same function, the Desktop tab in Windows XP also lets you configure additional items through the Customize Desktop button. Examples are changing which default icons to display on the Desktop and configuring web content for the Desktop.

Screen Saver   Sets up an automatic screensaver to cover your screen if you have not been active for a certain period of time. Originally used to prevent burned monitors, screensavers are now generally used for entertainment or to password-protect users' Desktops. The Screen Saver tab also gives you access to other power settings.

Appearance   Used to select a color scheme for the Desktop or to change the color or size of other Desktop elements.

Effects (Windows 9*x*/Me/2000 only)   Contains numerous assorted visual options. In Windows XP, some of these visual options are available via the Customize Desktop button on the Desktop tab.

Plus! (Windows NT only)   The Plus! Tab lets you configure various visual items, such as font smoothing and how to display icons. It also lets you configure which icon to use for Desktop items such as My Computer and Recycle Bin.

Web (Windows 9*x*/Me/2000 only)   Lets you configure Active Desktop settings. In Windows XP, you can access this tab via the Customize Desktop button on the Desktop tab.

Settings   Used to set the color depth or screen size. Also contains the Advanced button, which leads to graphics driver and monitor configuration settings.

FIGURE 12.3   The Display Properties screen

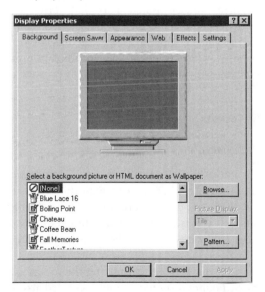

 In Windows 9*x*/Me/NT/2000 you can also access the Display Properties settings by using the Display Control Panel under Start ➢ Settings ➢ Control Panel. In Windows XP, you access the Display Control Panel under Start ➢ Control Panel.

EXERCISE 12.1

Changing a Screensaver

To change the Windows screensaver on Windows 9x/Me/NT/2000/XP, perform the following steps:

1. Right-click the Desktop.

2. Choose Properties from the context menu.

3. Click the Screen Saver tab.

4. Choose 3D Flower Box. Click Preview to see the new screensaver. Move the mouse to cancel the screensaver and return to the Display Properties dialog box.

5. Click the OK button or the Apply button. (OK performs two tasks—Apply and Exit window—whereas Apply leaves the window open.)

The Taskbar

The Taskbar (see Figure 12.4) is another standard component of the Windows interface. Note that although the colors and feel of the Desktop components, including the Taskbar, have changed in Windows XP, the components themselves are the same. The Taskbar contains two major items: the Start menu and the System Tray. The Start menu is on the left side of the Taskbar and is easily identifiable: It is a button that has the word *Start* on it. The System Tray is located on the right side of the Taskbar and contains only a clock by default, but other Windows utilities (for example, screensavers or virus-protection utilities) may put their icons here when running to indicate that they are running and to provide the user with a quick way to access their features.

FIGURE 12.4   The Taskbar

Windows also uses the middle area of the Taskbar. When you open a new window or program, it gets a button on the Taskbar with an icon that represents the window or program as well as the name of the window or program. To bring that window or program to the front (or to maximize it if it was minimized), click its button on the Taskbar. As the middle area of the Taskbar fills with buttons, the buttons become smaller so they can all be displayed.

You can increase the size of the Taskbar by moving the mouse pointer to the top of the Taskbar and pausing until the pointer turns into a double-headed arrow. Once this happens, click the mouse and move it up to make the Taskbar bigger. Or, move it down to make the Taskbar smaller. You can also move the Taskbar to the top or side of the screen by clicking the Taskbar and dragging it to the new location.

In Windows XP, once you've configured the Taskbar position and layout to your liking, you can configure it so that it can't be changed accidentally. To do so, right-click the Taskbar and select Lock The Taskbar. To unlock the Taskbar and make changes, right-click the Taskbar and select Lock The Taskbar again.

EXERCISE 12.2

Auto-Hiding the Taskbar

You can make the Taskbar automatically hide itself when it isn't being used (thus freeing that space for use by the Desktop or other windows):

1. Right-click the Taskbar.

2. Choose Properties, which will bring up the Taskbar Properties Screen (Windows 9x/NT) or the Taskbar And Start Menu Properties screen (Windows Me/2000/XP).

3. In Windows 9x/NT, check the Auto Hide option on the Taskbar Options tab. In Windows Me/2000, check the Auto Hide option on the General tab. In Windows XP, check the Auto-Hide The Taskbar option on the Taskbar tab.

4. Click OK.

5. In Windows 9x/Me/NT/2000, move your mouse to the top of the Desktop or click on the Desktop. The Taskbar will retract off the screen. In Windows XP, the Taskbar retracts as soon as you click OK.

6. Move the mouse pointer to the bottom of the screen, and the Taskbar will pop up and be available for normal use.

The Start Menu

Back when Microsoft officially introduced Windows 95, it bought the rights to use the Rolling Stones' song "Start Me Up" in its advertisements and at the introduction party. Microsoft chose that particular song because the Start menu was the central point of focus in the new Windows interface, as it has been in all subsequent versions.

To display the Start menu, click the Start button in the Taskbar. You'll see a Start menu similar to that shown in Figure 12.5 (pre–Windows XP) or Figure 12.6 (Windows XP). You'll notice that in Windows XP, the look of the Start menu has changed quite a bit from earlier versions of Windows. The Windows XP Start menu serves the same function (quick access to important features and programs); however, its layout and options have changed. Note that if you change the Desktop's appearance to the Windows Classic look, this only changes the color scheme, and so on—the options and layout of the Windows XP Start menu remain different from older versions of Windows. However, the way the Start menu works (the principles it applies) is essentially the same in Windows XP as in older versions.

FIGURE 12.5   The pre–Windows XP Start menu

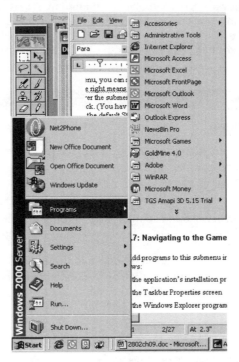

FIGURE 12.6   The Windows XP Start menu

From the Start menu, you can select any of the various options the menu presents. An arrow pointing to the right indicates that a submenu is available. To select a submenu, move the mouse pointer over the submenu title and pause. The submenu will appear; you don't even have to click. (You have to click to choose an option *on* the submenu, though.) We'll discuss each of the default Start menu's submenu options and how to use them.

One handy feature of the Start menu in pre–Windows XP versions of Windows is that it usually displays the name of the OS type along its side when you activate it. This provides an excellent way to quickly see whether you are on Windows 95, 98, Me, NT, or 2000. In Windows XP you don't see the name of the OS; however, the Start menu looks so different that you'll know you are using Windows XP. (The Windows XP Start menu also displays the name of the currently logged-in user at the top.)

In pre–Windows XP versions of Windows, you can also check which OS you are using by right-clicking the My Computer icon on the Desktop and selecting Properties. The OS type and version are displayed on the first tab. In Windows XP, the My Computer icon may not display on the Desktop by default. You can add the icon to the Desktop using the Display Properties (click Customize Desktop on the Desktop tab and select My Computer on the General tab and apply your changes), or you can click Start and then right-click the My Computer option and select Properties.

If you are attached to the look and feel of the pre–Windows XP Start menu, you can configure XP to use the old Start menu layout. To do so, right-click on the Taskbar and select Properties. Click on the Start Menu tab, select Classic Start Menu, and click OK.

Programs (Windows 9*x*/Me/NT/2000)/All Programs (Windows XP) Submenu

The Programs/All Programs submenu holds the program groups and program icons you can use. When you select this submenu, you will be shown another submenu, with a submenu for each program group, as shown in Figure 12.7. In Windows XP, the look is again a little different, but the functionality is the same. You can navigate through this menu and its submenus and click the program you wish to start.

New in Windows XP, after you install a program, the newly installed program or program group is highlighted on the Start menu so you can find it easily.

You can add programs to this submenu in many ways. The three most popular are as follows:

Using the Application's Installation Program   The installation program will not only copy the files for the program, but will also automatically make a program group and shortcuts for the programs under the Programs/All Programs submenu.

FIGURE 12.7 Navigating to the Games program group

 You can add shortcuts to the top of the Start menu by clicking a program or shortcut and dragging it onto the Start button. A shortcut for that item will then appear in the Start menu. In pre–Windows XP versions, the shortcut appears above a divider between the Programs option and the new shortcut. In Windows XP, the shortcut appears above a divider between shortcuts for frequently accessed programs and the new shortcut.

Using the Taskbar Properties Screen Another way to add programs to the Programs submenu is to use the Taskbar Properties (Windows 9x/NT) or Taskbar And Start Menu Properties screen (Windows Me/2000/XP). To get to this screen, right-click the Taskbar and choose Properties.

For pre–Windows XP versions, when the Taskbar Properties or Taskbar And Start Menu Properties screen appears, click the Start Menu Programs (Windows 9x/NT) or Advanced (Windows Me/2000) tab to bring it to the front. From here, you can click Add to add a new program or Remove to remove one. You can see the Windows 2000 Advanced tab in Figure 12.8. A *wizard* (a special sequence of screens designed to walk you through the necessary steps to accomplish certain tasks) will help you create or delete the shortcut(s).

In Windows XP, click the Start Menu tab to bring it to the front. You'll notice a Customize button next to each of the two available options, Start Menu and Classic Start Menu. You can add shortcuts to the Start menu through the Taskbar And Start Menu Properties screen in Windows XP only if you have selected the Classic Start Menu option. Click Customize, and you'll be able to add and delete shortcuts using a sequence of screens as mentioned earlier. However, if the default setting, Start Menu, is selected, you can use the Customize button to customize various aspects of the Windows XP Start menu (such as what Start menu items to display and how to display them), but you can't add shortcuts.

FIGURE 12.8   Use the Taskbar And Start Menu Properties screen to add and remove programs from the Programs submenu.

Using the Windows Explorer program   Finally, you can add programs to the Programs submenu by using Windows Explorer (EXPLORER.EXE). We will talk more about using Explorer later in the chapter.

Documents (Windows 9x/Me/NT/2000)/My Recent Documents (Windows XP) Submenu

The Documents/My Recent Documents submenu has only one function: to keep track of the last 15 data files you opened. Whenever you open a file, a shortcut to it is automatically made in this menu. To open the document again, click the document in the Documents menu to open it in its associated application. In Windows XP, this feature is not enabled by default. To enable it, in the Taskbar And Start Menu Properties screen, click the Start Menu tab and then click Customize next to Start Menu. Click the Advanced tab, select the List My Most Recently Opened Documents option, and then click OK. An option called My Recent Documents is added to the Start menu; it lists the 15 most recently opened data files.

To clear the list of documents shown in the Documents/My Recent Documents submenu, go to the Taskbar Properties or Taskbar And Start Menu Properties screen. Then, use the Clear button on the Start Menu Programs tab (Windows 9x) or Advanced tab (Windows Me/NT/2000/XP). (Remember that you access the Advanced tab in Windows XP via the Customize button on the Start Menu tab.)

Settings Submenu (Windows 9*x*/Me/NT/2000)

The Settings submenu provides easy access to the configuration of Windows. This menu has numerous submenus, including Control Panel, Printers, and Taskbar & Start Menu (Taskbar in Windows NT). Additional menus are available depending on which version of Windows you are using. These submenus give you access to the Control Panel, printer driver, and Taskbar configuration areas, respectively. You can also access the first two areas from the My Computer icon; they are placed together here to provide a common area to access Windows settings.

In Windows XP, you'll find Control Panel as an option directly off the Start menu (not below a submenu). You can add other options (such as Printers And Faxes) to the Start menu using the options on the Advanced tab of the Taskbar And Start Menu Properties screen (via the Customize button).

Search (Find) Submenu/Option

The name of this submenu (Windows 9*x*/Me/NT/2000) or Start menu option (Windows XP) differs between Search and Find in the various versions of Windows, but its purpose doesn't. In all cases, it's used to locate information on your computer or on a network.

In Windows 9*x*/Me/NT/2000, to find a file or directory, select the Find or Search submenu and then select Files or Folders (see Figure 12.9). In the Named field in this dialog box, type in the name of the file or directory you are looking for and click Find Now. Windows will search whatever is specified in the Look In parameter for the file or directory. Matches are listed in a window under the Find window. You can use wildcards (* and ?) to look for multiple files and directories. You can also click the Advanced tab to further refine your search.

FIGURE 12.9   Options in the Find submenu

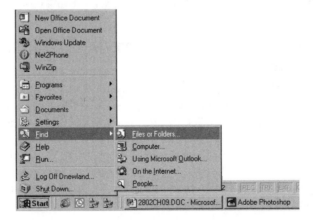

In Windows XP, to find a file or directory, click on the Search option in the Start menu. Doing so opens the Search Results dialog box shown in Figure 12.10. In the left pane, click on All Files And Folders, and then enter the appropriate information in the text fields. Expand the downward-pointing double arrows to access advanced search options. To start the search, click Search. The search results display in the right pane.

FIGURE 12.10   The Search Results dialog box in Windows XP

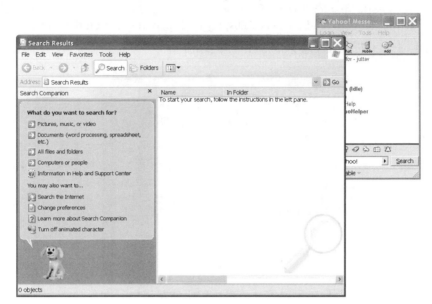

Help Command (Windows 9*x*/Me/NT/2000)/Help And Support Command (Windows XP)

Windows has always included a *very* good Help system. In addition, the Help system was updated with a new interface and new tools in Windows XP. Because of its usefulness and power, it was placed in the Start menu for easy access.

In Windows 9*x*/Me/NT/2000, when you select the Help command, it brings up the Windows Help screen (see Figure 12.11), which has several tabs. On the Contents tab, you can double-click a manual to show a list of subtopics and then click a subtopic to view the text of that topic.

FIGURE 12.11   Windows Help screen

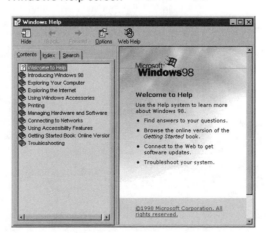

Or, you can click the Index tab to show an alphabetic listing of topics (see Figure 12.12). To select a topic, type the first few letters of the topic (for example, type **print** to move to the section that talks about printing), and then click Display to display the text on the topic.

FIGURE 12.12   The Index tab on the Help screen

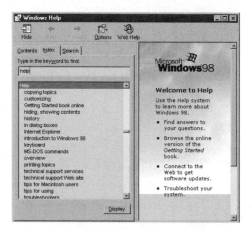

You can also click the Search tab—or the Find tab in Windows NT—to find any text you want in the help files. Simply type the text. As you type, Help will display a list of topics that contain the characters you are typing. The list of topics will get shorter as you type, because the more you type, the more you narrow your search. When the topic you want appears in the list, click the one(s) you want to read about, and then click Display.

In Windows XP, when you click Help And Support, the Help And Support Center home page opens. This screen may have been slightly customized by a hardware vendor if Windows XP was preinstalled on your machine. However, all the options and available tools will still be present. You can see an example of the Help And Support Center home page in Figure 12.13.

FIGURE 12.13   The Help And Support Center home page in Windows XP

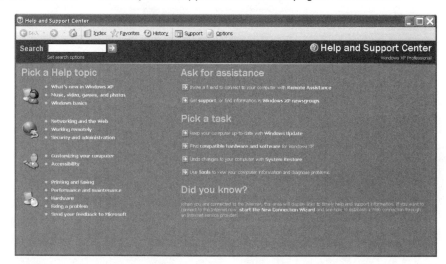

The available options on the main Help And Support Center screen are grouped into several sections. Here you can choose from items such as What's New In Windows XP; Music, Networking And The Web, Working Remotely, Customizing Your Computer Printing And Faxing, Performance And Maintenance, and so on.

Each available option is a link that provides a starting point into the Help system. If you click on a link, you're taken to another screen with a variety of subtopic links in the left pane. If you click on one of the subtopics in the left pane, you can then pick from a variety of related tasks or overviews, articles, and tutorials in the right pane, as shown in Figure 12.14. In addition, the left pane includes links to the Windows glossary, Windows keyboard shortcuts, various tools, and Windows newsgroups.

FIGURE 12.14 Links to topics, tasks, overviews, articles, and tutorials related to a Help subtopic

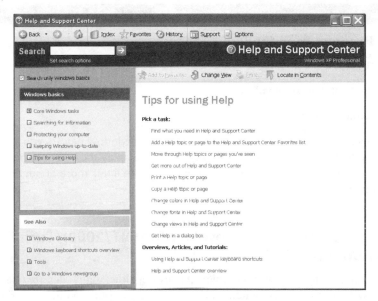

To perform a search on any of the Help And Support Center screens, enter your search text in the Search field and click the right-pointing arrow. To customize your search options, click Set Search Options. You can then specify where and how you want the Help system to look for information related to your search. Available options include Suggested Topics, Full-Text Search Matches, and Microsoft Knowledgebase. Each item has further options you can customize.

To see and use the Help system's index to find topics, click Index in the menu bar. To return to the home page, click the Home Page button in the menu bar.

Run Command

You can use the Run command to start programs if they don't have a shortcut on the Desktop or in the Programs submenu. When you choose Run from the Start menu, a screen similar to the one in Figure 12.15 appears. To execute a particular program, type its name and path in the Open field. If you don't know the exact path, you can browse to find the file by clicking the Browse button. Once you have typed in the executable name and path, click OK to run the program.

FIGURE 12.15 The Start menu's Run command

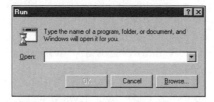

EXERCISE 12.3

Starting a Program from the Run Window

1. Click Start ➤ Run.

2. In the Open field, type **notepad**.

3. Click OK. Notepad will open in a new window.

If the program you want to run has been run from the Run window before, you can find it on the Open field's drop-down list. Click the down arrow to display the list, and then select the program you want by clicking its name and clicking OK. We'll talk more about starting and using applications later.

Shut Down Command (Windows 9x/Me/NT/2000)/Turn Off Computer Command (Windows XP)

Windows operating systems are very complex. At any one time, many files are open in memory. If you accidentally hit the power switch and turn off the computer while these files are open, there is a good chance they will be corrupted. For this reason, Microsoft has added the Shut Down (pre–Windows XP) or Turn Off Computer (Windows XP) command under the Start menu. Note that with a configuration called Fast User Switching, Windows XP also displays Shut Down, rather than Turn Off Computer. When you select this option, Windows presents you with several choices, an example of which is shown in Figure 12.16. Exactly which options are available depends on the Windows version you are running.

FIGURE 12.16 Turn Off Computer command options in Windows XP

The possible choices are as follows:

Shut Down (Windows 9x/Me/NT/2000)/Turn Off (Windows XP)   This option writes any unsaved data to disk, closes any open applications, and gets the computer ready to be powered off. Depending on whether the computer supports ACPI and other auto power off options, the computer is then powered down automatically, or you'll see a black screen with the message *It's now safe to turn off your computer*. In this case, you can power off the computer or press Ctrl+Alt+Del to reboot the computer.

Restart   This option works the same as the first option, but instead of shutting down completely, it automatically reboots the computer with a warm reboot.

Restart the Computer in MS-DOS Mode (Windows 9x only)   This option is special. It does the same tasks as the previous options, but upon reboot, Windows 9x executes the command prompt only and does not start the graphic portion of Windows 9x. You can then run DOS programs as though the machine were a DOS machine. When you are finished running these programs, type **exit** to reboot the machine back into the full Windows 9x with the GUI.

Stand By (Windows XP only)   This option places the computer into a low power state. The monitor and hard disks are turned off, and the computer uses less power. To resume working, press a key on the keyboard; the computer is returned to its original state. In this state, information in memory is not saved to hard disk, so if a power loss occurs, any data in memory will be lost. This option is also available if you are using a laptop under other versions of Windows.

If you enable Hibernation on a Windows XP machine, you can place the computer into hibernation by holding down the Shift key while clicking Stand By in the Turn Off Computer screen. Using the Hibernation feature, any information in memory is saved to disk before the computer is put into a low power state. Thus, if power is lost while the machine is in hibernation, your data is not lost. However, going into and coming out of hibernation takes more time than going into and coming out of stand-by mode.

Icons

Icons are not nearly as complex as windows can be, but they are very important nonetheless. Icons are shortcuts that allow a user to open a program or a utility without knowing where that program is located or how it needs to be configured. Icons consist of several major elements:

- Icon label
- Icon graphic
- Program location

The label and graphic simply tell the user the name of the program and give a visual hint about what that program does. The icon for the Solitaire program, for instance, is labeled *Solitaire*, and its icon graphic is a deck of cards. By right-clicking an icon once, you make that icon the active icon, and a drop-down menu appears. One of the selections is Properties. Clicking Properties brings up the icon's attributes (see Figure 12.17) and is the only way to see exactly which program an icon is configured to start and where the program's executable is located. You can also specify whether to run the program in a normal window or maximized or minimized.

FIGURE 12.17 The Properties window of an application with its icon to the left

In Windows XP, additional functionality has been added to an icon's Properties to allow for backward-compatibility with older versions of Windows. To configure this, click the Compatibility tab and specify the version of Windows for which you want to configure compatibility. Choices include Windows 95, Windows 98/Me, Windows NT 4.0 (Service Pack 5), and Windows 2000. This feature is helpful if you own programs that used to work in older versions of Windows but no longer run under Windows XP. In addition, you can specify different display settings that might be required by older programs.

Standard Desktop Icons

In addition to the options in your Start menu, a number of icons are placed directly on the Desktop. Three of the most important icons are My Computer, Network Neighborhood/My Network Places, and the Recycle Bin. In Windows XP, the My Computer and My Network Places icons no longer display by default on the Desktop; however, you might want to add them. Instructions on how to add My Computer were given earlier in the section "The Start Menu"; you can select My Network Places in the same place you select My Computer to display on the desktop.

The My Computer Icon

If you double-click the My Computer icon, it displays a list of all the disk drives installed in your computer. In pre–Windows XP versions of Windows, it also displays an icon for the Control Panel and Printers folders (see Figure 12.18), which can be used to configure the system.

In Windows XP, My Computer does not by default display an icon for Control Panel (although you can configure it to do so by going to Tools ➤ Folder Options and specifying to show Control Panel in My Computer on the View tab) or for printers; however, in addition to displaying disk drives, it also displays a list of other devices attached to the computer, such as scanners, cameras, mobile devices, and so on. In addition, in Windows XP, all the disk devices are sorted into categories such as Hard Disk Drives, Devices With Removable Storage, Scanners And Cameras, and so on. If you double-click a disk drive or device, you will see the contents of that disk drive or device.

FIGURE 12.18   Using My Computer to open folders

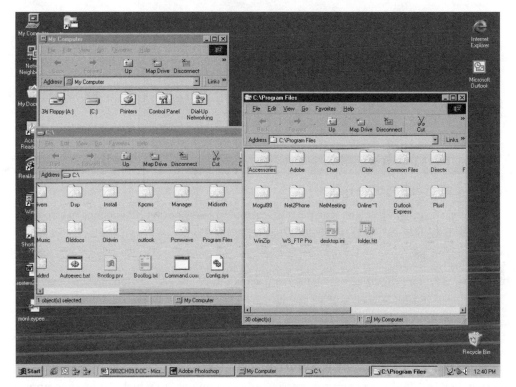

You can delve deeper into each disk drive or device by double-clicking it. The contents are displayed in the same window. You can use Tools ➤ Folder Options (View ➤ Folder Options in Windows NT) to configure each folder to open in a new window. Having multiple windows open makes it easy to copy and move files between drives and between directories using these windows.

In addition to allowing you access to your computer's files, the My Computer icon lets you view your machine's configuration and hardware, also called the System Properties, as shown in Figure 12.19. The following exercise shows you how to view these properties.

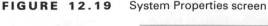

FIGURE 12.19 System Properties screen

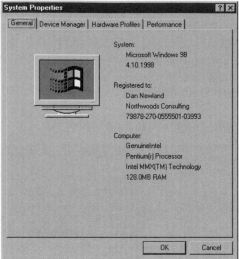

EXERCISE 12.4

Viewing System Properties

1. Right-click the My Computer icon (on the Desktop in pre–Windows XP versions of Windows and in the Start menu in Windows XP).

2. Choose Properties.

3. On the System Properties screen (General screen in Windows XP), look to see what type of processor your computer uses and how much RAM is installed. This screen also tells you what version of Windows is being used. We'll look at the System Properties in much more detail later in this chapter.

Network Neighborhood/My Network Places

Another icon in Windows relates to accessing other computers to which the local computer is connected. In Windows 9*x*/NT, this icon is called Network Neighborhood. In Windows Me/2000/XP, it's called My Network Places.

In Windows XP, the My Network Places icon may not display on the Desktop by default. You can add the icon to the Desktop through the Display Properties (in the same manner you can add the My Computer icon to the Desktop if it isn't there), or you can reach My Network Places by clicking Start ➢ My Network Places.

Opening Network Neighborhood/My Network Places enables you to browse for and access other computers and shared resources to which your computer is connected (see Figure 12.20). This might be another computer in a workgroup, domain, or other network environment (such as a Novell NetWare network). You can also use Network Neighborhood/My Network Places to establish new connections to shared resources.

FIGURE 12.20 My Network Places in Windows XP

Through the Properties of Network Neighborhood/My Network Places, you can configure your network connections, including LAN and dial-up connections. You will learn about networking, including Network Neighborhood/My Network Places, in detail in Chapter 16, "Windows Networking."

The Recycle Bin

All files, directories, and programs in Windows are represented by icons and are generally referred to as *objects*. When you want to remove an object from Windows, you do so by deleting it. Deleting doesn't only remove the object, though; it also removes the ability of the system to access the information or application the object represents. For this reason, Windows includes a special directory where all deleted files are placed: the Recycle Bin. The Recycle Bin holds the files until it is emptied and allows users the opportunity to recover files that they delete accidentally.

You can retrieve a file you have deleted by opening the Recycle Bin icon and then dragging the file from the Recycle Bin back to the disk it came from. Alternatively, you can right-click a file and select Restore.

If you have anti-virus software installed, option names in the Recycle Bin might change. For example, if you have Norton Antivirus installed and you right-click on a file, you'll see that the Restore option has been renamed to Recover.

To permanently erase files, you need to empty the Recycle Bin, thereby deleting any items in it and freeing the hard drive space they took up. If you want to delete only specific, but not all, files, you can select the file(s) in question in the Recycle Bin, right-click, and choose Delete. Or, you can select specific files and click Shift+Del. If the Recycle Bin has files in it, its icon looks like the full trash can shown on the left in Figure 12.21; after it is emptied, its icon reflects this fact, as shown on the right.

Deleting a file from the Recycle Bin frees up space on the drive by deleting the file's record from the drive's File Allocation Table (FAT). The information in the file actually remains on the drive until it has been overwritten by new information.

FIGURE 12.21 A full (left) and empty (right) Recycle Bin

EXERCISE 12.5

Emptying the Recycle Bin

1. Right-click the Recycle Bin.

2. Choose Empty Recycle Bin.

3. A window appears asking if you are certain you want to permanently delete the objects. Click Yes.

What's in a Window?

We have now looked at the nature of the Desktop, the Start menu, and the Taskbar. Each of these items was created for the primary purpose of making access to user applications easier, and these applications are in turn used and managed through the use of *windows*, the rectangular application environments for which the Windows family of operating systems is named. We will now examine how windows work and what they are made of.

A program *window* is a rectangular area created on the screen when an application is opened within Windows. This window can have a number of different forms, but most windows include at least a few basic elements.

Elements of a Window

Several basic elements are present in a standard window. Figure 12.22 shows the control box, title bar, Minimize button, Restore button, Close button, and resizable border in a text editor called Notepad (NOTEPAD.EXE) that has all the basic window elements—and little else.

FIGURE 12.22 The basic elements of a window

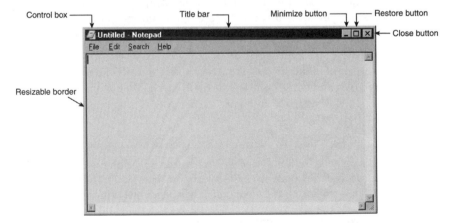

The basic window elements are as follows:

Control Box In the upper-left corner of the window. Used to control the state of the application. It can be used to maximize, minimize, and close the application. Clicking it once brings into view a selection menu. Double-clicking it closes the window and shuts down the application.

Minimize and Restore Buttons   Used to change the state of the window on the Desktop. They are discussed in the "States of a Window" section later in this chapter.

Close Button   Used to easily end a program and return any resources it was using to the system. It essentially does the same thing as double-clicking the control box, but with one less click.

Title Bar   The area between the Control box and the Minimize button. It states the name of the program and in some cases gives information about the particular document being accessed by that program. The color of the Title bar indicates whether a particular window is the active window.

Menu Bar   Used to present useful commands in an easily accessible format. Clicking one of the menu choices displays a list of related options you may choose from.

Active Window   The window that is currently being used. It has two attributes. First, any keystrokes that are entered are directed there by default. Second, any other windows that overlap the active window are pushed behind it.

Border   A thin line that surrounds the window in its restored state and allows it to be resized.

These elements are not all found on every window, because programmers can choose to eliminate or modify them. Still, in most cases they will be constant, with the rest of the window filled in with menus, toolbars, a workspace, or other application-specific elements. For instance, Microsoft Word, the program with which this book was written, adds an additional control box and Minimize and Maximize buttons for each document. It also has a menu bar, a number of optional toolbars, scroll bars at the right and bottom of the window, and a status bar at the very bottom. Application windows can become quite cluttered.

Notepad is a very simple Windows program. It has only a single menu bar and the basic elements seen previously in Figure 12.22. Figure 12.23 shows a Microsoft Word window. Both Word and Notepad are used to create and edit documents, but Word is far more configurable and powerful and therefore has many more optional components available within its window.

FIGURE 12.23   A window with more components

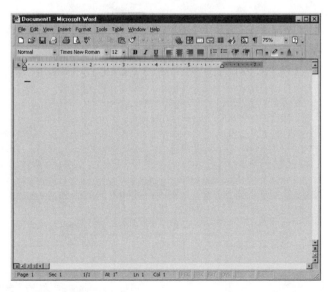

States of a Window

There is more to the Windows interface than the physical parts of a window. Windows also are movable, stackable, and resizable, and they can be hidden behind other windows (often unintentionally!).

When an application window has been launched, it exists in one of three states:

Maximized   A maximized window takes up all available space on the screen. When it is in front of other programs, it is the only thing visible—even the Desktop is hidden. In Figure 12.24, note that Microsoft Word is maximized; it takes up the entire space of the Desktop, and the middle button in the upper-right corner displays two rectangles rather than one. The sides of the window no longer have borders. The window is flush with the edges of the screen. Maximizing a window provides the maximum workspace possible for that window's application, and the window can be accessed actively by the user. In general, maximized mode is the preferred window size for most word-processing, graphics-creation, and other user applications.

FIGURE 12.24   Windows in different states

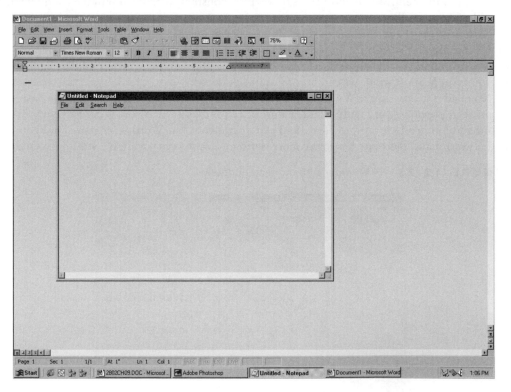

Restored   A restored window can be used interactively and is identical in function to a maximized window, with the simple difference that it does not necessarily take up the entire screen. Restored windows can be very small, or they can take up almost as much space as maximized windows. Generally, how large the restored window becomes is the user's choice. Restored windows display a restore box (the middle button in the upper-right corner) with a single rectangle in it; this is used to maximize the window. Restored windows have a border. Figure 12.24 shows an example of Notepad in a restored state.

Minimized   Minimized program windows are represented by nothing but an icon and title on the Taskbar, and they are not usable until they have been either maximized or restored. The only difference between a minimized program and a closed program is that a minimized program is out of the way but is still taking up resources and is therefore ready to use if you need it. It also leaves the content of the window in the same place when you return to it as when you minimized it. In Figure 12.24, Adobe Photoshop is minimized.

When a program is open and you need to open another program (or maybe you need to stop playing a game because your boss has entered the room), you have two choices. First, you can close the program and reopen it later. If you do this, however, your current game will be lost and you will have to start over. Minimizing the game window, on the other hand, removes the open window from the screen and leaves the program open but displays nothing more than an icon and title on the Taskbar, as with the PhotoShop icon in Figure 12.24. Later, you can restore the window to its previous size and finish the game in progress.

Using the Command Prompt

Although we're talking about the Windows Operating System in this book, its ancestor, the Microsoft Disk Operating System (MS-DOS), still plays a role in Windows today. MS-DOS was never meant to be extremely friendly. Its roots are in CP/M, which, in turn, has its roots in Unix. Both of these older OSs are command line–based, and so is MS-DOS. In other words, they all use long strings of commands typed in at the computer keyboard to perform operations. Some people prefer this type of interaction with the computer, including many folks with technical backgrounds (such as yours truly). Although Windows has left the full command-line interface behind, it still contains a bit of DOS, and you get to it through the command prompt.

We will look at a number of graphical utilities in the next few chapters and, believe it or not, the command prompt is one of them. Although you can't tell from looking at it (see Figure 12.25), the Windows command prompt is actually a 16- or 32-bit Windows program that is intentionally *designed* to have the look and feel of a DOS command line. Because it is, despite its appearance, a Windows program, the command prompt provides all the stability and configurability you expect from Windows.

FIGURE 12.25 The Windows command prompt

Running a Utility or Program from the Command Prompt

Windows includes a number of command-line utilities you can use to configure and maintain your system. Among these is the IPCONFIG utility of Windows NT/2000/XP. If you are running Windows NT/2000/XP, this utility allows you to check on the TCP/IP settings of the machine. (TCP/IP is the protocol that allows networked computers to use the Internet, and as such is something you will probably see a lot of. We will discuss it further in Chapter 16.)

You can access a command prompt by either running the 16-bit COMMAND.COM or the 32-bit CMD.EXE. CMD.EXE, however, is not available in Windows 9x/Me. It was first introduced in Windows NT and is now also available in Windows 2000 and XP. In fact, if in Windows NT, 2000, or XP you run COMMAND.COM and enter commands at the command prompt, they're actually sent to and handled by CMD.EXE.

There are few actual text-based applications in newer versions of Windows. However, for a taste of the old days, check out the EDIT program (See Figure 12.26), which is still provided free of charge with even the newest versions of Windows. EDIT is often used to modify batch files and text configuration files.

FIGURE 12.26 The EDIT program

EXERCISE 12.6

Using the *EDIT* Program

1. Open a command prompt. The quickest way to do this is to click Start ➢ Run, enter **Command** in the Open field, and click OK.

2. Type **EDIT** and press Enter.

3. The EDIT utility will open. In the text area, type **hello**.

4. To save the file, press Alt+F. This brings up the File menu. Press A.

5. In the Save As window, type **hello.txt** and click OK.

6. To exit from EDIT, press ALT+F and press X for Exit.

Issuing Text Commands

In general, older versions of Windows, such as Windows 98, use more *text-based commands* than newer versions, such as Windows 2000/XP. Look for a number of standard commands in the \\Windows\Command or \\Windows\System32 or \\WINNT\System32 directory, depending on the OS version. See Table 12.1 for a list of some of the available Windows text commands. Note that some of the commands are not available in Windows 2000 or XP and others are not available in earlier versions of Windows, such as Windows 98.

TABLE 12.1   Windows Text Commands

Command	Purpose
ATTRIB	Allows the user to set or remove file attributes.
CD	Changes your current folder to another folder.
CHKDSK	Examines the machine's hard drives.
CLS	Clears the screen.
COPY	Copies a file into another directory.
DEFRAG	Defragments (reorganizes) the files on your machine's hard drives, which can result in better performance.
DEL	Deletes a file from the folder.
DELTREE	Deletes files and subdirectories. A more powerful extension of the DEL command.

TABLE 12.1 Windows Text Commands *(continued)*

Command	Purpose
DIR	Displays the contents of the current folder.
DISKCOPY	Duplicates floppy disks.
DISKPART	Manages partitions on the computer's hard drives.
DOSKEY	Lists recently issued commands with a prompt session.
ECHO	Repeats typed text back to the screen. Can be used to send text to a file or device using redirection.
EXTRACT	Extracts data from Cabinet (.CAB) files.
FDISK	Creates, deletes, and manages hard-disk partitions.
FORMAT	Prepares a drive for use.
MD	Creates a new folder.
MEM	Provides information about how much memory is available to the system.
MOVE	Moves files from one folder to another.
MSCDEX	Loads CD-ROM driver and configures DOS access to CD-ROM devices.
PING	Establishes a connection to the specified host.
REN	Renames a file.
RD	Deletes a directory.
SCANDISK	Similar to CHKDSK.
SCANREG	Scans the Registry by starting a Windows application that checks for errors, and allows you to back up the Registry files.
SET	Sets, displays, and removes DOS environment variables.
SETVER	Sets the version and reports the version numbers of DOS utilities.
SYS	Prepares a drive to be used to start a computer.
TYPE	Displays the contents of text files.

TABLE 12.1 Windows Text Commands *(continued)*

Command	Purpose
VER	Checks the current version of the OS.
XCOPY	Duplicates files and subdirectories. An extension of the COPY command.

To issue a command from the command prompt, you need to know the structure the command uses, generally referred to as its *syntax*. You should also be familiar with the command's available *switches*. Switches enable you to further configure the command's actions. The following exercise shows you how to learn about a command's syntax and available switches and then run that command. The command in the exercise is ATTRIB, which is used to allow a user to set one of four attributes on a file: Read Only, Archive, System, or Hidden.

To identify the options or switches for a DOS command, you can use the built-in Help system. Type the command followed by a forward slash (/) and a question mark (?). Doing so displays all the options for that command and how to use them properly, as shown in Figure 12.27.

FIGURE 12.27 Options available for ATTRIB.EXE

EXERCISE 12.7

Changing a File Attribute on Windows XP

1. Open a command prompt. To do this, click Start ➢ Run, type **cmd** in the Open field and click OK.

2. In the command prompt window, type **CD C:** and press Enter.

3. Type **DIR** and press Enter. A list of all the files in the root of C: is shown.

4. Type **ATTRIB /?** and press Enter. Examine the available options.

EXERCISE 12.7 *(continued)*

5. Type **ATTRIB autoexec.bat** and press Enter. The current attributes of the file are displayed.

6. Type **ATTRIB autoexec.bat** +**R** and press Enter.

7. Repeat step 5 to view the changed attribute, and then repeat step 6 with the –**R** switch to return the file to its original attributes.

8. Type **Exit** to close the command prompt window.

You can use commands you've already typed at the command prompt again without having to type the same or a similar command over and over. To do so, press the up arrow on the keyboard. This steps backward one at a time through the commands you've entered, and can make working with command-prompt commands much quicker. When you've found the command you're looking for, you can either press Enter to execute it again or use the left and right arrow keys to navigate through the command to make minor modifications, such as specifying a different switch.

Windows Configuration

Simply navigating the Start menu and running EDIT at a command prompt does not an A+ certified tech make! Most of the tasks you will be called on to deal with are more complex than minimizing a window. The Windows OS provides numerous utilities to aid you in changing system configuration elements or identifying and diagnosing problems. Many of these are specific to the particular OS, but nonetheless their location and general usage is similar in the various versions of Windows. As a result, system management in Windows can be loosely grouped into the following areas:

- File management
- System tools
- Control Panel programs
- Task Manager
- Hardware Management
- Computer Management Console
- Virtual memory
- Disk management
- The Registry Editor

File Management

File management is the process by which a computer stores data and retrieves it from storage. Although some of the file-management interfaces in the Windows 9*x*/Me/NT/2000/XP platforms may have a different look and feel, the process of managing files is similar across the board.

Files and Folders

For a program to run, it must be able to read information off the disk and write information back to the disk. In order to be able to organize and access information—especially in larger new systems that may have thousands of files—it is necessary to have a structure and an ordering process.

Windows provides this process by allowing you to create *directories*, also known as *folders*, in which to organize files. Windows also regulates the way that files are named and the properties of files. Each file created in Windows has to follow certain rules, and any program that accesses files through Windows also must comply with these rules. Files created on a Windows system must follow these rules:

- Each file has a filename of up to 255 characters.

- Certain characters such as a slash (\ or /) are prohibited in the filename.

- An extension (generally three or four characters) can be added to identify the file's type.

- Filenames are not case sensitive. (You can create files with names that use both upper- and lowercase letters, but to identify the file within the filesystem, it is not necessary to adhere to the capitalization in the filename.) Thus, you cannot have a file named `working.txt` and another called `WORKING.TXT` in the same directory. To Windows, these filenames are identical, and you can't have two files with the same filename in the same directory. We'll get into more detail on this topic a little later.

- In Windows 3.*x* and DOS, filenames were limited to eight characters and a three-character extension, separated by a period. This is also called the *8.3* file-naming convention. With Windows 95, long filenames were introduced, which allowed the 255-character filename convention. Windows NT used long filenames from the get-go.

The Windows filesystem is arranged like a filing cabinet. In a filing cabinet, paper is placed into folders, which are inside dividers, which are in a drawer of the filing cabinet. In the Windows filesystem, individual files are placed in subdirectories that are inside directories, which are stored on different disks or different partitions.

Windows also protects against duplicate filenames, so no two files on the system can have exactly the same name and *path*. A path indicates the location of the file on the disk; it is composed of the logical drive letter the file is on and, if the file is located in a directory or subdirectory, the names of those directories. For instance, if a file named `AUTOEXEC.BAT` is located in the root of the C: drive—meaning it is not within a directory—the path to the file is `C:\AUTOEXEC.BAT`. If, as another example, a file called `FDISK.EXE` is located in the `Command` directory under Windows under the root of C:, then the path to this file is `C:\WINDOWS\COMMAND\FDISK.EXE`.

The *root directory* of any drive is the place where the hierarchy of folders for that drive begins. On a C: drive, for instance, C:\ is the root directory of the drive.

Common file extensions you may encounter are .EXE for executable files (applications), .DLL for Dynamic Linked Library (DLL) files, .SYS for system files, .LOG for log files, .DRV for driver files, .TXT for text files, and others. Note that DLL files contain additional functions and commands applications can use and share. In addition, most applications use specific file extensions for the documents created with each application. For example, documents created in Microsoft Word have a .DOC extension. You'll also encounter extensions such as .MPG for video files, .MP3 for music files, .TIF and .JPG for graphics files, .HTM or .HTML for web pages, and so on. Being familiar with different filename extensions is helpful in working with the Windows filesystem.

Capabilities of the Windows Explorer

Although it is technically possible to use the command-line utilities provided within the command prompt to manage your files, this generally is not the most efficient way to accomplish most tasks. The ability to use drag-and-drop techniques and other graphical tools to manage the filesystem makes the process far simpler, and the Windows Explorer is a utility that allows you to accomplish a number of important file-related tasks from a single graphical interface, as shown in Figure 12.28.

FIGURE 12.28 The Windows Explorer program

Some of the tasks you can accomplish using the Explorer include:

- Viewing files and directories
- Opening programs or data files
- Creating directories and files

- Copying objects (files or directories) to other locations
- Moving objects (files or directories) to other locations
- Deleting or renaming objects (files or directories)
- Searching for a particular file or type of file
- Changing file attributes
- Formatting new disks (such as floppy disks)

You can access many of these functions by right-clicking a file or folder and selecting the appropriate option, such as Copy or Delete, from the context menu.

Navigating and Using the Windows Explorer

Using the Windows Explorer is simple. A few basic instructions are all you need to start working with it. First, the Windows Explorer interface has a number of parts, each of which serves a specific purpose. The top area of the Windows Explorer is dominated by a set of menus and toolbars that give you easy access to common commands. The main section of the window is divided into two panes: The left pane displays the drives and folders available, and the right pane displays the contents of the currently selected folder. In pre–Windows XP versions, along the bottom of the window, the status bar displays information about the used and free space on the current directory. Some common actions in Explorer include the following:

Expanding a Folder   You can double-click a folder in the left pane to expand the folder (show its subfolders in the left pane) and display the contents of the folder in the right pane. Clicking the plus sign (+) to the left of a folder expands the folder without changing the display in the right pane (see Figure 12.29).

FIGURE 12.29   The Expand and Collapse symbols

Collapsing a Folder   Clicking the minus sign ( ) next to a folder unexpands/collapses it.

Selecting a File   If you click the file in the right pane, Windows highlights the file by marking it with a darker color.

Selecting Multiple Files   The Ctrl and Shift keys allow you to select multiple files at once. Holding down Ctrl while clicking individual files selects each new file while leaving the currently selected file(s) selected as well. Holding down Shift while selecting two files selects both of them and all files in between.

Opening a File   Double-clicking a file in the right pane opens the program if the file is an application; if it is a data file, it will open using whichever file extension is configured for it.

Changing the View Type   In Windows 9x, there are four different primary view types: Large Icons, Small Icons, List, and Details. Starting with Windows Me and 2000, the Thumbnail view was added. Then, in Windows XP, the Tiles view was added. In XP, you can still choose to view objects with icons, but you can no longer choose between large and small icons. You can move between these views by clicking the View menu and selecting the view you prefer.

Finding Specific Files   This option is accessed under Tools ➢ Find in Windows 9x/NT or by using the Search button in Windows Me/2000/XP. Either way, you can search for files based on their name, file size, file type, and other attributes, as shown in Figure 12.30.

FIGURE 12.30   Searching for a file in Windows

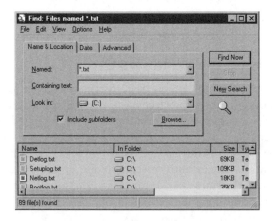

EXERCISE 12.8

Searching for a Type of File

1. In Windows 9x/NT, click Tools ➢ Find ➢ Files or Folders. In Windows Me/2000, click the Search button on the toolbar. In Windows XP, click the Search button on the toolbar and then click All Files And Folders in the left pane.

2. Either the Search window (Windows 9x/NT) or Search pane (Windows Me/2000/XP) appears. You are prompted for the Search information.

3. Type *.TXT in the field that asks for the name of the file(s).

4. In the Look In field, enter C:\, and click Find Now.

5. In Windows 98, make sure the Include Subfolders check box is checked. In Windows 2000, to include subfolders, click Search Options and then select Advanced Options. Once you select Advanced Options, Search Subfolders is automatically selected. In Windows XP, subfolders are searched by default. (To disable this function, click More Advanced Functions and deselect Search Subfolders.)

6. Click Find Now (Windows 98/NT), Search Now (Windows Me/2000), or Search (Windows XP).

7. Windows searches the C: drive and eventually displays a Search Results window with all the files it has found.

When you're searching, you can also use wildcards. *Wildcards* are characters that act as placeholders for a character or set of characters, allowing, for instance, a search for all files with a text (.TXT) extension. To perform such a search, you'd type an asterisk (*) as a stand-in for the filename: *.TXT. An asterisk takes the place of any number of characters in a search. A question mark (?) takes the place of a single number or letter. For example, AUTOEX??.BAT would return the file AUTOEXEC.BAT as part of its results.

Creating New Objects   To create a new file, folder, or other object, navigate to the location where you want to create the object, and then right-click in the right pane (without selecting a file or directory). In the menu that appears, select New and then choose the object you want to create, as shown in Figure 12.31.

FIGURE 12.31   Creating a new folder

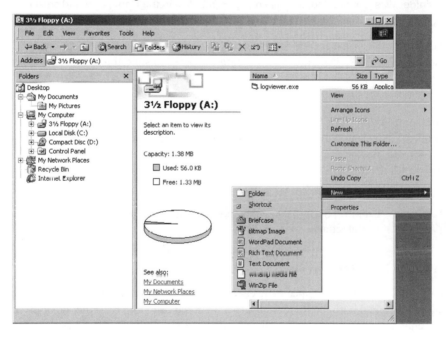

Deleting Objects   Select the object and press the Del key on the keyboard, or right-click the object and select Delete from the menu that appears.

 The simplicity of deleting in Windows makes it likely that you or one of the people you support will delete or misplace a file or a number of files that are still needed. In such a case, the Recycle Bin (mentioned earlier) is a lifesaver.

EXERCISE 12.9

Using Windows Explorer

1. Open Windows Explorer. In Windows 9x/NT, click Start ➢ Programs ➢ Windows (NT) Explorer. In Windows Me/2000, click Start ➢ Programs ➢ Accessories ➢ Windows Explorer. In Windows XP, click Start ➢ All Programs ➢ Accessories ➢ Windows Explorer.

2. To see what applications are installed in the Program Files directory, navigate the hierarchy from My Computer to C: to Program Files. You may need to click the + next to one or more of the folders to expand them and see their contents.

3. Navigate back to the root of C: and right-click in the right pane. Select New ➢ Folder and type **TEST** as the name of the folder.

4. Double-click the new **TEST** folder and examine the right pane after its contents are displayed. The folder was just created, so it is empty. Right-click in the right pane and select New ➢ Text Document. Give the file the name **NEW.TXT**.

5. To delete the file you just created, select it by clicking it once and then right-click it. Choose Delete. You are asked whether you are sure you want to send the file to the Recycle Bin; click Yes.

Besides simplifying most file-management commands as shown here, the Explorer also allows you to easily complete a number of disk-management tasks. You can format and label floppy disks and, in some cases, copy the Windows system files to a floppy so that you can use a disk to boot a machine.

Creating boot disks will be covered more fully in Chapter 13, "Major OS Architectures."

Changing File Attributes

File attributes determine what specific users can do to files or directories. For example, if a file or directory is flagged with the Read Only attribute, then users can read the file or directory, but not make changes to it or delete it. Attributes include Read Only, Hidden, System, and Archive, as well as Compression, Indexing, and Encryption. Not all attributes are available with all versions of Windows. We'll look at this subject in more detail in a moment.

You can view and change file attributes either with the Attrib command prompt command or through the Properties of a file or directory. To access the Properties of a file or directory in the Windows GUI, right-click the file or directory and select Properties. Figure 12.32 shows the Properties screen of a file in Windows XP. In Windows XP, you can view and configure the Read Only and Hidden file attributes on the General tab. To view and configure additional attributes, click Advanced.

System files are usually flagged with the Hidden attribute, meaning they don't appear when a user displays a directory listing. You should not change this attribute on a system file unless absolutely necessary. System files are required for the OS to function. If they are visible, users might delete them (perhaps thinking they can clear some disk space by deleting files they don't recognize). Needless to say, that would be a bad thing!

FIGURE 12.32 The General tab of a Windows XP file's Properties

Filesystem Advanced Attributes

Windows NT/2000/XP use the NT Filesystem (NTFS) filesystem, which gives you a number of options that are not available on earlier filesystems such as FAT or FAT32. You'll learn more about FAT/FAT32 and NTFS a little later in this chapter. A number of these options are implemented through the use of the Advanced Attributes window, shown in Figure 12.33. To reach these options in Windows 2000/XP, right-click the folder or file you wish to modify and select Properties from the menu. On the main Properties page of the folder or file, click the Advanced button in the lower-right corner.

FIGURE 12.33 The Advanced Options window in Windows 2000

On the Advanced Attributes screen you have access to the following settings:

Archiving   Identical to the Archive attribute on a FAT or FAT32 drive. This option tells the system whether the file has changed since the last time it was backed up. Technically it is known as the Archive Needed attribute; if this box is selected, the file should be backed up. If it is not selected, a current version of the file is already backed up.

Indexing   Windows NT/2000/XP implement an Index Service to catalog and improve the search capabilities of your drive. Once files are indexed, you can search them more quickly by name, date, or other attributes. Setting the index option on a folder causes a prompt to appear, asking whether you want the existing files in the folder to be indexed as well. If you choose to do this, Windows NT/2000/XP automatically reset this attribute on subfolders and files. If not, only new files created in the directory are indexed.

Compression   Windows 2000/XP support advanced compression options, which were first introduced in Windows NT. NTFS files and folders can be dynamically compressed and uncompressed, often saving a great deal of space on the drive. As with Indexing, turning on Compression for a folder results in your being prompted as to whether you want the existing files in the folder to be compressed. If you choose to do this, Windows 2000/XP automatically compress the subfolders and files. If not, only new files created in the directory are compressed.

Compression works best on files such as word-processing documents and uncompressed images. Word files and MS Paint bitmaps can be compressed up to 80 percent using compression. Files that are already packed well do not compress as effectively; EXE and Zip files generally compress only about 2 percent. Similarly GIF and JPEG images are already compressed (which is why they are used in Internet web pages), so they compress a little or not at all.

Encryption   First introduced in Windows 2000 and also available in Windows XP, encryption lets you secure files against anyone else's being able to view them, by encoding the files with a key that only you have access to. This can be useful if you're worried about extremely sensitive information, but in general, encryption is not necessary on the network. NTFS local file security is usually enough to provide users with access to what they need and prevent others from getting to what they shouldn't. If you want to encrypt a file, go through the same process you would for indexing or compression.

If a user forgets their password or is unable to access the network to authenticate their account, they will not be able to open encrypted files. By default, if the user's account is lost or deleted, the only other user who can decrypt the file is the Administrator account.

File Permissions

Windows NT/2000/XP also support the use of file permissions, because these OSs use the NTFS filesystem, which includes file-level filesystem security (rather than just share-level security, as is the case with Windows 9*x*/Me). You'll learn more about NTFS and other filesystem types later in this chapter. Permissions serve the purpose of controlling who has access and what type of access to what files or objects. Several permissions are available, such as Read, Write, Execute, Delete, Change Permissions, Take Ownership, Full Control, and so on. The list is quite extensive. For a complete list, consult the Windows Help files. These permissions are called *special permissions.*

Assigning special permissions individually could be a tedious task. To make it easier for administrators to assign multiple permissions at once, Windows incorporates *standard permissions.* Standard permissions are collections of special permissions, including Full Control, Modify, Read & Execute, Read, and Write. As we said, each of these standard permissions automatically assigns multiple special permissions at once. To see which special permissions are assigned by the different standard permissions, enter File Permissions (List) into the Help system's index keyword area.

Note that you can assign permissions to individual users or to groups. You assign standard permissions on the Security tab of a file or folder (see Figure 12.34), which you access through the file or folder's Properties.

FIGURE 12.34   The Security tab for a folder on a Windows 2000 Professional computer

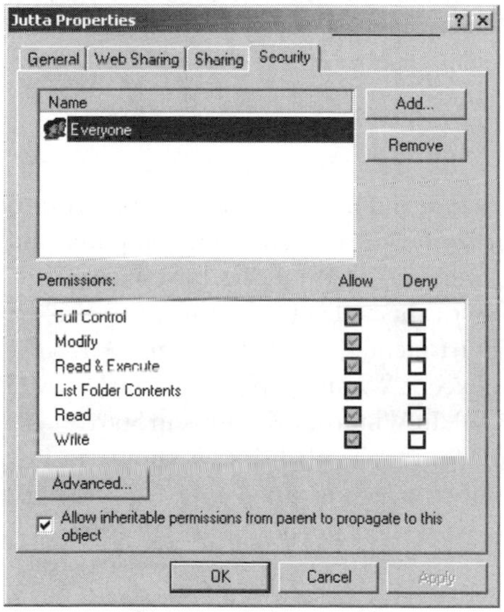

EXERCISE 12.10

Examining File Permissions

1. In Windows NT/2000/XP, open Windows Explorer.

2. Right-click a file or folder and choose Properties.

EXERCISE 12.10 *(continued)*

3. Select and then examine the Security tab. You'll see the users and/or groups to which permissions have been assigned. Select a user or group in the list and examine the list of standard permissions. (To add a new user or group, click Add and follow the prompts.) Any standard permissions that are checked in the Allow column are applied. If a check box is also grayed out, this means the permission was inherited. To revoke a set of standard permissions, click the appropriate check box in the Deny column. If you click the check box in the Deny column for the Full Control permission, all other standard permissions are denied also.

4. Click Advanced to examine advanced options.

5. Click Cancel twice to close the file or folder's Properties.

Be sure you don't accidentally make any changes you're not intending to make. Changing permissions without understanding the ramifications can have negative consequences, such as losing access to files or folders.

System Tools

All versions of Windows include a number of applications you can run to check on and improve the health and performance of a Windows computer and perform other tasks, such as disk management. Later versions of Windows have more of these gadgets, but earlier versions also have a number of them. Typically, these utilities, if installed, can be found in a particular folder on the Start menu: Start ➤ Programs ➤ Accessories ➤ System Tools for pre–Windows XP versions except Windows NT, and Start ➤ All Programs ➤ Accessories ➤ System Tools for Windows XP. In Windows NT, look in Start ➤ All Programs ➤ Administrative Tools (Common). A sample System Tools folder is shown in Figure 12.35. The available programs can be very useful to a technician. Table 12.2 lists some common Windows utilities found there, along with their purpose. Not all tools are available in all versions of Windows.

Windows 2000/XP also have a folder called Administrative Tools where many of their system configuration utilities are kept. Some of these tools are also available in earlier versions of Windows, but by different names or in different locations. For instance, Windows 98's System Monitor is expanded into a more powerful tool in Windows 2000/XP called Performance, which you can access by clicking Start ➤ Control Panel and then double-clicking the Administrative Tools folder.

FIGURE 12.35   The System Tools program group

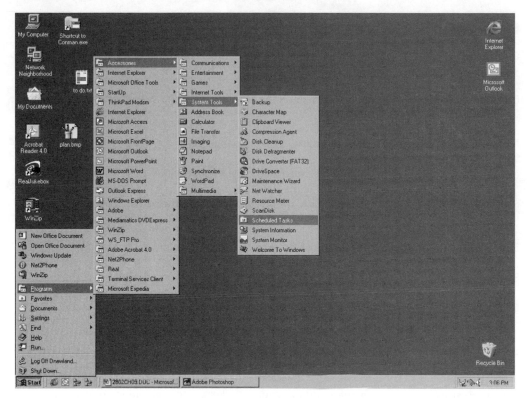

TABLE 12.2   System Tools

System Tool	Function
Backup	Makes archival copies of important files.
Character Map	Determines which type of letters, numbers, and nonalphanumeric characters the machine will use.
Clipboard Viewer	Allows you to see what has been copied onto the system Clipboard.
Drive Space 3	Allows you to compress the files on a drive to get more information onto the drive (although compressing files makes them slower to access).
Compression Agent	Used with Drive Space 3. Allows you to set up parameters for automatically determining which files to compress.

TABLE 12.2   System Tools *(continued)*

System Tool	Function
Disk Cleanup	A utility that goes through the system and deletes unneeded files to free up drive space.
Disk Defragmenter (DEFRAG.EXE)	Arranges data on the computer's disk drives so it is more easily available.
Maintenance Wizard	Sets up a system maintenance plan.
Net Watcher	Checks the performance of the network.
Resource Meter	Gives a quick, graphical display of how heavily basic system resources are being used.
Scandisk	Checks a disk drive for errors or problems.
Scheduled Tasks	Enables recurring tasks to be run automatically.
System Information	Finds information about the hardware and software installed on a PC.
System Monitor	A more complex version of Resource Meter. Monitors specific resources and watches how they are used in real time.
System Restore	Enables you to restore the system to a previous point in time without losing personal files.

EXERCISE 12.11

Scheduling a Disk Cleanup Task

1. In pre–Windows XP versions of Windows (except NT), click Start ➤ Programs ➤ Accessories ➤ System Tools ➤ Scheduled Tasks. In Windows XP, click Start ➤ All Programs ➤ Accessories ➤ System Tools ➤ Scheduled Tasks. In Windows NT, click Start ➤ Programs ➤ Administrative Tools (Common) ➤ Scheduled Tasks.

2. In the Scheduled Tasks window that appears, double-click the Add Scheduled Task icon.

3. In the Scheduled Task Wizard, read the introduction screen, and then click Next. (After filling out any screen in a wizard, you must click Next to continue. At the end of a wizard, you need to click Finish.) In the next screen, choose Disk Cleanup as the application to run, as shown in the graphic.

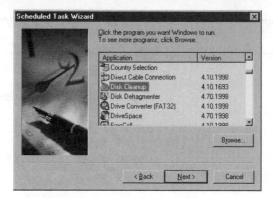

4. Choose to run it monthly.

5. Click the Day radio button and accept the default times.

6. If prompted, enter a password for the username provided.

7. Choose to view advanced properties, and click Finish.

8. Under the Settings tab, check the Wake The Computer To Run This Task option and click OK. Your task will now run on the first day of each month with the options you have selected.

9. If you do not want to keep this task, return to Scheduled Tasks (via the System Tools folder in the Start menu) and delete it.

Control Panel

Although for the most part the Windows system is functional from the time it is first installed, Microsoft realized that if someone were going to use computers regularly, they would probably want to be able to customize their environment so it would be better suited to their needs—or at least more fun to use. As a result, the Windows environment has a large number of utilities that are intended to give you control over the look and feel of the Desktop.

This is, of course, an excellent idea. It is also a bit more freedom than some less-than-cautious users seem to be capable of handling, and you will undoubtedly serve a number of customers who call you in to restore their configuration after botched attempts at changing one setting or another.

More than likely, you will also have to reinstall Windows yourself a few times because of accidents that occur while you are studying or testing the system's limits. This is actually a good thing, because no competent computer technician can say that they have never had to reinstall because of an error. You can't really know how to fix Windows until you are experienced at breaking it. So, it is extremely important to experiment and find out what can be changed in the Windows environment, what results from those changes, and how to undo any unwanted results. Toward this end, we will examine the most common configuration utility in Windows: Control Panel. The names of some panels are different in various versions of Windows; different names are indicated in parentheses. And, not all panels are available in all versions. You'll see some of the more popular panels described in Table 12.3.

TABLE 12.3   Selected Windows Control Panel Programs (Windows XP Names and other variations in Parentheses)

Program Name	Function
Add/Remove Hardware (Add Hardware in Windows XP; Add New Hardware in Windows 98)	Adds and configures new hardware.
Add/Remove Programs (Add Or Remove Programs)	Changes, adds, or deletes software.
Administrative Tools	Performs administrative tasks on the computer.
Date/Time (Date And Time)	Sets the system time and configures options such as time zone.
Display	Configures screensavers, colors, display options, and monitor drivers.
Folder Options	Configures the look and feel of how folders are displayed in Windows Explorer.
Fonts	Adds and removes fonts.
Internet Options	Sets a number of options that are discussed in more detail in Chapter 16.
Multimedia (Sounds And Multimedia; Sounds And Audio Devices; also Scanners And Cameras)	Configures audio, video, or audio and video options.
Network (Network And Dial-up Connections; Network Connections)	Sets options for connecting to other computers. Discussed further in Chapter 16.
Modems (Phone And Modem Options)	Sets options for using phone lines to dial out to a network or the Internet.
Power Options	Configures different power schemes to adjust power consumption.
Printers (Printers And Faxes)	Configures printer settings and print defaults.
System	Allows you to view and configure various system elements. We'll look at this in more detail later in this chapter.

In Windows XP, when you first open Control Panel, it displays in Category view. This view provides you with different categories to choose from, into which control-panel programs have been organized. Once you choose a category, you can pick a task, and the appropriate control-panel program is opened for you; or, you can select one of the control-panel programs that is part of the category. However, you can change this view to Classic View, which displays all the control-panel programs in a list, as in older versions of Windows (see Figure 12.36). We suggest that administrators of Windows XP computers change to this view. To do so, click Switch To Classic View in the left pane. Throughout this chapter, when we refer to accessing Control Panel programs, we will assume that you have changed the view to Classic View.

FIGURE 12.36   The Control Panel interface in Windows XP (using Classic View)

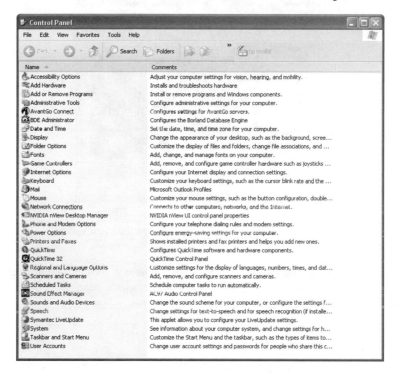

For a quick look at how the Control Panel programs work, the following exercise examines some of the settings in the Date/Time program. The Date/Time program is used to configure the system time, date, and time-zone settings, which can be important for files that require accurate timestamps or to users who don't have a watch. Because it is a simple program, it's a perfect example to use. In pre–Windows XP versions of Windows, the Date/Time program includes only two sets of *tabs* (Date & Time and Time Zone) and one option (whether to use Daylight Savings). Windows XP also has an Internet Time tab, which enables you to synchronize time on the computer with an Internet time server.

EXERCISE 12.12

Changing the Time Zone

1. In pre–Windows XP versions of Windows, click Start ➤ Settings ➤ Control Panel. In Windows XP, click Start ➤ Control Panel.

2. From Control Panel, double-click the Date/Time (Date And Time) icon (by default, the programs are listed alphabetically).

3. Click the Time Zone tab and use the drop-down menu to select (GMT –03:30) Newfoundland, as shown in the graphic.

4. Hop a plane to Newfoundland, secure in the knowledge that you will know what time it is once you get there.

5. If you skipped step 4, change the time zone back to where it should be before closing the window.

The System Control Panel

The System control panel (see Figure 12.37 for the Windows XP System control panel) is one of the most important control panels, and it's nearly all business. From within this one relatively innocuous panel, you can make a large number of configuration changes to a Windows machine. The different versions of Windows have different options available in this panel; as a general rule, the newer the OS, the more options you'll find. The System Properties panel is divided into tabs. They can include some of the following: General, Network Identification, Device Manager, Hardware, Hardware Profiles, User Profiles, Environment, Startup/Shutdown, Performance, System Restore, Automatic Updates, Remote, Computer Name, and Advanced. The General tab gives you an overview of the system, such as OS version, registration information, basic hardware levels (Processor and RAM), and the

Service Pack level that's installed, if any. For the rest of the tabs, we will look a bit more closely at their functionality. For each tab, we identify which versions of Windows contain the tab.

FIGURE 12.37   The System Properties control panel on a Windows XP computer with the Advanced tab selected

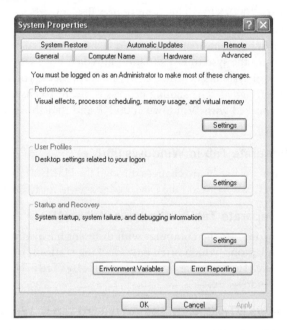

Network Identification (Windows 2000)/Computer Name (Windows XP)

This tab is used to define whether the machine is in a workgroup or a domain environment. We will talk more about networking in Chapter 16, but in general terms, the difference between a workgroup and a domain is this:

Workgroup   Loosely associated computers, each of which is its own security authority.

Domain   A group of computers that is tightly connected. Has a single authority (called a *domain controller*) that manages security for all the computers.

Hardware (Windows 2000/XP)

This tab includes a number of tools, all of which allow you to change how the hardware on your machine is used:

(Add) Hardware Wizard   The Hardware Wizard is used, as it says, to "install, uninstall, repair, unplug, eject, and configure" hardware in the system. Essentially, this means that if you want to add a new device to the system or uninstall drivers that are already there, this is the place to go. You can also use this tool to temporarily eject *PC Card* devices or other removable components.

WARNING Even in a Plug and Play system, it is important to properly unplug a device if you wish to remove it while the system is running. If you don't do this, nothing may go wrong, but you can sometimes damage the device or cause the system to become unstable.

Driver Signing (Windows 2000/XP)   This is an option first introduced in Windows 2000. In order to minimize the risks involved with adding third-party software to your Windows 2000 Professional machine, Microsoft has come up with a technique called *driver signing*. Installing new hardware drivers onto the system is a situation in which both viruses and badly written software can threaten your system's health. To minimize the risks, you can choose to only use drivers that have been *signed*. The signing process is meant to ensure that you are getting drivers that have been checked with Windows 2000/XP and that those drivers have not been modified maliciously.

Device Manager (Separate Tab in Windows 98/Me)

Although you can make many hardware changes through the Hardware Wizard, it is often easier to use the Device Manager. We'll discuss the Device Manager in more detail later in this chapter.

Hardware Profiles (Separate Tab in Windows 98/Me/NT)

A hardware profile lets you start the computer with different hardware configurations. This ability is most useful on laptops, which often have docking stations, or at the very least are moved from place to place. These are very similar to (in fact, exactly the same as) the hardware profiles discussed for Windows 9*x*.

User Profiles (Windows NT/2000; on the Advanced tab in Windows XP)

Unlike Windows 9*x*, where *user profiles* are an optional setting, in Windows NT/2000/XP every user automatically is given a user profile when they log on to the workstation. This profile contains information about the user's settings and preferences. Although this does not happen often, occasionally a user profile becomes corrupt or needs to be destroyed. Alternatively, if a particular profile is set up exceptionally well, you can copy it so that it is available for other users. To do either of these tasks, use the User Profiles tab to select the user profile you want to work with. At that point, you will be given three options:

Delete   Removes the user's profile entirely. When that user logs on again, they will be given a fresh profile taken from the system default. Any settings they have added will be lost, as will any profile-related problems they have caused.

Change Type   Configures a profile as local (the default) or roaming. If a user works at two machines, each of them will use a different profile. Updates to one machine will not be reflected on the other. If you have a network, roaming profiles can be configured to allow a user to have a single profile anywhere on the network. Further discussion of this topic is beyond the scope of this book.

Copy To   Copies a profile from one user to another. Often the source profile is a template set up to provide a standard configuration.

Advanced (Windows 2000/XP)

The Advanced tab has three subheadings, each of which can be configured separately. They're not identical in Windows 2000/XP, however. (This could also be called the Etc. tab rather than the Advanced tab.) Among its options are the following:

- Performance
- Environment Variables
- User Profiles
- Startup And Recovery
- We discussed User Profiles earlier, so we won't cover it again here.

Performance (Windows 2000/XP) Although it is hidden in the backwaters of Windows 2000/XP's system configuration settings, the Performance option holds some important settings you may need to configure on a 2000/XP Professional system. To access it in Windows 2000, on the Advanced tab, click Performance Options. In Windows XP, on the Advanced tab, click Settings in the Performance area.

Among the settings in the Performance window are the size of your virtual memory (we talk more about virtual memory later in this chapter) and how the system handles the allocation of processor time. In addition, in Windows 2000, this is the place to specify the maximum Registry size (through the Virtual Memory options). In Windows XP, you also use Performance to configure visual effects for the XP GUI.

Letting the Registry fill up is a serious problem. Although the default level is usually fine, if you think this may happen, you should change this option. An extra 10MB today could save a lot of pain tomorrow.

How resources are allocated to the processor is normally not something you will need to modify. It is set by default to optimize the system for foreground applications, making the system most responsive to the user who is running programs. This is generally best, but it means that any applications (databases, network services, and so on) that are run by the system are given less time by the system.

If the Windows machine will be working primarily as a network server, you may want to change this option to background services. Otherwise leave it as is.

Environment Variables (Windows 2000/XP; Environment Tab in NT) There are two types of *environment variables*, and each can be added through the Environment tab/Environmental Variables button:

User Variables Specify settings that are specific to an individual user, and do not affect others who log on to the machine.

System Variables Set for all users on the machine. System variables are used to provide information needed by the system when running applications or performing system tasks.

System and user variables were extremely important in DOS and Windows 3.1. If you are going to try to run DOS/Win3.1 applications on Windows, you will probably have to add variables in this window to support those applications.

Startup And Recovery (Windows 2000/XP; Startup/Shutdown Tab in Windows NT) The Windows NT/2000/XP Startup And Recovery options are relatively straightforward. They involve two areas: what to do during system startup and what to do in case of unexpected system shutdown:

System Startup The System Startup option defaults to the Windows OS you installed, but you can change this default behavior if you like. Unless you are *dual-booting*, only one option is available; but if you have another OS installed, you can change the Windows boot manager to load that as the default. You can also reduce the time the menu is displayed or remove the menu entirely. In Windows XP, you can also click Edit to edit the BOOT.INI file (more on this file in Chapter 13).

If you choose to completely disable the menu on a dual-boot system, you will find that doing so may cause you annoyance in the future when you want to boot into a different OS but no longer have a choice to do so. Thus, you should always let the boot menu appear for at least two to five seconds if you are dual-booting.

System Failure A number of options are available in the Startup And Recovery screen for use in the case of problems. These include writing an event about the problem, sending out an alert to the network, and saving information about the problem to disk. These options come into play only in case of a major system problem, though.

Your options for handling system failures will be covered along with the troubleshooting information in Chapter 18, "Windows Diagnostics and Troubleshooting."

System Restore (Windows XP)

The System Restore tab lets you disable/enable and configure the new System Restore feature in Windows XP. When it's enabled on one or more drives, Windows XP monitors the changes you make on your drives. From time to time it creates what is called a *restore point*. Then, if you have a system crash, it can restore your data back to the restore point. You can turn on System Restore for all drives on your system, or for individual drives. Note that turning off System Restore on the system drive (the drive on which the OS is installed) automatically turns it off on all drives.

Automatic Updates (Windows XP)

The Automatic Updates tab in Windows XP lets you configure how you want to handle updating the OS. You can specify that you want to automatically download updates, notify the user when updates are available (but not automatically install them), or turn off the feature. You can also specify that you want Windows XP to notify you again of updates you declined to download at an earlier point in time.

Remote (Windows XP)

The Remote tab in Windows XP lets you enable or disable Remote Assistance. Remote Assistance allows the local workstation to be used from a remote computer. This can help an administrator or other support person troubleshoot problems with the machine from a remote location.

Remote Assistance is enabled by default. It is handled at two levels. Just having Remote Assistance turned on only allows the person connecting to view the computer's screen. To let that person take over the computer and be able to control the keyboard and mouse, click Advanced and then, in the Remote Control section, click Allow This Computer To Be Controlled Remotely.

Task Manager

Another tool you can use to check on and control your Windows NT/2000/XP environment is the Task Manager. As we discussed in the section "The Taskbar," any time you run a program, it displays as a button on the Taskbar. Sometimes, however, you run into problems with running tasks. For example, a task (program) may hang. You'll know this has happened because you won't be able to use any of the program's functions—the program will be unresponsive. To deal with this situation, as well as for other reasons, you can use the Task Manager (see Figure 12.38).

FIGURE 12.38   The Task Manager in Windows XP

To access the Task Manager, press Ctrl+Alt+Del. In Windows NT/2000, you then have to click Task Manager on the Windows Security screen. In Windows XP, whether the Security screen displays depends on whether you're using the Windows XP Welcome screen (you can change this setting on the Screen Saver tab of the computer's Display Properties). By default, in Windows XP, the Windows Security screen does not display if you press Ctrl+Alt+Del; instead, Task Manager opens right away.

 To get to the Task Manager directly in any of the Windows versions that include it, you can press Ctrl+Shift+Esc.

In Windows NT/2000, the Task Manager has three tabs: Applications, Processes, and Performance. In Windows XP, the Task Manager has two additional tabs, Networking and Users. Let's look at these tabs in more detail:

Applications   The Applications tab lets you see what tasks are open on the machine. You also see the status of each task, which can be either Running or Not Responding. If a task/application has stopped responding (that is, it's hung), you can select the task in the list and click End Task. Doing so closes the program, and you can try to open it again. Often, although certainly not always, if an application hangs, you have to reboot the computer to prevent the same thing from happening again shortly after you restart the application. You can also use the Applications tab to switch to a different task or create new tasks.

Processes   The Processes tab lets you see the names of all the processes running on the machine. You also see the user account that's running the process, as well as how much CPU and RAM resources each process is using. To end a process, select the process in the list and click End Process.

Performance   The Performance tab contains a variety of information, including overall CPU Usage percentage, a graphical display of CPU usage history, page-file usage in MB, and a graphical display of page-file usage. This tab also provides you with additional memory-related information such as physical and kernel memory usage, as well as the total number of handles, threads, and processes. Total, limit, and peak commit-charge information also displays. Some of the items are beyond the scope of this book, but it's good to know that you can use the Performance tab to keep track of system performance. Note that the number of processes, CPU usage percentage, and commit charge always display at the bottom of the Task Manager window, regardless of which tab you have currently selected.

Networking (Windows XP Only)   The Networking tab provides you with a graphical display of the performance of your network connection. It also tells you the network adapter name, link speed, and state. If you have more than one network adapter installed in the machine, you can select the appropriate adapter to see graphical usage data for that adapter.

Users   The Users tab provides you with information about the users connected to the local machine. You'll see the username, ID, status, client name, and session type. You can right-click on any connected user to perform a variety of functions, including sending the user a message, disconnecting the user, logging off the user, and initiating a remote control session to the user's machine.

Windows 9*x*/Me has functionality that lets you close running programs, which is similar to the functionality offered by the Application tab in Task Manager. To access it, press Ctrl+Alt+Del. In the Close Program dialog box, select the program you want to close and click End Task.

Managing Hardware in Windows

On any Windows computer, you can configure the system's hardware. A number of tools and options let you install, update, and configure this hardware. We will first look at how you can examine the hardware that is installed on your machine, and then we'll examine how to install a new device.

Device Manager

The *Device Manager* is a graphical view of all the hardware installed in your computer that Windows has detected:

- In Windows 9*x*/Me, you can open Device Manager by right-clicking My Computer, choosing Properties, and then clicking the Device Manager tab. Or, you can open the System Control Panel program (from Start ➤ Settings ➤ Control Panel ➤ System) and choose Device Manager.

- In Windows NT, Device Manager is not included. Instead, you use a variety of programs in Control Panel to install and configure devices.

- To access Device Manager in Windows 2000/XP, right-click My Computer and choose Properties. Then select the Hardware tab and click Device Manager. In Windows 2000/XP, you can also access Device Manager through the System Control Panel program. In all of these cases, you will see a screen with information similar to that in Figure 12.39.

FIGURE 12.39 An example of a Device Manager screen

NOTE As you can see, one of the devices (COM 2) is marked with a red *X*. That is because the COM 2 port needed to be disabled so that the modem (which is installed to use COM 2) can use it.

The Device Manager displays all the hardware that Windows knows about and lets you configure the hardware settings of those devices. If you click the plus sign (+) next to a category of devices, it will "tree out" (expand) that category and allow you to see the devices in the category. If you then click a device and click Properties, you can view the information about that device. Figure 12.40 shows the result of selecting a network card and clicking Properties. Notice that there are three tabs: General, Driver, and Resources. Most devices have these tabs (although some devices may have only one or two, and others may have additional device-specific tabs). The General tab (shown in Figure 12.40) shows general information about the device and status information. It also allows you to disable or enable the device.

FIGURE 12.40 Displaying the properties of a device in the Device Manager

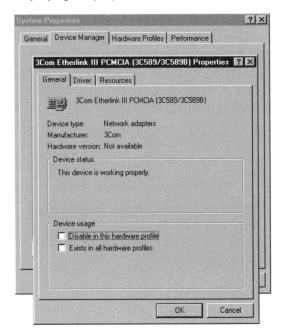

Updating a Device's Properties or Driver

The next tab is usually the Driver tab (Figure 12.41). This tab allows you to see the driver name, date, version, and provider for the device. In Windows XP, it also tells you the digital signer, if known. You can see in the figure that no drivers have been loaded for this device, or the drivers specified for the device are not compatible. If you need to load a driver (or update a driver), click the Update Driver button. Windows will present you with a list of drivers to select from or allow you to install your own from floppy disk or CD-ROM. In Windows 2000/XP, you can also click Uninstall to uninstall a driver. In Windows XP, you can further click Roll Back Driver to return to the previously used driver in case a new driver doesn't work. In all versions, you can click Driver Details (Driver File Details) to see additional information about the driver, such as where driver files are located.

FIGURE 12.41 The Driver tab of a device in the Device Manager

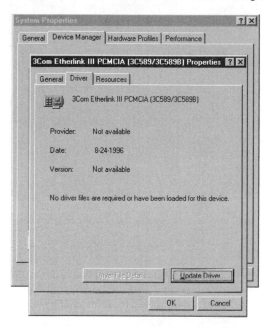

 To add drivers available on the Web, you usually must download the compressed driver files and then expand them onto a floppy disk or into a hard drive folder. At that point, you can run the update and point to the location you extracted the files to. My personal favorite site to obtain drivers is www.windrivers.com.

The rightmost tab is usually Resources. From this tab, you can view and configure the system resources the device is using (Figure 12.42). Most often, the check box next to Use Automatic Settings is checked, meaning that Windows Plug and Play has determined the settings for the device and is managing it. However, if the device is not a Plug-and-Play device and needs to be configured manually, uncheck the Use Automatic Settings check box. You can then select the setting (for example, the Interrupt Request) and click the Change Setting button to pick the correct setting from a list. When you configure settings manually, Windows lets you know if the setting you have chosen conflicts with another device. However, if you are in Safe mode, this feature can't be used.

FIGURE 12.42 The Resources tab of a device in the Device Manager

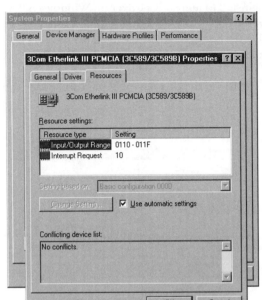

 Occasionally, Windows will not automatically detect a device you have installed. In such a case, you must install the device manually. To learn about more complex peripheral device installs, refer to Chapter 15, "Hardware Installation."

Computer Management Console

Windows 2000/XP includes a number of tools for administration and management of the system. These can be found in the *Administrative Tools* icon in Control Panel, which has a number of utilities. Component Services, Data Sources, and Telnet Server Administration are beyond the scope of this book, as is the local security policy. The rest of these tools are available through the Computer Management Console, and that is where we will examine them. Note that the Computer Management Console is a Microsoft Management Console (MMC) console. The Microsoft Management Console (MMC) is a tool used to create, save, and open administrative tools.

 You can also start the Computer Management Console using the compmgmt.msc command using Start ➤ Run. Or, you can right-click My Computer and choose Manage.

The Computer Management Console (see Figure 12.43) combines many Windows-based administrative tools into a single interface. Three basic classes of tasks are available from this console:

- System Tools

- Storage

- Services And Applications

FIGURE 12.43　The Computer Management interface

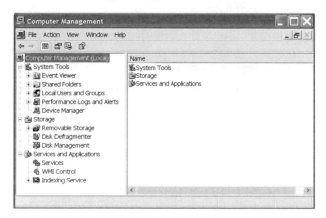

System Tools

The System Tools area provides access to a number of different utilities, many of which are also available elsewhere on the system. Not all items display in both Windows 2000 and XP. Even so, it provides a central interface for the following information:

Event Viewer　Logs data about computer events. Enables you to check for application, security, and system problems.

Local Users And Groups　The Windows 2000/XP Professional station maintains its own list of security accounts, and this is where those accounts are stored and modified. For a user to log onto a Windows 2000/XP Professional station, they must have a user account defined in the Local Users And Groups utility or they must use a *network security provider*, such as Microsoft's Active Directory or Novell's NDS.

System Information (Windows 2000 only)　Allows you to poll the system to find out information about installed hardware and software.

Shared Folders　Lets you take a quick look at the resources that are being shared on your computer.

Performance Logs And Alerts　Monitors system resource usage in real time or logs performance.

Device Manager Lets you view and modify information about system hardware. We already looked at Device Manager in detail earlier in this chapter.

Storage

The storage tools are used to manage and maintain the hard drives and other storage devices on your machine:

Removable Storage Allows you to manage a backup tape drive, optical drive, or Zip-type removable disk drive with your system. This also is the place to go to check up on your CD-ROM or DVD drive, which is also considered removable storage.

Disk Defragmenter Nearly identical to the Disk Defragmenter program in Windows 9*x*/Me. Checks the drive for errors and rearranges (*defragments*) files so they are more efficiently arranged on the drive, which improves performance.

Disk Management Known as Disk Administrator in Windows NT4; Windows 2000/XP's replacement for FDISK. You can use it to create or delete partitions and modify drive types. We'll look at Disk Management more a little later in this chapter.

Windows 2000/XP includes an enhanced disk type called a *dynamic disk*. You can use dynamic disks to create additional partitions and advanced disk configurations. Dynamic disks can only be used by Windows 2000/XP machines, so this change should be made only if Windows 2000/XP is the only OS that will be running on the machine.

Services And Applications

The last of the options, the Services And Applications tree, contains only one option that most of you will use: the Services option. WMI Control and Indexing Service almost never need to be modified:

Services Starts and stops services on the machine. A *service* is simply an application or function the computer runs in the background. Services are also accessible through Computer Management. If a service is unable to start, any of a number of things could be the problem. For more on this topic refer to Chapter 18.

WMI Control Configures and controls the Windows Management Instrumentation service.

Indexing Service Keeps an index of your drive, in order to speed searches of your drives or information. From this location, you can configure how the Indexing Service is carried out.

We don't have space to go into each of these tools in depth, but if you have access to a Windows 2000/XP Professional machine, we highly recommend that you go through and examine each of them.

Virtual Memory

Another thing you may need to configure is "*virtual memory.*" Virtual memory uses what's called a *swap* file, or *paging* file. A swap file is actually hard drive space into which idle pieces of programs are placed, while other active parts of programs are kept in or swapped into main memory. The programs running in Windows believe that their information is still in RAM, but Windows has moved the data into *near-line* storage on the hard drive. When the application needs the information again, it is swapped back into RAM so that it can be used by the processor.

Because the concept of virtual memory can sometimes be hard to grasp, here is an analogy. When you are working in your office and need a document, you may have to walk to a file cabinet to get it. You then return to your seat and read the document. When you have finished and are ready to go on to another task, you need to put down the current document. If you don't need it again in the near future, you should get up and put it back in the file cabinet. However, if you will need it again, you may just set it on your desk for easier access. When you need the document again, you have to pick it back up (unless you can remember what it said without looking again). Generally, you can think of a computer's disk drive as the file cabinet and virtual memory as the desk.

Random access memory (RAM) is the computer's physical memory. The more RAM you put into the machine, the more items it can remember without looking anything up. And, the larger the swap file, the fewer times the machine has to do intensive drive searches. The maximum possible size of your swap file depends on the amount of disk space you have available on the drive where the swap file is placed:

- If you don't make any changes to the swap file, in Windows 9*x*/Me, Windows automatically handles the size of the swap file dynamically, as shown in Figure 12.44. To configure the minimum and maximum swap file size, you must change the default setting.

FIGURE 12.44   The Windows 98 Virtual Memory window

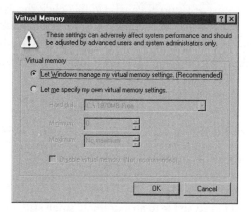

- In Windows XP, it's just the opposite. Windows XP configures the minimum and maximum swap file size automatically, but if you want Windows to handle the size of the swap file dynamically, you have to change the default setting by selecting System Managed Size in the Virtual Memory dialog box. We'll show you how to get there in a moment.

- In Windows NT/2000, Windows sets the minimum and maximum swap file size for you, and you can adjust these settings. However, you can't tell NT or 2000 to dynamically handle the swap file.

By default, on Windows 9x/Me, the swap file is called `WIN386.SWP`, and you'll find it in the `Windows` directory. On Windows NT/2000/XP, the file is called `PAGEFILE.SYS`, and it's located in the root directory of the drive on which you installed the OS files. The swap file is a hidden file, so to see the file in Windows Explorer you must have the folder options configured to show hidden files. (You'll learn how to do this in Chapter 13.) Typically, there's no reason to view the swap file in the filesystem, because you'll use Control Panel to configure it. However, you may want to check its size, and in that case you'd use Windows Explorer.

The moral of the story: As with most things virtual, a swap file is not nearly as good as actual RAM, but it is better than nothing!

To modify the default Virtual Memory settings:

- In Windows 9x/Me, click Start ➢ Settings ➢ Control Panel. Double-click the System icon and select the Performance tab. The Virtual Memory button is along the bottom of the window.
- In Windows NT, click Start ➢ Settings ➢ Control Panel. Double-click the System icon and select the Performance tab. Then, click Change in the Virtual Memory area.
- In Windows 2000, click Start ➢ Settings ➢ Control Panel. Double-click the System icon and select the Advanced tab. Then, click Performance Options and, in the Virtual Memory area, click Change.
- In Windows XP, click Start ➢ Control Panel. Double-click the System icon and select the Advanced tab. In the Performance area, click Settings. Next, click the Advanced tab (yes, another Advanced tab), and then, in the Virtual Memory area, click Change.

Note that in addition to changing the swap file's size and how Windows handles it, you can also specify the drive on which you want to place the file.

You should place the swap file on a drive with plenty of empty space. As a general rule, try to keep 20 percent of your drive space free for the overhead of various elements of the OS, like the swap file.

Do not set the swap file to an extremely small size. Another general rule would be that the swap file should be at least as big as the amount of RAM in the machine. If you make the swap file too small, the system can become unbootable, or at least unstable.

Disk Management

As we alluded to earlier, where there are files, there are disks. That is to say, all the files and programs we've talked about so far reside on *disks*. Disks are physical storage devices, and these disks also need to be managed. There are several aspects to disk management. One is concerned with getting disks ready to be able to store files and programs. Another deals with backing up your data. Yet another involves checking the health of disks and optimizing their performance. We'll look at these aspects in more detail.

Getting Disks Ready to Store Files and Programs

For a hard disk to be able to hold files and programs, it has to be partitioned and formatted. *Partitioning* is the process of creating logical divisions on a hard drive. A hard drive can have one or more partitions. *Formatting* is the process of creating and configuring a file allocation table (FAT) and creating the root directory. Several filesystem types are supported by the various versions of Windows, such as FAT16, FAT32, and NTFS. Windows 9*x*/Me use FAT32, but they recognize and support FAT16. Windows NT/2000/XP use a newer, more robust filesystem type called NTFS (NT Filesystem), and recognize and support FAT16 and FAT32.

To create a FAT16 or FAT32 partition, you can use the FDISK command. To format a partition, you can use the FORMAT command. FDISK.EXE is available with Windows 9*x*/Me, and you can run it from a command prompt. FORMAT.EXE is available with all versions of Windows. You can run FORMAT from a command prompt or by right-clicking a drive in Windows Explorer and selecting Format. However, when you install Windows, it performs the process of partitioning and formatting for you if a partitioned and formatted drive does not already exist.

 WARNING   Be extremely careful with the Format command! When you format a drive, all data on the drive is erased.

In Windows 2000/XP, you can manage your hard drives through the Disk Management component. (In Windows NT, this component is called Disk Administrator and looks somewhat different than in Windows 2000/XP.) To access Disk Management, access the Control Panel and double-click Administrative Tools. Then, double-click Computer Management. Finally, double-click Disk Management. The Disk Management screen looks similar to the one shown in Figure 12.45.

The Disk Management screen lets you view a host of information regarding all the drives installed in your system, including CD-ROM and DVD drives. In Figure 12.45, you can see that this computer has three disks (Disk 0, Disk 1, and Disk 2), one DVD (CD-ROM 0), and one CD-ROM (CD-ROM 1) drive installed. In this example, you can see that Disk 0 has four partitions. A different drive letter is assigned to each partition on Disk 0 (C:, D:, G:, and H:). The list of devices in the top portion of the screen shows you additional information for each partition on each drive, such as the filesystem used, status, free space, and so on. If you right-click a partition in either area, you can perform a variety of functions, such as formatting the partition and changing the name and drive-letter assignment. For additional options and information, you can also access the Properties of a partition by right-clicking it and selecting Properties.

FIGURE 12.45 The Disk Management screen

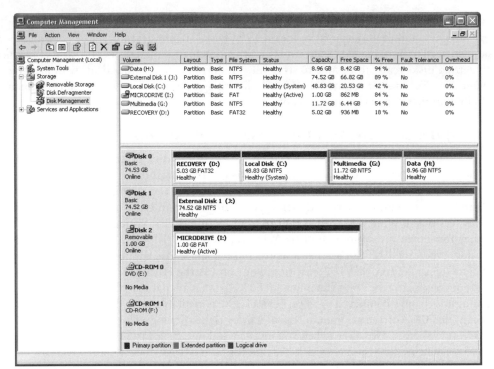

Backing Up the Data on Your Drives

Another very important aspect of disk management is backing up the data on your drives. Sooner or later, you can count on running into a situation where a hard drive fails or data becomes corrupted. Without a backup copy of your data, you're facing a world of trouble trying to re-create the data, if that's even possible or economically feasible. You also shouldn't rely on the Recycle Bin. Although it is a good utility to restore an occasional file or directory that a user has accidentally deleted, it will not help you if your drives and the data on them become unusable.

Toward that end, Windows has a built-in backup feature called, you guessed it, Backup. To access Backup, click Start ➤ Programs (All Programs) ➤ Accessories ➤ System Tools ➤ Backup. The following steps may also be necessary, depending on your version of Windows:

- If you don't see Backup in Windows 9x, open Control Panel and double-click Add/Remove Programs. Click the Windows Setup tab and select System Tools. Click Details, and select Backup in the list of Components. Click OK twice to install Backup. You will have to restart the computer for the installation to be complete.

- In Windows Me, the Backup utility is even more hidden. To install it, you have to run MSBEXP.EXE from the \\add-ons\MSBackup folder.

- In Windows NT, click Start ➤ Programs ➤ Administrative Tools ➤ Backup.

Figure 12.46 shows the Windows 2000 Backup utility with the Backup tab selected.

FIGURE 12.46 The Windows 2000 Backup utility with the Backup tab selected

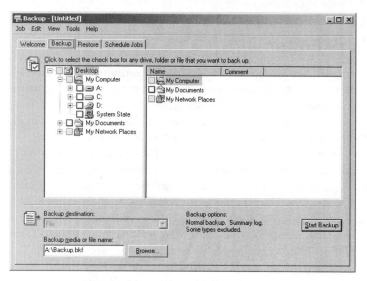

The Backup utility in each of the different versions of Windows has different capabilities, with newer versions having greater capabilities. In general, you can either run a wizard to create a backup job or manually specify the files to back up. You can also run backup jobs or schedule them to run at a specific time at a specific interval. Note that in Windows NT, you have to use the AT command to schedule backup jobs. Refer to the Windows Help system for in-depth information on how to use Backup.

Checking the Health of Hard Disks and Optimizing Their Performance

As time goes on, it's important to check the health Windows computers' hard disks and optimize their performance. Windows provides you with several tools to do so, some of which we've already mentioned in this chapter. One important tool is the Disk Defragmenter, which exists in all versions of Windows except Windows NT.

When files are written to a hard drive, they're not always written contiguously. As a result, file data is spread out over the disk, and the time it takes to retrieve files from disk increases. Defragmenting a disk involves analyzing the disk and then consolidating fragmented files and folders so they occupy a contiguous space, thus increasing performance during file retrieval.

To access the Disk Defragmenter, click Start ➢ Programs (All Programs) ➢ Accessories ➢ System Tools ➢ Disk Defragmenter. In the list of drives, select the drive you want to defragment, and then click Analyze. When the analysis is finished, Disk Defragmenter tells you how much the drive is defragmented and whether defragmentation is recommended. If it is, click Defragment. Be aware that for large disks with a lot of fragmented files, this process can take quite some time to finish.

In Windows 2000/XP, you can also access the Disk Defragmenter through the Properties of any partition listed in Disk Management. Click the Tools tab and then click Defragment.

The Registry Editor

Configuration information is also stored in a special configuration database known as the *Registry*. This centralized database contains environmental settings for various Windows programs. It also contains *registration* information that details which types of file extensions are associated with which applications. So, when you double-click a file in Windows Explorer, the associated application runs and opens the file you double-clicked.

The Registry was introduced with Windows 95. Most OSs up until Windows 95 were based on text files, which can be edited with almost any text editor. However, the Registry database is contained in a special binary file that can be edited only with the special Registry Editor provided with Windows. The Registry Editor's program in Windows 9*x*/Me is called REGEDIT.EXE, and its icon is not typically created during Windows installation—you must create the icon manually. You can also run the program manually by selecting Start ➢ Run, typing **REGEDIT**, and clicking OK.

Windows NT/2000/XP have two applications that can be used to edit the Registry, REGEDIT and REGEDT32 (with no *I*). They work similarly, but each has slightly different options for navigation and browsing. In addition, REGEDT32 allows you to configure security-related settings, such as assigning permissions.

The Registry is broken down into a series of separate areas called *hives* (see Figure 12.47). These keys are divided into two basic sections—user settings and computer settings:

- In Windows 9*x*, Registry information is stored in the user.dat and system.dat files.

- In Windows Me, it's stored in user.dat, classes.dat, and system.dat.

- In Windows NT/2000/XP, a number of files are created corresponding to each of the different hives. Most of these files do not have extensions and their names are system, software, security, sam, default. One additional file that does have an extension is NTUSER.DAT.

FIGURE 12.47 The Registry Editor

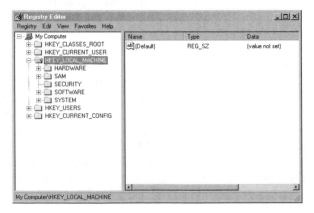

The basic hives of the Registry include:

HKEY_CLASSES_ROOT   Includes information about which file extensions map to particular applications.

HKEY_CURRENT_USER   Holds all configuration information specific to a particular user, such as their Desktop settings and history information.

HKEY_LOCAL_MACHINE   Includes nearly all configuration information concerning the actual computer hardware and software.

HKEY_USERS   Includes information about all users who have logged on to the system. The HKEY_CURRENT_USER hive is actually a subkey of this hive.

HKEY_CURRENT_CONFIG   Provides quick access to a number of commonly needed keys that are otherwise buried deep in the HKEY_LOCAL_MACHINE structure.

Modifying a Registry Entry

If you need to modify the Registry, you can modify the values in the database or create new entries or keys. You will find the options for adding a new element to the Registry under the Edit menu. To edit an existing value, double-click the entry and modify it as needed. On Windows NT/2000/XP systems, you need administrative-level access to modify the Registry.

WARNING   Windows uses the Registry extensively to store all kinds of information. Indeed, the Registry holds most, if not all, of the configuration information for Windows. Modifying the Registry in Windows is a potentially dangerous task. Control Panel and other configuration tools are provided so you have graphical tools for modifying system settings. Directly modifying the Registry can have unforeseen—and unpleasant—results. You should only modify the Registry when told to do so by an extremely trustworthy source or if you are absolutely certain you have the knowledge to do so without causing havoc in the Registry.

Restoring the Registry in Windows 9x/Me

As you may have noticed, the Registry is extremely important to the functioning of Windows. Because of this, any problems with the Registry can cause system-wide trouble. If your Windows 9x/Me Registry files (`system.dat`, `classes.dat`, and `user.dat`) become corrupted, there are two primary ways to repair them:

Automatically   Windows 9x/Me keeps backups of each of your Registry files and checks the current Registry for errors each time you boot the system. If errors are found, the backup copy of the Registry is located and used to replace the corrupt Registry. As long as you have not purposely deleted the Windows backup files, this process works fine.

Manually   In Windows 98/Me, you can perform manual restores either by restoring files previously backed up using a backup program, such as Windows Backup, or by using the command-line utility SCANREG. For the Windows 98/Me version of Windows Backup to back up the Registry, you have to select the Back Up Windows Registry option on the Advanced tab of a backup job (click Options on the Backup tab to access the Advanced tab). You can use SCANREG at a command prompt with the /restore switch to restore the previous day's Registry files. You can also use SCANREG to back up the Registry, using the /backup switch. If for some reason there are no backup files, you can try using SCANREG with the /fix switch to repair and optimize the Registry.

Restoring the Registry in Windows NT/2000/XP

Windows NT/2000/XP also store Registry information in files on the hard drive. You can restore this information using the Last Known Good Configuration option, which restores the Registry to a backup of its last functional state. To use this option:

- In Windows NT, press the spacebar when you see the message Press Space Bar For Last Known Good Configuration during bootup. Then, press L to invoke the Last Known Good Configuration.

- In Windows 2000/XP, press F8 during startup and then select Last Known Good Configuration from the menu that appears. You can also back up the Registry files to the systemroot\repair directory by using the Windows NT/2000/XP Backup program, or you can save them to tape during a normal backup. To repair the Registry from a backup, overwrite the Registry files in systemroot\system32\config.

- In Windows NT/2000, creating an Emergency Repair Disk (ERD) also backs up the Registry files (to floppy disk, in this case). To create an ERD, in Windows NT, use the RDISK command; in Windows 2000, use the Backup utility.

- In Windows XP, the ERD has been replaced with Automatic System Recovery (ASR), which is accessible through the Backup utility.

Note that ERD and ASR are considered last-resort options for system recovery. We'll talk more about ERD and ASR in Chapter 13.

Summary

In this chapter, you learned the basics of the Windows interface. Because Windows is a graphical system, the key to success in learning to use it is to click every option and examine every window. By exploring the system to find out what it can do, you will be better prepared to later decipher what a user has done.

First, we covered the Windows interface. We looked at the layout and components of the Desktop, the Taskbar, and the Start Menu, as well as at basic icons present in default Windows installations. Next, we covered what the component that gives Windows its name (the window) actually is and how windows are used.

We then went over using the command prompt under Windows. We showed you how to access the command prompt and how to run command-line utilities and issue text commands.

Last but not least, we covered basic configuration concepts. Concepts included how to perform and use file management, system tools, control panel programs, task manager, hardware management, the Computer Management Console, virtual memory, disk management and the registry editor.

With the basic knowledge gained in this chapter, we are now ready to look at the major OS architectures of Windows 98/Me, NT Workstation, 2000, and XP, which are covered in the next chapter.

Key Terms

Before you take the exam, be certain you are familiar with the following terms:

attribute	root directory
cluster	sector
directory	Start menu
disk	swap file (page file)
file allocation table (FAT)	switch
icon	syntax
Master File Table (MFT)	tab
partition	Taskbar
path	transactional logging
permission	window
platform	wizard
Registry	

Review Questions

1. What is the Desktop?

   A. The top of the desk where the computer sits

   B. The virtual desk upon which all of your other programs and utilities run

   C. A tool that keeps track of all the data on disk

   D. Where all of a computer's memory is stored

2. Which is *not* a common file extension?

   A. .EXE

   B. .DLL

   C. .RUN

   D. .LOG

3. The screensaver can be changed in the _____ dialog box.

   A. Display Properties

   B. Taskbar

   C. Menu Bar

   D. Shortcut Menu

4. In Windows XP, how can you start a search for files and folders?

   A. Click Start ➢ All Programs ➢ Search

   B. Run srch.exe at the command prompt

   C. Left-click a directory and choose Find

   D. Click Start ➢ Search

5. The Taskbar can be increased in size by _____.

   A. Right-clicking the mouse and dragging the Taskbar to make it bigger

   B. Left-clicking the mouse and double-clicking the Taskbar

   C. Moving the mouse pointer to the top of the Taskbar, pausing until the pointer turns into a double-headed arrow, and then clicking and dragging

   D. Highlighting the Taskbar and double-clicking in the center

6. Which file attributes are available in all versions of Windows?

   A. Hidden, Read Only, Archive, System

   B. Compression, Hidden, Archive, Encryption, Read Only

   C. Read Only, Hidden, System

   D. Indexing, Read Only, Hidden, System, Compression

7. What tool is used to check a machine for hard-drive errors?

   A. Disk Cleanup

   B. Disk Fragmenter

   C. SCANDISK

   D. System Monitor

8. The Windows Explorer program can be used to do which of the following? (Select all that apply.)

   A. Browse the Internet

   B. Copy and move files

   C. Change file attributes

   D. Create backup jobs

9. C:\ and D:\ are both examples of what?

   A. Network drives

   B. Root directories

   C. Share points

   D. Drive menus

10. Standard permissions are _____.

   A. The same as special permissions

   B. Only the R, W, and X permissions

   C. Permissions assigned to users, but not to groups

   D. Special permissions grouped together for easy assignment

11. In Windows 9x/Me/NT/2000, which submenu provides you with easy access to the configuration of Windows?

   A. Settings

   B. Programs

   C. Documents

   D. Find

12. Virtual memory is configured through which system tool?

   A. Taskbar

   B. System control panel

   C. Memory Manager

   D. Virtual Configuration

13. If a program doesn't have a shortcut on the Desktop or in the Programs submenu, you can start it by _____.

    A. Using the Shut Down command

    B. Typing **cmd** in the Start Run box

    C. Using the Run command and typing in the name of the program

    D. Typing **cmd** in the Start box followed by the program name

14. In all versions of Windows, the My Computer icon displays which of the following?

    A. All the disk drives installed in your computer

    B. Control Panel

    C. Dial-up Networking

    D. Printers

    E. Modems

15. What do you do if a program is hung?

    A. Open the System control panel and choose Performance to see what process is causing the problem.

    B. Add more memory.

    C. Press Ctrl+Alt+Del to reboot the computer.

    D. Open Task Manager, select the appropriate task, and click End Task.

16. In Windows, a deleted file can be retrieved using which of the following?

    A. My Computer icon

    B. Recycle Bin

    C. Control Panel

    D. Settings panel

17. To turn off a Windows 2000 machine, you should _____.

    A. Run the Shut Down (Turn Off) command at a command prompt.

    B. Turn off the switch and unplug the machine

    C. Press Ctrl+Alt+Del

    D. Select Start ➢ Shut Down, choose Shut Down, and turn off the computer

18. What type of resource do you configure in Device Manager?

    A. Hardware

    B. Files and folders

    C. Applications

    D. Memory

19. To back up the files on your disks in Windows, which Windows program can you use?

   A. Disk Management

   B. Backup

   C. My Computer

   D. Windows doesn't come with a backup program.

20. The Registry in Windows *9x* consists of which files?

   A. `User.dat, system.dat`

   B. `Classes.dat, sam, regedt.dat`

   C. `system, sam, default, users`

   D. `classes.dat, users.dat, system.dat`

Answers to Review Questions

1. **B.** By default, the Desktop contains the Start menu, the Taskbar, and a number of icons. Because it is the base on which everything else sits, how the Desktop is configured can have a major effect on how the GUI looks and how convenient it is for users.

2. **C.** There are many common file extensions, such as .EXE, .DLL, .DRV, .LOG, and so on. .RUN, however, is not one of them.

3. **A.** The screensaver can be changed in the Display Properties dialog box. To access the Display Properties dialog box, you can either right-click anywhere on the Desktop and choose Properties from the menu that appears or go to the Control Panel and click Display.

4. **D.** In addition to using the Start menu to start a search, you can also right-click a file or folder and choose Search, or you can click the Search button in the Windows Explorer toolbar.

5. **C.** You can increase the Taskbar's size by moving the mouse pointer to the top of the Taskbar, pausing until the pointer turns into a double-headed arrow, and then clicking and dragging.

6. **A.** The only attributes that all versions of Windows have in common are Read Only, Hidden, Archive, and System.

7. **C.** SCANDISK examines the drives on a machine for both file errors and physical defects in the drive itself.

8. **B, C.** The Windows Explorer program can be used to copy and move files and to change file attributes.

9. **B.** The top of any drive hierarchy is referred to as its root directory.

10. **D.** Standard permissions, unlike special permissions, have been grouped together to make it easier for administrators to assign permissions.

11. **A.** The Settings submenu in Windows 9x/Me/NT/2000 provides you with easy access to the configuration of these versions of Windows. To open it, select Start ➢ Settings.

12. **B.** Virtual memory settings are accessed through the Performance tab or area of the System control panel.

13. **C.** To run any program, select Start ➢ Run and type the name of the program in the Open field. If you don't know the exact path to the program, you can find the file by clicking the Browse button. Once you have typed in the executable name and path, click OK to run the program.

14. **A.** Any disks and partitions in your computer display in My Computer. In some versions of Windows, other items also display, such as Control Panel, Printers, and so on.

15. **D.** You use Task Manager to deal with applications that have stopped responding.

16. **B.** All deleted files are placed in the Recycle Bin. Deleted files are held there until the Recycle Bin is emptied. Users can easily recover accidentally deleted files from the Recycle Bin.

17. D.   To turn off a Windows 2000 machine, select Start ➢ Shut Down, choose Shut Down and turn the computer off.

18. A.   Device Manager is used in Windows to configure all hardware resources that Windows knows about.

19. B.   The Backup utility is provided with all versions of Windows, but it has different levels of functionality in the different versions.

20. A.   The Registry files for Windows *9x* include `user.dat` and `system.dat`.

Chapter 13

Major OS Architectures

THE FOLLOWING OBJECTIVES ARE COVERED IN THIS CHAPTER:

✓ 1.2 Identify the names, locations, purposes, and contents of major system files

✓ 2.3 Identify the basic system boot sequence and boot methods, including the steps to create an emergency boot disk with utilities installed for Windows 9x/Me, Windows NT 4.0 Workstation, Windows 2000 Professional, and Windows XP

When working with any operating system, it's imperative that you know the important files, know the files involved in the boot process, understand the boot process itself, and know how to prepare for a situation in which you have to perform an emergency boot. In this chapter, we will first look at the system files required to boot the Windows 9*x*/Me and Windows NT/2000/XP operating systems. We will then acquaint you with the various boot processes and sequences each OS goes through during bootup. Finally, we'll show how you can create emergency boot disks you can use to boot the OS to help you recover in the event of a system failure.

Listing the Important Files

Among the things you must be familiar with in preparation for the A+ exam are the startup and system files used by Windows 9*x* and Windows NT/2000/XP. We will look at each of them individually, but Windows makes nosing around in the startup environment difficult, and as such there is a change you need to make first.

To protect Windows system files from accidental deletion, and to get them out of the way of the average user, they are hidden from the user by default. Because of this, many of the files we are about to talk about will not be visible to you. To make them visible, you need to change the display properties of Windows Explorer. Follow these steps:

1. Open Windows Explorer.

2. Browse to the root of the C: drive. Look for the IO.SYS system file. It should be hidden and will not appear in the file list.

3. In Windows 9*x*, choose View ➢ Folder Options. In Windows NT, choose View ➢ Options. In Windows Me/2000/XP, choose Tools ➢ Folder Options. The Folder Options (Options) window opens.

4. Select the View tab, and in Windows 9*x*/2000/XP, scroll until you find the Hidden Files (Windows 9*x*), or Hidden Files And Folders (Windows Me/2000/XP) option (see Figure 13.1).

5. In Windows 9*x*/NT, select Show All Files. In Windows Me/2000/XP, select Show Hidden Files And Folders.

6. In Windows Me/2000/XP, deselect Hide Protected Operating System Files (Recommended).

7. Uncheck Hide File Extensions for Known File Types.

8. Click OK. You will now be able to see the Windows system files discussed in the following sections. For security reasons, you should set these attributes back after you've read this chapter.

FIGURE 13.1   The Windows Explorer View options

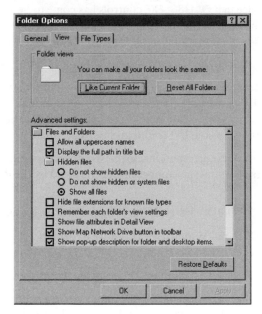

Important Files in Windows 9x

A number of files are stored in the root of C:, as well as in the WINDOWS directory, which can be used to modify your Windows 9x system's configuration and affect how your computer works. Some of the files listed in the following subsections are critical to the functioning of a Windows 9x computer, whereas others are holdovers from earlier OSs.

 Due to the fact that the Registry handles most of the startup tasks in Windows 9x, many system files are there mostly for compatibility with older programs; so, you may never use them. Regardless, many of these obsolete files are listed in CompTIA's test objectives, so you need to know about them!

Windows 9x Startup Files

Several files are necessary or used during the Windows 9x startup process. We'll look at these in detail in this section. Note that an asterisk appears next to the names of the files that are required to boot Windows 9x. Where files apply only to either Windows 9x or Windows Mc, this is pointed out in parentheses:

*MSDOS.SYS**   Functions primarily to handle disk I/O, hence the name *Disk Operating System (DOS)*. Just like IO.SYS, MSDOS.SYS is loaded into memory at bootup and remains in memory at all times.

EMM386.EXE (**Windows 9x Only**)   Provides the OS with a mechanism to see additional memory. The memory space that EMM386.EXE controls has come to be known as *upper memory*, and the spaces occupied by programs in that region are known as *upper memory blocks (UMBs)*. Note that in Windows Me, the functionality of EMM386 is built into the OS.

HIMEM.SYS (**Windows 9x Only**)   Used to access the High Memory Area (HMA).

IO.SYS*   Allows the rest of the OS and its programs to interact directly with the system hardware and the system BIOS. IO.SYS includes hardware drivers for common hardware devices. It has built-in drivers for such things as printer ports, serial or communication ports, floppy drives, hard drives, auxiliary ports, console I/O (input and output), and so on.

WIN.INI   Sets particular values corresponding to the Windows environment. It's used extensively by 16-bit Windows 3.x applications; it's almost entirely replaced by the Registry for Windows 9x 32-bit apps.

WIN.COM* (**Windows 9x Only**)   Initiates the Windows 9x protected load phase.

SYSTEM.INI   Used in DOS and Windows 3.1 to store information specific to running the OS. This and other INI files were used to configure 16-bit DOS and Windows apps.

COMMAND.COM   Called the *DOS shell* or the *command interpreter*. It provides the command-line interface that the DOS user sees. This is usually, but not always, the C:\> prompt.

CONFIG.SYS (**Processed by Windows 9x Only**)   Loads device drivers, some of which AUTOEXEC.BAT will use to configure the system environment. Memory-management tools and DOS peripheral drivers can be added here.

AUTOEXEC.BAT (**Processed by Windows 9x Only**)   Used to run particular programs during startup. Also declares variables (such as search paths).

A *batch file*, named with a .bat extension, is a set of commands that Windows can execute or run. These commands may run utilities, or they may point toward full-blown applications. AUTOEXEC.BAT is a batch file that is automatically executed when the system starts up.

CONFIG.SYS and AUTOEXEC.BAT aren't processed during the Windows Me startup, although the files still exist. Windows Me checks them for changes, and if any settings are added to these files, Windows Me extracts the settings during the next boot and adds them to the Registry.

System File Configuration Tools in Windows 9x

There are a number of ways to modify some of the startup files on a Windows 9x machine, such as INI files. You can open a copy of Notepad, or the text editor of your choice, and go to town. This is still probably the most common method of modifying configuration files. If you prefer to have things a bit easier, though, a couple of tools are provided with Windows 9*x* for dealing with these files. Both Windows 95 and Windows 98 allow you to use a tool called SYSEDIT.EXE to modify certain files, and Windows 98/Me have added MSCONFIG.EXE as well.

SYSEDIT

To run SYSEDIT, choose Start ➢ Run, enter **SYSEDIT**, and click OK. A window with a number of key configuration files will open, as shown in Figure 13.2.

FIGURE 13.2   Main SYSEDIT window

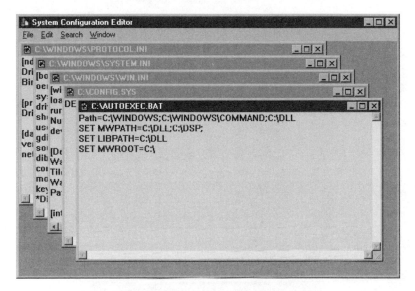

From here, you can examine, compare, and, if needed, modify any of these files. All that the SYSEDIT program really does is open multiple text editors, each of which contains one of the key text files.

You can use SYSEDIT to view and edit the PROTOCOL.INI (Windows 9*x* only), SYSTEM.INI, WIN.INI, CONFIG.SYS, and AUTOEXEC.BAT files.

MSCONFIG

Provided as a new addition to Windows 98/Me, the System Configuration Utility is accessed by opening a Run window, entering **MSCONFIG**, and clicking OK. The System Configuration Utility has a number of tabs, each of which has specific options you can manage (see Figure 13.3 for an example of the Windows 98 System Configuration Utility). Note that the tabs that are available are not identical in Windows 98/Me.

The thing that makes the System Configuration Utility different is that it lets you use your mouse to browse and modify settings that previously were accessible only through manual text configuration. You can also enable or disable Windows 98/Me–specific elements, such as those shown in Figure 13.4, by clicking Advanced on the General tab. The MSCONFIG utility therefore merges Windows 98/Me configuration information with a way for non–DOS-savvy users to work with DOS-era configuration files. Table 13.1 lists the tabs on the System Configuration Utility window.

FIGURE 13.3   The System Configuration Utility in Windows 98

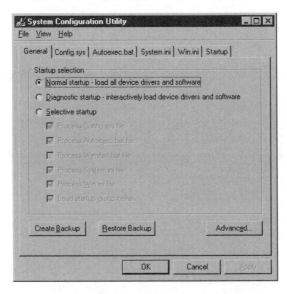

FIGURE 13.4   The Advanced window from the System Configuration Utility's General tab

TABLE 13.1   System Configuration Utility Tabs

Tab	Function
General	Used to set startup options, as well as to determine which files to load during startup. Also provides access to advanced startup options and (in Windows Me) System Restore.
Config.sys (Windows 98)	Used to graphically view and edit the CONFIG.SYS file.
Autoexec.bat (Windows 98)	Used to graphically view and edit the AUTOEXEC.BAT file.
System.ini	Allows you to modify the SYSTEM.INI file using a Registry-type interface.
Win.ini	Allows you to modify the WIN.INI file using a Registry-type interface.
Static VxDs (Windows Me)	Controls loading of static virtual device drivers (VxDs).
Startup	Can be used to enable or disable particular startup items.
Environment (Windows Me)	Controls the loading of various startup environment variables.
International (Windows Me)	Displays language and keyboard settings.

Note that the contents of the AUTOEXEC.BAT file are displayed in the copy of Notepad in Figure 13.5. The Autoexec.bat tab of the System Configuration Utility shows the same information. If you uncheck the last item and then reopen the AUTOEXEC.BAT file, the REM statement is added to block the execution of a line without actually deleting the command, in case you need it again later (Figure 13.6). This is very useful for troubleshooting.

The Windows Registry

In addition to being able to configure your startup environment, configuring other system parameters is equally as important. Many of those parameters and their values are configured through the Windows Registry. You already learned about the Windows Registry in Chapter 12, "Using the Microsoft Operating System GUI."

FIGURE 13.5   The AUTOEXEC.BAT file before modification

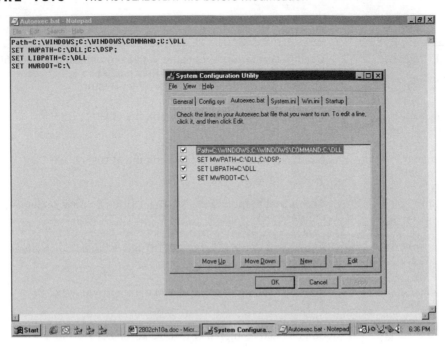

FIGURE 13.6   The AUTOEXEC.BAT file after modification

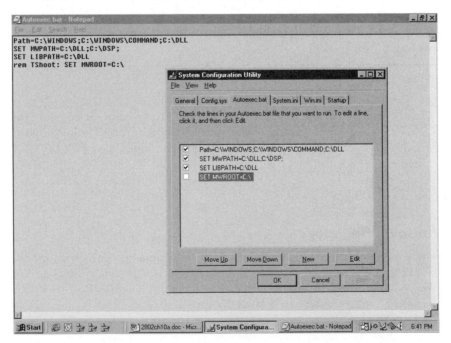

Important Files in Windows NT/2000/XP

Windows NT/2000/XP use different startup procedures and different startup files than Windows 9x. Windows 2000/XP are both based on Windows NT, and as such use the same key boot files as Windows NT. In this section, we will discuss these files.

Key Boot Files

Almost all the files needed to boot Windows 9x are unnecessary for Windows NT/2000/XP. Windows NT/2000/XP require only a few files, each of which performs specific tasks:

NTLDR   *Bootstraps* the system. In other words, this file starts the loading of an OS on the computer.

BOOT.INI   Holds information about what OSs are installed on the computer.

BOOTSECT.DOS   In a dual-boot configuration, keeps a copy of the DOS or Windows 9x boot sector so that the Windows 9x environment can be restored and loaded as needed.

NTDETECT.COM   Parses the system for hardware information each time Windows NT/2000/XP is loaded. This information is then used to create dynamic hardware information in the Registry.

NTBOOTDD.SYS   On a system with a SCSI boot device where the BIOS is disabled, used to recognize and load the SCSI interface. On EIDE systems, this file is not needed and is not even installed.

NTOSKRNL.EXE   The Windows NT/2000/XP OS kernel.

System Files   In addition to the previously listed files, all of which except NTOSKRNL.EXE are located in the root of the C partition on the computer, Windows NT/2000/XP also needs a number of files from its system directories, such as the hardware abstraction layer (HAL.DLL).

Numerous other DLL (dynamic link library) files are also required, but usually the lack or corruption of one of them produces a noncritical error, whereas the absence of HAL.DLL causes the system to be nonfunctional.

System Files Configuration Tools in Windows NT/2000/XP

The SYSEDIT configuration tool we discussed earlier in the section on Windows 9x also exists in Windows NT/2000/XP. Its usefulness is limited, however, because it opens the WIN.INI, SYSTEM.INI, AUTOEXEC.BAT, and CONFIG.SYS files for you to edit. WIN.INI and SYSTEM.INI contain information for application backward-compatibility reasons. AUTOEXEC.BAT and CONFIG.SYS are empty and should stay that way.

The MSCONFIG system-configuration tool also discussed earlier doesn't exist in Windows NT/2000. It is, however, included with Windows XP. In Windows XP, its functionality is similar to that of the Windows 9x version, but some additional functionality is available. Some tabs in the Windows XP version of MSCONFIG are the same as those in the Windows 9x version. These include General, System.ini, Win.ini, and Startup. They are used for the same functions in both versions. New tabs in the Windows XP version include Boot.ini and Services. The Boot.ini tab lets you modify the Boot.ini file and also specify other boot options. On the Services tab, you can view the Services installed on the system and their current status (running or stopped). You can also enable and disable services as necessary.

If you want to use the MSCONFIG configuration tool on a Windows NT/2000 computer, you can do so by copying MSCONFIG.EXE from a Windows XP computer to the Windows NT/2000 computer.

Boot Sequence

Now that you have an idea what the key boot files for each OS are, let's look at the process by which they are booted when the computer is turned on. Again, we'll consider Windows 9x and Windows NT/2000/XP separately.

The Windows 9x Boot Process

We'll first look at the process you use when you boot a Windows 9x system. When Windows 9x first starts up, it goes through a number of steps before presenting you with a Desktop. The basic elements of a Windows 9x startup are as follows:

System self-checks and enumerates hardware resources.   Each machine has a different startup routine, called the POST (power on self-test), which is executed by the commands written to the computer's motherboard. Newer Plug-and-Play (PnP) boards not only check memory and processors, they also poll the system for other devices and peripherals.

Master Boot Record (MBR) loads and finds the boot sector.   Once the system has finished with its housekeeping, the MBR is located on the first hard drive and loaded into memory. The MBR finds the bootable partition and searches it for the boot sector of that partition. Information in the boot sector allows the system to locate the root directory of C: and to find and load into memory the IO.SYS file located there.

IO.SYS **loads into memory and starts the processor in Real mode.**   The IO.SYS file performs a number of tasks, each of which is done in Real mode. Real mode is a method of accessing the processor in 16-bit mode. Drivers loaded through the CONFIG.SYS file therefore can continue to function in Real mode even after the next step, unless they are replaced by 32-bit Windows drivers. The IO.SYS file performs the following tasks:

- Provides basic filesystem access to allow the rest of the boot files to be found.
- Accesses the MSDOS.SYS file to obtain boot configuration parameters.
- Loads LOGO.SYS (Windows bitmap display) and DRVSPACE.BIN (compressed drive access) if they are present and needed.
- Loads the Registry file SYSTEM.DAT into memory, but does not access it.
- Selects a hardware profile (or allows the user to).
- In Windows 9x, processes the commands in the CONFIG.SYS and AUTOEXEC.BAT files if they are present. Windows Me no longer processes these files during startup. Instead, it checks them and, if they contain required information, extracts this information and transfers it to the Registry.

WIN.COM **loads and transfers the processor to Protected mode.** This file loads various drivers as instructed by the Registry. It also examines the SYSTEM.INI and WIN.INI files to obtain additional configuration information. Once the Registry files have been loaded, the processor is transferred into 32-bit Protected mode.

Virtual device drivers, the Windows kernel, and the GDI load. Various 32-bit virtual device drivers load to manage hardware resources, often replacing 16-bit real-mode drivers. The Windows kernel, which controls access to the processor from Windows 9*x*, is loaded into memory. After the graphical device interface (GDI) loads to manage screen I/O, the system is ready to accept customers.

The Explorer shell loads, and the user is presented with a Desktop. The last part of the boot process is the loading of the *shell* program: EXPLORER.EXE. The Explorer is the program that manages the graphical interface—the toolbar, the Desktop, and the Start menu. Once this loads, network connections are restored and programs in the STARTUP folder are run, all of which is determined by settings read out of the USER.DAT Registry settings for that user.

The Windows NT/2000/XP Boot Process

We'll now look at the Windows NT/2000/XP boot process. Aside from the first two steps, it is completely different from the Windows 9*x* boot process. It's also a lengthier, more complicated process, as these operating systems are more complex, providing you with a lot more functionality than Windows 9*x* offer:

System self-checks and enumerates hardware resources. Each machine has a different startup routine, called the POST (power on self-test), which is executed by the commands written to the motherboard of the computer. Newer PnP boards not only check memory and processors, they also poll the systems for other devices and peripherals.

MBR loads and finds the boot sector. Once the system has finished with its housekeeping, the Master Boot Record is located on the first hard drive and loaded into memory. The MBR finds the bootable partition and searches it for the boot sector of that partition.

MBR determines the filesystem and loads *NTLDR*. Information in the boot sector allows the system to locate the system partition and to find and load into memory the NTLDR file located there. (In Windows 9*x*, the MBR locates and loads IO.SYS at this point. A modification to the master boot sector was made in Windows NT to point to NTLDR instead of IO.SYS.)

NTLDR **switches the system from Real mode to Protected mode and enables paging.** Protected mode enables the system to address all of the available physical memory. It's also referred to as *32-bit Flat mode*. At this point, the filesystem is also started.

NTLDR **processes *BOOT.INI*.** BOOT.INI is a text file that resides in the root directory. It specifies what OSs are installed on the computer. During this step of the boot process, you may be presented with a list of the installed OSs (depending on how your startup options are configured and whether you have multiple OSs installed). If you're presented with the list, you can choose an OS; or, if you don't take any action, the default selection is chosen automatically. If you have multiple OSs installed and you choose a DOS-based OS from the list (such as

Windows 9*x*), NTLDR processes BOOTSECT.DOS and does a warm boot. The MBR code contained in BOOTSECT.DOS is run after the computer goes through the POST, and IO.SYS is loaded, starting the DOS-based OS's boot process. We will, however, continue with the NT/2000/XP boot process.

NTLDR loads and runs *NTDETECT.COM*.   NTDETECT.COM checks the system for installed devices and device configurations and initializes the devices it finds. It passes the information to NTLDR, which collects this information and passes it to NTOSKRNL.EXE after that file is loaded.

NTLDR loads *NTOSKRNL.EXE* and *HAL.DLL*.   NTOSKRNL.EXE holds the OS kernel, and also what's known as the *Executive subsystems*. Executive subsystems are software components that parse registry control set configuration information and start services and drivers. HAL.DLL enables communication between the OS and the installed hardware.

NTLDR loads the *HKEY_LOCAL_MACHINE\SYSTEM* registry hive and loads device drivers. The drivers that load at this time serve as boot drivers, using an initial value called a *Start value*.

NTLDR transfers control to *NTOSKRNL.EXE*.   NTOSKRNL.EXE initializes loaded drivers and completes the boot process.

Winlogon loads.   At this point, you are presented with the Logon screen. After you enter a username and password, you're taken to the Windows Desktop.

Advanced Startup Options

In addition to performing a regular boot into the OS of your choice, you can also make additional selections for advanced startup options. In Windows 9*x*, you access these options by pressing F8 when the computer starts booting. In Windows 2000/XP, you access the options by pressing the F8 key when you're presented with the list of OSs installed on the computer. If you don't have the system configured to display the list of OSs (for example, if you only have one OS installed), press F8 when a message on the screen tells you that you can do so. In Windows NT, there are only a couple of choices for special booting, and they're not on a menu. We'll cover how to access them later in this section.

If pressing F8 during bootup doesn't work in Windows 9*x*, you can try holding down the Ctrl key until the Windows 9*x* boot menu displays. Or, run MSCONFIG, click Advanced on the General tab, and specify that you want to enable the Startup menu. Doing so configures Windows 9*x* to always display the Startup menu during bootup.

In most cases you will be able to just boot into your OS without worrying about the advanced options. Occasionally, though, problems may arise. If you have a problem that makes it difficult to get Windows up and running, the advanced options offer a number of useful tools. The options are not identical on the various versions of Windows. We'll first look at the Windows 9*x* startup menu options and then at the Windows 2000/XP startup menu options. We'll then look at how you can perform special boots in Windows NT.

Advanced Options in Windows 9*x*

In this section we'll look at the special boot options available in Windows 9*x*. Even with these two OSs, the choices are not identical (although they're similar). We'll point out the differences as we look at each option:

 In Windows 9*x*, the special boot options display for only 30 seconds by default. If you don't make a choice by then, the OS continues to boot normally.

Normal   As the name implies, continues the boot process as it would normally occur. This is the default selection and is executed if you don't make a different choice during the 30-second time-out.

Logged (*BOOTLOG.TXT*)   Continues booting normally, but boot information is written to a file called BOOTLOG.TXT. This file is saved to the root directory. If Windows 9*x* doesn't finish booting, to be able to access the file, you have to be able to access a DOS prompt. To do so in Windows 9*x*, reboot the computer again and choose Command Prompt Only from the start-up menu. In Windows Me, boot the computer using the Windows Me emergency boot disk (startup disk). Once you're at the DOS prompt, you can use EDIT to examine the contents of BOOTLOG.TXT to identify the problem. Look for lines that contain LoadFailed, and then reinstall the file or driver that's causing the problem.

Safe Mode   Starts Windows 9*x* using only basic files and drivers (mouse, except serial mice; monitor; keyboard; mass storage; base video; default system services; and no network connections). Once in Safe mode, you can restore files that are missing or fix a configuration error.

Step-By-Step Confirmation   Causes startup to ask you to confirm each step of the process, such as whether drivers should be loaded or commands should be run. Press Y or Enter to load to the driver or run the command; press N or Esc to bypass the step in question. This method can be extremely useful in isolating where a startup problem is rooted.

Command Prompt Only (Windows 9*x* Only)   Causes only two files to be processed: AUTOEXEC.BAT and CONFIG.SYS. You're then taken to a command prompt. From there you can, for example, use Edit to inspect the BOOTLOG.TXT file if you created one to help troubleshoot a problem, or perform other command-line operations. When you're ready to start Windows again, you can enter win at the command prompt.

Safe Mode (Command Prompt Only) (Windows 9*x* Only)   Similar to Command Prompt Only, except that AUTOEXEC.BAT and CONFIG.SYS aren't processed. You're taken to a command prompt. This option can help you identify whether the problem you're experiencing is caused by AUTOEXEC.BAT or CONFIG.SYS.

Advanced Options in Windows 2000/XP

As we mentioned earlier, Windows 2000/XP also use an Advanced Options menu. However, with Windows 2000/XP, you have more options to choose from. Some of the options are equivalent to Windows 9*x* options; others are different. We'll look at each in more detail:

Safe Mode   Starts Windows 2000/XP using only basic files and drivers (mouse, except serial mice; monitor; keyboard; mass storage; base video; default system services; and no network connections). Once in Safe mode, you can restore files that are missing or fix a configuration error.

Safe Mode with Networking   Same as Safe mode, but tries to load networking components as well.

Safe Mode with Command Prompt   Similar to Safe mode, but doesn't load the Windows GUI. Presents the user with a Windows 2000/XP command-prompt interface.

Enable Boot Logging   Logs all boot information to a file called `ntbtlog.txt`. This file can be found in the \WINNT directory. You can then check the log for assistance in diagnosing system startup problems.

Enable VGA Mode   Starts Windows 2000/XP using the basic VGA driver, but loads the rest of the system as normal. If you happen to install an incorrect video driver or a video driver corrupts, this allows you to get into the system to fix the problem.

Last Known Good Configuration   Useful if you have changed a configuration setting in the Registry, which then causes the system to have serious problems, and you're not able to log in. Use Last Known Good Configuration to restore the system to a prior, functional state, which will allow you to log in again. It will not save you from a corrupt file or a deleted file error.

Directory Services Restore Mode   Used only with domain controllers. If chosen, boots into a mode that doesn't load directory services. This enables you to restore directory services, such as Active Directory, to the machine. (You can't restore directory services if directory services are running.)

Debugging Mode   A sort of advanced boot logging. Requires that another machine be hooked up to the computer through a serial port. The debug information is then passed to that machine during the boot process. This option is rarely used and should not be bothered with in most cases. If it comes to this, reinstalling is far faster!

Boot Normally (Start Windows Normally)   Continues the boot normally. It's equivalent to the Normal option in Windows 9x.

Reboot (Windows XP Only)   As the name implies, reboots the computer (warm boot).

Return to OS Choices Menu   Self-explanatory; returns you to the choice of installed OSs.

For more on Safe mode and Windows troubleshooting, refer to Chapter 18, "Windows Diagnostics and Troubleshooting."

Advanced Options in Windows NT

Windows NT is different from Windows 9x and Windows 2000/XP in that it does not have an Advanced Options menu. You can, however, invoke two different startup choices:

Last Known Good Configuration   Identical to the Last Known Good Configuration option in Windows 2000/XP. However, to access it, you have to press the spacebar when you see the message *Press spacebar now to use the Last Known Good Configuration* display during bootup. Then, on the Last Known Good Configuration menu, press L to invoke the last known good configuration.

Windows NT Workstation (VGA mode)   Displays on the menu that lets you choose which OS to run. It's essentially equivalent to Enable VGA Mode in Windows 2000/XP.

Creating a Startup Disk or Emergency Repair Disk

Most of the time, you won't bump into serious problems running any of the Windows versions we have been discussing. However, someday you might find yourself in a situation where the system won't boot up anymore, or where you are experiencing some other type of critical error. It is extremely important to be prepared for these types of scenarios. One thing you can do when the system is running smoothly is to create startup disks or emergency repair disks (depending on your OS). (You might also find these disks referred to as boot disks.) These disks typically enable you to at least boot the machine and access drives (and thus data) and also to troubleshoot the problem. In this section, we'll look at the different types of disks you can create in Windows 98/Me/NT/2000/XP.

Windows 98/Me Startup Disk

In a paradox every bit as difficult to resolve as the chicken-or-egg debate, you are only able to make the startup disk (a) during setup or (b) once 9x is installed. If you have lost your startup disk and need to boot and troubleshoot a Windows 9x machine that no longer boots or that displays other types of problems, or if you need to prepare a new drive, your best bet is to find a machine with an existing installation of Windows 9x and create a startup disk off of it. To do this, go to Start ≻ Settings ≻ Control Panel and double-click the Add/Remove Programs icon. Within Add/Remove Programs is a tab called Startup Disk (Figure 13.7).

Click the Startup Disk tab to bring it to the front. Click the Create Disk button to start the startup disk creation process. You will need a single floppy disk for this, and all information on it will be deleted and replaced. The Startup disk lets you boot the machine, as well as troubleshoot any problems you're experiencing. If you can't find a floppy disk and even a single machine already running Windows 9x, well, you may be in the wrong business. When you use the Startup disk to boot the machine, you can then choose to start the machine with or without CD-ROM support (more on this later). Once you make your choice, you're taken to the A: prompt. From here, you can enter **Help** to access a readme file on the various troubleshooting and configuration options available to you via the startup disk. This file also explains all of the files that have been copied to the disk, such as `fdisk.exe`, `ramdrive.sys`, and `config.sys`, along with their functions.

If you are performing the installation via CD, you must also make certain that the startup disk is capable of accessing the CD-ROM drive on your machine. In Windows 98/Me, the startup disk automatically loads standard CD-ROM drivers and presents you with an option to load

CD-ROM support on startup. Some Windows 95 startup disks also have this option, but if not, you can modify the AUTOEXEC.BAT and CONFIG.SYS to load a CD-ROM driver. The exact modifications you need to make depend on the type and manufacturer of your CD-ROM drive, but a sample CONFIG.SYS and AUTOEXEC.BAT follow:

```
CONFIG.SYS:
        Files=25
        Buffers=30
        DEVICE=C:\PANCD.SYS /B:25 /N:PANCD001
AUTOEXEC.BAT
        PATH=C:\;C:\DOS
        MSCDEX.EXE /D:PANCD001 /L:D /M:10
```

FIGURE 13.7   The Windows 98 Startup Disk tab

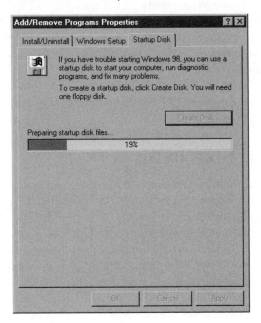

Notice that these aren't big changes, but they are crucial to make the CD-ROM functional under DOS; once Windows 9*x* is loaded, these files won't be needed because Windows has its own drivers for accessing the CD drive, and they will be loaded during the install. These lines can be added to and later removed from AUTOEXEC.BAT and CONFIG.SYS using any text editor.

Once you have a basic Windows startup disk, you can continue to make other small improvements to it by adding tools to allow you to perform common tasks more easily. SMARTDRV.EXE and XCOPY.EXE are two we recommend adding. Smart drive (SMARTDRV.EXE) increases file-copy speed, and XCOPY.EXE allows you to copy multiple files and directories easily.

Windows NT Workstation Boot Disks and Emergency Repair Disk (ERD)

In Windows NT, if you can't boot to the OS anymore, you can boot the machine using either the Windows NT CD or the three boot disks that came with your software when you purchased it or that you created during the Windows NT installation. If you don't have an NT CD, and you didn't create boot disks, go to the \i386 directory and run WINNT32 /OX to create the disks.

Beyond the boot disks, you should also create an *Emergency Repair Disk (ERD)* during the Windows NT installation. Then, if you run into trouble with the OS, you can first boot the machine as described above. Then, when prompted to either install Windows NT or repair a damaged installation, insert the ERD into the floppy drive and choose to repair a damaged installation. The ERD will then check registry files, system files, the startup environment, and the boot sector. If it finds problems, it will tell you what files to use to fix the problems. If you didn't create an ERD during the NT installation, you can run RDISK.EXE to create it later:

1. The RDISK.EXE file is located in \winnt\system32. It writes the emergency repair data to \winnt\repair and then prompts you to indicate whether you want to create an ERD.

2. Click Yes, and then place a blank floppy disk into the floppy drive. Click OK to create the disk. If the disk is not blank, all existing data on it will be erased, because RDISK.EXE formats the disk before it writes to it.

3. When it's finished, you'll see a message about the sensitive nature of the repair information. Click OK.

After you have created the disk, you should run RDISK.EXE again any time you successfully make system changes. Doing so will keep the disk up to date. To use the ERD in the event of a system crash, you must first run the Windows NT setup disks used to install Windows NT and then press R for Repair A Damaged System when given the choice on the setup menu.

To update the SAM and SECURITY databases when you run RDISK.EXE, you have to use the /s switch. Otherwise, these databases won't be updated.

In case you can't find your Windows NT setup disks, you can create new ones using the Windows NT installation CD-ROM. To do so, go to the i386 directory on the CD and run winnt.

Windows 2000 Boot Disks and ERD

To prepare for a Windows 2000 emergency, you need four OS boot disks, as well as an Emergency Repair Disk (ERD). To create the set of four boot disks, you need the Windows 2000 Operating System CD. To create an ERD, you need to use the Emergency Repair Disk utility in the Windows Backup utility (see Figure 13.8). Let's look at this process in more detail.

FIGURE 13.8   The Emergency Repair Disk utility in Windows 2000

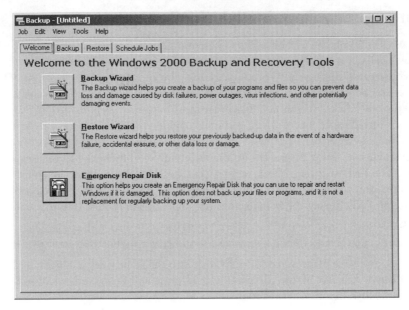

Creating Boot Disks and an ERD

To create the four Windows 2000 boot disks, insert the Windows 2000 Operating System CD into the CD-ROM drive. On the CD, browse to the Bootdisk directory and run MAKEBOOT.EXE. The program walks you through the process of creating the boot disks. Make sure you have four blank floppy disks ready. Once you have created the boot disks, you need to create an ERD (see Exercise 13.1).

EXERCISE 13.1

Creating a Windows 2000 ERD

1. Insert a blank floppy disk into the floppy drive.

2. Click Start ➤ Programs ➤ Accessories ➤ System Tools ➤ Backup.

3. On the Welcome tab, click the Emergency Repair Disk button.

4. In the Emergency Repair Diskette dialog box, select Also Backup The Registry To The Repair Directory. Click OK. The repair data is now copied to the floppy disk.

   Note: If you receive an error that the data couldn't be saved, you probably forgot to insert a blank floppy into the floppy drive. Do this now and start the process over.

5. When the process is done, you'll see a message advising you that the repair diskette was saved successfully. Click OK, and then close Backup.

Make sure you store these disks in a safe place. If you need to use them, use the boot disks to start the Windows 2000 Setup program. At some point, you'll be asked if you want to install or repair Windows 2000. Choose Repair. Windows 2000 Setup will continue and at a later point ask you for the ERD.

Automated System Recovery in Windows XP

In Windows XP, things are different. Windows XP introduces Automated System Recovery (ASR). As in Windows 2000, this feature is integrated into the Backup utility. It first creates a backup of your system partition, and then creates a recovery disk. Using these two components, you can recover from a system crash and restore the system back to a functional state. Follow these steps:

1. Click Start ➢ All Programs ➢ Accessories ➢ System Tools ➢ Backup. If Backup starts in Wizard mode, deselect Always Start In Wizard Mode and click Cancel. Then start Backup again. You're taken directly to the Backup interface.

2. Click the Automated System Recovery Wizard button. In the Welcome dialog box, click Next.

3. You're prompted for the Backup Destination. By default, this is `A:\BACKUP.BKF`. You need to change this location, because a backup of your system partition won't fit onto a floppy disk. Use a drive other than the C: drive, because this drive will be formatted as part of the recovery process. Click Next, and then click Finish.

4. The backup procedure starts. When it's finished, you're prompted to insert a floppy disk. Do so and click OK.

5. When the disk creation process has completed, click OK. Keep the ASR disk in a safe place.

To use ASR to recover from a system failure, run Setup from the Windows XP CD. During the text portion of the Setup program, you'll see a message to press F2; do so, and you'll be prompted to insert the ASR disk. The system then guides you through the rest of the process.

To obtain setup boot disks for Windows XP, you have to go to Microsoft's download website at `www.microsoft.com/download` and download them. These disks can be used to install XP if you can't boot from CD-ROM. You'll need six floppy disks during the download; they should be formatted and blank.

Summary

Before you ever get to use a Windows operating system, it has to boot up. If you're watching the screen it may seem like not much is happening during this process, but the opposite is true. Booting the OS is a complex process that involves many different phases. Without a successful boot, the OS won't be usable. If that's ever the case, it's important to know how to recover and regain access.

To that end, in this section, we first covered the boot process and boot files for the Windows 9x and Windows NT/2000/XP operating systems. We also showed you how to use system configuration tools to troubleshoot and configure booting-related options, and how to use advanced boot options. We then showed you how to create boot and startup disks in Windows 9*x*, and boot emergency repair disks in Windows NT/2000. Finally, we went over using Windows XP's Automated System Recovery feature.

Key Terms

Before you take the exam, be certain you are familiar with the following terms:

batch file	Master Boot Record (MBR)
cluster	Protected mode
command interpreter	Real mode
dual-boot	sector
Emergency Repair Disk (ERD)	upper memory
kernel	VxD (virtual device driver)

Review Questions

1. To be able to view hidden files, which utility do you use to change viewing options?

    A. MSCONFIG

    B. Windows Explorer

    C. SYSEDIT

    D. Internet Explorer

2. On Windows 9x, in which directories do you by default find the operating system startup files?

    A. C:\ and Windows

    B. Startup and C:\

    C. Windows and System32

    D. C:\ only

3. Which Windows 9x startup file enables the operating system to interact with the system BIOS?

    A. HIMEM.SYS

    B. WIN.INI

    C. NTLDR

    D. IO.SYS

4. In Windows 9x, what is WIN.COM responsible for during startup?

    A. Parses SYSTEM.INI

    B. Loads IO.SYS

    C. Initiates the Windows 9x protected load phase

    D. Sets particular values corresponding to the Windows 9x environment

5. Which is true for Windows Me?

    A. It processes AUTOEXEC.BAT and CONFIG.SYS

    B. It doesn't use AUTOEXEC.BAT and CONFIG.SYS files

    C. It adds startup configuration parameters to AUTOEXEC.BAT and CONFIG.SYS during startup

    D. It reads the contents of AUTOEXEC.BAT and CONFIG.SYS, extracts settings, and adds them to the Registry

6. Which is not a valid method of editing Windows 98/Me system files?

    A. Using the WINCONFIG utility.

    B. Using SYSEDIT

    C. Using the MSCONFIG utility

    D. Using Notepad

7. Which of the following versions of Windows do not include MSCONFIG?

    A. Windows 2000 and XP

    B. Windows XP

    C. Windows 95, NT, and 2000

    D. Windows Me

8. What happens in the Windows 9x boot sequence after the system self-checks and enumerates hardware resources?

    A. IO.SYS loads.

    B. AUTOEXEC.BAT and CONFIG.SYS are processed.

    C. SYSTEM.DAT loads.

    D. The Master Boot Record (MBR) loads and finds the boot sector.

9. In Windows NT/2000/XP, NTDETECT.COM _____.

    A. Parses the system for hardware information each time Windows NT/2000/XP is loaded

    B. Detects information about what OSs are installed on the computer

    C. Bootstraps the system

    D. Recognizes and loads the SCSI interface

10. HAL stands for _____.

    A. Hierarchical archive layer

    B. Hardware association layer

    C. Hardware abstraction layer

    D. HTML access legend

11. In the Windows NT/2000 boot sequence, which file loads NTOSKRNL.EXE?

    A. NTDETECT.COM

    B. NTLDR

    C. BOOT.INI

    D. IO.SYS

12. In Windows 9x/2000/XP, how do you access advanced startup options?

    A. By pressing the spacebar when prompted to do so

    B. By holding down Ctrl+Alt+Del after the Windows logo displays for the first time

    C. By pressing Esc after the OS menu displays

    D. By pressing F8 during the first phase of the boot process

13. What does Safe mode allow you to do?

    A. Run Windows without processing `AUTOEXEC.BAT` and `CONFIG.SYS`

    B. Boot the system without formatting drives

    C. Start Windows using only basic files and drivers

    D. Skip loading settings from the Registry

14. Which advanced startup option in Windows NT/2000/XP would you use to be able to return to a previously functioning environment?

    A. Command Prompt Only

    B. Safe Mode

    C. Step-By-Step Configuration

    D. Debugging Mode

    E. Last Known Good Configuration

15. In Windows 9*x*, what do you use to create a boot disk?

    A. Add/Remove Programs in Control Panel

    B. `MSCONFIG` utility

    C. Advanced Startup Options menu

    D. Backup utility

16. Which of the following is true if your startup disk doesn't provide CD-ROM support?

    A. Your disk is corrupted.

    B. You created the disk with Windows 95.

    C. You have to go to `www.Microsoft.com` to download updated startup disk files.

    D. You created the disk with Windows NT.

17. To create an Emergency Repair Disk in Windows NT, you need to do which of the following?

    A. Select Create Startup Disk from the OS Loader menu.

    B. Use the Backup utility.

    C. Run `RDISK.EXE`.

    D. Run `MAKEDSK` from the OS installation CD's root directory.

18. In Windows NT, what do you have to do to include the `SAM` and `SECURITY` databases when creating an ERD?

    A. They're included by default; no action is necessary.

    B. Select Include SAM and SECURITY databases in the What To Back Up section of the `RDISK.EXE` interface.

    C. Run `RDISKSS.EXE` instead of `RDISK.EXE`.

    D. Use the `/s` switch.

19. In Windows 2000, which utility do you use to create an ERD?

    A. Disk Management

    B. Backup

    C. SYSEDIT

    D. Windows 2000 doesn't support making an ERD.

20. What do you use in Windows XP to create a recovery disk?

    A. Automated System Recovery (ASR)

    B. RDISK.EXE

    C. Enhanced Startup Disk (ESD)

    D. Emergency Recovery System (ERS)

Answers to Review Questions

1. B. You use the Folder Options area of Windows Explorer to change the viewing options for hidden files.

2. A. Windows *9x* startup files are found in the `C:\` and `Windows` directories. Not all files are necessary for the system to run; some are there only for backward compatibility.

3. D. `IO.SYS` has built-in drivers for a variety of hardware devices, such as printer ports, hard drives, auxiliary ports, and so on.

4. C. The only task `WIN.COM` performs is initiating the Windows *9x* protected load phase.

5. D. Although `AUTOEXEC.BAT` and `CONFIG.SYS` still exist in Windows Me, they are not processed. Instead, the contents of these files are read and settings are added to the Registry.

6. A. `WINCONFIG` doesn't exist. `SYSEDIT`, `MSCONFIG`, and Notepad are all valid options for editing system files.

7. C. Windows 98/Me and XP are the only versions that include `MSCONFIG`. However, you can use a copy of `MSCONFIG` from a Windows XP computer on a Windows NT/2000 computer.

8. D. The MBR loads immediately after the system finishes its self-check and is done enumerating hardware resources. All other steps occur later in the startup sequence.

9. A. The information detected by `NTDETECT.COM` is used to create dynamic hardware information in the Registry.

10. C. HAL, the hardware abstraction layer, is required for a successful boot.

11. B. `NTLDR` loads `NTDETECT.COM`, `NTOSKRNL.EXE`, and `HAL.DLL`.

12. D. Pressing F8 during the first phase of the boot process brings up the Advanced Startup Options menu in Windows *9x*/2000/XP. In Windows NT, you can press the spacebar to access the Last Known Good Configuration.

13. C. Safe mode is a good option to choose to restore files that are missing, or to fix a configuration error. With only basic files and drivers loaded, you can more easily identify the source of the problem.

14. E. Last Known Good Configuration enables you to restore the system to a prior, functional state if a change was made to the Registry that turned out to be problematic.

15. A. Unlike in Windows 2000/XP, where you use the Backup utility to create a boot disk, in Windows *9x*, you use the Add/Remove Programs icon in Control Panel.

16. B. When you create a startup disk with Windows 95, it may not have CD-ROM support installed by default.

17. C. Windows NT uses the `RDISK.EXE` program to create an Emergency Repair Disk. `RDISK.EXE` is located in `\winnt\system32`.

18. D.   RDISK.EXE uses the /s switch to include the SAM and SECURITY databases.

19. B.   The Backup utility lets you create an ERD in Windows 2000.

20. A.   Windows XP introduced a new feature for system recovery, Automated System Recovery (ASR). It makes a backup of your system partition and creates a recovery disk.

Chapter

14

Installing and Upgrading Your OS

THE FOLLOWING OBJECTIVES ARE COVERED IN THIS CHAPTER:

✓ 2.1 Identify the procedures for installing Windows 9x/Me, Windows NT 4.0 Workstation, Windows 2000 Professional, and Windows XP, and bringing the operating system to a basic operational level.

✓ 2.2 Identify steps to perform an operating system upgrade from Windows 9x/Me, Windows NT 4.0 Workstation, Windows 2000 Professional, and Windows XP. Given an upgrade scenario, choose the appropriate next steps.

At some point, an operating system must be installed, reinstalled, or upgraded. Often, this is the case because you have built a new computer and need to install the OS to get the computer up and operating. Or, you may have an older OS and want to upgrade it to the newest version. In either case, the ability to install an OS and configure it properly is an important skill to have.

In this chapter, you will learn how to install the most popular Windows operating systems, as well as upgrade Windows to a newer version. You will also learn the procedures that must be followed, both pre- and post-installation.

Installing the Operating System

Usually, you install an OS from scratch—that is, you install it on a computer that currently has no OS. If the computer already has an OS, you will be essentially performing an OS upgrade. In this section, you will learn how to perform an installation of the five main Windows operating systems: Windows 98, Windows Me, Windows NT Workstation, Windows 2000 Professional, and Windows XP Professional. You will also learn the prerequisites for installation of each OS.

Installation Prerequisites

Before you can begin to install an OS, there are several items you must consider in order to have a flawless installation. You must perform these tasks before you even put the OS installation CD-ROM into your computer's CD-ROM drive. These items essentially set the stage for the procedure you are about to perform:

- Determining hardware compatibility and minimum requirements
- Determining installation options
- Determining the installation method
- Preparing the computer for installation

Let's begin our discussion by talking about hardware compatibility issues and requirements for installing the various versions of Windows.

Determining Hardware Compatibility and Minimum Requirements

Before you can begin to install any version of Windows, it is important that you determine whether the hardware you will be using is supported by the Windows version you will be running. That is, will the version of Windows have problems running any drivers for the hardware you have?

To answer this question, Microsoft has come up with several versions of its *Hardware Compatibility List (HCL)*. This is a list of all the hardware that works with Windows and which versions of Windows it works with. You can find this list at Microsoft's Hardware Driver Quality website: www.microsoft.com/whdc/hcl/search.mspx. Before you install Windows, you should check all your computer's components against this list and make sure each item is compatible with the version of Windows you plan to install.

In addition to general compatibility, it is important that your computer have enough "oomph" to run the version of Windows you plan to install. For that matter, it is important for your computer to have enough resources to run any software you plan to use. Toward that end, Microsoft (as well as other software publishers) publishes a list of both minimum and recommended hardware specifications that you should follow when installing Windows.

Minimum recommendations are the absolute minimum specifications for hardware you should have in your system in order to install and run the OS you have chosen. *Recommended* hardware specifications are what you should have in your system to realize useable performance. Always try to have the recommended hardware (or better) in your system. If you don't, you may have to upgrade your hardware before you upgrade your OS. Table 14.1 lists the minimum hardware recommendations for the versions of Windows tested on in the A+ exam. Table 14.2 lists the recommended hardware for the various versions of Windows. Note that in addition to these minimums, the hardware must be compatible with Windows. Also, additional hardware may be required if certain features are installed (for example, a NIC is required for networking support).

TABLE 14.1   Windows Hardware Minimum Requirements

Hardware	98 Requirement	Me Requirement	NT Workstation Requirement	2000 Professional Requirement	XP Professional Requirement
Processor	486DX66	Pentium 150Mhz	Intel Pentium, Alpha AXP, MIPS R4x00, or PowerPC or faster	Pentium 133	233MHz Pentium/Celeron or AMD K6/Athlon/Duron
Memory	16MB	32MB	16MB	64MB	64MB
Free Hard Disk Space	140MB, but can be as much as 335MB depending on disk format and options selected	320MB	110MB	650MB	1.5GB
Floppy Disk	One 3½" disk drive (if installing from floppy disks)	One 3½" disk drive	Required only if installing from boot disks	Required only if installing from boot disks	Not required

T A B L E   1 4 . 1   Windows Hardware Minimum Requirements *(continued)*

Hardware	98 Requirement	Me Requirement	NT Workstation Requirement	2000 Professional Requirement	XP Professional Requirement
CD-ROM	Required if installing from CD (preferred method)	Required	Required	Required	Required
Video	VGA or better	VGA or better	VGA or better	VGA	SuperVGA or better
Mouse	Required	Required	Required	Required (but not listed as a requirement)	Required
Keyboard	Required	Required	Required (but not listed as a requirement)	Required	Required

T A B L E   1 4 . 2   Windows Recommended Hardware

Hardware	98 Recommendation	Me Recommendation	NT Workstation Recommendation	2000 Professional Recommendation	XP Professional Recommendation
Processor	Pentium or higher	Pentium 150MHz or better	Intel Pentium, Alpha AXP, MIPS R4×00, or PowerPC or faster	Pentium II or higher	300MHz or higher Intel-compatible processor
Memory	24MB or more	32MB or more	16MB or more	128MB or more	128MB
Free Hard Disk Space	335 or more for a full install with all options	350MB or more	110MB or more	2GB plus what is needed for applications and storage	1.5GB
Floppy Disk	One 3$\frac{1}{2}$" disk drive (if installing from floppy disks)	One 3$\frac{1}{2}$" disk drive	One 3$\frac{1}{2}$" disk drive	Yes	Not Required

TABLE 14.2 Windows Recommended Hardware *(continued)*

Hardware	98 Recommen-dation	Me Recommen-dation	NT Workstation Recommen-dation	2000 Professional Recommen-dation	XP Professional Recommen-dation
CD-ROM	Required if installing from CD (preferred method)	Required	Required	Yes	Required
Video	SVGA or better	SVGA or better	SVGA or better	SVGA	SuperVGA or better
Mouse	Required	Required	Required	Required (but not listed as a requirement)	Required
Keyboard	Required	Required	Required but not listed as a requirement	Required	Required

If there is one thing to be learned from Tables 14.1 and 14.2, it is that Microsoft is nothing if not optimistic. For your own sanity, though, we *strongly* suggest that you always take the minimum requirements with a grain of salt. They are *minimums*. Even the recommended requirements should be considered minimums. Bottom line: Make sure you have a good margin between your system's performance and the minimum requirements listed. Always run Windows on *more* hardware, rather than less!

Other hardware—sound cards, network cards, modems, video cards, and so on—may or may not work with Windows. If the device is fairly recent, you can be relatively certain that it was built to work with the newest version of Windows. But if it is older, you may need to find out who made the hardware and check their website to see if they have drivers for the version of Windows you are installing.

Determining OS Installation Options

In addition to making sure you have enough and the right kind of hardware, you must determine a few of the Windows installation options. These options control how Windows will be installed, as well as which Windows components will be installed. Some of these options include:

- Installation type
- Network configuration
- Filesystem type
- Dual-boot support

Installation Type

When you install applications, OSs, or any software, you almost always have options as to how that software is installed. Especially with OSs, there are usually many packages that make up the software. You can choose how to install the many different components; these options are usually called something like Typical, Full, Minimal, and Custom:

- A *typical installation* installs the most commonly used components of the software, but not all of the components.

- A *full installation* installs every last component, even those that may not be required or used frequently.

- A *minimal installation* (also known as a *compact installation*) installs only those components needed to get the software functional.

- A *custom installation* usually allows you to choose exactly which components are installed.

Some Windows Setup programs include a *portable installation* type as well, which installs components needed for portable system installations on laptops. It includes features like power management and LCD display software.

All Windows versions use these, or derivations of these installation types, and you should decide ahead of time which method you are going to use (which may be dictated by the amount of disk space you have available).

Network Configuration

With many versions of Windows, you can choose whether to install networking options. If you do install networking, you can also choose (with some versions of Windows) which networking components you want installed. With later versions of Windows, like Windows 2000/XP, you also must know which workgroup or domain you are going to install.

You will learn more about workgroups and domains in Chapter 16.

File System Type

As Windows has evolved, a number of changes have been made to the basic architecture, as you might expect. One of the architecture items that has changed the most is the disk system structure. There have been multiple changes in the filesystem since DOS (the first Microsoft OS).

The following is a list of the major filesystems that are used with Windows and the differences among them:

File Allocation Table (FAT)   An acronym for the file on this filesystem used to keep track of where files are. It's also the name given to this type of filesystem, introduced in 1981. Many OSs have built their filesystem on the design of FAT, but without its limitations. A FAT filesystem uses the *8.3 naming convention* (eight letters for the name, a period, and then a three-letter file identifier). This later became known as *FAT16* (to differentiate it from FAT32) because it used a 16-bit binary number to hold cluster-numbering information. Because of that number, the largest FAT disk partition that could be created was approximately 2GB.

Virtual FAT (VFAT)   An extension of the FAT filesystem that was introduced with Windows 95. It augmented the 8.3 file-naming convention and allowed filenames with up to 255 characters. It created two names for each file: a *long name* and an 8.3-compatible name so that older programs could still access files. When VFAT was incorporated into Windows 95, it used 32-bit code for improved disk access while keeping the 16-bit naming system for backward compatibility with FAT. It also had the 2GB disk partition limitation.

FAT32   Introduced along with Windows 95 OEM Service Release 2. As disk sizes grew, so did the need to be able to format a partition larger than 2GB. FAT32 was based on VFAT, more than on FAT16. It allowed for 32-bit cluster addressing, which in turn provided for a maximum partition size of 2 terabytes (2048GB). It also included smaller cluster sizes to avoid wasted space (discussed later). FAT32 support is included in Windows 98/Me/Windows 2000, and Windows XP.

Older versions of Windows (Windows 3.*x* and Windows 95 original release) as well as all versions of DOS cannot read FAT32 partitions.

NT File System (NTFS)   Introduced along with Windows NT (and can be used on NT/2000/XP). NTFS is a much more advanced filesystem in almost every way than all versions of the FAT filesystem. It includes features like individual file security and compression, RAID support, as well as support for extremely large file and partition sizes and disk transaction monitoring. It is the filesystem of choice for higher-performance computing.

When you're installing any Windows OS, you will be asked first to format the drive using one of these disk technologies. Choose the disk technology based on what the computer will be doing and which OS you are installing.

Dual-Boot Support

Occasionally, a mission-critical program (one you can't do your business or function without) doesn't support the OS to which you are upgrading. There may be a newer release in the future, but at the present time, it isn't supported. In that case, you may have to install the new OS in a dual-boot configuration.

It is also possible, in some situations, to have a multiboot configuration where you can choose from a list of OSs. However, this setup makes it more difficult to choose compatible disk formats and often requires multiple disks to accomplish properly.

In a *dual-boot configuration*, you essentially have two OSs on the computer (Windows 98 and Windows 2000, for example). At boot time, you have the option of selecting which OS you want to use. Both OSs can share the same disk space (provided they use compatible formats, like FAT32 for 98/2000) or, in some cases, can use separate disks.

It is possible to multiple-boot to all Microsoft OSs, including DOS and Windows 95/98/Me/NT/2000/XP. Microsoft recommends that each installation be done to a separate disk in order to avoid conflicts with built-in programs like Internet Explorer. In addition, you should install the oldest OS first (usually MS-DOS or Windows 98), and then proceed in chronological order to the newest (Windows XP).

 For more information on dual-boot and multiboot configurations, visit the Microsoft support website at support.microsoft.com.

Determining the Installation Method

Another item you must determine is which method you are going to use to install Windows. Most versions of Windows come on a CD-ROM (which is bootable for every version after and including Windows 98 Second Edition). It was possible to install older versions of Windows (primarily Windows 95 and, to some degree, Windows 98) using floppy disks. Granted, there were several disks (the first Windows 95 installation used nineteen 3 ½-inch floppy diskettes). However, this isn't the most efficient method. CD-ROMs, because of their large storage capacity, are the perfect medium to distribute software.

Windows XP comes on a single CD-ROM (although there are companion CDs with other software, the OS still fits on one CD when compressed). It is possible to boot to this CD and begin the installation process. However, your system must have a system BIOS and CD-ROM capable of supporting bootable CDs.

If you don't have a bootable CD, you must first boot the computer using some other bootable media (usually a floppy disk of some sort), which then loads the CD-ROM driver so that you can access the installation program on the CD. With Windows 98/NT/2000, these bootable disks usually come with the packaged operating system (one for Windows 98, and usually three to five with NT/2000).

If you have many installs to do and installing by CD is too much work for many computers, you may want to do a *network install*. In a network installation, the installation CD is copied to a shared location on the network. Then, individual workstations boot and access the network share. The workstations can boot either through a boot disk or through a built-in network boot device known as a *boot ROM*. Boot ROMs essentially download a small file that contains an OS and network drivers and has enough information to boot the computer in a limited fashion. At the very least, it can boot the computer so it can access the network share and begin the installation.

The final method of installing Windows isn't really an installation method, per se. *Drive imaging* is a popular option among system manufacturers. In drive imaging, a system is installed completely, with all device drivers and software configured. Then, the system is booted to a floppy disk with a program such as Norton's Ghost installed. The drive is copied, sector by sector, to a file (usually stored on a network share or on several CD-ROMs). This file is known as an *image* because it is a duplicate or mirror image of the system being copied. Then, the image file is transferred to the computer without an OS. You boot the new system with the Ghost floppy and start the image download. The new system's disk drive is made into an exact sector-by-sector copy of the original system.

Imaging has major upsides. The biggest one is speed. In larger networks with multiple new computers, you can configure tens to hundreds of computers using imaging in just hours, rather than the days it would take to individually install the OS, applications, and drivers.

There are major downsides to imaging as well. The system being imaged and the system receiving the image should be identical. Although this requirement is not absolute (Windows automatically recognizes new hardware on reboot), if they are not identical, each machine must be separately reconfigured, and you lose the primary benefit of imaging.

Also, you must do a lot of preimaging work. For example, you must configure Windows so that on bootup after imaging, it asks for the license key (so you are not copying one copy of Windows to multiple machines, which violates the license agreement) to uniquely identify the computer. Also, it is a good idea to run a defragment routine before imaging, to reduce the amount of time spent imaging. If all the data is in contiguous sectors, the imaging process will take less time.

Preparing the Computer for Installation

Once you have verified that the machine on which you are planning to install Windows is capable of running it properly, you're sure all hardware is supported, and you have chosen your installation options, you need to make certain that the system is ready for the install. The primary question is whether you are planning to perform a fresh install of Windows or whether you are going to upgrade an existing system. We'll deal with upgrading later in the chapter; for now, we'll focus on new installations.

The Windows Startup Disk

If you are installing Windows onto a system that does not already have a functioning OS, you have a bit of work to do before you get to the installation itself. New disk drives need two critical functions performed on them before they can be used:

- *Partitioning* is the process of assigning part or all of the drive for use by the computer.

- *Formatting* is the process of preparing the partition to store data in a particular fashion.

You deal with these two procedures in Windows by using the FDISK.EXE and FORMAT.COM commands. Running any sort of command on a machine that has no OS is, well, impossible, though, so you need to boot the computer using a floppy disk that is bootable to MS-DOS or the Windows 9x command line. Windows 9x solves this problem through the use of a startup disk that allows you to boot a computer and run these and other basic commands. Windows NT/2000/XP can do these operations as part of the normal installation routine. These startup disks should be included in the Windows package you are installing from, but if not, you will need to make them.

PARTITIONING USING A WINDOWS 9*X* BOOT DISK

Once you have a DOS or Windows startup disk, it is time to boot the computer and prepare it for the Windows installation. When the computer first boots up, the Windows 95 boot disk will bring you to an A:\> prompt.

Partitioning refers to establishing large allocations of hard-drive space. A partition is a continuous section of sectors that are next to each other. In DOS and Windows, a partition is referred to by a drive letter, such as C: or D:. Partitioning a drive into two or more parts gives it the appearance of being two or more physical hard drives.

When a drive is partitioned in DOS, the first partition you create is a *primary partition*, which is marked *active*. The active partition is the location of the boot-up files for DOS or Windows. If there is more than one partition, the second and remaining DOS partitions are found inside another partition type called an *extended partition*. An extended partition contains one or more *logical partitions*; the logical partitions have drive letters associated with them. Only one primary and one extended partition can be created per disk using the Windows 95 disk utility, which is called FDISK. This two-partition limit is a characteristic of Windows 95, not a limitation of the hard drive.

When FDISK is executed, a screen appears that gives four or five options (Figure 14.1 shows the screen with four options). The fifth option, which allows you to select a hard drive, appears only when there is more than one physical hard drive. FDISK will partition only one hard drive at a time.

FIGURE 14.1   The introductory screen in FDISK.EXE

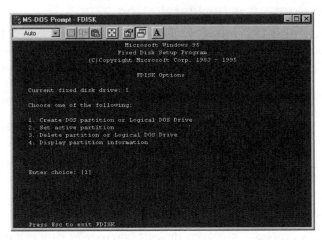

With FDISK, you can create partitions, delete partitions, mark a partition as active, or display available partitioning information. You must create a primary partition before you can create any other partitions. If space is still available on the drive, then you can create a second, extended partition. No drive letter is assigned to the extended partition. One or more logical partitions must be defined within the extended partition, and they can then have drive letters attached to them so users can access them.

WARNING   It is possible for no partitions to be marked active on a particular drive. In this case, the machine will not be able to boot to the drive. If this is the case, you must use FDISK to set an active partition before you can properly install Windows 9x. One and only one partition can be marked active.

FDISK creates a start and an end to a section of hard-drive space. At the beginning of that space, it creates a special file called the Master Boot Record (MBR). The MBR contains the partition information about the beginning and end of the primary and extended partitions. At the beginning of the partitions, this record is called the DOS Volume Boot Sector.

The size of a partition determines certain aspects of a file pointer table called the file allocation table (FAT). The larger the drive partition, the more space will be wasted on the drive.

FORMATTING THE HARD DRIVE

The next step in management of a hard drive is formatting, initiated by the FORMAT command. Technically, the sort of formatting we are talking about is high-level formatting. This should not be confused with low-level formatting, although it can be just as destructive to information on the hard drive. High-level formatting is, these days, normally the only formatting a technician will do. When high-level formatting is performed, the following actions take place:

- The surface of the hard drive platter is briefly scanned to find any possible bad spots, and the areas surrounding a bad spot are marked as bad sectors.

- Magnetic tracks are laid down in concentric circles. These tracks are where information is eventually encoded. These tracks, in turn, are split into pieces of 512 bytes called *sectors*. Some space is reserved in between the sectors for error-correction information, referred to as Cyclic Redundancy Check (CRC) information. The OS may use CRC information to re-create data that has been partially lost from a sector.

- A file allocation table (FAT) is created. This table contains information about the location of files as they are placed onto the hard drive. The FAT has a limited number of entries. Therefore, the space allocated for the partition may need to be divided into clusters of sectors, where a sector is the smallest part of a hard drive.

 Low-level formatting is the first step in preparing to install an OS into a computer. It is the process of getting the surface material of the hard drive platters prepared to accept information. Low-level formatting creates the tracks and sectors that higher-level processes look for. This formatting process destroys any information that is already present on the hard drive. For this reason, low-level formatting is rarely used on IDE hard drives, which contain some special information written at the factory. SCSI hard drives will occasionally be low-level formatted; on very rare occasions, an IDE drive will also be low-level formatted. Fortunately, these days hard drives are usually low-level formatted at the factory and never need to have this done to them again. For most technicians, this is a historical fact of past times.

OPTIMIZATION

Each FAT has a set number of entries; the number depends on the size of the hard drive. On a very small hard drive, the FAT could theoretically be large enough to track all the sectors, but in practice this never occurs. Only high-density floppy disks have FATs that track individual sectors. Sectors on hard drives are clumped together in what is called a *cluster* or *allocation unit*. In general, as the drive or drive partition increases in size, the number of sectors per cluster increases.

A drive between 16MB and 128MB has four sectors per cluster. A larger drive of up to 256MB has eight sectors per cluster. Every time you double the hard-drive size, you double the number of sectors per cluster. Thus, drives of up to 512MB have 16 sectors per cluster, drives of up to 1024MB have 32 sectors per cluster, and so on. Clusters of 32 sectors are 16KB in size.

Allocation units may not be used by two different files; thus any empty space in an allocation unit (any space not filled by the file assigned to that allocation unit) is wasted. Many files almost fill the last cluster allocated to them, but other files barely use this last allocated cluster. On average, files use half of the last cluster allocated to them.

Imagine large clusters with one cluster per file being only half filled. If these clusters are 16KB and there are 5,000 files, then roughly 40MB of hard-drive space is designated but unused. For example, if a hard drive has almost 25,000 files on one partition, that translates to 200MB of wasted space.

One solution to optimizing hard-drive space is to set up multiple partitions that are smaller in size and therefore use smaller clusters. It is not unusual for a 1GB drive to regain 200MB or more when split into two partitions. You should also avoid partition sizes that are just over the limit for cluster sizes. A 528MB partition has less available space on it than a 512MB partition does, because the clusters are large enough to waste more than the extra space on the larger partition. As new drives get larger, though, the difference between 528MB and 512MB becomes largely irrelevant. Because of this, a new filesystem—FAT32—solves many of these problems (and will be discussed later).

EXERCISE 14.1

Preparing a New Disk for Windows 9*x*

1. Insert the Windows 9*x* boot disk and start the computer.

2. At the prompt, type **FDISK** and press Enter.

3. In the main FDISK screen, select option 4, Display Partition Information.

4. If the drive is already partitioned properly, the partitions and their sizes will be listed.

5. Return to the main screen by pressing the Esc key on your keyboard. If the partitions were properly created already, press Esc again to leave FDISK.

6. If the disk is not yet partitioned, select 1, Create DOS Partition or Logical DOS Drive.

7. Select 1, Create a Primary DOS Partition. You will be asked if you want to use the maximum space available and make the partition startable. In most cases, this is best, but if you wish to make the partition a particular size, you can do so. *IMPORTANT: If there are partitions on the disk already, you must delete them to create new ones. If you do this, all information currently on those partitions will be lost!*

8. After you have created the new C: partition, press Esc until you are asked to reboot.

9. Reboot, and again use the startup disk to start the system. At the A: prompt, type **FORMAT C:** and press Enter to format the drive with the standard FAT filesystem.

10. You will be warned that all information on the drive will be deleted. Type **Y** and press Enter to confirm, and the format will begin. This can take some time. When the format is completed, you may begin the installation of Windows. You do not need to reboot after a format.

Using the Windows 98 Boot Disk

If you are using a Windows 98 boot disk to prepare a drive, you will notice that a few things are different. First, when the machine starts up, you are presented with two options: boot with CD-ROM support or boot without it. The default is to boot with CD support. If you are planning to install from CD-ROM, this option makes life easy, because most supported CD drives are loaded automatically.

Second, as you start the Windows 98 FDISK program, you are presented with the message about working with large hard drives. Standard FAT (FAT16) has problems dealing with large drives, both due to its maximum partition size of 2GB and because it uses extremely large cluster sizes for large partitions. As the size of computer hard drives increased, this became a serious problem, so Microsoft added support for a second format type—FAT32. As a comparison of how the new system saves you space, a 2GB drive with FAT16 has clusters of 32KB; with FAT32, the cluster sizes are 4KB. As a result, if you save a 15KB file, FAT needs to allocate an entire 32KB cluster. FAT32 would use four 4KB clusters, for a total of 16KB. FAT32 wastes an unused 1KB, whereas FAT wastes 15 times as much!

The disadvantage of FAT32 is that it is not compatible with older DOS, Windows 3.*x*, and Windows 95 OSs. This means that when you boot a Windows 95 Rev B or Windows 98 FAT32–formatted partition with a DOS boot floppy, you can't read the partition.

FAT32 supports drives of up to 2 terabytes. If you have a disk that is over 2,048GB in size, you must create multiple partitions on it.

Windows 9*x* Installation

If you have chosen to do a fresh installation of Windows 95, Windows 98, or Windows Millennium Edition (Me), the process is basically the same. The screens may look different and be in a slightly different order. To simplify things a bit, we will refer to them collectively as Windows 9*x*.

There are six parts to the Windows 9*x* installation process:

- Starting the installation
- Prefile copy phase
- File-copy phase
- Enumeration/detection phase
- Configuring system settings
- Configuring Internet Explorer settings

Starting a Windows 9*x* Installation

Once you have the drive prepared, you are ready to start the Windows install process. To do this, boot to the startup disk and put either the CD-ROM or the first setup disk into the machine.

The program that performs the installation is called SETUP.EXE, and it's located either in the root directory of Disk 1 of the set of installation floppies or in the WIN95 or WIN98 or WIN9*x* (for Windows ME) directory of the installation CD-ROM. It examines your hard disk and makes sure there is enough room to install Windows, and then copies a few temporary files to your hard disk. These temporary files are the components of the Installation Wizard that will guide you through the installation of Windows 9x.

 If you are booting to the CD, SETUP begins automatically with no switches. If you need to add switches, you can press F3 twice and exit to a command line to start SETUP.EXE manually as directed next.

You can use a few options with the Setup program. To use them, you place them after SETUP at the command line, separated by a single space. Table 14.3 details these Setup startup switches.

TABLE 14.3   Windows 9x SETUP Command-Line Options

Option	Function
/d	Tells Setup to ignore your existing copy of Windows. It only applies during an upgrade.
<filename>	Used without the < and >, specifies the preconfigured setup file that Setup should use (for example, SETUP MYFILE.INI causes Setup to run with the settings contained in MYFILE.INI).
/id	Tells Setup to skip the disk-space check.
/iq	Tells Setup to skip the test for cross-linked files.
/is	Tells Setup to skip the routine system check.
/it	Tells Setup to skip the check for Terminate and Stay Resident programs (TSRs) that are known to cause problems with Windows 95 Setup.
/l	Enables a Logitech mouse during setup.
/n	Causes Setup to run without a mouse.
/pi	Tells Setup to skip the check for any Plug-and-Play devices.
/T:C:\tmp	Specifies the directory (C:\tmp in this case) to which Setup will copy its temporary files. If this directory doesn't exist, Setup will create it.

In this portion of the chapter, we will look at the Windows 9x setup specifics. To start the installation, you change to the drive letter where the installation files are and enter **SETUP** (with the appropriate startup switches), like so:

```
C:>D:
D:>SETUP
```

Setup will tell you that it's going to check your system and that you must press Enter to continue. If you want to cancel the installation without continuing, you can press Esc. When you press Enter, Setup copies a very basic Windows system to your computer from the CD and starts it. Setup then executes in a Windows environment and welcomes you to the installation (Figure 14.2).

FIGURE 14.2   Windows 98 Setup

Prefile Copy Phase

Once you click Continue, you begin the prefile copy phase of the installation. During this phase, the Windows 9x setup program performs several operations to gather information about how Windows 9x should be installed:

- Runs ScanDisk to check for hard disk problems before installation
- Asks you to read and accept the *End User License Agreement (EULA)*
- Asks you a few questions about the installation (including which components to install, what you want to call this computer on the network, which network workgroup to install it in, and a computer description)
- Asks you what location you want this computer to operate in (which country settings you want this computer to use)
- Prompts you to make a startup disk (optional)

Once you have finished going through each of these screens, the Setup Wizard will tell you that it is ready to start copying files.

File-Copy Phase

During the file-copy phase, the Windows 9x Setup program copies all the files needed to get Windows operational. During the copy, you will see a screen similar to the one in Figure 14.3. Notice the progress bar in the lower-left hand corner of the screen; it advances according to how far along the file copy is.

FIGURE 14.3 Windows 98 Setup file-copy screen

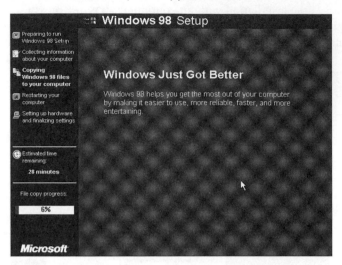

When the file copy is finished, the Windows 9x Setup program prompts you to remove all disks from any disk drives. When you click the OK button in the dialog box that appears, Windows 9x Setup displays another window and begin a countdown to the restart of the computer. You can wait for the countdown to finish, or click the Restart Now button to restart the computer. This ends the file-copy phase of Windows 9x installation.

Enumeration/Detection Phase

Once the computer reboots, the enumeration/detection phase of Windows 9x Setup begins. During the enumeration/detection phase of the Windows 9x installation process, Windows 9x Setup configures the installation of Windows 9x to run on your computer.

After the computer reboots, you will see Windows 9x splash screen shown in Figure 14.4. Notice it says that it is starting Windows for the first time. Now, follow these steps:

1. The computer runs the Setup program immediately and asks you to type in your name and a company name to uniquely identify you.

FIGURE 14.4 Getting ready to run Windows 98 for the first time

2. You are asked to read the EULA and indicate that you agree to its terms. Essentially, the EULA states that you won't give away or copy the OS and won't use it to do anything illegal (or if you do, that you won't blame Microsoft). It's an interesting read; if you have 20 minutes, read it sometime.

 You must agree to the EULA, or Setup won't continue the installation.

3. Enter the *Windows Product Key*. This 25-digit alphanumeric string uniquely identifies the installation of Windows. It can be found in one of a few places, including:

- Back cover of the Windows 9*x* manual

- Windows 9*x* CD-ROM case

- A label affixed to the computer (on most OEM installs)

Type in the characters exactly as found, and continue the installation.

4. Windows 9*x* detects and installs drivers for any hardware that you have. During this process, it may ask you for drivers that aren't on the Windows 9*x* installation CD. You must either insert a driver disk or cancel that request for drivers and install the drivers later (after Windows 9*x* is completely installed) using the installation CD that comes with the hardware in question.

During this process of detection and installation, Windows may need to reboot several times. Make sure the Windows 9*x* installation CD is not in the drive during bootup so that your computer boots to the partial installation of Windows 9*x*. Ideally, setup should only have to reboot once.

5. When all the hardware has been detected and the final reboot has occurred, Setup sets up any Plug-and-Play (PnP) devices and then presents you with a window to properly set the date and time.

You are now finished with this phase of the installation.

Configuring System Settings

The final phase of Windows 9*x* Installation that uses the Windows 9*x* Setup program is the configuring of the system settings. During this phase, the Setup program prompts you for the correct date and time as well as the time zone in which this computer will operate. You may have to click the Time Zone tab on the Date and Time window that appears in order to set the time zone. You can click OK when you're finished.

Windows 9*x* then updates system settings, including Control Panel items, items on the Start menu, Windows help files, and MS-DOS program settings, and updates the Registry. During this last step, a box appears (Figure 14.5) that indicates the progress of the system update. This takes some time.

Once the update is finished, you are prompted to reboot. This should be the last reboot before the system is completely operational. Also, this is the last time the Windows 9*x* Setup Wizard is used. After this reboot, you are presented with the Windows 9*x* Desktop.

FIGURE 14.5 System update progress

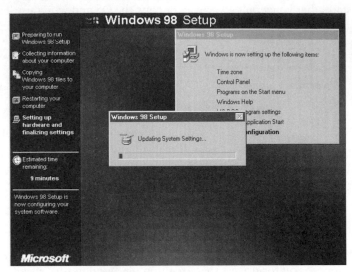

Configuring Internet Explorer Settings

When the computer boots, you see a regular Windows 9x startup screen. The computer should then detect any remaining hardware (like your monitor), as well as configure your personal settings for Internet Explorer. Windows 9x then continues to the login process. After login, you should be presented with the Windows Desktop, similar to the one in Figure 14.6. The Welcome screen is cool the first time you see it, but you may want to uncheck the Show This Screen Each Time Windows 9x Starts check box, lest the screen becoming annoying.

FIGURE 14.6 Windows 9x Welcome screen

You are now finished installing Windows 9x. You may have a few post-installation items to do (installing drivers, and so on), but they will be covered in the section "Post-Installation Routines" later in this chapter.

Windows NT Workstation Installation

The specific process for installing Windows NT Workstation is different from that for installing Windows 9x. This is partially because the OSs differ substantially in their basic architecture. Windows 9x is still based (at least in part) on the MS-DOS and Windows 3.x architecture. Windows NT is almost completely new, from the kernel on up.

However, the basic process is the same for Installing Windows NT: setup and partition the disk, start the install program, answer a few questions, copy the files, and install hardware drivers. As you go through this section on installing Windows NT, notice the similarities between the Windows NT installation process and the Windows 9x installation process.

Like Windows 9x, the Windows NT installation can be divided into phases:

- Starting the installation
- Text-based file-copy phase
- Graphical configuration and file copy phase
- First login

Notice that there are fewer stages with Windows NT than with other versions of Windows. This is because Microsoft wanted the installation of Windows NT to be simple and straightforward, without a lot of intervention. This trend continues with newer versions of Windows.

It is *extremely* important that the hardware used for Windows NT installations be compatible with Windows NT. If a component is not listed on the Windows NT Hardware Compatibility List (HCL), it will almost definitely not work with Windows NT and you should replace it before continuing with the installation.

Starting the Installation

Compared to installing Windows 9x, installing Windows NT should be easy. Most Windows NT Workstation CDs are bootable, and because most computers that support Windows NT also contain BIOSs that support bootable CD-ROMs, starting a Windows NT installation should also be simple.

Make sure your computer's BIOS has its boot order set to boot to the CD-ROM before booting to the hard disk, so that installation goes smoothly.

Power up the computer and immediately insert the Windows NT installation CD-ROM into the bootable CD-ROM drive. Depending on your BIOS, you may have to press a key to tell the BIOS to boot the computer from the CD-ROM. If everything goes well, you should see a screen like the one shown in Figure 14.7 that indicates the Windows NT installation process has started. If you didn't get your CD-ROM in the drive in time, or otherwise get an *Operating system not found* message, you didn't configure your computer properly. Leave the CD-ROM in the drive and try rebooting and see if you get the screen in Figure 14.7. If you don't, you'll have to change the boot setting in the BIOS as described.

FIGURE 14.7   Starting the Windows NT installation

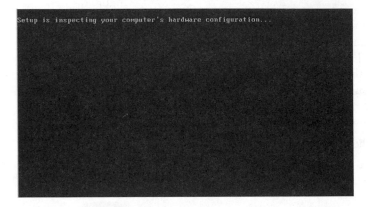

If Your Windows NT CD Is Not Bootable...

Some Windows NT CD-ROMs are not bootable. Also, some computers that support Windows NT don't support bootable CD-ROMs (although they might with a BIOS update). So, Microsoft includes three 3 1/2-inch diskettes in most Windows NT Workstation software packages. These disks contain the basic Windows NT system that will allow you to start the Windows NT installation process and, if necessary, use a third-party SCSI or CD-ROM driver. To begin a Windows NT installation using these disks, do the following:

1. Insert the disk marked Windows NT Setup Boot Disk in the boot floppy drive (your system should be set to boot to the floppy disk drive before the hard drive in your system's BIOS).

2. Insert the Windows NT CD-ROM in the CD-ROM drive.

3. Turn on the computer. The computer will boot to the first disk and start a basic version of Windows NT. At some point, the installation program will ask for the other two disks. Insert them as directed.

Text-Based File-Copy Phase

Now that Setup has started, it boots the computer to a black screen that says *Setup is inspecting your computer's hardware configuration*. This means Setup has started successfully and is examining your computer.

For the most part, you can press Enter from any screen during the text-based file-copy phase to accept the defaults and continue.

Setup then switches to a blue screen and starts loading files to bring up a basic Windows NT environment known as the *text-based Setup*; there are essentially no graphics or elements of a graphical interface during this part of the installation. During the text-based file-copy phase of the Windows NT installation, you will be asked to configure the disk onto which you are installing Windows NT, accept the EULA, select where you want Windows NT to be installed, and copy over the graphical portion of the Windows NT Setup wizard.

After starting Windows NT Setup, you are asked to press Enter to begin the installation. Now, follow these steps:

1. You are asked to confirm the type of mass-storage devices in your computer (Figure 14.8). Setup detects any storage adapters in your system, but if none are listed, you need a driver diskette from the manufacturer of your SCSI or ATA host adapter. Install that driver by pressing S and following the on-screen instructions. You need to do this before proceeding, or Windows NT Setup won't be able to see the disk drives in order to install to them.

FIGURE 14.8   Specifying a mass-storage device

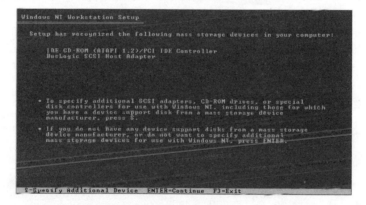

2. Windows asks you to accept the EULA. You must press Page Down twice to get to the end of the EULA and press F8 to accept that you have read the EULA before you can continue with Setup.

3. Setup asks you if the hardware it detected was correct (Figure 14.9). Most often the hardware it detects is the type of PC system you have as well as your display, keyboard, and mouse. Most often, these are detected correctly. However, if not, follow the on-screen instructions to change the incorrect setting. If it is correct, press Enter to continue.

4. Windows walks you through the configuration of the disk space on the computer. It asks how much space you want to allocate on the disk for Windows NT, whether you want that space to be formatted as NTFS (which is recommended) or FAT, and whether you want to format the partition you create as NTFS or FAT. Unless there is a specific reason for doing so (such as backward compatibility with Windows 98 or other), you should choose

NTFS—it is a much more secure and higher-performance filesystem. The on-screen instructions will tell you which keys to press in order to make the correct choices.

FIGURE 14.9   Detecting hardware for Windows NT

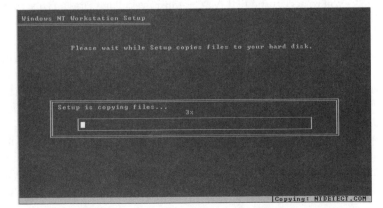

5. Setup asks where you want to install Windows NT. The standard location is \WINNT on the default partition (C:). Most often, you can accept this location by pressing Enter to continue, unless you have a good reason for changing it.

6. Setup examines the hard disk for errors and begins the text-based file copy for the graphical portion of Setup (discussed next). Figure 14.10 shows an example of the file-copy screen and progress bar. This file copy takes several minutes and is a good time to take a break.

If you don't want Setup to examine the disk block by block (Setup calls it an "exhaustive secondary examination"), you can press Esc when prompted. Doing so will cause Setup to do only a basic examination of the disks and decrease the amount of time this step takes.

FIGURE 14.10   Text-based file-copy screen

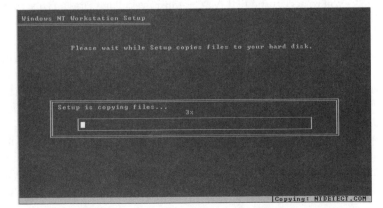

7. Remove all disks from the computer (including any floppy disks and the Windows NT CD-ROM) and press Enter. Doing so reboots the computer and starts the next phase of the Windows NT installation.

Graphical Configuration and File-Copy Phase

The final, and longest, phase of Windows NT installation is the graphical configuration and file-copy phase. During this phase, Windows NT Setup collects information about how you would like Windows NT installed, detects and configures hardware, and copies all the files and settings needed to get NT to a basic operational level.

After the reboot from the last phase, Windows NT has enough information to start Windows NT in a limited sense. The only thing running is the graphical Windows NT Setup (Figure 14.11). Windows NT first asks that you reinsert the Windows NT CD-ROM into the CD-ROM drive so that it can access the files it needs (as shown in Figure 14.11). Once you insert the CD-ROM and click OK, Windows NT Setup copies over several files it needs to continue the graphical portion of Setup.

FIGURE 14.11 Graphical Windows NT Setup

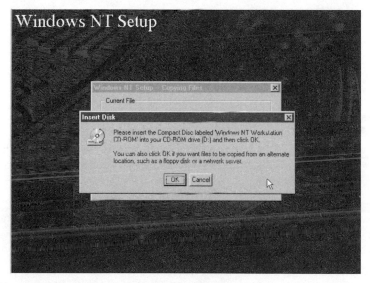

Once the file copy is complete, Setup presents you with a three-step approach. Step 1 gathers information about your computer; Step 2 installs Windows NT networking; and Step 3 finishes Setup by registering all components, building the Registry, and cleaning up temporary files. You can click Next to begin.

Step 1: Gathering Information about Your Computer

In this phase, follow these steps:

1. As with Windows 9*x*, Windows NT wants to know what kind of installation to perform (Typical, Portable, Compact, or Custom), as shown in Figure 14.12. This is almost identical to the setup selection screen for Windows 9*x*. A typical installation installs the most

commonly used components and is the one most often chosen, so leave it as the default selection and click Next to continue. The other options perform similarly to their Windows *9x* counterparts. You may want to choose Custom if you have many other options you wish to select.

FIGURE 14.12   Selecting the type of setup

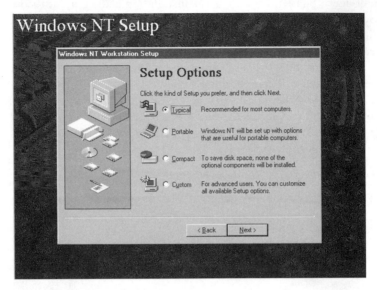

2.   Setup asks you to enter your name and organization to uniquely identify the person installing Windows NT. Then, Windows NT asks you to enter the product ID number (which can be found with Windows NT's packaging or manual, or on the computer itself if the computer originally came installed with Windows NT). Enter the number into the appropriate spaces and click Next to continue.

3.   Choose a computer name. You should choose a name that will be completely unique on the entire network. It is best to include only alphanumeric characters and stay away from punctuation and similar marks as part of the name, because they may be invalid (and Setup will tell you so if you try to include an invalid character). Click Next.

4.   Enter a password for the Administrator account. The Administrator account is the user account used to administrate the computer. Choose a password with alphanumeric characters and at least 1 symbol. A password like *five!dime* isn't bad, because it contains multiple characters and couldn't be guessed at random. Just don't use your name, or the word *administrator*, *admin*, or *password*. You must enter the password twice to ensure that you don't accidentally type it wrong and wind up not knowing your password.

5.   Windows NT Setup asks if you want to create an Emergency Repair Disk (ERD), as shown in Figure 14.13. I always recommend that people choose to do it later, because making an ERD increases the amount of time it takes to install Windows NT. An ERD allows you to repair a damaged Windows NT installation. You can always make one later (and should) using the RDISK utility. Select No here and continue.

FIGURE 14.13   Creating an ERD

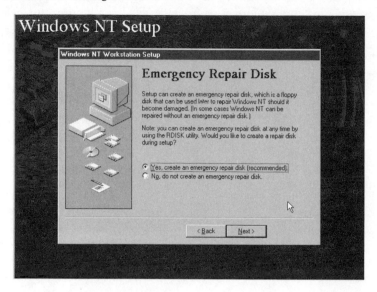

6. In a rather odd sequence, Microsoft put the component selection at this point in the install, rather than right after the selection of the type of installation. You can either let Setup choose the components to install, or you can choose them.

Step 2: Installing Windows Networking

At this point, you install Windows networking (dial-up, wired, or both). Windows NT is designed to function on a network, so this part of the installation is an integral part of the overall installation of Windows NT. Follow these steps:

1. Windows NT Setup asks if you want to start network setup. If you choose not to, you can always go back and install networking later, but you will have to add all the network components manually (which is much more difficult). In the same screen, you can tell Setup how it connects to a network—it's either wired to a network (as most computers are) or remotely connected to a network over some kind of dial-up connection.

2. Tell Setup to detect the network card(s), and then choose which protocols to install.

3. Setup installs the network card driver and protocol software and, if necessary, bring up dialogs to configure them. You might see a dialog asking for the network card's configuration (as shown in Figure 14.14) or a dialog asking if it's okay to use DHCP to configure the TCP/IP protocol. Answer each dialog with the appropriate configuration settings.

4. Setup installs the necessary components, binds the protocols to the adapters, and starts the network. If no errors appear, you can continue with the installation.

5. Once the network is operating, Setup asks you for a few final settings, including whether this computer will be participating in a domain or workgroup. Most Windows-based networks have a domain already set up, but if this computer won't be administrated by

a Windows network administrator, you will probably be installing it into a workgroup. Either way, you can get this information from the network administrator. Select the appropriate option (as shown in Figure 14.15) to finish the network setup.

FIGURE 14.14   Network card configuration dialog

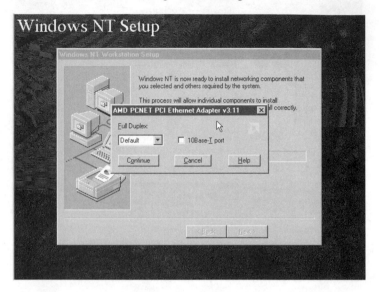

FIGURE 14.15   Setting the Domain or Workgroup option

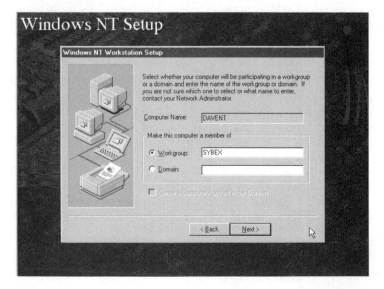

Step 3: Finishing the Setup

The last portion of the graphical configuration and file-copy phase of Windows NT installation is entitled "Finishing the Setup." In this portion, you will be asked to provide a few settings and test the video hardware. Follow these steps:

1. You are asked which time zone you live in. Select it by choosing your time zone from the drop-down list box. You can also adjust the time and date by clicking on the Time & Date tab and setting the exact time and date in the fields given. When you are finished selecting time and date options, click OK.

2. Configure your computer's display settings. Setup displays the video card it detected (as shown in Figure 14.16). Most often, Windows NT puts in a generic VGA driver for your video card. Before you can continue installation, you must test the video settings. Click the Test button and a test pattern (Figure 14.17) will appear. If it doesn't appear, you may have to change your video settings or install an appropriate video driver. Once you have tested your video driver, you should be able to click OK and continue the installation.

 After Windows NT is completely installed, you should install the actual driver for your video card to get the best performance from your system.

FIGURE 14.16   Display settings in Windows NT Setup

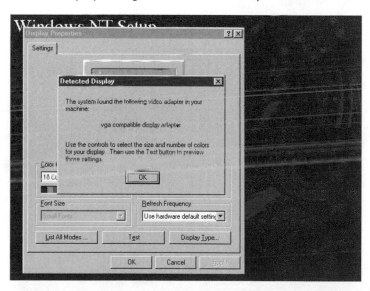

3. Setup copies the last of the Windows NT files, saves the configuration settings, and finalizes all items to prepare your computer to run Windows NT. It also cleans up any temporary files that may have been created during the installation process.

FIGURE 14.17 Video test pattern for testing Windows NT video drivers

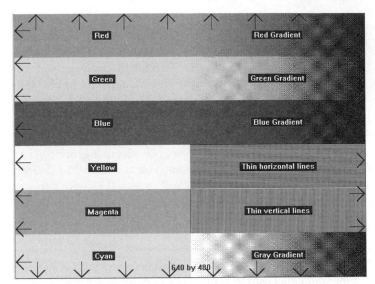

4. The last Setup screen tells you that Windows NT has been installed successfully. It also asks you to reboot (Figure 14.18). Click the button to reboot your computer, and Windows NT will be successfully installed.

FIGURE 14.18 Final Windows NT Setup screen

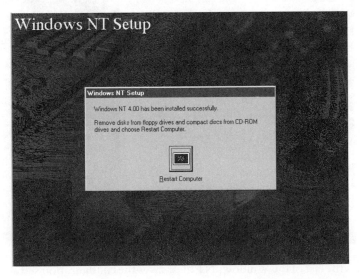

First Login

If everything goes correctly, once your computer reboots, you will see a login window (Figure 14.19). Press Ctrl+Alt+Del, and you are presented with a window asking you for your username and password. Enter **Administrator** and the password for the Administrator account that you gave Setup earlier. Click OK to log in.

FIGURE 14.19 Windows NT login screen

You will see a Windows NT Desktop (shown in Figure 14.20). You are now finished with the installation and can move on to post-installation routines (discussed later in this chapter).

FIGURE 14.20 Windows NT Desktop

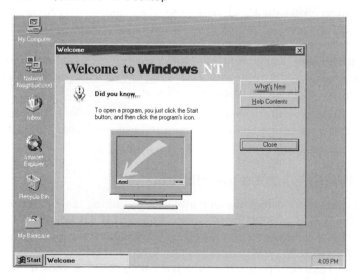

Windows 2000 Professional Installation

Windows 9x and Windows 2000 may look a lot alike when they are running, but one of the most important concepts you have to deal with in becoming a computer technician is that no two OSs are completely alike. As such, the installation process you use for Windows 9x is completely different than the installation process for Windows 2000. We will look next at the Windows 2000 installation process and, in doing so, cover the following topics:

- Installation requirements
- Accessing the Setup files
- Running the Setup program
- Partitioning
- Formatting
- Customizing Setup

Installation Prerequisites

As with earlier, we will start by looking at what you need to consider before installing or upgrading to Windows 2000. Because it is a power workstation, the hardware requirements for Windows 2000 are higher than those for Windows 9x, and Windows 2000 also is less forgiving of older, less efficient software.

Accessing the Setup Files

Unlike Windows 9x Setup, which must run from a functioning OS (an earlier version of DOS or Windows or a boot disk), Windows 2000 is generally a breeze to install on a machine. To start the install process, place the Windows 2000 Professional CD into the CD-ROM drive and restart the computer. After the POST routine for the computer has completed, a message appears that says *Press any key to boot from CD*. Hit a key, any key, and the Windows 2000 Setup program will start.

That is a "perfect world" situation, and sometimes reality intrudes. If the *Press any key* message does not appear, that generally means your PC is not configured to boot from CD-ROM or does not have that capability. In such a case, you need to do one of two things:

- Go into the BIOS to set the machine to boot to its CD drive. Consult your computer's user guide for more information about examining and making changes to the BIOS.
- Create and use Windows 2000 boot disks to start the setup.

Starting a Windows 2000 Installation

The startup options we've listed all eventually lead you to the same point: executing the Setup routine for Windows 2000 Professional. Professional has two different executables used to start Setup, depending on the OS you are using to start the install. These executables are WINNT (used from DOS or Windows 9x) and WINNT32 (used from Windows NT/2000). These commands have various options associated with them, as shown in Tables 14.4 and 14.5.

TABLE 14.4 Common WINNT.EXE Options

Option	Function
/s:*sourcepath*	Allows you to specify the location of the Windows 2000 source files.
/t:*tempdrive*	Allows you to specify the drive that Setup uses to store temporary installation files.
/u:*answer file*	Used in an unattended installation to provide responses to questions the user would normally be prompted for.
/udf:*id [,UDB_file]*	If you are installing numerous machines, each must have a unique computer name. This setting lets you specify a file with unique values for these settings.
/e:*command*	Allows you to add a command (such as a batch script) to execute at the end of Setup.
/a	Tells Setup to enable accessibility options.

TABLE 14.5 Common WINNT32.EXE Options

Option	Function
/s:*sourcepath*	Allows you to specify the location of the Windows 2000 source files.
/tempdrive:*drive_letter*	Allows you to specify the drive Setup uses to store temporary installation files.
/unattend	Used to run the install without user intervention.
/unattend*[num]:[answer_file]*	Allows you to specify custom settings for machines during an unattended installation.
/cmd:*command_line*	Executes a command (such as a batch file at the end of Setup).
/debug*[level]:[filename]*	Used to troubleshoot problems during an upgrade.
/udf:*id[,UDB_file]*	Allows certain values that need to be unique to be set separately for each machine installed.
/checkupgradeonly	Performs all the steps of an upgrade, but only as a test. The results are saved to an upgrade.txt file that can be examined for potential problems.
/makelocalsource	Specifies that the i386 installation directory from the CD should be copied to the hard drive, allowing for easier updates later.

If you start the install from CD-ROM or create the Windows 2000 boot disks, WINNT.EXE starts the install by loading a number of files, and then presents you with a screen that says, *Welcome to Setup.*

If you use a Windows 9*x* boot disk, change to the i386 directory and run WINNT from that directory.

Partitioning the Drive in Windows 2000

To start Setup, click Enter at the welcome screen, and you will be shown a list of the partitions currently configured on the machine. If one of them is acceptable, select that partition and click Enter. If you wish to create a new partition, you can do so using the Setup program itself, which replaces FDISK as a way to set up the system's hard drive(s).

To delete an existing partition, highlight the partition and press D. You will be asked to confirm your choice and will be reminded that all information on the partition will be lost. If the disk is new or if the old information is no longer needed, this is fine.

If you are not sure what is on the drive, find out before you repartition it!

To create a new partition, highlight some free space and click C. You will be asked how big you want the partition to be. Remember that Windows 2000 Professional wants you to have about 2GB as a minimum, but the partition can be as large as the entire drive.

Formatting the Partition in Windows 2000

Once you have created or decided on a partition to use, you are asked to format that partition. In doing so, you need to choose between NTFS and the FAT filesystem. FAT is the filesystem of DOS, and its advantages include the following:

- Compatible with DOS and Windows 9*x* dual-boot configurations
- Excellent speed on small drives
- Accessible and modifiable with many standard DOS disk utilities

NTFS, as you might expect, comes from Windows NT and is a more sophisticated filesystem that has a number of enhancements that set it apart from FAT:

- Supports larger partition sizes than FAT
- Allows for file-level security to protect system resources
- Supports compression, encryption, disk quotas, and file ownership

In most cases, you will find that it is better to go with the newer and more advanced NTFS.

When you choose one of the format options, the machine goes out and formats the installation partition. This generally takes a few minutes, even on a fast PC.

Installing Windows 2000

After the installation partition is formatted, the system checks the new partition for errors, and then begins to copy files. While the files are being copied, a progress indicator displays on the screen showing you how far along the process is. Windows installs files into temporary installation folders on the drive and asks you to reboot once the copy is complete. If you do not reboot within 15 seconds of the end of the file copy, the system automatically reboots for you.

WARNING   If Setup detects any problems during the partition check, it attempts to fix them and immediately asks you to reboot. At that point the install will need to start over. If problems are found, this often indicates problems with the hard drive, and you may want to run a full scandisk before returning to the install.

The Graphical Phase of Setup

When Windows 2000 Professional reboots, it automatically brings you into a graphical setup that resembles a massive Windows wizard (as shown in Figure 14.21). This is generally referred to as the graphical phase of Windows 2000 Setup, due to the contrast between this phase and the earlier blue-background-and-text nongraphical phase where you configured partitions and copied temporary files.

FIGURE 14.21   The Windows 2000 Setup Wizard

During this phase, Windows attempts to identify and configure the hardware in the computer, which may take a few minutes. One of the more unsettling parts of Setup occurs during this time, because the screen flickers—and often goes completely black—while monitor detection occurs.

> Windows 2000 comes packaged with an impressive array of drivers and is able to identify and load most modern hardware. Still, not all devices have compatible drivers on the Windows 2000 CD-ROM. If your hardware is not detected during startup, you can install additional device drivers after Setup completes, as shown later in the chapter.

After hardware detection is completed, the ever-polite Windows 2000 Setup Wizard welcomes you once again. To move through the wizard, click the Next and Back buttons along the bottom of the window. The screens of the setup process are as follows:

Regional Settings   The first screen rarely needs to be modified if you are configuring the machine for use in the U.S., but users in other countries will find that this is where they can change keyboard and language settings.

Personalize Your Software   Enter the name (required) and organization (optional) of the person to whom the software is registered. Both fields are just text boxes. Enter any values that apply.

Computer Name and Administrator Password   The *computer name* is the name by which a machine will be known if it participates on a network. This name is generally 15 characters or less. The administrator password is used to protect access to the powerful Administrator account. Unlike Windows 9*x*, where usernames and password security is optional, all users must log on with a username and password to use a Windows 2000 Professional Desktop.

Modem Dialing Information   If a modem has been detected, you are asked for country, area code, and dialing preference information. If you do not have a modem, this screen is skipped.

Date and Time Settings   The Date and Time dialog box also has time zone and daylight savings time information. Any data on this screen can easily be changed later.

Networking Settings/Installing Components   After you enter the date and time, you will wait a minute or two as Windows 2000 installs any networking components it has found and prepares to walk you through the network configuration. As you are waiting, the Status area shows you which components are being installed.

Performing Final Tasks   The Final Tasks page reports on the Setup's progress while it does the following:

Installs Start Menu Items   Shortcuts are created to the applications and options installed during Setup.

Registers Components   The Registry is updated with Setup information.

Saves Settings   Configuration information is saved to disk, and other defaults and user selections are applied (such as area code, time zone, and so on).

Removes Any Temporary Files Used   The temporary files saved to the hard drive at the start of Setup and used to install Windows are removed to free drive space.

This last screen can take quite a long time to complete. In general, the install of Windows 2000 takes about twice as long as an install of Windows 9x.

Eventually, the wizard completes, and you are asked to reboot by clicking the Finish button. When the system restarts, Windows 2000 Professional Setup is complete, and the standard 2000 boot process initiates.

Windows XP Installation

As of the writing of this book, Windows XP is the latest product in the Microsoft OS family. Installing it is a breeze compared to previous editions of Windows. As a matter of fact, you can install it with a minimum of user interaction. Microsoft has designed Windows XP to be the simplest OS to install yet.

As with the other versions, you will go through various phases of the installation:

- Starting the installation

- Text-based installation phase

- Graphical installation phase

Notice, however, that Windows XP does almost everything for you. It is a very quick OS installation.

This installation process assumes that there is no OS on the computer already. If there is, check out "Upgrading to Windows XP" later in this chapter.

Starting the Installation

During this phase, you begin the installation of Windows XP, configure the disk system to accept Windows XP, and start the graphical phase of Windows XP Setup.

In order to start a Windows XP installation, as with the other Windows OSs, you must first check your prerequisites (hardware support, available disk space, and so on). Plus, you must ensure that your computer supports booting to a CD-ROM (most do these days, especially those that are able to support Windows XP).

Once you do, to start the installation, power up the computer and quickly insert the Windows XP CD-ROM. If you don't do this quickly enough, you may get an *Operating system not found* message because the CD-ROM wasn't ready as a boot device (it hadn't spun up yet). If this happens, leave the CD in the drive and reboot the computer.

You may have to press a key on some systems. A phrase like *Press any key to boot from CD-ROM* may appear. If it does, press a key to do just that so you can begin the installation.

If the CD is inserted successfully, the screen clears and the words *Setup is inspecting your computer's configuration* appear. After that, the Windows XP Setup main screen appears (Figure 14.22).

FIGURE 14.22 Windows XP main Setup screen

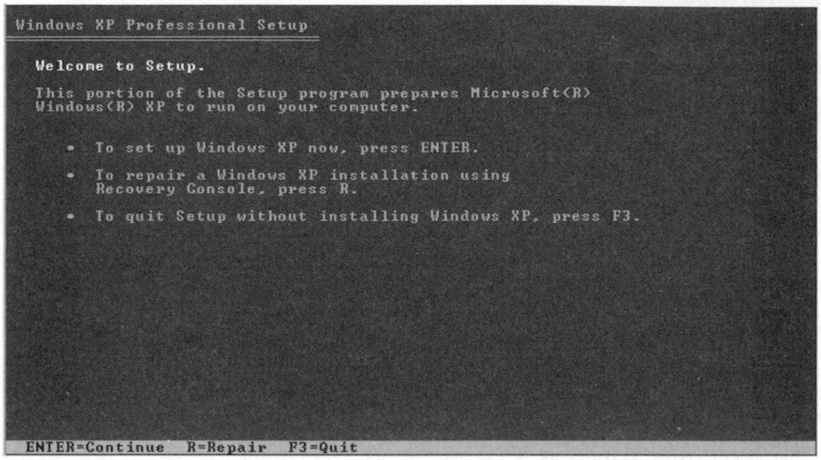

```
Windows XP Professional Setup

    Welcome to Setup.

    This portion of the Setup program prepares Microsoft(R)
    Windows(R) XP to run on your computer.

        • To set up Windows XP now, press ENTER.

        • To repair a Windows XP installation using
          Recovery Console, press R.

        • To quit Setup without installing Windows XP, press F3.

    ENTER=Continue   R=Repair   F3=Quit
```

If your computer was produced after the release of Windows XP and you need to install a third-party SCSI, IDE, or RAID driver in order to recognize the disk drives, press F6 as soon as the screen turns from black to blue (Setup will prompt you at the bottom of the screen).

Text-Based Installation Phase

When the Setup screen appears, you can press Enter to begin the installation. The EULA screen appears, which you must accept (otherwise you can't install Windows—as with other versions of Windows). Windows Setup then presents you with a series of screens similar to those in previous versions, where you can set up the disk to accept Windows XP using either FAT or NTFS. It is best to choose NTFS for performance reasons (as with other versions).

Windows Setup now formats the partition as you specified and copies the files needed to start the graphical portion of Setup. When it's finished copying and unpacking the files, Setup reboots the computer and starts the graphical portion of Windows XP Setup. If all is successful, you will see a screen similar to that in Figure 14.23.

Graphical Installation Phase

During the graphical installation phase, Windows XP Setup performs almost all of the actions necessary to bring Windows XP to a functional level. The first thing it does is copy files to the hard disk and begin installing devices (as shown in Figure 14.24). This process takes several minutes and should not be interrupted.

FIGURE 14.23 Windows XP Setup

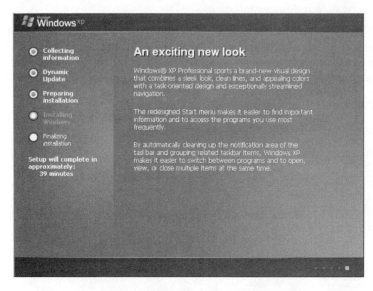

FIGURE 14.24 Installing devices in Windows XP Setup

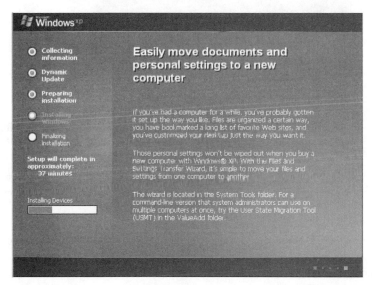

Now, follow these steps:

1. Setup asks you for regional and language settings. The defaults are English (United States) for the language, United States for the location, and US Keyboard Layout for the default text-input method. If you are in a different location or prefer a different input method, you can change either item by clicking the button next to that item (Customize for language and location, Details for text-input method). If you accept the displayed options, click Next to continue the installation.

2. Identify yourself to Windows XP Setup by entering your name and company (similar to other versions of Windows installation).

3. Windows asks you for the product key. You must enter the product key that comes with your version of Windows XP (a bogus key is shown in Figure 14.25). This product key can only be used on this computer. To prevent product key theft, Microsoft requires that you go through product activation after the installation is complete (see the upcoming sidebar).

FIGURE 14.25   Entering a Windows XP product key

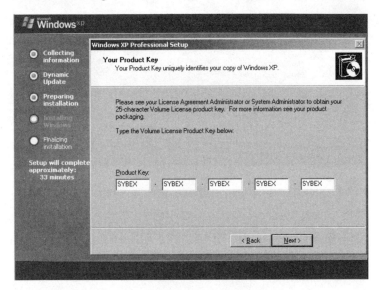

 The screen shown in Figure 14.25 is from a volume license installation (for corporate users). Individual retail and OEM installations have a different screen.

Activation

New to Windows XP is a process known as *product activation*. To curb software piracy, Microsoft requires that each copy of Windows XP be *activated* (either by phone or Internet) after installation. Without activation, you can run Windows XP, but you can only use it for 30 days. And, during that 30 days, Windows XP will constantly remind you to activate your product.

Additionally, the activation records what kind(s) of hardware are in your system, and if three or more pieces change, it requires you to activate again. It's somewhat of a hassle on the part of a system owner if they are constantly upgrading systems. However, some types of Windows XP distributions don't require activation (like those under volume license agreements with Microsoft).

The activation process is simple. After installation is complete, a wizard pops up, asking if you want to activate Windows. You can choose either the Internet or Phone option. If you have a connection to the Internet, the Activation Wizard asks you only which country you live in. No other personal information is required. You can then click Activate, and the Activation Wizard will send a unique identifier built from the different types of hardware in your system across the Internet to Microsoft's activation servers. These servers will send back a code to the Activation Wizard that activates your copy of Windows XP. The phone process is similar, but you must enter the code manually after calling Microsoft and receiving it.

For more information about the process, go to:

www.microsoft.com/windowsxp/pro/evaluation/overviews/activation.asp

4. Enter a computer name to identify this computer. Use something that will be completely unique on the entire network. Windows XP Setup suggests a name automatically, but you can overwrite it and choose your own. You also must enter a password for the Administrator user account (just as with Windows NT/2000).

5. Set the time, date, and time zone, as well as whether to adjust for daylight savings time. Click Next.

6. Setup prompts you for the network setup information. You can choose to either have Setup install the network for you or choose the settings yourself. My personal preference is to accept the Typical Settings option (Figure 14.26) and to go back and configure them later if they don't work. The typical settings include TCP/IP set to get its IP address automatically via DHCP (most networks are configured this way).

FIGURE 14.26   Network setup with typical settings

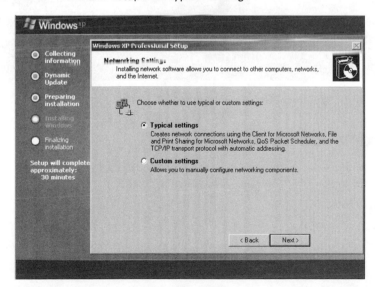

7. Setup asks you if you want to use a workgroup or a domain, similar to other installations of Windows (NT/2000). Select either choice and continue.

8. Windows finishes the installation by copying all the remaining necessary files, puts items on the Start menu, builds the Registry, and cleans up after itself. This last step should take several minutes to complete. When it's finished, Setup reboots the computer.

Upon reboot, Windows automatically adjusts the screen size for optimum use. You are presented with a screen welcoming you to Windows XP. It walks you through connecting your computer to the Internet and registering and activating your copy of Windows XP, asks you for the names of people who are going to use this computer, and then presents you with the login screen (Figure 14.27). Click on a username you want to log in as, and Windows XP will present you with a Desktop (Figure 14.28).

FIGURE 14.27   A Windows XP login screen

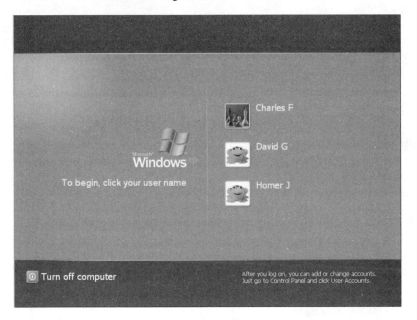

Congratulations: Windows XP is now installed.

Post-Installation Routines

Even though you have installed your OS, you are not quite finished. There are a few items you must do in order to be truly "finished." These items include:

- Updating drivers
- Restoring user data files

If you don't perform these tasks, you will find using the newly installed OS less than enjoyable.

FIGURE 14.28   A Windows XP Desktop

Updating Drivers

After you have gotten the OS up and running, you may find that a few items aren't configured or working properly. That is somewhat typical. The drivers for some hardware aren't found on the Windows installation CD. Or, more commonly, the drivers on the installation CD are horribly out of date. It's a good idea, then, to go back after an installation and update the drivers for your hardware.

You should check the version of drivers for the following hardware against their manufacturer's website and ensure you have the most current drivers for that item:

- Motherboard and chipset
- Video card
- Network card
- Sound card
- Disk controller

To update a driver, download the appropriate driver file package from the hardware manufacturer's website, extract it, and either run the setup utility that is included or use the Add Hardware wizard that comes with all versions of Windows.

Restoring User Data Files

After you have installed an OS, you will want to use the computer. This involves installing applications and (if applicable) restoring data from either an older computer, or this computer if you are reinstalling the OS.

Most often, restoring data files simply involves copying them from a different medium (like floppy disk, removable hard disk, magnetic tape, or other removable media). However, it can also involve copying the older data files from another computer. Windows XP includes a utility known as the *Files and Settings Transfer Wizard* that will transfer most of your files and individual application settings from an old computer to a new one. You connect the two computers (either by LAN or by null modem serial cable) and run the wizard on both computers. The files and settings are transferred to the new computer without much trouble.

 You can find out more about using this utility from Microsoft: www.microsoft.com/ windowsxp/expertzone/columns/crawford/november12.asp.

Upgrading the Operating System

In the previous sections, you have learned about installing an operating system from scratch. In this section, you will learn about upgrading an OS to a newer version of Windows. Microsoft is constantly releasing new versions of Windows. With each version, the hardware requirements go up; however, so does the amount of features that are included.

In this section you will learn about the various topics you must understand when upgrading an OS. For the most part, an upgrade is an installation. There are only a few differences, and we will explain them as they apply to the major OSs.

Upgrade Prerequisites

Before you can begin an upgrade, you must plan it so that it goes successfully. An OS upgrade is a major undertaking and shouldn't be taken lightly. You must consider several items, including:

- Upgrade path
- Hardware compatibility
- Application compatibility
- Service packs and updates
- Upgrade utility

In this section, you will learn about the various prerequisites that are necessary before beginning an upgrade.

Determining an Upgrade Path

Before you can upgrade your OS, you must determine if it is possible to upgrade directly to the OS you want from your current version. For example, if you have Windows 98 and wish to upgrade to Windows NT, it is possible to upgrade directly. However, upgrading from Windows 95 to Windows NT requires an intermediate upgrade to Windows 98 first.

Table 14.6 lists the source upgrades and possibilities of upgrading to the various existing versions of Windows. Start with your finger on the version of Windows you currently have on the left side of the table, and then slide it to the right into the column representing the version of Windows you want.

TABLE 14.6 Windows Upgrade Matrix

Your Current Version	Windows 98	Windows Me	Windows NT Workstation 4.0	Windows 2000	Windows XP
Windows 95	Yes	Yes	Yes	Yes	No
Windows 98	N/A	Yes	Yes	Yes	Yes
Windows Me	N/A	N/A	No	No	Yes
Windows NT Workstation 4.0	N/A	N/A	N/A	Yes	Yes
Windows 2000	N/A	N/A	N/A	N/A	Yes
Windows XP	N/A	N/A	N/A	N/A	N/A

Notice that you can only upgrade Windows Me to Windows XP. That's it! Because Windows Me came out after Windows NT/2000, it can't be upgraded to those versions. Also, this table assumes that the filesystems are compatible as discussed earlier in this chapter.

Determine Hardware Compatibility

As mentioned several times during this chapter, when you're doing any kind of installation, you must make sure the hardware onto which you are installing the software is compatible with that OS. Upgrades are no exception. Although the hardware might operate just fine under Windows 98, there's no guarantee it will do so under Windows 2000.

To be on the safe side, you should check the Microsoft Hardware Compatibility List (HCL) on the Microsoft website given earlier in this chapter for the hardware you have in your computer. Also, you may want to download the drivers that are compatible with the new version of the OS you will have and expand them into a directory on your computer so that they will be available if they are needed during the upgrade.

Determine Application Compatibility

In addition to hardware compatibility, you may have to deal with software application compatibility. Some older software may not work with the newer version of the OS that you are upgrading to. Thankfully, Microsoft has written standards for programmers to use, and if they follow those guidelines correctly, their applications will work on all versions of Windows.

However, programmers often need to take shortcuts to make deadlines, and their software may not be 100 percent compatible with certain versions of Windows.

Always make sure you have the most current patch level and version of your critical software before performing an OS upgrade. And, make sure all your applications will work properly after the upgrade.

Apply Service Packs and Updates

To ensure that your upgrade will work properly, you may need to update or patch your current OS before doing the upgrade. Most people take the "if it ain't broke, don't fix it" approach to OS patches. However, upgrades can bring out the worst in an OS. So, make sure your current OS is up to the most current patch level and that it will be compatible with the upgrade OS.

Determine the Correct Upgrade Utility

Finally, you must make sure which utility you need to use when upgrading your OS. For example, you can use the `WINNT32.EXE` program on the Windows 2000 upgrade disk to upgrade Windows NT to Windows 2000. There are three things to remember about the upgrade utilities:

- `SETUP.EXE` is for upgrading to Windows 9*x*.
- `WINNT.EXE` is for upgrading 16-bit OSs (Windows 9*x*) to a 32-bit OS (Windows NT/2000/XP).
- `WINNT32.EXE` is for upgrading a 32-bit OS to another 32-bit OS.

Upgrading to 98/Me

If you are currently running Windows 95 and want to upgrade to Windows 98 or ME, you're not alone. Most corporate and many home users have upgraded to Windows 98 at the time this book is being written in mid 2003. This is due, in part, to some of the features that Windows 98 added to enhance Windows 95. It can also be attributed to the fact that the upgrade process is very easy (almost painless, in fact) and to the fact that the Microsoft marketing machine did a great job of selling it as a significant upgrade. Some of the major enhancements with Windows 98 include the following:

- Better Internet support through the integration of Internet Explorer
- Year 2000 fixes
- Support for newer hardware, such as USB, AGP, and DVD
- FAT32
- DOS 7 (16-bit) is replaced by DOS32 (32-bit)
- Enhancements for MMX processors; better use of RAM and disk resources

In truth, Windows 98 is a relatively basic upgrade. Besides the fact that most of the changes were relatively modest, most of them were generally also available to interested Windows 95 users through free Internet updates. As you will see, for most configuration and troubleshooting tasks, Windows 95 and 98 are identical.

Still, time marches on, and if you are asked to upgrade a machine from Windows 95 to Windows 98, the procedure is relatively straightforward. Let's run through a typical upgrade.

Starting the Upgrade

For the most part, the major steps you need to follow when upgrading from an earlier version of Windows to Windows 98 are the same steps used to install Windows 98 on a machine without an OS. These are divided by Setup into the following areas:

1. Preparing to run Windows 98 Setup

2. Collecting information about your computer

3. Copying Windows 98 files to your computer

4. Restarting your computer

5. Setting up hardware and finalizing settings

The Windows 98 installation program, SETUP.EXE, performs these steps. In order to begin the upgrade, you need to start the SETUP.EXE program. If you are upgrading to Windows 98 using a CD-ROM with a working installation of Windows 95, things couldn't be much simpler. Insert the disk into the CD drive, and a window similar to the one in Figure 14.29 appears. In addition to this window, a box appears noting that you are using an earlier version of Windows and offering to upgrade you to Windows 98.

FIGURE 14.29   The Windows 98 autorun window

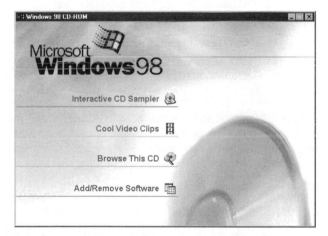

Click Yes, and the SETUP.EXE program will load. You will be able to see the progress of the setup process along the left side of the window as the Setup program shows which part of the install you are in and approximately how much time remains.

Preparing to Run Windows 98 Setup

The first part of the setup routine is pretty basic. All that happens during the initial preparation is that the drives are given a quick examination and the files needed to run the setup are loaded.

Windows checks for a couple of things at this time, such as whether you have enough free drive space for the install and whether any programs are running that may interfere with the upgrade.

> During a system upgrade, you should generally shut down all nonessential programs, including those that are sitting in your System Tray. Doing so will help avoid conflicts and make it more likely that the install will go smoothly.

Collecting Information about Your Computer

Once the Setup program is convinced that you are ready to install, it begins to gather the details needed for this install. A wizard appears and goes through the following screens:

License Agreement   Few people bother to read these agreements, and fewer still understand them. The most important thing that you need to remember is that if you don't accept the EULA, you can't complete the install. It's that simple.

Product Key   These keys just keep getting longer. Microsoft keys have gone from 10 characters in Windows 95 to 25 in Windows 98. Remember that if a user has purchased the software, you need to put in their actual key, not just any one you have handy.

Install Directory   Here you enter the directory in which the Windows 98 files will be stored. By default, this is the same directory the current version of Windows is in—generally `C:\WINDOWS`. You can change this directory, but if you do, the upgrade will no longer migrate existing programs, and you will have to install all programs and drivers over again (as in a new install).

At this point, Setup does some system checks and again checks for drive space. It also looks at the install directory you have specified. If you are upgrading over an existing Windows install, you're given the option to save your existing system files so that you can revert back if you have problems with Windows 98. If you decide to save these files, they are saved at this point.

> To save the files needed to revert back to Windows 95, you must have about 50MB of extra disk space. In most cases, you will not need these files and will choose not to save them. If you have any doubt about the compatibility of the hardware or software on the machine, though, this is a reassuring option.

Next you are presented with choices as to which Windows components you wish to install. There are four basic installation types, each of which gives you a different set of components:

Typical   If you are installing a system for someone else and are not sure which options to install, this is a good base install of most elements.

Portable   This type installs fewer components, but it includes a number of communication tools left out of the typical install, including Dial-Up Networking.

Compact   This no-frills install installs a minimal set of options.

Custom   This is the technician's special. It allows you to go in and choose exactly which components you want and which you don't from the component groups. Each group generally includes a number of options, and you can choose to install all, some, or none of any component group. The component groups are Accessibility (used to install options for those with mobility, hearing, or visual impairments), Accessories, Communications, Desktop Themes, Internet Tools, Microsoft Outlook Express, Multilanguage Support, Multimedia, Online Services, System Tools, and Web TV for Windows.

If a box is checked, all components for that group will be installed. If it is clear, none will be. If the box is gray, only some of the components will be installed. To see exactly which components are selected, use the Details button (see Figure 14.30).

FIGURE 14.30 The component check boxes

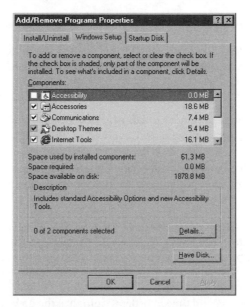

Once you have selected your components, you are asked for a computer name, a workgroup, and a description of the machine. The computer name can be up to 15 characters with no spaces, as can the workgroup name. The Description field can be longer and can include spaces. Their functions are as follows:

Computer Name Used to uniquely identify the machine on a Microsoft network. This name cannot be the same as any other machine's computer name.

Workgroup Used to organize computers. A workgroup is a group of machines that participate in a loose grouping on the network. If your workgroup name is different than everyone else's, you will be the only person in that workgroup.

Description A text field in which you can describe what the machine is, where the machine is, or why the machine is. It can also be left blank.

When these fields have been filled in, Setup confirms keyboard layout and regional settings, as well as country or regional information. You are then given the opportunity to make a Windows 98 startup disk. Because this is an upgrade, you may not have a Windows 98 startup disk, and this is an excellent time to create one. Click Next past the first screen, and then either

OK or Cancel, depending on whether you need a startup disk. If you choose to create one, place a floppy into the A: drive. Any data already on this disk will be completely erased.

After you have completed the startup disk screens, the information collection phase of the installation is over. The next phase of the install begins immediately.

Copying Windows 98 Files to Your Computer

Not a lot happens during this phase, at least as far as user interaction. Files are copied from the CD to the hard drive, and during this time, Microsoft marketing information about various Windows 98 features is displayed to keep you occupied. This is an excellent time to wander off and make coffee.

Restarting Your Computer

Once the file copy is complete, you are asked to reboot the machine. If you are off making coffee, the Setup program reboots for you after a 15-second delay.

Setting Up Hardware and Finalizing Settings

During the reboot, Windows collects information about the hardware installed in the machine, exactly as it did during an installation under Windows 95. Plug-and-Play devices are listed and activated if possible. Setup loads and tests drivers to detect other hardware.

Once your hardware has been detected, you are given the chance to specify driver locations for any devices that are not supported out of the box by Windows 98.

If you are upgrading, Windows 98 generally finds and uses the device drivers that were in use under Windows 95. This is good, in that it makes for an easy install, but you should check vendor websites to see if they have updated Windows 98 drivers. If so, you need to upgrade to the new drivers.

Windows now reboots a second time in order to initialize the new configuration and present your Desktop.

Windows 98 Setup

After the reboot, you're almost there. You can be pretty sure that you are nearing the end of the setup when you see in the Windows 98 Setup window that the basic settings for each of the following are being configured:

- Control Panel
- Programs on the Start menu
- Windows Help
- MS-DOS program settings
- Application start
- System configuration

These are user-based settings that are configured for each user the first time they use Windows 98. Windows 98 sets up the Desktop and other user-specific system elements according to the system defaults, after which point you are presented with a Windows 98 Desktop.

For more information about what to do when the setup doesn't go so well, check out Chapter 18.

If the computer seems to start up fine but Windows *9x* doesn't function properly, try rebooting in *Safe mode*. This mode of operation loads Windows 98 with a minimal set of drivers and can help you determine if the problem is hardware or software related. To boot the computer, turn it on and press the F8 key when you see the words *Starting Windows 98*. Doing so presents you with a list of boot-up choices, the third of which is Boot Computer in Safe Mode. Select this option (number 3) and press Enter. When Windows 98 comes up, it will be running in Safe mode, indicated by the words *Safe Mode* in all four corners of the screen. You can then check on drivers, conflicts, and so on, and make changes to the configuration as needed. To exit Safe mode, restart the computer. If you have fixed the problem, upon reboot, the computer will be operating normally.

For more on Safe mode, see Chapter 18 on troubleshooting.

Upgrading to NT Workstation 4.0

If you have Windows 95 or 98 and you want to upgrade to Windows NT, the process is basically the same as an installation. Providing you follow all of the previously mentioned prerequisites, all you need to do is install Windows NT:

1. You can either boot to the Windows NT Workstation 4.0 CD-ROM or insert it while Windows 98 is loaded. If you choose the former, you begin the same as when you are installing Windows NT. If you choose the latter, Setup first displays the Windows NT logo and allows you to click Windows NT Setup (as shown in Figure 14.31). It then asks you where the Windows NT Setup files are (usually D:\i386 or some other CD-ROM drive letter).

If you get an error at this stage like *Windows can't find the file location,* it's because Windows NT doesn't support FAT32 disks and it can't copy the files to a FAT32 partition.

2. Setup copies files to a temporary folder on the hard disk, just like during the regular Windows NT install.

3. Setup tells you to remove any disks or CD-ROMs from their drives, closes the window it was using, and reboots the computer.

You shouldn't need the Windows NT CD-ROM after this, because all files Setup should need (assuming they were all on the CD) are now on the hard disk.

FIGURE   14.31   Windows NT splash screen

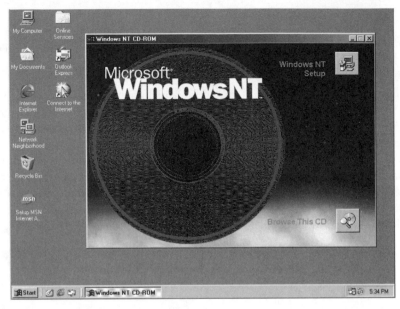

4. If you want to boot to the old version of Windows, choose Microsoft Windows from the menu; otherwise, choose Windows NT 4.0 Installation/Upgrade.

5. Setup starts, and begins with the standard *Press Enter to begin installation* message. You are asked to select a disk controller, agree to the EULA, and verify the installed hardware, just like a regular installation.

6. When you get to the section of Setup that deals with setting up the disks, you will notice that you have one more option when installing Windows NT to a FAT partition: converting the partition to NTFS, or leaving it as FAT (Figure 14.32). Unless you have a particular reason for not doing so, convert the partition to NTFS. You will gain much in performance and security.

FIGURE   14.32   Setup asking if you want to convert a partition to NTFS

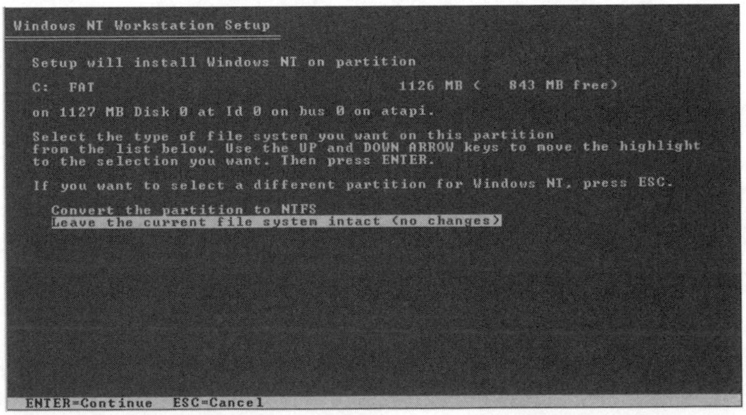

```
Windows NT Workstation Setup

  Setup will install Windows NT on partition

  C:  FAT                                1126 MB (   843 MB free)

  on 1127 MB Disk 0 at Id 0 on bus 0 on atapi.

  Select the type of file system you want on this partition
  from the list below. Use the UP and DOWN ARROW keys to move the highlight
  to the selection you want. Then press ENTER.

  If you want to select a different partition for Windows NT, press ESC.

      Convert the partition to NTFS
      Leave the current file system intact (no changes)

  ENTER=Continue   ESC=Cancel
```

The rest of an upgrade to Windows NT goes about the same as a standard Windows NT installation (except you now see an extra option in the boot menu, Microsoft Windows—in case you want to boot to the old OS).

Upgrading to Windows 2000

If the machine that you want to install Windows 2000 on already has Windows 9x/NT up and running, you may want to upgrade to the advanced security and performance of Windows 2000 without losing your installed programs or system configuration. Windows 2000 allows for this option by providing a sophisticated upgrade mechanism that can check your hardware and software and then update an existing Windows 9x install while preserving the look, feel, and functionality of your current environment.

 Windows 2000 cannot upgrade Windows 3.1 or DOS systems to 2000 Professional. Most machines running 3.1 or DOS probably will be running older hardware, but if you do want to upgrade such a system, you must perform a new full install rather than an upgrade. All programs or drivers that were installed on DOS or Windows 3.x will then need to be reinstalled under Windows 2000.

Starting Setup

Compared to the work involved in setting up a new Windows 2000 install, running the 2000 upgrade is almost effortless. The basic requirements are the same for an upgrade as for a new install, and again you have the option of doing either a CD-based install or a network-based install.

Generally, the simplest option is to place the Windows 2000 Professional disk into the CD-ROM drive of the machine to be upgraded. A window (see Figure 14.33) automatically appears, asking if you want to upgrade to Windows 2000.

FIGURE 14.33 The Windows 2000 upgrade autorun screen

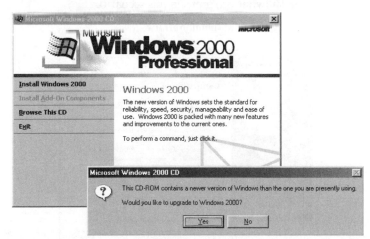

When a compact disc is inserted into a drive, it often automatically starts a program, such as an install routine. This is done through the *Autorun* option.

 Upgrading to Windows 2000 Professional from Windows 9*x* and Windows NT Workstation is essentially the same process—just pop the disk in and go. One of the big advantages of the Windows NT upgrade is that because it is a very similar OS to Windows 2000, you should have fewer compatibility issues. Also, Windows NT drivers can be used in Windows 2000, whereas Windows 9*x* drivers cannot, meaning more hardware may be automatically detected and installed.

If you click Yes to accept the offered upgrade, the Windows 2000 Setup Wizard begins. This wizard performs a number of preupgrade tasks and then starts the upgrade itself. The screens you may see during the Upgrade Wizard include the following:

Welcome to the Windows 2000 Setup Wizard   The first choice in the wizard is also probably the most important. This screen (shown in Figure 14.34) is where you decide whether to perform an upgrade to your existing system or install a fresh copy of Windows 2000 onto the drive. Both options have their advantages:

Upgrade to Windows 2000 (Recommended)   The upgrade allows you to keep your existing programs, but it also retains any existing *problems*. Because of this, any system configuration glitches or files that are no longer used will continue to plague you in the new install, just like they did in Windows 9*x*.

Install a New Copy of Windows 2000 (Clean Install)   A clean install has two major advantages. First, it allows you to start fresh without the baggage of your Windows 9*x* setup. Second, it allows you to dual-boot back to your original Windows 9*x* OS. The disadvantage, of course, is that you have to reinstall all your programs in this scenario.

FIGURE 14.34   The upgrade and install options

Windows 2000 and Windows 9x can exist on the same FAT32 partition in a dual-boot scenario. However, because certain drive locations (such as the location of Internet Explorer and Outlook Express) are hard-wired to the same directory for both, software problems can occur. To install a new copy of Windows 2000 and dual-boot to Windows 9x, it is recommended that you have a second partition on your disk or a second disk. Windows 9x should be installed on the C partition first, and then Windows 2000 can be installed afterward on the D partition. The installation of Windows 9x after Windows 2000 is not supported as a dual-boot scenario.

If you choose to upgrade, you will continue through the wizard. If you choose to install a new copy of the OS, you will be immediately funneled into the process described in the "Windows 2000 Professional Installation" section.

In most cases, I use upgrades as an opportunity to clean up a system. In order to do this, I generally back up any needed data and then reformat the machine's drives and start over from ground zero. It takes a bit more time but is often worth it. Before doing this, though, make sure you still have installation disks for all the applications and other software you will need to reinstall.

License Agreement and Product Key   Assuming you have continued the upgrade, you're required to complete the next two screens, License Agreement and Product Key. They allow you to accept the Microsoft licensing terms and ask you for a Windows 2000 *product key*. As with the regular install, this key is 25 characters in length and can usually be found on the case of the CD.

Preparing to Upgrade to Windows 2000   With the bookkeeping out of the way, you can now get down to the business of the upgrade itself. Before you start copying files, the Upgrade Wizard examines your existing configuration to see whether there are any problems that will make upgrading difficult (Figure 14.35). The Upgrade Wizard provides a link to Microsoft's Windows Compatibility website for product updates and compatibility information.

FIGURE 14.35   Preparing to upgrade to Windows 2000

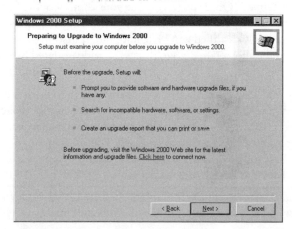

During the upgrade, Setup tries to contact Microsoft's website for information and updates, including the upgrade packs it's looking for on the next page of the wizard. If you do not have a connection to the Web as you are upgrading, you will be asked to connect, but you can choose to continue to work offline. If you do work offline, any updates must be applied manually later. If you have an Internet connection, it is recommended that Setup go out to the website and look for updates.

Provide Upgrade Packs   If you choose to work offline, you may need to provide application upgrade packs. Most 32-bit applications will continue to function without any problems. If you have any 16-bit DOS or Windows 3.*x* applications, though, they may not work. Also, any new or odd hardware may not be upgraded properly, as you will see in the next section. If you have been to the Microsoft upgrade site or a vendor site and have obtained updated files for 2000, you can add them now by choosing the Yes, I Have Upgrade Packs option. If not, select the No, I Don't Have Any Upgrade Packs option. In such a case, you can still apply upgrades later if applications do not function after the upgrade.

Upgrading to the Windows 2000 NTFS Filesystem   Another upgrade option you are given is to upgrade your drive's filesystem to Windows 2000's advanced NTFS. The upgrade to NTFS enables increased file security, disk quotas, and disk compression. NTFS also makes better use of large drives by using a more advanced method of saving and retrieving data.

To enable NTFS and sever all ties to Windows 9*x*, select the Yes, Upgrade My Drive option. To retain your links to the past and allow for dual-boot scenarios, select the No, Do Not Upgrade My Drive option.

Although upgrading to NTFS has a number of advantages, this filesystem is only understood by Windows NT/2000. If you want to reinstall Windows 9*x* on the drive, you will have to completely reformat.

Preparing an Upgrade Report   Once you have made your choices, Setup finally goes through and examines your system for compatibility issues. This involves checking to be sure all hardware and software that is currently installed can be found, and it also involves creating a detailed upgrade report. You will be allowed to do two things: provide updated files for any incompatible hardware and view a report of what the compatibility check has found.

Provide Updated Plug-and-Play Files   In upgrading any system, there is a chance that incompatible hardware may be found. In upgrading certain systems, such as older machines or laptops, the chances are even greater. IBM's ThinkPad series, for example, has hardware support for DVD playback available through an MPEG-2 Decoder Card. This is an optional piece of hardware that is specifically built by IBM for IBM, and as such it is not common enough to be recognized by the Setup process. In order for this device to work, you must obtain updated files from IBM.

If you don't have updated files at present for any unsupported hardware, you can continue with the install, but you will have to update the files before the hardware will function under

Windows 2000. If the functioning of the hardware is essential to the operation of the system (network card, video card, and so on), you may want to stop the install and get the new drivers before continuing. For nonessential hardware such as a DVD decoder, you can continue and fix the problem later; but it is a good idea to at least verify that the hardware is compatible with Windows 2000, so you won't be surprised later.

 As noted earlier, you cannot use the same Windows 9*x* drivers that are currently installed.

Upgrade Report   The Setup Wizard now provides you with a detailed report (see Figure 14.36) of what it thinks may cause you issues as you upgrade. The following topics are included:

Hardware   Any devices that cannot be confirmed as compatible with Windows 2000 are listed here.

Software   Programs that do not work with Windows 2000 are listed here. The ThinkPad upgrade discussed earlier, for instance, finds that not only is the DVD decoder not supported, but the installed DVD player also will not work. In these cases you are directed to uninstall the program before the upgrade, because it will not function and may not uninstall properly after the upgrade.

FIGURE 14.36   The completed upgrade report

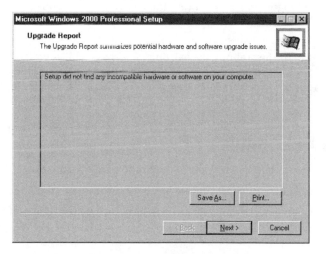

 This particular IBM DVD player should be expected to fail, because it was designed to link directly to the IBM DVD decoder card. Such direct access of hardware is explicitly restricted in Windows NT/2000, and as such this software will be prevented from executing without an acceptable Windows 2000 driver.

Program Notes   Some programs need to be reconfigured to work with Windows 2000. The Program Notes area details some of these known issues, such as the fact that Microsoft Outlook 2000 works with Windows 2000 but must be reinstalled after the upgrade.

General Information   This section details information best described as "other." Some of the upgrade issues that came up during a recent upgrade included notes on issues concerning hardware profiles, backup files, and the Recycle Bin.

If you wish to save the upgrade report information for later use, you have two options: print it or save it to a file. If you feel that the machine has major compatibility issues, you should probably save or print the report, and visit `www.microsoft.com/windows2000/compatible` and `www.hardwareupdate.com` for information or updates.

Once you have checked out the upgrade report, you have to choose whether to proceed with the upgrade immediately or to exit from the upgrade in order to regroup and obtain needed updates. If you are ready to proceed, click Next to continue with the install. If you would rather wait, click Cancel, and the upgrade will end without affecting your existing Windows 9*x* or NT install.

Ready to Install Windows 2000   If you have made it this far, the tough part is over. As the wizard states, *This process is completely automatic, and you will not have to answer any additional questions.*

All you need to do is click the Next button and head off to get some coffee, or preferably some lunch. About one hour and three restarts later, you should find that the process has completed and a Windows 2000 logon screen is waiting for you when you return.

After the first reboot, the existing Windows install is deleted and Windows 2000 files are copied to the drive. After that, a second graphical setup starts, and your settings from Windows 9*x*/NT are automatically reapplied.

Upgrading to Windows XP

Upgrading to XP is probably the simplest OS upgrade of all:

1. Insert the CD and choose Install Windows XP from the menu that appears (Figure 14.37).

2. The Setup program detects that you already have an OS installed and presents you with a menu that says Upgrade (Recommended) (Figure 14.38). Click Next to begin the upgrade.

3. Setup asks you to agree to the EULA, enter the product key, and download an updated version of the Setup program (if necessary).

4. Setup copies several files over, reboots a couple of times, and continues like a standard Windows XP installation.

FIGURE 14.37   Windows XP installation menu

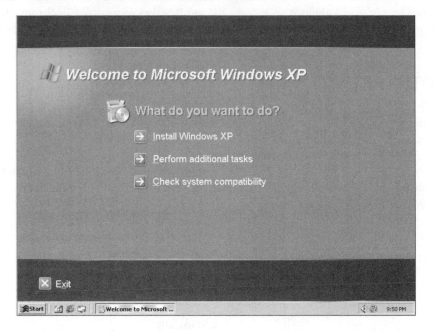

FIGURE 14.38   Windows XP upgrade menu

Once you have finished the installation, you must activate it (like a standard Installation of Windows XP), but that's about it. Windows XP Setup makes most of the decisions about the upgrade for you so only a minimal amount of interaction is necessary.

Summary

In this chapter, you learned the different methods of installing and upgrading the various Windows operating systems. For each type of OS installation, you learned the installation prerequisites and how to install that OS.

You also learned the methods used to upgrade one OS to another, as well as which OSs can be upgraded to one another. Finally, we explained the steps necessary to upgrade to each different type of OS and how an upgrade differs from a standard installation.

Key Terms

8.3 naming convention

active

allocation unit

autorun

boot ROM

cluster

compact installation

computer name

custom installation

drive imaging

dual-boot configuration

End User License Agreement (EULA)

extended partition

FAT16

FAT32

File Allocation Table (FAT)

Files and Settings Transfer Wizard

full installation

Hardware Compatibility List (HCL)

image

logical partitions

minimal installation

network install

NT File System (NTFS)

portable installation

primary partition

product activation

product key

Safe mode

typical installation

Virtual FAT (VFAT)

Windows product key

Review Questions

1. Which of the following is *not* a possible upgrade?

   A. Windows 98 to Windows NT

   B. Windows Me to Window 2000

   C. Windows 2000 to Windows XP

   D. Windows NT to Windows 2000

2. Which of the following is *not* a requirement to install Windows 98?

   A. 386 or higher processor; Pentium recommended

   B. 16MB to 32MB memory

   C. 140MB free hard-disk space

   D. One 3½-inch disk drive

   E. CD-ROM

   F. VGA or better video card

   G. Mouse and keyboard

3. Which of the following upgrade paths are *not* possible?

   A. Windows 95 to Windows 98

   B. Windows NT to Windows 2000

   C. Windows Me to Windows NT

   D. Windows 98 to Windows XP

4. What is the first step when installing Windows 9*x* onto a system that doesn't already have a functioning operating system?

   A. Formatting

   B. Partitioning

   C. Redirecting

   D. Installing the OS

5. The DOS command that partitions the hard drive is called what?

   A. FORMAT.COM

   B. XCOPY.EXE

   C. FDISK.EXE

   D. FDISK.COM

6. When a drive is partitioned, what is the first partition that is created called?

   A. Secondary partition

   B. Extended partition

   C. Expanded partition

   D. Primary partition

7. Using Windows 9*x*'s FDISK utility, how many primary partitions and extended partitions can be created?

   A. Two

   B. Three

   C. One

   D. Four

8. Which option on the FDISK utility allows you to select the hard drive and appears only when there is more than one physical hard drive?

   A. First option

   B. Second option

   C. Third option

   D. Fifth option

9. Which of the following is *not* performed by formatting the hard drive?

   A. Formatting scans the surface of the hard-drive platter to find bad spots and marks the areas surrounding a bad spot as bad sectors.

   B. High-level formatting lays down magnetic tracks in concentric circles.

   C. The tracks are split into pieces of 512 bytes called sectors.

   D. Low-level formatting creates a file allocation table that contains information about the location of files.

10. A 2GB FAT32 partition has a cluster size of _____KB.

    A. 4

    B. 16

    C. 32

    D. 64

11. A 2GB FAT partition has a cluster size of _____KB.

    A. 4

    B. 16

    C. 32

    D. 64

12. When you use a Windows 98 boot disk when the machine first starts up, what is the first option?

    A. Boot with CD-ROM support or without it

    B. Boot from a floppy disk

    C. Boot from the hard drive

    D. Format the hard drive

13. What is the disadvantage of FAT32?

    A. It supports drives up to 2 terabytes.

    B. It's not compatible with older versions of DOS or with Windows 3.*x* and Windows 95 OSs.

    C. It is compatible with all versions of DOS and other OSs.

    D. You don't have to create multiple partitions.

14. The program that performs the Windows 9*x* installation is called _____.

    A. `INSTALL.BAT`

    B. `SETUP.DAT`

    C. `SETUP.EXE`

    D. `INSTALL.DAT`

15. Which switch tells Windows 95's Setup program to ignore settings from your current copy of Windows?

    A. `/is`

    B. `/it`

    C. `/id`

    D. `/d`

16. Which switch causes Setup to run without a mouse?

    A. `/n`

    B. `/l`

    C. `/pi`

    D. `/iq`

17. Which utility is used to upgrade Windows 98 to Windows XP?

    A. `SETUP.EXE`

    B. `WINNT32.EXE`

    C. `WINNT.EXE`

    D. `WINXP.EXE`

18. Where is the best place to find Windows hardware compatibility information?

  A. Windows manuals

  B. Hardware manuals

  C. Microsoft website

  D. Manufacturer's website

19. How many different Ways of installing Windows are there (according to the Setup Wizard)?

  A. One

  B. Two

  C. Three

  D. Four

20. Which installation type allows Setup to choose the most popular options?

  A. Typical

  B. Portable

  C. Compact

  D. Custom

Answers to Review Questions

1. B.   Because Windows Me was released *after* Windows 2000, the Setup program doesn't know about the particulars of Windows Me and therefore can't upgrade.

2. A.   To install Windows 98, you must have a 486DX or higher processor; Pentium is recommended.

3. C.   Because Windows Me was released *after* Windows NT, it is not possible to properly upgrade to Windows NT from Windows Me.

4. B.   New disk drives or PCs with no OS need to have two critical functions performed on them before they can be used: partitioning and formatting. These two functions are performed by using two commands, FDISK.EXE and FORMAT.COM, which can be copied to a bootable floppy.

5. C.   FDISK is usually performed on a computer that has no OS or has a new hard drive. FDISK creates a start and an end to a section of hard-drive space. At the beginning of that space, it creates a special file called the Master Boot Record (MBR). The MBR contains the partition information about the beginning and end of the primary and extended partitions.

6. D.   When a drive is partitioned, the first partition that is created is called the primary partition. The primary partition must be named drive C:, must contain the system files, and must be marked active for the system to boot up.

7. A.   FDISK is a DOS-derived utility, and DOS can access only two partitions per drive. Other disk utilities allow up to four partitions per drive.

8. D.   The fifth option on the FDISK utility allows you to select the hard drive and appears only when there is more than one physical hard drive. The fifth option is Select Hard Drive.

9. D.   The file allocation table is created by high-level formatting, not low-level formatting.

10. A.   FAT32 uses smaller cluster sizes on large drives and, therefore, is able to more efficiently store files.

11. C.   FAT was designed for small drives (as small as 16MB), and as drive size increases, FAT handles it relatively inefficiently.

12. A.   When you use a Windows 98 boot disk when the machine first starts up, the first option is whether to boot with CD-ROM support or without it. The default is to boot with CD-ROM support.

13. B.   The disadvantage of FAT32 is that it's not compatible with older versions of DOS or with Windows 3.*x* and early Windows 95 OSs.

14. C.   The program that performs the Windows 9*x* installation is called SETUP.EXE.

15. D.   The /d switch in Windows 95 ignores the setup of your existing copy of Windows. The /id switch tells Setup to skip the disk-space check, /it tells it to skip the check for Terminate and Stay Resident programs (TSR) that are known to cause problems with Windows 95 Setup, and /is skips the routine system check.

16. A.   The /n switch causes Setup to run without a mouse. Use /l if you have a Logitech mouse and want it enabled during setup. The /pi switch tells Setup to skip the check for any Plug-and-Play devices, and /iq tells Setup to skip the test for cross-linked devices.

17. C.   The upgrade utility for all 16-bit versions of Windows (including Window 98 and Me) is WINNT.EXE. The WINNT32.EXE is used to upgrade 32-bit versions of Windows like Windows NT/2000.

18. C.   Although D might seem like a good answer (and you might find the information), the best (and most current) place to find hardware compatibility information for Windows is the Microsoft Hardware Control List on the Microsoft website.

19. D.   Windows has four different types of setups: Typical, Portable, Compact, and Custom.

20. A.   The Typical option allows Setup to choose the most popular options.

Chapter

15

Hardware Installation

THE FOLLOWING OBJECTIVES ARE COVERED IN THIS CHAPTER:

✓ **2.4 Identify procedures for installing/adding a device, including loading, adding, and configuring device drivers, and required software.**

Hardware devices come in all shapes and sizes, adding a variety of capabilities to your computer system. In this chapter, you will learn the specifics of installing device drivers for many different types of peripherals. You will learn the different methods of connecting a peripheral as well as the steps required to install a driver on the most popular Windows operating systems.

As a technician, one task you will constantly be asked to perform is to install a device driver. A *device driver* (or just *driver* for short) is a small piece of software that allows the OS to communicate directly with a specific piece of hardware. Without the driver, the OS wouldn't know the special commands to send to the device to make it do what you want.

Let's begin with an overview of the steps necessary to install a hardware device in Windows.

Overview of Windows Device Installation

Most often, you will be adding a device or component to your computer in order to expand the computer's capabilities. Regardless of function, devices that you can install can be divided into two primary groups:

Plug-and-Play   *Plug-and-Play (PnP)* is a standard set of specifications that was developed by Intel to enable a computer to detect a new device automatically and install the appropriate driver. PnP makes a technician's job easier because the system already knows what hardware settings are in use, and it sets the new device's hardware settings (IRQ, I/O address, and so on) to appropriate, nonconflicting settings. Almost every new device introduced since 1995 is a PnP device.

Non–Plug-and-Play   If you have to configure a device's hardware settings manually in order to install it, the device can be considered a non-PnP device. These devices are becoming rarer as manufacturers embrace PnP methods.

The basic process for installing these devices is the same for all versions of Windows. There are simply some minor differences in procedures and the appearance of the dialog boxes.

Rights and Security Issues

Whenever you are installing a new device, Windows (in the case of those versions with local security settings, namely NT/2000/XP) may consider that process a security threat. After all, you might be installing some kind of snooping or monitoring device. As such, you must have certain permissions to be able to install a new piece of hardware in Windows.

The primary requirement is that in most cases, in order to install a device, you must be logged in either as an administrator or as a user who is a member of the Administrators group. However, if the device driver has a digital signature, Windows may consider it okay to install without Administrators permission. A *digitally signed driver* is a driver that has been digitally "signed" by Microsoft with a special value that only Windows can read. This signature tells the Windows installer that the driver being installed has been tested for security and stability on the chosen Windows platform and that the driver is from a reputable source. Using digitally signed drivers increases the stability and reliability of your system.

Another requirement to installing hardware without the administrator's permission is if the device can be installed without user interaction. That is, a window does not have to be displayed that requires the user to make a choice of some kind.

Basic Procedure for Device Installation

The basic procedure for installing any device into a Windows computer is the same no matter what version of Windows you are using or whether the device is PnP compliant. The process is as follows:

1. Locate drivers for the device.
2. Connect the device to your computer (either internally or externally).
3. Load or install the proper drivers.
4. Configure the device.

The last two steps will not require your intervention if the device you are installing is PnP compliant.

Keep in mind that these are general steps. Whenever possible, it is advisable to follow the manufacturer's exact instructions when installing any piece of hardware. Failure to do so may possibly damage the device and void the device's warranty.

Locating Drivers for the Device

Device drivers are software, and they are distributed much like any other software. Usually, a CD-ROM or floppy disk comes with whatever hardware you are installing. On that CD-ROM is the device driver for the OS version you have. Most driver CD-ROMs contain drivers for all possible compatible OSs (usually the version for each different OS is in its own directory). However, the drivers on these CDs aren't always the most up-to-date ones.

To find more up-to-date drivers, there are many places you can go. Often, if the OS you have installed is newer than the hardware in your computer, a more current driver may be on the OS CD-ROM. The most current driver can often be found on the device manufacturer's support website. Go to that company's main website. Usually, the main page has a link to Support, Product Support, Download Drivers, or something similar.

Once on the support website, you download an archive file that contains all the driver files needed for your device (including any setup program and supporting utilities). Download it to a directory on your computer, and then double-click on the archive to open it and extract all the files (this may also start the installation program).

Connecting the Device

Connecting devices to your computer can be accomplished in many ways. There are many different ports and interfaces to your computer. Each one of them may be used to add a new device to your computer (or upgrade an existing device).

Generally speaking, when you are connecting a device to the inside of your computer (either in an expansion slot, or connecting to an existing expansion bus), you should power down the computer, unplug it, and wait at least 30 seconds before attempting to install or remove any device. This is necessary because power in the newer ATX-style motherboards remains supplied to the motherboard for at least that long until the capacitors in the power supply drain completely. Some motherboards have a small LED that indicates whether the board has power (even if the power switch is off). If your motherboard has one of these LEDs, wait until it goes out (usually 20 to 30 seconds) before attempting to add or remove a device.

 The procedure for USB devices is contrary to this rule. Generally, you install the driver and software for the USB device first, and then plug in the device *while the computer is on*. Doing so allows the computer to recognize the new component and configure it properly.

To connect the device, follow the manufacturer's instructions and insert the card, plug in the cable, or connect the device in whatever method it uses. Make sure it is firmly secured before you attempt to power up the computer.

 Chapters 6 ("Building a PC") and 8 ("Upgrading PC Components") discuss in more detail the process of connecting these devices.

Loading or Installing the Proper Drivers

There are two main methods of installing device drivers: You can either use the Setup program that comes with the hardware driver CD-ROM (or downloaded file) or use the Windows hardware installation wizard. Either method will get the software installed. However, if the driver is for a device that requires a monitoring utility (like a webcam utility for a webcam), you *must* use the Setup utility that comes with the driver software. Often, if you try to install hardware that requires such a utility with the Windows Add New Hardware Wizard, the wizard will tell you exactly that and halt the installation.

 We'll cover the steps necessary to install a device in the next section.

Often, after installing a device, you must reboot the computer so that Windows will recognize and load the driver properly. Even if Windows doesn't ask you to reboot, you should anyway, just to ensure that the device works properly.

Configuring the Device

Once the device has been installed, you must configure its various options so that it functions the way you want it to. In the case of a video card, you must ensure that it is set to the right resolution for the monitor you are using, so you get the highest possible performance out of the system.

Often, this step is overlooked. Some people install the driver, and if the device works, that's the key. However, you can often obtain the best performance with only a few more minutes of adjustment.

Usually, in order to configure the device, you must either go to the System control panel in Windows and view the properties of the device you are concerned with, or use the utility that comes with the device. The latter method is more common with many peripherals and complex expansion cards.

Windows Version-Specific Installation Items

For the most part, installing a new device is similar among the different versions of Windows. However, there are a few areas where installation differs. In this section, you will learn the differences between adding hardware on the different Windows platforms, including Windows 9x/NT/2000/XP.

Adding a New Device under Windows 95/98/Me (a.k.a. Windows 9x)

Adding new hardware devices is simple under Windows 9x. When you start Windows after installing a new hardware device, Windows will normally detect the new device using PnP and automatically install the software for it. If it doesn't, you need to run the Add New Hardware Wizard.

The screens for this section were taken from Windows 98. The version of Windows 9x you are using (98, Me, and so on) may show slightly different screens, but the process will be the same for the most part.

To add the new device, follow these steps:

1. Double-click the My Computer icon and then double-click Control Panel.

2. To start the wizard, double-click the Add New Hardware icon in the Control Panel window (Figure 15.1).

You can also bring up this window by choosing Start ➤ Settings ➤ Control Panel.

3. Once you have started the wizard, you will see a screen similar to the one in Figure 15.2. This is the introduction to the wizard. To start the configuration of the new hardware, click Next.

FIGURE 15.1 The Control Panel window

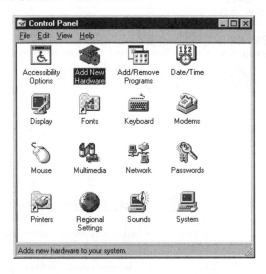

FIGURE 15.2 Add New Hardware Wizard

4. The next screen that is presented (Figure 15.3) allows you to select whether the wizard should search for the hardware. If you click Yes, then in the next step, Windows will search for the hardware and install the drivers for it automatically. This is the easiest method (especially if the hardware is PnP compliant) and the least complex. If you click No, the wizard will present a screen in which you select the type, brand, and settings for the new hardware. For this example, click Yes and then click Next.

5. The next screen tells you that Windows is ready to search for the new hardware. To begin the detection, click Next. Windows makes an intensive scan of the hardware (you should notice that the hard disk light is on almost constantly and you hear the hard disk thrashing

away). During this scan, you will see a progress bar at the bottom of the screen (Figure 15.4) that indicates Windows' progress with the detection. You can stop the detection at any time by clicking the Cancel button.

FIGURE 15.3 Telling Windows to search for the new hardware

FIGURE 15.4 Detecting new hardware

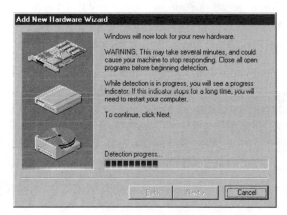

6. When the progress indicator gets all the way to the right, Windows tells you that it has found hardware it can install (Figure 15.5). You can see which hardware it found by clicking the Details button. To finish the setup of the new hardware, click the Finish button.

7. Windows copies the drivers from the installation disks or CD for the device (you may be prompted for the location of the driver). It may ask you for configuration information, if necessary.

8. To finish the hardware setup, Windows asks you to reboot so the changes take effect and Windows can recognize (and use) the new hardware.

FIGURE 15.5 Finishing new hardware installation

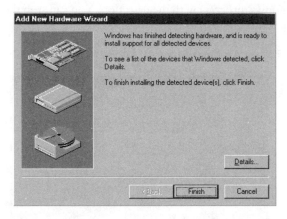

Installing Hardware in Windows NT

Installing drivers in Windows NT is quite a bit different than in all other versions of Windows to date. There is no Add New Hardware Wizard. Instead, you can either use the Setup program that comes with the device you are installing, or you can open Control Panel and hunt for the applet to use to install the device. Windows NT doesn't center device-driver installation around one applet; instead, device installation is spread out among the Control Panel applets for different hardware.

For example, to install a new sound card, you must follow these steps:

1. Go to Start ➢ Settings ➢ Control Panel. Open the Multimedia Control Panel applet (Figure 15.6).

FIGURE 15.6 Multimedia Control Panel applet

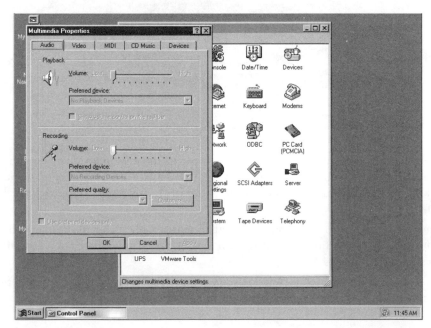

You would think that in order to install a device driver, you would go to the Devices applet. But, that is not the case. The Devices applet is used to see which device drivers are loaded and how they are loaded (at startup or manually).

2. Click on the Devices tab (Figure 15.7). Notice that it shows you all the devices that are installed in this computer. From this window, you can add, remove, or change the settings of multimedia devices.

FIGURE 15.7   Devices tab in the Multimedia Control Panel applet

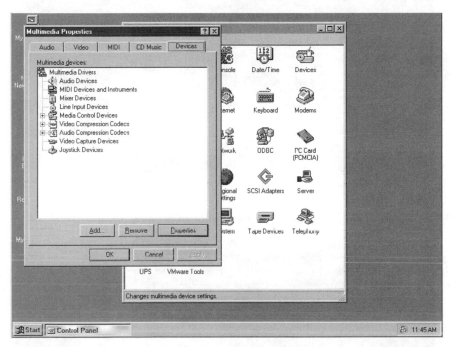

3. To add a new device, click the Add button. The window in Figure 15.8 appears and asks what kind of device to add. This list includes all the drivers that the Windows NT CD-ROM comes with, in addition to other drivers that have been installed. If the driver you are installing is not in the list, click Unlisted Or Updated Driver (the first item on the list) and click OK.

4. Windows asks you to put in the CD-ROM or disk that contains the driver you are trying to install (Figure 15.9). You can either type it in or click the Browse button to navigate to the location of the new or updated driver. The driver may be located on a CD-ROM or disk from the manufacturer, on a network share, or in a local directory you have created to store a downloaded driver. Once you have selected the proper device driver file, click OK.

 If the file you need is on the Windows NT CD-ROM (and you have an Intel-based installation of Windows NT), the files are located in <CD-ROM drive letter>:\i386 as shown in Figure 15.9.

FIGURE 15.8   Adding a new device driver

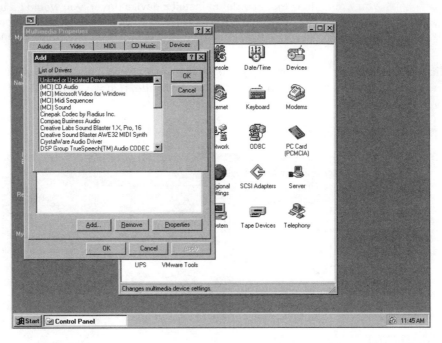

FIGURE 15.9   Windows asking for the location of the new driver

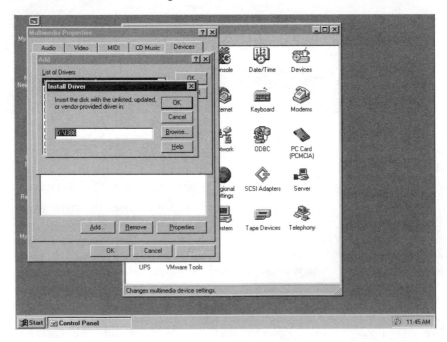

5. Windows installs the driver and brings up a configuration window asking you for the proper settings for the device. Configure the settings correctly and click OK, and the device will be installed (other dialogs may open, depending on the driver being installed).

This process is basically the same for other types of hardware. However, some people use the hardware/vendor selection screen shown in Figure 15.10. To select a particular driver, you select the vendor from the list on the left and then select the device model on the right. If the model isn't listed, you must click the Have Disk button in the lower-right corner. A window will appear asking you where the new driver is located (similar to Figure 15.9). If you don't know the exact location, you can click the Browse button and navigate to the location of the new driver.

FIGURE 15.10   Device driver selection screen

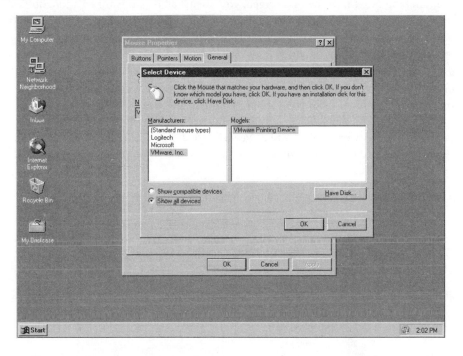

 The process for upgrading a driver is almost identical. The only difference is that instead of clicking Add to add a new device, you click the device you want to upgrade, click Properties to open the Properties page, click the Driver tab, and then click Update Driver. Windows asks you for the location of the updated driver. Provide the location as described previously, and Windows will install the updated driver.

Adding New Hardware in Windows 2000

There are very few differences between adding a new piece of hardware in Windows 9x and in Windows 2000. However subtle the differences, though, they are important to note. First,

Windows 2000 relies heavily on PnP. Installing a piece of hardware in a Windows 2000 computer basically involves physically installing the device, booting the computer, and letting Windows 2000 automatically install the driver for that device. If it can't find the driver, it will ask you for the location. Additionally, the screens have the Windows 2000 look and feel. Finally, you can use the Add/Remove Hardware Wizard to both add new hardware and update drivers for existing hardware.

Follow these steps:

1. Just as with Windows 9x, begin the process by double-clicking the Add/Remove Hardware icon (found in Start ➤ Settings ➤ Control Panel). Doing so starts the Add/Remove Hardware Wizard, which is similar to the wizard in Windows 9x.

2. After clicking Next past the first screen, you are asked if you want to add/troubleshoot a device or uninstall/unplug a device. The latter choice allows you to prepare Windows to completely remove a device or temporarily disable a device. To continue adding a hardware device, choose Add/Troubleshoot A Device and click Next.

3. Windows 2000 searches for any uninstalled PnP devices. It also searches for a list of currently installed devices that may or may not need new drivers. The wizard then presents you with a list of devices so you can choose the device for which you want to install a new driver (either a new device or an existing one), as shown in Figure 15.11. If you are installing a new device, choose Add A New Device. If you are updating a driver for an existing device, choose the device whose driver you want to update. When you've made your choice, click Next.

FIGURE 15.11   Choosing a device for which to install a driver

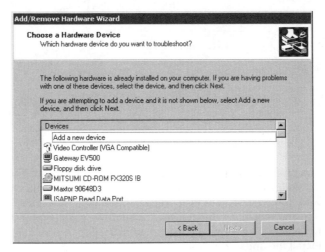

4. From this point on, the Add/Remove Hardware Wizard works almost exactly the same as the Windows 9x wizard. You choose whether you want Windows to search for the hardware or whether you'll select from a list. The wizard then installs the hardware driver or asks you for the appropriate driver, and the installation finishes.

One final difference between installing new hardware on *9x* and installing it on 2000 is that if the device driver can't be found or won't install correctly, Windows 2000 starts a trouble-shooting wizard to help you finish installing the new hardware.

Adding Hardware under Windows XP

You will notice that Microsoft changed the name of the Windows 2000 Add/Remove Hardware Wizard to Add Hardware under Windows XP. As in previous versions of Windows, to install hardware you can let Windows XP recognize new hardware on boot-up and install drivers then, use the manufacturer's installation program, or manually install hardware using the Add Hardware Wizard.

When you install some hardware under Windows XP, XP will warn you to install software before installing the device. You will notice this requirement mainly on USB devices and some other PnP devices.

To begin installing a driver for a new piece of hardware, follow these steps:

1. Install the hardware (either insert the expansion card or plug in the device).

2. Boot the computer and wait for Windows XP to recognize the new hardware. If XP recognizes the new hardware, it displays a screen similar to the one shown in Figure 15.12, which asks if you want Windows to install the driver automatically for you or if you want to pick the driver from a list (as you did in earlier versions). If you go with the default choice of having Windows XP install the driver automatically, XP locates the driver in its database of drivers that come with XP or that have already been installed. It then proceeds to install the driver and activate the new hardware.

FIGURE 15.12   XP detecting new hardware

You may see a warning telling you that if your hardware came with an installation CD, you should insert it now. That way, XP can find the driver automatically.

3. Once XP has found the driver, it determines whether the driver is properly signed (and gives you the chance to stop the installation if it's not).

4. XP tells you that the device has been installed.

Clearly, Microsoft has streamlined the hardware-installation process for Windows XP.

Peripheral Connection Methods

Just as there are many different types of peripherals, there are many types of peripheral connection methods. The A+ exam will test your knowledge of these methods, including:

- Serial
- Parallel
- SCSI
- USB
- FireWire (IEEE 1394)

In this section, you'll learn about the different types of methods to connect peripherals. You'll also learn how to differentiate them from one another by their properties.

Serial

Of all the peripheral connection methods, none is as popular as serial. It's a simple, effective way to connect a peripheral to a PC. It is also cheap to manufacture, which is probably the main reason it's so popular. Serial connections transfer data one bit at a time, one right after another. The maximum speed of a serial connection is 128Kbps, so it isn't good for transferring large amounts of data, but it works great for synchronizing two data sources. The most popular application of a serial connection is connecting an external modem to a PC.

Parallel

The next most popular peripheral connection method is parallel. Parallel connections transfer data 8 bits at a time as opposed to 1 bit at a time (as serial connections do). The most common peripheral connected via a parallel connection is a printer. Hence, parallel ports are often called printer ports. Additionally, newer parallel ports can connect devices like scanners and Zip drives to computers. Unfortunately, the parallel connection doesn't work as well as other types of connection methods (such as USB) because it wasn't designed to connect devices other than printing devices. Parallel was designed to connect only one peripheral at a time.

SCSI

The *Small Computer System Interface (SCSI)* is the best choice for peripherals that require high-speed connections, as well as those that transfer large amounts of data, because it can transfer data either 16 or 32 bits at a time. For example, you could use a SCSI connection to connect a scanner, which might have to transfer megabytes of image data in a short period of time. The most popular use for SCSI is to connect disk drives to computers.

Although it is most often found in server systems, SCSI can be added to desktop systems through the use of an expansion card.

USB

In the last few years, a high-speed bus has been developed specifically for peripherals. That bus is the *Universal Serial Bus (USB)*. The serial bus can only connect a maximum of two external devices to a PC. USB, on the other hand, can connect a maximum of 127 external devices. In addition, USB is a much more flexible peripheral bus than either serial or parallel. USB supports connections to printers, scanners, and many other input devices (such as joysticks and mice).

When connecting USB peripherals, you must connect them either directly to one of the USB ports on the PC or to a USB hub that is connected to one of those USB ports. Hubs can be chained together to provide multiple USB connections. Although you can connect up to 127 devices, doing so is impractical in reality. Most computers will support around 12 USB devices.

Let's take a look at connecting a digital camera as an example. Here are the steps to connect a USB digital camera to a PC to download the images from the camera:

Keep in mind that most USB devices require that you install the driver *first*, before you install the hardware. And, if you use the device's installation utility, it will walk you through plugging in the device as well.

1. With the PC powered on, connect the USB cable from a digital camera to an open USB port, either on a hub or a USB port on the back of the computer. Windows PnP recognizes that a new device is attached and automatically starts the Add New Hardware Wizard.

2. Follow the prompts on the screen to install the driver for your digital camera.

3. Install the image-manipulation software that came with your digital camera.

As you can see, the combination of USB and Windows PnP allows devices to be configured very easily.

FireWire (IEEE 1394)

With the advent of digital video, a new peripheral connection method was needed in order to download large video files into a PC. *IEEE 1394* was the standard developed to meet this need. This standard was developed from work done by Apple and others. The standard is more commonly known as *FireWire*, after the moniker given to it by Apple.

FireWire is a leap in technology over USB because it can transfer data at a maximum of 400Mbps. It has become the peripheral connection method of choice for connecting digital video cameras to PCs.

IEEE 1394 ports can be found on many different types of computers, but they are most common on Apple iMac computers. As a matter of fact, Apple has made a special version of the iMac called the iMac DV that is specifically set up for digital video.

Windows Printing Configuration

Now that we've gone over the general system for connecting hardware, let's look at configuring one specific piece of hardware you'll often be asked to install: the printer. Probably the most troublesome aspect of a technician's job is configuring Windows printing properly. As such, the A+ exam will test your ability to do so.

There are two ways to configure Windows printing: with a local printer or a network printer. In this section, you will learn about topics related to each.

When it comes to configuring a printer, the steps for Windows 9*x* and 2000 are essentially the same, but we'll make note of the important differences in the following sections.

Local Printing Configuration

One of the most common devices to add to computer system is a printer. Whether you are installing a dot-matrix printer or a laser printer, the configuration is basically the same. In this section, we'll examine how to set up a Windows computer to print to a locally attached printer. Setting a workstation to print to a network printer is covered later in this chapter. We'll explain how to perform the various steps for each Windows OS. As you learn the different methods, pay close attention to the differences between the methods for the various Windows versions.

Connecting Printers in Windows 9*x*

In the various versions of Windows 9*x*, the process for installing printers is close to the same. There a few differences, but they are very slight. The A+ exam covers two areas regarding printers and Windows 9*x*:

- Adding a printer
- Managing an existing printer

Adding a Printer

Microsoft was thoughtful enough to provide a wizard to help us install printers. It's named the Add Printer Wizard (neat, huh?). It guides you through the basic steps of installing a printer by asking you questions about how you would like the printer configured:

1. To start the Add Printer Wizard (APW), open the PRINTERS folder by either going to Start ➤ Settings ➤ Printers or double-clicking the Printers icon in Control Panel.

2. In the PRINTERS folder, double-click the Add Printer icon. Doing so displays a screen that tells you the wizard will help you install your printer quickly and easily. Let's hope so. Click Next to begin the configuration.

3. The first question the APW ask is where this printer is (Figure 15.13). If it is connected to the network, click the Network Printer button. If the printer is connected to your PC, click Local Printer. We will discuss using network printers later, so for right now, click Local Printer and click Next.

FIGURE 15.13   Telling the APW where the printer is

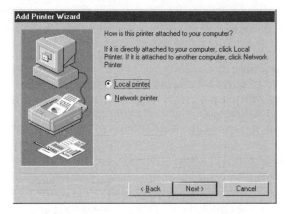

In Windows 2000, there is an extra option to allow Windows to automatically detect and install the printer for you. If you want, you can leave this option selected (which is the default), and Windows will automatically install and configure the printer. The rest of these steps will then be moot.

4. The next screen the APW presents allows you to choose the driver for your printer by selecting the manufacturer from the list on the left and the model from the list on the right (Figure 15.14). You may need to scroll on either side, because the lists can get rather long. If your printer is not listed, or if you would like to install a more current driver, you can click the Have Disk button; the APW will prompt you to insert the disk and type in the path to the directory where the driver is located. Either way, select your driver and click Next.

Make sure you select the correct driver for your model of printer. Most printing problems can be traced to a corrupt or out-of-date printer driver.

FIGURE 15.14 Selecting a printer driver to install

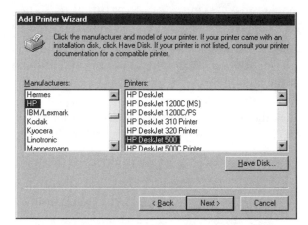

 Some printer drivers can't be installed using the Add Printer Wizard. You must run SETUP or INSTALL from the disk to install the printing software. These programs will not only install the correct printer drivers, they will also set up the printer for use with Windows. In this case, you won't have to run the APW (in fact, it won't work, because you can't select the right driver).

5. The next screen (Figure 15.15) allows you to choose which port the printer is hooked to. It presents a list of ports that Windows knows about, including parallel (LPT), serial (COM), and infrared (IR) ports, and asks you to choose the port to which the printer is connected. Click the port name on the list and click Next. If necessary, you can click Configure Port to configure any special port settings the printer may require.

FIGURE 15.15 Picking the printer port

6. In the next step, the APW asks you to give the printer a name (Figure 15.16) so that you can choose the printer by name when you select Print from any program. By default, the APW

supplies the name of the print driver in this field. You can change it by clicking in the field and typing in a new name. Additionally, you can select whether you want this printer to be the default that Windows selects when you don't select a specific printer. If you want this printer to be the default, click Yes. If not, click No. When you're finished changing these settings, click Next.

FIGURE 15.16   Naming the printer

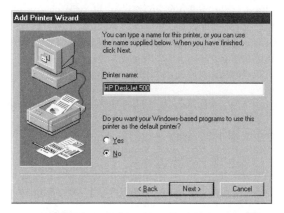

7. The final step in setting up a new printer is to indicate to the APW whether you'd like to print a test page (Figure 15.17). If you say Yes and click Finish, Windows copies the driver and any support files and then tries to print a test page. When the test page is printed, Windows presents you with a screen asking you if the page printed correctly. If you click Yes, the APW is finished and you know the printer works. If you select No, APW launches Windows Help and brings you to the Printing Troubleshooting page. If you don't want to print a test page, select No (from the APW screen) and click Finish, and APW copies the files and brings you back to the desktop.

FIGURE 15.17   Finishing setting up a printer

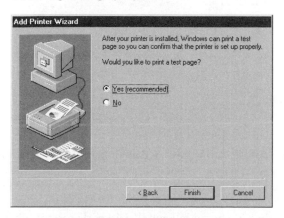

Managing an Existing Printer

If you have a printer installed on your Windows computer, there will be times where you need to change the way the printer functions. For this reason, you should know how to manage an existing printer under Windows. Managing a printer involves knowing how to configure the printer object after you have used the APW to set it up.

Most of what you need to configure is centered around the printer icon (in the PRINTERS folder) that represents the printer you want to configure. You can configure most items from the printer's property page by double-clicking the icon of the printer you want to configure. Doing so will also show you the print queue.

If you right-click a printer's icon in the PRINTERS folder and choose Properties, you will see a screen similar to the one in Figure 15.18. There may be more options, depending on the type of printer it is. Each tab is used to configure different properties. Table 15.1 lists the tabs and describes their functions.

You can print a test page from this page at any time by clicking the Print Test Page button.

FIGURE 15.18 The Properties page for a printer

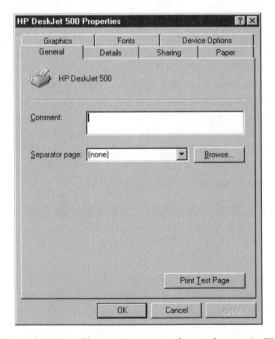

If you select the Details tab, you will see a screen similar to the one in Figure 15.19. From here you can configure how Windows communicates with the printer. For example, you can select a different port to print to for this printer. Additionally, you can install a new or updated driver from this screen. Click the New Driver button, and Windows presents you with a driver selection screen (similar to the one shown in Figure 15.14 earlier in this chapter).

TABLE 15.1   Printer Properties Tabs and Functions

Tab	Description
General	Displays the printer's name as well as any comments you want to enter to describe the printer's functions (or eccentricities).
Details	Used to configure how Windows communicates with the printer.
Sharing	Used to share the printer on the network to which the machine is connected.
Paper	Used to configure what kind of paper the printer is using (size-wise) as well as its orientation when printing.
Graphics	Used to configure the resolution of the printer. Lower resolutions use less toner.
Fonts	Displays the installed fonts. Also used to install other fonts.
Device Options	Changes depending on the kind of printer. Used to set the printer's device-specific settings.

FIGURE 15.19   The Details tab of a Windows printer's Properties page

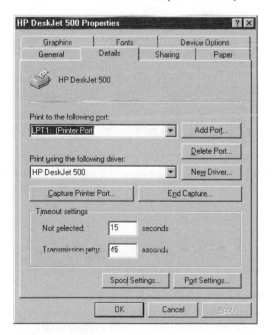

CONFIGURING PRINTER SPOOLING

One of the most important options on this screen is the Spool Settings button. This button allows you to configure whether Windows spools print jobs. If print jobs are spooled, every time you click Print in a program, the job is printed to a spool directory (usually a subdirectory of the `C:\WINDOWS\SPOOL` directory) by a program called `SPOOL32.EXE`. Then the job is sent to the printer in the background while you continue to work. If you don't want print jobs to be spooled (it is the default), click the Spool Settings button. From the screen shown in Figure 15.20, you can choose either Spool Print Jobs or Print Directly to the Printer. Choose the appropriate option and click OK. Once you have made changes to a printer, click OK on the Properties page to save them.

FIGURE 15.20 Changing a printer's spool settings

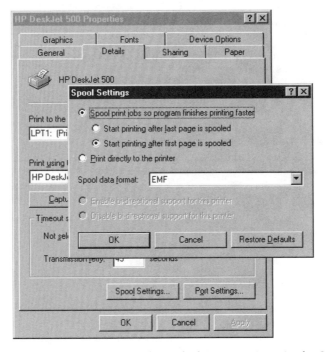

The other way to configure a printer is through the printer item in the System Tray (Figure 15.21). When you print a document, an icon of a printer appears in the System Tray. By double-clicking it, you can open it so that you can manage the print jobs.

FIGURE 15.21 The printer icon in the System Tray

MANAGING PRINT JOBS

When you double-click the printer icon, you will see the screen shown in Figure 15.22. From here you can see any pending print jobs listed as well as their statistics. Notice that one print job currently is being printed. If you want to stop the printer, you can choose Printer ➢ Pause Printing, and Windows will stop sending print jobs to the printer. If you want to delete a job, click the job in the list of jobs and press the Delete key on your keyboard.

FIGURE 15.22 Printer job list

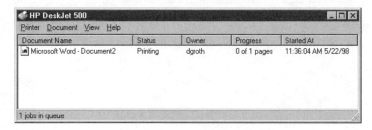

 To delete all jobs in this list, choose Purge Print Jobs from the Printer menu. All jobs that are currently spooled will be deleted.

Printer Configuration in Windows NT

Adding a printer using the Add Printer Wizard in Windows NT is very similar to doing so in Windows 9x. Microsoft knows a good thing when it sees one and made only a few changes. However, those changes are mostly for the increased functionality and network capabilities of Windows NT. As before, the two main areas you need to know are how to add a printer and manage an existing printer.

Adding a Printer

To add a printer under Windows NT Workstation 4.0, follow these steps:

1. Go to Start ➢ Settings ➢ Printers to open the Printers folder. You can also go to the Printers folder shortcut in Control Panel.

2. Double-click the Add Printer icon to start the Add Printer Wizard (APW). This wizard is similar in nature to the one in Windows 9x; however, it includes a few new screens.

3. First you see a screen similar to the one in Figure 15.23. As before, you can select either a printer connected directly to your computer or one connected to the network. We'll cover network printers later, so leave the default My Computer selected and click Next.

4. The next screen (Figure 15.24) asks which port this printer is connected to. Click the checkbox next to the correct port. If the printer is connected to a parallel port, it will be one of the LPT ports; if the printer is connected to a serial port, it will be one of the COM ports. If you need to configure any options (such as data bits, parity, and so on for a serial port connection), you can configure those options by clicking on the port to configure and clicking Configure Port. Click Next.

FIGURE 15.23   Selecting the printer connection type

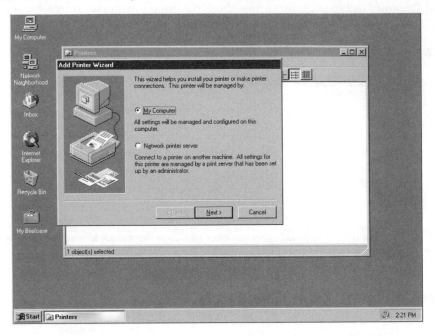

FIGURE 15.24   Selecting the local printer connection port

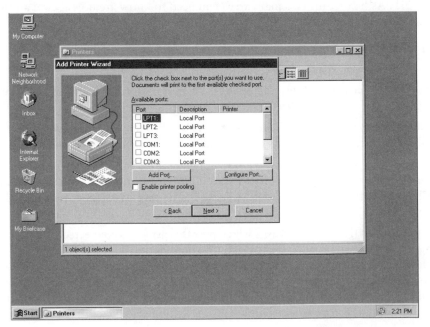

> Some network printing software (Lexmark and HP for example) installs a vir-
> tual network port that can be selected from this screen. If you have accidentally
> deleted your printer icon, but you haven't removed the software, you can use
> the NT APW to reinstall the driver and connect to the network printer.

> You'll notice an Enable Printer Spooling option on this screen. If for any
> reason you have one printer that is extremely busy (for example, a receipt
> or warehouse printer), you can hook two or more printers (they must be
> *identical*) to your computer and set up one print icon (and print queue) to
> serve them both. To do so, select this option, and then select the two or more
> ports that have the printers attached. When one printer is busy, the next
> printer will service the print job.

5. Windows NT asks you to pick the driver that NT will use to print to this printer (Figure 15.25). If the printer is older than Windows NT 4.0, you should be able to choose
   it from the list by selecting the manufacturer in the left window and selecting from a list
   of that manufacturer's printers on the right. You can also click the Have Disk button
   if you have a disk or location with a new or updated driver. Once you have chosen a
   driver, click Next.

FIGURE 15.25   Selecting the Windows NT printer driver

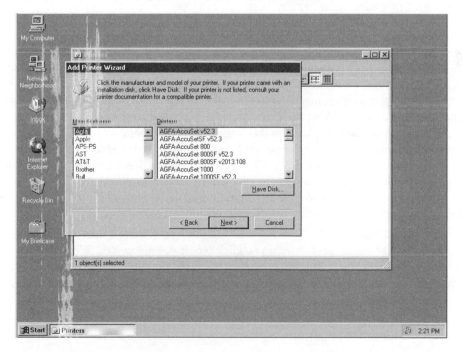

6. The NT APW asks you to name this printer. It selects a name for you automatically, as shown in Figure 15.26, but you can also choose your own name for this printer by typing it in the field provided.

FIGURE 15.26 Choosing a printer name

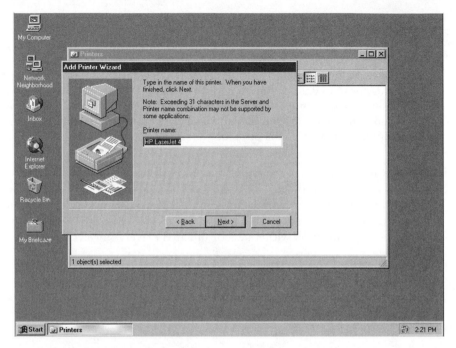

7. Because Windows NT is designed to be a networked OS, it assumes you may want to share this printer with others on the network (Figure 15.27). However, the default is not to share it. If you don't want to share it with others, fine. Leave the default selection (Not Shared) and click Next to continue. However, if you do want to share the printer, click Shared, and then type in a name for the shared printer (NT suggests an eight-character name; you may want to use it or choose your own). Select from the list all the platforms on which you want this printer to work. Doing so makes Windows NT copy all the printer driver files for those OSs to its hard drive; when someone connects to your shared printer, Windows NT will automatically install those drivers on the client's OSs. This technology is known as *Point and Print*. Once you have configured all these items, click Next to continue.

8. You can tell Windows NT if you want to print a test page (Figure 15.28). The default is Yes, but you can choose to do so later if you click No. If you select Yes, Windows NT sends a test page to the printer after it has been installed so you know if the printer is configured properly. Personally, I don't like to waste the paper. I test the printer with a print job I may want to keep. Select either option and click Finish.

9. Windows NT copies some files (and prompts you for appropriate locations for those files, if necessary), and the installation is complete.

FIGURE 15.27 Configuring printer sharing

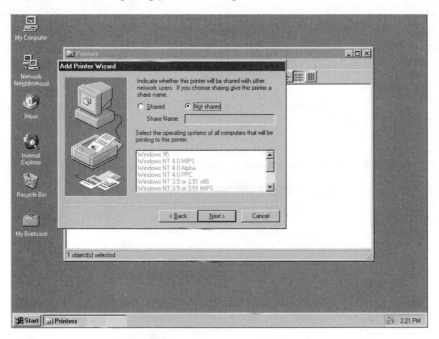

FIGURE 15.28 Selecting a test-page option

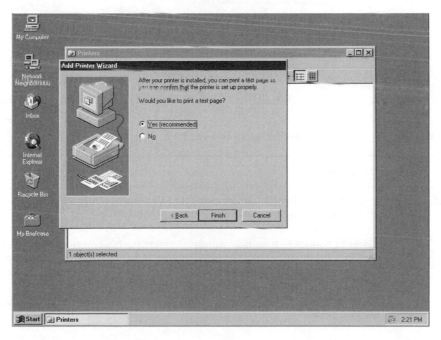

Managing an Existing Printer

Once you have installed the printer, you can manage its settings, just as with Windows 9*x*. To accomplish this, you begin by right-clicking on the printer icon in the Printers folder that represents the printer you want to manage, and then click Properties. Doing so brings up the window shown in Figure 15.29. From these tabs, you can manage the printer and its behavior.

As with Windows 9*x*, you can print a test page from this window at any time by clicking the Print Test Page button.

FIGURE 15.29 Printer Properties window

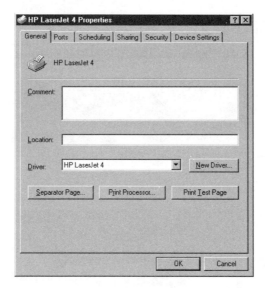

As before, each tab has a specific function. Table 15.2 lists the tabs and their basic functions.

TABLE 15.2 Printer Properties Tabs and Functions

Tab	Description
General	Displays the printer's name as well as any comments you want to enter to describe the printer's functions (or eccentricities).
Ports	Used to configure how this printer connects to this computer as well as the settings for those ports. This tab works exactly like setting up the ports during the installation of the printer.
Scheduling	Used to configure when the printer is available to print as well as spooling for this printer.

TABLE 15.2 Printer Properties Tabs and Functions *(continued)*

Tab	Description
Sharing	Used to share the printer on the network to which the machine is connected.
Security	Used to set security for who has access to this printer and what those users can do with the printer.
Device Settings	Changes depending on the kind of printer. Used to set the printer's device-specific settings (paper types it supports, accessory options, and so on).

CONFIGURING PRINTER SPOOLING

Printer spooling for Windows NT is handled by the SPOOLSS.EXE process. To configure how Windows NT handles print spooling, click the Scheduling tab (Figure 15.30) from within the printer's Properties window. From this window, you can select the same options for print spooling (Print Directly to the Printer or Spool Print Documents, and so on) as with Windows *9x*.

FIGURE 15.30 Configuring printer spooling

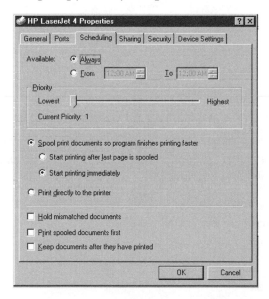

However, with Windows NT, the spool directory is located in the *%SYSTEMROOT%*\SYSTEM32\ SPOOL directory (where *%SYSTEMROOT%* is where Windows NT is installed, usually C:\WINNT).

If the volume where the spool directory is located happens to be full, you will not be able to print until space is freed on that volume. Or, you could change the printer's spool setting to Print Directly to the Printer.

PRINTER SECURITY

New to Windows NT is file and printer security. You will learn more about sharing security in Chapter 16. However, just a note about it here. In order to configure printer security, you click the Security tab (Figure 15.31) from the printer Properties window. Then, click the Permissions button to view or change which users have rights to print to or manage this printer.

FIGURE 15.31 Printer Security tab

Another note is that there are no individual permissions for printer security—only access levels. These access levels control what a user can do with a particular printer. These levels are:

Full Control The user can change settings, manage print documents, and even delete the printer.

Manage Documents The user can print to the printer and manage (change the order of, stop, and resume) all print jobs on this printer.

Print A user can print to this printer, as well as manage their own print jobs.

No Access A user cannot use this printer at all.

When you're setting these access levels, you use the standard Windows method of setting permissions, as discussed in Chapter 16.

MANAGING PRINT JOBS

Managing print jobs works exactly the same as it does in Windows 9x. Double-click on the printer to access all the same functions for controlling the print jobs.

Printers in Windows 2000

With Windows 2000, Microsoft changed the process of adding printers significantly, because it added the capability of true Plug-and-Play. Windows can detect the printer and install it with very little user interaction.

The A+ exam tests your knowledge of printer installation on the Windows 2000 platform as well, including adding a printer and managing an existing printer.

Adding a Printer

You will notice only a few similarities between adding a printer under Windows 2000 and doing the same for Windows NT (as discussed earlier):

1. To begin, as with other versions, open the Printers folder by going to Start ➢ Settings ➢ Printers.

2. To add a new printer, double-click the Add Printer icon. As before, doing so starts the Add Printer Wizard, which helps you install the printer (Figure 15.32). Click Next to begin the installation.

FIGURE 15.32   The Windows 2000 Add Printer Wizard

3. The first step in the installation is to tell the APW if the printer is attached locally or to the network (Figure 15.33) and, if the printer is attached directly to the computer, whether you want Windows 2000 to detect it automatically. If you do, Windows 2000 connects to the printer, determines where it's attached and what kind of printer it is, and automatically installs a driver (if possible). If the printer can't be detected, Windows lets you know, and manual installation continues. For the purposes of this section, uncheck the detection option and proceed with a manual installation. Click Next to continue.

4. Tell the Windows 2000 APW which port the printer is connected to (Figure 15.34). As in previous versions, you select the port from the list. If the port is not listed, you must click the Create a New Port option and specify the type of port you are adding. Once you have selected the port that this new printer is connected to, click Next.

5. The next screen asks you to select the driver for the printer you are connecting (Figure 15.35). You can select it from the list of printer drivers that Windows 2000 already has by selecting the printer manufacturer on the left and the printer model on the right. If the printer is not listed, click the Have Disk button and supply the APW with the location of the printer driver. When you're finished selecting the printer driver, click Next.

FIGURE 15.33 Telling APW how the printer is connected

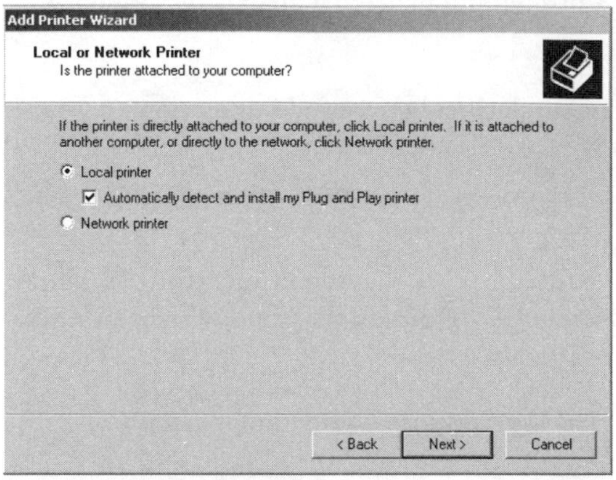

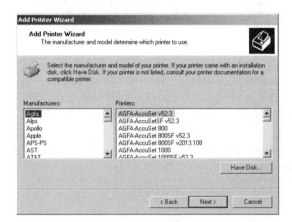

FIGURE 15.34 Selecting the printer's port

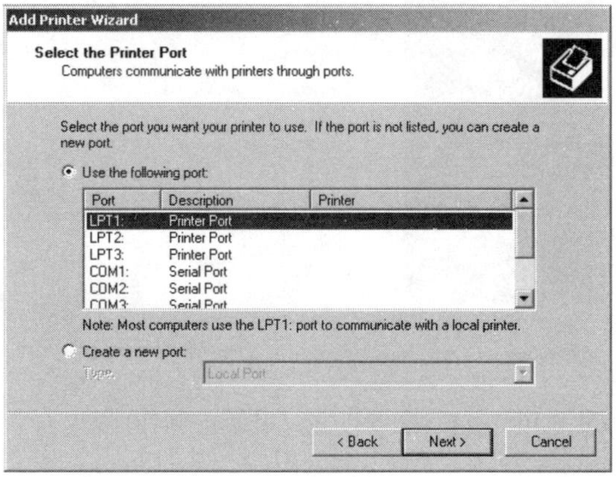

FIGURE 15.35 Selecting the proper printer driver

6. The next step is to name the printer (Figure 15.36). As with other versions of the Windows APW, give the printer a name that you will remember (Windows will suggest one for you). Click Next.

FIGURE 15.36 Naming the printer

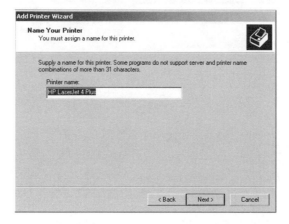

7. Like Windows NT, Windows 2000 is a networked OS. So, it is possible to share files and printers with Windows 2000. As in Windows NT, the APW asks you if you want to share this printer (Figure 15.37). If you want to share it, select Share As and type in a name that the printer should be shared as. If you don't want to share the printer, select Do Not Share This Printer. Click Next to continue.

 If you select Share As at this step, the APW brings up one more screen that asks you to give a location and description for the shared printer. Doing so will help users who are browsing for this printer identify whose printer it is.

FIGURE 15.37 Selecting printer share options

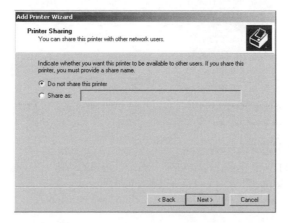

8. As with the other versions, the APW asks if you want to print a test page (Figure 15.38). Select either option and click Next.

FIGURE 15.38   Selecting the test page option

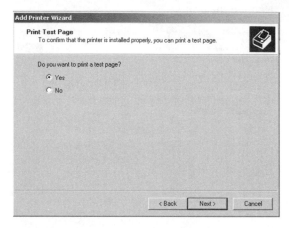

9. The APW presents a final screen displaying the options you have selected (Figure 15.39). Review the choices and, if everything looks correct, click Finish. Windows installs the printer drivers and prints the test page (if selected).

FIGURE 15.39   Printer option review

If the installation goes smoothly, there will be a new icon in the Printers folder representing the printer you have just installed.

Managing an Existing Printer

As with Windows NT and, to some degree, Windows 98, you can manage all of the new printer's printing options. The A+ exam will test your knowledge of managing a printer under Windows 2000. As you might expect by now, there are quite a few similarities between

Windows 2000 printer management and Windows NT/98 printer management. The main differences are the names of the tabs on the printer Properties window.

As with the other versions, you begin managing your printer by opening the Printers window (Start ➢ Settings ➢ Printers) and then right-clicking on the printer and choosing Properties. The printer Properties window for this printer will appear (Figure 15.40).

 You can print a test page from this window, just as with the other versions.

FIGURE 15.40   Printer Properties window in Windows 2000

Each tab shown in Figure 15.40 has a specific function. Table 15.3 lists the tabs and their basic functions.

TABLE 15.3   Printer Properties Tabs and Functions

Tab	Description
General	Displays the printer's name as well as any comments you want to enter to describe the printer's functions (or eccentricities).
Sharing	Used to share the printer on the network to which the machine is connected.
Ports	Used to configure how this printer connects to this computer as well as the settings for those ports. This tab works exactly like setting up the ports during the installation of the printer.

TABLE 15.3 Printer Properties Tabs and Functions *(continued)*

Tab	Description
Advanced	Used to configure when the printer is available to print as well as spooling for this printer.
Security	Used to set security for who has access to this printer and what those users can do with the printer.
Device Settings	Changes depending on the kind of printer. Used to set the printer's device-specific settings (paper types it supports, accessory options, and so on).

CONFIGURING PRINTER SPOOLING

Printer spooling for Windows 2000 is handled by the SPOOLSV.EXE process. To configure how Windows 2000 handles print spooling, click the Advanced tab (Figure 15.41) from within the printer Properties window. From this window, you can select the same options for print spooling (Print Directly to the Printer, Spool Print Documents, and so on) as in Windows 9x/NT. (Notice that this tab is called Advanced rather than Scheduling, as it is with NT.)

FIGURE 15.41 Configuring printer spooling

However, as with Windows NT, the spool directory is located in the *%SYSTEMROOT%*\SYSTEM32\ SPOOL directory (*%SYSTEMROOT%* is where Windows 2000 is installed, usually C:\WINNT).

PRINTER SECURITY

As with Windows NT, Windows 2000 has printer security. And, as with Windows NT, in order to configure printer security, you must click the Security tab (Figure 15.42) from the printer Properties window. However, you don't have to go any further than that. From this window, you can view or change which users have rights to print to or manage this printer.

FIGURE 15.42   Printer Security tab

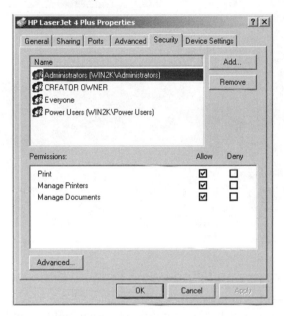

As with NT, when you're setting these access levels, you use the standard Windows method of setting permissions, as discussed in Chapter 16.

MANAGING PRINT JOBS

The process of managing print jobs (deleting, and so on) works exactly as it does for Windows 9x/NT. However, with Windows 2000, a new feature has been added: You now have the ability to work with the printer offline. In Figure 15.43, you'll notice a new Use Printer Offline menu option (third from the bottom) under the Printer menu. When you select this option, Windows no longer sends print jobs to the printer. It treats the printer as being offline and keeps the print jobs stored on disk, ready to be printed. When the printer comes back online, you just need to deselect the Use Printer Offline option, and Windows will send the print jobs to the printer.

This option is handy for laptop users who don't always carry a printer with them. They can print their print jobs offline while away from the printer. Then, when they return, they can connect to the printer and send all their jobs at once.

FIGURE 15.43   Use Printer Offline option

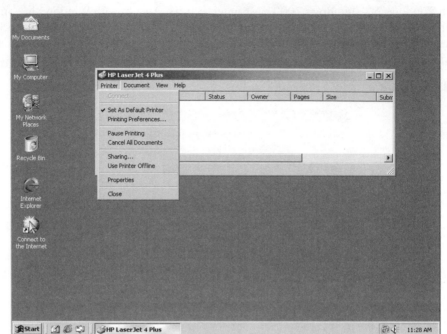

Printer Configuration in Windows XP

With the introduction of Windows XP, Microsoft changed the look and feel of Windows significantly, as you may already have noticed. As a result, adding and managing printers is somewhat different as well, although it is still decidedly Microsoft-style.

Because the A+ exam tests your knowledge of installing and configuring printing software from within all versions of Windows, in this section you will learn about installing and configuring printers for the latest version of Windows, Windows XP.

Installing a New Printer

As already mentioned, installing a printer on Windows XP is a bit different than installing one on other OSs:

1. To begin the installation, go to Start ➢ Printers and Faxes. Click the Add Printer Wizard on the left of the Printers and Faxes window. This will start the Add Printer Wizard (Figure 15.44).

> You will not need to use the Windows XP APW if you are using a USB printer. Simply install the software on the CD-ROM that comes with the printer and connect the printer to the computer with the provided USB cable. Windows XP will detect the printer and install it. The APW will remind you of this as well when you run it.

FIGURE 15.44 Windows XP Add Printer Wizard

2. Once you have started the APW, click Next to begin the installation of the printer. The APW asks whether the printer is local or network (Figure 15.45) and whether it should be automatically detected, as it did with Windows 2000. For the purposes of this section, choose Local and uncheck the Automatically Detect and Install My Plug and Play Printer option so that you can run through all steps of the installation manually. Click Next to continue the installation.

FIGURE 15.45 Selecting a local or network printer connection

3. From this point forward, the installation continues as with Windows 2000 or other versions of Windows. To continue, choose the printer port your computer will use to connect to the printer and click Next.

4. Choose the driver your computer will use to communicate with the printer and click Next.

5. On the screen that appears, choose a name for the printer, enter it in the space provided, and pick whether you want it to be the default printer. Click Next.

6. Choose whether you want to print a test page, then click Next.

7. Finally, review all the settings. If you want to change any setting, click Back to the page you want to change. If everything is correct, click Finish.

Managing an Existing Printer

Just as with previous versions of Windows, managing printers in Windows XP is done through the icon that represents the printer. However, as previously mentioned, the folder that contains the icons is now named Printers and Faxes and can be found directly under the Start menu. To open the Printers and Faxes window, go to Start ➤ Printers and Faxes. In the resulting window, you can manage any of the installed printers by right-clicking its icon and choosing Properties. From the printer Properties window (Figure 15.46), you can manage most of a printer's settings.

FIGURE 15.46 The printer Properties window for Windows XP

As with previous versions, each tab shown in Figure 15.46 has a specific function. Table 15.4 lists the tabs and their basic functions.

TABLE 15.4 Printer Properties Tabs and Functions

Tab	Description
General	Displays the printer's name as well as any comments you want to enter to describe the printer's functions (or eccentricities).

TABLE 15.4 Printer Properties Tabs and Functions *(continued)*

Tab	Description
Sharing	Used to share the printer on the network to which the machine is connected.
Ports	Used to configure how this printer connects to this computer as well as the settings for those ports. This tab works exactly like setting up the ports during the installation of the printer.
Advanced	Used to configure when the printer is available to print as well as spooling for this printer.
Security	Used to set security for who has access to this printer and what those users can do with the printer.
Device Settings	Changes depending on the kind of printer. Used to set the printer's device-specific settings (paper types it supports, accessory options, and so on).

CONFIGURING PRINTER SPOOLING

Printer spooling for Windows XP is handled by the SPOOLSV.EXE process. To configure how Windows XP handles print spooling, click the Advanced tab (Figure 15.47) from within the printer Properties window. From this window, you can select the same options for print spooling (Print Directly to the Printer, Spool Print Documents, and so on) as with Windows 9*x*/NT/2000. Notice this tab is called Advanced, as in Windows 2000.

FIGURE 15.47 Configuring printer spooling

However, as with Windows NT, the spool directory is located in the *%SYSTEMROOT%*
SYSTEM32\SPOOL directory (*%SYSTEMROOT%* is where Windows XP is installed, usually
C:\WINDOWS).

MANAGING PRINTER SECURITY

As with Windows NT/2000, Windows XP has printer security. In order to configure printer
security, click the Security tab (Figure 15.48) from the printer Properties window. However,
you don't have to go any further than that. From this window, you can view or change which
users have rights to print or manage this printer.

FIGURE 15.48   Printer Security tab

 With Windows XP Professional, the Security tab is visible only if you have
turned off the Use Simple File Sharing option for Windows. To disable this
option, open the Windows Explorer program, go to Tools ➢ Folder Options,
click on the View tab, and uncheck Use Simple File Sharing.

As with NT, when you're setting these access levels, you use the standard Windows method
of setting permissions, as discussed in Chapter 16.

MANAGING PRINT JOBS

The process of managing print jobs (deleting, and so on) works exactly as it does for Windows 2000. To manage printers in Windows XP, open the Printers and Faxes folder (Start ➢
Printers and Faxes), and then double-click on the printer you want to manage. You will see
a Window similar to the one in Figure 15.49 (the Printer menu has been pulled down to show
the options available).

FIGURE 15.49   Managing print jobs in Windows XP

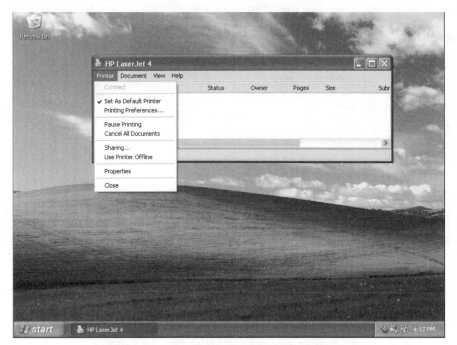

Network Printing

Network printing is a lot like local printing except that you are introducing a degree of separation between the computer and the printer. That degree of separation is a network. Configuring network printing is very similar to configuring local printing except you must configure the Windows printer driver to print to the network instead of to a local printer port. Usually, this involves installing network software that comes with the printer; the software makes a virtual printer port that points to the specified network printer.

For the A+ exam, you will not be expected to know everything about connecting network printers (after all, that is what the Network+ exam is for). However, you should know the basic steps. In this section, you'll learn how to configure network printing for each of the Windows OSs.

Network Printing in Windows 9x

To set up the printer on your Windows 9x workstation, you most likely will use the Point and Print option for Windows printing. This option allows you to click and drag a printer to the PRINTERS folder and run a shorter version of the Add Printer Wizard, which sets up the printer icon and the right drivers on your machine automatically. Follow these steps:

1. Using the Network Neighborhood icon on the desktop, browse to the computer that hosts the printer you want to set up and double-click the computer name. You'll see a window with a list of resources the computer is hosting.

2.   Open the PRINTERS folder (choose Start ➤ Settings ➤ Printers). Arrange these windows so you can see both at the same time (Figure 15.50).

FIGURE 15.50   Preparing for the Point and Print process

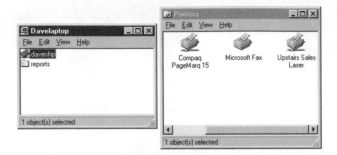

3.   To start the Add Printer Wizard, drag the printer you want to set up from the list of resources the computer is hosting to the Printers window. As soon as you release the mouse button, the wizard will start, and it will display the window shown in Figure 15.51. You can also locate the printer in Network Neighborhood and double-click on it. You are asked if you want to install this networked printer on your computer.

FIGURE 15.51   Starting the Add Printer Wizard

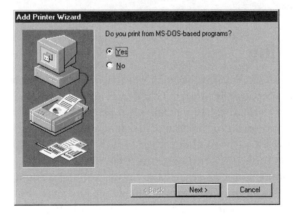

4.   The wizard asks you a series of questions to help you configure the printer. The first question it asks is, *Do you print from MS-DOS–based programs?* The reasoning behind this question is similar to the reason we map drive letters. Most older DOS programs (and to a lesser extent, Windows programs) don't understand the UNC path syntax for access to a shared resource. Instead, they understand a name for a local hardware resource (like LPT1, for the first local parallel port). So, you must point out a local printer port name to the network in a process known as *capturing*. If you need to capture a printer port, answer Yes to this question; otherwise leave it set to the default (No). For this example, click Yes and click Next to move to the next step of the wizard.

5. The next step in the APW captures the printer port (Figure 15.52). This screen allows you to capture a printer port so that DOS programs can print to the network printer. Click the Capture Printer Port button to bring up the screen (shown in Figure 15.53) in which you choose which local port you want to capture.

FIGURE 15.52   Capturing a printer port

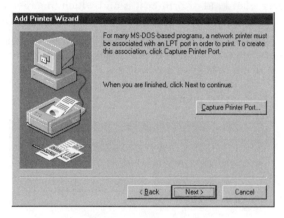

FIGURE 15.53   Picking which local port to capture

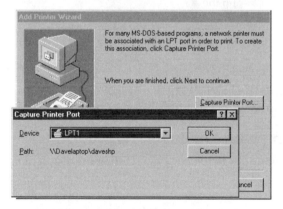

6. From the drop-down list, choose the local port you want to capture (any port from LPT1 to LPT9). Remember two things about capturing ports:

- The port doesn't have to be installed physically in your computer in order to be captured. The capture process just associates a port name with a shared printer.

- If the port you capture *is* installed in your computer and you capture it, all print jobs sent to that port name will be sent to the network printer, not out the local port (which is the way it is supposed to work). If you have a printer attached to that port, you will not be able to print to it.

  Click OK to accept your choice and return to the wizard screen. Then, click Next to continue running the wizard.

7. Choose the printer's manufacturer and model. This choice, in effect, selects the driver. If the model of printer you are connecting to is not listed, click the Have Disk button, specify the location of the driver, and click OK to accept it. When you have chosen a printer model, click Next.

8. The next step is to give the printer instance a name. You should give a network printer a name that reflects what kind of printer it is and which machine is hosting it. In this example, the printer is labeled HP LaserJet III (the default name of the driver), but it could have been named Laser on Bob's PC. Type in the name that makes sense to you (Figure 15.54). You can also choose whether you want the printer to be the default printer that is used by all Windows applications.

FIGURE 15.54   Naming the printer

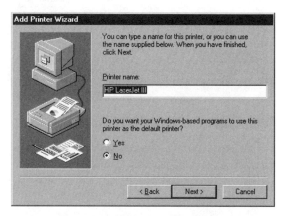

From here on, network printer installation is exactly the same as installing a local printer. We covered this process earlier, so we won't discuss it further here.

Network Printing with Windows NT/2000/XP

These OSs include support for *Point and Print*. During the installation of a printer on a host computer (as you saw earlier), you are asked which platforms should be supported (that is, which versions of the drivers should be copied). This step places the driver files for the supported OSs into a directory on the host computer. When a client connects to the host computer and tries to use the shared printer, Windows sends the appropriate driver, and it is automatically installed.

To install a Point and Print printer, do the following:

1. Use Network Neighborhood to browse to the printer that is hosting the shared printer.

2. Right-click on the printer and choose either Install (for Windows NT clients) or Connect (for Windows 2000/XP clients).

3. Windows copies all necessary drivers from the host computer. If the host computer doesn't have the proper driver for the client you are using, the client OS prompts for an installation disk for that printer model.

4. Windows automatically finishes the installation of the printer. The network printer appears in the Printers folder (Printers and Faxes for Windows XP) as a network printer.

This feature of these versions of Windows makes configuring network printers extremely easy for the client. The process is easiest when all the appropriate drivers are installed on the host computer.

 It is also possible to install a printer using the Add Printer Wizard. Choose Network printer at the first screen instead of Local printer, and then browse for the network printer.

Summary

In this chapter, you learned how to use and configure peripherals. A peripheral is any device that is not part of the computer itself. Examples of peripherals include modems, printers, scanners, and so on.

In the first section of this chapter, you learned about the most popular methods of connecting peripherals to host computers. These methods include serial, parallel, USB, FireWire, and SCSI. We discussed the advantages and disadvantages of each connection method as well as the best application for each.

In the final section, you learned about the proper methods of setting up Windows printing for both locally connected printers and network-connected printers. We showed you how to use the Add Printer Wizard to connect both of these types of printers as well as how to add printer drivers and configure printing properties for each type of printer in each type of Windows OS.

Key Terms

Before you take the exam, be certain you are familiar with the following terms:

device driver	Plug-and-Play (PnP)
digitally signed driver	Point and Print
driver	Small Computer System Interface (SCSI)
FireWire	Universal Serial Bus (USB)
IEEE 1394	

Review Questions

1. You've successfully completed an upgrade to Windows 2000 Professional. Several days later, you add your old printer, using the driver that originally came with it. Now the printer, which has never had a problem, won't print. What do you need to do to fix the problem?

    A. Older printers are often not compatible with Windows 2000. You may need to replace the printer.

    B. Your printer driver is out of date. Contact the vendor or visit its website for an updated driver.

    C. Uninstall, and then reinstall the printer using the original driver.

    D. None of the above.

2. You've set up a network printer. However, you cannot print from your DOS-based programs. What did you do wrong during printer setup?

    A. Nothing. You cannot print from DOS-based programs within Windows 2000.

    B. You have an incorrect printer driver and need an update.

    C. During setup, you did not capture the printer port. Rerun the Add Printer Wizard and make the appropriate changes.

    D. Run the Add Printer Wizard again and accept all defaults.

3. When you print in Windows 2000, you cannot perform any other task until the print job is complete. What can you do?

    A. Your printer driver is corrupt. Replace it.

    B. There is nothing you can do. That is the normal printing mode.

    C. Change your printer settings back to the default mode.

    D. Your computer needs more RAM.

4. Which of the following methods correctly adds new hardware to a Windows 9x system if Plug and Play does not work? (Select all that apply.)

    A. Choose Start ➢ Settings ➢ Control Panel and then double-click the Add New Hardware icon.

    B. Exit to DOS and use the software that came with the device to run the installation.

    C. If Plug and Play does not work, there is no way to get the hardware working in the Windows 9x environment.

    D. On the Desktop, double-click the My Computer icon, double-click the Control Panel icon, and then double-click the Add New Hardware icon.

5. The most popular connection method is serial. Which of the following are characteristics of a serial connection? (Select all that apply.)

   A. Transfer rate of one data bit at a time.

   B. Maximum speed of 128Kbps.

   C. Although it's popular, it's expensive to manufacture.

   D. All of the above.

6. Which of the following is a difference between installing new hardware on a Windows 9x system versus a Windows 2000 system?

   A. There is no difference.

   B. With Windows 9x, if the proper device driver cannot be found or won't install properly, a troubleshooting wizard helps finish the task.

   C. With Windows 2000, if the proper device driver cannot be found or won't install properly, a troubleshooting wizard helps finish the task.

   D. With Windows 9x, if the proper device driver cannot be found or won't install properly, then the device cannot be installed at all.

7. The Small Computer System Interface (commonly known as SCSI) is yet another method for connecting peripherals. Which of the following are characteristics of SCSI? (Select all that apply.)

   A. SCSI is the best choice for high-speed connectivity.

   B. SCSI, when properly linked, can support up to 127 peripheral devices.

   C. SCSI can transfer either 16 or 32 bits of data at a time.

   D. SCSI can be added to desktop systems with an expansion card.

8. Which of the following are peripheral connection methods for Windows 9x and Windows 2000? (Select all that apply.)

   A. Parallel

   B. Serial

   C. SCSI

   D. USB

   E. IEEE 1394

9. You're using your USB port for your scanner. What is the preferred method for swapping your scanner with a previously configured digital camera?

   A. Shut down the computer, disconnect the scanner, connect the digital camera, and then turn your computer back on.

   B. With USB, you can hot-swap devices. Therefore, just disconnect the scanner, hook up the digital camera, and you're done.

   C. Turn off the scanner and disconnect it. Connect the digital camera. Reboot. You can now use your digital camera.

   D. None of the above. Digital cameras will not work on a USB port.

10. Which of the following are accepted methods for initiating the Add Printer Wizard (APW)? (Select all that apply.)

   A. Choose Start ➢ Settings ➢ Printers and double-click the Add Printer icon.

   B. Type **APW.EXE** at the DOS prompt.

   C. Double-click the Printers icon in Control Panel and double-click the Add Printer icon.

   D. Choose Start ➢ Run, type **APW.EXE**, and click OK.

11. Serial connections are very popular. One of the most popular applications of a serial connection is _____.

   A. Synchronizing two data sources

   B. Linking multiple peripherals

   C. Transferring large amounts of data at high speeds

   D. All of the above

12. What is the final step in setting up a newly installed printer?

   A. Configure the port settings

   B. Create a unique printer identification name

   C. Configure the Graphics setting

   D. Print a test page

13. FireWire, or IEEE 1394, is a relatively new peripheral connection method. What is FireWire used for?

   A. It is primarily used to download large video files to a PC.

   B. It is the preferred method for linking multiple peripherals.

   C. It provides direct access to the Internet, bypassing the modem.

   D. It is used to activate explosives via computer.

14. A previously installed Windows 9x printer needs to be modified for higher resolution. How can this be accomplished?

   A. Uninstall and then reinstall the printer, making your changes during the installation process.

   B. Right-click the printer icon, choose Properties, click the Graphics tab, and make your changes.

   C. Right-click the printer icon, choose Change Graphics, and make your changes.

   D. Right-click the printer icon, choose Properties, click Change Graphics, click Resolution, and make your changes.

15. One of the most popular connection methods is parallel. Which of the following are characteristics of a parallel connection? (Select all that apply.)

A. Transfer rate of 8 data bits at a time.

B. Usually used to connect printers.

C. New parallel ports can connect scanners and Zip drives.

D. Can connect multiple devices at the same time.

16. Plug-and-Play includes a troubleshooting wizard on which operating system?

A. Windows 95

B. Windows 98

C. Windows NT

D. Windows 2000

17. Which icon will allow you to manage print jobs as well as printer properties?

A. PRINTERS folder

B. Printer icon in the PRINTERS folder

C. Printer icon in the System Tray

D. Spooler control panel

18. In addition to the Add Printer Wizard, which other method(s) can be used to configure a printer? (Select all that apply.)

A. Copy the new driver to the C:\WINDOWS\PRINTERS directory

B. INSTALL on the manufacturer's disk

C. PSETUP in the C:\WINDOWS directory

D. SETUP on the manufacturer's disk

19. The Universal Serial Bus (USB), is a relatively new connection device. Which of the following are characteristics of USB?

A. Can connect a maximum of 127 external devices

B. Supports printers, scanners, joysticks, digital cameras, and mice

C. Faster data transfer rate than a serial port

D. All of the above

20. You've installed a printer for network use, but no one on the network is able to print to it. Which of the following would be a viable solution to fix the problem?

A. Right-click the Printer icon, click Network, and configure the printer as needed.

B. Right-click the Printer icon, click Properties, click the Sharing tab, and configure the printer as needed.

C. Open Control Panel, double-click the Printer icon, click Network, and configure the printer as needed.

D. Only a reinstall of the printer will enable it for network use.

Answers to Review Questions

1. **B.**   When installing a printer, you must always be sure to have an updated driver. Many printing problems originate with out-of-date printer drivers.

2. **C.**   During setup, you must point out a local printer port name to the network. This process is known as *capturing*. During normal setup, the default to capture a printer port is No. If you run the Add Printer Wizard again and change the answer to the Capture Printer Port question to Yes, your printer should then be able to print from DOS-based programs.

3. **C.**   The default setting for printing enables a feature that allows your printing to be done in the background while you work on other tasks. Spool Print Jobs is a property of most printers and if turned off will cause the behavior described in the question.

4. **A, D.**   Plug and Play will automatically detect new hardware and install the proper software. If it is not successful, you can use the Add New Hardware Wizard. You can access that program by the methods indicated in answers A and D.

5. **A, B.**   Serial connections have a transfer rate of one data bit at a time, a maximum speed of 128Kbps, and are very inexpensive to manufacture.

6. **C.**   One major difference between installing new hardware on a Windows 9*x* system versus a Windows 2000 system is that, if the proper device driver cannot be found or won't install properly, a Windows 2000 troubleshooting wizard helps to finish the task.

7. **A, C, D.**   SCSI offers an array of benefits, including high speeds, 16- or 32-bit data transfer rates, and ease of use via an expansion card, but it cannot support 127 peripheral devices. Only USB can do that.

8. **A, B, C, D, E.**   All of the options are peripheral connection methods.

9. **B.**   With USB, you can hot-swap devices. With the PC powered on, disconnect the scanner from the USB cable and connect the cable to the digital camera. There is no need to shut down the computer or reboot.

10. **A, C.**   As with most functions within Windows, there is more than one way to accomplish a task. To initiate the Add Printer Wizard, options A and C are equally correct.

11. **A.**   Serial connections are popular because they are so inexpensive to manufacture. But their transfer rate is slow, and only one peripheral can be connected to a serial port. They are, however, an excellent way to synchronize two data sources.

12. **D.**   Printing a test page is the final step in setting up a new printer.

13. **A.**   With a maximum data transfer rate of 400MBps, FireWire is primarily used to download large video files.

14. **B.**   It is relatively easy to make changes to installed printers. Right-clicking the printer icon and choosing Properties opens a series of printer property pages and functions.

15. A, B, C.   Parallel connections have a transfer rate of 8 data bits, they are primarily used to connect printers, and new parallel ports can connect other devices. However, they can connect only one device at a time.

16. D.   When Plug-and-Play does not work, Windows 2000 has a troubleshooting wizard to assist the user. The Add New Hardware Wizard in Windows 2000 can also be used to add new hardware and update drivers for existing hardware.

17. C.   While a document is printing, a printer icon appears in the System Tray. By double-clicking it, you can open it and manage your print jobs as well as the printer properties from menus within it.

18. B, D.   There are printers for which the APW does not work. In such instances, you will need to run SETUP or INSTALL from the vendor printer disk to install the appropriate printing software.

19. D.   The Universal Serial Bus (USB) connects up to 127 external devices, supports most peripherals (including printers, scanners, digital cameras, mice, and so on), and provides a high data-transfer rate.

20. B.   One of the tabs on the printer Properties page is Sharing. That tab is used to share the printer on the network.

Chapter

16

Windows Networking

THE FOLLOWING OBJECTIVES ARE COVERED IN THIS CHAPTER:

✓ 4.1 Identify the networking capabilities of Windows. Given configuration parameters, configure the operating system to connect to a network.

✓ 4.2 Identify the basic Internet protocols and terminologies. Identify procedures for establishing Internet connectivity. In a given scenario, configure the operating system to connect to and use Internet resources.

When the first version of this book appeared, we noted, "It seems that everywhere you look today, someone is talking about the Internet." Well, we hadn't seen anything at that point. Having toppled into the new millennium, we really need to modify that statement to "It seems that everywhere you look today, someone is *using* the Internet."

In the space of just a few years, computer networking has gone from an obscure technology to a part of everyday life. Computers are being connected to networks and to each other at a flabbergasting rate, and as a computer professional, one of your primary jobs over the next decade may be to connect your clients' PCs to a network or to manage their access resources on their local network or the Internet.

Just look at the preponderance of website addresses on radio and television commercials today. The Web has become a hot button that advertising companies love to exploit. But few people realize what the Internet actually is. Some people think it's a public thoroughfare for information (hence the moniker *information superhighway*). Others believe it to be some kind of new high-tech toy. In reality, however, the *Internet* is a mesh of interconnected private networks that spans the globe. Whether it is the Internet or a local network at your school or place of work, the basic concepts remain the same. Because of this, to understand the Internet, you must understand its underlying infrastructures: networks.

Simply put, a *network* is a number of devices (not just computers) connected together for the purpose of sharing resources, such as printers or disk space. Networks provide the physical path upon which computers communicate. When two networks connect to each other, they form a single larger network called an *internetwork*. The largest of these internetworks is the Internet, which spans the globe and reaches into nearly every major business in the world, as well as into millions of homes. Networking software is written to be used by several people at once and to perform a variety of functions such as e-mail, collaboration, and business management, whereas networking hardware includes the machines that make that collaboration possible.

The A+ exam includes information about basic networking concepts, the Internet, and setting up computers to access both regular business networks and the Internet. We will discuss the installation and configuration of connecting to local area networks (LANs) and to the Internet from both Windows 9x, Windows 2000, and XP. Luckily, much of this information is similar in both systems, but as always, there are some significant differences.

The networking software business includes quite a few major players (like Novell, Microsoft, IBM, and Seagate). However, there are clearly two leaders in the game: Novell (whose company headquarters is in Provo, UT) and Microsoft (headquartered in Redmond, WA). Each company produces several software products for networks, but in the following sections, we'll focus on the different ways that Windows 9x/NT/2000/XP connect to the networking operating systems (NOSs) made by these two companies.

Even as Microsoft was creating both clients and servers, other companies were specializing in one or the other. One of the most successful was Novell (www.novell.com), which has been a market leader in providing networking and network management software for the last decade. Novell has developed a NOS called NetWare (currently at version 6.0). NetWare has been the 800-pound gorilla of the networking world for over a decade; however, Microsoft's Windows 2000 Server and Windows 2003 Server is following on the heels of the immensely successful Windows NT 4 Server and has made substantial gains over the last few years. Both NetWare and Windows 2000 Server and Windows 2003 Server are extremely common at this time. Other systems, such as Sun's Solaris or the open-source Linux variants, will not be specifically discussed here.

 The Internet is still very much a Unix world, so our discussion of how to access the Internet is in some ways a look at how to attach to everything that isn't NetWare or Windows.

Other than making sure you know what they are, we won't discuss the NOS servers themselves. Rather, we will look at how Windows implements various networking elements and examine their networking capabilities when they're hooked up to other systems. Also, because the A+ exam deals only with the client side of networking (that is, getting to resources that are already on the network), we won't talk extensively about how any particular version of Windows works as a network server. Nonetheless, both OSs can act as servers; if you are interested in learning more about this topic, refer to *Network+ Study Guide* (Sybex, 2001).

Windows Networking Basics

When MS-DOS was developed, it was designed to be a simple, stand-alone operating system. So, it didn't contain any network software except SHARE.EXE. SHARE.EXE was designed as an add-on to popular networking software that allowed two users to edit the same file at the same time on a network. Without SHARE.EXE, when a second user tried to open a file that the first user had opened, they got an error message. With SHARE.EXE installed, when the second user tried to open the file, they received a message saying that the file was being used by someone else and offering to provide a copy of the file.

DOS could run client software for Novell and Microsoft networks. Most client software for DOS (and Windows 3.x) falls into the category of redirection software. This software redirects requests bound for *local resources* out to network resources (Figure 16.1). For example, with network client software installed, you could point a DOS drive letter to some disk space on the network. When you saved a file to that drive letter, you were really saving that file to a server. But, as far as DOS was concerned, it was accessing a local drive letter.

FIGURE 16.1 Network client software redirects local requests to the network.

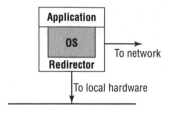

 With *client software*, a computer can connect to a server and access the network resources hosted by that server.

As discussed earlier, Windows 3.1 was little more than a pretty face sitting on top of the MS-DOS OS; as a result, Windows 3.1 networking was every bit as limited as DOS networking. In an effort to help, Microsoft brought out Windows 3.11, which has an add-on called Windows for Workgroups. This add-on allows a machine running DOS and Windows 3.11 to participate in a peer-to-peer network and share its files and any local printers with the rest of the network. Windows for Workgroups also allows a user to add 32-bit TCP/IP networking. However, although it was far better than before, even Windows 3.11 was relatively limited in its networking capacities.

Microsoft was working on more than its clients, though. They had released Microsoft LAN Manager, a relatively primitive network server that allowed users to access centralized resources on the network. LAN Manager evolved into Windows NT; as part of that evolution, the LAN Manager networking software was integrated into the Windows NT Workstation client, giving Microsoft its first really effective network client.

 Servers are computers that offer up resources (files, printers) or services (name resolution, time synchronization) to other machines on the network. They use special software to detect and respond to client requests.

Windows 95 and Beyond

When Windows 95 was released in late 1995, it wasn't the first Microsoft OS to contain built-in networking. Both the Windows NT OS and, to a lesser extent, Windows for Workgroups already had provided networking functionality. However, Windows 95 was similar to the Monolith from the movie *2001*, in that it issued in a new age of PC networking by providing built-in networking that was easy to use and configure. Suddenly, normal people could get their modems to work and corporate users could use the network without constantly getting sharing errors (SHARE.EXE was no more). Improved support for all phases of the networking process rounded out the package.

Installing Networking Hardware and Software

Before you can begin the configuration of your network, you must have a network card installed in the machine. Installing a network card is a fairly simple task if you have installed any expansion card before; a network interface card (NIC) is just a special type of expansion card. To install a NIC, follow these steps:

1. Move jumpers or flip DIP switches on the expansion card to set it to the correct IRQ/DMA/IO port settings as per the factory instructions. If the card uses a software setup program, you can ignore this step. Most newer NICs do not have jumpers and are entirely software configured.

2. Power off the PC, remove the case cover, and insert the expansion card into an open slot.

3. Secure the expansion card with the screw provided.

4. Put the case cover back on the computer and power it up (you can run the software configuration at this step, if necessary). If there are conflicts, change any parameters so that the NIC doesn't conflict with any existing hardware.

5. Install a driver for the NIC for the type of OS that you have. Windows should auto-detect the NIC and install the driver automatically. It may ask you to provide a copy of the necessary driver if it does not recognize what type of NIC you have installed. If the card is not detected at all, run the Add New Hardware Wizard by double-clicking Add New Hardware in Control Panel.

After installing a NIC, you must hook the card to the network using the cable supplied by your network administrator. Attach this patch cable to the connector on the NIC and to a port in the wall, thus connecting your PC to the rest of the network.

Sometimes older NICs conflict with newer Plug-and-Play (PnP) hardware. Additionally, some newer NICs with PnP capability don't like some kinds of networking software. To resolve a PnP conflict of the latter type, disable PnP on the NIC either with a jumper or with the software setup program. In this chapter, we will assume that your NIC is installed and the drivers are loaded. For more information on resolving hardware issues, refer to Chapter 18.

Configuring Windows 9*x* as a Network Client

The configuration of Windows 9*x* networking centers on Control Panel's Network program. From this single interface, you configure client software, protocols, NICs, and the network services you want this machine to perform. To access the Network program, select Start ➢ Settings ➢ Control Panel and double-click Network in the Control Panel window that appears.

Windows *9x* will display the Network window. The Network window has three areas of interest: the components list, the primary logon list, and the File And Print Sharing button.

 If you already have some networking components installed, you can right-click the Network Neighborhood icon on your Desktop and choose Properties from the pop-up menu.

Windows *9x* Network Components

Let's review the four basic types of networking components that can be added in the Network panel, as shown in Figure 16.2. You can reach this screen by clicking Add on the Configuration tab.

FIGURE 16.2 The Select Network Component Type window

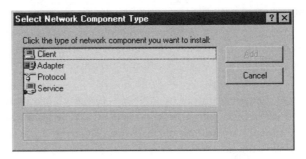

The networking components are as follows:

Client As mentioned before, the *client* is software that allows your machine to talk to servers on the network. Each server vendor uses a different way of designing its network access, though; so if a computer needs to get to both a Novell and a Microsoft network, the computer must have two pieces of client software installed—one for each type of server. The three network client groups supported by Windows *9x* are for Microsoft, Novell, and Banyan servers.

Adapter The *adapter* is technically the peripheral hardware that installs into your computer, but in this case, it refers to the software that defines how the computer talks to that hardware. If you do not have the proper adapter software installed, your PC will not be able to talk properly to the NIC, and you will not be able to access the network until you change the adapter to one that is compatible with the hardware. It is often best to think of an adapter as a network driver, which is what it is. Windows *9x* supports a long list of adapters; with support for more recent hardware. Adapter drivers can also be downloaded from most NIC vendors' websites.

Protocol Once the client service and the adapter are installed, you have cleared a path for communication from your machine to network servers. The *protocol* is the computer language you use to facilitate communication between the machines. If you want to talk to someone, you have to speak their language. Computers are no different. Among the languages available to Windows *9x* are NetBEUI, NWLink, and *TCP/IP*.

Service A *service* is a component that gives a bit back to the network that gives it so much. Services add functionality to the network by providing resources or doing tasks for other computers. In Windows 9*x*, services include file and printer sharing for Microsoft or Novell networks.

Installing Components in Windows 9*x*

Suppose you want to connect to Microsoft servers on your network (including Windows 2000 Server, 2000 Professional, or Windows 9*x* with sharing enabled). To connect to this network, you must have at least three components (no services, the fourth component, are required at this point):

- A client, such as Client for Microsoft Networks
- A protocol (whichever protocol is in use on the network; generally TCP/IP)
- An adapter (whatever is in the PC)

To install a client and protocol for use with your network adapter, follow these steps:

1. Click the Add button toward the bottom of the Network window to display the screen shown in Figure 16.2.

2. Choose the type of item you are going to install. In this example, you're installing the Client for Microsoft Networks, so click Client and then click Add.

3. You will see a screen similar to the one in Figure 16.3. It is the standard "pick your component" screen that Windows 9*x* uses. On the left, select the company whose software (or driver) you want to install (in this example, Microsoft). When you have selected a manufacturer, a list of the software that Windows 9*x* can install from that company appears on the right.

FIGURE 16.3   Selecting the software you want to install

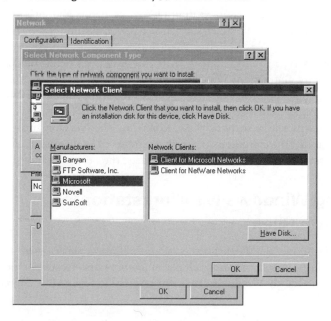

4. Click Client For Microsoft Networks when it appears in the right pane, and then click OK. Windows 9x will bring you back to the Configuration tab of the Network program.

5. Once the client is installed, you can verify that the protocol you need is present. TCP/IP generally installs by default, but this is not always so. If it is not present, click Add on the Configuration tab. In the Select Network Component Type window, select Protocol and then click Add. In the Select Network Client window, select Microsoft in the Manufacturers list and TCP/IP in the Network Protocols list. Click OK to complete the installation.

WARNING   When it is first installed, TCP/IP is configured to expect that a special server called a *Dynamic Host Configuration Protocol (DHCP)* server is available on the network to provide it with information about the network. If a DHCP server is not available, the protocol will not function properly. Consult your administrator to see whether the network uses DHCP or static addressing. In static addressing, all TCP/IP settings must be manually added, and in this case, you will need additional information from the administrator. TCP/IP will be discussed in more detail later in this chapter.

The list of components should reflect your additions and show which network components are currently installed on this machine. If there are a number of components, a scroll bar appears on the right-hand side. The scroll bar allows you to see all the clients, network adapters, protocols, and services that might be installed. Once the client and protocol are installed, you have all the software you need to connect to the network. At that point, just a few choices remain. Don't close that Network program yet!

Primary Network Logon

A Windows 9x workstation can support multiple simultaneous network types. For example, a user can log on to both Novell and Microsoft networks, assuming they have both network clients installed and configured correctly. The Primary Network *Logon* drop-down list determines which network type you log on to first. If you have not yet installed a network client, this list gives you only one option: Windows Logon.

You have installed a Microsoft network client, so select the Client for Microsoft Networks as the primary logon, as displayed in Figure 16.4.

After you make this selection, click the OK button. The Network program closes, and you are asked to restart the computer so the new settings can take effect. Until you reboot, the network will not function. When the machine restarts, the network should be available.

Configuring Windows NT Workstation as a Network Client

For a long time, Windows NT Workstation was the Windows platform of choice for corporate network workstations. It is stable and includes many network-aware components. Today it is quickly being replaced by Windows 2000 Professional (and to some degree, Windows XP Professional).

FIGURE 16.4   Choosing a Primary Network Logon

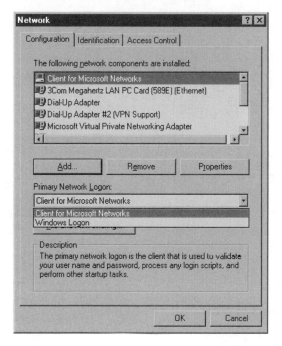

NT Network Components

The Windows NT Workstation network software contains items similar to those in Windows 9*x* networking, clients, adapters, protocols, and services. However, in Windows NT it is much easier to configure complex networking environments. As with Windows 9*x*, the network is configured through the Network control panel applet, which can be accessed by going to Start ➢ Settings ➢ Control Panel and double-clicking on Network. You can also access it by right-clicking on the Network Neighborhood icon on the Desktop and choosing Properties. Both options display the window shown in Figure 16.5.

As with Windows 9*x*, you must have three things in order to network: a client (which is installed under the Services tab), a protocol, and an adapter. In addition, the protocol must be bound (logically associated with) to both the adapter and the client. The workstation must be running the same protocol as the rest of the network and be configured similarly. By default, the Workstation service (together with the NetBIOS Interface service) provides access to Microsoft networking servers.

    The default protocol that is installed when you install the network is TCP/IP.

In addition, Windows NT Workstation must be part of either a domain or workgroup in order to properly participate on the network.

FIGURE 16.5   Windows NT Network control panel applet

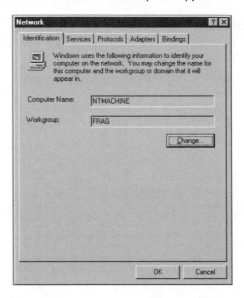

Installing Components in NT

Because the network adapter driver is installed automatically when you boot the computer after physically installing it, you must install and configure the other components (either client or protocol). To install networking components, use the following procedure:

1. Open the Network control panel applet as described earlier.

2. Click on the tab that represents the software you wish to install (Services for clients; Protocols for protocols).

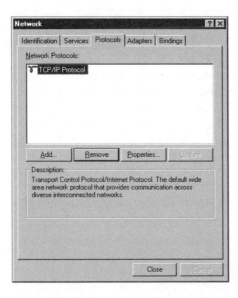

3. Click Add to add a new entry to the list of drivers already configured for this computer (in this example, we will show protocols). A window appears, asking you which component (in this case, which protocol) you wish to install. This list includes the protocols Windows NT already has on the installation CD. If the item you wish to add is not listed, you can add it by clicking the Have Disk button and telling Windows NT where to find the installation files for the item you are installing. Once you have selected the item you are going to install, click OK to begin the installation.

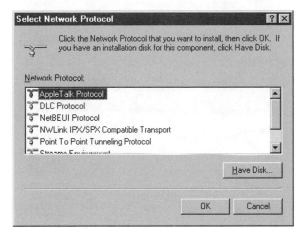

4. Windows asks you for the location of the Windows NT Setup files (if you chose an item from the Windows list, instead of the Have Disk option). It automatically displays the location from which Windows NT was installed. Insert the Windows NT installation CD-ROM and click Continue. If you want Windows to copy the Windows NT files from a different location, type it in the space given and then click Continue.

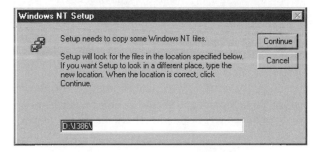

5. Windows NT copies the files necessary to install the item from the CD-ROM or other installation location and then returns you to the Network control panel applet. Click OK to accept the newly installed item. Windows completes the installation by storing all the binding information and reconfiguring the network with the new settings.

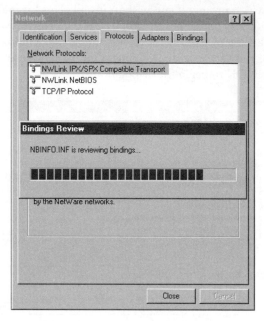

6. Windows tells you that the new network settings won't take effect until you reboot the system, and asks whether would you like to do this. If you answer Yes, Windows shuts down and reboots the system. If you answer No, Windows returns you to the Desktop, but you will still need to reboot before the settings take effect.

 Once you've rebooted, you should be able to use the new network component. If you experience any problems, check the Event Viewer.

Logging On in Windows NT

The logon procedure for Windows NT is much different than it is for other OSs. Upon system boot, you see a screen similar to the one shown in Figure 16.6. To begin the logon process, press Ctrl+Alt+Del (a.k.a. The Three Finger Salute) simultaneously. On previous versions of Windows, doing so might reboot the computer, but on Windows NT, it begins the logon procedure (providing you are not already logged on).

FIGURE 16.6   Beginning logon screen

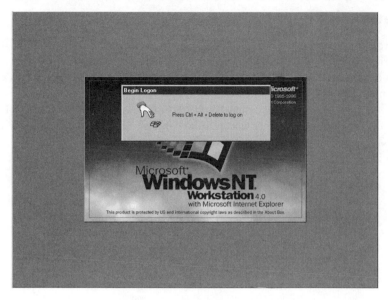

You will now see the window shown in Figure 16.7. The window may be slightly different if the Windows NT Workstation you are using is a member of a domain (it asks you which domain you want to use to authenticate the user you are logging on with). Enter your username and password, and then click OK to log on. If you enter the information properly, you will be presented with a Desktop.

FIGURE 16.7   Logon screen

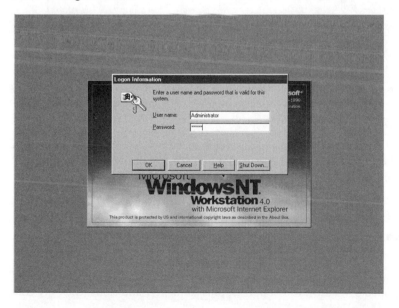

Configuring Windows 2000 and Windows XP Professional as a Network Client

For the most part, the concepts behind configuring Windows 9x are the same as the concepts for configuring in Windows 2000/XP. You still need a client, a protocol, and an adapter, for instance. The difference is in the way they are configured, because Microsoft has changed a few things in Windows 2000/XP.

The Network program is now called Network and Dial-up Connections (NDC) (or in Windows XP, Network and Internet Connections) and is organized differently. When you first access the NDC window, instead of a list of all components, you are greeted by a Make New Connection icon and a Local Area Connection icon, as shown in Figure 16.8.

FIGURE   16.8   The Network and Dial-up Connections window

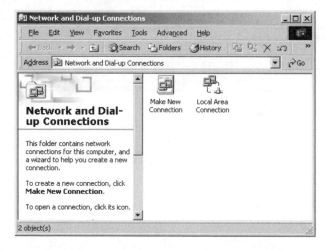

 WARNING If you do not see a Local Area Connection icon, your NIC or modem is not present or is not functioning properly. If you see more than one LAN connection, it means you have multiple NICs installed (Windows 2000/XP can support multiple NICs).

To add client software and protocols, right-click the LAN connection and select Properties. You should find that everything you need is in place, because the MS client and IP are installed by default on the LAN adapter.

 WARNING File and Printer Sharing for Microsoft Networks is also installed by default. To disable it, click the check mark next to the service. To remove it completely, click Uninstall.

You can also add additional clients, protocols, and services. Windows 2000/XP support the same components Windows 9x supports, plus some new additions (the only component not

supported in 2000 that is in 9*x* is the Banyan client). Once you have verified that the Client for Microsoft Networks and TCP/IP are installed, click OK. You should not have to reboot after making changes to the network settings in Windows 2000/XP, but in Windows 9*x* you do have to reboot.

 It should be noted that NetBEUI is not supported in Windows XP by default.

Logging On to Windows 2000

As shown in Figure 16.9, users are presented with a number of options when they start Windows 2000. The user logon system comes up immediately at the end of the Windows 2000 startup process; the system requires, at the very least, a username and password, but it allows for other choices. This is due to the fact that its security structure requires *every* user on a Windows 2000 Professional system to have a unique name and password to identify them and their configuration.

FIGURE 16.9   The Windows 2000 logon screen

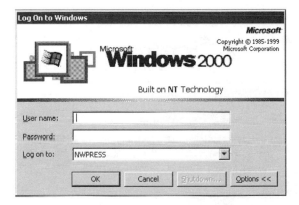

The options available on this screen include the following:

User Name   The *username* defines a particular individual on the computer. Each user has their own Desktop and personal settings and can be given or restricted from particular files or tasks. This field displays letters as you type them and is not case sensitive. You may enter a username of any length less than or equal to 20 characters (for both Windows 2000 and Windows XP).

Password   A *password* is a personal identifier that is used to verify that users are who they say they are. Without a verified username and password set, a user cannot log on to a Windows 2000 Professional workstation. The password field displays only asterisk (*) characters as you type, and the field is case sensitive. The password can be up to 127 characters in length (although some utilities limit what can be entered).

Log On From   This field allows the user to set the security context from which they will be authenticated. Windows 2000 Professional workstations have their own user database, but they can also authenticate using a shared database, such as the Windows 2000 Server Active Directory.

You cannot type new information into the Log On To field, but if you have multiple authentication options configured, you can select from among them using the down arrow.

Log On Using Dial-Up Networking This option allows a user to establish a dial-up connection to a remote network and then authenticate against a database over that connection. It is rarely used, but it may be needed in high-security environments. It only shows up if you don't currently have a network connection but do have a dial-up connection.

In order to log on, you need to enter valid credentials. You may have created an administrator account and password during setup, or you may need to get this information from a network administrator.

Once you have entered your credentials, Windows 2000 configures your Desktop and loads any personal settings and user policy settings associated with your account. At that point, you can begin using Windows 2000.

If it is your first time logging on to the system as a particular user, it may take a minute or two for your initial system environment to be set up. A number of wizards will run, and an introduction screen will be displayed, as in Figure 16.10.

FIGURE 16.10   The Getting Started screen

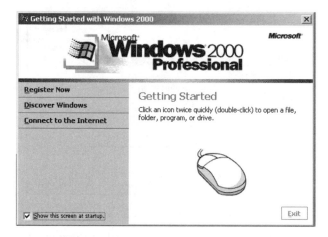

Logging On to Windows XP

Even though the networking components are mostly the same as Windows 2000, the logon process is slightly different. At bootup, Windows XP displays a list of users configured for that machine. To log on, all you need to do is click on the user you wish to log on as. Enter the password (if prompted), and Windows XP will log you on and display the Desktop.

This method is based on the Fast User Switching mode (the default) which allows user's programs to stay running while switching users. This option can be turned on and off in the Control Panel. If turned off, a user must completely log out and close all their programs before another user can log on.

Configuring Clients for NetWare Network Access

Windows 9*x*/NT/2000/XP handle the addition of a network client for NetWare in similar ways. Add (9*x*) or install (2000/NT/XP) the client, and it automatically installs the NetWare-compatible NWLink (IPX/SPX) protocol for you (Figure 16.11). Once you have these, you are presented with a NetWare logon option screen on startup, where you can choose the NetWare server or tree you wish to log on to (Figure 16.12).

FIGURE 16.11   Microsoft Novell Client with the NetWare client and NWLink installed

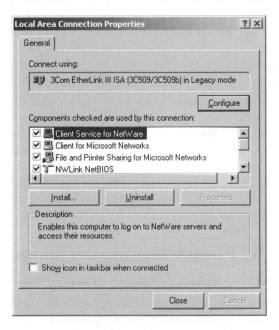

FIGURE 16.12   The NetWare default server/tree option screen

The *tree* is a group of machines that share security and configuration information. Both Novell's NetWare and Microsoft's Active Directory use tree structures to store information and authenticate users. To access the NetWare tree more efficiently, frequent NetWare users should download the newest version of NetWare's own client software for 9x/NT/2000/XP. It is available at `http://download.novell.com/filedist/pages/PublicSearch.jsp`.

Configuring Windows to Share Files and Printers

As noted before, it is possible to set up both Windows 9x and Windows 2000 Professional to share files and printers with other users on the network. Networking in which users share each other's resources is called *peer-to-peer networking*; each computer acts as both a client and a server.

You have already completed the client configuration. This is a must, actually, because file and printer sharing is possible only if the proper client and protocol are already set up. Now they are, so all you need to do is turn on file and printer sharing and then specify which resources you wish to share. Even after file and printer sharing is enabled, you must specifically share any directory or printer that you want to make available on the network.

Enabling File and Printer Sharing on Windows 9x

To add file and printer sharing services, perform the following steps:

1. Open the Network program and click the File And Print Sharing button. You will see a screen that lets you select which services you want to share (Figure 16.13).

2. Click the box next to the I Want To Be Able To Give Others Access To My Files option if you want to share files on your machine with someone else on the network. If you want others to be able to print to a printer hooked to your machine, click the box next to the I Want To Be Able To Allow Others To Print to My Printer(s) option.

3. The service called File and Printer Sharing for Microsoft Networks now appears in the list of installed network components. In addition to specifying what you are going to share, you must specify how security will be handled. There are two options: Share-Level Access Control and User-Level Access Control. With share-level control, you supply a username, password, and security settings for each resource you share. With user-level control, there is a central database of users (usually administered by the network administrator) that Windows 9x can use to specify security settings for each shared resource. Most of the time, share-level access control is fine. User-level control is needed in only a few cases (such as in a network where the administrator has said you will do it this way). To specify these settings, choose the Access Control tab in the Network window (Figure 16.14) and select the appropriate option.

FIGURE 16.13   Enabling file and printer sharing

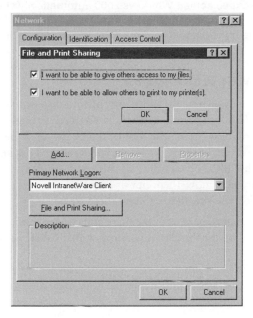

FIGURE 16.14   Specifying the access control method

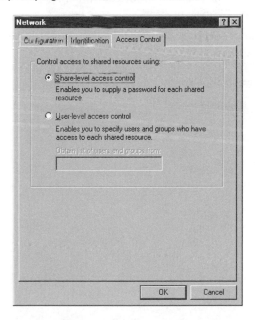

4. Click OK to save all of these new settings.

5. Windows 9*x* copies some files and asks you to reboot (big surprise, huh?). Reboot your computer to begin sharing files and printers.

As described earlier, Windows 2000 automatically starts and installs File and Printer Sharing when a network connection is created. Unless you have disabled it, no additional configuration is required to begin sharing resources.

Sharing Folders with Windows 9*x*

If you have a folder on your machine that contains information everyone should be able to see, you need to enable *file sharing*. Sharing is generally enabled through Windows Explorer.

Any folder can be shared (including the root of the C: drive). When you share a folder, the person you share it with can see not only the folder you've shared but also any folders inside that folder. Therefore, you should be certain that all subfolders under a share are intended to be shared as well. If they are not, move them out of the share path.

Once you have decided what to share, follow these steps:

1.   Right-click the folder that is the start of the share and choose Sharing from the menu that pops up. This option brings up the Properties window of that folder with the Sharing tab in front.

You can also access the Sharing tab by right-clicking a folder, choosing Properties, and clicking the tab.

2.   To start the share, click the Shared As radio button. Two previously grayed-out fields become visible (Figure 16.15):

Share Name   The name used to access this folder. It should accurately represent what you are sharing. (Required.)

FIGURE 16.15   Enabling a share

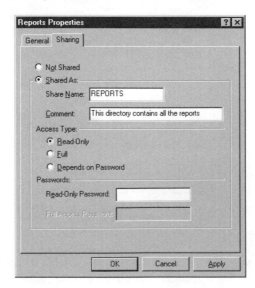

Comment   Allows you to enter a description of the share as a comment that helps identify the contents of the share to users. (Optional.)

3.   You may specify the access rights and password(s) for the share. There are three options for access rights when you're using the share-level security scheme. Click the radio button next to the option you want to use:

Read-Only   With this option selected, anyone accessing the share can only open and read the files inside the folder and any subfolders. You must specify a password that users can use to access the share in read-only mode.

Full   In full access mode, everyone accessing the share has the ability to do anything to the files in the folder as well as any subfolders. This includes being able to delete those files. You must specify a password that the users can use to access this share.

Depends On Password   This option is probably the best option of the three. With this option, users can use one password to access the share in read-only mode and a different password to access it in full-access mode. You can give everyone the read-only password so they can view the files and give the full-access password only to users who need to change the files.

By default, the group Everyone has full control permissions to the share in Windows NT/2000/XP. This means anyone on the network can come in and view, modify, or even delete the files in the share. Often this situation is a bit too dangerous, and as such, you will probably want to use a read-only or depends-on password security setting. (A Windows 9*x* share is read-only by default. Anyone on the network can view files in the share.)

4.   Click OK to share the folder. Notice that the folder now has a hand underneath it, indicating that it is being shared (Figure 16.16).

FIGURE 16.16   The Reports folder after being shared

In Windows 2000, sharing is enabled in exactly the same way as in Windows 9x. The only difference is that in 2000, you can enable NTFS and use it to secure files and folders. At that point, all you have to do is create a share on Windows 2000 Professional to the directories you wish to allow the network access to, and the permissions set at the file level will be enforced. Share-level permissions control how the resource is accessed from the network, and NTFS permissions control the access to the files and folders themselves both locally and through the network.

Sharing Printers with Windows 9x

Sharing printers is similar to sharing folders. The procedure is as follows:

1. You must have the printer correctly set up to print on the machine that will be hosting it.

2. Right-click on the printer in the `Printers` folder and click Sharing. The printer property page appears with the Sharing tab selected to allow you to share the printer.

3. Click Shared As and specify a name for the share (Figure 16.17). The name defaults to a truncated version of the name you gave the printer when you installed it. The name you give this share (called the *share name*) should be something that everyone will recognize when they see it on the network and that accurately describes the printer. This one is called DavesHP so people will know that it's next to Dave's workstation and that it's an HP printer.

FIGURE 16.17   Sharing a printer

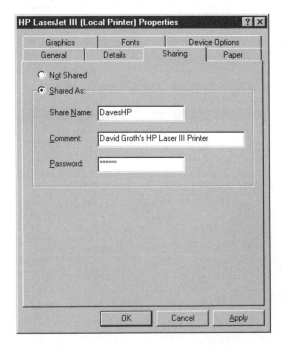

4. In addition to specifying the name of the printer share, you can enter a comment that describes the printer accurately.

5. Specify a password that users must enter in order to install this printer on their workstations (they won't have to enter it every time they print).

6. Click OK. Windows *9x* prompts you for the password again, just to verify that you know what it is and that you didn't misspell it. Retype the password in the box that appears and click OK, and the share will be active. Notice that the printer in the `Printers` folder in Figure 16.18 has a hand under it, indicating that it is shared.

FIGURE 16.18   The printer is now shared

Enabling Sharing in Windows NT

Because Windows NT was designed to be a networked OS, it has more robust features, including user-based security. That is, different users that connect to a shared folder can have different permissions on that folder.

Unlike in Windows *9x*, sharing is installed in Windows NT by default, so you don't have to install it. You must, however, set up the user accounts that will be accessing resources from this computer. By default, all users have all rights to any folder you share, so it is necessary to first create user accounts and set up security for those accounts. You must then share them out and select which permissions to use. A *permission* is a specific type of security ability that you assign to a user for a specific object. Permissions define who can do what to any object within Windows.

Creating User Accounts in NT

In order to assign different security to different users, you must create user accounts within Windows NT. That way, you can assign permissions for a particular resource based on the user account a user logs on with. You create user accounts in Windows NT Workstation with User Manager. To start User Manager, click Start ➤ Programs ➤ Administrative Tools ➤ User Manager. You will see a screen like the one in Figure 16.19.

FIGURE 16.19   User Manager for Windows NT Workstation

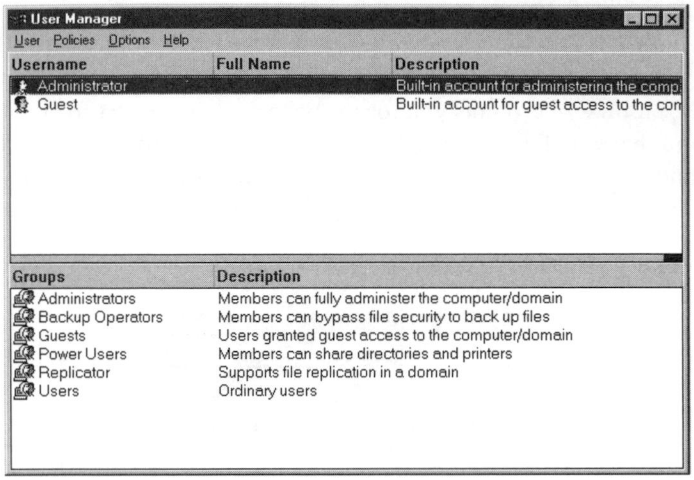

To add a new user, follow these steps:

1.   Click the User menu and select New User. Doing so brings up the screen in Figure 16.20.

FIGURE 16.20   Creating a new user

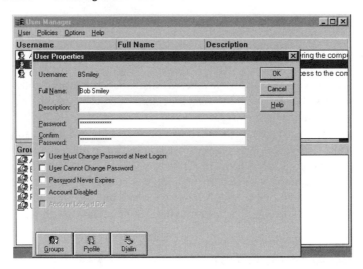

2.   In the fields provided, enter the username the user will log on with and type in a password (you must enter it again in the Confirm Password field to make sure you didn't type it wrong).

3.   You can now select various account behavior options using the check boxes (you can set the same options after creating the user by entering User Manager and double-clicking on the user):

User Must Change Password At Next Logon   Allows the user to choose their own password, once they log on using the password you supplied. They are forced to change it right then and there in order to continue the logon process.

User Cannot Change Password   Prevents a user from changing their own password. This is a useful feature if you have a generic account used for dial-up or some other access and you don't want different users changing the password.

Password Never Expires   Causes the user's password to never expire. It is possible to set up account policies so that a password expires every so often (every 30 days, for example), thus forcing the user to change it.

Account Disabled   Prevents a user from logging on using this account. You may want to disable an account when a user will be gone for an extended period of time, but will be returning.

4. You can now add the user to a user group. *User groups* associate users of like security settings or types so that permissions can be assigned at the group level for all users within that group. For example, if you want this user to be an administrator, add them to the Administrators group. All permissions assigned to the Administrators group will also be given to this user. To assign a user to a group, click the Groups button; the window shown in Figure 16.21 will appear. The groups of which this user is a member are shown in the left column (all new users are members of the Users group by default), and the available groups are shown on the right. Click the group in the Not Member Of list and click the Add button. The group name pops over to the Member Of list, and the user is now a member of that group. Click OK to accept the new group membership.

You can add a user to a group at any time. Just start User Manager, double-click the user you want to add to a group, and then click the Groups button.

FIGURE 16.21   Adding a user to a group

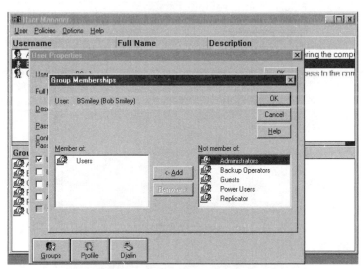

5. Click OK until you are back at the user listing screen. Notice in Figure 16.22 that a new user is shown in the list. You are now ready to share folders and printers with this new user.

FIGURE 16.22   New user added

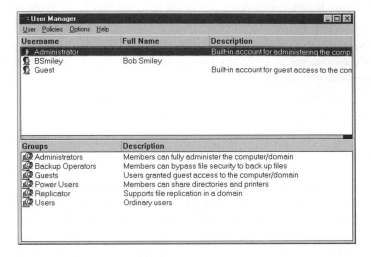

Sharing Folders in NT

Sharing folders in Windows NT is similar to sharing folders in Windows 9*x*. Use Explorer to navigate to the folder you want to share, right-click on it, and choose Sharing. Once this is done, you'll see a window like the one in Figure 16.23. The default setting for all folders is Not Shared. To share the folder, click the Shared As radio button. The display changes to allow you to change the settings. The most important setting is Share Name. By default, Windows chooses a share name for you, based on the name of the folder. You can accept this name or choose your own, but keep it simple.

FIGURE 16.23   Folder sharing setup

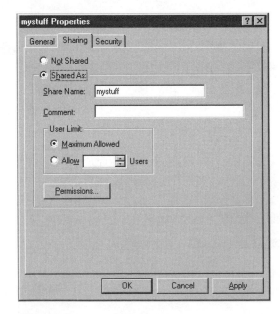

Once you have chosen to share a folder, you should examine the permissions for the share. Two types of permissions are used with Windows NT:

Share Permissions   Control access to the information through the share and are simpler.

NTFS Permissions   Control access to the information stored on the disk, accessed from either the local computer or the network. The share permissions control access through the network, while NTFS permissions control the ultimate access to the file or folder. Think of share permissions as the window through which you access the file or folder through the network. If the window is closed, you can't access the files through the network, even if you do have all the NTFS permissions in the world.

In this chapter, you will only learn about the share permissions, for the purposes of the A+ exam.

 If a Windows NT drive has been formatted with NTFS, you will see a Permissions option under the Security tab of the folder's properties. These are NTFS permissions.

Windows NT uses four types of share permissions:

Full Control   Gives the user full control over the folder and the files within it. They can add files, delete files, rename them, and so on. By default, the group Everyone has Full Control permissions for every new share.

Change   Allows a user to do everything that Full Control allows, except administrative permissions (like changing the share permissions for other users).

Read   Allows a user to see files within the folder and open them, including executing any programs within that folder. However, they cannot delete or change the files in any way.

No Access   Prevents a user from having any access to the share.

You can change the permissions for a share as follows:

1. Click the Permissions button as shown earlier in Figure 16.23. You will see a window like the one in Figure 16.24. In this window, you can see that the Everyone group has been assigned the Full Control permission.

FIGURE 16.24   Setting access through share permissions

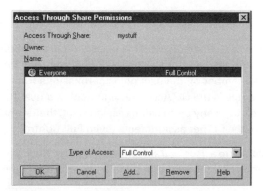

2. To add permissions for a user or group, click the Add button at the bottom of this window. You are presented with a list of groups (Figure 16.25). You can also see a list of users by clicking the Show Users button (it adds all the users to the list of groups and allows you to select them).

FIGURE 16.25   Add Users and Groups permissions window

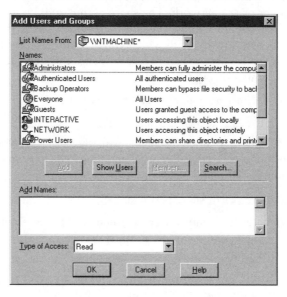

3. Select the user or group for which you wish to add permissions, and then click Add. The user or group pops into the area below the user list.

4. While the user or group is selected, choose the permission(s) you want them to have from the drop-down list and click OK to accept it.

5. Click OK to close the Access Through Share Permissions window.

Real World Scenario

Server, May I?

When you're setting up share permissions, you need to understand a few basic rules:

-   *Permission assignments are cumulative.* If you assign one set of permissions to a user account for a share, and then assign another set of permissions for the same share to a group the user is a member of, the user gains permissions from both assignments. The exception to this rule is the No Access assignment. If a user has been assigned the No Access permission from any permissions assignment, their rights for that share are No Access, regardless of their other assignments (even Full Control).

-   *If you don't specify access to a user for a share, no access is implied.* So, if you don't specifically assign a user rights to a share (either through a user or group assignment), they can't access it.

- *You cannot permanently lock out an administrator from a resource on a Windows NT computer.* The administrator can always take ownership of a resource and reassign permissions to it.

- *Directories and files within a share inherit the permissions assigned to the parent.* When you access a share, you gain whatever permissions have been set for that share for your user. However, NTFS may restrict these permissions further.

Sharing Printers in Windows NT

Sharing printers is almost the same in Windows NT as in Windows 9*x*: Open the Printers folder (Start ➤ Settings ➤ Printers), right-click on the printer you wish to share, and choose Sharing from the pop-up menu. From there you can share the printer by changing the Not Shared radio button to Shared and entering a share name for the printer.

The two main differences are the automatic driver download and security. With automatic driver download, you highlight which drivers should be managed for this printer (that is, which platforms). When you click OK to begin sharing the printer, Windows NT copies drivers for the printer to the computer's hard drive and distributes them automatically when users connect to the share. It may require that you have multiple platform driver disks available when you share the printer so that you can copy the driver files.

To enable automatic driver download, you only need to select the platforms you wish to support under the Alternate Drivers list (shown in Figure 16.26). Then, click OK and insert the driver disk(s) for your printer for the platforms you specify.

FIGURE 16.26   Alternate Drivers list in Windows NT printer sharing

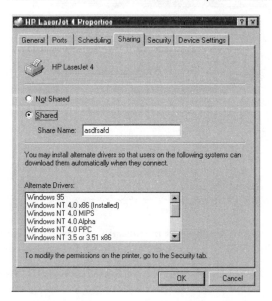

Security is set under the Security tab, shown in Figure 16.27.

FIGURE 16.27 The Security tab of the printer Properties window

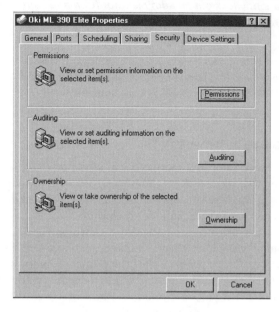

To set permissions for printing, click the Permissions button. You will see a screen similar to that shown in Figure 16.28.

FIGURE 16.28 Setting permissions on a printer

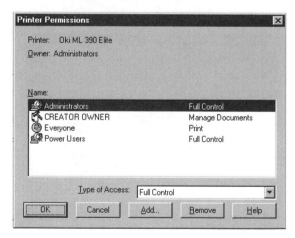

In this window, you can see who has permissions to use the printer and what those permissions are. Windows NT printing security includes four permissions:

No Access Similar to the folder sharing No Access permission. Users and groups with this permission can't access the printer.

Print   Users and groups can print to this printer and manage (delete and pause) their own print jobs.

Manage Documents   Users and groups can print to this printer, manage their own documents, and manage other users' print jobs (reorder them, delete them, pause them, and so on).

Full Control   Similar to the folder sharing Full Control permission. Users and groups can do everything they can with the Manage Documents permission, and they can also set security on the printer.

To set security, similar to the way you set security on a folder, click Add, select the user or group you want to give permissions to (as shown in Figure 16.29), select the permission from the drop-down list, and then click OK to accept it. Finally, click OK to close the printer Properties window.

FIGURE 16.29   Selecting user or group permissions for printing security

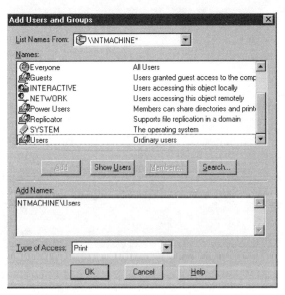

Once shared, the printer appears in the Printers folder with a blue-sleeved hand supporting it on its printer icon.

Sharing in Windows 2000

With the introduction of Windows 2000, Microsoft added several features to Windows and also made changes to the way sharing is done. Microsoft simplified the process and added support for Active Directory (Microsoft's directory structure that centrally manages users, groups, and security). However, because Windows 2000 is still Windows, no doubt the look and feel of the sharing process will be familiar as you review the methods necessary to share resources in Windows 2000.

Creating User Accounts in Windows 2000

You create user accounts in Windows 2000 through the Users and Passwords control panel applet, which can be started by going to Start ➤ Settings ➤ Control Panel and double-clicking on Users And Passwords. Doing so brings up the window shown in Figure 16.30.

FIGURE 16.30   Users and Passwords applet

 You can also use the Local Users and Groups section in Computer Management to add users.

To add a new user, follow these steps:

1. Click Add. You will see the Add New User Wizard (Figure 16.31). In this window, you must first type in a username. You can also enter the full name and description for this user. Click Next to continue.

 You will not be able to click Add unless Users Must Enter A User Name And Password To Use This Computer is checked. Otherwise, Windows 2000 will automatically log in at startup and not ask for a username.

FIGURE   16.31   Entering a username and full name

2. In the next window (Figure 16.32), you can enter a password for the user. You'll have to enter it twice the same way, to prevent mis-entering the password and locking the user out of their own account. Click Next.

FIGURE   16.32   Entering a password for the new user

3. The final step in adding the user is selecting which group they will initially be a member of (and thus receive permissions from). A user can be a member of more than one group, of course, but to simplify things, only one group is specified during the creation process. There are three options: Standard User, Restricted User, and Other (see Figure 16.33):

-   Standard users are placed in the Power Users group and are allowed to do just about anything on this computer. For the most part, unless you are creating users for network access only, this may be the option to choose for new users.

-   Users in the Restricted Users group are allowed to log in, but they are very limited in what they can do and see on this computer.

-   The Other option allows you to make the new user a member of any group on the system, including Administrators.

    Choose an option and click Finish to complete the creation of the new user.

FIGURE 16.33   Granting access to the new user

4. You are returned to the screen shown earlier in Figure 16.30. To create more users, click the Add button again and repeat the process described. If you are finished creating users, click OK to close the Users and Passwords control panel applet.

Sharing Folders in Windows 2000

Sharing folders in Windows 2000 follows a similar process to sharing folders under Windows NT:

1. Use Explorer to navigate to a folder you want to share. Right-click on that folder and choose Sharing from the pop-up menu. The folder Properties window will appear with the Sharing tab shown (Figure 16.34). By default, the share settings is Do Not Share This Folder.

FIGURE 16.34   Sharing tab in Windows 2000

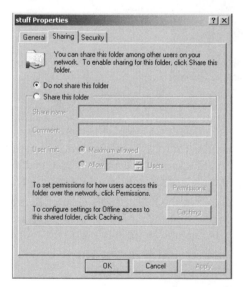

2. As with Windows NT, to share the folder, click the Share This Folder radio button and specify a name for the share in the field provided. Windows suggests a name for the share based on the name of the folder (Figure 16.35).

FIGURE 16.35   Sharing a folder

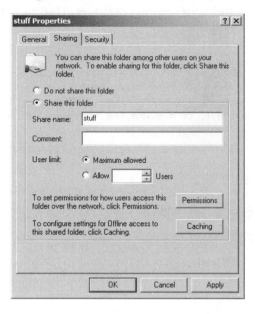

3. Now you must set up the share permissions for the folder. Click the Permissions button to add or change the permissions for this share. (If you want to accept the default settings of letting the Everyone have Full Control, you can skip this step.) From the window in Figure 16.36, you can see that the Everyone group has been allowed the Full Control permission.

FIGURE 16.36   Viewing permissions for the share

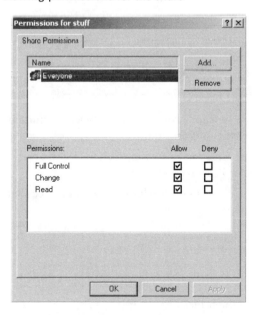

To change the permissions, use the check boxes under the user list. In the top window, click the user whose permissions you want to change. Then click the check box next to the permission you want to allow or deny.

You'll notice there's no No Access permission. This is the case because in Windows NT and 2000, No Access mean no access at all. Instead of being able to deny someone a single permission, you deny them all. This function primarily works with NTFS permissions, but it carries over to share permissions as well.

4. To add another user, click Add, select the user(s) or group(s) from the window that appears (Figure 16.37) by double-clicking them (they will pop into a list at the bottom of the window), and click OK.

FIGURE 16.37   Adding users and groups to the permissions list

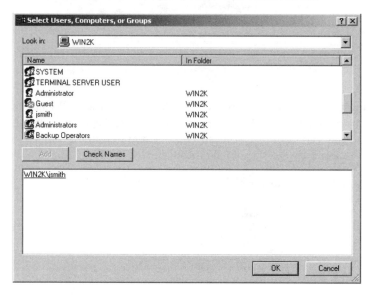

5. Once you have added users and groups, you may select permissions for them as well. Keep in mind that share permissions are additive.

6. When you are finished selecting permissions, click OK to accept the permission changes and return to the folder Properties window.

7. Click OK to finish the creation of the share. You will notice that the folder now has the share hand underneath it (Figure 16.38).

FIGURE 16.38   A shared folder

stuff

Sharing Printers in Windows 2000

Sharing printers in Windows 2000 is almost identical to doing so in Windows NT, with the important exception of the elimination of the No Access permission. To share a printer, open the `Printers` folder (Start ➤ Settings ➤ Printers), right-click on the printer you wish to share, and select Sharing from the pop-up menu. As with other versions, you will see the Sharing tab of the printer Properties windows (Figure 16.39). You enable sharing by selecting the Shared As radio button.

FIGURE 16.39   Printer sharing

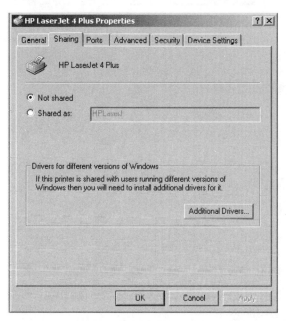

Setting permissions for printing in Windows 2000 is very similar to doing so in Windows NT. The share permissions are still found under the Security tab, but the look and feel is similar to folder sharing, as discussed earlier. Adding a user and changing the printing permissions are the same as they are for changing permissions on a folder under Windows 2000; the permissions are different (such as Print instead of Write), but they work in a similar fashion.

Sharing in Windows XP

Windows XP is not all that different from all other versions of Windows when it comes to sharing files and printers. Microsoft has buried the complexity of sharing files and printers in order to make the process simpler for most users. As with the other versions of Windows, in this section you will learn the steps necessary to share files and printers, including the creation of user accounts.

Creating User Accounts in XP

Creating user accounts in Windows XP is as simple as it gets. Open the Windows Control Panel by going to Start ➢ Control Panel. To begin adding users, double-click on the User Accounts control panel applet. You will see a window similar to the one in Figure 16.40. At the bottom of this window are listed all the accounts that currently exist. A wizard will guide you through the process of creating a user.

FIGURE 16.40 User Accounts control panel applet

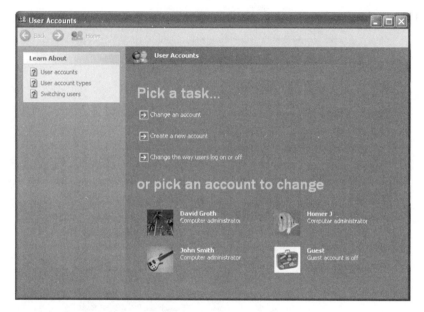

To begin creating a user, click on Create A New Account. The wizard will start. Use the following steps to create the account:

1. Type in a username for the new account. Do not use special characters or spaces. Click Next.

2. Select Limited for the type of computer account for a normal user by clicking the proper radio button. Select Computer Administrator if you want this user to have administrative abilities on this computer.

3. Click Create Account.

You will now see an icon for the user you just created in the User Accounts window. You should now create a password for the new account:

1. Select Change An Account from the User Accounts window.

2. Select the account for which you want to assign a password by clicking on it.

3. Click Create A Password in the list of tasks that appears.

4. Type the password twice (as you did in the other versions of Windows) in the fields provided, and then type in a word or phrase as the password hint.

5. Click Create Password.

Once you have added the password for the new user, you are returned to the Change Account screen. You can then close the User Accounts window.

Sharing Folders in XP

Sharing folders works exactly the same as in Windows 2000. To share a folder, navigate to it using Windows Explorer, right-click on it, enable sharing, type a share name, and select the permissions you want the share to have. The main difference is that when you are changing share permissions and you are adding users or groups to specify their permissions, you must use a new interface (shown in Figure 16.41). This is probably the worst thing Microsoft ever did to Windows XP. You can't easily browse for users or groups from this window. Instead, when selecting users or groups, you must already know their names (or part of the name) and have the utility search for them.

FIGURE 16.41   Selecting users or groups interface

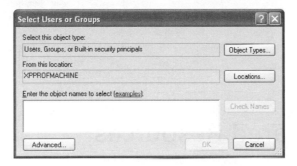

To do this, type the name (or a portion of it) into the Enter The Object Names To Select field. You can enter multiple object names separated by a semicolon (;). Click the Check Names button; Windows checks the names against the list of names and shows them in the Enter The Object Names To Select field if it finds them. Click OK to accept the names of users and groups. Windows will list them in the Group or User Names box in the Permissions window so you can set the permissions as in Windows 2000. (Personally, I would have thought a simple list of names and groups would be easier, but I don't make those decisions.)

Sharing Printers in XP

Sharing printers under Windows XP works exactly as it does under Windows 2000, with three exceptions:

- The printers are located under Printers and Faxes in the Start menu.
- The radio buttons in the Sharing tab (Figure 16.42) are labeled Share This Printer and Do Not Share This Printer.
- The Additional Drivers section of the Sharing tab is located on a separate window accessed through a button called Additional Drivers (shown in Figure 16.42).

Apart from that, the process of sharing printers is identical: Locate the printer, right-click, choose Sharing, enable sharing, name the share, set up security, click OK.

FIGURE 16.42   Additional Drivers section

Using Shared Resources

To access shared folders and printers, we'll turn to the Network Neighborhood icon. When you double-click this icon, you can browse the network for resources. Figure 16.43 shows an example of a Network Neighborhood browse window. As you can see, there are several entities on this network. The little icons that look like computers are just that—computers on the network. However, the icons aren't different for a Novell server, an NT server, or a Windows 9x machine sharing out part of its hard disk; they all look the same to Windows 9x. The icon that looks like a tree is an NDS tree that represents a Novell network.

Through this screen, you can double-click any computer to see the resources that are hosted by that computer. Using a shared folder is just like using any other folder on your computer, with two exceptions: First, the folder exists on the network, so you have to be connected to the network to use it. Second, for some programs to work properly, you must map a local drive letter to the network folder. This is because the Windows 9x reference to a share on the network uses the Universal Naming Convention (UNC) path. The UNC path uses the format *servername**share*\. So, a directory called JULY98 under a share called REPORTS on a machine called DAVELAPTOP would be written as \\DAVELAPTOP\REPORTS\JULY98.

 In Windows 9x, if you know the name of the computer that hosts the resource you are looking for, you can use the Find command instead of browsing. Go to Start ➢ Find ➢ Computer and type in the name of the computer preceded by two backslashes (the beginning of a UNC path).

FIGURE 16.43   A sample Network Neighborhood window

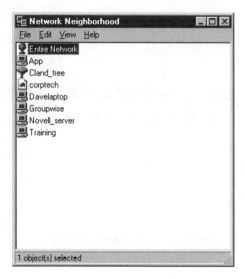

If there is a space in the name of any item, be careful. Some DOS utilities can't interpret spaces.

To connect to a network folder share, double-click the computer that's hosting it to view the list of shares (Figure 16.44). Notice that both the folder and printer that were shared in the previous examples are shown. To use the folder share, double-click it to see its contents (and copy files to and from it if necessary).

FIGURE 16.44   Viewing the resources a computer is hosting

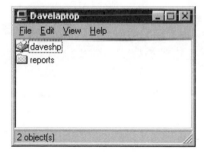

You can also map a drive letter to the folder share so that all your applications will be able to use it. To do so, right-click the folder (Reports in this case) and choose Map Network Drive. This will cause the screen shown in Figure 16.45 to appear. Pick a drive letter (one that is not being used) and click OK to map the drive. Remember that most Windows applications can use UNC paths and don't need drive mappings, but even some newer applications still require a drive letter. Now that you have a drive mapped, you can use the files and directories in the share you mapped to.

For the most part, these options for Windows 9*x*/NT work with other versions of Windows, with a few minor differences.

FIGURE 16.45 Mapping a drive letter to a network share

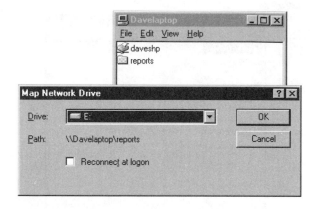

Sharing Options with Windows 2000

Windows 2000 is very similar to Windows 9x when it comes to accessing network resources, but there are a few modifications. First, Network Neighborhood is renamed My Network Places in Windows 2000. Second, to search for computers by name, you no longer go to the Find menu (now renamed Search). Instead, when you double-click My Network Places, the Search For Computers and Search For Files Or Folders options appear in the left part of the window (Figure 16.46). Click the Entire Contents link to display the network contents; everything will be displayed as it is in Windows 9x, and you can view and map network drives.

FIGURE 16.46 The initial Entire Network window

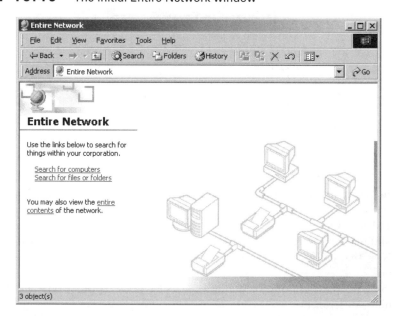

Another option for mapping a drive in 9*x*/2000 is to use Windows Explorer. In Explorer, click the Tools menu and select Map Network Drive. You will need to either enter the UNC path (*server**share*) or navigate to the folder using the Browse button. Drives can be disconnected using the Tools ➢ Disconnect Network Drive option.

Sharing Options with Windows XP

Using shared folders with Windows XP is similar to Windows 2000 and earlier versions. You use the My Network Places folder. However, anytime a network share is used, a shortcut is placed in the My Network Places folder automatically, so that it can be easily accessed later.

To locate a network resource using Windows XP, follow these steps:

1. Open My Network Places by going to Start ➢ My Network Places.

2. From the window that appears, you can connect to any of your network places by double-clicking, or browse to a new one using the Network Tasks list or the Other Places list.

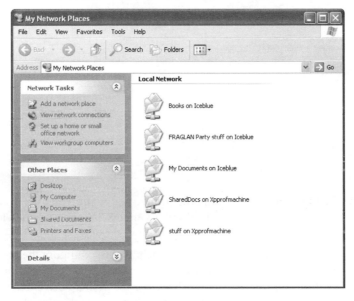

3. To locate a network resource on your entire local Windows-based network, click View Workgroup Computers under Network Tasks.

4. Click Microsoft Windows Network under Other Places.

5. Double-click the workgroup you want to browse.

6. Double-click the computer that hosts the resource you want to use (log in if necessary).

7. Double-click on the share you want to open. Or, to assign a drive letter to the share, right-click on the share and choose Map Network Drive, select a drive letter to map to and whether to automatically reconnect at logon, and then click Finish.

Using a Shared Printer

In this section, we'll discuss the way to set up a Windows 9*x*/NT/2000/XP client to print to a shared printer. Accessing shared printers is very similar to accessing shared resources; in both cases, you are accessing a resource that has been shared on the host computer. Additionally, in both cases, you are pointing a local resource (in this case, a printer icon) to a network resource (a shared printer).

To set up the printer on your workstation, you most likely will use the Point and Print option for Windows 9*x*/2000 printing. This option allows you to click and drag a printer to the Printers folder and run the Add Printer Wizard, which sets up the printer icon and the correct drivers on your machine. Follow these steps:

1. Browse to the computer that hosts the printer you want to set up and double-click the computer name so you can see the printer you want to install.

2. Open the Printers folder under Start ➢ Settings ➢ Printers. Arrange these windows so you can see both at the same time (Figure 16.47).

FIGURE 16.47   Preparing to configure the Point and Print option

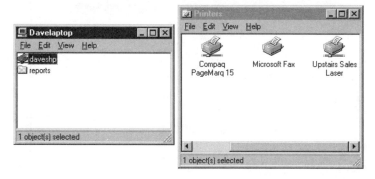

3. To start the Add Printer Wizard, drag the printer you want to set up from the list of resources the computer is hosting to the Printers window. As soon as you release the mouse button, the wizard will start. It displays the window shown in Figure 16.48.

4. The wizard asks you a series of questions that help you to configure the printer. If you are using Windows 9*x*, the wizard asks *Do you print from MS-DOS–based programs?* The reasoning behind this question is similar to the reason we map drive letters. Most older DOS programs (and, to a lesser extent, Windows programs) don't understand the UNC path syntax for access to a shared resource. Instead, they understand a name for a local hardware resource (like LPT1: for the first local parallel port). So, you must point a local printer port name out to the network in a process known as *capturing*. If you need to capture a printer port, answer Yes to this question; otherwise leave it set to the default (No). For this example, click Yes and then click Next to move to the next step of the wizard.

Although Windows 2000 allows you to map LPT: ports, 2000 does not have much interest in DOS, and so it does not make any special mention of it.

FIGURE 16.48   Starting the Add Printer Wizard

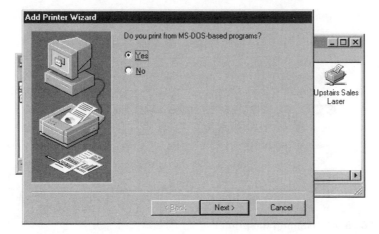

5. If you choose Yes in the preceding step, the next step is to capture the printer port. You will see the screen in Figure 16.49. It allows you to capture a printer port so that DOS programs can print to the network printer. Click the Capture Printer Port button to bring up the screen in Figure 16.50, which lets you choose which local port you want to capture. Select a port (generally LPT1).

FIGURE 16.49   Capturing a printer port

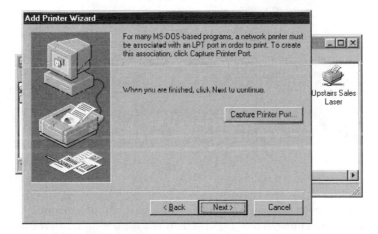

6. The next step is to give the printer instance a name. You should give a network printer a name that reflects what kind of printer it is and which machine is hosting it. In this example, the printer is labeled HP LaserJet III (the default name of the driver), but we could have named it Laser on Bob's PC. Whatever name makes sense to you, type it in the screen the wizard presents (Figure 16.51). You can also choose whether you want the printer to be the default printer that is used by all Windows applications.

From here on, printer installation is exactly the same as installing a local printer.

FIGURE 16.50   Picking which local port to capture

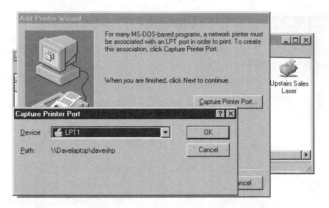

FIGURE 16.51   Naming the printer

Network Protocol Overview

One of the procedures today's technicians perform most often is setting up a computer to connect to the Internet. The Internet is no longer just a buzzword, it's a reality. It has been estimated that over 50 percent of the homes in America have computers and that over 50 percent of those computers are connected to the Internet. It's is no wonder that most computers come with software to connect them to the Internet.

Before we can discuss connecting Windows to the Internet, we need to talk about the Internet itself. There are some common terms and concepts every technician must understand about the Internet. First, the Internet is really a bunch of private networks connected together using public telephone lines. These private networks are the access points to the Internet and are run by companies called Internet Service Providers (ISPs). They sell you a connection to the Internet for a monthly service charge (like your cable bill or phone bill). Your computer talks to the ISP using public phone lines, or even using technologies such as cable or wireless.

Network technologies are covered in more detail in Chapter 5, "Networking Fundamentals."

Two major protocols are used on Windows networks: Transmission Control Protocol/Internet Protocol (TCP/IP) and Internetwork Packet eXchange/Sequenced Packet eXchange (IPX/SPX; NWLink). Each has benefits over the other for particular situations (although TCP/IP has become the de facto standard for most networks because of its use on the Internet). In this section you will learn the differences between the two as well as how they are configured for use with Windows.

TCP/IP

Regardless of which network type you choose, you will probably be running TCP/IP over the top of it. Because the Internet is a network, everyone on it needs to be running the same protocol in order to communicate. The protocol of the Internet is TCP/IP, and increasingly, the protocol of the Internet is becoming the primary protocol of all networks. Named for two of its most commonly used components, TCP/IP is actually a suite of protocols rather than just being a single monolithic creation.

Created in 1969 as a part of DARPAnet (the Defense Advanced Research Projects Administration Network), TCP/IP evolved over time. DARPAnet evolved also, eventually moving out of government hands and becoming the Internet that we know and love. Currently the Internet is managed by the Internet Society (www.isoc.org), which develops new standards for the Internet and for the TCP/IP suite.

When you're starting to work with TCP/IP, the first thing to note is that it is generally managed by using two independent hierarchical structures. The first is the IP address hierarchy. Each computer that runs TCP/IP must have a unique IP address assigned to it, and that address must fall within a specific range. IP addresses are composed of a set of four numbers, each of which must be in the range from 0 to 255. The IP address can either be automatically assigned to the machine or an administrator can specifically assign it. Aside from its IP address, a machine also has a *host name*, which identifies it on the network. Host names are friendly names by which computers can be more easily located, and they are managed using a worldwide naming system called the *Domain Name System (DNS)*. DNS allows a user to type in http://www.yahoo.com and be connected directly to a computer hundreds or thousands of miles away. The same user could use an IP address such as http://200.50.172.14 (not Yahoo!'s actual address), but most people find that the domain name (yahoo.com) is far easier to remember. Table 16.1 includes a list of other common Internet terms with which you will want to be familiar.

TABLE 16.1   Internet Terminology

Term	What It Means
ISP	Internet Service Provider. A company that provides access to the Internet.
Host	A computer on a TCP/IP network such as the Internet.

TABLE 16.1 Internet Terminology *(continued)*

Term	What It Means
WWW	World Wide Web (or just Web). This graphical extension of the Internet allows users to search for and view information easily through the use of a browser. Users navigate the Web by jumping from one page to the next through hyperlinks.
Hyperlink	Text or an image on a web page that, when clicked, takes the user to another place on the page or to a different page.
Browser	Software made to understand and interpret HTTP content.
HTTP	A TCP/IP protocol that defines how World Wide Web content is downloaded and displayed in your browser. HTTP stands for Hypertext Transfer Protocol.
FTP	File Transfer Protocol; another TCP/IP protocol. Used to transfer large files over the Internet. Users can use either a graphical client or a command line.
E-mail	Electronic mail. A way of sending and receiving messages over the Internet.
DHCP	Dynamic Host Configuration Protocol. Used to automatically configure TCP/IP information for hosts on the network.
WINS	Windows Internet Name Service. Manages Microsoft NetBIOS-based names and makes it easier to find resources on a Microsoft network.
DNS	Domain Name System. Manages Internet host and domain names and makes it easier to find resources on TCP/IP networks.
HTML	Hypertext Markup Language. The programming language in which web pages are designed. This simple language describes what items are on the page; the web browser interprets the HTML when loading the page and displays it.
HTTPS	*Hypertext Transport Protocol—Secure.* One method of securing HTTP connections between web server and web browser.

TCP/IP Addressing

All stations on a TCP/IP-based network need their own unique address, just like every home in a town must have a house address. TCP/IP requires that you have three major addresses configured before you can connect to a TCP/IP network. These addresses are as follows:

Host Address The unique, 32-bit number (actually four eight-bit numbers known as *octets*) that identifies the host. It is most often in the format *xxx.xxx.xxx.xxx*, where *xxx* is any decimal number from 0 to 254. One example of a host address is 192.168.1.36.

Subnet Mask   Indicates which portion of the host address refers to the host itself (known as the *node portion* of the address), and which portion refers to the address of the network (known as the *network portion*). The number is in the same format as the host address, except the numbers in the octets are usually larger numbers (usually something like 255.255.255.0).

Default Gateway   The address of the router to which the client sends all TCP/IP traffic that is not addressed to a specific station on the local network. The default gateway address should be entered on any client PC that is connected to a network that is connected to the Internet via a router. The address of the default gateway is another piece of configuration information that can be distributed using a DHCP server.

These addresses can be assigned in two major ways: static and automatic.

Static IP Addressing

Static IP addressing means that the TCP/IP address is just that: static. It is assigned, and then it doesn't change. Typically, the network administrator gives a static TCP/IP address to each network entity. Each network entity with an IP address is known as a *host*. Hosts can include not just computers, but also router interfaces, printers, and so on.

Once the administrator has assigned an IP address to that entity, the entity must be told about its address. Configuring a static IP address is different for each entity, but for Windows machines, you must tell the Windows network configuration utility that you are going to specify an IP address. Then, you type in the appropriate values for the IP address for that station, the subnet mask for the network it will be on, and the default gateway the station should use.

Automatic IP Addressing

Because manually configuring TCP/IP addresses is rather complex, there are methods of configuring TCP/IP addresses automatically. The two most common methods are DHCP and Automatic Private IP Addressing (APIPA).

DHCP

DHCP is a protocol that delivers workstation configuration information from a central server. That way, IP addresses, along with other workstation configuration information (such as subnet masks, DNS server addresses, and so on) are automatically assigned to the workstation.

DHCP works like this:

1. A workstation boots up and enables TCP/IP.

2. The host OS notices that the configuration of TCP/IP addressing has been set to auto (or something similar). The TCP/IP stack sends out a DHCP query (known as a DHCPDISCOVER packet) asking the network where a DHCP server is.

3. A DHCP server responds with an offer, which is a possible IP address for the workstation to use, and sends the offer back to the requesting workstation.

4. The workstation receives the offer and configures itself with the IP address (and other associated information). In turn, it makes a formal DHCP request to permanently (at

least for the duration of the DHCP address lease) use the offered IP address and sends it to the DHCP server.

5. The DHCP server responds with each an acknowledgement (*ACK*) or a negative acknowledgement (*NAK*). An ACK means the station is free to go on using the address; a NAK means the station must give up the address and repeat the request.

6. Once configured, the station can use the given IP address for a limited period of time known as the *address lease period*. This period of time indicates exactly how long the station may keep the selected address. It can range from a few minutes to several days. The lease time is sent along with the address during the offer of an address from a DHCP server. When half the lease time has expired, the station begins the DHCP address request all over again.

APIPA

Windows 98/2000/XP have a feature called *Automatic Private IP Addressing (APIPA)*. Using APIPA, DHCP clients can automatically self-configure an IP address and subnet mask when their DHCP server can't be found. When Windows is booting, if it can't find a DHCP server, APIPA configures an IP address for the computer automatically. This address is in the range 169.254.0.1 to 169.254.255.254 with a Class B subnet mask of 255.255.0.0. The client uses this address until the DHCP server becomes available.

During the time that the workstation is using the APIPA address, DHCP continues to check for a DHCP server on the network (by default, every 5 minutes). If a DHCP server is found, a DHCP request is made, and if it's successful, the newly obtained IP address replaces the APIPA address.

Computer Name Resolution

Early TCP/IP Windows networks used NetBIOS for name resolution. When Microsoft first began producing network-capable OSs, such as DOS with networking, LAN Manager, and Windows NT 3.1, the Internet was nothing but a group of mainframe computers connecting selected military and university campuses. At that time, it seemed that the thing to do when you created network software was to also create your own proprietary protocol and assume that no one would ever connect to any network but yours. Novell had IPX/SPX, Apple had AppleTalk, and Microsoft, came up with NetBEUI.

The NetBEUI protocol is insufficient on so many levels that discussing its faults is too big a job for this chapter. Nonetheless, it is an extremely fast protocol for allowing a few computers on a single network to communicate. It just doesn't scale very well, which doomed it as networks grew and began to interconnect.

The death knell of NetBEUI wasn't a problem, because TCP/IP and other protocols were ready to take over. The one thing that has continued to cause confusion and trouble, though, is that NetBEUI was based on another Microsoft protocol called NetBIOS, which has been far more difficult to replace.

NetBEUI and NetBIOS

NetBEUI and NetBIOS are obviously similar-looking terms, and unfortunately, there has been a certain amount of confusion surrounding them. Here is a brief explanation of what each does:

NetBEUI A transport protocol. It is responsible for how data is transmitted between two computers. It is not routable and is rarely used in modern computing.

NetBIOS A name resolution system. It allows a computer to search for another computer on the network by its Microsoft computer name. It must be used on every Microsoft-based network up to Windows 2000.

Computer Names and Host Names

The continuing presence of NetBIOS makes for some interesting confusion in that a Microsoft 9*x* machine with TCP/IP installed actually has two distinct names. Its NetBIOS computer name is set in the Identification tab of the Network program (Figure 16.52), whereas its host name is set in the TCP/IP DNS Configuration tab (Figure 16.53). In the figures, both names are set to Coyote; the computer and host name are usually the same because they are set that way by default. If you are having trouble reaching a 9*x*/NT machine, though, you may want to check this setting.

FIGURE 16.52   The NetBIOS computer name

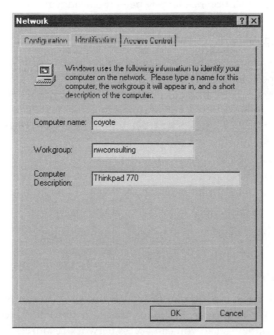

FIGURE 16.53   The TCP/IP host name

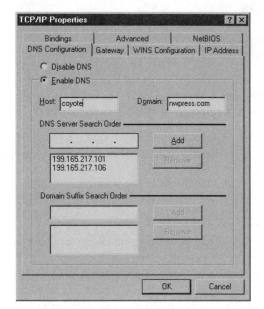

In Windows 2000, Microsoft has finally started to make a break from this nonsense. Computer and host names in 2000 must be the same, and NetBIOS name resolution has largely been replaced with DNS naming resolution.

What Is Resolution?

In order for a computer to talk to another computer, it must be able to access it using an IP address. Computers speak in numbers, not letters. So, the friendly names that we use to make computers easy to remember and find must be *resolved* to find out what IP address the machine is using. There are a number of methods of doing this, but WINS servers and DNS servers are the most common. WINS resolves NetBIOS computer names to IP addresses, and DNS does so for host names. (More on this in a minute.)

Another way of resolving names is to use either the LMHOSTS file (computer names) or the HOSTS file (host names). These are text files into which you can put entries that specifically tell your machine the address of another machine, as in the following line:

```
192.168.1.250        NTSERVER
```

Although these files work fine, they require a lot of maintenance and are not used regularly in modern networking.

Configuring TCP/IP

NetBEUI and NWLink are protocols that need little tuning. You can pretty much install them and go, without needing to configure anything. Not so with TCP/IP, which has a number of settings that must be configured so you can access network resources.

First, there are two settings that are absolutely crucial. Without an IP address and a subnet mask, TCP/IP will not function. In addition, a number of other settings may also be needed, depending on what you are planning to access. The settings are listed in Table 16.2 (settings needed for Internet access are marked with an asterisk).

TABLE 16.2   TCP/IP Configuration Settings

Setting	Example	Purpose
IP address*	192.168.1.75	Uniquely identifies the computer on the network.
Subnet mask*	255.255.255.0	Used to determine whether other IP addresses are on the same network or on another network. Sadly, there is no easy explanation for subnet masks. Suffice it to say that you need it, and it has to be right! The network administrator should give you the subnet mask setting (and all other necessary information).
Default gateway*	192.168.1.1	The address of the router your machine uses to access the outside world.
Host	Coyote	The name used to refer to the machine in DNS.
Domain	Sybex.com	The name of the organization you are in. Similar to a workgroup, but for TCP/IP.
DNS server*	192.168.1.250	The machine that resolves names for the network. This machine answers a question such as *What IP address does coyote.sybex.com have?* with an answer of 192.168.1.75.
WINS server	192.168.1.250	Serves the same purpose as DNS, but deals with computer names, not host names. Answers questions such as *What IP address does COYOTE have?*

Managing TCP/IP

There are two ways to manage TCP/IP. The manual way involves going to each machine and setting upward of 10 separate values. This is also known as the hard way of configuring IP. Another possibility is the use of DHCP. If your network is using DHCP, all you have to do is install IP and reboot. A special server called a *DHCP server* then provides your machine with all the values it needs when it starts up again. Machines are given leases to the IP addresses that the server manages and must periodically renew these leases. If you are using DHCP, your TCP/IP settings in the Network program should be grayed out, as shown in Figure 16.54.

If you are wondering what a machine's IP settings are, there are a number of utilities you can use to find out. The primary options are listed in Table 16.3.

FIGURE 16.54   TCP/IP auto-configured by DHCP

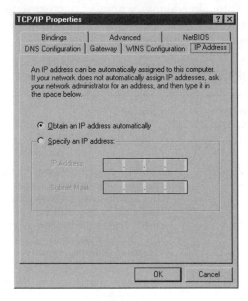

TABLE 16.3   TCP/IP Utilities

Utility	Function
WINIPCFG	A graphical utility on Windows 9*x* that allows you to get information about your IP configuration. It also allows you to release a DHCP lease and request a new one.
IPCONFIG	Does the same thing as WINIPCFG, but for Windows NT/2000/XP. IPCONFIG is also different in that it is a command-line utility.
PING	Allows you to test connectivity with another host by typing a command like **PING www.sybex.com** or **PING 192.168.1.250**.
Tracert	Trace route utility that allows you to watch the path information takes to get from your machine to another one.
NSLOOKUP	A utility that allows a user to perform a manual DNS query of any DNS database to see if DNS name resolution is functioning properly.

Using these utilities is straightforward. For an example, follow these steps to view TCP/IP information on Windows NT/2000/XP:

1. Choose Start ➢ Run.

2. Type **CMD** and press Enter to bring up a command prompt.

3. At the prompt, type **IPCONFIG**. Basic information about your TCP/IP configuration will be displayed.

4. Type **IPCONFIG** again, this time adding the **/A** switch: **IPCONFIG /A**. The /ALL switch tells the system to display additional information. Other options can be found using the IPCONFIG /? command. The additional options are also run using switches, and are run in the same fashion as the /ALL switch—you type them in after the command.

Other TCP/IP Protocols

In addition to TCP and IP, the TCP/IP protocol suite has provisions for several different protocols, each of which has a different function. The A+ exam will test your basic knowledge of these protocols. The other TCP/IP protocols include (but are not limited to):

- HTTP
- FTP
- POP3
- SMTP
- NNTP
- LPR
- LDAP
- Telnet
- Gopher

Many of these protocols are covered in more detail in other chapters, but in the following list, you'll gain a basic understanding of what each one does:

Hypertext Transfer Protocol (HTTP) The command and control protocol used to manage communications between a web browser and a web server. When you access a web page on the Internet or on a corporate intranet, you see a mixture of text, graphics, and links to other documents or other Internet resources. HTTP is the protocol that initiates the transport of each of the components of a web page.

File Transfer Protocol (FTP) A TCP/IP protocol that provides a mechanism for single or multiple file transfers between computer systems; when written in lowercase, ftp is also the name of the client software used to access the FTP server running on the remote host. The ftp package provides all the tools needed to look at files and directories, change to other directories, and transfer text and binary files from one system to another. FTP uses TCP port 21 to actually move the files.

Simple Mail Transfer Protocol (SMTP) The protocol responsible for moving messages from one e-mail server to another. It is also the protocol used to send e-mail from a client to an e-mail server. Most e-mail servers run either Post Office Protocol (POP3) or Internet Mail Access Protocol (IMAP) to distribute e-mail messages to users. All e-mail servers that send e-mail to the Internet must be using TCP/IP and an e-mail program that can send e-mail using SMTP.

Post Office Protocol 3 (POP3)   Used to download mail from an Internet (SMTP) mail server. POP3 servers provide a storage mechanism for incoming mail. When a client connects to a POP3 server, all the messages addressed to that client are downloaded; messages cannot be downloaded selectively. Once the messages are downloaded, the user can delete or modify messages without further interaction with the server. In some locations, POP3 is being replaced by another standard, Internet Mail Access Protocol (IMAP).

Network News Transfer Protocol (NNTP)   Used to transport Internet news (also called Usenet news) between news servers. It is also the protocol used to transport these news articles between news servers and news clients. This protocol is often confused with the Network Time Protocol (NTP), which serves a different purpose.

Line Printer (LPR) Protocol   Used primarily on Unix system, although Windows NT uses it as well. It is the protocol used to send commands to network printers over TCP/IP. Its name suggests it works only for line printers (also called dot-matrix printers). That's mainly because, when it was being developed, the majority of the printers in use were line printers.

Lightweight Directory Access Protocol (LDAP)   Used to make simple requests of a network directory (like NDS, X.500, or Active Directory). This protocol is being used more often as network directories see increased use. LDAP requests can consist of requests for names, locations, and other information like phone numbers and e-mail addresses. Many web browsers (including Navigator and Internet Explorer) contain LDAP clients so they can request information from directory servers.

Telnet   A terminal emulation protocol that allows a workstation to perform a remote logon to another host over the network. It is used primarily to let users at workstations access a Unix server and run commands just as if they were sitting at the server's console.

Gopher   A text-based utility that was used in the early years of the Internet to search for data and news. It presented selections in a hierarchical format. Gopher was developed from work done at the University of Minnesota; their mascot was the gopher, so they named this technology Gopher. It was the best way to search for information before the Web came along and made everything friendly.

IPX/SPX (NWLink)

Internetwork Packet eXchange/Sequenced Packet eXchange (IPX/SPX) protocol is the main protocol suite used on Novell NetWare networks. NetWare was one of the first network OSs for PCs. It still is used in major corporations as their backbone infrastructure. Because of NetWare's popularity, Microsoft began to include IPX/SPX support in Windows versions as early as Windows 3.*x*. However, Microsoft developed its own version of the IPX/SPX protocol stack and called it NWLink.

IPX/SPX is a very efficient LAN protocol. However, it isn't as efficient when traversing a WAN. As a result, Novell NetWare has switched from running only on the IPX/SPX protocol to running in a mixed environment of both IPX/SPX and TCP/IP, and it now includes support to run completely on TCP/IP, thus eliminating the need for IPX/SPX.

In this section, you will learn the following concepts related to IPX/SPX:

- Addressing

- Name resolution
- Configuring/managing IPX/SPX

IPX Addressing

Implementing an IPX/SPX-based network requires that you understand the network address concepts that exist for IPX. An IPX network is fairly easy to implement because the addressing scheme is reasonably easy to understand. Three types of addresses exist on an IPX/SPX-based network:

- IPX network address
- Station IPX address
- Socket identifier

IPX Network Address

IPX network addresses are 8-digit hexadecimal numbers (for example, A3F2451B) that uniquely identify the network segment (Figure 16.55). They are used to make IPX internetwork routing possible. When you configure IPX on a server, you tell the server what IPX network number should be assigned to that network segment. Additionally, each segment's IPX number must be unique on the network. A duplicated network address can cause problems with routing IPX packets.

FIGURE   16.55   IPX network number assignments

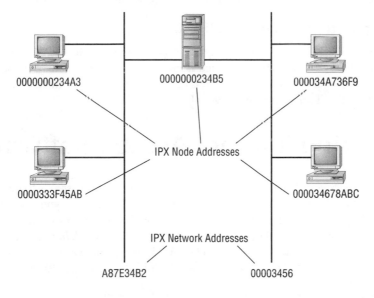

0000000234A3   0000000234B5   000034A736F9

IPX Node Addresses

0000333F45AB   000034678ABC

IPX Network Addresses

A87E34B2   00003456

The addresses 00000000, FFFFFFFF, and FFFFFFFE are reserved for special use on an IPX network and cannot be used for network addresses.

You can pick any 8-digit hexadecimal number for an IPX address.

Station (Node) IPX Address

The station (node) address is a 12-digit (6-byte) hexadecimal number. To make configuration easy, the node address for IPX was designed to use the hardware (MAC) address of the network interface card as the IPX node address.

Each device on a segment must have a unique node address. If there are duplicates, neither station will be able to communicate with the rest of the network.

Socket Identifiers

Within each server or station, several processes can be running. When a sending workstation is addressing an IPX packet, it needs to specify which service the packet is destined for on the server. It does this using special addresses called *socket identifiers* (also called *socket IDs* or socket numbers). Each service is given a unique socket ID. These IDs are usually assigned not by an administrator but by the designers of the various services and protocols.

IPX/SPX Name Resolution

IPX/SPX can use many different services for binding station names to an IPX/SPX address. But, IPX/SPX networks don't use name resolution (apart from NetBIOS names) in Windows networks. That function is handled by higher-layer protocols. However, services are located on the network using a protocol known as the Service Advertising Protocol (SAP).

Configuring and Managing IPX/SPX

Apart from installing IPX/SPX, nothing needs to be done to configure IPX/SPX on a workstation. The network number is automatically obtained from the network itself, and the node portion of the address is obtained from the MAC address of the NIC and incorporated by IPX/SPX in its transmissions. It is also a self-managing protocol.

Configuring Internet Access Software

If you want to connect your Windows machine to the Internet, the first step is to get an account with an ISP. The ISP will give you all the information you need to connect your machine. In some cases, the ISP will give you a disk with a preconfigured connection and browser—all you have to do is install the software, and you'll be ready to connect to the Internet. A *browser* is a piece of software used to access the World Wide Web, and a Dial-Up Networking (DUN) connection holds the settings needed to access an ISP. In this section, we will look at how to install and use each of these.

Although in most cases you need to make a DUN connection to use the Internet, it is important to note that some service providers, such as AOL and Prodigy, create their own connections. Don't try to make the connection for these programs, and don't delete these connections!

Some connections, such as cable or DSL, do not use a modem and as such are configured through the use of network cards and standard network clients. Configuring Internet access for DSL is very similar to configuring access on a company network: You install TCP/IP, configure it properly, and then skip ahead to connecting to the Internet. You will need information from the ISP when configuring these systems.

Creating a Windows 9x DUN Connection

You must create a new DUN connection to connect to the Internet. To do so, first open the Dial-Up Networking folder under Start ➢ Programs ➢ Accessories. The resulting window shows all the DUN connections that are configured. To create a new DUN connection, follow these steps:

1. Double-click the Make New Connection item to bring up the screen shown in Figure 16.56. From this screen, you can give the connection a name. As with other names in Windows 9x, use one that reflects what it is (in this case, a connection to the Internet). Additionally, this screen allows you to select which modem you want to use to dial this connection (if you have only one configured in Windows 9x, it defaults to that one).

FIGURE 16.56 Making a new connection and naming it

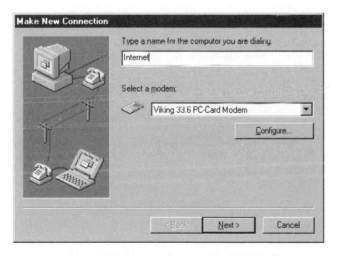

2. Enter the phone number of the system you are dialing (Figure 16.57). Type in the area code and phone number of your ISP and click Next to continue. When it dials, Windows 9x automatically determines if the number is long-distance and either adds or omits the 1 and the area code.

If you live in a country other than the U.S., select your country under Country Code to change the way Windows 9x interprets phone number syntax.

FIGURE 16.57 Entering the ISP's phone number

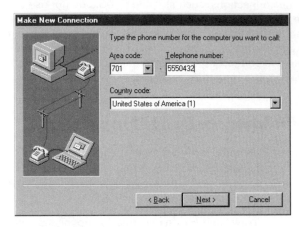

3. In the final screen, click the Finish button to finish creating the connection.

Configuring the Properties of a Windows 9x DUN Connection

Now that you have a DUN connection, you need to configure the settings specific to your Internet connection:

1. Right-click the connection in the Dial-Up Networking folder (Figure 16.58). From the menu that appears, you can choose to use the connection to connect (the Connect option), or you can choose the Properties option to configure the connection. Because you aren't ready to connect yet, choose the Properties item from the menu.

FIGURE 16.58 Choosing the DUN connection to configure

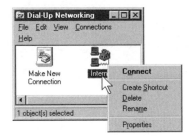

2. You should now see a screen similar to the one in Figure 16.59. Here, you can configure the same properties you configure in the Make New Connection Wizard (telephone number, connection name, and modem). This screen has two more tabs that you can use to configure the other properties (such as protocol settings).

3. Click the Server Types tab, and you will see the settings for the type of server you are dialing in to (Figure 16.60). For an Internet connection, this is usually set to PPP: Windows 95, Windows NT 3.5, Internet (unless your ISP instructs you to use another setting). Notice also that there are check boxes for several other settings, including which protocol(s) this

dial-up connection will use. TCP/IP must be selected in order for an Internet connection to work. Configure these settings according to your ISP's instructions and click OK to accept them.

FIGURE 16.59   Properties of the Internet DUN connection

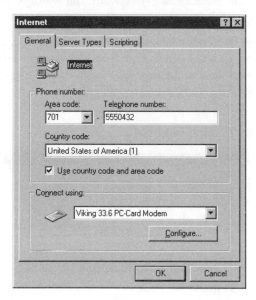

FIGURE 16.60   Configuring the server type parameter

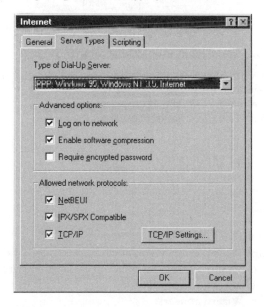

The Scripting tab is used if your ISP doesn't support any type of automatic username and password authentication protocol like *Password Authentication Protocol (PAP)* or *Challenge Handshake Authentication Protocol (CHAP)*. If in doubt, ask your ISP. This tab allows you to specify a file that automatically enters your username and password. The Windows 9*x* Help file documents how to use this feature.

You can also configure DUN parameters in the Connect screen of the Internet connection. To access this area, double-click the connection. You will see a screen similar to the one in Figure 16.61. Enter the username and password your ISP has assigned you. Additionally, double-check the phone number you entered to make sure it's correct. Once you've finished configuring the phone number, you're ready to connect to the Internet.

FIGURE 16.61 The Connect To screen

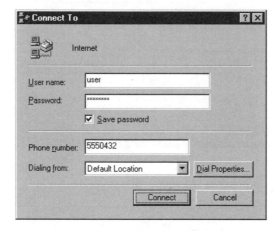

 If you want to save the password so you don't have to type it in every time, click the Save Password check box. Be careful, though. If you save your password, anyone can get onto the Internet from your computer (using your username) without having to enter a password.

Installing DUN on Windows 2000

With Windows 2000, wizards are used everywhere, including the creation of a DUN connection:

1. Choose Start ➤ Settings ➤ Network and Dial-up Connections.

2. In the window that appears, double-click Make New Connection.

3. If this is the first time you have created a network connection, the Location Information window appears. You cannot escape this window without entering an area code, so enter it and click OK. You will get another location screen as well. Click OK again, and the Network Connection Wizard appears.

4. Choose Dial Up To The Internet. The Welcome to the Internet Connection Wizard (ICW) window appears (Figure 16.62). That makes three nested wizards. (A bit extreme, no?)

FIGURE 16.62   The first screen of the Internet Connection Wizard

5. In the ICW, you are led through a long series of choices. Click through and enter the values that apply to your Internet setup. You are asked what type of device (modem or network) you are using, what number you need to dial, and what your username and password are. At the end, you can even set up your mail account, and the wizard offers to connect you when you are finished.

6. A new icon appears in the Network and Dial-Up Connections window, showing that your new connection has been added (Figure 16.63). You can view the status of a connection by double-clicking it or change its settings by right-clicking and selecting Properties.

FIGURE 16.63   The finished dial-up connection

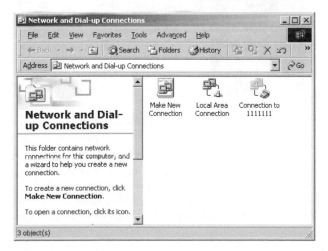

The Windows 2000 Internet setup is typical of the sort of straightforward, easy-to-use tools that we as technicians have to hope do not become common. If everything gets this easy, it's going to be tough to make a living in this business!

Making a Dial-Up Connection in Windows XP

Windows XP doesn't call its dial-up networking, *dial-up networking*. Instead, it's called just *networking*, and you are just making another network connection as far as Windows XP is concerned—except you're using a modem instead of a NIC.

To make a dial-up connection to an ISP in Windows XP, follow these steps:

1. Open the Network Connections tool by clicking Start ➢ Control Panel and then clicking on Network and Internet Connections.

2. Click Create A New Connection. You will see the New Connection Wizard (Figure 16.64).

You can also access the Network Connections tool by going to Start ➢ All Programs ➢ Accessories ➢ Communications ➢ Network Connections.

FIGURE 16.64   New Connection Wizard

A screen under Internet Options in Internet Explorer allows you to configure an Internet connection, but the order of the screens in the wizard is different from those described here. You also may be presented with slightly different screens. However, the information you are required to enter is virtually the same.

3. If this is the first time you've made any kind of connection (aside from the default LAN network connection), you are asked to enter information about your location (Figure 16.65). This information indicates to Windows how to dial the number, including whether to dial a 1, what prefix to use when dialing an outside number (such as 9 or 8), and so on. Click OK.

FIGURE 16.65   Setting up dialing properties

4. Choose the type of network connection you are making (Figure 16.66). There are four types of connections you can create:

Connect To The Internet   Allows you to set up an Internet connection with all the settings appropriate to connect your computer to the Internet.

FIGURE 16.66   Choosing the network connection type for a new connection

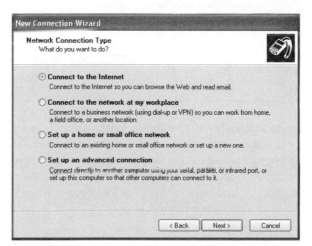

Connect To The Network At My Workplace   Configures the new connection to connect your computer to a network at your workplace, either through a dial-up connection or by VPN over an Internet connection.

Set Up A Home Or Small Office Network   Configures the new connection to work on a small office or home office network. This is primarily a LAN connection type.

Set Up An Advanced Connection   If the other three options aren't specific enough for what you want to do, you can set up an advanced connection. Within this option, you can set up connections directly to other computers (to establish a peer-to-peer type connection between them) using a parallel, serial, or laplink-type cable.

Because you are setting up a dial-up Internet connection, choose the first option (which is already selected, because it's the default) and click Next.

5. The next screen (Figure 16.67) asks how you want to connect to the ISP. You can choose one of the following options:

Choose From A List Of Internet Service Providers (ISPs)   Choose this option if you have not already set up an Internet account with an ISP. The New Connection Wizard helps you set up an account with an ISP with service in your area and configure your computer to use that account.

FIGURE 16.67   Configuring an ISP connection method

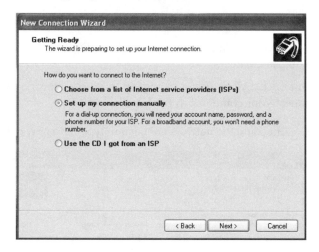

Set Up My Connection Manually   If you already have a connection account with an ISP and just need to set up this computer to use it, select this option. You need the ISP's connection phone number (the phone number your modem will dial), a username and password, and possibly some other information (like DNS server addresses, mail server addresses, and so on). This information is typically supplied to you on a piece of paper when you sign up. You need that piece of paper handy when you select this option.

Use The CD I Got From An ISP   If you already have a connection account with an ISP, and the ISP has supplied you with a CD-ROM with an ISP-specific configuration on it, select this option. The New Connection Wizard sets up this computer to use your ISP, using the settings and files found on the CD-ROM. You must have the CD-ROM available (or the files found on it).

For the purposes of this discussion, you are setting up a dial-up connection to an ISP you already have an account with. So, choose the second option.

6. In the next screen (Figure 16.68) of the New Connection Wizard, you must specify how you will connect to the ISP. There are three options:

Connect Using A Dial-Up Modem   Select this connection type if you are going to use a regular dial-up modem (not a cable or DSL modem) via a phone line to connect to the ISP. You must have a modem connected (either internally or externally) in order to use this option.

Connect Using A Broadband Connection That Requires A Username And Password   Select this option if you have a broadband connection (cable, DSL, satellite, or other) that requires a username and password. This is sometimes referred to as a *PPPoE connection*. You must have the username and password the ISP assigned you handy when selecting this option.

Connect Using A Broadband Connection That Is Always On   Many broadband connections don't require a username and password. If you are using such a broadband connection, select this option.

You are making a dial-up connection, so select the first option and click Next.

FIGURE 16.68   Selecting the ISP connection method

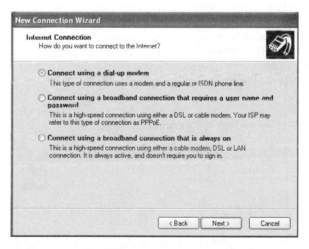

7. Give the connection a name (Figure 16.69). You should enter a name that will help you remember which ISP this connection connects you to. In Figure 16.69 we chose *My ISP*, but you can enter any text here as long as it helps you remember. Click Next to continue.

8. Have your ISP's connection phone number handy. The wizard asks you to enter the phone number your computer must dial to connect to your ISP (Figure 16.70). You can get this number from your ISP (it's most likely on the sheet they gave you with your connection

information, username, password, and so on). Enter the ISP's phone number with the area code. Click Next to continue.

FIGURE 16.69 Naming the connection

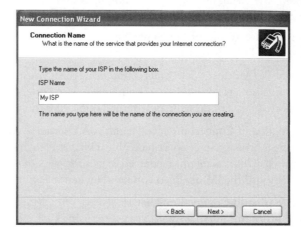

 Remember that when you set up your location, you entered your local area code. If necessary, Windows will dial it long distance if you set up another location when you travel. Let's say you live in Minnesota, and your local area code is 612. Let's also pretend that you need to travel to North Dakota (area code 701). Before you leave, you can set up a location called North Dakota; then, switch it to be your default location when you leave. Your computer will dial your home ISP with the correct area code and long-distance codes (although this may not be the most efficient way to dial your ISP).

FIGURE 16.70 Entering the ISP's phone number

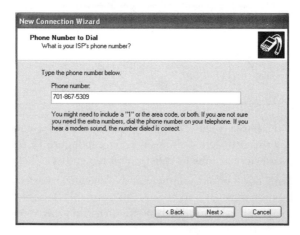

9. Don't put away that ISP data sheet just yet; you still need it. It's time to enter the username and password for your Internet account (Figure 16.71). This may or may not be the username and password you use to get your e-mail from the same ISP. Enter them in the spaces provided (you'll have to enter the password twice to ensure you've entered it correctly). You can also select from three other options:

    Use This Account Name And Password When Anyone Connects To The Internet From This Computer   Because Windows XP is a multiuser OS, different users can have different Internet connections. However, there are situations where you might want to force everyone who uses the computer to use the same Internet connection (a single computer for a family, for example). By checking this option, anyone who connects to the Internet from this computer will be able to use this user account and password.

    Make This The Default Internet Connection   If you have only one Internet connection and this new connection will be the primarily connection, make sure this option is checked. But if, for example, you have a broadband connection and this new connection is a backup or auxiliary connection (like in a laptop), make sure this option remains unchecked.

    Turn On Internet Connection Firewall For This Connection   This option, when checked, enables the *Internet Connection Firewall (ICF)* for this connection. You will learn more about ICF later in this chapter.

    Click Next.

FIGURE 16.71   Entering the username, password, and options for the ISP connection

10. The wizard summarizes the options you have selected (Figure 16.72). If any of the options are incorrect, click Back and correct them. Also, if you want the wizard to place a shortcut on the Desktop, mark the check box (it's off by default). If everything is correct, click the Finish button to finish the setup of the connection.

    If you selected the option to create a shortcut for this connection on the Desktop, a new icon appears on your Desktop, labeled with the name of the new connection. You can double-click on this connection to dial the new connection and test it.

FIGURE 16.72   New connection summary screen

Installing and Configuring Firewall Protection under Windows XP

Windows XP includes a new feature known as the Internet Connection Firewall (ICF). The ICF is a *firewall*, or barrier, built into Windows XP that stands between your computer and the possible security problems on the Internet. It is enabled on a LAN connection that is *directly* connected to the Internet to protect that connection (and the computer it's connected to). It isn't as effective as a dedicated router or firewall, and is not really necessary on connections that connect to the Internet via a router or other computer running Internet Connection Sharing (although the computer running ICS is an excellent candidate for ICF).

WARNING   If ICF is enabled on a LAN connection, it blocks file and printer sharing on that LAN connection. This is a major source of frustration for Windows XP users and is a common problem.

It is possible to enable or disable ICF separately on every dial-up, LAN, or other high-speed Internet connection within the Windows XP Network Connections folder. However, it is important to note that ICF only protects against *incoming* traffic; it doesn't do anything with outgoing traffic.

You can enable ICF during the setup of the connection as discussed earlier, or you can enable it from the properties of a network connection. You must be logged in as a member of the Administrators group. Follow these steps:

1.   Open the Network Connections folder by going to Start ➢ Control Panel and double-clicking on the Network Connections folder.

2.   Right-click on the connection for which you wish to enable the ICF and choose Properties. Doing so brings up the network connection Properties window (Figure 16.73). In this window you can see the various protocols and so on that are installed. Ensure that TCP/IP appears in the list under This Connection Uses The Following Items.

FIGURE 16.73   Network connection Properties

3. You enable the ICF on the Advanced tab of the network connection Properties. Click on the Advanced tab (Figure 16.74) and click the Protect My Computer And Network… check box in the Internet Connection Firewall box.

FIGURE 16.74   The Advanced tab of the network connection Properties

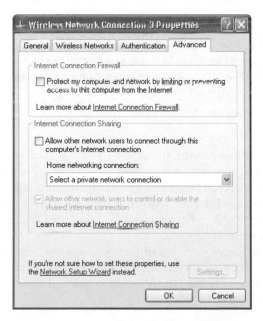

4. After you have enabled the ICF, you can configure it by clicking the Settings button at the bottom of the window. Tell the ICF which applications and service can pass through the ICF and which are blocked.

Other Internet Software

Connecting to the Internet is simple once you get the connection configured. Double-click the connection, enter the password (unless you chose the Save Password button previously), and click Connect. A window appears that allows you to follow the status of the connection (Figure 16.75). You should hear the modem dial and then connect. When it connects, the status screen says Verifying Username and Password, and then says Connected. Once you are connected, the status screen closes and you see an icon on the Taskbar (the same icon that's on the status screen). At this point, you are connected to your ISP and, through it, to the rest of the world. You can fire up your favorite web browser and start surfin'.

FIGURE 16.75   Connection status screen

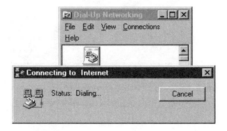

 If you are configuring the system for someone who just wants to click and go, you can right-click the Internet Explorer icon on the Desktop and use the Connection tab of the Internet Settings window to configure auto-dial. Set the connection you have created as the default and specify that the system should Always Dial My Default Connection. Any time an application needs to access the Internet, it can initiate the DUN connection automatically.

Browsers

The first, and probably the most important, thing you need is a web browser. This piece of software allows you to view web pages from the Internet. The two browsers with the largest market share are Netscape Navigator and Microsoft Internet Explorer (IE). Both work equally well for browsing the Internet. Microsoft includes its IE browser (Figure 16.76) with Windows 9*x*/NT/2000/XP, whereas Netscape Navigator (Figure 16.77), which is free, must be downloaded separately.

If you are looking for a newer version of Internet Explorer, you can go to Microsoft's website, `www.microsoft.com/windows/ie`. For Navigator, go to `www.netscape.com`. Select the version you want and specify the type of machine you will be using it on. You can then download and install the software.

FIGURE 16.76   The main window of Microsoft Internet Explorer

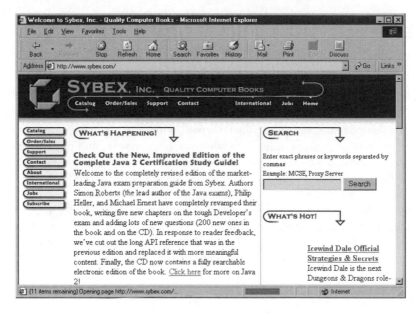

FIGURE 16.77   The main window of Netscape Navigator

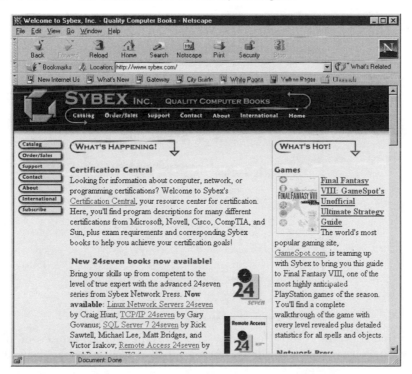

Configuring IE

The A+ exam tests your knowledge of several primary configuration tasks for Internet Explorer. These tasks include:

- Configuring security settings and enabling/disabling script support
- Configuring proxy settings

CONFIGURING SECURITY SETTINGS AND ENABLING/DISABLING SCRIPT SUPPORT

With IE, security is a major concern. Many of the Internet security problems that have been discovered are related to the way that IE interacts with Windows. There are scripts on the Internet that, when run, modify your Windows installation in some way, and possibly allow the introduction of a virus. To prevent against that possibility, you should change IE's security settings as well as disable script support (although it may be necessary to re-enable it from time to time).

To change security settings for IE, go to Start ➤ Settings ➤ Control Panel (or, in XP, Start ➤ Control Panel). In the Control Panel window, double-click on the Internet Options applet. In the Internet Properties Window (Figure 16.78), you can change many of the settings of IE, including how it functions, how it loads pages, which page it loads at startup, security, and so on.

 You can also open this window by going to Tools ➤ Internet Options from within Internet Explorer.

FIGURE 16.78 Internet Properties Window

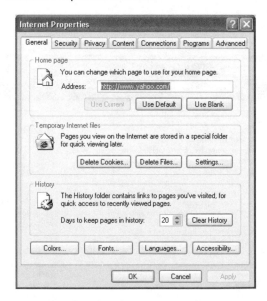

The tab that concerns us most for this discussion is the Security tab. From this tab (Figure 16.79), you can view the security settings for IE as well as change them. IE divides network security into four different security zones. Each zone is one group of sites that IE accesses; security is controlled separately for each zone:

Trusted Sites   Websites you put into this domain are those that you completely trust. Therefore, you can set the security settings lower for this domain. You can add sites to the trusted list by clicking the Sites button and entering the URLs for the trusted sites.

Restricted Sites   This zone defines a security area for all those sites that could potentially damage your computer or install malicious code onto your computer. You must add sites to the restricted site list manually by clicking the Sites button and specifying the URLs.

Local Intranet   This zone contains any websites you access using UNC names (such as \\server) or website URLs without dots (such as http://server).

Internet   This zone contain all sites that don't fit into any of the other zones.

FIGURE 16.79   Security tab of the Internet Properties window

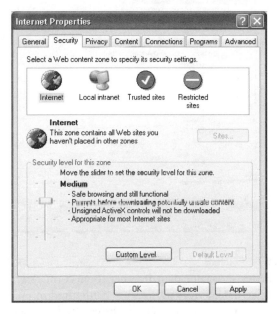

Click on the zone title to view the security settings for that zone. There are four default security levels (they are the same for each zone):

- High
- Medium
- Medium-Low
- Low

You'll notice a vertical slider that indicates the security level. To change the security settings on a zone, click on the zone you wish to change, and then move the slider up or down to raise or lower the protective measures and thus the security level.

There may be cases where the default security levels don't exactly fit your needs. It is possible to change individual security settings, such as enabling or disabling script support for a particular set of default security settings. To do that, set the default security level for the zone as close as possible to the security settings you want, and then click the Custom Level button. You will see a window like the one in Figure 16.80. From this window, you can scroll up and down and enable, disable, or have Windows prompt your for each security setting. For example, to disable ActiveX script support, scroll down until you see the Run ActiveX controls and plug-ins. Click the Disable radio button and click OK. When you are finished setting custom security settings, click OK to close the Internet Options control panel applet.

FIGURE 16.80   Setting custom security settings

CONFIGURING PROXY SETTINGS

Many networks use a proxy server for their Internet connection. A *proxy server* sits between a network and the Internet. Client workstations are configured to use the proxy server. The proxy server makes Internet requests on behalf of the client. Then, when the response comes back, the proxy server keeps a copy of the data stored on its own hard disks. The next time any-one makes a request for the same website, the data is retrieved from the proxy server, instead of from the Internet connection. A proxy server can greatly increase the perceived speed of an Internet connection, especially if users on a network all go to similar websites.

To configure IE to use a proxy server, you must first open the Internet Options control panel applet (Tools ➢ Internet Options) from within IE. Then, click on the Connections tab (Figure 16.81).

On the Connections tab, click LAN Settings to open the LAN Settings window (Figure 16.82). At the bottom of this window you will see the Proxy Server configuration section. In this section, you can configure the various parameters that control how this client uses (or doesn't use) a proxy server. To enable the use of a proxy server, check the Use A Proxy Server... check box and type in the TCP/IP or DNS address of the proxy server and the port address on which it operates. These addresses can be obtained from your network administrator.

FIGURE   16.81   Connections tab in the Internet Properties window

FIGURE   16.82   LAN Settings window

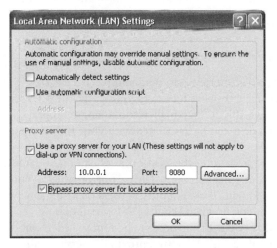

Your network administrator may also require you to configure a client with the bypass proxy server for local addresses. That means any requests for web servers on your same network are not sent first to the proxy server to save time (and to prevent DNS resolution problems). To add this option, click Bypass Proxy Server For Local Addresses check box.

When you're finished configuring proxy server options, click OK to close the LAN Settings window, and then click OK to close the Internet Properties window and save the settings.

In addition to a browser, you probably need to use at least two other critical Internet functions: FTP and e-mail. Both are supported natively in Windows 9*x*/2000.

FTP

The File Transfer Protocol is available to you either through the command-line FTP client or through your browser. To access the Microsoft FTP site through the command prompt, open a prompt and type **FTP ftp.microsoft.com**. The site will respond with a request for your e-mail address, and you will then be given access. You can use standard DOS navigation commands to move between directories, and you can retrieve and send files using the GET <*filename*> and PUT <*filename*> commands, respectively. When you are finished with your session, type **QUIT**.

IE also supports FTP. If you type in **http://www.microsoft.com**, you are taken to a web page. If you change the first part of the name to ftp://, though, the system knows to look for an FTP resource instead. Typing **ftp://ftp.microsoft.com** also takes you to the Microsoft website, and you can then use all of the standard Explorer GUI file-management techniques, just as you would if you were connecting to any other network drive.

Because Microsoft's FTP site is a public site, it allows you to use a special anonymous account that provides access. If you go to a site where that account has been disabled, you must provide another username and password, which should be provided by the site's administrator, or you will not be allowed into the site. In addition, most FTP sites only allow visitors to download data, so PUT commands generally are rejected unless you have a real (nonanonymous) account on the server.

E-Mail

Another common use of the Internet is to send and receive electronic mail. E-mail allows you to quickly and inexpensively transfer messages to other people. To send and receive e-mail, you need to have only two things: an e-mail account and an e-mail client. The account can be provided by a company, or it can be associated with your ISP account. Either way, you will have an address that looks like username@domain.com.

The last part of this address (after the @) identifies the domain name of the company or ISP that provides you with your e-mail account. The part before the @ is your username. A username must be unique on each domain. Two Bill the Cat users on a single network, for instance, might be billthecat@domain.com and billthecat1@domain.com.

As with other TCP/IP services, e-mail needs to be configured. (Nothing in TCP/IP networking ever just works by itself, it seems.) Windows provides a service called *Messaging Application Programming Interface (MAPI)* to make configuring e-mail easier; overall, configuring e-mail is relatively straightforward.

Your MAPI settings can be defined in Control Panel's Mail applet. Figure 16.83 shows just a few of the many Internet e-mail settings you can define. Among these are the *Post Office*

Protocol v3 (POP3) and *Simple Mail Transport Protocol (SMTP)* server settings, which an administrator will give you. A POP3 server is a machine on the Internet that accepts and stores Internet e-mail and allows you to retrieve that mail when you are online. An SMTP server accepts mail you want to send and forwards it to the proper user. In order to send and receive mail, you need both.

If you are using Windows XP and you have your Control Panel view set to Category View, you won't see the Mail applet (as well as several others). Simply click the Switch to Classic View option in the task pane on the left to switch to Classic view so you can see the Mail applet.

FIGURE 16.83   Internet e-mail properties

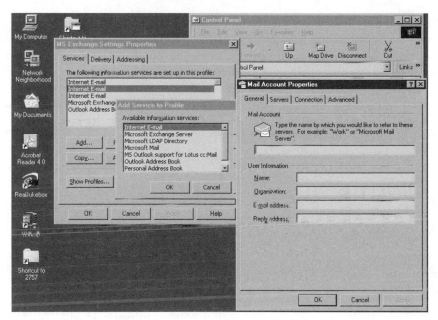

Once you have configured the settings, you need to install an e-mail client or use the built-in client included with Windows 98/NT/2000/XP. That client is called Outlook Express, and it's a good basic e-mail application.

Monitoring and Disconnecting from the Internet

To see information (such as speed and quantity) about the data you have transferred during your Internet session, you can double-click the connection icon in the System Tray (lower-right portion of the screen) to bring up a status window. In this window, you can see the number of bytes sent and received, and you can disconnect from the Internet. You can also disconnect by right-clicking the connection icon and choosing Disconnect.

Summary

At one time, computer repair technicians and computer network engineers had distinctly different job descriptions, and techs rarely needed to deal with network issues. As documents have become larger, and networking and the Internet have become more basic parts of both home and office computer use, understanding networking is no longer an optional part of a computer technician's job description. Whether you need to access drivers on the Internet or set up a client's machine to share files on the network, PC techs now need to learn about networking.

In this chapter, we looked at a number of the basic issues you may come across, including how to set up a Windows machine to use a particular protocol and client software. We also looked at how a Windows client can access file or print resources on the network and how a Windows 9x/2000 machine can be configured to provide file or print services to other machines on the network.

Last, we looked at the special case of the TCP/IP protocol, and the Internet, because configuring TCP/IP and installing and using Internet applications are crucial tasks for both network and Internet configurations.

Key Terms

Before you take the exam, be certain you are familiar with the following terms:

browser	host
client software	host name
default gateway	Hypertext Transfer Protocol (HTTP)
domain	Internet
Domain Name System (DNS)	Internet Service Provider (ISP)
Dynamic Host Configuration Protocol (DHCP)	internetwork
e-mail	IP address
file sharing	IPCONFIG
File Transfer Protocol (FTP)	local resources

Logon

Messaging Application Programming
Interface (MAPI)

network

network adapter

peer-to-peer networking

PING

Post Office Protocol v3 (POP3)

protocol

server

share name

Simple Mail Transport Protocol (SMTP)

subnet mask

TCP/IP

Tracert

Windows Internet Name Service (WINS)

WINIPCFG

World Wide Web (WWW)

Review Questions

1. Using a Windows workstation, which of the following components do you need to connect to a Microsoft network server? (Select all that apply.)

   A. Protocol

   B. Client

   C. Adapter

   D. Sharing

2. Which of the following can be used to automatically assign an IP address to a Windows XP workstation?

   A. APIPA

   B. DNS

   C. DHCP

   D. WINS

3. Transmission Control Protocol/Internet Protocol (TCP/IP) is a collection of protocols that help manage Internet communication. Each computer running TCP/IP must have a unique IP address assigned to it. Which of the following statements best describes an IP address?

   A. An IP address is no more than your dial-up telephone number.

   B. An IP address is a set of four numbers, each of which must be in the range from 0 to 255. These numbers can be automatically provided or assigned by a system administrator.

   C. An IP address is a set of three numbers, each of which must be in the range from 0 to 255. An IP address is a unique name that identifies the computer within a network. This name can be automatically provided or assigned by a system administrator.

   D. IP addresses are composed of four numbers, each of which is between 1 and 256. These numbers can be automatically provided or assigned by a system administrator.

4. You've enabled file and printer sharing on your Windows 9x system. You must now specify how security will be handled. What are your options? (Select all that apply.)

   A. Share-Level Access Control

   B. System-Wide Access Control

   C. Remote-Access Control

   D. User-Level Access Control

5. TCP/IP is installed on each PC within a network. You can communicate within the network but are unable to access the Internet. Which of the following TCP/IP settings must be properly configured for Internet access? (Select all that apply.)

    A. IP address

    B. Subnet mask

    C. Default gateway

    D. DNS server

6. A Windows 9x workstation includes default support for which of the following network types? (Select all that apply.)

    A. Microsoft's Windows Networking

    B. Sun's Solaris

    C. Novell's NetWare

    D. Apple's Macintosh Networking

7. You've installed an older NIC in a Windows 9x system. During the Plug-and-Play (PnP) process, you encounter a conflict. Which of the following methods would you use to resolve the conflict?

    A. Disable PnP on the NIC either with a jumper or with the software setup program.

    B. Run PnP again. The conflict should be resolved the second time around.

    C. Older NICs are prone to this problem. Remove the older NIC and buy a new one.

    D. None of the above.

8. Configuring a Windows 2000 system as a network client requires three elements: a client, an adapter, and _____.

    A. A host name

    B. An IP address

    C. A protocol

    D. A gateway

9. You've set up a network whereby each computer acts as a client and a server and in which each user shares each other's resources, including printers. What is the correct term for such an arrangement?

    A. Enterprise Services

    B. Sharing & Caring

    C. Server-client linking

    D. Peer-to-peer networking

10. In a Windows 9x system, which of the following statements involving NetBEUI and NetBIOS is true?

A. NetBEUI is a name resolution system, whereas NetBIOS is a transport protocol.

B. NetBEUI and NetBIOS are subprotocols of TCP/IP.

C. NetBEUI is a transport protocol, and NetBIOS is a name resolution system.

D. NetBEUI and NetBIOS are not used within a Windows 9x system.

11. Sending and receiving electronic mail (e-mail) is a common benefit of the Internet. Assuming a user has access to the Internet on a properly configured PC, which of the following items are required before a user can begin using e-mail?

A. An e-mail account and a domain

B. An e-mail account and an e-mail client

C. An e-mail account and e-mail permissions

D. None of the above

12. You can map a network drive in Windows using which of the following commands?

A. Map Network Drive

B. Connect to Network Share

C. Connect Network Share

D. Map Network Share

13. You've been granted the right to use a shared folder and printer in a Windows 9x system. What do you need to do to gain access to them?

A. From the Desktop, double-click the Network icon. Click the Shared Resources tab. Any resources you have access to are listed.

B. Double-click the My Computer icon on your Desktop. Click Web Folders. Your shared resources are listed.

C. From the Desktop, double-click the Network Neighborhood icon, which allows you to browse for shared resources.

D. Open Control Panel and click on the Network Neighborhood icon. Browse for shared resources.

14. Computers communicate using IP addresses. The address can be a series of numbers or a host name such as Bob's PC. Obviously, it is easier for humans to remember the host name, but computers communicate with numbers. Which of the following methods help locate a computer's numeric IP address when a human searches for it using only the host name? (Select all that apply.)

A. NRP (Name Resolution Protocol)

B. WINS (Windows Internet Name Service)

C. DNS (Domain Name System)

D. None of the above

15. Which of the following types of networking components can be added in the Network program on a Windows 9*x* system? (Select all that apply.)

  A. Protocol

  B. Adapter

  C. Client

  D. Service

16. Which of the following is the correct way to use the protocol utility IPCONFIG in a Windows 2000 environment?

  A. IPCONFIG does not work with Windows 2000.

  B. Choose Start ➢ Run and type **IPCONFIG**.

  C. Open a browser window and type **IPCONFIG** in the address line.

  D. Choose Start ➢ Run, type **CMD**, and press Enter. At the command prompt, type **IPCONFIG**.

17. What would you need to do to create a new Dial-Up Networking (DUN) connection within a Windows 9*x* system?

  A. Open Control Panel and click the Dial-Up Networking icon. Click Make New Connection. Choose a name for your connection. Select which modem you are using. Enter the dial-in telephone number. Click the Finish button.

  B. Choose Start ➢ Programs ➢ Accessories ➢ Choose Dial-Up Networking. Doing so opens a window that shows all current DUN connections. Double-click Make New Connection. Choose a name for your connection. Select which modem you are using. Enter the dial-in telephone number. Click the Finish button.

  C. Open Control Panel and click the Make New Connection icon. Choose a name for your connection. Select which modem you are using. Enter the dial-in telephone number. Click the Finish button.

  D. None of the above.

18. Which of the following TCP/IP protocols is used to send mail on the Internet?

  A. HTTP

  B. SMTP

  C. POP3

  D. FTP

19. In a Windows *9x* environment, if you don't know the name of the computer that is acting as the host for a resource you are looking for, you can use the _____ command.

   A. Map

   B. Run

   C. Find

   D. Search

20. You have just granted someone share-level access to a folder in your Windows *9x* system. Which access rights are available? (Select all that apply.)

   A. Full Access

   B. Depends on Password

   C. Depends on IP Address

   D. Read-Only

Answers to Review Questions

1. **A, B, C.** Three initial components—adapter, client, and protocol—are required to connect to a Microsoft network server.

2. **A, C.** DHCP and APIPA are used to assign IP addresses automatically to workstations.

3. **B.** Every computer running TCP/IP must have a unique IP address; that address is in the format *x.x.x.x*, where *x* is a number from 0 to 255. These numbers can be automatically provided or assigned by a system administrator. The machine also has a host name, which identifies the machine on the network.

4. **A, D.** There are two security options in a Windows *9x* system. Share-level access control involves supplying a username, password, and security setting for each shared resource. User-level access control means Windows *9x* uses a central database of users to specify security settings for each shared resource.

5. **A, B, C, D.** A proper IP address and subnet mask are essential for any sort of network communication. However, to reach the Internet, a default gateway, which is the IP address of the router your machine uses to access the Internet, must be configured. You also need the Domain Name System (DNS) server, so you can type **www.yahoo.com** instead of having to remember the numeric IP address.

6. **A, C.** Within a Windows *9x* workstation, clients are provided for both Microsoft and Novell networks.

7. **A.** Conflicts between older NICs and the Plug-and-Play installation process can occur. However, as indicated in option A, if PnP is disabled either with a jumper or with the software program, the device can be successfully installed.

8. **C.** Windows requires three elements: a client, an adapter, and a protocol. The way each element is configured is slightly different between the two OSs, however. Host names, IP addresses, and gateways may also be necessary, but only if the chosen protocol is TCP/IP.

9. **D.** Networking in which users share each other's resources is called peer-to-peer networking.

10. **C.** NetBEUI is a transport protocol, managing data transmission between two computers. NetBIOS is a name resolution system, allowing a computer to search for another computer on a network by its Microsoft computer name.

11. **B.** To send and receive e-mail, all that are required are an e-mail account and an e-mail client.

12. **A.** This is one of those technicality questions, but knowing proper terminology is important when taking technical exams. Questions like this crop up regularly.

13. **C.** The Network Neighborhood icon, located on the Desktop, provides easy access to any shared resources. Network Neighborhood is not accessible from Control Panel or from My Computer.

14. B, C.   Although a number of services are available for resolving names, the most common are WINS and DNS. WINS resolves NetBIOS computer names to the appropriate IP address, and DNS does the same for host names.

15. A, B, C, D.   There are four basic types of networking components in a Windows *9x* system. They are protocol, adapter, client, and service.

16. D.   The IPCONFIG protocol utility is a good way to find basic information about your TCP/IP configuration. It can be used at the command prompt. If you type **IPCONFIG /A**, the system displays additional information.

17. B.   You can create a new DUN connection as indicated in option B. The Dial-Up Networking icon can also be accessed by double-clicking My Computer from the Desktop.

18. B.   The only protocol listed that is used to send mail on the internet is SMTP. POP3 is used to download mail, but never to send it. The other protocols are not mail protocols at all.

19. C.   The Find command can be used to search your machine for files or the network for other machines. Search is used on Windows 2000 to do the same tasks.

20. A, B, D.   Read-Only, Full Access, and Depends on Password are the three options for access rights. These options are accessible by right-clicking the shared folder and choosing Sharing.

Chapter

17

Windows Optimization

THE FOLLOWING OBJECTIVE IS COVERED IN THIS CHAPTER:

✓ 2.5 Identify procedures necessary to optimize the operating system and major operating system subsystems.

Anyone who's run a Windows computer for any length of time has experienced it: Your computer runs faster than anything when you first get it, but after a while, it seems to slow down. It gets slower and slower until it's almost unusable. This particular problem is partially a result of poor Windows optimization. Windows *optimization* is the process of making Windows run at its best with a given hardware platform.

You can perform several tasks to make your system run better. The most common tasks that will affect performance significantly include:

- Managing virtual memory
- Defragmenting disks
- Using files and buffers
- Using caches
- Managing temporary files

In this chapter, you will learn how to use these common tasks to optimize Windows performance.

Managing Virtual Memory

Let's face it. Windows is a resource hog. The more hardware a computer has (memory, hard disk space, and so on), the more resources Windows will use. You can never have enough memory. Toward that end, Microsoft developed for Windows its own virtual memory technology. *Virtual memory* is the general term for a type of computer technology where hard disk space is used as a kind of backup memory.

The *swap file* is used to provide virtual memory to the Windows system. The swap file is hard drive space where idle pieces of programs are placed, while active parts of programs are kept in or swapped into main memory. The programs running in Windows believe that their information is still in RAM, but Windows has moved it into near-line storage on the hard drive. When the application needs the information again, the data is swapped back into RAM so it can be used by the processor.

Throughout this section, you will see the terms swap file, page file, and paging file. They are all synonyms.

When you are working in your office and need a document, you may have to walk over to a file cabinet to get it. You then return to your seat and read the document. When you have finished and are ready to go on with another task, you put down the current document. If you don't need it again in the near future, you should get up and put it back in the file cabinet. If you will need it again, though, you may just set it on your desk for easier access. When you need it again, you have to pick it back up (unless you can remember what it said without looking). Generally, you can think of a computer's disk drive as the file cabinet and virtual memory as the desk.

Real memory (RAM) is the computer's memory. The more RAM you put into the machine, the more things it is able to remember without looking anything up. The larger the swap file, the fewer times the computer has to do intensive drive searches.

The moral of the story: As with most things virtual, a swap file is not nearly as good as actual RAM, but it is better than nothing!

In this section, you will learn how the different versions of Windows handle virtual memory and how it can be used to optimize system performance.

Operating systems besides Windows use virtual memory in one form or another. Unix, Linux and Macintosh OSs all use some kind of virtual memory (although they may call it something different).

Virtual Memory in Windows 9*x*

As shown Figure 17.1, the default behavior for virtual memory is that Windows 9*x* handles it for you. This is a good thing, and unless you have a particular need to modify the file, you are best served by letting the computer handle it. If a particular application does require extensive virtual memory, you can modify it easily, though. To find the Virtual Memory button, choose Start ➢ Settings ➢ Control Panel. Double-click the System icon and select the Performance tab. The Virtual Memory button is along the bottom of the window.

Locate the swap file on a drive with plenty of empty space. As a general rule, try to keep 20 percent of your drive space free for the overhead of various elements of the operating system, like the swap file.

If you want to change the swap file, click the Let Me Specify My Own Virtual Memory Settings radio button. You can then enter values for the drive on which you would like the swap file to reside, as well as the minimum and maximum sizes for the swap file. The minimum size should be at least as much RAM as you currently have in the system. Windows will automatically increase the size as it needs to. If you change the swap file, Windows 98 requires that you reboot afterward.

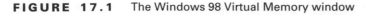

FIGURE 17.1   The Windows 98 Virtual Memory window

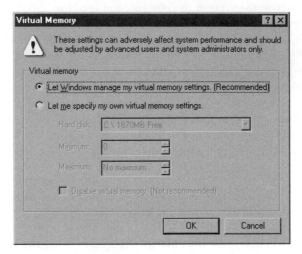

WARNING   As mentioned in Chapter 12, do not set the swap file to an extremely small size. Another general rule is that the minimum swap file size should be at least as big as the amount of RAM in the machine (ideally 2.5 to 3 times as much). If you make the swap file too small, the system can become unbootable, or at least unstable.

Virtual Memory in Windows NT

The procedure for managing virtual memory on Windows NT is almost the same as for Windows 9x, although, generally speaking, you will have more flexibility with Windows NT. In addition, you should try to keep your swap file at least three times as big as the amount of memory present in your system.

To manage the virtual memory settings, open the System control panel (found in Start ➢ Settings ➢ Control Panel, as with Windows 9x) and click the Performance Tab (Figure 17.2). There, you can view the current size of the *paging file* (what Windows NT calls the swap file). During installation, Windows NT will modify the virtual memory settings to give an adequate level of performance; however, these settings are a bit conservative.

TIP   You can also access the System control panel by right-clicking on My Computer and choosing Properties.

To change the virtual memory settings, click the Change button to bring up the Virtual Memory settings window (Figure 17.3). Under the section labeled Paging File Size For Selected Drive, you can view and change some settings of the swap file. To increase the size of the swap file (and thus increase your swap-file performance), you must increase the Initial Size value to at least three times the amount of memory installed in your computer (for example, if your system has 128MB of RAM, you should make your swap file's initial size at least 384MB). The maximum size should be a value approximately twice that.

FIGURE 17.2   Performance tab of the System control panel

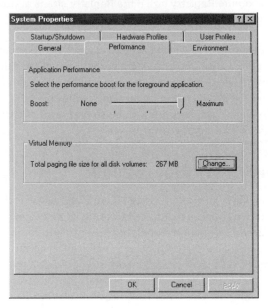

FIGURE 17.3   Changing virtual memory settings in Windows NT

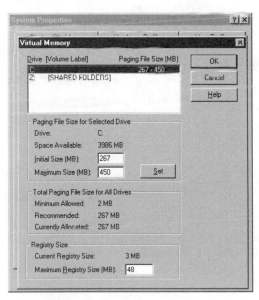

> While you are in this screen, you may want to ensure that your Registry file has enough space to work with. As you can see in Figure 17.3, this machine has a way to go before it fills the Registry. However, on systems that have been running for a while, the Registry file may become fairly large. Feel free to adjust the maximum Registry size if the Registry size is approaching the maximum allowed by this setting.

Once you change the minimum and maximum sizes, click Set to set the changes, click OK to accept them, and then click Close on the System control panel. Windows NT will ask you to reboot, because it has to delete and re-create the file, and it can't do that while Windows NT is running. Click Yes to reboot the system and complete the change.

You may have to change the numbers a few times to find settings that work for your system. This will be something of a trial-and-error process.

Virtual Memory in Windows 2000

The virtual memory settings in Windows 2000 (see Figure 17.4), as with other versions of Windows, tell you how much hard-drive space is allocated to the system as a swap file. Windows 2000 recommends a particular virtual-memory level, but you can add to or subtract from this value as necessary. Often, certain applications (SQL Server, for instance) need you to raise Windows 2000 Professional's virtual-memory limit in order to work properly. Graphics and CAD applications also require you to raise the virtual-memory level, but if this is the case, the setup instructions for the application will generally tell you what modifications need to be made.

FIGURE 17.4   The Virtual Memory window in Windows 2000

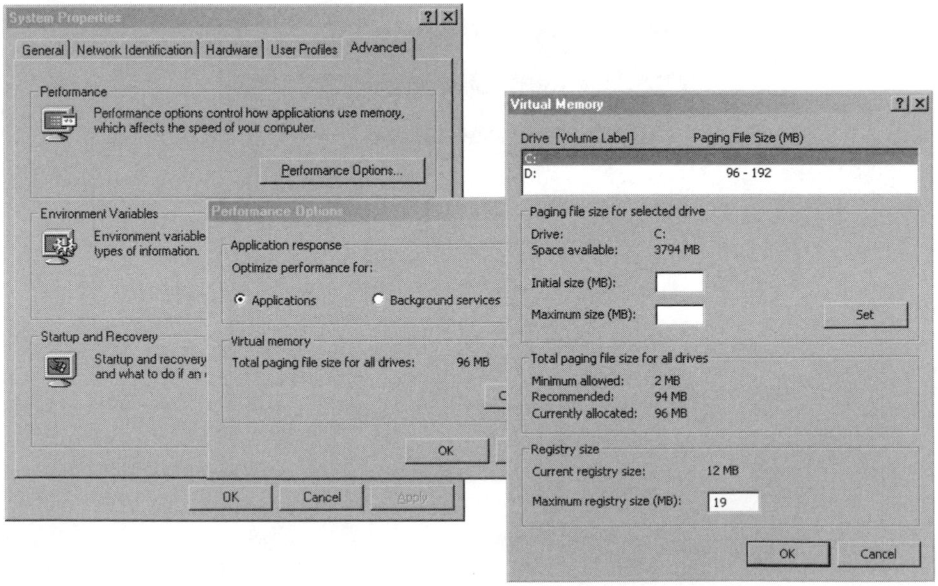

WARNING Adding to the swap-file size is not always helpful and can sometimes slow down the system. Modify this setting only if you have been instructed to or if you are testing to see whether the change speeds up or slows down the computer. Reducing the page-file size is generally not recommended and can have serious consequences on performance.

As you can see in Figure 17.4, to change the virtual memory settings under Windows 2000, the process is almost identical to earlier versions of Windows. The major difference is the location of the virtual memory settings. To access them, open the System control panel as with the other versions of Windows, click the Advanced tab, and then click the Performance Options button. Doing so will bring up the Performance Options window, where you can view the current virtual memory settings.

To change the size of the paging file, you must be logged on as Administrator. To begin, click Change under the size of the current page file. Doing so will bring up a window almost identical to the Windows NT virtual memory settings window (as shown earlier in Figure 17.3). This window works the same as the one in Windows NT: Type in values for the maximum and minimum sizes of the page file (Microsoft recommends a value at least 1.5 times the amount of RAM as in your system), click Set, and then click OK.

NOTE If you reduce the minimum or maximum size of the page file, you will have to reboot your computer. However, unlike in Windows NT, in Windows 2000 increases don't require a restart.

TIP If you need to delete a paging file, set both the minimum and maximum sizes to zero.

Virtual Memory in Windows XP

Setting the swap-file size and location in Windows XP is almost identical to the process in Windows 2000. The major differences are how you get to the controls and what the screen looks like.

As in Windows 2000, you must be logged on as an administrator. However, the screen that allows you to change your virtual memory settings is a bit more buried. To begin, open the System control panel, as shown in Figure 17.5. Click the Advanced tab. On this tab, click the button labeled Settings in the Performance section to access the Performance Options window. Click the Advanced tab.

On this tab are various performance-tuning options. At the bottom of the displayed tab are the virtual memory settings (Figure 17.6). This area tells you the total paging-file size for all drives. If you have multiple swap files on multiple drives, the number listed tells the total size for all swap files.

FIGURE 17.5 Windows XP System control panel

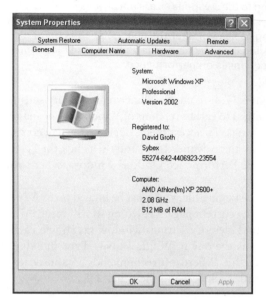

FIGURE 17.6 Advanced performance settings

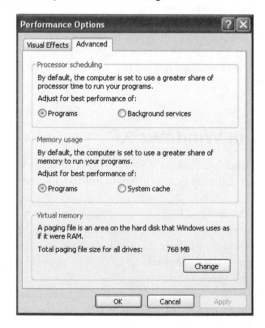

To change the size of your swap files, click the Change button to open the screen in Figure 17.7. In the Drive [Volume Label] section, select the drive that contains the swap file you want to change. Then, in the paging section, change the minimum and maximum numbers as in Windows 2000. Click Set to make the changes, and click OK in each open window. Windows may ask you to reboot to complete the changes, but (as in Windows 2000) only if you've reduced the swap-file size.

To let Windows manage the swap-file size (as in Windows 98), choose the System Managed Size option on the screen shown in Figure 17.7.

FIGURE 17.7 Changing the Windows XP paging-file size

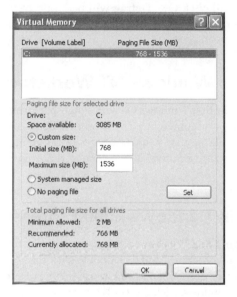

Defragmenting Disks

When Windows is installed on a new disk, all the full clusters are contiguous. That is, they are located one after another rotationally on the disk. However, as files and programs are installed and deleted, the blocks of disk space get less and less contiguous. This can hinder Windows' performance, because it has to constantly go looking for more sections of different files. You've probably seen a symptom of a fragmented disk: the hard-drive light flickers madly, and the system seems slow as a snail when switching programs, starting a new program, or opening a file. This symptom is known as *disk thrashing*.

To solve this problem, Microsoft includes a utility with Windows for reorganizing, or *defragmenting*, the hard disk. With earlier versions of Windows, this was a separate utility you ran to defragment your disk; in later versions, it is integrated into the operating system.

Defragmenting in Windows 9*x*

In Windows 9*x*, the defragmenting utility is known as DEFRAG.EXE. You can access this program from the properties of the disk drive you want to defragment (it's found on the same option page as SCANDISK). You can also run it by using the Start ➤ Run command and typing in **DEFRAG**, or by going to Start ➤ Programs ➤ Accessories ➤ System Tools ➤ Disk Defragmenter.

The utility asks you which disk you want to defragment. Choose the appropriate disk from the drop-down list and click OK. Defrag will begin defragmenting the drive. This process may take several minutes or several hours, depending on how badly the drive is fragmented.

Defragmenting in Windows NT Workstation

Because Windows NT was the first Windows OS with a high-performance file system (specifically, NTFS), Windows NT does not come with a version of Microsoft Defrag. However, many third-party utilities are available that you can use to defragment a Windows NT hard disk. Symantec (http://www.symantec.com) is one vendor that provides such a utility (namely Speed Disk).

Defragmenting in Windows 2000 Professional

The procedure for defragmenting Windows 2000 is very similar to that in Windows 98. To begin defragmenting, close all programs, and then double-click the My Computer icon. Right-click on the hard disk you want to defragment and choose Properties to bring up the Local Disk Properties window. In this Windows, click the Tools tab (shown in Figure 17.8), and then click the Defragment Now button to start the defragmentation program.

NOTE   You can also start the program by going to Start ➤ Programs ➤ Accessories ➤ System Tools ➤ Disk Defragmenter.

Once you have started the Disk Defragmenter, you can do one of two things: analyze a disk to see whether it needs defragmentation (by clicking the Analyze button) or go ahead with the defragmentation (by clicking the Defragment button). If you click the Defragment button to begin the defragmentation, Disk Defragmenter will analyze the disk to get a map of where files are stored, and then rearrange them into contiguous disk space. This process will take some time, and it may be best to start it in the evening before you go to bed. Figure 17.9 shows what the defragmentation process looks like while it's proceeding.

FIGURE 17.8   Disk Properties window

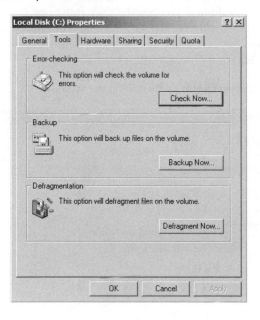

FIGURE 17.9   Defragmenting a disk using the Windows 2000 Disk Defragmenter

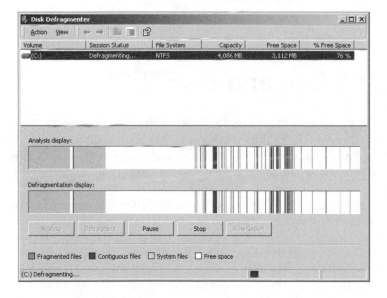

Defragmenting in Windows XP Professional

As in other operations that modify key parts of the Windows installation or hardware (especially disk drives), you must be logged in as an administrator in order to perform a defragmentation on Windows XP. However, the process for starting the Disk Defragmenter is exactly the same as in previous versions of Windows. To open the Disk Defragmenter, go to Properties in My Computer on any drive you want to defragment, click the Tools tab, and then click Defragment Now. As with Windows 2000, click Defragment to begin the process. Figure 17.10 shows an example of the defragmentation process in Windows XP.

FIGURE 17.10   Defragmenting a disk using the Windows XP Disk Defragmenter

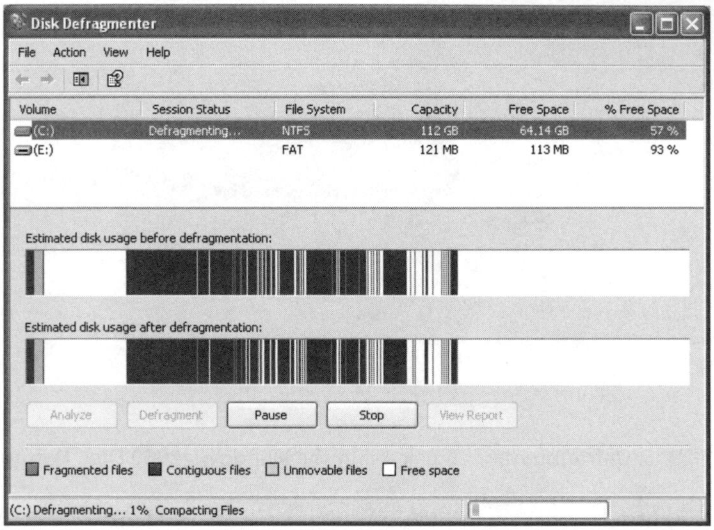

Using *FILES=* and *BUFFERS=*

At startup, MS-DOS uses the FILES= and BUFFERS= settings in the CONFIG.SYS configuration file to specify how many file handles and memory buffers should be allocated during that session of DOS. For the most part, this optimization setting doesn't directly affect the performance of most versions of Windows. It does, however, affect the command-line performance for backward compatibility with MS-DOS applications.

The FILES command describes how many *file handles* DOS can keep track of simultaneously. A file handle is simply another name for an open file. If DOS discovers that a program exceeds this limit as it tries to open a file, DOS responds by saying that too many files are open. In light of that, it would seem logical to assign FILES the highest value the system will allow (255), but the memory available to the system is reduced slightly when this number is increased. Setting FILES to 30 is typical. Documentation that comes with programs often specifies the minimum FILES setting.

The syntax for the FILES command is as follows:

FILES=*n*

Here is an example of the FILES command:

FILES=30

Not unlike the FILES command, the BUFFERS command determines the number of buffers DOS creates, so that it can store disk information in RAM rather than on disk. This lessens the need to constantly access the hard drive, reduces the number of reads and writes, and speeds up the computer's overall operation. As with the FILES command, the higher this value is set, the more memory it will use. Setting BUFFERS to 50 is typical on a hard drive of 120MB or more.

The BUFFERS value should be reduced on systems running a disk-caching program such as SMARTDRV. In this case, you should set BUFFERS to a lower number, such as 15. Windows 3.*x* automatically installs SMARTDRV in the AUTOEXEC.BAT file, so a Windows computer should have BUFFERS set to a low value.

The syntax for the BUFFERS command is

BUFFERS=*n*

where *n* is the number of buffers you want to set. An example of this command in use is as follows:

BUFFERS=50

The different versions of Windows handle these settings differently. Let's take a quick look at how to configure these settings for backward compatibility with DOS programs.

FILES= and BUFFERS= in Windows 9*x*

The most common use of the FILES= and BUFFERS= settings is in Windows 9*x*. Windows 9*x* uses a file called IO.SYS for the functions formerly performed by CONFIG.SYS under MS-DOS. However, some applications will not run under Windows 9*x* if they don't see CONFIG.SYS and certain parameters in it.

The CONFIG.SYS file is located at the root of the boot drive (usually C:\). If you need to place an entry for either FILES or BUFFERS into CONFIG.SYS, you can edit it directly using Windows Notepad and insert lines, like so:

FILES=60
BUFFERS=60

 The DOS application you are trying to run under Windows 9*x* should have documentation that indicates what these settings need to be in order for the program to run properly.

Once you've added the lines, save the file and reboot.

FILES= and BUFFERS= in Windows NT/2000/XP

In Windows NT/2000/XP, the CONFIG.SYS file and the FILES and BUFFERS settings play less of a role. With these operating systems, you are essentially starting a small 16-bit MS-DOS session each time you run an old MS-DOS application, so they must still have a way to make these settings available. However, these are just settings for DOS mode (for compatibility purposes), which are not needed for any other purpose.

The CONFIG.SYS file doesn't exist in these OSs. Instead, they use a file called CONFIG.NT. This file is located in C:\WINNT\SYSTEM32 (C:\WINDOWS\SYSTEM32 in the case of Windows XP) and can be edited with Windows Notepad.

Using Disk Caches

A *disk cache* is a small amount of memory that is used to hold data that is frequently accessed from the hard disk. Various utilities and software handle disk caching for the different versions of Windows. The A+ exam tests your knowledge of disk caching as it applies to increasing system performance. If you use disk caching and it is configured properly, you can greatly increase the performance of Windows and, thus, your system.

In this section, you will learn how to configure disk caching for the various versions of Windows.

> It's important to remember that because disk caching uses system RAM to increase performance, any RAM dedicated to the disk cache cannot be used by applications. So, if you adjust the disk cache too far, you may decrease performance, because there isn't enough memory for applications and they must be swapped to virtual memory (which will *really* hurt your system's performance).

Disk Caching in Windows 9*x*

Disk caching in Windows 9*x* is no longer handled by SMARTDRIVE, as it was in earlier versions of Windows. Instead, Windows 9*x* uses a 32-bit caching program called VCACHE, which was originally introduced with Windows 3.11. This protected-mode driver runs more efficiently than its real-mode predecessor, SMARTDRIVE. It uses a more efficient set of rules for predicting the needed hard-drive data. Further, it caches data from the network and from the CD-ROM; thus it is able to speed up the access to data from these devices.

In order to configure the VCACHE program, you must use Notepad and edit the SYSTEM.INI file, which can be found in the C:\WINDOWS directory. Search for the section that starts with [vcache]. Modify the two entries MinFileCache=*n* and MaxFileCache=*n*, replacing *n* with the minimum and maximum sizes (in kilobytes), respectively, for the file cache. If the section or these entries do not exist, add them.

Here are some general guidelines for modifying these parameters:

- If your machine has 16MB of RAM, set Minimum to 1024 (1MB) and Maximum to 4096 (4MB).

- If your machine has 32MB of RAM, set Minimum to 2048 (2MB) and Maximum to 6144 (6MB).

- If your machine has 64MB of RAM, set Minimum to 4096 (4MB) and Maximum to 16384 (16MB).
- If your machine has 128MB of RAM or more, set Minimum to 4096 (4MB) and Maximum to 32768 (32MB).

Disk Caching in Windows NT/2000/XP

Windows NT/2000/XP take care of most of their own disk caching. However, you can modify one disk-cache setting by changing the Large System Cache entry in the Registry. This option, when enabled, takes all memory not being used by applications, the system, or data, and uses it for disk caching. Otherwise, only 4MB of memory is used for disk caching. This option is off by default in Windows NT Workstation, Windows 2000 Professional, and Windows XP Professional (it's on by default in Windows NT Server and Windows 2000 Server).

 You should normally enable this setting only if you have at least 96MB of RAM or more in your computer. Otherwise, you may hamper performance.

You can enable this feature by changing one key:

1. Launch either `Regedit.exe` or `Regdt32.exe`.
2. Navigate to the Registry key `HKey_Local_Machine\System\CurrentControlSet\Control\Session Manager\Memory Management`.
3. Double click on the item labeled `LargeSystemCache`.

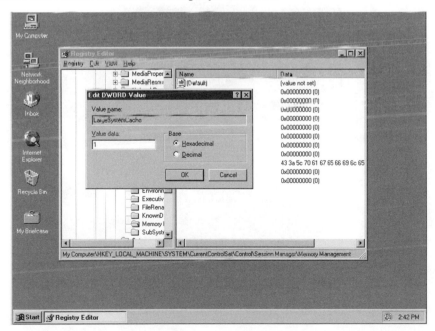

4. The Value Data field should have a 0 in it. Change it to a 1 and click OK.

5. Close Regedit and reboot the computer to enable the settings.

Cached Internet Explorer Files

The other type of disk caching you can tweak to increase your system's performance is the cache of often-visited web pages in Internet Explorer. IE copies to your hard disk any images or HTML files from websites you visit frequently. That way, the next time you visit the website, you don't need to redownload the images for that web page; IE instead gets them from its local disk cache. IE's local disk cache is also known as the *Temporary Internet Files* directory, which is a special directory set up for storing these images and pages.

However, this disk cache can become too large or contain outdated information. Therefore, you can modify some settings to change how this feature works from within IE.

This procedure is for IE 5.*x* and 6.*x* for Windows. Other versions have this feature, but it looks slightly different.

To configure IE's disk cache settings, do the following from within IE:

1. Select Tools ➤ Internet Options to open the Internet Options control panel. (You can also open it by choosing Start ➤ Settings ➤ Control Panel and double-clicking Internet Options.)

2. Click the Settings button in the Temporary Internet Files section. The settings on the window that appears allow you to modify how IE's disk cache works.

By default, IE uses automatic settings. Each time a page is requested, the local page is compared to the page from the web server to determine if a redownload is necessary. If the pages are the same, IE uses the local version. For the most part, this provides the best performance. However, if you are constantly getting older pages, you may want to modify the settings.

3. You can change the size of the disk cache by either moving the slider or modifying the numbers next to the slider. Increasing these numbers or moving the slider to the right increases the amount of disk space used for caching Internet pages.

4. You can also put this disk cache on a different disk, thus reducing the burden on your boot hard disk. Click the Move Folder button, navigate to the drive and directory where you would like the cache to be, and click OK. IE will move the cache to the new location and use it from there.

If you ever need to clear the disk cache (for example, if you always get the same outdated page and you know there is a new version), you can delete all the temporary files. To do so, open the Internet Options control panel and click the Delete Files.

Managing Temporary Files

A *temporary file (temp file)* is just that—temporary. It is designed to store information for a short period of time and then be deleted. Almost every program of any size today uses temp files. There is one problem, however: Often, the temp files remain more permanent. Eventually, they begin taking up considerable disk space.

One thing you can do to improve system performance is to delete any temporary files that exist on your system. Temp files can be found in a variety of locations, including:

`C:\TEMP`

`C:\TMP`

`C:\WINDOWS\TEMP`

`C:\WINDOWS\TMP`

The way to know for sure where they're located is to determine what values the `TEMP` and `TMP` environment variables are set to. An *environment variable* is a setting that stays permanent throughout a Windows or DOS session. It is set by an entry in an INI file, the Registry, or one of the MS-DOS configuration files (`CONFIG.SYS` or `AUTOEXEC.BAT`).

To find out where the temporary files are stored in your machine, start a command-line session (choose Start ➢ Run and type in either **CMD** or **COMMAND**). At the command prompt, type **SET**. This command returns all the environment variables for your system. Look for `TEMP=` or `TMP=` (or both). These variables point to directories on your hard disk; in these locations, you will find the temporary files.

Once you have found the temporary files, use Windows Explorer to delete them. You may need to reboot, and then try to delete the temp files. Otherwise, some of them may be in use, and you won't be able to delete them.

Summary

In this chapter, you learned about the methods used to optimize system performance on the various Windows platforms. We explained some little tricks you can use to bump up speed and efficiency.

You first learned about the methods used to manage virtual memory and swap files on the Windows platforms. You learned that for the most part, Windows manages virtual memory on its own, but sometimes you can tweak by increasing the size of the page file.

You then learned that Windows disks frequently become fragmented, thus causing disk thrashing to occur. We described how to solve this problem using the built-in Disk Defragmenter program that comes with many versions of Windows (except NT).

You also learned about the `FILES=` and `BUFFERS=` settings that are used for backward compatibility with MS-DOS applications. You learned where to put these settings in all versions of Windows.

Finally, you learned about disk caches and how to manage temporary files. We explained how to manage the disk caches not only in Windows, but in Internet Explorer as well. You also learned how to locate the temporary files that Windows uses and how to delete them when they begin causing problems.

Key Terms

Before you take the exam, be certain you are familiar with the following terms:

BUFFERS=	paging file
defragmenting	SMARTDRIVE
disk cache	swap file
disk thrashing	temporary file (temp file)
environment variable	Temporary Internet Files
file handles	VCACHE
FILES=	virtual memory

Review Questions

1. Which version of Windows does *not* come with a disk-defragmentation utility?

   A. 9*x*

   B. NT

   C. 2000

   D. XP

2. If you have 64MB of RAM in your Windows 98 computer, a Pentium II 450MHz processor, and a 20GB hard disk, what should the `MinFileCache=` and `MaxFileCache=` values be set to in the `SYSTEM.INI` for optimum performance of the disk cache?

   A. 1024, 2048

   B. 2048, 8092

   C. 4096, 16384

   D. 16384, 32768

3. The _____ is hard-drive space in which idle pieces of programs are placed, while other active parts of programs are kept in or swapped into main memory.

   A. Swap file

   B. Location file

   C. Temporary file

   D. Program file

4. Where do Windows NT, 2000, and XP keep the disk cache setting?

   A. `WIN.INI`

   B. `SYSTEM.INI`

   C. Registry

   D. `Regedit.exe`

5. What file holds the `FILES=` and `BUFFERS=` settings on Windows 2000 for backward compatibility with MS-DOS applications?

   A. `CONFIG.SYS`

   B. `CONFIG.2k`

   C. `CONFIG.DOS`

   D. `CONFIG.NT`

6. Where is the file that specifies the settings for MS-DOS application backward compatibility in Windows XP? This file can be modified with any text editor, including Windows Notepad.

   A. `C:\WINXP\`

   B. `C:\WINDOWS\SYSTEM32`

   C. `C:\WINNT\SYSTEM32`

   D. `C:\WINDOWS\`

7. How do you start the Disk Defragmenter program in Windows 9*x*?

   A. Start ➤ Settings ➤ Control Panel ➤ Disk Defragmenter

   B. Start ➤ Programs ➤ Accessories ➤ Disk Defragmenter

   C. Start ➤ Programs ➤ Accessories ➤ System Tools ➤ Disk Defragmenter

   D. None of the above

8. How do you start the Disk Defragmenter program in Windows NT?

   A. Start ➤ Settings ➤ Control Panel ➤ Disk Defragmenter

   B. Start ➤ Programs ➤ Accessories ➤ Disk Defragmenter

   C. Start ➤ Programs ➤ Accessories ➤ System Tools ➤ Disk Defragmenter

   D. None of the above

9. How do you start the Disk Defragmenter program in Windows 2000 Professional?

   A. Start ➤ Settings ➤ Control Panel ➤ Disk Defragmenter

   B. Start ➤ Programs ➤ Accessories ➤ Disk Defragmenter

   C. Start ➤ Programs ➤ Accessories ➤ System Tools ➤ Disk Defragmenter.

   D. None of the above

10. The swap file is called a _____ in Windows NT.

   A. Swap file

   B. Paging file

   C. Page file

   D. Swapping file

11. If you have 128MB of RAM in a Windows 98 machine, what is the ideal size for the swap file?

   A. 128MB

   B. 256MB

   C. 384MB

   D. 1024MB

12. Which of the following is *not* a known location for Windows temporary files?

   A. C:\TEMP

   B. C:\WINDOWS\TEMP

   C. C:\TMP

   D. None of the above

13. Which operating systems require a reboot after you increase the swap-file size? (Select all that apply.)

   A. Windows 98

   B. Windows 2000

   C. Windows NT

   D. Windows XP

Answers to Review Questions

1. B.   Windows NT does not come with a version of either DEFRAG or Disk Defragmenter. All other versions of Windows include some kind of disk-defragmentation utility.

2. C.   For best results, if you have 64MB of RAM or greater (up to 128MB), you should set MinFileCache to 4096 and MaxFileCache to 16384.

3. A.   A swap file is a file used for virtual memory. It is where the information that was swapped from main memory resides on the hard disk.

4. C.   The settings for LargeSystemCache are located in the Windows Registry.

5. D.   The CONFIG.NT file is executed for all command-line environments for backward compatibility with older MS-DOS programs.

6. B.   For Windows XP, the CONFIG.NT file is located in C:\WINDOWS\SYSTEM32.

7. C.   The proper sequence for Windows 9x is Start ➢ Programs ➢ Accessories ➢ System Tools ➢ Disk Defragmenter.

8. D.   Windows NT does not include a Disk Defragmenter.

9. C.   Windows 2000 Professional puts the program in the same place as Windows 9x.

10. B.   In most screens and utilities, Microsoft refers to the swap file as a paging file in Windows NT.

11. C.   An ideal swap-file size under Windows 98 is three times the amount of physical RAM. $3 \times 128 = 384MB$.

12. D.   All of the listed options are known to be places where Windows temporary files are located.

13. A, C.   Windows 2000 and XP only require a reboot when you decrease the size of a swap file.

Chapter

18

Windows Diagnostics and Troubleshooting

THE FOLLOWING OBJECTIVES ARE COVERED IN THIS CHAPTER:

✓ 3.1 Recognize and interpret the meaning of common error codes and startup messages from the boot sequence, and identify steps to correct the problems.

✓ 3.2 Recognize when to use common diagnostic utilities and tools. Given a diagnostic scenario involving one of these utilities or tools, select the appropriate steps needed to resolve the problem.

✓ 3.3 Recognize common operational and usability problems and determine how to resolve them.

Troubleshooting involves asking a lot of questions of yourself and of other people. Beginners (and yes, I was a beginner once upon a time) like the trial-and-error method of fixing things, but in the long run, a methodological approach works better. The reason beginners often choose trial and error is that they don't yet have a good enough background to analyze problems.

NOTE *Analysis* is the act of breaking down a structure or system into its component parts and their relationships.

More than occasionally, a technician will unwittingly create new problems in an attempt to fix a real problem. For example, if a program will not run and displays an *Out of Memory* error, it might seem logical to add more memory.

But certain types of memory currently on the market will not work in older 486 computers—what happens if the memory the technician installs is the wrong type for the computer? Now there are two problems.

And what if the computer with the mismatched memory actually starts up, but eventually locks up because of the memory problem? The lockups could create an interruption in writing information to the hard drive, and a program could become corrupted. That would make three problems total.

Once the technician has sorted out all the problems, it's time to repair whatever went wrong. In this example, it is quite likely that the source of the original *Out of Memory* error was corrupted program code. Many times, a Windows program with damage to one or more components will cause that error to be displayed.

In this chapter, we'll go over the steps to methodically go about troubleshooting Windows and other applications.

Troubleshooting Steps

In a computer system, you need to consider at least four main parts, each of which is in turn made up of many pieces:

1. A *collection of hardware pieces* integrated into a working system. As you know, the hardware can be quite complex, what with motherboards, hard drives, video cards, and so on. Software can be equally perplexing.

2. An *operating system*, which in turn is dependent on the hardware. Remember that the DOS and Windows operating systems have kernels, internal commands, and external commands, which may interact with the hardware in different ways.

3. An *application* or software program that is supposed to do something. Programs such as Microsoft Word and Excel are bundled with a great many features.

4. A *computer user*, ready to take the computer system to its limits (and beyond). A technician can often forget that the user is a very complex and important part of the puzzle.

Effective troubleshooting requires some experience just for the background required to analyze the problem at hand, but you also need to remember some other logical steps. Ask yourself, "Is there a problem?" Perhaps it is as simple as a customer expecting too much from the computer. If there is a problem, is it just one problem, or multiple issues? To help during the troubleshooting process, follow these steps.

Step 1: Talk to the Customer

Talking to the user is an important first step. Your first contact with the computer that has a problem will usually be through the customer, either directly or by way of a work order that contains the user's complaint. Often, the complaint will be something straightforward, such as, "There's a disk stuck in the floppy drive." At other times, the problem will be complex, and the customer will not have mentioned everything that has been going wrong.

The act of diagnosis starts with the art of customer relations. Go to the customer with an attitude of trust: *Believe* what the customer is saying. At the same time, go to the customer with an attitude of hidden skepticism, meaning *don't* believe that the customer has told you everything. This attitude of hidden skepticism is not the same as distrust. Most customers are not going to lie, but they may inadvertently forget to give a crucial detail.

A customer once complained that his CD-ROM drive didn't work. What he failed to say was that it had never worked and that he had installed it himself. It turned out that he had mounted it with screws that were too long, and these screws prevented the tray from ejecting properly.

The most important part of this step is to have the customer show you what the problem is. The best method I've seen of doing this is to ask them, "Show me what 'not working' looks like." That way, you see the conditions and methods under which the problem occurs. The problem may be a simple matter of an improper method. The user may be performing an operation incorrectly or doing the steps in the wrong order. During this step, you have the opportunity to observe how the problem occurs, so pay attention.

Step 2: Gather Information

The user can give you vital information. The most important question is, "What changed?" Problems don't usually come out of nowhere. Was a new piece of hardware or software added?

Did the user drop some equipment? Was there a power outage or a storm? These are the types of questions you can ask a user in trying to find out what is different.

If nothing changed, at least outwardly, then what was going on at the time of failure? Can the problem be reproduced? Can the problem be worked around? The point here is to ask as many questions as you need to in order to pinpoint the trouble.

Step 3: Eliminate Possibilities

Once the problem(s) have been clearly identified, your next step is to isolate possible causes. If the problem cannot be clearly identified, then further tests will be necessary. A common technique for hardware and software problems alike is to strip the system down to bare-bones basics. In a hardware situation, this could mean removing all interface cards except those absolutely required for the system to operate. In a software situation, this may mean booting up with the CONFIG.SYS and AUTOEXEC.BAT files disabled.

Generally, you can gradually rebuild the system toward the point where it started. When you reintroduce a component and the problem reappears, then you know that component is the one causing the problem.

Step 4: Document Your Work

We need to make one last point in this brief introduction to troubleshooting: You should document your work. If the process of elimination or the process of questioning the user goes beyond two or three crucial elements, start writing it down. Nothing is more infuriating than knowing you did something to make the system work but not being able to remember what it was.

Windows File-Related Problems

The first set of specific Windows problems we'll discuss are those that can be traced to missing, corrupt, or misconfigured files. These issues can cause consternation to no end because they can be troublesome to fix. Thankfully, the error message usually gives an indication of which file is the problem.

In this section, you will learn about some of the various file-related problems that can occur in Windows, as well as their solutions. These problems can be categorized into four main areas:

- System files not found
- Configuration file issues
- Swap file issues
- Boot issues

Because the most easily fixed problems are related to missing system files, that's the next topic we'll cover.

System Files Not Found

Every operating system or operating environment (such as Windows 9*x* or Windows NT) has certain key system files that must be present in order for it to function. If these files are missing or corrupt, the OS will cease to function properly. Files can be deleted by accident rather easily, so it's important to know what these system files are, where they are located, and how to replace them.

 The major system files for the different versions of Windows are covered in Chapter 13, "Major OS Architectures."

When you boot Windows 9*x*/NT, the presence of the system files (HIMEM.SYS, COMMAND.COM, and so on) is checked, and each file is loaded. If you remember, the computer's BIOS first checks the PC's hardware, and then looks for a boot sector on one of the disks and loads the OS found in that boot sector. However, if the computer can't find a boot sector with an OS installed on any of the disks, it displays an error similar to the following:

No operating system found

This error means the computer's BIOS checked all the drives it knew about and couldn't find any disk with a bootable sector. This could be due to any number of reasons, including:

- An operating system wasn't installed.
- The boot sector has been corrupted.
- The boot files have been corrupted.

Thankfully, there are a couple of solutions to these problems. First, if the file or files are missing, copy them from the original setup diskettes or CD-ROM, or copy them from a backup (assuming you have one). The same holds true if you have a corrupt file, except you must delete the corrupt file(s) first, and then replace them with new copies.

 When deleting and/or replacing system files, you must use the ATTRIB command to remove the hidden, system, and read-only attributes before you replace these files.

These same concepts hold true for other system file–related problems, such as:

Bad or missing COMMAND.COM
Bad or missing command interpreter
Missing NTLDR
HIMEM.SYS not loaded
Missing or corrupt HIMEM.SYS

These errors mean that the specified files (COMMAND.COM, HIMEM.SYS) are either missing or corrupt. Just replace them with fresh copies. The error should go away, and the computer will function properly. Most often, an OS reinstall should take care of these issues.

Configuration File Issues

As discussed in Chapter 13, Windows 9*x*/NT contain several files that hold configuration data for Windows, such as the Registry, SYSTEM.INI, WIN.INI, and CONFIG.SYS. Because users can edit these files, the possibility for introduction of invalid configurations is more likely. Additionally, most software installation programs modify these files when a new program is installed. These files are modified so frequently, in fact, that it's a wonder they aren't corrupted more often.

Some of the more commonly seen errors in Windows that are related to configuration files are as follows:

```
A device referenced in SYSTEM.INI can not be found
A device referenced in WIN.INI can not be found
A device referenced in the Registry can not be found
Error in CONFIG.SYS line XX
```

These errors are basically the same and mean that an item that refers to a piece of hardware or software that wasn't installed was placed into a configuration file. The difference is the file in which the error is contained. Again, with missing things, the solution is simple: add the missing item. In *Error in CONFIG.SYS line xx*, the error message tells you which line contains the error—you can go directly to that line and fix the problem. With the SYSTEM.INI and WIN.INI file errors, you must search through the files using your favorite text editor to find the invalid line. It may be as difficult as finding an additional backslash put in the wrong place, or as easy as finding a string of corrupt characters.

The process is the same for the Registry except that you must use the Registry Editor (REGEDIT.EXE or REGEDT32.EXE, for Windows 9*x* and Windows NT/2000/XP, respectively) to search for corrupt or invalid entries. You will learn more about the Registry later in this chapter.

Swap File Issues

As mentioned in earlier chapters, Windows uses swap files (also called page files or paging files in Windows NT/2000/XP) to increase the amount of usable memory by using hard-disk space as memory. However, sometimes problems can occur when a computer doesn't have enough disk space to make a proper swap file. Because Windows relies on swap files for proper operation, if a swap file isn't big enough, Windows will slow down and start running out of usable memory. All sorts of memory-related problems can stem from swap files that are incorrect or too small. Symptoms of swap-file problems include an extremely slow system speed and a disk that is constantly being accessed. This condition, known as hard disk *thrashing*, occurs because Windows doesn't have enough memory to contain all the programs that are running, and there isn't enough disk space for a swap file to contain them all. This situation causes Windows to swap between memory and the hard disk.

The solution to this problem is to first free up some disk space. With IDE hard-disk sizes at tens of gigabytes available for around $100, the easiest thing to do is install a bigger hard disk. If that solution isn't practical, you must delete enough unused files that the swap file can be made large enough to be functional.

Windows Boot Issues

Troubleshooting Windows boot issues is another type of Windows troubleshooting that is commonly performed. To understand Windows boot issues, you must first understand the Windows boot process, which was described in Chapter 13.

Let's take a brief look at some common Windows NT/2000/XP boot errors, what might be causing them, and how to solve them:

Invalid Boot Disk   You get the *Invalid boot disk* error when the BIOS finds a partition that could be bootable but is missing the essential system files. You can correct this problem by reinstalling the OS.

Operating System Not Found   This error means exactly what it says. Essentially, the system could not find an OS, or even a valid boot partition, on any of the boot devices (floppy, hard disk, or CD-ROM). You will get this error on a brand-new computer that you have just built, until you install the OS.

Inaccessible Boot Device   This error applies primarily to Windows NT/2000/XP. If, on boot-up, you receive an error that states *STOP: 0x0000007B Inaccessible Boot Device*, you may have one of several problems. The most common is that Windows could not load the driver for the disk controller on the boot device. This could be because it is the wrong driver, or because the disk controller is conflicting with some other hardware in the system.

 This issue could also be caused by a unique installation procedure. If you are trying to run Windows NT/2000/XP Setup from a SCSI CD-ROM, Setup will not allow you to install a third-party SCSI driver when you boot from the SCSI CD-ROM. You will have to try using the boot disks to install NT/2000/XP.

Missing NTLDR   As you've learned, NTLDR is relied on heavily during the boot process. If it is missing or corrupted, Windows NT will not be able to boot, and you'll get an error similar to *Can't find NTLDR*.

On the other hand, if you get an error such as *NTOSKRNL.EXE missing or corrupt* on boot-up, it may be an error in the BOOT.INI file. This is a common occurrence if you have improperly used the multi(0)disk(0)rdisk(0)partition(1)\WINNT="Windows NT Server" syntax for partition entries or had the partition table modified in a multi-disk setup. If these entries are correct, the NTOSKRNL.EXE file may be corrupt or missing. Boot to a startup disk and replace the file from the setup disks or CD-ROM.

Bad or Missing Command Interpreter   When Windows 9*x* can't find COMMAND.COM, it displays this statement. This file is required for Windows 9*x* to boot, so you must replace it with a fresh copy from the setup disk or CD in order to properly boot Windows. This error will also sometimes appear when COMMAND.COM is corrupt, or when you have a nonbootable floppy disk in the floppy drive and the system is looking to boot from the floppy drive before the hard disk.

Troubleshooting Windows Printing Problems

Another major category of problems you might be asked to troubleshoot are those problems that occur during printing. If a printer is not printing at all, then you should start with the DOS troubleshooting method. First, reboot the computer in Safe mode from the DOS Prompt. (See the section "Troubleshooting Tools: Windows-Based Utilities" for more information on Safe mode.) Then, copy a file or a directory listing to the printer port. If the file or directory listing doesn't print, the cause is most likely a hardware failure or loose cable. If it *does* print, then you can assume the printing problems are associated with the Windows printer drivers.

One common source of printer-driver errors is corruption of the driver. If a printer doesn't work, you can delete the printer from the printer settings window and reinstall it. If this method fails, the problem may be that related printer files were not replaced. Delete all printers from the computer and reinstall them. If this second method fails, then the printer driver is not compatible with Windows or with the printer, and you will need to obtain an updated driver.

A quick way to test the printer functionality is to use the Print Test Page option. This option is presented to you as the last step when setting up a new printer in Windows. Always select this option when you're setting up a new printer so you can test its functionality. To print a test page for a printer that's already set up, look for the option on the Properties menu for the particular printer.

After the test page is sent to the printer, the computer will ask if it printed correctly. The first few times, you'll probably want to answer No and use the troubleshooting wizard that appears; but after you have troubleshot a few printer problems, you may prefer to answer Yes and bypass the wizard, which is rather simplistic and annoying.

Troubleshooting Other Common Problems

Some common Windows problems don't fall into any category other than "common Windows problems." They include the following:

General Protection Faults (GPFs)   This is probably the most common and most frustrating error. A *General Protection Fault (GPF)* happens in Windows when a program accesses memory that another program is using or when a program accesses a memory address that doesn't exist. Generally, GPFs are the result of sloppy programming. To fix this type of problem, a simple reboot will usually clear memory. If GPFs keep occurring, check to see which software is causing the error. Then, find out if the manufacturer of the software has a patch to prevent it from GPFing.

Windows Protection Error   A Windows protection error (Windows $9x$ only) is a condition that usually happens on either startup or shutdown. Protection errors occur because Windows $9x$

could not load or unload a virtual device driver (VXD) properly. Thankfully, this error usually tells which VXD is experiencing the problem so you can check to see if the specified VXD is missing or corrupt. If it is, you can replace it with a new copy. If it is one of the Windows *9x* built-in VXDs, you must re-run Windows *9x* SETUP.EXE with the /p I option.

Illegal Operation   Occasionally, a program will quit, apparently for no reason, and present you with a window that says *This program has performed an illegal operation and will be shut down. If the problem persists, contact the program vendor.* An *illegal operation error* usually means that a program was forced to quit because it did something Windows didn't like. Windows then displays this error window. The name of the program that quit appears at the top of the window, along with three buttons: OK, Cancel, and Details. The OK and Cancel buttons do the same thing: dismiss the window. The Details button opens the window a little farther and shows the details of the error, including which module experienced the problem, the memory location being accessed at the time, and the registers and flags of the processor at the time of the error.

System Lock-Up   It is obvious when a system lockup occurs. The system simply stops responding to commands and stops processing completely. System lockups can occur when a computer is asked to process too many instructions at once with too little memory. Usually, the cure for a system lockup is to reboot. If the lockups are persistent, it may be a hardware-related problem instead of a software problem.

Dr. Watson   Windows NT 4, Windows 2000, and Windows XP includes a special utility known as Dr. Watson. This utility intercepts all error conditions and, instead of presenting the user with a cryptic Windows error, displays a slew of information that can be used to troubleshoot the problem. Additionally, Dr. Watson logs all errors to log files stored in the WINNT\DRWATSON directory.

Failure to Start GUI   Occasionally, the Windows GUI won't appear. The system will hang just before the GUI appears. Or, in the case of Windows NT, 2000, or XP, the *Blue Screen of Death (BSOD)*—not a technical term, by the way—appears. The BSOD is another way of describing the blue-screen error condition that occurs when Windows NT fails to boot properly or quits unexpectedly. In Windows *9x*, instead of a BSOD, you get a black screen (usually with a blinking cursor in the upper-left corner) that indicates there is a problem. Because it is at this stage that the device drivers for the various pieces of hardware are installed, if your Windows GUI fails to start properly, more than likely the problem is related to a misconfigured driver or misconfigured hardware. Try booting Windows in Safe mode to bypass this problem. (See the section "Troubleshooting Tools: Windows-Based Utilities" for more information on Safe mode.)

If you happen to get a BSOD with a *Fatal Exception error 0D* message, chances are that the culprit is a problem relating to the video card.

Option (Sound Card, Modem, SCSI Card, or Input Device) Will Not Function   When you are using Windows, you are constantly interacting with pieces of hardware. Each piece of hardware has a Windows driver that must be loaded in order for Windows to be able to use it.

Additionally, the hardware must be installed and functioning properly. If the device driver is not installed properly or the hardware is misconfigured, the device won't function properly.

TSR (Terminate and Stay Resident) Programs and Viruses   In the days of DOS, there was no easy way to run a utility program in the background while you ran an application. Because necessity is the mother of invention, programmers came up with Terminate and Stay Resident (TSR) programs. These programs were loaded from AUTOEXEC.BAT and stayed resident in memory until called for by a key combination. Unfortunately, while that approach worked for DOS, Windows 95 had its own method of using background utilities. If any DOS TSR programs are in memory when Windows 9x is running, they can interfere with the proper operation of Windows programs. Before you install Windows 9x, make sure that any DOS TSRs (like DOS anti-virus programs or e-mail notification programs) are disabled in AUTOEXEC.BAT.

Cannot Log On to the Network (Option—NIC Not Functioning)   If your computer is hooked up to a network (and more and more computers today are), you need to know when your computer is not functioning on the network properly and what to do about it. In most cases, the problem can be attributed to either a malfunctioning network interface card (NIC) or improperly installed network software. The biggest indicator in Windows that some component of the network software is nonfunctional is that you can't log on to the network or access any network service. To fix this problem, you must first fix the underlying hardware problem (if one exists), and then properly install or configure the network software.

 Networking software is covered in Chapter 16, "Windows Networking."

Applications Don't Install   We've all experienced this frustration. You are trying to install the coolest new program, and, for whatever reason, it just won't install properly. It may give you one of the previously mentioned errors or a cryptic installation error. If a software program won't install and it gives you any of the errors we've mentioned (such as a GPF or illegal operation), use the solutions for those errors first. If the error that occurs during install is unique to the application being installed, check the application manufacturer's website for an explanation or update. These errors generally occur when you're trying to install over an application that already exists, or when you're trying to replace a file that already exists but that another application has in use. When you're installing an application, it is extremely important that you first quit all running programs so the installer can replace any files it needs to.

Application Will Not Start   Once you have an application successfully installed, you may run across a problem getting it to start properly. This problem can come from any number of sources, including an improper installation, a software conflict, or system instability. If your application was installed incorrectly, the files required to properly run the program may not be present, and the program can't function without them. If a shared file that's used by other programs is installed, it could be a different version than should be installed that causes conflicts with other already-installed programs. Finally, if one program GPFs, it can cause memory problems that can destabilize the system and cause other programs to crash. The solution to these problems is to reinstall the offending application, first making sure that all programs are closed.

Invalid Working Directory   Some Windows programs are extremely processing intensive. These programs require an area on the hard disk to store their temporary files while they work. This area is commonly known as a *working directory*, and its location is usually specified during that program's installation. However, if that directory changes after installation and the program still thinks its working directory is in the same location, the program will issue an error that says something such as *Invalid working directory*. The solution is to reinstall the program with the correct parameters for the working directory.

For this reason, many programs use the Windows TEMP directory as their working directory. You will see this error only if the programmer chose to use a user-settable working directory.

Bad Network Connection   When you're troubleshooting network problems, as with other problems, never fail to check the simple stuff. Although the issue could be something difficult like weird driver conflicts, more often than not, problems sending and receiving data with the network can be attributed to bad physical connections. Bad network connections are the result of a problem with the cabling system and its connections. Things to check when looking for cable problems include:

- Broken or loose connectors
- Wires pulled free from a connector
- Kinked wires
- Unplugged patch cables

Remember that there are two universal solutions to Windows problems: rebooting and obtaining an update from the software manufacturer.

Preemptive "Troubleshooting": Guarding against Virus Attacks

One type of troubleshooting is best done before you ever have problems. That type of troubleshooting is virus checking. A computer *virus* is a small, deviously genius program that replicates itself to other computers, generally causing those computers to behave abnormally. Generally speaking, a virus's main function is to reproduce. A virus attaches itself to files on a hard disk and modifies those files. When the files are accessed by a program, the virus can infect the program with its own code. The program may then, in turn, replicate the virus code to other files and other programs. In this manner, a virus may infect an entire computer.

When an infected file is transferred to another computer (via disk or modem download), the process begins on the other computer. Because of the frequency of downloads from the Internet, viruses can run rampant if left unchecked. For this reason, antivirus programs were developed. They check files and programs for any program code that shouldn't be there and either eradicate it or prevent the virus from replicating. An antivirus program is generally run in the background on a computer and examines all the file activity on that computer. When it detects a suspicious activity, it notifies the user of a potential problem and asks them what to do about it. Some antivirus programs can also make intelligent decisions about what to do. The process of running an antivirus program on a computer is known as *inoculating* the computer against a virus.

For a listing of most of the viruses that are currently out there, refer to Symantec's Anti-Virus Research Center (SARC) at www.symantec.com/avcenter/index.html.

But Where Do I Stick the Needle?

You may notice that a lot of the language surrounding computer viruses sounds like language we use to discuss human illness. The moniker *virus* was given to these programs because a computer virus functions much like a human virus, and the term helped to anthropomorphize the computer a bit. Somehow, if people can think of a computer as getting sick, it breaks down the computer phobia that many people have.

There are two categories of viruses: benign and malicious. The benign viruses don't do much besides replicate themselves and exist. They may cause the occasional problem, but it is usually an unintentional side effect. Malicious viruses, on the other hand, are designed to destroy things. Once a malicious virus (for example, the Michelangelo virus) infects your machine, you can usually kiss the contents of your hard drive goodbye.

To prevent virus-related problems, you can install one of any number of antivirus programs (McAfee Anti-Virus, for example). These programs will periodically scan your computer for viruses, monitor regular use of the computer, and note any suspicious activity that might indicate a virus. In addition, these programs have a database of known viruses and the symptoms each one causes.

These databases should be updated frequently (about once a week, although the more often, the better) to keep your antivirus up-to-date with all the possible virus definitions. New viruses are released every week.

Troubleshooting Tools: Windows-Based Utilities

In addition to learning about the many common problems and troubleshooting techniques for Windows, you should know about the different tools that Microsoft provides with Windows to troubleshoot Windows. These resources are the best to use if you have no other troubleshooting tools available. They can also be used as a starting point for troubleshooting a computer. The built-in Windows tools that the A+ exam tests you on include:

- SCANDISK
- Device Manager
- Computer Management
- Event Viewer—Event log is full
- MSCONFIG.EXE
- REGEDIT.EXE (view information/back up Registry) and REGEDT32.EXE
- ATTRIB.EXE
- EXTRACT.EXE
- EDIT.COM
- FDISK.EXE
- SYSEDIT.EXE
- SCANREG.EXE
- WSCRIPT.EXE
- HWINFO.EXE
- ASD.EXE (Automatic Skip Driver)
- CVI1.EXE (Drive Converter FAT16 to FAT32)
- MSD.EXE
- WinMSD
- Safe modes
- Recovery CD
- ConfigSafe

SCANDISK

You can use the Windows SCANDISK utility to correct problems with corrupt files or disk errors, like cross-linked files. There are two ways you can use SCANDISK. First, if you suspect a particular hard disk is having problems or you have a corrupt file on a particular disk, you can manually start SCANDISK by right-clicking the problem disk and selecting Properties.

This will bring up the Properties window for that disk, which shows the current status of the selected disk drive, as shown here.

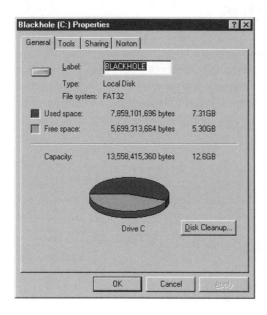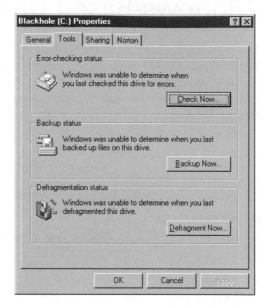

Click the Tools tab at the top of the screen, and then click the Check Now button in the Error-Checking Status section to start SCANDISK.

Once you start SCANDISK, you begin the scanning process by selecting the type of scan you want to perform (Standard or Thorough) and clicking Start. SCANDISK will scan the disk looking for corrupt files and fix or delete them, as shown. Additionally, if you choose the Thorough option, SCANDISK will scan the surface of the disk for defects and mark them as unusable.

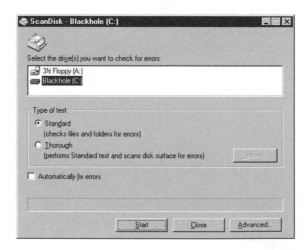

You can also run SCANDISK automatically. When you turn off a Windows computer without choosing the Shut Down command, Windows 95 OSR2 and Windows 98 automatically run SCANDISK when the computer is restarted. SCANDISK checks to see if any of the Windows files are corrupt so that Windows can be started.

Device Manager

With Windows 9*x*, Microsoft provides the Device Manager, a tool that analyzes hardware-related problems. The Device Manager displays all of the devices installed in a computer (as shown in Figure 18.1). If a device is malfunctioning, a yellow circle with an exclamation point inside it is displayed (as with the Iomega Parallel Port Interface in Figure 18.1).

FIGURE 18.1   The Windows 9*x* Device Manager

With this utility, you can view the devices installed in a system and any of those devices that are failing, and also double-click on a device and view and set its properties (as shown in Figure 18.2). On the General tab, you will see the status of the device (whether it's working). The other tabs are used to configure the individual devices, add or update drivers, and verify the version of drivers installed.

When you're troubleshooting a specific Windows-related hardware problem, you can access the Device Manager in two different ways. First, and quickest, you can right-click the My Computer icon and choose Properties. This brings up the General tab by default. To access the

Device Manager from here, click the Device Manager tab. You can then use the Device Manager to troubleshoot your system. Windows NT does not use Device Manager, but in Windows 2000 and XP, you can access the Device Manager by right clicking the My Computer icon, choosing Properties, and then clicking the Hardware tab. On the Hardware tab are many buttons, but to access the Device Manager, click the Device Manager button.

FIGURE 18.2   Properties of a network card

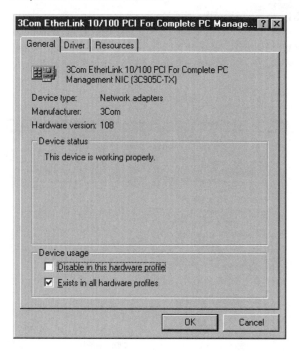

Computer Management

Windows 2000/XP includes a new piece of software to manage computer settings: the Computer Management Console. Because Windows 2000 is more advanced as a platform, the Computer Management Console can manage more than just the installed hardware devices. In addition to a Device Manager that functions almost identically to the one in Windows 9x, the Computer Management Console can also manage all the services running on that computer. It contains an Event Viewer to show any system errors and events, as well as methods to configure the software components of all the computer's hardware. Figure 18.3 shows an example of the Computer Management Console running on Windows 2000.

To access the Computer Management Console, go to Start ➢ Settings ➢ Control Panel ➢ Administrative Tools ➢ Computer Management. You will see all of the computer management tools, including the Device Manager. You can then use the Computer Management Console to manage hardware devices and software services.

FIGURE 18.3   Windows 2000 Computer Management Console

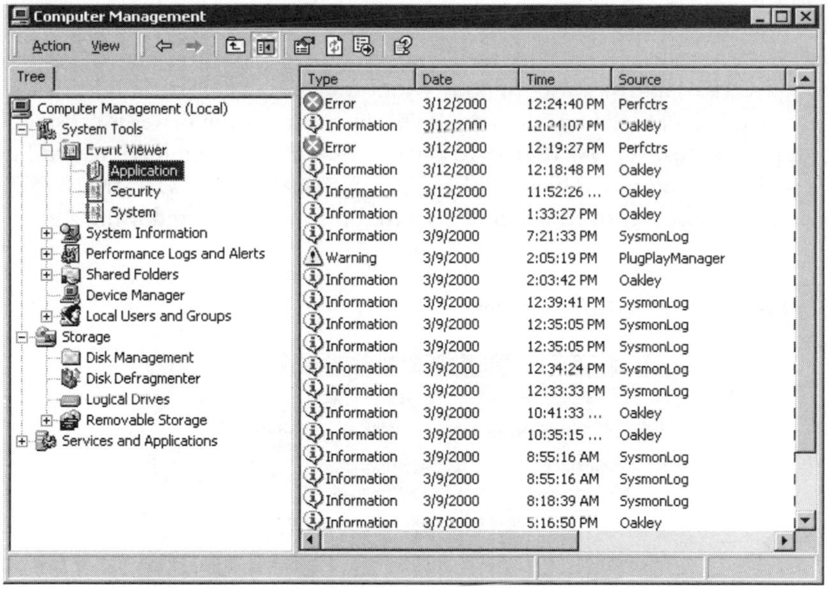

Event Viewer

Windows NT/2000/XP, like other network operating systems, employs comprehensive error and informational logging routines. Every program and process theoretically could have its own logging utility, but Microsoft has come up with a rather slick utility, Event Viewer, which, through log files, tracks all events on a particular Windows NT/2000/XP computer. Normally, though, you must be an administrator or a member of the Administrators group to have access to Event Viewer.

To start Event Viewer, log in as an administrator (or equivalent) and go to Start ➢ Programs ➢ Administrative Tools ➢ Event Viewer. From here, you can view the System, Application, and Security log files:

- The System log file displays alerts that pertain to the general operation of Windows.

- The Application log file logs server application errors.

- The Security log file logs security events such as login successes and failures.

These log files can give a general indication of a Windows computer's health.

One situation that does occur with the Event Viewer is that the Event Viewer log files get full. Although this isn't really a problem, it can make viewing log files confusing because there are many entries. Even though each event is time- and date-stamped, you should clear the Event Viewer every so often. To do this, open the Event Viewer and choose Clear All Events from the Log menu. Doing so erases all events in the current log file, allowing you to see new events more easily when they occur.

MSCONFIG.EXE

A new utility was introduced with Windows 98: MSCONFIG.EXE *(a.k.a. the System Configuration Utility)*. It allows a user to manage their computer system's configuration. MSCONFIG.EXE (shown in Figure 18.4) allows a user to boot Windows 98 in diagnostic mode, in which they can select which drivers to load interactively. If you suspect a certain driver is causing problems during boot, you can use MSCONFIG.EXE to prevent that driver from loading. Additionally, each of the major configuration files (CONFIG.SYS, AUTOEXEC.BAT, WIN.INI, SYSTEM.INI) and the programs loaded at startup can be reconfigured and reordered using a graphical interface.

FIGURE 18.4   MSCONFIG.EXE screen

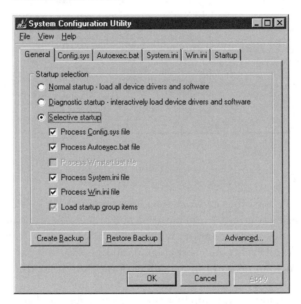

If you want to prevent a particular driver from loading, you can go to the tab that represents the file from which the driver is loaded and uncheck the box in front of the driver you want to eliminate. Or, from the General tab, check Diagnostic Startup in the Startup Selection area and then reboot the computer. Upon reboot, as each driver loads, you will be able to choose whether a particular driver loads during this boot cycle.

REGEDIT.EXE

The most flexible (and possibly the most dangerous) utility in the Windows troubleshooting arsenal is the Registry Editor, also known by its executable names REGEDIT.EXE (for Windows 9x) and REGEDT32.EXE (for Windows NT/2000). The Registry stores all Windows configuration information. If you edit the Registry, you are essentially changing the configuration of Windows. The Registry Editor is used to manually change settings that are usually changed by other means (such as through Setup programs and other Windows utilities).

In addition to changing Windows settings, you can use REGEDIT to back up and restore the Registry. To back up the Registry, choose the Export Registry File command under the Registry menu (or File ➤ Export in later versions). This command allows you to save the Registry file to a backup media. You can restore it later by choosing the Import Registry File command under the Registry menu.

ATTRIB.EXE

Every OS since DOS provides four attributes that can be set for files to modify their interaction with the system. These attributes are as follows:

Read-only Prevents a file from being modified, deleted, or overwritten.

Archive Used by backup programs to determine whether the file has changed since the last backup and needs to be backed up.

System Used to tell the OS that this file is needed by the system and should not be deleted.

Hidden Used to keep files from being seen in a normal directory search. This attribute is useful to prevent system files and other important files from being accidentally moved or deleted.

You set attributes for files using the external DOS command ATTRIB.EXE, which uses using the following syntax:

ATTRIB `<filename>` [+ or -][attribute]

To set the read-only attribute on the file TESTFILE.DOC, use the following series of commands:

ATTRIB TESTFILE.DOC +r

Occasionally, it is necessary to remove various attributes and replace them. To do this, use the ATTRIB command. You can also modify these attributes using the Windows GUI.

EXTRACT.EXE

All Windows setup files come compressed in Cabinet (CAB) files. These files are extracted during the Windows Setup process by the EXTRACT.EXE utility. You can also use this utility to extract one or multiple files from a CAB file to replace a corrupt file. If you have one Windows file that is corrupt, you can extract a replacement from the Windows setup CAB files. If you don't know which CAB file contains a particular Windows system file, you can look it up in the CABS.TXT file.

For example, to extract the UNIDRV.DLL file from the Win95_10.CAB file on a CD-ROM in drive D: to the C:\WINDOWS\SYSTEM directory, use the following command syntax:

EXTRACT D:\WIN95_10.CAB UNIDRV.DLL /L C:\WINDOWS\SYSTEM

The new file will be extracted to the new location and replace the old corrupt version in that location.

EDIT.COM

Occasionally, you need to quickly edit a configuration file or other text file (such as CONFIG.SYS or AUTOEXEC.BAT). For this purpose, a simple editor named EDIT.COM has been included with all Microsoft OSs since DOS version 6. To edit a file, start a command-line session and type in the following:

EDIT *<filename>*

Replace *<filename>* with the name of the file you wish to edit. Once EDIT comes up, it works like any other word processor or text editor. When you are finished editing the file, save it, and it will be saved as a standard ASCII text file.

You can also use the Windows NOTEPAD.EXE for the same function.

FDISK.EXE

If you have already installed the disk drives and now need to configure unused space on your drive for use, you will need to use the FDISK command. FDISK.EXE is a DOS program that allows you to access and modify information about your fixed disks (hence the name). It is used for four major tasks:

- Viewing the current partition configuration
- Creating DOS partitions or logical DOS drives
- Setting active partitions
- Deleting partitions or logical DOS drives

These functions can be used on any of the physical disks in your machine, as long as those disks are considered to be permanent (that is, *fixed*) drives. Hard drives, whether they are SCSI, IDE, or EIDE, are all fixed. Once installed, they are expected to be permanently attached to the system, and if one is removed, extensive reconfiguration may need to be done on the system. Floppy drives and CD-ROM drives are designed to support removable, interchangeable media, and as such are not configurable under FDISK.

To run the FDISK utility, boot to a bootable disk that has the FDISK program on it and type **FDISK**.

You must run FDISK from a bootable disk, *not* from a command prompt within Windows. This is the case because Windows may not represent the disk drives correctly.

Following the prompts on screen, you can then view, add, or delete partitions.

SYSEDIT.EXE

The *System Editor* (SYSEDIT.EXE) is a holdover from Windows 3.*x*. With this utility, you can view and edit the CONFIG.SYS, AUTOEXEC.BAT, WIN.INI, SYSTEM.INI, PROTOCOL.INI, and MSMAIL.INI files. Although it is not as efficient as MSCONFIG.EXE, you can still use SYSEDIT to edit these files quickly and to easily remove an offending driver entry or software configuration.

To run this program in Windows 9*x*, go to Start ➢ Run and type in **SYSEDIT**. Doing so brings up the window shown in Figure 18.5, in which you can click on a window and edit any of the particular files just as if you were using EDIT.COM. You can then save the changes and restart the computer to make them take effect.

FIGURE 18.5 SYSEDIT screen

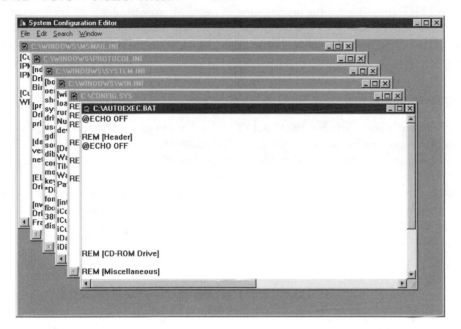

SCANREG.EXE

The Windows Registry Checker, SCANREG.EXE (9x only), is a quick and simple utility you can use to check the Registry for consistency and to make a backup of the Registry. To start SCANREG, go to Start ➢ Run, type **SCANREG**, and click OK. Doing so starts SCANREG, which initiates an immediate scan and fixes the Registry (Figure 18.6).

FIGURE 18.6 SCANREG.EXE screen

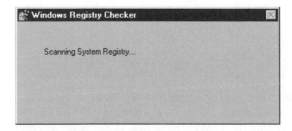

After the Registry scan is complete, SCANREG will prompt you to back up your Registry. You can use this backup to restore the Registry in case of a problem.

WSCRIPT.EXE

The Windows Scripting Host (WSCRIPT.EXE) is a service that allows programmers to write Windows scripts that can perform any number of automated tasks. Unfortunately, because WSCRIPT can also work with Internet Explorer, if it's allowed to run unchecked it is a major security hole that can potentially allow malicious scripts to be run without the user's knowledge.

This tool is responsible for the propagation of weird Microsoft-only bugs such as the fairly recent I Love You virus. If you see WSCRIPT present in the task list on Windows NT, make sure it is supposed to be running. Or, if you are sure you won't need it for scripts of any kind, completely delete it.

HWINFO.EXE

Windows 9*x* and above include a HWINFO.EXE utility that can give a text report of all the hardware configuration information for Windows. It includes the driver name, version, company name, Registry information, and other file-related information for the driver. You can save or print this text report for later reference on this system.

To view this file, you must start the HWINFO.EXE utility by selecting Start ➢ Run, typing **HWINFO /UI**, and clicking OK. Doing so runs the HWINFO utility and produces a report similar to the one in Figure 18.7. You can then either save this file as an ASCII text file or print the file to a printer by using the Save or Print command, respectively, under the File menu.

FIGURE 18.7   The HWINFO screen

This utility is useful when you're trying to track down a hardware problem you suspect may be due to an outdated driver. You can examine the file this utility produces for the versions of all drivers and compare them to the newest possible drivers on the hardware vendors' websites.

ASD.EXE (Automatic Skip Driver)

It never fails: Eventually, you will have a driver that hangs the system on boot-up. We've already discussed several methods for troubleshooting this problem, and this is yet another one. The Automatic Skip Driver (ASD.EXE) utility is used to automatically skip loading a driver during boot that failed to load at the last boot.

To use ASD, in Windows 9*x* go to Start ➢ Run, type **ASD**, and click OK. Doing so brings up the ASD utility (Figure 18.8). From this screen, you can see which tasks failed to respond. If you check a box next to a particular task, the next time you boot Windows, that task won't load. In this way, ASD can prevent lockups during boot.

FIGURE 18.8   ASD.EXE main screen

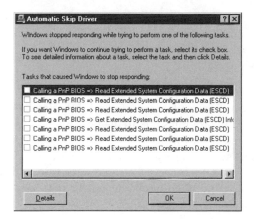

CVT1.EXE

With the release of Windows 95 OSR2 came a new feature: a 32-bit FAT table, also known as FAT32. Until that point, the FAT system was a 16-bit system (now known as FAT16). The new FAT32 system allowed for faster access and larger drive sizes. With newly installed systems, FAT32 was the FAT type of choice. However, older systems still used FAT16. The FAT32 Upgrade Wizard, also known as CVT1.EXE, allows you to convert a FAT16 disk system to a FAT32 system. To do this, you must first run the Drive Converter by clicking Start ➢ Run, typing in **CVT1.EXE**, and clicking OK. This will start the Drive Converter Wizard (Figure 18.9). In this wizard, you follow the prompts and continue clicking Next to convert your drive from FAT16 to FAT32.

A Few Warnings about Converting to FAT32

- Once you convert to FAT32, you can't go back to FAT16.

- You may not be able to convert a compressed drive.

- Removable disks formatted with FAT32 may not work with other systems.

- Dual-boot to older systems will not be possible after a conversion to FAT32.

FIGURE 18.9 FAT32 Drive Converter Wizard

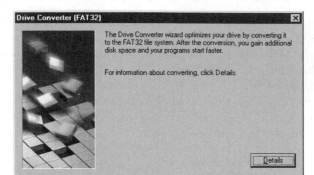

MSD.EXE

The best way to determine a PC's available resources is by using hardware configuration discovery utilities. These software programs talk to the PC's BIOS as well as the various pieces of hardware in the computer and display which IRQ, DMA, and memory addresses are being used. Numerous commercial packages do a very good job of determining which resources are in use and which are available. Most OSs, however, include some way of determining this information. MS-DOS, Windows 3.*x*, and Windows 95 included a tool named MSD.EXE. Windows 98 has a graphical utility called the Device Manager. Windows NT/2000/XP includes a program known as NT Diagnostics. Because all of these tools report the same type of information, we'll use MSD.EXE as our example.

One advantage of MSD.EXE over the other programs listed is that it can be included on a boot floppy. In the event that a resource conflict is preventing your system from booting properly, you can boot to the DOS floppy and troubleshoot your problem.

When you run MSD.EXE, it can display information about the computer's memory, I/O ports, IRQs that are being used, and many other PC resources you want to see. Figure 18.10 shows the main menu that appears when you first run the program.

From the main menu, you can use the menu options to display information about the various resources. For example, if you want to find out if any IRQ channels are available, press Q to bring up a screen similar to the one in Figure 18.11 (your screen may show something different).

As you can see, the computer in Figure 18.11 has IRQs 3, 5, 10, 11, 12, and 15 available. (You can tell because either the Detected column indicates No or the Description column indicates Reserved for these IRQ channels.) If you want to install a device that requires an IRQ channel, you can set it to any of these channels, and there should be no IRQ conflicts. You perform the same procedure to find out if any of the other resources are available.

FIGURE 18.10   The main menu of MSD.EXE

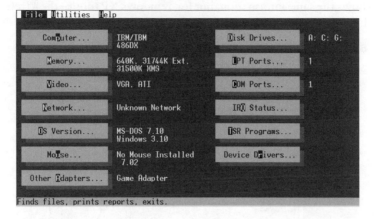

FIGURE 18.11   MSD IRQ Status screen

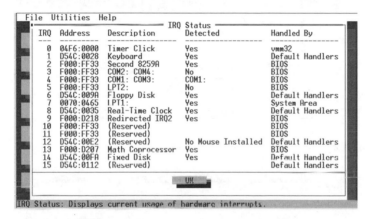

Don't rely completely on the report you get from MSD if you're running it under Windows 3.*x*/95). In that situation, MSD simply gives the information it gets from Windows. This information may be somewhat incorrect and could prove to be a problem. For best results, run MSD in DOS only (or in MS-DOS mode under Windows 95). Regardless of which OS you're using, the OS can color the performance of a software diagnostic program. For this reason, it's best to always *verify* the settings the program reports against the settings as published in your computer documentation and device manuals.

WinMSD

Windows NT/2000/XP have a version of MSD, as well: WinMSD. You can start it by going to Start ➢ Run, typing in **WinMSD**, and clicking OK. WinMSD is a graphic version of MSD that can show settings and information for the same categories of information. In Figure 18.12, you can see WinMSD running on Windows NT and displaying the IRQs in use for the system. Figure 18.13 shows the same information, but for Windows XP (notice the WinMSD program is called System Information in Windows XP).

FIGURE 18.12   WinMSD running on Windows NT

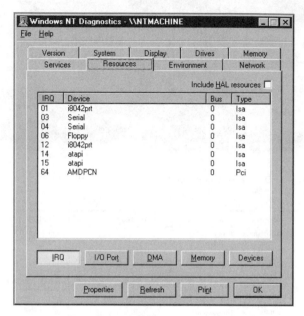

FIGURE 18.13   WinMSD running on Windows XP

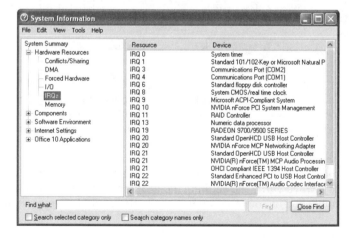

Safe Modes

Windows can be started in many different ways. Normally, if you don't press any keys at start-up, Windows starts normally, loads all its drivers, and does not prompt for any interaction (apart from login in Windows NT/2000/XP). However, occasionally Windows may not load properly, or a device may not function properly.

When Windows won't start properly, it is probably due to a driver or other piece of software not loading correctly. To fix problems of this nature, you should boot Windows in *Safe mode*. In Safe mode, Windows loads a minimal set of drivers (including a VGA-only video driver) so that you can disable the offending driver. To start Windows in Safe mode, press the F8 key when you see the Starting Windows display during Windows boot-up. Doing so brings up a menu that allows you to choose to start Windows in Safe mode. Once you've booted in Safe mode, you can uninstall any driver you suspect is causing a Windows boot problem. Upon reboot, the system should go back to normal operation (non-Safe mode).

A few other options can be accessed through the F8 menu. These will be different for the different versions of Windows, but they include the following:

Safe Mode with Command Prompt   Windows starts with only the most basic drivers. After boot, instead of displaying a Windows Desktop, Windows leaves you with a command prompt.

Safe Mode with Networking   Windows boots with the same minimal set of networking drivers, but this time Windows has network support.

Step by Step/Single Step Mode   Windows prompts you to go through each line of AUTOEXEC.BAT and CONFIG.SYS (for Windows 9*x*) as it boots. You can choose whether to load each item.

You can also use the F8 menu to select other boot options, such as logging all messages to a log file during boot.

Recovery CD

Many times, a computer will have more problems than can be fixed easily, or the fix may only result in a temporary solution. Usually, such a case calls for a complete format and reinstall of the OS and applications, and restoration of data. However, many new computers today don't come with a true OS CD-ROM. Instead, they come with one or more recovery CDs. A *recovery CD* is a CD-ROM that comes with a particular model and brand of computer. The CD-ROM contains an image of the entire Windows installation, along with applications, utilities, and drivers specifically for that computer. In the case of a serious system failure, you can insert this CD-ROM into the CD-ROM drive of your computer, boot to it, and completely restore the system back to the way it was when you bought it.

These CDs are also known as *restoration CDs.*

However, these CDs will *erase the hard drive first*! Therefore, any data and settings you've created will be gone, including data files, e-mail configuration settings, Internet favorites, and so on. The computer will be *exactly* as it was out of the box.

If you ever need to use a recovery CD-ROM, *back up your data* before booting to the CD. Most recovery CDs don't give you the option of backing up before the restoration. You *will* lose all your data when you do a recover using one of these CDs.

ConfigSafe

One utility that has become popular for keeping the stability of Windows in check is ConfigSafe. ConfigSafe, by ImagineLan, is a utility that technicians and IT professionals use when they are installing new, untested software, or to keep their systems stable.

ConfigSafe works by taking a snapshot of the current system configuration, including file lists, Registry settings, icons, and so on, and storing that information in a file. Then, if you install a new piece of software or a driver, or make other configuration changes, and that change causes your system to stop functioning, you can roll back to the last good configuration.

Windows XP includes a utility similar to ConfigSafe known as System Restore, which allows you to roll back to the last known good configuration.

Diagnostic Resources

In addition to the many diagnostic tools you have available, there are some diagnostic resources you should use to make troubleshooting easier. Although most people don't necessarily think of these resources as a tool, they aid in the troubleshooting process. These resources include:

- Manuals
- Internet resources
- Training materials

User/Installation Manuals

Technicians are the most guilty of not using this readily available resource when troubleshooting a system. In fact, most often, a technician will rely on their own experience and try to install a new component without reading the manual. Then, when the installation doesn't work, they might go back and look at the manual after spending time looking for the solution to a problem that might have been avoided in the first place.

Typically, in addition to the steps needed to install software or a device, a manual includes a section on the most common problems and the solutions to those problems. This area of the manual would be especially useful for the technician we just described.

Internet/Web Resources

Possibly the most useful resource to the technician is the Internet. As mentioned throughout this book, a manufacturer's website is the best place to get the most current drivers, fixes, and technical information. Often, you can search a hardware or software vendor's website for a problem you might be having with that hardware or software, and find the fix for it. In addition, Microsoft's website contains a wide variety of known problems and issues with Windows and its interaction with other software. Sometimes an issue that can't be solved at the software vendor's website can be solved by viewing the Microsoft support website, because Microsoft has a larger staff and has been able to document a larger variety of problems. If you can't find an answer at the manufacturer's or Microsoft's website, you might try entering your problem into one of the many search engines, like Yahoo (`www.yahoo.com`) or Google (`www.google.com`).

There are websites dedicated to communities of technical individuals (such as yourself) that can be a great source of information. Chances are, if you're having a computer or technical problem, someone else, somewhere in the world, has the solution—and the Internet can bring you together. You can post your problem to any number of website bulletin boards and newsgroups and receive a response, possibly within minutes.

Training Materials

The final resource is one that most people overlook. Individuals do not acquire knowledge magically—they either learn it by themselves with self-study materials, or are taught by an experienced instructor. In either case, books and other training materials (like the one you are reading right now) are excellent sources of information. Although training materials don't often contain patches or updates, they can and do teach concepts you can apply to help you with troubleshooting. After all, if you had not read this book, you might not have gotten the information you needed to pass the A+ exam.

Now ask yourself: Did I learn anything? Will the information I learned be able to help me troubleshoot a computer problem?

Summary

In this chapter, we gave you some tips for troubleshooting the Windows environment. Just as with troubleshooting hardware, it is important that you know how to troubleshoot software problems. However, troubleshooting software is actually more difficult, because the problems can appear to be more phantom-like.

In the first section, you learned the basic steps to troubleshooting software problems. You also learned how to apply these troubleshooting steps to problems. These steps are:

1. Talk to the customer.
2. Gather information.
3. Eliminate possibilities.
4. Document the solution.

In the next section, you learned how to troubleshoot file-related problems. We described some of the more common file-related problems and their solutions. Some of the problems you learned about include missing or corrupt system files, missing application DLL files, Windows NT/2000/XP boot problems, and swap-file issues.

In the next section, you learned about some of the printing problems that are commonly found in the Windows environment (such as the wrong driver installed). We explained how to use the Windows printing troubleshooting utilities (Print Test Page and the Troubleshooting Wizard) to troubleshoot these problems.

You learned in the next section how to troubleshoot Windows problems that don't fall into any particular category. Some of these issues include General Protection Faults, invalid page faults, and applications that won't install. We explained how to recognize the symptoms of each of these problems and how to solve them when they occur.

Next, you learned how to use the various built-in Windows troubleshooting utilities. You learned what each utility is for and how to use it. We also discussed when to apply a particular utility to a problem and when *not* to use a utility.

Finally, we ended this chapter by considering some resources for troubleshooting that are often overlooked but are potentially very helpful: user guides, web resources, and training materials (like the book you are holding now!).

Key Terms

Before you take the exam, be certain you are familiar with the following terms:

Blue Screen of Death (BSOD)	restoration CD
Fixed	Safe mode
General Protection Fault (GPF)	System Editor (SYSEDIT.EXE)
illegal operation error	thrashing
inoculating	virus
MSCONFIG.EXE (a.k.a. System Configuration Utility)	working directory
recovery CD	

Review Questions

1. All of the following are considered to be Windows-based utilities except _____.

   A. SYSEDIT

   B. PSCRIPT

   C. HWINFO.EXE

   D. ASD.EXE

   E. CVT1.EXE

2. All of the following are common problems faced in troubleshooting Windows and applications except _____.

   A. General Protection Faults

   B. Valid working directory

   C. System lockup

   D. Application will not start or load

3. What is the first step in the troubleshooting process?

   A. Talk to the customer.

   B. Gather information.

   C. Eliminate possibilities.

   D. Document your work.

4. All of the following are Windows file-related problems except _____.

   A. System files not found

   B. Configuration file issues

   C. AUTOEXEC.BAT issues

   D. Swap-file issues

   E. NT boot issues

5. Which files are checked upon boot-up of Windows 9x/NT?

   A. Config files

   B. AUTOEXEC.BAT files

   C. System files

   D. Swap files

6. The *No Operating System Found* error message means that the computer's BIOS checked all the drives it knew about and couldn't find a disk with a bootable sector. This could occur because of all the following reasons except _____.

   A. An OS wasn't installed

   B. There is no problem with the boot sector

   C. The boot files have been corrupted

   D. The boot sector has been corrupted

7. All of the following are commonly seen errors in Windows that are related to configuration files except _____.

   A. *Device referenced in Info.INI file cannot be found*

   B. *Device referenced in WIN.INI cannot be found*

   C. *Device referenced in the Registry cannot be found*

   D. *Error in CONFIG.SYS line XX*

8. In order to delete and/or replace system files, which command must you use to remove the hidden, system, and read-only attributes on the file before you replace the file?

   A. UNDELETE

   B. ERASE

   C. ATTRIB

   D. DELETE

9. Symptoms of swap-file problems include extremely slow system speed and a disk that is constantly being accessed, which is referred to as _____:

   A. Clocking

   B. Thrashing

   C. Booting

   D. Filtering

10. Which of the following are solutions to thrashing? (Select all that apply.)

    A. Formatting the disk

    B. Buying a new hard disk

    C. Freeing up disk space

    D. Deleting all files

11. What is the solution to a corrupt NTOSKRNL.EXE file?

    A. Reinstall Windows NT

    B. Replace the corrupt file with a new one

    C. Delete the NTOSKRNL.EXE file and modify the BOOT.INI file

    D. Boot to a startup disk and replace the file from the setup disks or CD-ROM

12. After connecting to a printer and installing the print drivers, what is the best way to test the printer's functionality? (Select all that apply.)

    A. Go to Word and print a document.

    B. Print a test page from Printer Properties.

    C. Go to the printer and run diagnostics.

    D. Wait until someone prints a document and complains.

13. Which of the following are the most common Windows printing problems? (Select all that apply.)

    A. Print spool is stalled

    B. Incompatible printer model

    C. Incorrect/incompatible driver for the printer

    D. Incorrect parameter

14. A condition that usually happens on either startup or shutdown and that results because Windows 9x could not load or unload a virtual device driver properly is called _____.

    A. General Protection Fault (GPF)

    B. Windows protection error

    C. Illegal operation

    D. System lockup

15. Which of the following is the most common error in Windows, and happens when a program accesses memory another program is using or when a program accesses a memory address that doesn't exist?

    A. General Protection Fault

    B. Windows protection error

    C. Illegal operation

    D. System lockup

16. Which Windows error message is displayed when a program is forced to quit because it did something Windows didn't like?

    A. General Protection Fault

    B. Windows protection error

    C. Illegal operation

    D. System lockup

17. What error occurs when the system stops responding to commands and stops processing completely?

   A. General Protection Fault

   B. Windows protection error

   C. Illegal operation

   D. System lockup

18. What error occurs when the Windows GUI won't appear?

   A. Illegal operation

   B. Dr. Watson

   C. Failure to start GUI

   D. Option sound card, modem, SCSI card, or input device will not function

Answers to Review Questions

1. **B.** PSCRIPT is not considered to be a Windows-based utility. SYSEDIT, HWINFO.EXE, ASD.EXE, and CVT1.EXE are all utilities used to troubleshoot Windows.

2. **B.** A valid working directory is not a common problem faced in troubleshooting Windows and applications.

3. **A.** The first step in the troubleshooting process is to talk to the customer. It is best to obtain as much information as possible from the user so you have an idea of where to begin your troubleshooting.

4. **C.** Windows file-related problems do not include AUTOEXEC.BAT issues. AUTOEXFC.BAT is a DOS batch file that is automatically executed during boot-up if the file is present.

5. **C.** The files that are checked upon boot-up of Windows 9x/NT are the system files. Every OS or operating environment has certain key system files that must be present in order for it to function.

6. **B.** The *No Operating System Found* error means an OS wasn't installed, the boot sector has been corrupted, or the boot files have been corrupted.

7. **A.** *Device referenced in Info.INI file cannot be found* is not a commonly seen error in Windows related to configuration files.

8. **C.** In order to delete and/or replace system files, you must use the ATTRIB command to remove the hidden, system, and read-only attributes on the file.

9. **B.** *Thrashing* means an extremely slow system speed and a disk that is constantly being accessed. This condition occurs because Windows doesn't have enough memory to contain all the programs that are running.

10. **B, C.** The solution to thrashing is to free up some disk space. However, it may be easiest to install a bigger hard disk. If that solution isn't practical, you must delete enough unused files that you can make the swap file large enough to be functional.

11. **D.** The solution to a corrupt NTOSKRNL.EXE file is to boot to a startup disk and replace the file from the setup disks or CD-ROM.

12. **A, B.** You should go to Word and print a document or print a test page in Printer Properties. Printing diagnostics only tests whether the printer is able to print if it is connected to a device with the correct drivers.

13. **A, C, D.** The most common Windows printing problems are a stalled print spool, an incorrect/ incompatible driver, or an incorrect parameter. Windows will support almost any type of printer model.

14. **B.** A Windows protection error usually happens on startup or shutdown and results because Windows 9x could not load or unload a virtual device driver properly.

15. A. A General Protection Fault is the most common error in Windows. It happens when a program accesses memory that another program is using or when a program accesses a memory address that doesn't exist. Generally, GPFs are the result of sloppy programming; they can often be fixed by clearing the memory with a reboot.

16. C. *Illegal operation* is the Windows error message displayed when a program is forced to quit because it did something Windows didn't like. The error's details include which module experienced the problem, the memory location being accessed at the time, and the registers and flags of the processor at the time of the error.

17. D. The system lockup error occurs when the system stops responding to commands and stops processing completely. System lockups can occur when a computer is asked to process too many instructions at once with too little memory. Usually, the cure for a system lockup is to reboot. If the lockups are persistent, it may be a hardware-related problem.

18. C. If your Windows GUI fails to start properly, the "Failure to start GUI" error message will appear.

Glossary

386 enhanced mode   In Microsoft Windows, the most advanced and complex of the different operating modes. 386 enhanced mode lets Windows access the protected mode of the 80386 (or higher) processor for extended memory management and multitasking for both Windows and non-Windows application programs.

3-pin fan connector   The connector usually used for PC fans. The first two wires are for power and ground, and the third wire (usually a yellow wire) is for speed sensing.

802.3   An IEEE standard that defines a bus topology network that uses a 50-ohm coaxial baseband cable and carries transmissions at 10Mbps. This standard groups data bits into frames and uses the Carrier Sense Multiple Access with Collision Detection (CSMA/CD) cable access method to put data on the cable.

8.3 naming convention   A method of file naming that uses eight letters for the name, a period, and then a three-letter file extension. The FAT filesystem uses 8.3 naming.

8-bit bus   The type of expansion bus used with the original IBM PC. The bus can transmit 8 bits at a time.

AC adapter   A device that allows notebook computers to use AC power.

Accelerated Graphics Port (AGP) bus   A type of 32-bit expansion bus that runs at 66MHz. It is a very high-speed bus used primarily for video expansion cards; it can transfer data at a maximum throughput of 508.6MBps.

access point (AP)   The device that allows wireless devices to talk to each other and the network. It provides the functions of network access as well as security monitoring.

access time   The period of time that elapses between a request for information from disk or memory and when the information arrives at the requesting device. Memory access time refers to the time it takes to transfer a character from memory to or from the processor, and disk access time refers to the time it takes to place the read/write heads over the requested data.

ACK (acknowledgment)   A special packet that acknowledges receipt of some kind of packet.

active   The designation of the partition that is the location of the boot-up files for DOS or Windows.

Active Directory   A feature of Windows 2000 that stores information about users, computers, and network resources. The Active Directory is stored in databases on special Windows 2000 Server computers called domain controllers.

active hub   A type of hub that uses electronics to amplify and clean up the signal before it is broadcast to the other ports.

active-matrix screen   A liquid crystal display (LCD) mechanism that uses an individual transistor to control each pixel on the screen. Active-matrix screens are characterized by high contrast, a wide viewing angle, vivid colors, and fast screen refresh rates, and they do not show the streaking or shadowing that is common with cheaper LCD technology.

active termination   A method for terminating a daisy chain of SCSI devices in which the terminator contains (in addition to terminating resistors) voltage regulators that actively take terminator power from the SCSI bus itself and use it for powering the termination of the bus.

actuator arm   The device inside a hard disk drive that moves the read/write heads as a group in the fixed disk.

adapter   See *adapter card*.

adapter card   A circuit board that is installed into a computer to increase the computer's capabilities. Also known as an *expansion card*.

address   The precise location in memory or on disk where a piece of information is stored. Every byte in memory and every sector on a disk has its own unique addresses.

address bus   The internal processor bus used for accessing memory. The width of this bus determines how much physical memory a processor can access.

address lease period   During the DHCP process, the period of time that indicates exactly how long the station may keep the selected address.

allocation unit   A portion of the hard drive that is used by the computer when saving information to the drive. Smaller allocation units are generally more efficient, because they result in less wasted space.

analog   Describes any device that represents changing values by a continuously variable physical property such as voltage in a circuit, fluid pressure, liquid level, and so on. An analog device can handle an infinite number of values within its range.

antistatic bag   A bag designed to keep static charges from building up on the outside of a computer component during shipping. The bag collects some of the charges, but does not drain them away as ESD mats do.

antistatic wrist strap (ESD strap)   A specially constructed strap worn as a preventive measure to guard against the damages of ESD. One end of the strap is attached to an earth ground and the other is wrapped around the technician's wrist.

antivirus program   An application program you run to detect or eliminate a computer virus or infection. Some antivirus programs are Terminate and Stay Resident (TSR) programs that can detect suspicious activity on your computer as it happens, whereas others must be run periodically as part of your normal housekeeping activities.

AppleTalk   A proprietary network protocol for Macintosh computers.

Application layer   The seventh, or highest, layer in the International Organization for Standardization's Open Systems Interconnection (ISO/OSI) model for computer-to-computer communications. This layer uses services provided by the lower layers, but is completely insulated from the details of the network hardware. It describes how application programs interact with the network operating system, including database management, e-mail, and terminal emulation programs.

ASCII (American Standard Code for Information Interchange) A standard coding scheme that assigns numeric values to letters, numbers, punctuation marks, and control characters, to achieve compatibility among different computers and peripherals.

asynchronous Describes a type of communication that adds special signaling bits to each end of the data. The bit at the beginning of the information signals the start of the data and is known as the start bit. The next few bits are the actual data that needs to be sent; they are known as the data bits. Stop bits indicate that the data is finished. Asynchronous communications have no timing signal.

AT Attachment 3 (ATA-3) Interface A minor revision of the ATA-2 interface specification that introduced several improvements over ATA-2, including SMART.

AT Attachment Interface (ATA) The original specification for how two IDE hard disks connect together and communicate with the host computer. Also known as ATA-1.

AT Attachment Interface with Packet Interface (ATAPI) Extension An extension to the ATA interface specification that allows devices besides hard drives (like CD-ROM drives) to communicate with the computer using the same cabling as ATA hard drives.

AT Attachment with Packet Interface-5 (ATA/ATAPI-5) Version 5 of the ATA standard (with ATAPI support) that includes support for all features of the ATA standards before (versions 1 through 4) as well as new UltraDMA modes, mandatory 80 conductor cable, and the removal of outdated ATA commands.

AT Attachment with Packet Interface (ATA/ATAPI-6) Version 6 of the ATA standard (with ATAPI support) that includes support for the features of all earlier versions of the ATA standard and includes support for new features such as 100MBps (UltraDMA/100) and a 48-bit LBA address length.

AT bus A 16-bit bus designed for the IBM AT processor. Another name for the ISA bus. See also *ISA (Industry Standard Architecture)*.

AT system connector The power connector on either a power supply cable or a motherboard that allows an AT power supply to be connected to an AT motherboard.

ATA version 2 (ATA-2) The second version of the original IDE (ATA) specification that allowed drive sizes of several gigabytes and overcame the limitation of 528MB. It is also sometimes generically known as Enhanced IDE (EIDE).

ATA/ATAPI-4 Fourth revision of the ATA standard. Includes ATA features, plus support for ATAPI and a new cable design (80-wire, as opposed to the 40-wire cable used on earlier revisions of the standard).

ATA/ATAPI-7 The newest, proposed ATA/ATAPI standard (proposed as of spring 2003). To include such features as serial ATA and a 150MBps transfer rate.

ATA-2 The second revision of the ATA standard. Includes support for logical block addressing (LBA), which allows for drives larger than 528MB, support for PIO modes 3 and 4, and multi-word DMA modes 1 and 2.

Attached Resource Computer Network (ARCNet)   A network technology that uses a physical star, logical ring and token passing access method. It is typically wired with coaxial cable. It was developed in 1977 for IBM mainframe networks.

ATX motherboard   A motherboard type that has the processor and memory slots at right angles to the expansion cards, allowing the installation of full-length expansion cards. This arrangement also puts the processor and memory in line with the fan output of the power supply, allowing the processor to run cooler.

ATX system connector   Also known as the ATX motherboard power connector. This type of power connector feeds an ATX motherboard. It provides the six voltages required and delivers them all through a single 20-pin connector.

AUTOEXEC.BAT   A contraction of AUTOmatically EXECuted BATch. AUTOEXEC.BAT is a special DOS batch file located in the root directory of a startup disk. It runs automatically every time the computer is started or restarted.

Automatic Private IP Addressing (APIPA)   A feature of Windows 98/2000/XP that enables DHCP clients to automatically self-configure an IP address and subnet mask when their DHCP server can't be found.

auto-ranging multimeter   A multimeter that automatically sets its upper and lower ranges depending on the input signal. These multimeters are more difficult to damage by choosing the wrong range setting. See also *multimeter*.

Autorun   On a CD-ROM, an option that allows the CD to automatically start an installation program or a menu screen when it is inserted into the CD-ROM drive.

B channel   See *bearer channel*.

baby AT   A type of motherboard form factor wherein the motherboard is smaller than the original AT form factor.

backside bus   A set of signal pathways between the CPU and Level 2 cache memory (if present).

backup   A duplicate copy made so that you can recover from an accidental loss of data.

bandwidth   In communications, the difference between the highest and the lowest frequencies available for transmission in any given range. In networking, the transmission capacity of a computer or a communications channel stated in megabits or megabytes per second; the higher the number, the faster the data transmission takes place.

Basic Rate Interface (BRI)   An ISDN line with two B channels and one D channel. Each B channel is 64Kbps, for a total of 128Kbps for data and/or voice. The D channel is 16Kbps for management.

basis weight   A measurement of the "heaviness" of paper. The number is the weight, in pounds, of 500 17" × 22" sheets of that type of paper.

batch file   A file with a .bat extension that contains DOS commands. If you type the name of the batch file at a DOS command line and press Enter, DOS processes all of the batch file commands, one at a time, without needing any additional user input.

baud rate   In communications equipment, a measurement of the number of state changes (from 0 to 1 or vice versa) per second on an asynchronous communications channel.

bearer channel   The ISDN channel that carries 64Kbps of data.

Berg connector   A type of connector most commonly used in PC floppy drive power cables. It has four conductors arranged in a row.

bias voltage   The high-voltage charge applied to the developing roller inside an EP cartridge.

bidirectional   A satellite connection wherein the satellite is used for both uploads and downloads.

binary   Any scheme that uses two different states, components, conditions, or conclusions. In mathematics, the binary (base-2) numbering system uses combinations of the digits 0 and 1 to represent all values.

BIOS (basic input/output system)   The ROM-based software on a motherboard that acts as a kind of interpreter between an operating system and a computer's hardware.

BIOS CMOS setup program   A program that modifies BIOS settings in the CMOS memory. You access this program at system startup time by pressing a key combination such as Alt+F1 or Ctrl+F2.

BIOS shadow   A copy of the BIOS in memory.

bit   Contraction of BInary digiT. A bit is the basic unit of information in the binary numbering system, representing either 0 (for off) or 1 (for on). Bits can be grouped together to make up larger storage units, the most common being the 8-bit byte. A byte can represent all kinds of information including the letters of the alphabet, the numbers 0 through 9, and common punctuation symbols.

blackout   A power drop from 110 volts to zero volts in a very short period of time. It is a complete loss of power for anywhere from a few seconds to several minutes or longer. Blackouts are typically caused by a power failure somewhere in your area. Computer systems need to be prepared to deal with blackouts.

blank   A piece of plastic that is removed when a removable media drive is installed in a computer.

blocker   A key in PCI buses that prevents a +3.3VDC card from being plugged into a +5.5VDC bus slot and vice versa.

Blue Screen of Death (BSOD)   A typical way of describing the blue-screen error condition that occurs when Windows NT, 2000, or XP fails to boot properly or quits unexpectedly.

Bluetooth   A wireless technology that is used to replace the myriad of interface cables that run between a computer and all its peripherals.

BNC   A type of connector used to attach stations to a Thinnet network.

bonding   Combining two bearer channels into one 128Kbps data connection to maximize throughput.

boot   To load an operating system into memory, usually from a hard disk, although occasion-ally from a floppy disk. This is an automatic procedure begun when you first turn on or reset your computer. A set of instructions contained in ROM begin executing, first running a series of power on self-tests (POSTs) to check that devices such as hard disks are in working order, then locating and loading the operating system, and finally passing control of the computer over to that operating system.

boot ROM   A chip installed into a NIC that will allow the workstation to boot from an operating system installed onto a special boot server. The boot ROM will contact the boot server, download an operating system into memory, then allow the computer to boot from the downloaded OS.

bootable disk   Any disk capable of loading and starting the operating system, although most often used when referring to a floppy disk. In these days of increasingly larger operating sys-tems, it is less common to boot from a floppy disk. In some cases, all the files needed to start the operating system will not fit on a single floppy disk, which makes it impossible to boot from a floppy.

bps (bits per second)   A measurement of how much data (how many bits) is transmitted in one second. Typically used to describe the speed of asynchronous communications (modems).

bridge   A type of connectivity device that operates in the Data Link layer of the OSI model. It is used to join similar topologies (Ethernet to Ethernet, Token Ring to Token Ring) and to divide traffic on network segments. This device passes information destined for one particular workstation to that segment, but it does not pass broadcast traffic.

broadband   The general designation for higher-speed Internet connections. It uses analog signals across multiple frequencies to send data.

broadcast   To send a signal to all entities that can listen to it. In networking, it refers to sending a signal to all entities connected to that network.

brouter   In networking, a device that combines the attributes of a bridge and a router. A brouter can route one or more specific protocols, such as TCP/IP, and bridge all others.

brownout   A short period of low voltage often caused by an unusually heavy demand for power.

browser   A piece of software used to access the Internet. Common browsers are Netscape's Navigator and Microsoft's Internet Explorer.

bubble-jet printer   A type of sprayed ink printer. It uses an electric signal that energizes a heating element, causing ink to vaporize and be pushed out of the pinhole and onto the paper.

buffer   A special area of memory set aside to receive data from the expansion card.

BUFFERS=   Settings used by MS-DOS in the CONFIG.SYS configuration file at startup to specify how many memory buffers should be allocated during that session of DOS.

bug   A logical or programming error in hardware or software that causes a malfunction of some sort. If the problem is in software, it can be fixed with changes to the program. If the fault is in hardware, new circuits must be designed and constructed. Some bugs are fatal and cause the program to hang or result in data loss, others are just annoying, and many are never even noticed.

bus   A set of pathways that allows information and signals to travel between components inside or outside of a computer.

bus clock   A chip on the motherboard that produces a type of signal (called a clock signal) that indicates how fast the bus can transmit information.

bus connector slot   A slot made up of several small copper channels that grab the matching "fingers" of the expansion circuit boards. The fingers connect to copper pathways on the motherboard.

bus mastering   A technique that allows certain advanced bus architectures to delegate control of data transfers between the Central Processing Unit (CPU) and associated peripheral devices to an add-in board.

bus topology   A type of physical topology that consists of a single cable that runs to every workstation on the network. Each computer shares that same data and address path. As messages pass through the trunk, each workstation checks to see if the message is addressed to that workstation. This topology is difficult to reconfigure, because reconfiguration requires you to disconnect and reconnect a portion of the network (thus bringing down the whole network).

byte   Contraction of BinarY digiT Eight. A group of 8 bits that, in computer storage terms, usually holds a single character, such as a number, letter, or other symbol.

cable   A medium used to connect another devices to a computer using multiple copper or fiber optic conductors inside a common wrapping or sheath.

cable access methods   Methods by which stations on a network get permission to transmit their data.

cable modem   A device that is used to connect computers and other devices to a cable television data network.

cache   Pronounced "cash." A special area of memory, managed by a cache controller, that improves performance by storing the contents of frequently accessed memory locations and their addresses. When the processor references a memory address, the cache checks to see if it holds that address. If it does, the information is passed directly to the processor; if not, a normal memory access takes place instead. A cache can speed up operations in a computer in which RAM access is slow compared with its processor speed, because the cache memory is always faster than normal RAM.

cache memory   Fast SRAM memory used to store, or cache, frequently used instructions and data.

caliper   The thickness measurement of a given sheet of paper, which can affect a printer's feed mechanism.

card services   Part of the software support needed for PCMCIA (PC Card) hardware devices in a portable computer, controlling the use of system interrupts, memory, or power management.

When an application wants to access a PC Card, it always goes through the card services software and never communicates directly with the underlying hardware.

carpal tunnel syndrome   A form of wrist injury caused by holding the hands in an awkward position for long periods of time.

carriage belt   The printer belt placed around two small wheels or pulleys and attached to the printhead carriage. The carriage belt is driven by the carriage motor and moves the printhead back and forth across the page during printing.

carriage motor   A stepper motor used to move the printhead back and forth on a dot-matrix printer.

carriage stepper motor   The printer motor that makes the printhead carriage move.

CAS latency   The length of time (measured in clock cycles) between the request for information from memory and receipt of the information. The most common markings for CAS latency are CL3 and CL2. CL2 is a lower latency (meaning a faster access time) than CL3.

case   The plastic cover that surrounds the computer components and provides protection from the elements.

case fan   A small fan that is used to bring air into, or take air out of, the computer's case.

case frame   The metal reinforcing structure inside a laptop that provides rigidity and strength and that most components mount to.

cathode ray tube   See *CRT (cathode ray tube)*.

CCD (charge-coupled device)   A device that allows light to be converted into electrical pulses.

CD-R   A CD drive that allows you to create (or *burn*) a CD. Also known as a CD burner.

CD-ROM (compact disc read-only memory)   A high-capacity optical storage device that uses compact disc technology to store large amounts of information, up to 650MB (the equivalent of approximately 300,000 pages of text), on a single 4.72-inch disk.

CD-RW (rewritable)   A CD drive that allows you to create (or *burn*) or re-create a CD. Also known as a CD burner.

Central Processing Unit (CPU)   The computing and control part of the computer. The CPU in a mainframe computer may be contained on many printed circuit boards, the CPU in a mini-computer may be contained on several boards, and the CPU in a PC is contained in a single extremely powerful microprocessor.

centralized processing   A network processing scheme in which all "intelligence" is found in one computer and all other computers send requests to the central computer to be processed. Mainframe networks use centralized processing.

Centronics parallel interface   A standard 36-pin interface in the PC world for the exchange of information between the PC and a peripheral, such as a printer, originally developed by the printer manufacturer Centronics, Inc. The standard defines eight parallel data lines, plus additional lines for status and control information.

CGA (Color Graphics Adapter)   A video adapter that provided low-resolution text and graphics. CGA provided several different text and graphics modes, including 40- or 80-column by 25-line, 16-color text mode, and graphics modes of 640 horizontal pixels by 200 vertical pixels with 2 colors, or 320 horizontal pixels by 200 vertical pixels with 4 colors. CGA has been superseded by later video standards, including EGA, VGA, SuperVGA, and XGA.

Challenge Handshake Authentication Protocol (CHAP)   A security authentication protocol used in conjunction with PPP and remote access to validate the identity of the originator of the connection during connection or any time thereafter.

charge-coupled device   See *CCD (charge-coupled device)*.

charging corona   The wire or roller that is used to put a uniform charge on the EP drum inside a toner cartridge.

charging step   The step in EP printing at which a special wire in the toner cartridge gets a high voltage from the HVPS. It uses this high voltage to apply a strong, uniform negative charge (around –600VDC) to the surface of the photosensitive drum.

checksum   A method of providing information for error detection, usually calculated by summing a set of values.

checksumming   An error checking routine that runs a mathematical equation against a set of data and comes up with a result, called a checksum. The data is transmitted, and the receiver then runs the same formula against the data transmitted and compares the result to the checksum. If they are the same, the transmission is considered successful.

chip creep   The slow self-loosening of chips from their sockets on the system board as a result of the frequent heating and cooling of the board (which causes parts of the board—significantly, the chip connector slots—to alternately expand and shrink).

chip puller   A tool that is used on older (pre-386) systems to remove the chips without damaging them.

chipset   A collection of chips or circuits that perform interface and peripheral functions for the processor.

clamshell design   A laptop design that is made up of two halves, hinged together at the back.

cleaning cycle   A set of steps that a bubble-jet printer goes through in order to purge the printheads of any dried ink. It uses a special suction cup and sucking action to pull ink through the printhead, dislodging any dried ink and clearing stuck passageways.

cleaning step   The step in the EP print process at which excess toner is scraped from the EP drum with a rubber blade.

client   A network entity that can request resources from the network or server.

client computer   A computer that requests resources from a network.

client software   Software that allows a device to request resources from a network.

clock doubling   Technology that allows a chip to run at the bus's rated speed externally, but still be able to run the processor's internal clock at twice the speed of the bus. This technology improves computer performance.

clock multiplier   The number used to change the working speed of the processor relative to the speed of the external clock.

clock rate   See *clock speed*.

clock signal   A built-in metronome-like signal that indicates how fast the components can operate.

clock speed   Also known as the clock rate. The internal speed of a computer or processor, normally expressed in MHz. The faster the clock speed, the faster the computer can perform a specific operation, assuming the other components in the system, such as disk drives, can keep up with the increased speed.

clock tripling   A type of processor design wherein the processor runs at one speed externally and at triple that speed internally.

cluster   The smallest unit of hard disk space that DOS can allocate to a file, consisting of one or more contiguous sectors. The number of sectors contained in a cluster depends on the hard disk type.

CMOS (Complementary Metal Oxide Semiconductor)   An area of nonvolatile memory containing settings that determine how a computer is configured.

CMOS battery   A battery used to power CMOS memory so that the computer won't lose its settings when powered down.

CMOS setup program   A program that modifies the computer's settings in the CMOS memory that stores the configuration information for the computer. It is accessed by a special key or key combination at startup.

CMYK   A color inking system that mixes cyan, magenta, yellow, and black inks to make the desired colors.

coaxial cable   A medium for connecting computer components that contains a center conductor, made of copper, surrounded by a plastic jacket, with a braided shield over the jacket.

command interpreter   The Windows startup file, also known as the DOS shell or COMMAND.COM, that provides the command-line interface the DOS user sees.

COMMAND.COM   Takes commands issued by the user through text strings or click actions and translates them back into calls that can be understood by the lower layers of DOS. It is the vital command interpreter for DOS.

Communication Network Riser (CNR)   Slots on Intel motherboards that allow a mother-board designer to design a chipset with certain integrated features, which allow the addition of a CNR riser card to enhance onboard capabilities.

compact installation   A procedure that installs only those components needed to get the software functional.

Complementary Metal Oxide Semiconductor   See *CMOS (Complementary Metal Oxide Semiconductor)*.

computer name   The name by which a Microsoft computer is known on the network. This is a NetBIOS name (up to 15 characters in length) that must be unique on the network. In Windows 2000, the computer name is always the same as the machine's host name, whereas in Windows 9*x* the two names can be different.

conditioning step   The step in the EP print process at which a uniform charge is applied to the EP drum by the charging corona or charging roller.

conductor   Any item that permits the flow of electricity between two entities.

conduit   A piece of software that facilitates the communication between software on the PC (like Microsoft Outlook) and the applications on a PDA.

CONFIG.SYS   In DOS, some versions of Windows, and OS/2, a special text file containing set-tings that control the way the operating system works. CONFIG.SYS must be located in the root directory of the default boot disk, normally drive C:, and is read by the operating system only once as the system starts running. Some application programs and peripheral devices require you to include special statements in CONFIG.SYS, whereas other commands may specify the number of disk-read buffers or open files on your system, specify how the disk cache should be configured, or load any special device drivers your system may need.

connectivity device   Any device that facilitates connections between network devices. Some examples include hubs, routers, switches, and gateways.

Control Program for Microcomputer (CP/M)   A computer operating system that was an early competitor of Microsoft's DOS system. CP/M was a command-line system developed by Gary Kildall.

conventional memory   The amount of memory accessible by DOS in PCs using an Intel pro-cessor operating in real mode (normally the first 640KB).

cooperative multitasking   A form of multitasking in which all running applications must work together to share system resources.

core voltage   The voltage that a processor uses internally while running at a separate voltage externally.

corona roller   A type of transfer corona assembly that uses a charged roller to apply charge to the paper.

corona wire   A type of transfer corona assembly. Also, the wire in that assembly that is charged by the high voltage supply. It is narrow in diameter and located in a special notch under the EP print cartridge.

CPU   See *Central Processing Unit (CPU)*.

CPU clock   A type of clock signal that dictates how fast the CPU can run.

CPU clock speed   The setting, in MHz, of how fast the CPU's clock "ticks."

crosstalk   A problem related to electromagnetic fields when two wires carrying electrical signals run parallel and one of the wires induces a signal in the second wire. If these wires are carrying data, the extra unintended signal can cause errors in the communication. Crosstalk is a problem especially in unshielded parallel cables that are longer than 10 feet.

CRT (cathode ray tube)   A display device used in computer monitors and television sets. A CRT display consists of a glass vacuum tube that contains one electron gun for a monochrome display, or three (red, green, and blue) electron guns for a color display. Electron beams from these guns sweep rapidly across the inside of the screen from upper-left to lower-right. The inside of the screen is coated with thousands of phosphor dots that glow when they are struck by the electron beam. To stop the image from flickering, the beams sweep at a rate of between 43 and 87 times per second, depending on the phosphor persistence and the scanning mode used—interlaced or noninterlaced. This is known as the refresh rate and is measured in Hz. The Video Electronics Standards Association (VESA) recommends a vertical refresh rate of 72Hz, noninterlaced, at a resolution of 800 × 600 pixels.

custom installation   An installation procedure that allows the installer to choose exactly which components are installed.

cutover   A condition in which the line voltage drops below a preset threshold, causing sensors to detect the situation and switch the power from the wall to the internal battery. When the power comes back above the threshold, the sensors detect the restoration of power and switch the power source back to the line voltage.

Cyclical Redundancy Check (CRC)   An error-checking routine that runs a mathematical formula against the data being transmitted. A result is computed and sent with the data. When the data arrives at its destination, the same formula is run against the data. If the results are the same, the transmission is considered successful.

cylinder   The collective name for all the tracks at the same concentric position on a disk. A hard disk consists of two or more platters, each with two sides. Each side is further divided into concentric circles known as tracks.

Cylinder, Head, Sector (CHS) addressing   A method of accessing each block of data by its cylinder, head, and sector address. Compare to *LBA address size expansion*.

D channel   A channel used for call setup and link management. This channel has only 16Kbps of bandwidth.

daisy-chaining   A pattern of cabling wherein the cables run from the first device to the second, second to the third, and so on. If the devices have both an "in" and an "out," the in of the first device of each pair is connected to the out of the second device of each pair.

daisy-wheel printer   An impact printer that uses a plastic or metal print mechanism with a different character on the end of each spoke of the wheel. As the print mechanism rotates to the correct letter, a small hammer strikes the character against the ribbon, transferring the image onto the paper.

DAT   See *digital audio tape (DAT)*.

data bits   In asynchronous transmissions, the bits that make up the data. Usually, 7 or 8 data bits make up the data word.

data bus   A bus used to send data to and receive it from the microprocessor.

data compression   Any method of encoding data so that it occupies less space than in its original form.

Data Link layer   The second of seven layers of the International Standards Organization's Open Systems Interconnection (ISO/OSI) model for computer-to-computer communications. The Data Link layer validates the integrity of the flow of data from one node to another by synchronizing blocks of data and by controlling the flow of data.

Data Over Cable Service Interface Specification (DOCSIS)   The standard used by most cable systems for transmitting Internet traffic to a subscriber via television cable.

data set ready   See *DSR (data set ready)*.

data terminal equipment   See *DTE (data terminal equipment)*.

data terminal ready   See *DTR (data terminal ready)*.

data transfer rate   The speed at which a disk drive can transfer information from the drive to the processor, usually measured in megabits or megabytes per second.

datagrams   Chunks of data organized at the Network layer.

daughterboard   A printed circuit board that attaches to another board to provide additional functions.

DB connector   Any of several types of cable connectors used for parallel or serial cables. The number following the letters *DB* (for data bus) indicates the number of pins the connector usually has.

de facto   Latin translation for "by fact." Any standard that is a standard because everyone is using it.

de jure   Latin translation for "by law." Any standard that is a standard because a standards body decided it should be so.

debouncing   A keyboard feature that eliminates unintended triggering of keystrokes. It works by having the keyboard controller constantly scan the keyboard for keystrokes. Only keystrokes that are pressed for more than two scans are considered keystrokes. This prevents spurious electronic signals from generating input.

dedicated server   The server that is assigned to perform a specific application or service.

default CMOS settings   The settings programmed by the factory that allow the computer to become functional at a basic level.

default gateway   The path taken by all outgoing traffic unless another path is specified. If you need to communicate by TCP/IP with a computer that is not on your subnet (the local network segment), the computer needs to use a gateway to access this remote network.

defragmentation   The process of reorganizing and rewriting files so that they occupy one large continuous area on your hard disk rather than several smaller areas.

delta channel   See *D channel*.

Desktop   Contains the visible elements of Windows and defines the limits of the graphic environment.

desktop case   A computer case designed to lie horizontally, with at least three $5^1/_4$-inch bays oriented horizontally and the $3^1/_2$-inch bays oriented vertically.

Desktop Control Panel   Windows control panel applet that is used to configure the system so it easier to use. Control Panel contains the settings for the background color and pattern as well as screen saver settings.

desktop replacement laptop   A laptop designed to replace a standard desktop computer for day-to-day use. Thus it is more full featured than other laptops.

developing roller   The roller inside a toner cartridge that presents a uniform line of toner to help apply the toner to the image written on the EP drum.

developing step   The step in the EP print process at which the image written on the EP drum by the laser is developed—that is, it has toner stuck to it.

device bay   A large slot on the computer into which an expansion device fits (usually a disk drive of some sort).

device driver   A small program that allows a computer to communicate with and control a device.

Device Manager   A utility in Windows 9*x*/2000 that allows you to view and modify hardware settings. Device drivers can be installed or upgraded, and problems with devices can be found and dealt with here.

diagnostic program   A program that tests computer hardware and peripherals for correct operation. In the PC, some faults are easy to find; these are known as hard faults, and the diagnostic program diagnoses them correctly every time. Others, such as memory faults, can be difficult to find; these are called soft faults because they do not occur every time the memory location is tested, but only under very specific circumstances.

dialer   A special program for dial-up networking that initiates the connection with the ISP, takes the phone off hook, dials the ISP's access number, and establishes the connection.

dial-up   An Internet connection wherein the computer connecting to the Internet uses a modem to connect to the ISP over a standard telephone line.

dial-up networking   The built-in dialer present in most versions of Windows.

die   The small chip in the center of the big CPU chip package.

differential backup   Backup files that have changed since the last full backup.

differential signaling   A method of signaling that uses two wires, each carrying the electrical opposite of the other. The receiving device takes the difference (subtracts one from the other), and the resulting value is used.

digital audio tape (DAT)   A method of recording information in digital form on a small audio-tape cassette. Many gigabytes of information can be recorded on a cassette, so a DAT can be used as a backup medium. Like all tape devices, however, DATs are relatively slow.

digital camera   A *camera* that works much like a standard camera, except that a *charge-coupled device* replaces the film and records the picture as a pattern of bits.

digital signal   A signal that consists of discrete values. These values do not change over time; in effect, they change instantly from one value to another.

digital signed driver   A driver that has been digitally "signed" by Microsoft with a special value that only Windows can read. This signature tells the Windows installer that the driver being installed has been tested for security and stability on the chosen Windows platform and that the driver is from a reputable source.

Digital Subscriber Line (DSL)   A broadband Internet access technology that uses the existing phone line from your home to the phone company to carry digital signals at higher speeds.

DIMM (Dual Inline Memory Module)   A memory module that is similar to a SIMM (Single Inline Memory Module), except that a DIMM is double-sided. There are memory chips on both sides of the memory module. DIMMs have since been introduced with chips on one side of the memory stick.

DIN-*n*   A circular type of connector used with computers. (The *n* represents the number of connectors.)

DIP (Dual Inline Package)   A standard housing constructed of hard plastic, commonly used to hold an integrated circuit. The circuit's leads are connected to two parallel rows of pins designed to fit snugly into a socket; these pins may also be soldered directly to a printed-circuit board. If you try to install or remove DIPs, be careful not to bend or damage their pins.

DIP switch   A small switch used to select the operating mode of a device, mounted as a Dual Inline Package (DIP). DIP switches can be either sliding or rocker switches and are often grouped together for convenience. They are used on printed-circuit boards, dot-matrix printers, modems, and other peripherals.

Direct Memory Access   See *DMA (Direct Memory Access).*

Direct Rambus   A memory bus that transfers data at 800MHz over a 16-bit memory bus. Direct Rambus memory models (often called *RIMMs*), like DDR SDRAM, can transfer data on both the rising and falling edges of a clock cycle.

directory   Used to organize files on the hard drive. Another name for a directory is a folder. Directories created inside or below others are called subfolders or subdirectories.

direct-solder method   A method of attaching chips to the motherboard. The chips are soldered directly to the motherboard.

disk cache   An area of computer memory where data is temporarily stored on its way to or from a disk. A disk cache mediates between the application and the hard disk; when an application asks for information from the hard disk, the cache program first checks to see whether that data is already in the cache memory. If it is, the disk-cache program loads the information from the cache memory rather than from the hard disk. If the information is not in memory, the cache program reads the data from the disk, copies it into the cache memory for future reference, and then passes the data to the requesting application.

disk-caching program   A program that reads the most commonly accessed data from disk and keeps it in memory for faster access.

disk controller   The electronic circuitry that controls and manages the operation of floppy or hard disks installed in the computer. A single disk controller may manage more than one hard disk; many disk controllers also manage floppy disks and compatible tape drives.

disk drive   A peripheral storage device that reads and writes to magnetic or optical disks. When more than one disk drive is installed on a computer, the operating system assigns each drive a unique name—for example A: and C: in DOS, Windows, and OS/2.

disk duplexing   In networking, a fault-tolerant technique that writes the same information simultaneously onto two different hard disks. Disk duplexing is offered by most of the major network operating systems and is designed to protect the system against a single disk failure; it is not designed to protect against multiple disk failures and is no substitute for a well-planned series of disk backups.

disk mirroring   In networking, a fault-tolerant technique that writes the same information simultaneously onto two different hard disks, using the same disk controller. In the event that one disk fails, information from the other can be used to continue operations. Disk mirroring is offered by most of the major network operating systems and is designed to protect the system against a single disk failure; it is not designed to protect against multiple disk failures and is no substitute for a well-planned series of disk backups.

Disk Operating System   See *DOS.*

disk sector   The part of a hard disk track that falls in a particular section of the "pie slice" on the disk.

disk thrashing   See *thrashing.*

diskette   An easily removable and portable floppy disk $3^1/_2$ inches in diameter and enclosed in a durable plastic case that has a metal shutter over the media access window.

display   The screen element in a laptop computer.

distributed processing   A computer system in which processing is performed by several separate computers linked by a communications network. The term often refers to any computer system supported by a network, but more properly refers to a system in which each computer is chosen to handle a specific workload and the network supports the system as a whole.

DIX Ethernet   The original name for the Ethernet network technology. Named after the original developer companies: Digital, Intel, and Xerox.

DMA (Direct Memory Access)   A method of transferring information directly from a mass-storage device such as a hard disk or from an adapter card into memory (or vice versa), without the information passing through the processor.

DMA channels   Dedicated circuit pathways on the motherboard that make DMA possible.

DMA transfer modes   Data transfers during which the ATA interface manages the data transfer directly to the rest of the system (typically direct to memory).

docking port   A port used to connect the laptop to a special laptop-only peripheral known as a *docking station*.

docking station   A hardware system into which a portable computer fits so that it can be used as a full-fledged desktop computer. Docking stations vary from simple port replicators (that allow you access to parallel and serial ports and a mouse) to complete systems (that give you access to network connections, CD-ROMs, a tape backup system, and/or PCMCIA ports).

domain   1. The security structure for Windows NT Server and Windows 2000 Active Directory. 2. The namespace structure of TCP/IP's DNS structure.

Domain Name System (DNS)   Allows TCP/IP-capable users anywhere in the world to find resources in other companies or countries by using their domain name. Each domain is an independent namespace for a particular organization, and DNS servers manage requests for information about the IP addresses of particular DNS entries. DNS is used to manage all names on the Internet.

dongle   A special cable that provides a connector to a circuit board that doesn't have one. For example, a motherboard may use a dongle to provide a serial port when there is a ribbon cable connector for the dongle on the motherboard, but there is no serial port.

dongle connection   A connector on a motherboard where a dongle can connect.

DOS   1. Acronym for Disk Operating System, an operating system originally developed by Microsoft for the IBM PC. DOS exists in two very similar versions: MS-DOS, developed and marketed by Microsoft for use with IBM-compatible computers; and PC-DOS, supported and sold by IBM for use only on computers manufactured by IBM.

2. A DOS `CONFIG.SYS` command that loads the operating system into conventional memory, extended memory, or upper-memory blocks on computers using the Intel 80386 or later processor. To use this command, you must have previously loaded the `HIMEM.SYS` device driver with the `DEVICE` command in `CONFIG.SYS`.

DOS prompt   A visual confirmation that DOS is ready to receive input from the keyboard. The default prompt includes the current drive letter followed by a right angle bracket (for example, C>). You can create your own custom prompt with the `PROMPT` command.

DOS shell   An early graphic user interface for DOS that allowed you to manage files and run programs through a simple text interface and even use a mouse. It was soon replaced by Windows.

dot pitch   In a monitor, the vertical distance between the centers of like-colored phosphors on the screen of a color monitor, measured in millimeters (mm).

dot-matrix printer   An impact printer that uses columns of small pins and an inked ribbon to create the tiny pattern of dots that form the characters. Dot-matrix printers are available in 9-, 18-, or 24-pin configurations.

dots per inch (dpi)   A measure of resolution expressed by the number of dots that a device can print or display in one inch.

double-density disk   A floppy disk with a storage capacity of 360KB.

DRAM   See *dynamic RAM (DRAM)*.

drawing tablet   A pointing device that includes a pencil-like device (called a stylus) for drawing on its flat rubber-coated sheet of plastic.

drive bay   An opening in the system unit into which you can install a floppy disk drive, hard disk drive, or tape drive.

drive geometry   Term used to describe the number of cylinders, read/write heads, and sectors in a hard disk.

drive hole   The hole in a floppy disk that allows the motor in the disk drive to spin the disk. Also known as the hub hole.

drive imaging   A procedure whereby a system is installed completely, with all device drivers and software configured. Then, the system is booted to a floppy disk that has a program such as Norton's Ghost installed. The drive is copied, sector by sector, to a file (usually stored on a network share or on several CD-ROMs).

drive letter   In DOS, Windows, and OS/2, a designation used to specify a particular hard or floppy disk. For example, the first floppy disk is usually referred to as drive A:, and the first hard disk as drive C:.

driver   See *device driver*.

driver signing   A Windows 2000 process that allows companies to digitally sign their device software. It prevents viruses and poorly written drivers from damaging your system and also allows administrators to block the installation of unsigned drivers.

driver software See *device driver*.

D-Shell See *DB connector*.

DSL endpoint The device used to access DSL, commonly referred to mistakenly as a DSL modem.

DSR (data set ready) A hardware signal defined by the RS-232-C standard to indicate that the device is ready.

D-Sub See *DB connector*.

DTE (data terminal equipment) In communications, any device, such as a terminal or a computer, connected to a communications channel or public network.

DTR (data terminal ready) A hardware signal defined by the RS-232-C standard to indicate that the computer is ready to accept a transmission.

dual booting An option offered by a boot manager that presents you with a choice of which operating system to use at startup. If a single machine must be used for many tasks, it may be necessary for it to have multiple operating systems installed simultaneously. To use a different operating system, you shut down the system, restart it, and select the other operating system.

Dual Inline Memory Module See *DIMM (Dual Inline Memory Module)*.

Dual Inline Package See *DIP (Dual Inline Package)*.

dumb terminal A combination of keyboard and screen that has no local computing power, used to input information to a large, remote computer, often a minicomputer or a mainframe. This remote computer provides all the processing power for the system.

duplex In asynchronous transmissions, the ability to transmit and receive on the same channel at the same time; also referred to as full duplex. Half-duplex channels can transmit only or receive only. Most dial-up services available to PC users take advantage of full-duplex capabilities, but if you cannot see what you are typing, switch to half duplex. If you are using half duplex and you can see two of every character you type, change to full duplex.

duplex printing Printing a document on both sides of the page so that the appropriate pages face each other when the document is bound.

dynamic electricity See *electricity*.

Dynamic Host Configuration Protocol (DHCP) A protocol that manages the automatic assignment of TCP/IP addressing information (such as the IP address, subnet mask, default gateway, and DNS server). It can save you a great deal of time when you're configuring and maintaining a TCP/IP network.

Dynamic Link Library (DLL) files Windows component files containing small pieces of executable code that are shared between multiple Windows programs. They are used to eliminate redundant programming in certain Windows applications. DLLs are used extensively in Microsoft Windows, OS/2, and Windows NT. DLLs may have the filename extension .dll, .drv, or .fon.

dynamic RAM (DRAM)   A common type of computer memory that uses capacitors and transistors storing electrical charges to represent memory states. These capacitors lose their electrical charge, and so they need to be refreshed every millisecond, during which time they cannot be read by the processor. DRAM chips are small, simple, cheap, easy to make, and hold approximately four times as much information as a static RAM (SRAM) chip of similar complexity. However, they are slower than static RAM. Processors operating at clock speeds of 25MHz or more need DRAM with access times of faster than 80 nanoseconds (80 billionths of a second), whereas SRAM chips can be read in as little as 15 to 30 nanoseconds.

Each operating system contains a standard set of device drivers for the keyboard, the monitor, and so on, but if you add specialized peripherals (such as a CD-ROM disk drive) or a network interface card, you will probably have to add the appropriate device driver so that the operating system knows how to manage the device. In DOS, device drivers are loaded by the DEVICE or DEVICEHIGH command in CONFIG.SYS.

edge connector   A form of connector consisting of a row of etched contacts along the edge of a printed circuit board that is inserted into an expansion slot in the computer.

EDO (Extended Data Out) RAM   A type of DRAM that increases memory performance by eliminating wait states.

EEPROM (Electrically Erasable Programmable Read-Only Memory)   A memory chip that maintains its contents without electrical power, and whose contents can be erased and reprogrammed either within the computer or from an external source. EEPROMs are used where the application requires stable storage without power but may have to be reprogrammed.

EGA (Enhanced Graphics Adapter)   A video adapter standard that provides medium-resolution text and graphics. EGA can display 16 colors at the same time from a choice of 64, with a horizontal resolution of 640 pixels and a vertical resolution of 350 pixels. EGA has been superseded by VGA and SVGA.

EISA (Extended Industry Standard Architecture)   A PC bus standard that extends the traditional AT-bus to 32 bits and allows more than one processor to share the bus. EISA has a 32-bit data path and, at a bus speed of 8MHz, can achieve a maximum throughput of 33MBps.

EISA Configuration Utility (EISA Config)   The utility used to configure an EISA bus expansion card.

Electrically Erasable Programmable Read-Only Memory   See *EEPROM*.

electricity   The flow of free electrons from one molecule of substance to another. This flow of electrons is used to do work.

electromagnetic drawing tablet   Type of drawing tablet that has grids of wires underneath the rubberized surface. The stylus contains a small sensor that is sensitive to electromagnetic fields. At timed intervals, an electromagnetic pulse is sent across the grid. The sensor in the stylus picks up these pulses.

electromagnetic interference (EMI)   Any electromagnetic radiation released by an electronic device that disrupts the operation or performance of any other device.

electron gun   The component of a monitor that fires electrons at the back of the phosphor-coated screen.

electronic stepper motor   A special electric motor in a printer that can accurately move in very small increments. It powers all of the paper transport rollers as well as the fuser rollers.

electrostatic discharge (ESD)   The exchange of electrons that occurs when two objects of dissimilar charge come in contact with one another, to standardize the electrostatic charge between the objects. This exchange, or discharge, can sometimes be seen as a spark or arc of electricity. Even when it cannot be seen it is damaging to electronic components.

e-mail   Electronic mail, generally sent across the Internet using protocols named SMTP (for sending) and POP3 (for receiving).

EMI   See *electromagnetic interference (EMI)*.

EMM386.EXE   A reserved memory manager that emulates expanded memory in the Extended Memory area (XMS) and provides DOS with the ability to utilize upper memory blocks to load programs and device drivers.

encoding   A process by which binary information is changed into flux transition patterns on a disk surface.

Enhanced Capabilities Port (ECP)   A port designed to transfer data at high speeds to printers. It uses a DMA channel and a buffer to increase printing performance.

Enhanced Graphics Adapter   See *EGA (Enhanced Graphics Adapter)*.

enhanced keyboard   A 101- or 102-key keyboard introduced by IBM that has become the accepted standard for PC keyboard layout. Unlike earlier keyboards, it has 12 function keys across the top, rather than 10 function keys in a block on the left side; it has extra Ctrl and Alt keys; and it has a set of cursor control keys between the main keyboard and the numeric keypad.

Enhanced Parallel Port (EPP)   A port that meets IEEE standard 1284, designed to provide greater data transfer speeds and the ability to send memory addresses as well as data through a parallel port.

envelope feeder   A special device for feeding envelopes into a printer.

environment variables   Variables used to set certain system-wide parameters that can then be used by applications running on the system. For instance, a system's temporary directory can be set to a specific location using an environment variable.

EP drum   A device coated with a photosensitive material that can hold a static charge when not exposed to light. The drum contains a cleaning blade that continuously scrapes the used toner off the photosensitive drum to keep it clean.

EP print process   The six-step process an EP laser printer uses to form images on paper. In order, the steps are charging, exposing, developing, transferring, fusing, and cleaning.

EP printer (electrophotographic printer)   A printer that uses high voltage, a laser, and a black carbon toner to form an image on a page.

EPROM (Erasable Programmable Read-Only Memory)   A memory chip that maintains its contents without electrical power, and whose contents can be erased and reprogrammed by removing a protective cover and exposing the chip to ultraviolet light.

ergonomics   Standards that define the positioning and use of the body to promote a healthy work environment.

Error Correcting Code (ECC) memory   Memory that uses a special algorithm that can detect and correct single-bit errors.

ESD   See *electrostatic discharge (ESD)*.

ESD mat   A preventive measure to guard against the effects of ESD. The excess charge is drained away from any item that comes in contact with it.

Ethernet   A network technology based on the IEEE 802.3 CSMA/CD standard. The original Ethernet implementation specified 10MBps, baseband signaling, coaxial cable, and CSMA/CD media access.

Ethernet port   A port attached to the motherboard that allows an Ethernet connection.

EULA (End User License Agreement)   An agreement displayed during software setup whereby you confirm that you understand the terms of usage.

even parity   A technique that counts the number of 1s in a binary number and, if the total number of 1s is not even, adds a digit to make it even. See also *parity*.

exit roller   Found on laser and page printers, the mechanism that guides the paper out of the printer into the paper-receiving tray.

expanded memory page frame   See *page frame*.

Expanded Memory Specification (EMS)   The original version of the Lotus-Intel-Microsoft Expanded Memory Specification (LIM EMS) that lets DOS applications use more than 640KB of memory space.

expansion bus   An extension of the main computer bus that includes expansion slots for use by compatible adapters, such as memory boards, video adapters, hard disk controllers, and SCSI interface cards.

expansion card   A device that can be installed into a computer's expansion bus.

expansion slot   One of the connectors on the expansion bus that gives an adapter access to the system bus. You can add as many additional adapters as there are expansion slots inside your computer.

extended DOS partition   A further optional division of a hard disk, after the primary DOS partition, that functions as one or more additional logical drives. A logical drive is an area of a larger disk that acts as though it were a separate disk with its own drive letter.

Extended Graphics Array   See *XGA (Extended Graphics Array)*.

Extended Industry Standard Architecture   See *EISA (Extended Industry Standard Architecture)*.

extended memory manager   A device driver that supports the software portion of the extended memory specification in an IBM-compatible computer.

Extended Memory System (XMS)   Memory above 1,024KB that is used by Windows and Windows-based programs. This type of memory cannot be accessed unless the `HIMEM.SYS` memory manager is loaded in the DOS `CONFIG.SYS` file with a line like `DEVICE=HIMEM.SYS`.

extended partition   A second partition that can be created out of the remaining space if all the space on a drive is not used in the creation of the drive's primary partition. This extended partition can hold one or more logical drives.

external bus   An external component connected through expansion cards and slots that allows the processor to talk to other devices and vice versa.

external cache memory   A separate expansion board that installs in a special processor-direct bus containing cache memory.

external hard disk   A hard disk packaged in its own case with cables and an independent power supply, as opposed to a disk drive housed inside and integrated with the computer's system unit.

external modem   A stand-alone modem, separate from the computer and connected by a serial cable. LEDs on the front of the chassis indicate the current modem status and can be useful in troubleshooting communications problems. An external modem is a good buy if you want to use a modem with different computers at different times or with different types of computer.

FAQ (Frequently Asked Questions)   A document that lists some of the more commonly asked questions about a product or component. When you're researching a problem, the FAQ is usually the best place to start.

FAT   See *file allocation table (FAT)*.

fax modem   An adapter that fits into a PC expansion slot and provides many of the capabilities of a full-sized fax machine, but at a fraction of the cost.

FC-PGA package   The Flip Chip-PGA. A processor form-factor type in which the internal processor die in the package is put in with the die toward the top so that the heatsink and thermal grease that are normally applied to the insulation of a package can be used directly on the part that is putting out the heat. It makes for much more efficient cooling of the processor.

FDDI   See *fiber distributed data interface (FDDI)*.

FDISK.EXE   The DOS utility that is used to partition hard disks for use with DOS.

feed roller   The rubber roller in a laser printer that feeds the paper into the printer.

feeder   A device that feeds paper or other media into a printer.

Fiber Distributed Data Interface (FDDI)   A specification for fiber optic networks transmitting at a speed of up to 100Mbps over a dual, counter-rotating, Token Ring topology. FDDI is suited to systems that require the transfer of very large amounts of information, such as medical imaging, 3D seismic processing, oil reservoir simulation, and full-motion video.

fiber optic cable   A transmission technology that sends pulses of light along specially manufactured optical fibers. Each fiber consists of a core, thinner than a human hair, surrounded by a sheath with a much lower refractive index. Light signals introduced at one end of the cable are conducted along the cable as the signals are reflected from the sheath.

Field Replaceable Unit   See *FRU (Field Replaceable Unit)*.

file allocation table (FAT)   A table maintained by DOS or OS/2 that lists all the clusters available on a disk. The FAT includes the location of each cluster, as well as whether it is in use, available for use, or damaged in some way and therefore unavailable. The FAT also keeps track of which pieces belong to which file.

file compression program   An application program that shrinks program or data files so that they occupy less disk space. The file must then be extracted or decompressed before you can use it. Many of the most popular file compression programs are shareware, like WinZip, PKZIP, LHA, and StuffIt for the Macintosh, although utility packages like PC Tools from Central Point Software also contain file compression programs.

file corruption   Process whereby a file's information becomes unreadable, due to an improper shutdown, a virus, or a random problem. This unreadable file is referred to as corrupt, and it must be either repaired or replaced.

file locking   A feature of many network operating systems that "locks" a file to prevent more than one person from updating the file at the same time.

file server   A networked computer used to store files for access by other client computers on the network. On larger networks, the file server may run a special network operating system; on smaller installations, the file server may run a PC operating system supplemented by peer-to-peer networking software.

file sharing   In networking, the sharing of files via the network file server. Shared files can be read, reviewed, and updated by more than one individual. Access to the file or files is often regulated by password protection, account or security clearance, or file locking, to prevent simultaneous changes from being made by more than one person.

File Transfer Protocol (FTP)   A protocol used to transfer large files across the Internet or any TCP/IP network. Special servers, called FTP servers, store information and then transfer it back to FTP clients as needed. FTP servers can also be secured with a username and password to prevent unauthorized downloading (retrieval of a file from the server) or uploading (placing of a file on the server).

finger mouse   See *Touchpoint*.

finisher   A printer device that finishes sets of documents being printed, by folding, stapling, hole-punching, sorting, or collating them into their final form.

FireWire   See *IEEE-1394.*

firmware   Any software stored in a form of read-only memory—ROM, EPROM, or EEPROM—that maintains its contents when power is removed.

fixed disk   A disk drive that contain several disks (also known as platters) stacked together and mounted through their centers on a small rod. The disks rotate as read/write heads floating above the disks make, modify, or sense changes in the magnetic positions of the coatings on the disk.

fixed resistor   A type of resistor that is used to reduce the current by a certain amount. Fixed resistors are color coded to identify their resistance values and tolerance bands.

flash memory   A special form of nonvolatile EEPROM that can be erased at signal levels normally found inside the PC, so that you can reprogram the contents with whatever you like without pulling the chips out of your computer. Once flash memory has been programmed, you can remove the expansion board it is mounted on and plug it into another computer if you wish.

flatbed scanner   An optical device that can be used to digitize a whole page or a large image.

flat-panel display   In laptop and notebook computers, a very narrow display that uses one of several technologies, such as electroluminescence, LCD, or thin-film transistors.

floating-point calculation   A calculation of numbers whose decimal point is not fixed but moves or floats to provide the best degree of accuracy. Floating-point calculations can be implemented in software, or they can be performed much more quickly by a separate floating-point processor.

floating-point processor   A special-purpose, secondary processor designed to perform floating-point calculations much more quickly than the main processor.

floppy disk   A flat, round, magnetically coated plastic disk enclosed in a protective jacket. Data is written onto the floppy disk by the disk drive's read/write heads as the disk rotates inside the jacket. It can be used to distribute commercial software, to transfer programs from one computer to another, or to back up files from a hard disk. Floppy disks in personal computing are of two physical sizes, $5^1/_4$-inch and $3^1/_2$-inch, and a variety of storage capacities. The $5^1/_4$-inch floppy disk has a stiff plastic external cover, whereas the $3^1/_2$-inch floppy disk is enclosed in a hard plastic case. IBM-compatibles use $5^1/_4$-inch and $3^1/_2$-inch disks, and the Macintosh uses $3^1/_2$-inch disks.

floppy disk controller   The circuit board that is installed in a computer to translate signals from the CPU into signals the floppy disk drive can understand. Often it is integrated into the same circuit board that houses the hard disk controller; however, it can be integrated into the motherboard in the PC.

floppy disk drive   A device used to read and write data to and from a floppy disk. Floppy disk drives may be full-height drives, but more commonly these days they are half-height drives.

floppy drive cable   A cable that connects the floppy drive(s) to the floppy drive controller. The cable is a 34-wire ribbon cable that usually has three connectors.

floppy drive interface   A connector on a motherboard used to connect a floppy drive to the motherboard.

floppy drive power connector   A small, flat connector, also known as a *Berg connector*, commonly used to power floppy disk drives and other small form factor devices.

flux transition   The presence or absence of a magnetic field in a particle of the coating on the disk. As the disk passes over an area, the electromagnet is energized to cause the material to be magnetized in a small area.

font   The typestyle used for printing a document. The font can be loaded onto the hard drive of the computer or the onboard memory of the printer.

footprint   The amount of desktop or floor space occupied by a computer or display terminal. By extension, it also refers to the size of software items such as applications or operating systems.

form factor   The physical characteristics and dimensions of a drive style.

form feed (FF)   A printer command that advances the paper in a printer to the top of the next page. You issue this command by pressing the FF button on the printer.

FORMAT.COM   An external DOS command that prepares the partition to store information using the FAT system as required by DOS and Windows 9*x*.

formatter board   A type of circuit board that takes the information a printer receives from the computer and turns it into commands for the various components in the printer.

formatting   1. To apply the page-layout commands and font specifications to a document and produce the final printed output.
   2. The process of initializing a new, blank floppy disk or hard disk so that it can be used to store information.

fragmentation   A disk storage problem that exists after several smaller files have been deleted from a hard disk. The deletion of files leaves areas of free disk space scattered throughout the disk. The fact that these areas of disk space are located so far apart on the disk causes slower performance, because the disk read/write heads have to move all around the disk's surface to find the pieces of one file.

free memory   An area of memory not currently in use.

Frequently Asked Questions   See *FAQ (Frequently Asked Questions)*.

friction feed   A paper-feed mechanism that uses pinch rollers to move the paper through a printer, one page at a time.

frontside bus   A set of signal pathways between the CPU and main memory.

FRU (Field Replaceable Unit)   The individual parts or whole assemblies that can be replaced to repair a computer.

Full Control permission   A share permission in NT that gives you full control over the folder and the files within it.

full installation   An installation procedure that installs every component, even those that may not be required or used frequently.

full tower case   A computer case that stands approximately 20 to 254 inches tall, has at least five $5^1/_4$-inch drive bays, and is designed to stand vertically on the floor next to a desk (instead of on the desk).

full AT   A type of motherboard form factor wherein the motherboard is the same size as the original IBM AT computer's motherboard.

full-duplex communications   Communications where both entities can send and receive simultaneously.

function keys   The set of programmable keys on the keyboard that can perform special tasks assigned by the current application program.

fuser   A device on an EP printer that uses two rollers to heat the toner particles and melt them to the paper. The fuser is made up of a halogen heating lamp, a Teflon-coated aluminum fusing roller, and a rubberized pressure roller. The lamp heats the aluminum roller. As the paper passes between the two rollers, the rubber roller presses the paper against the heated roller. This causes the toner to melt and become a permanent image on the paper.

fusing assembly   See *fuser*.

fusing step   The step in the EP printing process during which the toner image on the paper is fused to the paper using heat and pressure. The heat melts the toner, and the pressure helps fuse the image permanently to the paper.

game port   A DB-15 connector used to connect game devices (like joysticks) to a computer.

gateway   In networking, a shared connection between a local area network and a larger system, such as a mainframe computer or a large packet-switching network. Usually slower than a bridge or router, a gateway typically has its own processor and memory and can perform protocol conversions. Protocol conversion allows a gateway to connect two dissimilar networks; data is converted and reformatted before it is forwarded to the new network.

GDI.EXE   A Windows core component that is responsible for drawing icons and windows in Windows 3.*x*.

General Protection Fault (GPF)   A Windows error that typically occurs when a Windows program tries to access memory currently in use by another program.

gigabyte   One billion bytes. However, bytes are most often counted in powers of 2, so a gigabyte becomes 2 to the thirtieth power, or 1,073,741,824 bytes.

GPF   See *General Protection Fault (GPF)*.

graphical user interface (GUI)   A graphics-based user interface that allows you to select files, programs, or commands by pointing to pictorial representations on the screen rather than by typing long, complex commands from a command prompt. Application programs execute in windows, using a consistent set of pull-down menus, dialog boxes, and other graphical elements such as scroll bars and icons.

graphics accelerator board   A specialized expansion board containing a graphics coprocessor as well as all the other circuitry found on a video adapter.

graphics mode   A mode of a video card that allows the video card to display graphics.

GUI   See *graphical user interface (GUI)*.

half-duplex communications   Communications that occur when only one entity can transmit or receive at any one instant.

half-height drive   A space-saving drive bay that is half the height of the 3-inch drive bays used in the original IBM PC. Most of today's drives are half-height drives.

handheld PC (HPC)   A handheld device that is basically a shrunken laptop. HPCs run on an operating system called Windows CE.

handheld scanner   A type of scanner that is small enough to be held in your hand. Used to digitize a relatively small image or artwork, it consists of the controller, CCD, and light source contained in a small enclosure with wheels on it.

hard disk controller   An expansion board that contains the necessary circuitry to control and coordinate a hard disk drive. Many hard disk controllers are capable of managing more than one hard disk, as well as floppy disks and even tape drives.

hard disk drive   A storage device that uses a set of rotating, magnetically coated disks called platters to store data or programs. A typical hard disk platter rotates at up to 7200rpm, and the read/write heads float on a cushion of air from 10 to 25 millionths of an inch thick so that the heads never come into contact with the recording surface. The whole unit is hermetically sealed to prevent airborne contaminants from entering and interfering with these close tolerances. Hard disks range in capacity from a few tens of megabytes to several gigabytes of storage space; the bigger the disk, the more important a well-thought-out backup strategy becomes.

hard disk interface   A connector on a motherboard that makes it possible to connect a hard disk to the motherboard.

hard disk system   A disk storage system containing the following components: the hard disk controller, hard disk, and host adapter.

hard memory error   A reproducible memory error that is related to hardware failure.

hard reset   A system reset made by pressing the computer's reset button or by turning the power off and then on again.

hardware   All the physical electronic components of a computer system, including peripherals, printed-circuit boards, displays, and printers.

Hardware Compatibility List (HCL)   A list (maintained and regularly updated by Microsoft for each of its Windows operating systems) of all hardware currently known to be compatible with a particular operating system. Windows 98/NT/2000 all have their own HCL.

hardware interrupt An interrupt or request for service generated by a hardware device such as a keystroke from the keyboard or a tick from the clock. Because the processor may receive several such signals simultaneously, hardware interrupts are usually assigned a priority level and processed according to that priority.

hardware port See *I/O address*.

head The electromagnetic device used to read from and write to magnetic media such as hard and floppy disks, tape drives, and compact discs. The head converts the information read into electrical pulses sent to the computer for processing.

header Information attached to the beginning of a network data frame.

heat spreaders Two aluminum sheaths that cover the chips on a DIMM/RIMM to help prevent overheating.

heatsink A device attached to an electronic component that removes heat from the component by induction. It is often a plate of aluminum or metal with several vertical fingers.

hermaphroditic data connector A connector that is both male and female.

hertz Abbreviated Hz. A unit of frequency measurement; 1 hertz equals one cycle per second.

hexadecimal Abbreviated hex. The base-16 numbering system that uses the digits 0 to 9, followed by the letters A to F (equivalent to the decimal numbers 10 through 15). Hex is a very convenient way to represent the binary numbers computers use internally, because it fits neatly into the 8-bit byte. All of the 16 hex digits 0 to F can be represented in 4 bits, and so two hex digits (one digit for each set of 4 bits) can be stored in a single byte. This means 1 byte can contain any one of 256 different hex numbers, from 0 through FF. Hex numbers are often labeled with a lowercase *h* (for example, 1234h) to distinguish them from decimal numbers.

High Memory Area (HMA) In an IBM-compatible computer, the first 64KB of extended memory above the 1MB limit of 8086 and 8088 addresses. Programs that conform to the extended memory specification can use this memory as an extension of conventional memory, although only one program can use or control HMA at a time.

High Voltage Differential (HVD) Support for differential signaling added to SCSI-2.

high-density disk A floppy disk with more recording density and storage capacity than a double-density disk.

high-level format The process of preparing a floppy disk or a hard disk partition for use by the operating system. In the case of DOS, a high-level format creates the boot sector, the file allocation table (FAT), and the root directory.

high-voltage power supply (HVPS) A component that provides the high voltages used during the EP print process. It converts house AC currents into higher voltages that the two corona assemblies can use.

high-voltage probe A device used to drain away voltage from a monitor before testing. It is a pencil-shaped device with a metal point and a wire lead with a clip.

HIMEM.SYS   The DOS and Microsoft Windows device driver that manages the use of extended memory and the high memory area on IBM-compatible computers. HIMEM.SYS not only allows your application programs to access extended memory, it oversees that area to prevent other programs from trying to use the same space at the same time. HIMEM.SYS must be loaded by a DEVICE command in your CONFIG.SYS file; you cannot use DEVICEHIGH.

HMA   See *High Memory Area (HMA).*

home page   On the Internet, an initial starting page. A home page may be related to a single person, a specific subject, or a corporation, and is a convenient jumping-off point to other pages or resources.

host   The central or controlling computer in a networked or distributed processing environment, providing services that other computers or terminals can access via the network. Computers connected to the Internet are also described as hosts, and can be accessed using FTP, Telnet, Gopher, or a browser.

host adapter   A device that translates signals from the hard drive and controller to signals the computer's bus can understand.

host name   The name by which a computer is known on a TCP/IP network. This name must be unique within the domain the machine is in. In Windows 2000, the computer name is always the same as the machine's host name, whereas in Windows 9x the two can be different.

hub   A connectivity device used to link several computers together into a physical star topology. A hub repeats any signal that comes in on one port and copies it to the other ports.

HVPS   See *high-voltage power supply (HVPS).*

hybrid topology   A mix of more than one topology type used on a network.

Hypertext Transfer Protocol (HTTP)   The protocol of the World Wide Web, used to send and receive web pages and other content from an HTTP server (web server). HTTP uses of linked pages accessed via hyperlinks, which are words or pictures that, when clicked on, take you to another page.

I/O address   Lines on a bus that allow the CPU to send instructions to the devices installed in the bus slots. Each device is given its own communication line to the CPU. These lines function like one-way (unidirectional) mailboxes.

I/O port   See *I/O address.*

I/O voltage   The external voltage of the processor.

IBM data connector   A unique, hermaphroditic connector commonly used with IBM's Token Ring technology and Type 1 or 2 STP cable.

IBM PC   A series of personal computers based on the Intel 8088 processor, introduced by IBM in mid-1981. The PC was released containing 16KB of memory, expandable to 64KB on the motherboard, and a monochrome video adapter incapable of displaying bitmapped graphics.

The floppy disk drive held 160KB of data and programs. There was no hard disk on the original IBM PC; that came later, with the release of the IBM PC/XT.

IBM PS/2   A series of personal computers using several different Intel processors, introduced by IBM in 1987. The main difference between the PS/2 line and earlier IBM personal computers was a major change to the internal bus. Previous computers used the AT bus, also known as industry-standard architecture, but IBM used the proprietary micro channel architecture in the PS/2 line instead. Micro channel architecture expansion boards do not work in a computer using ISA. See *IBM-compatible computer*.

IBM-compatible computer   Originally, any personal computer compatible with the IBM line of PCs. With the launch of IBM's proprietary micro channel architecture in the PS/2 line of computers, which replaced the AT bus, two incompatible standards emerged, and so the term became misleading. Now, it is more common to use the term *industry-standard computer* when referring to a computer that uses the AT or ISA bus, and the term *DOS computer* to describe any PC that runs DOS and is based on one of the Intel family of chips.

IC   See *integrated circuit (IC)*.

icons   On-screen graphics that act as doors through which programs are started and therefore used to spawn windows. They are shortcuts that allow you to open a program or a utility without knowing where that program is or how it needs to be configured.

IDE (Integrated Drive Electronics)   A hard disk technology that can connect multiple drives together. These drives integrate the controller and drive into one assembly. This makes them very inexpensive. As a result, IDE drives are the most commonly used disk technology installed in computers today.

IEEE-1394   A high-speed digital interface most commonly used to transfer data between computers and digital video cameras. It has a maximum data transfer rate of over 400MBps.

illegal operation error   A Windows error that occurs when a program does something Windows wasn't expecting or doesn't know how to do.

image   The mirror image of the system copied when you perform drive imaging.

impact printer   Any printer that forms an image on paper by forcing a character image against an inked ribbon. Dot-matrix, daisy-wheel, and line printers are all impact printers, whereas laser printers are not.

incremental backup   A backup of a hard disk that consists of only those files created or modified since the last backup was performed.

Industry Standard Architecture   See *ISA (Industry Standard Architecture)*.

Infrared Data Association (IrDA)   The organization that outlines a standard way of transmitting and receiving information via infrared so that devices can communicate with each other.

infrared transmission   Wireless transmission between devices that use radiation in the infrared range of the electromagnetic spectrum.

INI file   A text file created by an installation program when a new Windows application is installed. INI files contain settings for individual Windows applications as well as for Windows itself.

initialization commands   A set of commands sent to a modem to prepare it to function.

ink cartridge   A reservoir of ink and a printhead, in a removable package.

inoculation   The process of protecting a computer system against virus attacks by installing antivirus software.

input/output address   See *I/O address*.

integrated circuit (IC)   Also known as a chip. A small semiconductor circuit that contains many electronic components.

Integrated Drive Electronics   See *IDE (Integrated Drive Electronics)*.

Integrated Services Digital Network   See *ISDN (Integrated Services Digital Network)*.

integrated system board   A system board that has most of the computer's circuitry attached, as opposed to the circuitry's having been installed as expansion cards.

Intel OverDrive   A processor that can increase application performance by an estimated 40 to 70 percent. OverDrive chips boost system performance by using the same clock multiplying technology found in the Intel 80486DX-2 and DX4 chips.

intelligent hub   A class of hub that can be remotely managed on the network.

interface   Any port or opening that is specifically designed to facilitate communication between two entities.

interface circuitry   Printer circuits that make the physical connection to whatever signal is coming from the computer (parallel, serial, SCSI, network, infrared, and so on) and connect the interface to the control circuitry. The interface circuitry converts the signals from the interface into the datastream the printer uses.

interface software   The software for a particular interface that translates software commands into commands a printer can understand.

interlacing   A display technique that uses two passes over the monitor screen, painting every other line on the screen the first time and then filling in the rest of the lines on the second pass. It relies on the physiological phenomenon known as persistence of vision to produce the effect of a continuous image.

interleaving   A process that involves skipping sectors to write the data, instead of writing sequentially to every sector. This evens out the data flow and allows the drive to keep pace with the rest of the system. Interleaving is given in ratios. If the interleave is 2:1, the disk skips 2 minus 1, or 1 sector, between each sector it writes (it writes to one sector, skips one sector, and then writes to the next sector following). Most drives now use a 1:1 interleave, because today's drives are very efficient at transferring information.

International Standards Organization (ISO)   An international standards-making body, based in Geneva, that establishes global standards for communications and information exchange.

Internet   The global TCP/IP network that now extends into nearly every office and school. The World Wide Web is the most visible part of the Internet, but e-mail, newsgroups, and FTP (to name just a few) are also important parts of the Internet.

Internet address   An IP or domain address that identifies a specific node on the Internet.

Internet Control Message Protocol (ICMP)   An element of the TCP/IP protocol suite that transmits error messages and network statistics.

Internet Protocol   See *IP (Internet Protocol)*.

Internet Service Provider (ISP)   A company that provides Internet access and e-mail addresses for users. Generally, ISPs are local or regional companies.

internetwork   Any TCP/IP network that spans router interfaces. Anything from a small office with two subnets to the Internet itself can be described as an internetwork.

Internetwork Packet eXchange/Sequenced Packet eXchange (IPX/SPX) protocol   The main protocol suite used on Novell NetWare networks. Microsoft's version of the protocol stack is called NWLink.

interrupt   A signal to the processor generated by a device under its control (such as the system clock) that interrupts normal processing. An interrupt indicates that an event requiring the processor's attention has occurred, causing the processor to suspend and save its current activity and then branch to an interrupt service routine. This service routine processes the interrupt (whether it was generated by the system clock, a keystroke, or a mouse click) and, when it's complete, returns control to the suspended process. In the PC, interrupts are often divided into three classes: internal hardware, external hardware, and software interrupts. The Intel $80x86$ family of processors supports 256 prioritized interrupts, of which the first 64 are reserved for use by the system hardware or by DOS.

interrupt request (IRQ)   Signals that an event has taken place that requires the processor's attention, and may come from the keyboard, the input/output ports, or the system's disk drives. In the PC, the main processor does not accept interrupts from hardware devices directly; instead interrupts are routed to an Intel 8259A Programmable Interrupt Controller. This chip responds to each hardware interrupt, assigns a priority, and forwards it to the main processor.

interrupt request (IRQ) lines   Hardware lines that carry a signal from a device to the processor.

inverse multiplexing   See *bonding*.

IP (Internet Protocol)   The underlying communications protocol on which the Internet is based. IP allows a data packet to travel across many networks before reaching its final destination.

IP address   A unique address each machine must have in order to communicate on a TCP/IP network. This address is in the form $x.x.x.x$, where x is a number from 0 to 255.

IPCONFIG   Used on Windows 2000 to view current IP configuration information and to manually request updated information from a DHCP server.

IPX network address   An eight-digit hexadecimal number used by IPX addresses for the network portion. This number can be assigned randomly by the installation program or manually by the network administrator.

IRQ   See *interrupt request (IRQ)*.

ISA (Industry Standard Architecture)   A 16-bit bus design first used in IBM's PC/AT computer in 1984. ISA has a bus speed of 8MHz and a maximum throughput of 8MBps. EISA is a 32-bit extension to this standard bus.

ISDN (Integrated Services Digital Network)   A worldwide digital communications network emerging from existing telephone services, intended to replace all current systems with a completely digital transmission system. Computers and other devices connect to ISDN via simple, standardized interfaces, and when complete, ISDN systems will be capable of transmitting voice, video, music, and data.

ISDN terminal adapter   The device that connects a computer to an ISDN line.

joystick port   See *game port*.

jumper   A small plastic and metal connector that completes a circuit, usually to select one option from a set of several user-definable options. Jumpers are often used to select one particular hardware configuration rather than another.

kernel file   A Windows core component responsible for managing Windows resources and running applications.

keyboard/mouse port   A combination port on a laptop that allows for the connection of an external keyboard or mouse.

kilobit   Abbreviated Kb or Kbit. 1024 bits (binary digits).

kilobits per second   Abbreviated Kbps. The number of bits, or binary digits, transmitted every second, measured in multiples of 1024 bits per second. Used as an indicator of communications transmission rate.

kilobyte   Abbreviated K, KB, or Kbyte. 1024 bytes.

L1 cache   Any cache memory that is integrated into the CPU.

L2 cache   Any cache memory that is external to the CPU.

LAN   See *local area network (LAN)*.

lapping   A process by which the heatsink or water block surface is sanded flat using a very flat surface (like a sheet of glass) and progressively finer grits of sandpaper until the surface is as flat as it can get. This helps minimize the very small air gaps that occur between the processor and heatsink due to the uneven metal surface of the heatsink, thus creating the largest possible surface area for the greatest heat transfer efficiency.

laser printer   A generic name for a printer that uses the electrophotographic (EP) print process.

laser scanner   The assembly in an EP process printer that contains the laser. This component is responsible for writing the image to the EP drum.

latency   The time that elapses between issuing a request for data and starting the data transfer. In a hard disk, this translates into the time it takes to position the disk's read/write head and rotate the disk so that the required sector or cluster is under the head. Latency is just one of many factors that influence disk-access speeds.

LBA address size expansion   The increase of the LBA address size in ATA/ATAPI-6 to 48 bits, which means a maximum of 281474976710656 separate blocks. A 48-bit address length means a maximum drive size of 144115188075855360 bytes, or 137438953472GB.

LCD   See *liquid crystal display (LCD)*.

LCD monitor   A monitor that uses liquid crystal display technology. Many laptop and notebook computers use LCD displays because of their low power requirements.

least significant bit (LSB)   In a binary number, the lowest-order bit. That is, the rightmost bit. In the binary number 0001, the 1 is the least significant bit.

LED page printer   A type of EP process printer that uses a row of LEDs instead of a laser to expose the EP drum.

legacy   A component that is still functional but is out of date.

letter quality (LQ)   A category of dot-matrix printer that can print characters that look very close to the quality a laser printer might produce.

levels   In RAID, the various methods used for writing to disks to ensure redundancy. Each level is designed for a specific purpose.

line conditioner   A device that produces "perfect" power of 110V/60Hz. These devices remove most of the stray EMI and RFI signals from the incoming power. They also reduce any power overages down to 110V.

line power   Electrical power that comes out of the standard wall socket.

link light   A light that indicates when a basic electrical connection to the network has been made.

liquid cooling   Technology whereby a water block is used to conduct heat away from the processor (as well as chipsets). Water is circulated through this block to a radiator, where it is cooled.

liquid crystal display (LCD)   A display technology common in portable computers that uses electric current to align crystals in a special liquid. The rod-shaped crystals are contained between two parallel transparent electrodes, and when current is applied, they change their orientation, creating a darker area. Many LCD screens are also backlit or side-lit to increase visibility and reduce the possibility of eyestrain.

lithium ion (Lilon)   The latest type of laptop battery that can't be overcharged, has a longer life, and provides more power than NiMH or NiCad.

local area network (LAN)   A group of computers and associated peripherals connected by a communications channel, capable of sharing files and other resources among several users.

local bus   A PC bus specification that allows peripherals to exchange data at a rate faster than the 8MBps allowed by the ISA (Industry Standard Architecture) and the 32MBps allowed by the EISA (Extended Industry Standard Architecture) definitions. Local bus can achieve a maximum data rate of 133MBps with a 33MHz bus speed, 148MBps with a 40MHz bus, or 267MBps with a 50MHz bus.

local resources   Files or folders that are physically located on the machine the user is sitting at. Windows 2000 has the ability to enforce local security, but Windows 9*x* does not.

logic board   The sturdy sheet or board to which all other components on the computer are attached. These components consist of the CPU, underlying circuitry, expansion slots, video components, and RAM slots, just to name a few. Also known as a motherboard or planar board.

Logical Block Addressing (LBA)   A method of overcoming the 528MB maximum drive size design limitation of the combination of ATA and the BIOSs of the time. Rather than accessing each block of data by its cylinder, head, and sector address (known as *Cylinder, Head, Sector (CHS) addressing*), LBA specifies that each block on the disk be given its own unique ID number, which is 28 bits long (a maximum of 137GB worth of addresses).

logical drive   A drive created within an extended partition, which is used to organize space within the partition. It can be accessed through the use of a drive letter.

logical memory   The way memory is organized so it can be accessed by an operating system.

logical partitions   Partitions on a hard disk that have drive letters associated with them.

logical topology   The topology that defines how the data flows in a network.

logon   The process of logging on submits your username and password to the network and gives you the network credentials you will use for the rest of that session. Users can either log on to a workgroup or to a network security entity (such as the Active Directory).

Low Voltage Differential (LVD)   A feature set introduced with SCSI-3 that increases the maximum SCSI bus length to 25 meters (82 feet) and increases the maximum possible throughput to 80MBps (on Ultra3 Wide LVD).

low-level format   The process that creates the tracks and sectors on a blank hard disk or floppy disk; sometimes called the physical format. Most hard disks are already low-level formatted; however, floppy disks receive both a low- and a high-level format (or logical format) when you use the DOS or OS/2 command FORMAT.

LPT*x* port   In DOS, the device name used to denote a parallel communications port, often used with a printer. DOS supports three parallel ports: LPT1, LPT2, and LPT3; and OS/2 adds support for network ports LPT4 through LPT9.

MAC address   The unique physical address for each NIC.

main motor   A printer stepper motor that is used to advance the paper.

master drive   The primary drive in an IDE master/slave configuration.

math coprocessor   A processor that speeds up the floating decimal point calculations needed in algebra and statistical calculations.

MCA (Micro Channel Architecture)   An architecture incompatible with expansion boards that follow the earlier 16-bit AT bus standard, physically because the boards are about 50 percent smaller and electronically as the bus depends on more proprietary integrated circuits. MCA was designed for multiprocessing, and it also allows expansion boards to identify themselves, thus eliminating many of the conflicts that arose through the use of manual settings in the original bus.

megabit (Mbit)   Usually 1,048,576 binary digits or bits of data. Often used as equivalent to 1 million bits.

megabits per second (Mbps)   A measurement of the amount of information moving across a network or communications link in 1 second, measured in multiples of 1,048,576 bits.

megabyte (MB)   Usually 1,048,576 bytes. Megabytes are a common way of representing computer memory or hard-disk capacity.

megahertz (MHz)   One million cycles per second. A processor's clock speed is often expressed in MHz. The original IBM PC operated an 8088 running at 4.77MHz; the more modern Pentium processor runs at speeds of 1000MHz and higher.

memory   The primary random access memory (RAM) installed in the computer. The operating system copies application programs from disk into memory, where all program execution and data processing takes place; results are written back out to disk again. The amount of memory installed in the computer can determine the size and number of programs it can run, as well as the size of the largest data file.

memory address   The exact location in memory that stores a particular data item or program instruction.

memory effect   The condition that results when a laptop battery is discharged partially, and then charged. The next time the battery is discharged, it doesn't last as long. Eventually, the battery gets so bad that it is unusable.

memory map   The organization and allocation of memory in a computer. A memory map gives an indication of the amount of memory used by the operating system and the amount remaining for use by applications.

memory optimization   The process of making the most possible conventional memory available to run DOS programs.

memory refresh   An electrical signal that keeps the data stored in memory from degrading.

mesh topology   A type of logical topology in which each device on a network is connected to every other device on the network. This topology uses routers to search multiple paths and determine the best path.

Messaging Application Programming Interface (MAPI)   An interface used to control how Windows interacts with messaging applications such as e-mail programs. MAPI makes most of the functions of e-mail transparent and allows programmers to write just the application, not the whole messaging system.

MFT (Master File Table)   Describes all the other metadata files and holds a recoverable list of every other file and directory on an NFS partition.

MicroDIMM   An extremely small RAM form factor, only 45.5 millimeters (about 1.75 inches) long and 30 millimeters (about 1.2 inches, a bit bigger than a quarter) wide. It was designed for the ultralight, portable subnotebook style of computer. The module has 144 pins and is similar to a DIMM in that it uses 64-bit memory modules.

Microsoft Diagnostics   See *MSD (Microsoft Diagnostics)*.

Microsoft Disk Operating System   See *MS-DOS (Microsoft Disk Operating System)*.

mid tower case   A computer case that stands between 16 and 19 inches tall, has at least three $5^1/_4$-inch drive bays, and is designed to stand vertically on either on the floor or on a computer users desk next to their monitor. They don't have quite as much room as a full tower case, but still have significant room for airflow and component layout.

midi tower case   A term used to describe a computer case between a mid tower and mini tower in size.

mini tower case   A computer case that stands about 12 to 15 inches tall, has one or two $5^1/_4$-inch drive bays, and is designed to stand next to a computer monitor. It was designed to keep the small form factor of a desktop case, but the look of a tower, which is more visually appealing.

minimal installation   See *compact installation*.

modem   Contraction of modulator/demodulator. A device that allows a computer to transmit information over a telephone line. The modem translates between the digital signals the computer uses and analog signals suitable for transmission over telephone lines. When transmitting, the modem modulates the digital data onto a carrier signal on the telephone line. When receiving, the modem performs the reverse process and demodulates the data from the carrier signal.

Molex connector   See *standard peripheral power connector*.

monitor   A video output device capable of displaying text and graphics, often in color.

monochrome monitor   A monitor that can display text and graphics in one color only, such as white text on a green background or black text on a white background.

mopier (multiple original copier)   A laser printer that includes copier-like functions (coalition, stapling, and so on), so each "copy" is essentially an original.

most significant bit (MSB)   In a binary number, the highest-order bit. That is, the leftmost bit. In the binary number 10000000, the 1 is the most significant bit.

motherboard   The main printed circuit board in a computer that contains the central processing unit, appropriate coprocessor and support chips, device controllers, memory, and also expansion slots to give access to the computer's internal bus. Also known as a logic board or system board.

mouse   A small input device with one or more buttons used as for pointing or drawing. As you move the mouse in any direction, an on-screen mouse cursor follows the mouse movements; all movements are relative. Once the mouse pointer is in the correct position on the screen, you can press one of the mouse buttons to initiate an action or operation; different user interfaces and file programs interpret mouse clicks in different ways.

MSBACKUP   A DOS program that allows you to make backup copies of all the programs and data stored on the hard disk. This program is menu-driven and allows you to set up options that can be used each time you back up the hard drive.

MSCONFIG   A utility introduced with Windows 98 that allows you to manage your computer system's configuration. Also known as the System Configuration Utility.

MSD (Microsoft Diagnostics)   A program that allows you to examine many different aspects of a system's hardware and software setup.

MS-DOS (Microsoft Disk Operating System)   A single-user, single-tasking operating system, with either a command-line interface or a shell interface. MS-DOS, like other operating systems, allocates system resources (such as hard and floppy disks, the monitor, and the printer) to the applications that need them.

multifunction printer   A peripheral that is essentially a printer, copier, scanner, and fax machine all in one.

multimedia   A computer technology that displays information by using a combination of full-motion video, animation, sound, graphics, and text with a high degree of user interaction.

multimeter   An electronic device used to measure and test ohms, amperes, and volts.

multiplexer   A network device that combines multiple data streams into a single stream for transmission. Multiplexers can also break out the original data streams from a single, multiplexed stream.

multipurpose server   A server that has more than one use. For example, a multipurpose server can be both a file server and a print server.

multistation access unit (MAU)   The central device in a Token Ring network that provides both the physical and logical connections to the stations.

multisync monitor   A monitor designed to detect and adjust to a variety of different input signals. By contrast, a fixed-frequency monitor must receive a signal at one specific frequency.

multitasking   A feature of an operating system that allows more than one program to run simultaneously.

multithreading   The ability of a program to send multiple tasks to the processor at the same time. This allows an application to execute more quickly, but it requires the support of a multithreaded operating system.

multiword DMA mode   A data transfer mode that transfers several words at a time in a kind of burst. Multiword transfer is used more with later ATA specifications because of the inefficiency of setting up a connection to transfer a single word each time. It sets up the connection, transfers multiple words of data, and then closes the connection.

NAK (negative acknowledgment)   A special packet used during data communications. The packet is sent by a receiving station back to the sending station to indicate the data that was received was either incomplete or corrupt.

near letter quality (NLQ)   A category of dot-matrix printer that can come close to the quality of a laser printer, but still is lacking somewhat in print quality.

NetBEUI (NetBIOS Extended User Interface)   A network device driver for the transport layer supplied with Microsoft's LAN Manager.

NetBIOS (Network Basic Input/Output System)   In networking, a layer of software, originally developed in 1984 by IBM and Sytek, that links a network operating system with specific network hardware. NetBIOS provides an application program interface (API) with a consistent set of commands for requesting lower-level network services to transmit information from node to node.

NetBIOS Extended User Interface   See *NetBEUI (NetBIOS Extended User Interface)*.

network   A group of computers and associated peripherals connected by a communications channel capable of sharing files and other resources between several users. A network can range from a peer-to-peer network (that connects a small number of users in an office or department) to a local area network (that connects many users over permanently installed cables and dial-up lines) or to a wide area network (that connects users on several different networks spread over a wide geographic area).

network adapter   Expansion hardware designed to interface with a network. In order to access network resources, a physical connection to the network must be made, generally via a network adapter.

Network Basic Input/Output System   See *NetBIOS (Network Basic Input/Output System)*.

network client software   The software that enables a computer to communicate on the network.

network install   An installation procedure during which the installation CD is copied to a shared location on the network. Individual workstations boot and access the network share.

network interface card (NIC)   In networking, the PC expansion board that plugs into a personal computer or server and works with the network operating system to control the flow of information over the network. The network interface card is connected to the network cabling (twisted-pair, coaxial, or fiber optic cable), which in turn connects all the network interface cards in the network.

Network layer   The third of seven layers of the International Standards Organization's Open Systems Interconnection (ISO/OSI) model for computer-to-computer communications. The Network layer defines protocols for data routing to ensure that the information arrives at the correct destination node.

network portion   The part of the IP address that refers to the address of the network.

network security provider   Centralized user ID and password storage in a network environment, which often makes it easier to manage the network. Examples of this type of centralized system are Windows 2000's Active Directory and NetWare's NDS.

NIC   See *network interface card (NIC)*.

Nickel-Cadmium (NiCad)   The most popular battery for laptops in use today. They last approximately 700 charge cycles (a charge cycle is one cycle from full charge to complete discharge). They hold a charge well, but don't function well when overcharged or undercharged.

Nickel Metal Hydride (NiMH)   A laptop battery type. NiMH batteries don't suffer from the memory effect, and they are made from nontoxic metals, so they are more environmentally friendly than their NiCad counterparts. They provide about 10 percent more power, but they only last for about 400 charge cycles and cost more.

node   In communications, any device attached to the network.

node portion   The part of the IP address that refers to the host.

nonconductor   Any material that does not conduct electricity.

nondedicated server   A computer that can be both a server and a workstation. In practice, by performing the functions of both server and workstation, this type of server does neither function very well. Nondedicated servers are typically used in peer-to-peer networks.

nonintegrated system board   A type of motherboard wherein the various subsystems (video, disk access, and so on) are not integrated into the motherboard, but rather placed on expansion cards that can be removed and upgraded.

noninterlaced   Describes a monitor in which the display is updated (refreshed) in a single pass, painting every line on the screen. Interlacing takes two passes to paint the screen, painting every other line on the first pass, and then sequentially filling in the other lines on the second pass. Noninterlaced scanning, although more expensive to implement, reduces unwanted flicker and eyestrain.

Northbridge   A subset of a motherboard's chipset or circuitry that manages high-speed peripheral communications. The Northbridge subset is responsible primarily for AGP communications and processor-to-memory communications.

NOS (network operating system)   Software that runs on the server and controls and manages the network. The NOS controls the communication with resources and the flow of data across the network.

notebook computer   A small portable computer, about the size of a computer book, with a flat screen and a keyboard that fold together. A notebook computer is lighter and smaller than a laptop computer. Some models use flash memory rather than conventional hard disks for program and data storage, whereas other models offer a range of business applications in ROM. Many offer PCMCIA expansion slots for additional peripherals such as modems, fax modems, or network connections.

NTFS (NT File System)   Created to provide enhanced security and performance for the Windows NT operating system. It has been adopted and improved upon in Windows 2000. NTFS provides Windows 2000 with local file security, file auditing, compression, and encryption options. It is not compatible with Windows 9x or DOS.

null modem   A short RS-232-C cable that connects two personal computers so they can communicate without the use of modems. The cable connects the two computers' serial ports, and certain lines in the cable are crossed over so the wires used for sending data by one computer are used for receiving data by the other computer and vice versa.

numeric keypad   A set of keys to the right of the main part of the keyboard, used for numeric data entry.

NWLINK   The Microsoft version of the IPX/SPX protocol.

octet   An eight-bit number, four bits of which make up the TCP/IP host address.

odd parity   A technique that counts the number of 1s in a binary number and, if the total number of 1s is not odd, adds a digit to make it odd. See also *parity*.

ohm   A unit of electrical resistance.

OLGA on Interposer (OOI)   A form factor package type most often found on Pentium II processors with 423 pins. OLGA is short for *Organic Land Grid Array*, which is the way the pins are laid out on this type of package.

Open Systems Interconnection model   See *OSI (Open Systems Interconnection) model*.

operating system (OS)   The software responsible for allocating system resources, including memory, processor time, disk space, and peripheral devices such as printers, modems, and the monitor. All application programs use the operating system to gain access to these system resources as they are needed. The operating system is the first program loaded into the computer as it boots, and it remains in memory at all times thereafter.

optical disk   A disk that can be read from and written to, like a fixed disk; but, like a CD, is read with a laser.

optical drive   A type of storage drive that uses a laser to read from and write to the storage medium.

optical mouse   A mouse that uses a special mouse pad and a beam of laser light. The beam of light shines onto the mouse pad and reflects back to a sensor in the mouse. Special small lines crossing the mouse pad reflect the light into the sensor in different ways to signal the position of the mouse.

optical scanner   See *scanner*.

optical touch screen   A type of touch screen that uses light beams on the top and left side and optical sensors on the bottom and right side to detect the position of your finger when you touch the screen.

option diskette   A diskette that contains the device-specific configuration files for the device being installed into a MCA bus computer.

opto-mechanical mouse   A type of mouse containing a round ball that makes contact with two rollers. Each roller is connected to a wheel that has small holes in it. The wheel rotates between the arms of a U-shaped mechanism that holds a light on one arm and an optical sensor on the other. As the wheels rotate, the light flashes coming through the holes indicate the speed and direction of the mouse, and these values are transmitted to the computer and the mouse-control software.

Organic Land Grid Array   See *OLGA on Interposer*.

OSI (Open Systems Interconnection) model   A protocol model, developed by the International Standards Organization (ISO), that was intended to provide a common way of describing network protocols. This model describes a seven-layer relationship between the stages of communication. Not every protocol maps perfectly to the OSI model, as there is some overlap within the layers of some protocols.

Overclocking   The process of forcing a computer to operate faster by increasing the clock multiplier or overall clock frequency.

packet   A group of bits ready for transmission over a network. It includes a header, data, and a trailer.

page description language   Describes the whole page being printed. The controller in the printer interprets these commands and turns them into laser pulses or firing print wires.

page frame   The special area reserved in upper memory that is used to swap pages of memory into and out of expanded memory.

page printer   A type of printer that handles print jobs one page at a time instead of one line at a time.

pages   16KB chunks of memory used in expanded memory.

paging   The process of swapping memory to an alternate location, such as to and from a page frame in expanded memory or to and from a swap file.

paper feed mechanism   The mechanism that picks up paper from the paper drawer and feeds it into a printer.

paper feed sensors   The mechanism that tells a printer when it is out of paper, as well as when a paper jam has occurred during the paper-feed process.

paper feeder   See *feeder*.

paper pickup roller   A D-shaped roller that rotates against the paper and pushes one sheet into a printer.

paper registration roller   A roller in an EP process printer that keeps paper movement in sync with the EP image-formation process.

paper transport assembly   The set of devices that moves the paper through a printer. It consists of a motor and several rubberized rollers that each perform a different function.

paper tray   The tray that holds paper until it is fed into a printer.

parallel interface   A medium that transfers data 8 bits at a time over eight separate transmit wires inside a parallel cable (1 bit per wire).

parallel port   An input/output port that manages information 8 bits at a time; often used to connect a parallel printer.

parallel processing   A processor architecture wherein a processor essentially contains two processors in one. The processor can then execute more than one instruction per clock cycle.

parity   A simple form of error-checking used in computers and telecommunications. Parity works by adding an additional bit to a binary number and using it to indicate any changes in that number during transmission.

parked   The locked rest position of the printhead when the print process is finished.

partition   A portion of a hard disk that the operating system treats like a separate drive.

partition table   In DOS, an area of the hard disk containing information about how the disk is organized. The partition table also contains information that tells the computer which operating system to load; most disks contain DOS, but some users divide their hard disk into different partitions, or areas, each containing a different operating system. The partition table indicates which of these partitions is the active partition—the partition that should be used to start the computer.

passive hub   A type of hub that electrically connects all network ports together. This type of hub is not powered.

passive termination   A method of SCSI bus termination wherein you must install terminating resistor packs on the ends of the buses.

passive-matrix screen   An LCD display mechanism that uses a transistor to control every row of pixels on the screen. This is in sharp contrast to active-matrix screens, where each individual pixel is controlled by its own transistor.

password   A means of user identification. In order to identify themselves on the network, users must provide two credentials: a username and a password. The username says, "This is who I am," and the password says, "And here's proof!" Passwords are case sensitive and should be kept secret from other users on the network.

path   A description of where a file on a computer's hard drive exists within the directory structure. If a file is on the D: drive in a folder named TEST, its path is `d:test\`.

PC Card   A peripheral device that uses the PCMCIA specification; also known as a PCMCIA card or a credit-card adapter. PC Cards have the advantage of being small, easy to use, and fully Plug-and-Play compliant.

PC Card slot   An opening in the case of a portable computer intended to receive a PC Card; also known as a PCMCIA slot.

PC Card socket services   See *socket services.*

PCB   See *printed-circuit board (PCB).*

PC-DOS 1.0   A slight modification of Microsoft's Disk Operating System (MS-DOS) that was packaged with IBM's personal computers.

PCI (Peripheral Component Interconnect)   A specification introduced by Intel that defines a local bus that allows up to 10 PCI-compliant expansion cards to be plugged into the computer. One of these 10 cards must be the PCI controller card, but the others can include a video card, network interface card, SCSI interface, or any other basic input/output function. The PCI controller exchanges information with the computer's processor at either 32- or 64-bits at a time and allows intelligent PCI adapters to perform certain tasks concurrently with the main processor by using bus-mastering techniques.

PCMCIA (PC Memory Card International Association)   A standard that defines a laptop expansion bus with small form factor expansion cards. Expansion cards developed for this standard are now called PC Cards.

peer-to-peer network   A network in which the computers act as both workstations and servers and that has no centralized administration or control.

Pentium   The evolution of the 80486 family of microprocessors. The Pentium adds several notable features, including 8KB instruction code and data caches, a built-in floating-point processor and memory-management unit, as well as a superscalar design and dual pipelining that allow the Pentium to execute more than one instruction per clock cycle.

Pentium Pro   A 32-bit processor (also known as the P6) that has a 64-bit data path between the processor and the cache and that is capable of running at clock speeds up to 200MHz. Unlike the Pentium, the Pentium Pro's secondary cache is built into the CPU itself, rather than on the motherboard, meaning that it accesses cache at internal speed, not bus speed.

peripheral   Any hardware device attached to and controlled by a computer, such as a monitor, keyboard, hard disk, floppy disk, CD-ROM drives, printer, mouse, tape drive, or joystick.

Peripheral Component Interconnect   See *PCI (Peripheral Component Interconnect).*

peripheral interface   A method of connecting a peripheral or accessory to a computer, including the specification of cabling, connector type, speed, and method of communication used.

Personal Digital Assistant (PDA)   A small handheld device that has some computing power and can be attached to a PC as a peripheral.

PGA (Pin Grid Array)   A type of IC package that consists of a grid of pins connected to a square, flat package.

phase-change cooling   A cooling system wherein the cooling effect resulting from the change of a liquid to a gas is used to cool the inside of a PC.

photosensitive drum   See *EP drum*.

Physical layer   The first and lowest of the seven layers in the International Standards Organization's Open Systems Interconnection (ISO/OSI) model for computer-to-computer communications. The Physical layer defines the physical, electrical, mechanical, and functional procedures used to connect the equipment.

physical topology   A description that identifies how the cables on a network are physically arranged.

pickup roller   See *paper pickup roller*.

pickup stepper motor   The motor that turns the pickup roller in a printer.

Pin Grid Array   See *PGA (Pin Grid Array)*.

PING   A utility used to send a short message to another computer on a TCP/IP network. PING can be useful to test connectivity between networks or to see if a particular machine is communicating with the network.

PIO modes   A method of data transfer in which the computer's CPU and supporting hardware directly control the transfer of data between the hard disk and the rest of the computer. Most often, DMA is used in favor of PIO modes (especially on PCI-based systems).

pixel   Contraction of *picture element*. The smallest element that display software can use to create text or graphics. A display resolution described as being 640 × 480 has 640 pixels across the screen and 480 down the screen, for a total of 307,200 pixels. The higher the number of pixels, the higher the screen resolution. A monochrome pixel can have two values, black or white; this value can be represented by 1 bit as either 0 or 1. At the other end of the scale, true color is capable of displaying approximately 16.7 million colors, requires 24 bits of information for each pixel.

planar board   See *motherboard*.

Plastic Pin Grid Array (PPGA)   A form factor package type that has pins arranged so the processor can be inserted only one way into its socket. It also has a nickel-plated copper heatsink on top. This package type is used primarily by early Intel Celeron processors with 370 pins that fit into a Socket 370.

platform   An operating system. It is the basic software that runs on a computer, and is the base on which all other software sits. As such, the operating system is the "platform" on which applications and utilities run.

platters   Several disks within the hard drive that are stacked together and mounted through their centers on a small rod called a *spindle*. As the platters rotate, one or more read/write heads float above the disk surfaces and make, modify, or sense changes in the magnetic positions of the coatings on the disks.

plenum rated   When referring to coaxial covering, a designation that means the coating does not produce toxic gas when burned (as PVC does) and is rated for use in air plenums that carry breathable air.

Plug and Play (PnP)   A standard that defines automatic techniques designed to make PC configuration simple and straightforward.

Point and Print   A printer-sharing technology whereby Windows NT copies all the printer driver files for those operating systems specified during the sharing of the printer to its hard drive. When someone connects to a shared printer, Windows NT automatically installs those drivers on the client's operating systems.

port   A generic term for any connector on a computer that allows a cable to be plugged into it.

port replicator   A separate type of dock or an integrated part of the docking station that reproduces the functions of the ports on the back of a laptop. Components like monitors, keyboards, and printers that don't come with the laptop on the road can remain connected to the dock and don't have to all be physically unplugged each time the laptop is taken away.

portable computer   Any computer that contains all the functionality of a desktop computer system but is portable.

portable installation   An installation procedure that installs components needed for portable system installations on laptops. This includes features like power management and LCD display software.

POST   See *power on self-test (POST)*.

Post Office Protocol v 3 (POP3)   A protocol used to accept and store e-mail and to allow users to connect to their mailbox and access their mail. SMTP is used to send mail to the POP3 server.

PostScript   A page-description language used when printing high-quality text and graphics. Desktop publishing or illustration programs that create PostScript output can print on any PostScript printer or imagesetter, because PostScript is hardware-independent. An interpreter in the printer translates the PostScript commands into commands the printer can understand.

potentiometer   See *variable resistor*.

POTS line   The Plain Old Telephone Service line that supplies telephone service to most houses.

power circuits   The set of conductive pathways that converts 110V or 220V house current into the voltages a bubble jet printer uses (usually 12V and 5V) and distributes those voltages to the other printer circuits and devices that need it.

power on self-test (POST)   A set of diagnostic programs, loaded automatically from ROM BIOS during startup, designed to ensure that the major system components are present and operating. If a problem is found, the POST software writes an error message on the screen, sometimes with a diagnostic code number indicating the type of fault located. These POST tests execute before any attempt is made to load the operating system.

power supply   A part of the computer that converts the power from a wall outlet into the lower voltages, typically 5 to 12 volts DC, required internally in the computer.

power surge   A brief but sudden increase in line voltage, often destructive, usually caused by a nearby electrical appliance (such as a photocopier or elevator) or when power is reapplied after an outage.

power user   Someone who either does administrative-level tasks on their machine or needs to have additional access to the system to do their work. The Power Users group on a Windows 2000 Professional station has abilities somewhere between normal users and administrators.

preemptive multitasking   A form of multitasking wherein the operating system executes an application for a specific period of time, according to its assigned priority and need. At that time, it is preempted and another task is given access to the CPU for its allocated time. Although an application can give up control before its time is up, such as during input/output waits, no task is ever allowed to execute for longer than its allotted time period.

Presentation layer   The sixth of seven layers of the International Standards Organization's Open Systems Interconnection (ISO/OSI) model for computer-to-computer communications. The Presentation layer defines the way data is formatted, presented, converted, and encoded.

preventive maintenance   The process of performing various procedures on a computer to prevent future data loss or system downtime.

primary DOS partition   In DOS, a division of the hard disk that contains important operating system files. A DOS hard disk can be divided into two partitions, or areas: the primary DOS partition and the extended DOS partition. If you want to start your computer from the hard disk, the disk must contain an active primary DOS partition that includes the three DOS system files: MSDOS.SYS, IO.SYS, and COMMAND.COM. The primary DOS partition on the first hard disk in the system is referred to as drive C:. Disk partitions are displayed, created, and changed using the FDISK command.

Primary Rate Interface (PRI)   An ISDN interface known as 23B+D, which means it has 23 B Channels and one D channel.

print buffer   A small amount of memory (typically 512KB to 16MB) on a printer used to store print jobs as they are received from the printing computer.

print consumables   Products a printer uses in the print process that must be replaced occasionally. Examples include toner, ink, ribbons, and paper.

print media   Another name for the media being printed on. Examples include paper, transparencies, and labels.

printed-circuit board (PCB)   Any flat board made of plastic or fiberglass that contains chips and other electronic components. Many PCBs are multilayer boards with several different sets of copper traces connecting components together.

printer control assembly   A large circuit board in a laser printer that converts signals from the computer into signals for the various parts in a printer.

printer control circuits   Usually, one small circuit board that contains all the circuitry to run the stepper motors the way the printer needs them to work (back and forth, load paper and then stop, and so on). It is also responsible for monitoring the health of the printer and reporting that information back to the PC.

printer resident fonts   Fonts that are housed in a printer's onboard memory.

printer ribbon   A fabric strip that is impregnated with ink and wrapped around two spools encased in a cartridge. This cartridge is used in dot-matrix printers to provide the ink for the print process.

printhead   The part of a printer that creates the printed image. In a dot-matrix printer, the printhead contains the small pins that strike the ribbon to create the image, and in an ink-jet printer, the printhead contains the jets used to create the ink droplets as well as the ink reservoirs. A laser printer creates images using an electrophotographic method similar to that found in photocopiers and does not have a printhead.

printhead alignment   The process by which the printhead is calibrated for use. A special utility that comes with the printer software is used to do this.

printhead carriage   The component of a bubble-jet printer that moves back and forth during printing. It contains the physical as well as electronic connections for the printhead and (in some cases) the ink reservoir.

processor form factor   A term that describes how the package of a processor is laid out, including how many pins it has and what its size and composition are.

processor socket (or slot)   The device that physically holds the processor in place through the use of clips and/or friction and allows the motherboard to electrically connect to the processor.

product activation   A process that Microsoft requires, to curb software piracy. Each copy of Windows XP must be "activated" (either by phone or Internet) after installation. Without activation, you can run Windows XP, but you can use it for only 30 days. During that 30 days, Windows XP will constantly remind you to activate your product.

product key   An anti-piracy feature. Software piracy is a serious problem in the industry, so many programs include a product key that must be typed in for the software to install properly. This key is then submitted if the user registers for technical support.

Program Manager   The primary interface to Windows 3.x that allows you to organize and execute numerous programs by double-clicking an icon in a single graphical window.

Programmed I/O (PIO)   See *PIO modes*.

propagation delay   In satellite Internet, the delay caused by the length of time required to transmit data and receive a response via satellite.

proprietary design   A design style for computer components that is unique to a particular manufacturer and is not licensed to other manufacturers.

protected mode   A processor operating mode wherein every program's memory is protected from every other program. If one program crashes, it doesn't bring down the other programs.

protocol   In networking and communications, the specification that defines the procedures to follow when transmitting and receiving data. Protocols define the format, timing, sequence, and error-checking systems used.

protocol stack   In networking and communications, the several layers of software that define the computer-to-computer or computer-to-network protocol. The protocol stack on a Novell NetWare system will be different from that used on a Banyan VINES network or a Microsoft LAN Manager system.

PS/2 mouse interface   A type of mouse interface that uses a round, DIN-6 connector. It gets its name from the first computer it was introduced on, the IBM PS/2.

puck   The proper name for the mouse-like device used with drawing tablets.

push-in standoffs   Spacers made of nylon plastic with a small one-way barb the fits into any of the mounting holes in the motherboard. To install them, you push the barb into the motherboard and slide the small tab on the bottom into a pre-cut hole in the mounting plate.

QSOP (Quad Small Outline Package)   A type of IC package that has all leads soldered directly to the circuit board. Also called a surface-mount chip.

Quick-and-Dirty Disk Operating System (QDOS)   The basis of MS-DOS; created by Tim Patterson of Seattle Computer Products. QDOS was purchased by Microsoft and renamed MS-DOS.

radio frequency interference (RFI)   Electromagnetic radiation produced by many electronic devices, including computers and peripherals, that can interfere with other signals in the radio-frequency range. This is normally regulated by government agencies in each country.

rag stock   Paper made from cotton.

RAM (random access memory)   The main system memory in a computer, used for the operating system, application programs, and data.

RAM disk   An area of memory managed by a special device driver and used as a simulated disk. Anything stored on a RAM disk is erased when the computer is turned off; therefore, the contents must be saved onto a real disk.

Rambus Inline Memory Module (RIMM)   A type of memory module that uses Rambus memory. See *Direct Rambus*.

random access memory   See *RAM*.

rasterizing   The process of converting signals from the computer into signals for the various assemblies in a laser printer.

read-only memory   See *ROM (read-only memory)*.

read/write head   That part of a floppy- or hard-disk system that reads and writes data to and from a magnetic disk.

real mode   A processor operating mode whereby a processor emulates an 8086 processor.

recovery CD   A CD-ROM that comes with a particular model and brand of computer. It contains an image of the entire Windows installation, as well as applications, utilities, and drivers specifically for that computer. In the case of a serious system failure, you can insert this CD-ROM into the CD-ROM drive of your computer, boot to it, and completely restore your system back to the way it was when you bought it.

reference disk   A special disk that is bootable and contains a program that is able to send special commands to MCA bus devices to configure their parameters.

refresh rate   In a monitor, the rate at which the phosphors that create the image on the screen are recharged.

registered jack (RJ)   A type of connector, most often used in telecommunications. RJ-11 connectors are most commonly used in household telephone hookups.

registration roller   See *paper registration roller*.

Registry   Used in Windows 9*x*/NT/2000 to store configuration information about the machine, including individual user settings and global system settings.

***REM* statement**   A command placed at the beginning of a line in a DOS batch file to prevent that line from executing.

removable mass storage   Any high-capacity storage device inserted into a drive for reading and writing, and then removed for storage and safekeeping.

removable media   Any storage media that can be removed from the system.

repeater   In networking, a simple hardware device that moves all packets from one local area network segment to another.

resistor   An electronic device used to resist the flow of current in an electrical circuit. See also *fixed resistor* and *variable resistor*.

resistor pack   A combination of multiple resistors in a single package. Often used to terminate SCSI buses.

resource   Anything on a network that clients might want to access or use.

resource discovery expansion card   A card that, when installed into any expansion slot, tells you what resources are being used in the computer and indicates any possible conflicts.

restoration CD   See *recovery CD*.

restore   The process of getting data from a backup restored to the computer it originally came from.

retaining clips   The two white or brown levers on the sides of the socket in which memory is installed.

revision number   The first number to the right of the decimal point in a software version number. Revision numbers increment until the software developers decide to release another major release.

RFI   See *radio frequency interference (RFI)*.

rheostat   See *variable resistor*.

ribbon cartridge   The container that holds the printer ribbon.

RIMM   See *Rambus Inline Memory Module*.

ring topology   A type of physical topology in which each computer connects to two other computers, joining them in a circle and creating a unidirectional path where messages move from workstation to workstation. Each entity participating in the ring reads a message, regenerates it, and then hands it to its neighbor.

riser card   An expansion card that adds further capabilities to an existing expansion card or bus. The riser card may also allow an expansion bus to change direction (e.g., from horizontal to vertical).

RJ-11/RJ-45   A commonly used modular telephone connector. RJ-11 is a four- or six-pin connector used in most connections destined for voice use; it is the connector used on phone cords. RJ-45 is the eight-pin connector used for data transmission over twisted-pair wiring and can be used for networking; RJ-45 is the connector used on 10BaseT Ethernet cables.

ROM (read-only memory)   A type of computer memory that retains its data permanently, even when power is removed. Once data is written to this type of memory, it cannot be changed.

root directory   In a hierarchical directory structure, the directory from which all other directories must branch. The root directory is created by the FORMAT command and can contain files as well as other directories. This directory cannot be deleted.

rounded cables   Cables that are rounded to prevent the airflow impedance that can be caused by flat ribbon cables.

router   In networking, an intelligent connecting device that can send packets to the correct local area network segment to take them to their destination. Routers link LAN segments at the Network layer of the International Standards Organization's Open Systems Interconnect (ISO/OSI) model for computer-to-computer communications.

RS-232 cables   See *serial cables*.

RS-232-C   In asynchronous transmissions, a recommended standard interface established by the Electrical Industries Association. The standard defines the specific lines, timing, and signal characteristics used between the computer and the peripheral device and uses a 25-pin or 9-pin DB connector. RS-232-C is used for serial communications between a computer and a peripheral such as a printer, modem, digitizing tablet, or mouse.

RS-422/423/449 In asynchronous transmissions, a recommended standard interface established by the Electrical Industries Association for distances greater than 50 feet but less than 1000 feet. The standard defines the specific lines, timing, and signal characteristics used between the computer and the peripheral device.

RTS (request to send) A hardware signal defined by the RS-232-C standard to request permission to transmit.

Safe mode A Windows operating mode that loads only a basic set of drivers and a basic screen resolution. It can be activated using the F8 key at boot time.

sag A momentary drop in voltage, after which a computer experiences disorientation. A computer's normal response to this kind of disorientation is to reboot itself.

satellite Internet A type of Internet connection that uses a satellite dish to receive data from a satellite and a relay station that is connected to the Internet.

scanner An optical device used to digitize images such as line art or photographs, so that they can be merged with text by a page-layout or desktop publishing program or incorporated into a CAD drawing.

screen saver A program originally designed to prevent damage to a computer monitor from being left on too long. These programs usually include moving graphics so that no one pixel is left on all the time. Screen savers detect computer inactivity and activate after a certain period.

screw-in standoff Spacers, usually made of brass, that screw into the mounting plate into a pre-drilled and -tapped hole.

SCSI (Small Computer System Interface) A high-speed, system-level parallel interface defined by the ANSI X3T9.2 committee. SCSI is used to connect a personal computer to several peripheral devices using just one port. Devices connected in this way are said to be daisy-chained together, and each device must have a unique identifier or priority number.

SCSI adapter A device used to manage all the devices on the SCSI bus as well as to send and retrieve data from the devices.

SCSI address A unique address given to each SCSI device.

SCSI bus Another name for the SCSI interface and communications protocol.

SCSI chain All the devices connected to a single SCSI adapter.

SCSI terminator A terminator on the SCSI interface. The SCSI interface must be correctly terminated to prevent signals echoing on the bus. Many SCSI devices have built-in terminators that engage when they are needed. With some older SCSI devices, you have to add an external SCSI terminator that plugs into the device's SCSI connector.

sector The smallest unit of storage on a disk, usually 512 bytes. Sectors are grouped together into clusters.

seek time   The time it takes the actuator arm to move from rest position to active position for the read/write head to access information. Often used as a performance gauge of an individual drive. The major part of a hard disk's access time is actually seek time.

semiconductor   Any material that, depending on some condition, is either a conductor or nonconductor.

separator pads   Rubber patches that help keep the paper in place so that only one sheet goes into a printer.

Serial ATA   An implementation of the ATA interface that works over much smaller cables and operates serially (as opposed to the current implementation that operates via parallel signal lines). It is possible to buy Serial ATA controllers and drives, but they are not necessarily an implementation of ATA/ATAPI-7.

serial cables   Cables used for serial communications. See *serial communications*.

serial communications   The transmission of information from computer to computer or from computer to a peripheral, one bit at a time. Serial communications can be synchronous and controlled by a clock or asynchronous and coordinated by start and stop bits embedded in the data stream.

serial mouse   A mouse that attaches directly to one of the computer's serial ports.

serial port   A computer input/output port that supports serial communications in which information is processed one bit at a time. RS-232-C is a common serial protocol used by computers when communicating with modems, printers, mice, and other peripherals.

serial printer   A printer that attaches to one of the computer's serial ports.

server   In networking, any computer that makes access to files, printing, communications, or other services available to users of the network. In large networks, a server may run a special network operating system; in smaller installations, a server may run a personal computer operating system.

service   Any program that runs in the background on a computer and performs a task for that computer or other machines on the network.

Session layer   The fifth of seven layers of the International Standards Organization's Open Systems Interconnection (ISO/OSI) model for computer-to-computer communications. The Session layer coordinates communications and maintains the session for as long as it is needed, performing security, logging, and administrative functions.

share name   A name used to identify a network access point. Share names can be the same as the directory they are sharing or different.

share permission   In Windows NT, the type of permission that controls access to information through the network.

shell   A program that controls how an operating system's interface works. The interface allows users to navigate the system. For MS-DOS, the Windows Program Manager was its most popular shell. For Windows 9x/2000, Explorer (`explorer.exe`) is the standard shell program.

shielded twisted-pair   See *STP (shield twisted-pair)*.

signal channel   See *D channel*.

signal pathways   The routes that allow information and signals to travel between internal and external computer components.

Simple Mail Transport Protocol (SMTP)   A protocol used to send mail from a client to an e-mail server. SMTP servers do not store mail for users to pick up; they send the mail out, and another server (such as a POP3 server) is used to store incoming mail.

Single Edge Contact Cartridge (SECC)   A processor packaging type similar to a SEPP, except the entire expansion card is placed inside a plastic case to protect it. See also *Single Edge Processor Package (SEPP)*.

Single Edge Processor Package (SEPP)   A processor packing type where the processor is placed on a special expansion card, which then fits into a Slot 1 connector.

Single Inline Memory Module (SIMM)   Individual RAM chips soldered or surface-mounted onto small narrow circuit boards called carrier modules, which can be plugged into sockets on the motherboard. These carrier modules are simple to install and occupy less space than conventional memory modules.

Single Inline Package (SIP)   A type of semiconductor package wherein the package has a single row of connector pins on one side only.

single-purpose server   A server that is dedicated to one purpose (for example, a file server or a printer server).

single-word DMA mode   A data transfer mode whereby data is transferred one word at a time, in contrast to multiword DMA transfer.

site license   A software license that is valid for all installations at a single site.

slave drive   The secondary drive in an IDE master/slave disk configuration.

slocket   A circuit board that plugs into a slot 1, but has a socket (typically a Socket 370) on it. It allows Socket 370-based chips to be plugged into to slot 1 motherboards.

slot 1 connector   A slot similar to an expansion slot, which functions like a processor socket into which the daughterboard is inserted.

slot A   A card and slot-processor interface developed by AMD. The slot A allows for a higher bus rate than a Socket 7 or Super 7 and is used primarily with the AMD K7 processor family.

Small Computer System Interface   See *SCSI*.

Socket 370   A 370-pin motherboard socket developed by Intel to address people's aversion to the slot. Users could buy a version of the CPU that worked in a socket.

Socket 423   A motherboard CPU socket style that arrived with the Pentium 4.

Socket 478 A motherboard CPU socket style that is currently used with the Pentium 4. It's similar to the Socket 423 but with more pins for extra capabilities.

Socket 7 A motherboard processor socket that supports Intel Pentium Processors and AMD processors with 321 pins in a Zero Insertion Force (ZIF) socket.

Socket 8 The physical and electrical specification for the 387-pin Zero Insertion Force (ZIF) socket used by various Intel Pentium Pro and Pentium II overdrive processors. The pins are arranged in a 24 × 26 matrix.

Socket A A socket style that consists of 462 pins and looks similar to other socket types. The Socket A primarily supports AMD Athlon, Duron, and Athlon XP processors.

socket ID A special IPX address that specifies which service a packet is destined for on the server.

socket services Part of the software support needed for PCMCIA hardware devices in a portable computer, controlling the interface to the hardware. Socket services is the lowest layer in the software that manages PCMCIA cards. It provides a BIOS-level software interface to the hardware, effectively hiding the specific details from higher levels of software. Socket services also detect when you insert or remove a PCMCIA card and identify the type of card it is.

software An application program or an operating system that a computer can execute. Software is a broad term that can imply one or many programs, and it can also refer to applications that may actually consist of more than one program.

software driver Software that acts as the liaison between a piece of hardware and the operating system and allows the use of a component.

solenoid An electromechanical device that, when activated, produces an instant push or pull force.

solid ink printer A printer that uses ink is in a waxy solid form, rather than in liquid form. This allows the ink to stay fresh and eliminates problems like spillage.

source The code that defines what a program is and how it works. All computer programs—operating system or application—are nothing but a collection of program code. The open source movement is involved with allowing you to see and even modify this source code.

Southbridge The subset of the chipset that is responsible for providing support to the myriad of onboard peripherals (PS/2, parallel, IDE, and so on), managing their communications with the rest of the computer and the resources given to them.

spike An electrical power overage condition that exists for an extremely short period of time and can damage some computer.

spin speed An indication of how fast the platters on a fixed disk are spinning.

spindle The rod onto which platters are mounted in a hard disk drive.

SRAM See *static RAM (SRAM)*.

ST506 interface   A popular hard-disk interface standard developed by Seagate Technologies, first used in IBM's PC/XT computer and still popular today, with disk capacities smaller than about 40MB. ST506 has a relatively slow data transfer rate of 5Mbps.

stabilizer bar   A small metal bar on a printer that holds the printer carriage as it crosses the page.

stack   Another name for the memory map, or the way memory is laid out.

standard peripheral power connector   A type of connector used to power various internal drives. Also called a Molex connector.

standard serial cable   A cable used to hook various peripherals like modems and printers to a computer.

standby power supply   The backup power supply that kicks in when the power drops below a preset threshold. See *cutover*.

standoffs   Small metal or plastic spacers that hold the motherboard away from the motherboard mounting plate in the case and prevent the components of the motherboard from touching the mounting plate and shorting out.

star network   A network topology in the form of a star. At the center of the star is a wiring hub or concentrator; the nodes or workstations are arranged around the central point and represent the points of the star.

start bit   In asynchronous transmissions, the bit transmitted to indicate the beginning of a new data word.

Start menu   The main focus of the Windows 9*x*/NT/2000 user interface. The Start menu allows program shortcuts to be placed for easy and organized access.

static RAM (SRAM)   A type of computer memory that retains its contents as long as power is supplied. It does not need constant refreshment like dynamic RAM chips.

static-charge eliminator strip   The device in EP process printers that drains the static charge from the paper after the toner has been transferred to the paper.

stepper motor   A very precise motor that can move in very small increments. Often used in printers.

stick of memory   A slang term for any memory module that is long (SIMM, DIMM, RIMM, etc.).

stop bit(s)   In asynchronous transmissions, bits transmitted to indicate the end of the current data word. Depending on the convention in use, one or two stop bits are used.

STP (shielded twisted-pair)   Cabling that has a braided foil shield around the twisted pairs of wire to decrease electrical interference.

stylus   A pen-like pointing device used in pen-based systems and Personal Digital Assistants (PDAs).

subnet mask   A required part of any TCP/IP configuration, used to define which addresses are local and which are on remote networks.

superscalar   See *parallel processing*.

SuperVGA (SVGA)   An enhancement to the Video Graphics Array (VGA) video standard defined by the Video Electronics Standards Association (VESA).

surface mount   See *QSOP (Quad Small Outline Package)*.

surge   An electrical power overage condition that exists for up to several seconds and can cause some computer damage.

surge suppressor   Also known as a surge protector. A regulating device placed between the computer and the AC line connection that protects the computer system from power surges.

SVGA   See *SuperVGA (SVGA)*.

swap file   On a hard disk, a file used to store parts of running programs that have been swapped out of memory temporarily to make room for other running programs. A swap file may be permanent, always occupying the same amount of hard disk space even though the application that created it may not be running; or it may be temporary, created only as and when needed.

synchronization   The timing of separate elements or events to occur simultaneously.

   1. In a multimedia presentation, synchronization ensures that the audio and video components are timed correctly, so they make sense.

   2. In computer-to-computer communications, the hardware and software must be synchronized so that file transfers can take place.

   3. The process of updating files on both a portable computer and a desktop system so that they both have the latest versions is also known as synchronization.

synchronous DRAM   A type of DRAM memory module that uses memory chips synchronized to the speed of the processor.

synchronous transmission   In communications, a transmission method that uses a clock signal to regulate data flow. Synchronous transmissions do not use start and stop bits.

syntax   The proper way of forming a text command for entry into the computer. Many commands have a number of different options, each of which requires a particular format.

system attribute   An attribute of DOS that tells the operating system that this file is needed by the operating system and should not be deleted. It marks a file as part of the operating system and also protects the file from deletion.

system board   The sturdy sheet or board to which all other components on the computer are attached. These components consist of the CPU, underlying circuitry, expansion slots, video components, and RAM slots, just to name a few. Also known as a logic board, motherboard, or planar board.

system bus   See *expansion bus*.

system disk   A disk that contains all the files necessary to boot and start the operating system. In most computers, the hard disk is the system disk; many modern operating systems are too large to run from floppy disk.

system editor (*SYSEDIT.EXE*)   A utility that allows you to view and edit the `CONFIG.SYS`, `AUTOEXEC.BAT`, `WIN.INI`, `SYSTEM.INI`, `PROTOCOL.INI`, and `MSMAIL.INI` files. You can use `SYSEDIT` to edit these files and remove an offending driver entry or software configuration.

system resources   On a Windows 3.*x* or 95/98 machine, those components of the PC that are being used (memory, CPU, and so on).

system software   The programs that make up the operating system, along with the associated utility programs, as distinct from an application program.

SYSTEM.INI   In Microsoft Windows, an initialization file that contains information about your hardware and the internal Windows operating environment.

tablet PC   A laptop designed to be held like a pad of paper.

tabs   A display element found on many windows, to save space. A single window can have many tabs, each of which can be selected to display particular information.

tape cartridge   A self-contained tape storage module, containing tape much like that in a video cassette. Tape cartridges are primarily used to back up hard disk systems.

tape drive   A removable media drive that uses a tape cartridge containing a long polyester ribbon coated with magnetic oxide and wrapped around two spools with a read/write head in between.

Taskbar   The area of the Windows 9*x*/NT/2000 interface that includes the Start button and the System Tray, as well as icons for any open programs.

TCP/IP (Transmission Control Protocol/Internet Protocol)   A set of computer-to-computer communications protocols that encompasses media access, packet transport, session communications, file transfer, e-mail, and terminal emulation. TCP/IP is supported by a very large number of hardware and software vendors and is available on many different computers from PCs to mainframes.

temporary file (temp file)   A file designed to store information for a short period of time and then be deleted.

Temporary Internet Files   A special directory on the local disk cache set up to store Internet images and pages so they don't need to be downloaded.

temporary swap file   A swap file that is created every time it is needed. A temporary swap file does not consist of a single large area of contiguous hard disk space, but may consist of several discontinuous pieces of space. By its very nature, a temporary swap file does not occupy valuable hard disk space if the application that created it is not running. In a permanent swap file, the hard disk space is always reserved and is therefore unavailable to any other application program.

terminal A monitor and keyboard attached to a computer (usually a mainframe), used for data entry and display. Unlike a personal computer, a terminal does not have its own central processing unit or hard disk.

Terminate and Stay Resident (TSR) A DOS program that stays loaded in memory, even when it is not running, so that you can invoke it quickly to perform a specific task.

terminating resistor pack A small package of resistors used for terminating SCSI drives. See also *terminator*.

terminator A device attached to the last peripheral in a series or the last node on a network. A resistor is placed at both ends of a coax Ethernet cable to prevent signals from reflecting and interfering with the transmission.

text mode A video display mode for a video card that allows it to only display text. When running DOS programs, a video card is in text mode.

thermal contact patch A tape-like substance attached to the heatsink or water block to facilitate the best contact with the processor.

thermal grease A compound used to allow the heatsink or water block to make the best contact with the processor.

thermal interface material (TIM) Material used to allow the heatsink or water block to make the best contact with the processor. Includes thermal grease and thermal contact patches.

thermal printer A nonimpact printer that uses a thermal printhead and specially treated paper to create an image.

thick Ethernet Connecting coaxial cable used on an Ethernet network. The cable is 1cm (approximately 0.4 inch) thick and can be used to connect network nodes up to a distance of approximately 3300 feet. Thick Ethernet is primarily used for facility-wide installations. Also known as 10Base5.

thin Ethernet Connecting coaxial cable used on an Ethernet network. The cable is 5mm (approximately 0.2 inch) thick, and can be used to connect network nodes up to a distance of approximately 1000 feet. Thin Ethernet is primarily used for office installations. Also known as 10Base2.

thrashing A slang term for the condition that occurs when Windows must constantly swap data between memory and hard disk. The hard disk spins continuously during thrashing and makes a lot of noise.

token passing A media access method that gives every NIC equal access to the cable. The token is a special packet of data that is passed from computer to computer. Any computer that wants to transmit has to wait until it has the token, at which point it can add its own data to the token and send it on.

Token Ring network A local area network with a ring structure that uses token-passing to regulate traffic on the network and avoid collisions. On a Token Ring network, the controlling computer generates a token that controls the right to transmit. This token is continuously passed from one node to the next around the network. When a node has information to transmit, it captures the token, sets its status to busy, and adds the message and the destination address. All other nodes continuously read the token to determine if they are the recipient of a message; if they are, they collect the token, extract the message, and return the token to the sender. The sender then removes the message and sets the token status to free, indicating that it can be used by the next node in sequence.

tolerance band   Found on a fixed resistor, a colored band that indicates how well the resistor holds to its rated value.

toner   A black carbon substance mixed with polyester resins and iron oxide particles. During the EP printing process, toner is first attracted to areas that have been exposed to the laser in laser printers and is later deposited and melted onto the print medium.

toner cartridge   The replaceable cartridge in a laser printer or photocopier that contains the electrically charged ink to be fused to the paper during printing.

topology   A way of laying out a network. Can describe either the logical or physical layout.

Torx screwdriver   A tool for the little screws found on Compaq and Apple computers. The Torx type of screw has the most surfaces to turn against and therefore has the greatest resistance to screw-head damage.

touchpad   A device that has a pad of touch-sensitive material. You draw with your finger on the touchpad, and the onscreen pointer follows your finger motions. Included with the touchpad are two buttons for left- or right-clicking (although with some touchpads it is possible to perform the functions of the left-click by tapping on the touchpad).

Touchpoint   A pointing device that uses a small rubber-tipped stick. When you push the Touchpoint in a particular direction, the onscreen pointer goes in that same direction. The harder you push, the faster it goes. It allows fingertip control of the onscreen pointer, without the reliability problems associated with trackballs.

touch screen   A special monitor that lets you make choices by touching icons or graphical buttons on the screen.

Tracert   A utility used to trace the path of a packet across a TCP/IP network.

trackball   An input device used for pointing, designed as an alternative to the mouse.

track   The concentric circle unit of hard disk division. A disk platter is divided into these concentric circles.

transfer corona assembly   The part of an EP process printer that is responsible for transferring the developed image from the EP drum to the paper.

transferring step   The step in the EP print process when the developed toner image on the EP drum is transferred to the print medium using the transfer corona.

transistor   Abbreviation for transfer resistor. A semiconductor component that acts like a switch, controlling the flow of an electric current. A small voltage applied at one pole controls a larger voltage on the other poles. Transistors are incorporated into modern microprocessors by the million.

Transmission Control Protocol/Internet Protocol   See *TCP/IP (Transmission Control Protocol/Internet Protocol)*.

Transport layer   The fourth of seven layers of the International Standards Organization's Open Systems Interconnection (ISO/OSI) model for computer-to-computer communications. The Transport layer defines protocols for message structures and supervises the validity of the transmission by performing some error checking.

TSR   See *Terminate and Stay Resident (TSR)*.

twisted-pair cable   Cable that comprises two insulated wires twisted together at six twists per inch. In twisted-pair cable, one wire carries the signal and the other is grounded. Telephone wire installed in modern buildings is often twisted-pair wiring.

typical installation   An installation procedure that installs the most commonly used components of software. Not all the components are installed.

UART (Universal Asynchronous Receiver/Transmitter)   An electronic module that combines the transmitting and receiving circuitry needed for asynchronous transmission over a serial line. Asynchronous transmissions use start and stop bits encoded in the data stream to coordinate communications rather than the clock pulse found in synchronous transmissions.

UltraDMA IDE   Also known as ATA version 4 (ATA-4). A technology that can transfer data at 33Mbps or faster, so it is also commonly seen in motherboard specifications as UltraDMA/33, Ultra66, Ultra100, or UDMA.

unidirectional   A form of satellite Internet wherein the satellite is used for only one part of the connection: downloading from the Internet.

uninstall   To remove a program from a computer. This process generally involves removing the program's configuration information from the Registry, its icons from the Start menu, and its program code from the filesystem.

uninterruptible power supply (UPS)   A system whereby a battery is always running off a continually recharged battery. When power fluctuates, only the charging circuit is affected. The battery continues to provide power to the equipment uninterrupted.

universal data connector (UDC)   Another name for an IBM data connector.

Universal Serial Bus   See *USB (Universal Serial Bus)*.

Unix   Pronounced "you-nix." A 32-bit, multiuser, multitasking, portable operating system.

upper memory area   See *reserved memory area*.

upper memory block (UMB)   Free area of memory that can be used for loading drivers and programs into the upper memory area.

USB (Universal Serial Bus)   A technology used to connect peripheral devices to a computer. Each USB channel supports 127 devices and has a total transfer rate of up to 12Mbps.

user group   A designation used to associate users of like security settings or types together so that permissions can be assigned at the group level for all users within that group.

user profile   A means of saving a particular user's desktop appearance and preferences so that when they log on they always have their own desktop, even if they share the machine with others. This allows each user to customize their Windows experience.

USER.EXE   Windows core component that allows you to interact with Windows. It is the component responsible for interpreting keystrokes and mouse movements and sending the appropriate commands to the other core components.

User Datagram Protocol (UDP)   Part of the TCP/IP suite that performs a similar function to TCP, with less overhead and more speed, but with lower reliability.

username   A means of user identification. In order to identify themselves on the network, users must provide two credentials: a username and a password. The username says, "This is who I am," and the password says, "And here's proof!" Each username must be unique on the network and is generally used by only one person.

UTP (unshielded twisted pair)   A type of unshielded network cable that contains multiple conductors in pairs that are twisted around each other.

vacuum tube   An electronic component that is a glorified switch. A small voltage at one pole switches a larger voltage at the other poles on or off.

variable resistor   A resistor that does not have a fixed value. Typically, the value is changed using a knob or slider.

VCACHE   The virtual cache program in Windows.

version   A number used by computer programmers to tell modified programs apart. Each time computer software is modified, new features are added and old problems are fixed. The version is incremented by one digit (for example, from 1.0 to 2.0) for major revisions, or by a tenth of a digit (for example, from 2.0 to 2.1) for minor modifications. Higher version numbers mean newer versions.

VGA (Video Graphics Array)   A video adapter. VGA supports previous graphics standards and provides several different graphics resolutions, including 640 pixels horizontally by 480 pixels vertically. A maximum of 256 colors can be displayed simultaneously, chosen from a palette of 262,114 colors. Because the VGA standard requires an analog display, it is capable of resolving a continuous range of gray shades or colors. In contrast, a digital display can only resolve a finite range of shades or colors.

video (SVGA) port   A port on a motherboard with built-in video circuitry to allow the computer to display images on the monitor.

video adapter   An expansion board that plugs into the expansion bus in a DOS computer and provides for text and graphics output to the monitor. The adapter converts the text and graphic signals into several instructions for the display that tell it how to draw the graphic.

Video Graphics Array   See *VGA (Video Graphics Array)*.

video RAM (VRAM)   Special-purpose RAM with two data paths for access, rather than just one as in conventional RAM. These two paths let a VRAM board manage two functions at once—refreshing the display and communicating with the processor. VRAM doesn't require the system to complete one function before starting the other, so it allows faster operation for the whole video system.

virtual FAT (VFAT)   An extension of the FAT filesystem that was introduced with Windows 95. It augmented the 8.3 file-naming convention and allowed filenames with up to 255 characters. It created two names for each file: a *long name* and an 8.3-compatible name so that older programs could still access files.

virtual memory   A memory-management technique that allows information in physical memory to be swapped out to a hard disk. This technique provides application programs with more memory space than is actually available in the computer. True virtual-memory management requires specialized hardware in the processor for the operating system to use; it is not just a question of writing information out to a swap file on the hard disk at the application level.

virus   A program intended to damage your computer system without your knowledge or permission. A virus may attach itself to another program or to the partition table or the boot track on your hard disk. When a certain event occurs, a date passes, or a specific program executes, the virus is triggered into action. Not all viruses are harmful; some are just annoying.

VL bus   Also known as VL local bus. Abbreviation for the VESA local bus, a bus architecture introduced by the Video Electronics Standards Association (VESA), in which up to three adapter slots are built into the motherboard. The VL bus allows for bus mastering.

VLSI (Very Large Scale Integration)   A technology used by chip manufacturers to integrate the functions of several small chips into one chip.

voltage ID (VID) programmable   A processor's ability to tell the Voltage Regulator Module what voltage it needs.

Voltage Regulator Module (VRM)   A small module that regulates the voltage fed to the processor.

volt   A unit of electrical potential.

volume   A named chunk of disk space. This chunk can exist on part of a disk, can exist on all of a disk, or can span multiple disks. Volumes provide a way of organizing disk storage.

VRAM   See *video RAM (VRAM)*.

VXD (virtual device driver)   A special device drive that has direct access to the Windows operating system kernel.

wait state   A clock cycle during which no instructions are executed because the processor is waiting for data from a device or from memory.

WAN (wide area network)   A network that expands LANs to include networks outside of the local environment and also to distribute resources across distances.

warm boot   The process of pressing Ctrl+Alt+Del to reboot the computer. This type of booting doesn't require the computer to perform all the hardware and memory checks that a cold boot does.

water block   An aluminum device mounted to the processor with two small connectors for a water inlet and outlet, which are in turn connected to a small pump and radiator for processor cooling.

water cooling   Using water to cool a computer processor. See *water block*.

watt   A single unit of power.

wide area network   See *WAN (wide area network)*.

WIN.INI   A file that contains Windows environmental settings that control the environment's general function and appearance.

window   In a graphical user interface, a rectangular portion of the screen that acts as a viewing area for application programs. Windows can be tiled or cascaded and can be individually moved and sized on the screen. Some programs can open multiple document windows inside their application window to display several word-processing or spreadsheet data files at the same time.

Windows 2000   A Windows operating system version that incorporates the look and feel of Windows 9*x* with the power of Windows NT and some additional interface enhancements.

Windows 95   A 32-bit, multitasking, multithreaded operating system capable of running DOS, Windows 3.1, and Windows 95 applications. It supports Plug and Play (on the appropriate hardware) and adds an enhanced FAT filesystem in the virtual FAT that allows long filenames of up to 255 characters while also supporting the DOS 8.3 file-naming convention.

Windows 98   The home PC operating system released by Microsoft as the successor to the popular Windows 95 operating system. Basically the same as Windows 95, it offers a few improvements. For example, Windows 98 improves the basic look and feel of Windows 95 with a browser-like interface. It also contains bug-fixes and can support two monitors simultaneously. In addition to new interface features, it includes support for new hardware, including Universal Serial Bus devices.

Windows ME   The last version of Windows to use the Windows 95/98 "look and feel" as well as the Windows 9*x* operating system kernel.

Windows Desktop   See *Desktop*.

Windows Installer   A method Microsoft Windows uses to allow users to customize application installations more easily. The Windows Installer also makes it easier for users to install approved software on secured workstations and can automatically repair damaged installs.

Windows Internet Name Service (WINS)   A service that provides a database for the storage and retrieval of NetBIOS computer names. Each client must register with the WINS server to be able to be added to and query the database.

Windows NT   A 32-bit multitasking, portable operating system developed by Microsoft. Initial versions ran on Intel 80386 (or later) processors and RISC processors, such as the MIPS R4000 and the DEC Alpha. Windows NT contains the graphical user interface from Windows 3.1 and can run Windows 3.1 and DOS applications as well as OS/2 16-bit character-based applications and new 32-bit programs specifically developed for Windows NT. Multitasking under Windows NT is preemptive, and applications can execute multiple threads. Security is built into the operating system at the U.S. Government–approved C2 security level. Windows NT supports the DOS FAT filesystem, the OS/2 HPFS, installable filesystems such as CD-ROM systems, and a native filesystem called NTFS. Windows NT also supports multiprocessing, OLE, and peer-to-peer networking.

Windows XP   The latest release of Windows that includes an interface redesign and updated security features. It is based on the Windows NT kernel and platform and, as such, is fully 32-bit and includes multitasking.

Windows product key   A 25-digit alphanumeric string that uniquely identifies an installation of Windows.

WINIPCFG   In Windows $9x$, the utility that allows you to view your current TCP/IP configuration. It also lets you request a new IP configuration from a DHCP server.

wireless access point (AP)   See *access point*.

wireless Internet   An Internet access technology that uses radio frequency signals to communicate between ISP and user. It allows the user to roam about a particular area while remaining connected to the Internet.

wizard   A preprogrammed utility that walks you through a particular task. Each wizard generally includes a number of different pages, each of which allows you to enter information or choose particular options. At the finish of the wizard, the computer performs the requested task based on the information it has gathered.

word   In binary communications, multiple bytes associated together.

workgroup   A group of individuals who work together and share the same files and databases over a local area network. Special groupware such as Lotus Notes coordinates the workgroup and allows users to edit drawings or documents and update the database as a group.

working directory   A special directory used by programs that need to save temporary files or configuration data while they are running. Users can also have a working directory to save their temporary files.

workstation   1. In networking, any personal computer (other than the file server) attached to the network.
   2. A high-performance computer optimized for graphics applications such as computer-aided design, computer-aided engineering, or scientific applications.

World Wide Web (WWW)   The graphical extension of the Internet that features millions of pages of information accessed though the use of the Hypertext Transfer Protocol (HTTP).

write-protect   To prevent the addition or deletion of files on a disk or tape. Floppy disks have write-protect notches or small write-protect tabs that allow files to be read from the disk but prevent any modifications or deletions. Certain attributes can make individual files write-protected so they can be read but not altered or erased.

write-protect tab   The small notch or tab in a floppy disk that is used to write-protect it.

writing step   The step in the EP print process during which the items being printed are written to the EP drum. In this step, the laser is flashed on and off as it scans across the surface of the drum. The area on which the laser shines is discharged to almost ground (–100V).

***x*86 series**   The general name given to the Intel line of IBM-compatible CPUs.

XGA (Extended Graphics Array)   A video standard available only as a micro channel architecture expansion board, not in ISA or EISA form. XGA supports resolution of 1024 horizontal pixels by 768 vertical pixels with 256 colors, as well as a VGA mode of 640 pixels by 480 pixels with 65,536 colors; and, like the 8514/A, XGA is interlaced. XGA is optimized for use with graphical user interfaces. Instead of being very good at drawing lines, it is a bit-block transfer device designed to move blocks of bits like windows or dialog boxes.

zero wait state   Describes a computer that can process information without wait states. A wait state is a clock cycle during which no instructions are executed because the processor is waiting for data from a device or from memory.

ZIF processor socket   Abbreviation for Zero Insertion Force socket. A specially designed chip socket which makes replacing a chip easier and safer. It doesn't require you to snap the chip into the socket. Rather, you set the chip into the ZIF socket and push down a bar to secure it.

Index

Note to the Reader: Throughout this index **boldfaced** page numbers indicate primary discussions of a topic. *Italicized* page numbers indicate illustrations.

O

V